Understanding War and Peace

Second edition

Written for undergraduate students studying the politics of conflict and cooperation, *Understanding War and Peace* considers the roots of global conflicts and the various means used to resolve them. Edited by Dan Reiter with contributing authors who are all leading scholars in the field, it balances approachable, engaging writing with a conceptually rigorous overview of the most important ideas in conflict studies.

Focusing on concepts, policy, and historical applications, the text minimizes literature reviews and technical jargon to engagingly present all major topics in international conflict, including nuclear weapons, peacekeeping, terrorism, gender, alliances, nuclear weapons, environment and conflict, civil wars, and public opinion. Enriching the textbook pedagogy, each chapter concludes with a summary of a published quantitative study to introduce students with no prior quantitative training to quantitative analysis. Online resources for instructors include an instructor manual, a test bank, and contemporary case studies for each chapter topic regarding the conflict in Ukraine.

Dan Reiter is the Samuel Candler Dobbs Professor of Political Science at Emory University. He is one of the leading scholars in international relations, having published across the breadth of conflict topics, including the causes of war, bargaining and war, alliances, terrorism, nuclear weapons, gender and conflict, military effectiveness and war outcomes, IR decision-making, domestic politics and foreign policy, the democratic peace, military strategy, foreign-imposed regime change, and others. He has won many scholarly awards, served on the editorial boards of leading journals in political science and international relations, and taught undergraduates for decades.

"*Understanding War and Peace* is an outstanding textbook that offers an insightful and comprehensive introduction to the complex world of international conflict. Written by a team of leading scholars in the field, it delivers an engaging and accessible overview of the most important concepts and historical applications in the study of war, making it an ideal resource for undergraduate students. The book's focus on policy and real-world examples, coupled with its innovative pedagogy, including quantitative analysis, and valuable online resources, make it an indispensable tool for anyone seeking a deeper understanding of global conflicts and their resolutions."

Professor Allan C. Stam, *University of Virginia*

"*Understanding War and Peace* is an exceptional textbook that thoroughly prepares students for further analysis and coursework in international conflict. Its highly innovative structure is unique and extremely valuable as a teaching tool. Finally, a hallmark of this book is that it is exceptionally well-written, and therefore easily engages the reader and maintains the reader's interest."

Professor Hein Goemans, *University of Rochester*

"This concise text is a fantastic resource for engaging international relations students. It draws on first-rate scholarship to teach complex, important topics in an accessible manner. *Understanding War and Peace* is a valuable addition to any syllabus and is sure to promote learning, spur discussion, and provoke thought among those entering the field."

Professor Caitlin Talmadge, *Georgetown University*

"*Understanding War and Peace* is an accessible but comprehensive guide to the complex and fundamental issue of conflict in the contemporary international system which can be used as an introductory textbook but may also be useful to the concerned public."

Professor Filippo Andreatta, *University of Bologna*

"Cleverly conceived and lucidly written, this book relies on leading scholars to provide a sweeping education about the field of international relations: its topics, methods, and debates."

Professor Jennifer M. Lind, *Dartmouth College*

Understanding War and Peace

Second edition

Edited by

Dan Reiter
Emory University, Atlanta

CAMBRIDGE
UNIVERSITY PRESS

Shaftesbury Road, Cambridge CB2 8EA, United Kingdom

One Liberty Plaza, 20th Floor, New York, NY 10006, USA

477 Williamstown Road, Port Melbourne, VIC 3207, Australia

314–321, 3rd Floor, Plot 3, Splendor Forum, Jasola District Centre, New Delhi – 110025, India

103 Penang Road, #05-06/07, Visioncrest Commercial, Singapore 238467

Cambridge University Press is part of Cambridge University Press & Assessment,
a department of the University of Cambridge.

We share the University's mission to contribute to society through the pursuit of
education, learning and research at the highest international levels of excellence.

www.cambridge.org
Information on this title: www.cambridge.org/highereducation/isbn/9781009123365

DOI: 10.1017/9781009127721

First edition © Dan Reiter, Kyle Beardsley, Kathleen Gallagher Cunningham, Christopher Gelpi, Cullen S. Hendrix,
Michael C. Horowitz, Sarah E. Kreps and Paul Poast. The first edition was published as an online, modular textbook at
www.understandingwarandpeace.com

Second edition 2024

A catalogue record for this publication is available from the British Library.

Library of Congress Cataloging-in-Publication Data
Names: Reiter, Dan, 1967– editor.
Title: Understanding war and peace / Dan Reiter.
Description: Cambridge, United Kingdom ; New York, NY : Cambridge University Press, 2023. |
    Includes bibliographical references and index.
Identifiers: LCCN 2023003026 (print) | LCCN 2023003027 (ebook) | ISBN 9781009123365 (hardback) |
    ISBN 9781009125031 (paperback) | ISBN 9781009127721 (epub)
Subjects: LCSH: War. | Peace.
Classification: LCC U21.2 .U64 2023 (print) | LCC U21.2 (ebook) | DDC 355.02–dc23/eng/20230515
LC record available at https://lccn.loc.gov/2023003026
LC ebook record available at https://lccn.loc.gov/2023003027

ISBN 978-1-009-12336-5 Hardback
ISBN 978-1-009-12503-1 Paperback

Additional resources for this publication at www.cambridge.org/reiter.

....

Contents

Extended Contents

Part II: Domestic Politics and War

3 Domestic Political Institutions and War
Jessica L. P. Weeks

4 Public Opinion and the Conduct of Foreign Policy
Christopher Gelpi

Part IV: Diplomacy and Conflict

List of Contributors

Dan Reiter, Samuel Candler Dobbs Professor of Political Science, Emory University

Kyle Beardsley, Professor of Political Science, Duke University

Kathleen Gallagher Cunningham, Professor of Government and Politics, University of Maryland

Christopher Gelpi, Professor and Director and Chair of Peace Studies and Conflict Resolution, Mershon Center for International Security Studies, Ohio State University

Cullen S. Hendrix, Senior Fellow at the Peterson Institute for International Economics

Michael C. Horowitz, Richard Perry Professor of Political Science and Director of Perry World House, University of Pennsylvania

Valerie M. Hudson, University Distinguished Professor and George H. W. Bush Chair, Professor of International Affairs, Bush School of Government and Public Service, Texas A&M University

Sarah E. Kreps, John L. Wetherill Professor of Government, Cornell University

Paul Poast, Associate Professor of Political Science, University of Chicago

Philip B. K. Potter, Associate Professor of Politics and Policy and Director of the National Security Policy Center, University of Virginia

Jessica L. P. Weeks, Professor and H. Douglas Weaver Chair in Diplomacy and International Relations, University of Wisconsin

Preface

DAN REITER

Understanding War and Peace (second edition) is a textbook for use in lower and upper level undergraduate classes in international relations, conflict, and war. The textbook covers leading ideas about the causes, prosecution, termination, consequences, and prevention of many kinds of violent conflicts, including wars between states, civil wars, insurgency, drone warfare, terrorism, violence against girls and women, and others.

The chapters are all specifically written with undergraduate readers in mind. That is, they are not reprinted or abbreviated journal articles. Chapters focus on concepts without being too heavy on jargon, they keep literature review to a minimum, and they make liberal use of policy and historical applications. Each chapter is written by a leading scholar with expertise in that field, ensuring that the content reflects the cutting edge of academic research, and each is designed as a stand-alone chapter, meaning that no chapter presumes that the student has read any other chapter, though the chapters do cross-reference each other. The chapters also do not presume that the student has taken any other relevant coursework, such as an introduction to international relations course or courses in research methods or statistics.

Each chapter contains three sections of content. The first chapter section is the main body of content, working through the main concepts with plenty of historical and policy examples as illustrations. The second chapter section is a case study of a historical episode, designed to illustrate some of the main concepts from the chapter. The third chapter section contains a nontechnical summary of a previously published quantitative study on some proposition from the chapter. This third section is designed to be readable for any student, even those without any background in statistics or math, and is intended in part to introduce students to the approach of using quantitative empirical methods. Both the second and third sections are independent of the first section, meaning that the first section can be assigned with or without assigning either the second or third sections.

There are also separate, chapter-specific content modules available online, on the textbook website. For example, there are chapter-specific modules on the Ukraine War. Instructors can assign a Ukraine War module to help illustrate conceptual ideas presented in an assigned chapter.

Each chapter contains several pedagogical tools. Students are provided with a list of key terms, all of which are discussed in the chapter. There are review questions, all of which are answered within the chapter. There is also a list of discussion questions which can be used to generate discussion in class, or as shorter writing assignments. Each chapter also includes a list of suggested additional readings for students. Lastly, instructors have secure online access to a bank of multiple choice test questions, thirty questions per chapter.

The Introduction that follows this Preface serves two functions. First, it provides a general survey of war itself, touching on a few scholarly debates such as whether or not the frequency or intensity of war is in decline. Second, it introduces the essentials of the scientific method, defining terms such as hypothesis, independent variable, dependent variable, and spurious correlation. Knowing these terms will help students work through the summaries of quantitative research presented in the chapters. The discussion of research method is completely nonquantitative.

The book's substantive chapters that follow the Introduction cover many aspects of war and are grouped into five parts. The first offers broad perspectives on war. Chapter 1, "Bargaining and War" by Dan Reiter, presents the broad theoretical perspective of thinking about war as an exercise in bargaining, or more specifically that international relations is in general all about bargaining, and war is part of that bargaining process. This chapter tries to solve perhaps the most central puzzle in the entire study of war: if war is so costly, why do actors sometimes stumble into war?

Chapter 2, "Sex, Gender, and Violence" by Valerie Hudson and Dan Reiter, examines the relationships between the biological category of sex, the social category of gender, and violent behavior. It examines a number of possible causal pathways among sex, gender, and violence, and then discusses several different possible forms of violence caused by sex and/or gender dynamics, including conflict between states, civil wars, terrorism, violence against women and girls, and others.

The chapters in Part II examine the many possible connections between domestic politics and war. Chapter 3, "Domestic Political Institutions and War" by Jessica Weeks, begins Part II's examination of the relationships between politics within states and politics between states. The chapter touches on very well-established debates on the "democratic peace," the proposition that countries with democratic political institutions are significantly less likely to fight each other. But its primary focus is on contemporary ideas and debates, exploring in particular whether variation in authoritarian political institutions, such as whether an autocratic regime is ruled by a personalist dictator, a single political party, or a military junta, affects a state's likelihood of starting and winning interstate wars.

Chapter 4, "Public Opinion and War" by Christopher Gelpi, focuses on domestic politics within democratic settings, and in particular on how public opinion might shape decisions for war. What kinds of factors shape public support for or opposition to war? Does public opinion drive the decisions of elected leaders for war, or are those leaders able to ignore public beliefs? The chapter draws on survey research aimed at answering these questions, as well as ideas from political psychology that seek to understand opinion formation.

Chapter 5, "Leaders and War" by Michael Horowitz, builds on Chapters 3 and 4 by examining national leaders, and in particular whether the background and profile of national leaders might affect the likelihood of war. It also unpacks whether national leaders can act with impunity, or whether they are constrained by the domestic political institutions of their countries, linking with the discussion in Chapter 3. Last, it examines national leader decisionmaking. When leaders must choose whether or not to go to war, are they acting with clear heads and vision, or are their choices clouded by cognitive or other biases?

Chapter 6, "Economics and War" by Paul Poast, pushes the discussion of domestic politics and war in a new direction, examining the connections between economics and war. One important way that wars affect domestic societies is through the economic cost required to pay for them. The average citizen is materially affected: more guns means less butter. How do leaders pay for wars? Are some means of paying for wars easier to sell to skeptical publics than others?

Part III of the book shifts the focus towards conflict within states. Chapter 7, "Civil Wars" by Kathleen Gallagher Cunningham, lays important foundations for thinking about how civil wars break out. The outbreak of civil war means the government has failed in its most central function, the maintenance of order. How does this happen? What factors make the onset of civil war more likely?

Chapter 8, "Terrorism" by Philip Potter, examines the ultimate weapon of the weak, terrorism. It discusses the concept and definition of terrorism, and asks a series of questions, such as: Why do groups turn to terrorist tactics? Why do people join terrorist groups? Are terrorist groups more likely to emerge and thrive in some domestic political environments than others? What policy tools might be useful against terrorism?

Part IV examines two important forms of international diplomacy related to conflict. Chapter 9, "International Alliances" by Dan Reiter, concerns agreements between states to fight or work together when their security is threatened. The course of international diplomatic history has been powerfully shaped by alliances, from the Grand Coalitions that eventually defeated Napoleon Bonaparte in 1815 to the victories of the Allies in the World Wars in the first half of the twentieth century, to the emergence of the North Atlantic Treaty Organization and Warsaw Pact alliances that created the structure of the Cold War, to the enduring relevance of many alliances into the 2020s. The chapter develops several important concepts concerning the form, origins, consequences, and compliance patterns of alliances.

Chapter 10, "Third-Party Peacemaking and Peacekeeping" by Kyle Beardsley, describes how third-party actors such as the United Nations and others sometimes try to end wars both within and between states through mediation. These actors also sometimes try to strengthen postwar peace through efforts such as the dispatch of peacekeeping troops to war-torn regions. The chapter examines the thinking behind these efforts to produce lasting solutions to conflict, and then also the conditions under which they might or might not work.

The fifth and final part examines three specific forms of contemporary conflict. Chapter 11, "Nuclear Weapons" by Michael Horowitz, discusses the most destructive technology of any kind developed by humans. It covers several of the core theoretical ideas about nuclear deterrence developed during the Cold War, concepts which remain important into the 2020s. It also examines contemporary questions of nuclear proliferation, examining the causes and consequences of, and possible policy solutions to, nuclear proliferation.

Chapter 12, "Drone Warfare" by Sarah Kreps, addresses the use of nonpiloted aircraft by states and nonstate actors in the new century. Drones emerged in the 2000s as a critical tool for the United States in its war on terror and insurgency, and since then has come to be used globally. What are the battlefield advantages and disadvantages of drones? Is drone use ethical or legal? Is it popular? Has drone use violated norms of democratic governance? What is the future of drones? This chapter addresses these questions and more.

Chapter 13, "Environment and Conflict" by Cullen Hendrix, unpacks the highly complex relationships between environmental degradation, natural resource depletion, and violent conflict. The chapter presents basic ideas about natural resources, and why they get depleted. It also examines several concepts connecting the depletion of natural resources and environmental degradation to a variety of forms of violent conflict, examining issues such as drought, transboundary water resources, climate change, and others.

Introduction

DAN REITER

This book is about war, and peace. Its goal is to try to broaden your understanding of many forms of violent conflict, as well as approaches to preventing and healing the wounds of war.

War is full of paradoxes, and one of the biggest ones underlies why we wish to understand it. On one hand, we want to learn about war because it is so destructive, killing thousands, millions, tens of millions of people. Any effort to improve the human condition must prioritize reducing war. On the other hand, despite the horrors, we may also find ourselves fascinated by the many puzzles of war, the aspects of war that at first glance cannot be easily explained. If war is so destructive, why can't actors avoid it? Why do some belligerents attack civilians during war, and some do not? Is it the case that the most destructive tools of war ever invented, nuclear weapons, are also among the most useful in preventing wars? And yet, however intense our intellectual curiosity, we cannot wish away the terror of war, its absolute destructiveness. The Confederate States of America rebel general Robert E. Lee captured the flavor of this paradox when he remarked, "It is well that war is so terrible, or else we would love it too much."

This introductory chapter lays out some basic ideas about war, and sets the table for the rest of the book. It seeks to accomplish three goals. First, it discusses the nature of war, and describes what we mean by the concept of war. Second, it considers the possibility that the practice and frequency of war has changed over time. Third, it describes the scientific approach to understanding war and peace.

What Is War?

Some of us might think about war as the clash of national armies. In our mind's eye, we see masses of soldiers wearing their nations' uniforms, marching together, driving tanks, flying jets to fight across a fixed battlefield line. Modern history has been shaped by such wars, including World Wars I and II, the Korean War, the Arab–Israeli Wars, and others. Contemporary policy debates focus on possible future wars between states, such as on the Korean peninsula, between India and Pakistan perhaps over Kashmir, between Russia and Eastern European states, between China and its South China Sea neighbors, and so on.

Though wars between states have been, are, and will continue to be important, this book deliberately employs a broader conception of war, beyond just conflict between states to include other forms of violent conflict. The book looks at civil wars, conflicts between rebel groups and their national governments, and sometimes between subnational ethnic groups. It looks at terrorist campaigns. It also examines some forms of interpersonal violence, especially interpersonal violence against girls and women. It describes war as *violence between people pursued for political or social ends*. This overlaps with the famous proposition by Carl von Clausewitz on interstate war, that war is "politics by other means," that war is a tool in service of political goals (see Chapter 1).

The book uses this broader conception of war for two reasons. First, and most simply, we need to understand the causes and dynamics of wars beyond just wars between states. Civil wars, for example, routinely become slaughterhouses, imposing gigantic human suffering. Since 1945, the Chinese Civil War, the Second Congo War, and the 1980s Afghanistan Civil War each led to the deaths of more than a million people, to say nothing of bloody conflicts such as the Colombian Civil War, the Syrian Civil War, and others. Further, many kinds of violence beyond wars between states have very substantial political or social consequences. The September 11, 2001, terrorist attacks completely changed US foreign policy, and the politics of the Muslim world. The 1930s Spanish Civil War reshaped European politics and set the stage for World War II. Violence against women and girls reinforces male power structures (see Chapter 2). And so on.

Second, these different kinds of wars overlap with each other; it's not accurate to think of wars between states as residing only in one bin, civil wars in another bin, and so on. There is not a clean division between terrorism and civil wars, as some terrorists seek the overthrow of governments, and some rebel groups employ terrorist tactics. Many civil wars, such as the Syrian Civil War and the post-2003 insurgency in Iraq, are international because they draw in other states. Further, sometimes we can improve our understanding by comparing different kinds of wars to each other, focusing on commonalities rather than differences. Resource shortages can cause wars between states, wars between ethnic groups, and violence of men against women. The international community uses peacekeeping and mediation techniques to resolve conflicts both between states and within states. Drone strikes can be used in interstate wars, by governments against terrorist groups, and by terrorist groups against governments. In other words, we are better off keeping our minds open to connections across different kinds of conflict, rather than constructing conceptual walls between categories of conflict.

Plus ça change, plus c'est la même chose: Has War Changed over Time?

War is as old as human society. Some of humanity's oldest surviving art, cave paintings perhaps 30,000 years old, depicts people being pierced with arrows. Cultures from across the world have centered on violent conflict of all kinds, glorifying violence in service of honor, celebrating the annihilation of enemies, and so forth. Certainly, ancient texts from the Judeo-

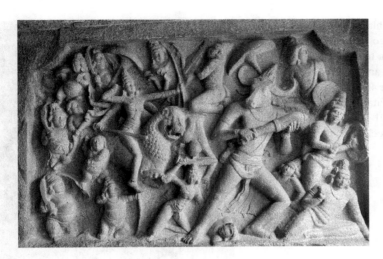

Figure i.1. Female warriors and Hindu goddess Durga slaying buffalo demon, from Indian cave temple. War is inextricably interwoven with the very beginnings of human civilization and culture.
©Hi/iStock / Getty Images Plus via Getty Images.

Christian Old Testament to the Greek *Iliad* to the Hindu *Bhagavad Gita* to the Muslim Koran all describe and often exalt gods, people, nations, and armies killing each other. Figure i.1 shows an ancient carving of an epic Hindu tale found in a cave in India. The carving illustrates a famous legend, when the three most powerful Hindu gods – Shiva, Brahma, and Vishnu – combined their energies to form the goddess Durga, who was tasked with slaying Mahisha, a terrible demon who (here in the form of a buffalo) was terrifying the universe. In contemporary social science, the evolution of political and social phenomena such as ethnic identity and the nation state cannot be separated from war. As one sociologist once wrote of the emergence of modern states in Europe, "War made the state, and the state made war" (Tilly 1975, 45).

We might ask, what has changed about war over time, and what has not changed? On the surface, the means of fighting wars has changed tremendously over the decades, centuries, millennia. Humanity has gone from fighting with swords to muskets to tanks to computers.

But in some ways war has changed perhaps less than you might think. Governments have faced terrorism and insurgency for millennia. The Jewish holiday of Chanukah celebrates the insurgent rebellion of Hebrews against the ancient Greeks. Governments have always sought to acquire economic resources through the use of force, from ancient Rome seizing iron deposits from the barbaric island of Britain, to twenty-first-century China flexing its military muscle to secure the oil and natural gas located under the South China Sea. Sex and gender have been interwoven with war across time, at least as far back as the ancient Greek play *Lysistrata* in which Greek women refused sexual relations with their husbands in an effort to stop the Peloponnesian War between the Greek superpowers of Athens and Sparta. Indeed, this storyline was revived in the 2015 American film *Chi-Raq*, in which women in modern Chicago refuse to have sex with their partners in order to stop raging gang violence there (Figure i.2). Modern leaders still look to the ancient. Members of the Trump White House frequently discussed the ancient Greek historian Thucydides. Modern military academies continue to read *The Art of War*, by the ancient Chinese thinker Sun Tzu. Past wars continue to echo.

And, sometimes contemporary wars can look surprisingly ancient. In some modern genocides such as in 1995 Rwanda, civilians were slaughtered with simple weapons such as knives.

Figure i.2. Poster for 2015 film *Chi-Raq*. In this Spike Lee film, women in Chicago refuse to have sex with their partners in an attempt to stop the gang violence there, echoing a plot from an ancient Greek play. In the 2010s there were about 400 murders per year in Chicago, a higher annual fatality rate than US forces experienced during the 2001–2021 Afghanistan War. TCD/Prod.DB / Alamy Stock Photo.

When fighting flared up between China and India in 2021, by common agreement troops from the two sides fought without weapons in hand-to-hand combat, to limit escalation risks. And, very sadly, the horrifying mechanics of sexual assault have changed very little over time, if at all.

Consider the February 2022 Russian invasion of Ukraine. The prospect of one country openly and without provocation invading another country seemed like a return to a pattern of international relations going back decades, centuries, millennia. And yet there were of course aspects of this war that distinguished it from earlier interstate wars. Russian military attacks on Ukrainian territory were preceded by cyberattacks on Ukrainian targets. Satellites and other sources of intelligence made the Russian military buildup on the Ukrainian border so transparent that US President Joe Biden predicted the invasion days before it occurred, and satellite photos of the Russian buildup were publicly available online. Ukrainian traffic jams displayed on Google Maps marked the advance of Russian tanks.

Let's ask a different question: Has the *frequency* of war changed over time? There was great hope in 1989 that the end of the Cold War might also mark the "End of History," and a global embrace of peace, democracy, and market capitalism. Unfortunately, these hopes were quickly dashed by the 1991 Gulf War, the early 1990s wars in the former Yugoslavia, the 1999 Kargil and Kosovo Wars, the 2001 Afghanistan War, the 2003 Iraq War, the 2020 Nagorno-Karabakh War between Azerbaijan and Armenia, and other conflicts.

But maybe there are narrower patterns to be seen, if we look closer. Perhaps it might be too optimistic to forecast a long-term decline in civil wars, insurgency, or terrorism, or even some kinds of conventional wars. But there might be a reduction, though not elimination, of high intensity wars between major powers. The last open conflict between major powers was the Korean War (the US and China), and since then the major powers have avoided overt war with each other, though occasionally fighting each other secretly, as occurred between Chinese and US forces in the Vietnam War. Some have described the decades of quasi-peace between the major powers as the "Long Peace," arguably the longest stretch of peace between major powers for centuries. There are several arguments as to why the likelihood of major power wars may have declined, many of which are described in this book, including that nuclear-armed states avoid conflict with each other, higher levels of trade (as between the US and China) reduce conflict, the greater transparency of the satellite/internet/social media era reduces potential war-causing uncertainty, and others.

But even if trends seem to be moving in the right direction, we should be careful about concluding that even major power war has been eliminated. In 1910, Norman Angell published a book called *The Great Illusion*, in which he forecast that war between the major powers would be so economically costly that major power war was very unlikely, and if it did break out, it would end quickly. Four years later, Angell sadly watched the outbreak of World War I, a conflict that tore Europe to pieces over four long years and became the deadliest war yet in the history of humanity.

What Is the Scientific Approach to Studying War?

You may have been assigned this text for a political science class. Perhaps you have wondered, what's so scientific about politics? Where are the Bunsen burners, the microscopes, or the petri dishes?

This book takes a scientific approach to studying war. A scientific approach means basically three things:

- Asking general rather than specific questions
- Developing theories
- Testing theories on data

What does each of these three parts mean? First, the scientific approach means focusing on general rather than specific questions. Though a historian might ask the more specific question, "What were the causes of World War I?" a political scientist asks the more general question, "What are the causes of war?" It's not that political scientists are not also interested in specific historical and policy questions, such as what were the causes of the 1995 Rwanda genocide or what is the likelihood of a war between the US and China in the twenty-first century. The political science view is that the best way to get a handle on specific questions such as these is to ask and answer general questions, just as the best way to prevent your grandmother from getting diabetes is to understand the causes of diabetes in general.

Each chapter in this book asks and tries to answer a different set of general questions about war. These include questions such as: If two states sometimes disagree, such as on where to place a national border, why do they sometimes resort to the use of force? Are men on average more violent than women? Do nuclear weapons help prevent war? What kinds of wars, if any, do citizens tend to support? How can environmental threats make violent conflict more likely? Can international organizations such as the United Nations help build peace after civil wars? What kinds of dictatorships are prone to war, and why? How do states pay for their wars? Do drone strikes help reduce militant violence? Can international alliances help keep the peace? We imagine that you will find at least some of these questions intriguing, if not fascinating.

The second element of the scientific approach is the development of theory. Theories are clusters of ideas that together provide a general description of how some element of the natural or human world works. In the natural world, the theory of evolution proposes that organisms ill-suited to survive their environments die off and are replaced by organisms that are fitter and more likely to survive. The Freudian theory of psychology assumes that the human psyche contains three central elements, the id, the ego, and the superego. And so on.

Theories of war are clusters of assumptions mostly about human behavior and society, trying to understand the causes, prosecution, and/or consequences of war. Some theories of war describe people as "rational" actors, meaning they assess the costs and benefits of different actions, account for available information without cognitive bias, and then act so as to best advance their goals. Some theories of war try to understand strategic interactions between actors, describing how actors make choices in anticipation of how other actors will react or are behaving. Other theories draw on different ideas, describing possible biological impulses to aggression, outlining social forces such as nationalism pushing people to engage in violence, and others. What ties all of these theories together is that they are general, trying to describe a class of events or behavior rather than something specific.

The third element of the scientific approach is testing theories with data. The basic premise is that we cannot be confident of any theory or idea about the way the world works unless we test it with data. Part of the reason is that sometimes data shows that ideas that sound pretty plausible are actually incorrect. For example, maybe you drink a lot of coffee (is that your third coffee of the day on your desk right now?), and you might fret that drinking too much coffee might be bad for you. It turns out that coffee consumption actually has health benefits, and most of us can safely drink up to five or more cups of coffee per day without risks to our health. So, go ahead and enjoy that third latté!

How do we go about testing theories with data? We first draw hypotheses from theory. The theory is the general picture of the way the world works, and the hypothesis is the narrower prediction drawn from the theory. For example, if our general theory is that genes determine personal characteristics, a hypothesis might be that a human is more likely to be taller if her parents are taller.

What is the structure of a hypothesis? A hypothesis is an if–then proposition that describes a relationship between phenomena called variables, the cause being the independent variable and the effect being the dependent variable. For example, for the hypothesis, "People who smoke are more likely to experience lung cancer," smoking is the independent variable (the cause), and lung cancer is the dependent variable (the effect). A typical international relations hypothesis might be, "Democracies fight fewer wars than dictatorships," the independent variable being type of political system (democracy or dictatorship), the dependent variable being fighting wars.

Hypotheses need to be falsifiable, meaning that it must be possible to collect data that would disprove the hypotheses. For example, if our data showed that democracies were as likely to fight wars as compared with dictatorships, then this would falsify the democracy/war hypothesis above. Non-falsifiable hypotheses are those which are difficult or impossible to falsify. For example, the hypothesis, "Higher levels of trade might or might not strengthen peace between states" is impossible to falsify, because whatever data one collects, whether trading states fight or do not fight, could be used to support the hypothesis.

After falsifiable hypotheses are crafted, the next task is to collect data to test the hypotheses. We collect data on the independent and dependent variables to see if changes in the independent variable correlate with changes in the dependent variable. So, for the democracy–war hypothesis, we might collect data on all countries in the world, assessing which countries are democracies and which are not, and then also which countries are at war and which are not, aiming to see whether democracies tend to be more peaceful than dictatorships. If we have data on enough cases, then we can use statistical methods to test our hypotheses, to see if we can be confident that the independent variables are significantly correlated with the dependent variables.

Another approach is to provide a deeper dive into a smaller number of cases. Instead of collecting a small amount of information on each of a larger number of cases, we could collect a larger amount of information on each of a smaller number of cases. Using that larger amount of information, we can more directly examine what actually happened inside of the historical episode, whether for example the relevant decision-makers were thinking about their options in the manner described by the theory. Our theory might forecast that drought makes civil war more likely, and a deep case study of the Syrian Civil War (see Chapter 13) will help us understand whether the Syrian drought actually caused the Syrian Civil War.

There are many sources of data we can use. We might of course look at history books and even primary sources like archival records to unpack what actually happened in historical episodes like the 1962 Cuban Missile Crisis. Survey data helps us answer questions such as: What factors might cause the public to be more likely to support the use of force (see Chapter 5)? The Internet and social media offer tremendous data opportunities. If we propose that external threats cause citizens to feel more patriotic, then we might see if people make more patriotic social media posts when their country is at war. Experiments of different kinds offer opportunities to collect data. If the hormone testosterone is proposed to cause aggressive behavior, then we can see if injecting subjects with testosterone causes them to be more aggressive (see Chapter 2). If we think that visual images such as memes or political advertisements affect public attitudes, we can see if exposing subjects to patriotic images causes them to have more hostile attitudes towards foreigners. We might also engage in "field experiments" out in the real world, for example randomly assigning peacekeepers to some areas of a post-conflict country but not others, to see if peacekeepers help maintain peace in areas to which they are deployed.

One task of all data is to try to find out if variation in the independent variable is actually *causing* variation in the dependent variable. The trap we wish to avoid is observing correlation between two variables, that one variable goes up when the other goes up, and falsely inferring that movement in one is actually causing movement in the other. If two variables are moving together but one is not causing the other to move, this is called spurious correlation. For example, we might observe that people who eat ice cream are more likely to experience heat stroke, so there is a correlation between ice cream consumption and heat stroke. But the correlation is likely spurious, as ice cream consumption is not causing heat stroke, but hot temperatures are likely causing both ice cream consumption and heat strokes. Figuring out whether correlations are spurious is important. For example, if you were a policymaker and you wanted to reduce heat stroke, you would want to know if banning ice cream would reduce heat stroke (if the ice cream was actually causing heat stroke), or not (if the observed correlation was spurious).

The good news is that there are different ways of figuring out whether or not a correlation is causal or spurious. One general approach is to collect data on other possible explanations. So, in our ice cream example, we might also collect data on air temperature, assessing whether heat rather than ice cream is causing heat stroke. Data on other possible explanations of the dependent variable are sometimes called "control variables." Another angle is to conduct an experiment, to assign randomly which subjects get the "treatment." In our ice cream example, it would mean randomly choosing who gets to eat ice cream and who does not, across hot and cold days. That kind of random assignment is often used in studies on drug effectiveness, with half the subjects being given the drug in question, and the other half being given a placebo drug.

This book will expose you to different kinds of data, and different kinds of studies. Each chapter will provide a case study of a single episode that delves deeply into details to examine whether or not the dynamics described in the theory did actually occur. Each chapter will also provide a brief summary of a quantitative study of one of the ideas presented in the chapter. The idea is to give you an idea of what that kind of research looks like, even if you have never taken a course in statistics, or maybe even just don't like math much at all.

A Final Note

We'd like to leave you with one final thought. An ancient Roman once declared, "If you want peace, prepare for war." Maybe. But if there is one central idea across the entire book, it would be a slight revision of that ancient aphorism. This book declares: "If you want peace, understand war."

KEY TERMS

Theory
Hypothesis
Independent variable
Dependent variable

Falsifiability
Spurious correlation
Causal correlation
Control variables

ADDITIONAL READING

Braumoeller, B. F. (2019). *Only the Dead: The Persistence of War in the Modern Age*. Oxford: Oxford University Press.
Fukuyama, F. (1992). *The End of History and the Last Man*. New York: Free Press.
Pinker, S. (2012). *The Better Angels of Our Nature*, New York: Penguin.

REFERENCES

Tilly, C. (1975). Reflections on the history of European state-making. In C. Tilly (ed.). *The Formation of National States in Western Europe*. Princeton: Princeton University Press.

Part I

Broad Perspectives

1   Bargaining and War

DAN REITER

Introduction

What is war? Some view it as a scourge on humanity, one of the many curses we must endure along with poverty, disease, crime, and starvation. Others see it as an inevitable expression of human nature. Biology, original sin, or patriarchy condemn us to violence.

An alternative perspective is that war is fundamentally political. As the nineteenth-century Prussian general Carl von Clausewitz put it, war is politics by other means. Now, Clausewitz was not glibly equating fighting war with more benign activities like giving speeches or running campaign ads. Rather, he meant that war is a means to accomplish political goals like capturing territory. War, both between states and within states, is part of politics, and specifically it is a way of resolving political disputes.

This chapter frames the insight that war is political by describing war as part of a **bargaining** process, envisioning actors like states or rebel groups as unitary and rational (Schelling 1960) This may seem like a strange approach, as we usually think about bargaining in economic contexts, like a buyer and a seller bargaining over the price of a used car, or a labor union and corporate management bargaining over workers' wages. Bargaining is also an important part of international relations, as states bargain over the terms of treaties, where to place borders, and so forth. This chapter describes war as part of the bargaining process in two ways. First, war occurs when peacetime bargaining fails, when actors such as states or opposition groups fail to come to a peaceful agreement settling a political dispute. Second, bargaining happens during wartime, and wars end when the two sides reach a settlement each prefers to continuing to fight.

This chapter will use the bargaining perspective to answer some of the most important questions about war, namely: If war is so costly, why does it ever happen? Why do some wars drag on longer than others? Why do some wars end in total victory for one side, and others do not, ending in more limited victory?

What Do States Fight Over?

International relations are fundamentally about disagreements between actors. The Israeli government wishes to control all of Jerusalem, and the Palestinian Authority wishes to control at least East Jerusalem, if not all of Jerusalem. North Korea wishes to possess nuclear weapons, and most of the rest of the world wishes it does not. Exporter nations sometimes want to price their goods at artificially low levels in import markets, and importer nations oppose such practices. Countries like Norway and Germany desire to combat climate change more aggressively, and the United States, or at least some groups in the United States, wishes to combat climate change less aggressively.

All of these disputes have something in common: the actors involved cannot all get their way. Israel cannot control all of Jerusalem at the same time that the Palestinian Authority controls half of Jerusalem. North Korea cannot both have and not have nuclear weapons. China cannot sell its solar panels in the United States both at an artificially low price and at a higher price that reflects market forces. That is, these disputes are over what we might call **scarce goods**. They are goods because they are items that actors desire, and they are "scarce" in the sense that everyone cannot simultaneously get all that they wish.

When two sides dispute how to divide up a scarce good, they often first try to settle on a mutually agreeable division of the disputed scarce good. Such deals are often difficult to strike, for the simple reason that the more one side gets, the less the other side gets. The more of Jerusalem that Israel controls, the less of it that the Palestinian Authority controls. Map 1.1 is a map of another territorial conflict, the dispute between India and Pakistan over control of Kashmir, a region that the two states have been in conflict over since they became independent in 1947. Each side currently controls only a portion of the region, but both sides demand control over the entire region.

One way to represent how two adversaries negotiate over a disputed good is to use a number line. The number line represents all the possible ways that the disputed good can be divided up. Figure 1.1 is a number line describing all the possible ways that Kashmir could be divided up between India and Pakistan. The line is scaled from 0 to 100. So, on the left side of the line, the number 0 indicates that Pakistan controls none of Kashmir and India controls 100 percent of it, and on the right side of the line, the number 100 indicates that Pakistan controls 100 percent of Kashmir and India controls none of it.

For convenience, we label the 0 point "India's Ideal Point" and the 100 point "Pakistan's Ideal Point," the numbers indicating the percentage of Kashmir Pakistan would receive. (Ideally, India would like Pakistan to have 0, and Pakistan would like to have 100.) Generally, an actor's **ideal point** is its optimal possible division of the good, among all of the possible divisions. So, 0 is India's ideal point because at the 0 point Pakistan gets 0 percent of Kashmir, and India gets 100 percent. Note also that if you compare possible settlements along the number line, India prefers settlements that are closer to its ideal point; that is, India would prefer a "20" settlement (Pakistan gets 20, India gets 80) to a "50" settlement (each side gets 50). Accordingly, Pakistan prefers settlements closer to its ideal point of 100.

Two sides negotiate over a disputed good by exchanging offers on how to split the disputed good. India might offer a 50–50 split of Kashmir, and Pakistan might counter by offering a 60–40 split, providing Pakistan with 60 percent of the territory and India with 40 percent. As

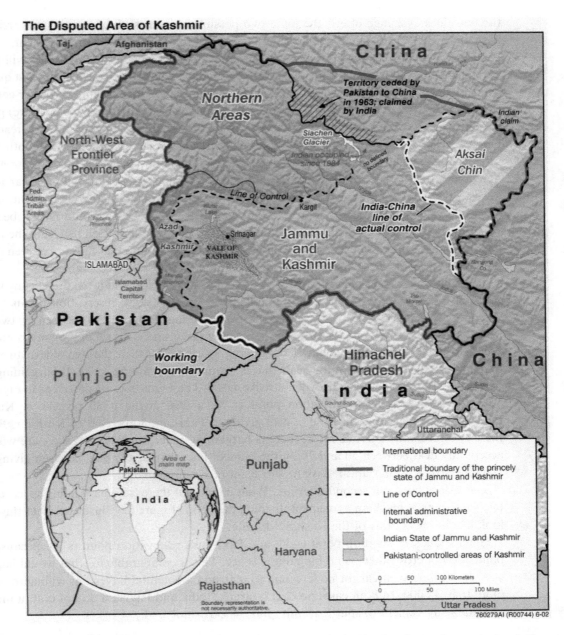

Map 1.1. India and Pakistan bargaining and fighting over Kashmir. For decades, each country has had varying degrees of control of the areas of Kashmir (sometimes called Jammu and Kashmir), and either side could go to war to try to gain more or all of Kashmir. Library of Congress, Geography and Map Division.

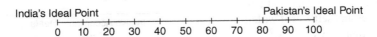

Figure 1.1. The Kashmir dispute, on a number line. The numbers on the number line represent the percentage of Kashmir owned by Pakistan.

the two sides exchange offers, there are two possible outcomes: the two sides can arrive at a bargain to split the disputed good, or they might fail to arrive at such an agreement.

Next, we need to ask two questions: How can we predict whether the two sides will reach a bargain? And what happens if the two sides do not reach a bargain? Consider the first question. Remember that as an offer gets farther away from one side's ideal point, that offer gets to be less and less attractive to that side. A side can identify the worst (from its perspective) possible bargain that it would be willing to accept compared with the outcome of not reaching a bargain. That worst possible bargain is called that side's **reservation point**. If the other side's offer is less attractive than the first side's reservation point, then the first side prefers the outcome of no bargain and rejects the offer. For example, if you are selling a car and the lowest price you would be willing to accept for the car is $3,000, then your reservation point would be $3,000. If someone offered to buy the car for $2,999, you would refuse, because if your choice is to sell the car for $2,999 or not sell it, you would not sell it. Using the number line, we can say that a side would be willing to accept any bargain that falls in between its ideal point (best possible deal) and its reservation point (worst possible acceptable deal).

The other side also has its reservation point and its ideal point, and it too prefers any bargain between those two points. A bargain is possible if the two sides' reservation points "cross," meaning that the two ranges of acceptable bargains overlap. That overlap between the two sides' range of acceptable bargains is called the **bargaining space**, and is the set of bargains both would prefer to reaching no agreement. If bargaining space exists, then the two sides can reach a bargain, which will be one of the deals that is within the bargaining space. If bargaining space does not exist, then the two sides will not strike a deal. These concepts are described in Figure 1.2.

In Figure 1.2, India's reservation point is 70, a deal giving it 30 percent of Kashmir. Pakistan's reservation point is 30, a deal giving it, Pakistan, 30 percent of Kashmir. Because these two reservation points cross, there is bargaining space, and the two sides are willing to accept any deal between 30 and 70 on the number line, that is, any deal between giving India 70 percent of Kashmir and Pakistan 70 percent of Kashmir.

This brings us to our second question: What happens if there is no bargaining space, and the two sides cannot reach an agreement dividing the good? Figure 1.3 illustrates what this would look like in the context of the Kashmir dispute.

Here, India's reservation point is 30, and Pakistan's reservation point is 70. Because these points do not cross, there is no bargaining space. This is comparable to what would happen if you were selling your car for no less than $3,000, and a potential buyer was willing to offer no more than $2,000. In both cases no deal is struck. India and Pakistan do not craft a mutually acceptable agreement to split Kashmir, and the car is not sold.

Figure 1.2. Kashmir number line with bargaining space. Bargaining space is the space between the two sides' reservation points, and both sides prefer any settlement within that bargaining space rather than war.

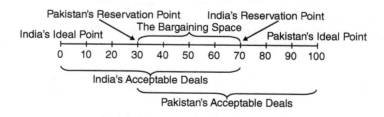

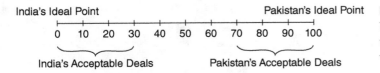

Figure 1.3. Kashmir number line without bargaining space. Without bargaining space, there is no possible settlement that both sides would prefer to going to war.

In general, when two sides fail to reach a deal dividing the scarce good, they instead reach a **reversion outcome**. Now, in many economic interactions, the reversion outcome is simply the lack of a sale, like the seller keeping her car. In international relations, the reversion outcome can mean the endurance of the status quo. When talks between Israel and the Palestinian Authority over the status of Jerusalem break down (or fail to take place), the reversion outcome is the status quo, Israeli control of all of Jerusalem. In the Kashmir conflict, the breakdown of talks means the persistence of the Line of Control, the de facto border between Indian-controlled and Pakistani-controlled Kashmir (see Map 1.1).

However, the reversion outcome can mean something worse than the persistence of the status quo. It can mean war, as following the breakdown of negotiations to divide a scarce good, each side has the option of starting a war. War is potentially attractive because it might provide an opportunity to achieve a preferable division of the good. Let's say, for example, that an adversary is offering a country a 50–50 split of the good. However, the country being offered the 50–50 split believes that if it goes to war, then at the end of the war it will control 75 percent of the good. Or, it has a 75 percent chance of controlling all of the good (which is comparable to having a 100 percent chance of controlling 75 percent of the good). Under these circumstances, war looks attractive, as a 75–25 split is better than a 50–50 split.

This dynamic occurred in the 1980s regarding the Falkland Islands (also known as the Malvinas), a remote group of islands in the South Atlantic (see Map 1.2). Though the United Kingdom (UK) controlled the Falklands, Argentina also claimed ownership. In the early 1980s, the UK refused to hand the islands over to Argentina. In 1982, in response to negotiation failure, Argentina invaded the Falklands, hoping to achieve a division of the good (Argentine control of the Falklands) superior to either the reversion outcome of the status quo (British control of the Falklands) or any of the peacetime offers the UK had been making. As it happened, Argentina lost the war, and Britain retained control of the Falklands.

This asks the question: Why don't states go to war all the time to get (more of) what they want? One answer is that fighting war is costly, in blood and money. Both sides in a war lose the lives of their soldiers and spend money on military equipment. Importantly, victory does not allow a side to escape paying these costs. For example, though Germany enjoyed a tremendously lopsided victory when it conquered Poland in 1939, it still suffered costs, including some 16,000 German soldiers killed. So, any actor considering starting a war to get what it wants must weigh the costs of fighting against the benefits it would expect to gather from winning the war.

This then presents another puzzle. To demonstrate, let's return to the Kashmir example. Imagine that India and Pakistan both knew that if they went to war, the war would end with India controlling 60 percent of Kashmir, and both sides would suffer the painful human and financial costs of fighting (in a 1965 war over Kashmir, for example, India experienced about 3,700 killed, and Pakistan suffered perhaps 1,500 killed). Under these circumstances, India and

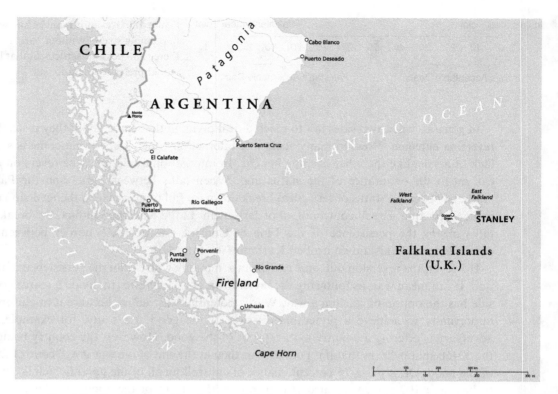

Map 1.2. The Falklands War between Britain and Argentina. The islands, called the Malvinas by Argentina, are in the South Atlantic Ocean, off the coast of Argentina, and far from Britain. ©PeterHermesFurian/iStock / Getty Images Plus/Getty Images.

Pakistan could either: go to war and receive the 60/40 split of Kashmir; or strike a peaceful, prewar bargain establishing a 60/40 split, knowing that that is what would happen anyway if they fought. Given that in both circumstances the Kashmir split is the same but the war choice would mean human and financial costs for both sides, why don't the two sides choose the peaceful 60/40 split? Both sides would benefit from choosing a peaceful 60/40 deal as compared with war, as the peace deal offers the same fraction of Kashmir as each would get if war occurred, but the peace deal enables both to avoid the human and financial costs of war.

Actors sometimes avoid war by agreeing to divide a good based on what would occur if war were fought. For example, in April 1940, Nazi Germany was poised to invade its much smaller northern neighbor, Denmark. Both Germany and Denmark agreed on two things: that in a war, Germany would easily conquer Denmark, and that war would impose costs on both sides. Recognizing its grim and unavoidable fate, Denmark agreed to surrender its sovereignty to German occupation peacefully, providing each side the same political outcome that would have occurred if war had broken out (German conquest of Denmark), but enabling each side to avoid the costs of fighting.

The Denmark example suggests a larger puzzle. Why don't actors do this all the time, agree to split the scarce good peacefully in the manner that would have occurred if war had broken out? In short, *why does war ever happen?* Three potential answers to this question are lack of information, the incredibility of actors' commitments to their agreements, and issue indivisibility (Fearon 1995).

Why States Fight: Lack of Information

The puzzle is: If both sides agree on what would happen if war were to occur, then war should never occur, and yet, war does sometimes happen. How can we solve this puzzle, how can we explain the occurrence of war?

One solution is to challenge the puzzle's assumption that both sides agree on what would happen if war did break out. It seems reasonable to think that this assumption might not be valid, as global politics are frequently clouded by uncertainty, secrecy, and misinformation. Foreign policy is often conducted in shadows and darkness, with leaders and entire societies making only rough guesses as to the consequences of different policy choices. Another way to frame it is that one or both might lack the information, perhaps the raw intelligence data, needed to assess accurately who would win a potential war. In such a case, the two sides might disagree as to what would happen if war were to break out. Perhaps each side thinks it would win, a condition we might describe as mutual optimism.

How might disagreement about how a war would unfold make the outbreak of war more likely? We can frame the costs and benefits of war in terms of money. Imagine that two sides are in dispute over a single American dollar. The two sides agree that if they fought, the outcome would provide 63 cents to the first side and 37 cents to the other side. (Analogously, if it was a dispute over territory, both agree that the war would end with one side controlling 63 percent of the disputed territory.) We will also assume that the costs of fighting are strictly financial, costing each side 5 cents. So, if war occurs, the first side will gain a total of 58 cents (63 − 5 = 58), and the other side will gain a total of 32 cents (37 − 5 = 32). Each side has incentive to settle peacefully on a 63–37 split of the dollar through peaceful negotiations, rather than fight a war and get a 58–32 split.

But what if the two sides disagree about what might happen? For example, what if the first side thinks the outcome will be a 63–37 split, but the other side thinks that the outcome will be a 50–50 split? In this case, the first side offers a 63–37 split to the second side, but the second side believes that fighting a war would provide a return of 45 cents (50 − 5 cent cost for fighting). The second side prefers the expected war payoff of 45 to the first side's offer of 37, so it rejects the first side's offer of 37, and war becomes possible.

If the two sides disagree about how a war would turn out, two related factors would affect the likelihood of war erupting: how much the two sides disagree about the likely war outcome, and the expected costs of war. As the disagreement about the likely war outcome decreases, war becomes less likely. To get a sense of this dynamic, imagine that the difference of opinion was smaller, such as one side expecting an outcome of 63–37 and the other side expecting an outcome of 60–40. Now, the second side faces the following choice: accept the first side's offer of 37, or reject that offer and go to war, providing a payoff of 35 (40 − 5 = 35). Here, even though the two sides disagree on the likely outcome of war, the disagreement is sufficiently small such that there remains a peaceful split of the good both sides prefer to war. (In particular, the second side prefers an offer of 37 to the expected war outcome payoff of 35.) Bargaining space exists, and the two sides can avoid war.

Regarding costs, as the expected costs of war increase, the likelihood of war goes down. Regarding the 63–37 example, consider what would happen if the cost of war was 20 cents rather than 5 cents. In this case, even if the two sides still disagreed about the likely outcome of war (the first state expects a 63–37 outcome, and the second state expects a 50–50 outcome), the second state will take the first state's offer of 37 rather than go to war, because now its expected payoff from war is 30 ($50 - 20 = 30$), and it prefers 37 to 30. The deep irony is that the more awful (and, therefore, costly) war becomes, the easier it is to maintain peace. This is the fundamental logic behind the idea that nuclear weapons can bolster peace through mutual assured destruction. Because the gigantically high costs of fighting a nuclear war dwarf any benefits a state could hope to gain, states become very unwilling to start wars. As Winston Churchill put it in 1955, nuclear weapons mean that "safety will be the sturdy child of terror, and survival the twin brother of annihilation" (Churchill 1955).

Let's explore more deeply exactly why two sides might disagree about the likely outcome of a war. Consider these five different sources of disagreements that could make war more likely: military capabilities, military strategy, military technology, resolve, and third-party intervention.

Military Capabilities

An important part of determining who wins wars pertains to sizes of military forces, how many tanks, soldiers, planes, and so forth each side has, as well as less material factors contributing to military power like morale and quality of training. If the two sides disagree about the balance of capabilities of the two sides, they are likely to disagree about a war's likely outcome, eliminating bargaining space and making war more likely (Reed 2003).

This dynamic can help explain Nazi Germany's ultimately doomed June 1941 decision to invade the Soviet Union. The German high command expected rapid victory, but soon discovered that it had underestimated the size of the Soviet Red Army. Adolf Hitler himself remarked to one of his generals that August, "If I had known that the figures for Russian tank strength which you gave in your book were in fact the true ones, I would not – I believe – ever have started this war" (quoted in Guderian 1952, 190). That is, if Hitler had had an accurate sense of Soviet military capabilities, he would not have ordered the invasion.

Military Strategy

The outcomes of wars are determined not just by the sizes of armies, but also by belligerents' military strategies, the plans for actually using armies in battle. A state can substantially improve its chances for winning if it selects the right military strategy, even if it does not have a larger army or better military technology. If one side has a military strategy that gives it a better chance of winning the war, its confidence in victory may push it to demand more of the disputed good. However, because the other side is unaware of the first side's military strategy, it will view the first side's demand as unacceptable. The lack of bargaining space creates the conditions for war.

Military strategy played a tremendously important role in the German decision to invade France in May 1940. In spring 1940, Germany's army was very roughly the same size as the British, Belgian, and French forces arrayed against it in the West. Both sides had advanced aircraft, tanks, and other weaponry. Given this balance, who would win? Britain and France believed they could blunt a German attack on Belgium and France, as occurred during World War I some twenty-five years earlier. However, unbeknownst to the Allies, Germany had developed a secret military strategy that promised rapid victory, luring Anglo-French forces into northern Belgium while the bulk of German forces would crash through the Ardennes forest in Luxembourg and southern Belgium, en route to Paris. Britain and France refused to make concessions to Hitler, and Germany attacked on May 10, executing its strategy successfully and shocking the world by conquering France in six weeks.

Military Technology

Advanced military technology can sometimes help a belligerent fight more effectively. However, two sides can disagree about how military technology might affect fighting power, especially if the technology is untested or if one state is keeping its technology secret. That is, one side might be confident of victory because of its technology, but the other side views the first side's confidence as misplaced because it is unaware of or dismisses the significance of the technology. With disagreement over who would win a war, the two sides' reservation points might not overlap, no bargaining space appears, and war becomes possible.

Consider the 1991 Gulf War. Iraqi leader Saddam Hussein thought his army could raise the costs of war to a sufficiently high level through massive, bloody conventional battles that the casualty-sensitive United States might be deterred from trying to liberate Kuwait by force. Saddam promised the United States that in the event of war it would face the "mother of all battles," and he bluntly told an American diplomat early in the crisis, "Yours is a society which cannot accept ten thousand dead in one battle" (quoted in Stein 1992, 175). However, along with other factors, American military technological advantages such as air superiority and superior tank firing ranges encouraged American decisionmakers to come to a more optimistic assessment of their abilities to defeat Iraqi forces with limited casualties, leading them to go to war. American decisionmakers proved correct, and the United States and its coalition partners defeated an Iraqi force of 300,000 troops in 100 hours, suffering less than 150 combat fatalities.

Resolve

Some wars are less about the conquest of territory and more about inflicting human and economic costs on the other side. Each side in such a war focuses on killing the other side's soldiers and civilians and perhaps destroying its economy, and the war ends when one side has suffered enough and makes concessions sufficient to end the war. Such conflicts are sometimes called "wars of attrition." A key factor determining who will win a war of attrition is each side's **resolve**, its willingness to absorb costs in the pursuit of victory. Other things being equal, the side with the higher resolve will win, as it will be able to hold out longer than the less resolved side.

Now, if the two sides understood clearly which side had higher resolve, they would know more about who would win a war. Perhaps both sides know that once war started, the less resolved side would be first to be ready to make concessions to end the war. Each side would then have an incentive to divide peacefully the scarce good to reflect the outcome that would have occurred if they had fought, enabling each to avoid paying the costs of fighting.

However, sometimes two sides disagree about each other's resolve, about which side would be the first to lose its will to continue fighting and make concessions aimed at ending the war.

Figure 1.4. Vietnam War Memorial in Washington, DC. It is inscribed with the names of the more than 50,000 Americans who died in the war. Its solemnity expresses the pain the American nation feels at these deaths from the war. ©vmbfoto/iStock Editorial/Getty Images.

These conditions mean that the two sides would disagree about the likely outcome of war, preventing the appearance of bargaining space and making war more likely.

The Vietnam War demonstrated this dynamic in bloody fashion. The United States wanted North Vietnam to recognize and leave alone an independent, non-Communist South Vietnam, and North Vietnam wanted to spread Communism to South Vietnam and to fold South Vietnam in to a single Vietnamese state. The military fundamentals of this conflict were, in important respects, about mass killing. The US strategy was to kill enough Viet Cong insurgents, North Vietnamese soldiers, and North Vietnamese civilians (through strategic bombing) to push North Vietnam to its breaking point, to get it to make concessions at the negotiating table. Conversely, the North Vietnamese strategy was to kill enough American soldiers to cause the American public to tire of the war and to withdraw, which would then leave South Vietnam vulnerable to conquest; the Vietnam War Memorial in Washington, DC (see Figure 1.4) lists the names of 58,318 Americans who died in the Vietnam War. War occurred because the two sides disagreed about which side would be the first to give in, the first to make concessions in an effort to stop the killing. The USA thought North Vietnam would be the first to "break," and North Vietnam thought the USA would submit first.

The evolution of the war revealed that the United States vastly underestimated North Vietnamese resolve, as North Vietnam proved willing to absorb titanic levels of casualties in its mission to spread Communism to South Vietnam. As former Secretary of State Dean Rusk commented towards the end of the war in 1971, "I personally underestimated the resistance and the determination of the North Vietnamese. They've taken over 700,000 killed which in relation to population is almost the equivalent of – what? Ten million Americans? And they continue to come" (quoted in Reiter 2009, 13). North Vietnam accurately assessed that American resolve was lower than its own resolve. The American population eventually tired of the war, making possible a peace deal in January 1973. That deal involved the withdrawal of US forces from South Vietnam, allowing North Vietnam in April 1975 to conquer South Vietnam.

Third-Party Intervention

Sometimes a war's outcome can be determined if a third party enters the conflict, helping one side against the other. However, before the war begins, the two sides might disagree about the likelihood of this third party joining the war, with perhaps one side being more confident that the third party will enter the war on its behalf, the other side being more confident that the third party will remain neutral. Diverging beliefs about the likely actions of a third party in the event of war can lead the sides to disagree about who would win a war, as the first side thinks it will win because the third party will provide assistance during war, and the second side thinks it will win because the third party will remain neutral. These diverging assessments can prevent the emergence of bargaining space, making war more likely.

This process was demonstrated in the 1999 conflict between the North Atlantic Treaty Organization (NATO) and Serbia. The Serb government had been mistreating a small ethnic group residing within its borders in the south of Serbia, the ethnic Albanian Kosovars. NATO demanded that the oppression cease. Though NATO was much stronger than Serbia, the Serb government hoped that if war broke out, Russia would come to its aid, thereby balancing out NATO's military power, enabling it to win. NATO was more confident it could keep Russia out of the conflict. In early 1999, Serbia refused to concede to NATO's demands for better treatment of the Kosovars, and war broke out in March. A few weeks into the war, as it became clearer to Serbia that Russia would not enter the war, Serbia made the concessions NATO had demanded, and the war ended. Put differently, the war began because the two sides disagreed about whether or not Russia would intervene, and once both sides agreed that Russia was unlikely to do so, Serbia offered concessions, bargaining space appeared, and the war ended.

Why Not Share Information?

We have now considered five areas of possible disagreement – meaning, the two sides having different information – about the likely outcome of a possible war: balance of capabilities; strategy; technology; resolve; and third-party intervention. When two sides disagree about at least one of the above five areas, the outbreak of war becomes more likely. However, remember that war is costly for all who fight, and both sides disputing a scarce good would be better off if they could avoid war and divide the good according to how it would have unfolded had they fought. This begs a question: if there is disagreement about who would win a war, and war is costly, why don't the two sides just reveal all of their information to each other? Doing so would reduce disagreement about who would win a hypothetical war between them, which would then allow the two sides to sign a war-avoiding peace deal, leaving both sides better off. So why not do it?

There are two answers to this question. First, a state sometimes has incentives *not* to reveal information about its military power, especially regarding strategy and technology. The reason is straightforward: military strategy and technology often provide the biggest advantage if they are kept secret until war breaks out. Regarding military strategies, nearly all strategies have a best counterstrategy, and if one side knows the other side's strategy, it can implement the optimal counterstrategy, nullifying the other side's strategic advantage. Germany's 1940 invasion plan against France would have been easily thwarted if the Allies had known the German strategy and positioned their forces in the Ardennes to best counter the German attack. There are also ways to blunt superior military technology, if one side recognizes the other side's technology. During the October 1973 War, for example, Egypt enjoyed initial combat successes against Israel because of secret, Soviet-supplied surface-to-air missiles (SAMs). There are useful countermeasures to blunt the effectiveness of SAMs, and had Israel implemented these countermeasures at the outset of the war, Egypt would not have been able to experience its early successes. These secrecy incentives present a paradox: states would like to reveal the power provided by factors like strategy and technology to push their adversaries to make deep concessions, but the very act of revealing this power actually *reduces* that power. That is, if a state tries to cash in on the advantage provided by a brilliant military strategy by revealing that strategy (hopefully causing the other side to offer concessions), revealing that advantage actually eliminates the advantage, preventing the first state from cashing in. So, the state keeps the secret rather than reveal the strategy, counting on the military advantage it will provide if war comes, but making war more likely.

Another reason why states cannot successfully reveal their true power to each other involves bluffing, lying about oneself. A low-resolve state would like to lie about its resolve, claiming it is a high-resolve state, hoping to persuade the other side that it might not experience a favorable outcome should war come, pushing the other side to make concessions during bargaining. Leaders sometimes do this in international relations, making (likely) exaggerated claims about their resolve. For example, in 1957, Chinese leader Mao Tsetung declared his willingness to accept nuclear devastation, stating, "I'm not afraid of nuclear war. . . . China has a population of 600 million; even if half of them are killed, there are still 300 million people left" (quoted in Beinart 2017). However, the success of American nuclear threats in persuading Mao to leave Taiwan alone suggests that Mao likely had an aversion to nuclear war, a lower resolve than he attempted to portray.

Making matters worse, there is no legal barrier preventing states from lying, no world government that can punish a state for lying. Because low-resolve states have the motive and means to lie about their resolve, both low- and high-resolve states will describe themselves as high-resolve, and therefore a state's description of itself as high-resolve is not a believable signal about its level of resolve, even if the description is true. That is, if one state hears a second state declare itself to be high-resolve, the first state can't tell whether the second state is telling the truth. Communications that cannot be believed are sometimes called **cheap talk**, echoing the common saying, "Talk is cheap." Because statements about resolve are unlikely to be believed, communicating about resolve will not reduce disagreement about the balance of resolve between the two states, and will not reduce the likelihood of war.

Why States Fight: Commitment

Once sides agree peacefully on how to divide a scarce good, ostensibly they will adhere to that deal into the future. That is, after agreeing on how to divide the scarce good, the two sides agree not to attack each other, and not to demand more of the scarce good than the agreement allows. However, sides might not abide by agreements to divide disputed goods. Sometimes sides break such agreements, either demanding more of the disputed good or going to war. For example, though North Korea signed the 1994 Agreed Framework calling on it to scale back its nuclear weapons program, it violated this commitment over the next several years by expanding its nuclear arsenal. Germany agreed to accept its border with the new state of Poland with its signature to the 1919 Treaty of Versailles, and then violated that agreement when it invaded Poland in September 1939.

This begs the question, what factors might make a state more willing to break a deal dividing the good? Put differently, what factors might make a state's **commitment** to an agreement dividing a good not **credible**? Let's return to our earlier discussion of two sides seeking to divide a good peacefully and avoid war. Assume that the two sides agree on who would win if war broke out between them. The argument presented so far proposes that the two sides would agree to divide the good as if the two had fought, but without fighting and paying the costs of war.

Now, imagine that after such a war-avoiding peace deal has been struck, the balance of power changes, and one side becomes stronger in relation to the other side. This might happen for different reasons. Most simply, one side might enjoy faster economic or population growth and build a bigger military. It might secure a massive military aid deal from an ally. Or it might develop a new superweapon or military strategy, making its army more powerful.

Another way in which the balance of power might change is if the peace deal itself shifts the balance. Specifically, if the scarce good itself contributes to a state's power, then a deal that gives one side more of the good can make that side more powerful. For example, imagine that two states are in dispute over a piece of territory that contains resources that can boost military power, such as population to serve in the military or arms factories that can produce weapons. If the two sides peacefully reach a deal that transfers the territory from one side to the other, then that will make the side gaining the territory more powerful, shifting the balance of power. This happened in October 1938, when as part of a negotiated deal Germany peacefully annexed from Czechoslovakia a piece of territory called the Sudetenland. This transaction boosted German military power, both because Sudetens were now Germans who could serve in the German army, and because some of the biggest arms factories in Europe were located in Sudetenland.

If the balance of power shifts after a peace deal is struck, what happens next? The side that is growing in power now has an incentive to demand more of the divided good, because the balance of power has shifted in its favor. That is, it might renege on its previous commitment to an agreed-upon division of the good. Think about a very simple example. Two sides agree that if war occurs, each side has a 50 percent chance of winning. If the disputed good is a dollar, then reflecting this assessment each side would agree peacefully to take 50 cents, and avoid paying the costs of fighting a war, perhaps five cents. Now, imagine that after the two sides make the deal, the balance of power shifts, such that now one side has a 70 percent chance of winning the war. That side now has an incentive to demand a redivision of the good, asking for a shift from a 50–50 split to a 70–30 split. It declares to the other side, "Either redivide the good to a 70–30 split, or else we will go to war, and you will end up worse off because you will still end up with only 30 percent of the good, and you will also have to pay the five cent cost of fighting." This is what occurred in German–Czech relations. Six months after Germany acquired the Sudetenland in 1938, a more powerful Germany demanded the annexation of the rest of a now weakened Czechoslovakia. The Czechs gloomily complied, and the entirety of Czechoslovakia became part of Germany, without a shot being fired.

The possibility of one side breaking a deal in turn affects the prospects of a deal being struck in the first place. Sometimes, states can see that such a shift in the balance of power is coming.

Both sides know that though there is a 50–50 balance of power now, in the future the balance of power will be 70–30. Even if the side growing stronger offers the other side a 50–50 split now, the side growing weaker fears that in the future the side growing stronger might either demand more or start a war, taking advantage of its growth in power. What looks like a reasonable deal is likely to be broken in the future.

Does the side growing weaker have any other options? One possibility is that the weakening side might reject an offer to split the good peacefully, and instead start a war under the assumption that victory in war will solve the credible commitment problem. Even though this occurs under circumstances in which both sides agree on what will happen if they fight, it might still make sense for the side growing weaker in power to launch a war. Think about the example just described. If the state growing weaker fights now, then its expected payoff will be a 50–50 split of the divided good, minus the five cents for fighting, 45 cents (50 minus 5). If it does not fight now, then in the future when the other side grows in power, the other side will demand a 70–30 split, an accurate reflection of the new balance of power. Because 45 is bigger than 30, the side that is becoming weaker over time will attack now to get the 45 cents, rather than wait for later when the state growing in power will either demand greater concessions, or will start a war that provides the weakening state a payoff of only 30 cents.

Many wars, sometimes called preventive wars, have started because of this dynamic, of one side fearing that it will grow weaker in the future. In the summer 1914 crisis that escalated to World War I, Germany was willing to accept war with Russia because it feared that Russia would grow stronger in the years to come, modernizing its army and its railroad network, the latter critical for rapid military mobilization in the event of war. In 2003, the George W. Bush administration decided to invade Iraq because it thought Iraq was only a few years away from acquiring nuclear weapons, a development that would make Iraq much more powerful and more difficult to defeat in war.

Why States Fight: Issue Indivisibility

Up until now, we have considered the disputed issue as if it could easily be divided up. There are an infinite number of ways that assets like territory can be divided up, and many ways that money can be divided up. However, what if the disputed good does not lend itself to division, or, put differently, what if dividing the good would destroy its value? Regarding our earlier discussion of a dispute over a dollar's worth of money, consider if the two sides are in dispute over a single paper dollar rather than a digital dollar. A paper dollar is essentially worthless if it is cut into two pieces. This insight emerges in brutal fashion in an Old Testament fable. Two women are in dispute over who is the mother of a baby, and the true mother is shocked when King Solomon suggests cutting the baby in half, as of course doing so would kill the baby. A good is **indivisible** if it cannot be divided, or if actors believe that dividing the good would destroy its value.

There are a few possible examples of indivisible goods in international relations. A state's first nuclear weapon is an indivisible good. A nuclear weapon no longer functions if it is cut in half. More commonly, some disputed goods are physically divisible, but the relevant actors may claim the good is de facto indivisible, in the sense that it is worthless to them if they do not receive all of the good. That is, at least one of the claimant actors "socially constructs" the good to be indivisible (Hassner 2009). Israel has controlled all of Jerusalem since 1967, and has formally declared Jerusalem to be its "eternal and indivisible" capital since 1980.

Indivisible goods can make war more likely, even when both sides agree on the likely outcome of war. Imagine if two sides agree that they each have an equal chance of winning a war. With a divisible good, the sides could arrive at a 50–50 split of the good. With an indivisible good, however, the only two possible divisions are 0–100 or 100–0, and a side facing a deal giving it nothing would rather go to war with a 50 percent chance of seizing the entire good, even if it means paying the costs of fighting.

Bargaining and the Termination of Wars

However, what happens once war starts? One perspective might be that the start of war is the end of politics, if bargaining stops once the guns erupt. This was the sentiment of one nineteenth-century Prussian general who famously declared, "The politician should fall silent the moment that mobilization [for war] begins" (quoted in Brodie 1973, 11).

Another perspective is that war remains unavoidably political, even after it begins. Just as two sides peacefully bargain over a disputed good before war starts, they continue to bargain over the disputed good during war. Indeed, war ends when the two sides reach an agreement on how to split the disputed good, that is, an agreement that outlines a division of the good that both prefer to continuing the war. Haggling over how to split the disputed good is the essence of wartime diplomacy, as the two sides exchange **war termination offers**, propositions to end the war on the basis of a specific division of the disputed good, and the war ends when one side makes a war termination offer that the other side accepts or, less frequently, when one side completely vanquishes the other in an "absolute war."

The information and commitment ideas developed in the previous section on the *causes* of war provide important insights into the *termination* of war.

Information and the Termination of Wars

From the previous section, we know that wars sometimes begin because of disagreement about who will win if war starts. This disagreement blocks the appearance of bargaining space. All wars, of course, eventually end, through agreement on a war termination offer. If two sides reach a negotiated settlement, then this means bargaining space must have emerged, as the existence of the settlement means that the two sides agreed there is a division of the good that both prefer to continuing the war.

How does this happen? How does the process of fighting war help two sides go from having no bargaining space to having some bargaining space? Fighting helps create bargaining space by producing information about the balance of power, the balance of resolve, or both. Consider the balance of power. When war starts, each side makes estimates about the balance of power, estimates that are driven by guesses about the size of the other side's force, strategy, its technology, and the likelihood of third parties intervening on either side. Actual fighting starts to provide information about these parameters to both sides. Fighting forces states to reveal the sizes of their armies by deploying troops in battle, to reveal their strategies by initiating war plans, and to reveal secret weapons by using them. Third parties reveal their true intentions by choosing to intervene or remain neutral. Further, as a belligerent continues to fight and suffer costs without giving in, this provides a clear and credible signal that that side has high resolve.

These streams of information help reduce disagreement between the two sides about who will eventually win the war. The "fog of war" lifts, and the two sides begin to come to a common understanding about how the war will turn out. As that common understanding emerges, the two sides' reservation points move towards each other and eventually cross, creating bargaining space that permits the war to end. Put differently, once the two sides agree on who will win the war, they are able to strike a war-ending peace deal to divide the disputed good, allowing each to stop paying the costs of fighting.

Commitment Credibility and War Termination

An earlier discussion described the argument that war can happen if a belligerent believes that war now is more attractive than war later, perhaps because the balance of power is shifting. Importantly, this argument assumes that not only is war motivated by the credible commitment problem, but that war *solves* the credible commitment problem. That is, if you are growing weaker over time, you are motivated to go to war now because it avoids the possibility of the adversary growing stronger in the future and reneging on an earlier deal to divide the disputed good. But why exactly might war address the credible commitment problem?

Consider two possible ways that war might do so. First, war might enable the attacking state to shift the balance of power back in its favor, by capturing elements of the disputed good that are sources of military power. In World War I, Germany solved the problem of incredible Russia commitments, caused by the long-term growth in Russian power, by capturing Russian military–economic resources. Germany forced Russia to give up millions of square kilometers of populated, economically productive territory in western Russia in the (ultimately short lived) March 1918 Treaty of Brest-Litovsk. In 1967, Israel was concerned that Syria could not credibly commit to stop attacking northern Israeli territory, and the Israeli capture of the strategically critical Golan Heights from Syria during the 1967 Six Day War helped secure the safety of northern Israel from future Syrian aggression, allowing the war to end.

A second way that war can solve the credible commitment problem is by pursuing the complete surrender of the opponent – what von Clausewitz referred to as "absolute war." It is a simple if inelegant solution: you prevent the other side from breaking a commitment by eliminating its ability to do so, that is, its ability to launch a war. If a state achieves an absolute war outcome, then war ends not when bargaining space between the two sides has appeared, but rather when one side has inflicted decisive military defeat on the other. In terms of allocating the disputed good, achieving an absolute war outcome permits the victor to seize all of the disputed good.

Absolute war can take a number of forms. At its limit, it can involve genocide, the annihilation of the other side's population. This very rarely actually occurs (the closest modern example being perhaps the Paraguayan War in the 1860s, during which Paraguay lost as much as 70 percent of its adult male population). However, it is sometimes discussed, as when for example in World War II a December 1944 public opinion poll revealed that 13 percent of Americans supported murdering the entire Japanese population *after* the war ended (Dower 1986, 53–54).

Other forms of absolute war are more common. Victors sometimes annex defeated states, as when North Vietnam annexed South Vietnam in 1975, and Iraq (temporarily) annexed Kuwait in 1990. Victors also sometimes impose regime change on the defeated state, ousting its government and installing either a puppet leader or democratic institutions, often hardwiring pacifism into the defeated state's postwar constitution. This was the approach taken by the Allies against Japan, Germany, and Italy after World War II.

America's wars in Iraq and Afghanistan demonstrate this dynamic. In the early 2000s, the George W. Bush administration perceived both the Iraqi and the Afghan leadership to be engaging in actions threatening to US interests: Iraq under Saddam Hussein developing weapons of mass destruction and supporting anti-American terrorist groups like al-Qaeda, and Afghanistan under the Taliban providing safe haven and support for al-Qaeda. The Bush administration did not trust either Saddam or the Taliban, perceiving that neither could make a credible commitment to stop its dangerous actions. In both cases, the United States saw absolute war through imposed regime change as the only way to eliminate the threats posed by Saddam and the Taliban. The United States attacked both countries, overthrew both governments, helped install new, democratic institutions, supported pro-American politicians in both, and helped write new constitutions for each country banning them from supporting terrorist groups or acquiring weapons of mass destruction. Of course, not all attempts to impose an absolute war outcome succeed: twenty years after it overthrew the Taliban government in Afghanistan, the United States withdrew its forces and the Taliban returned to power.

Fears about commitment credibility can be so severe that they might cause a belligerent to pursue absolute victory even in the face of battlefield setbacks. This is surprising, as battlefield defeats ought to cause a belligerent to become more pessimistic about its eventual chances of winning. Such pessimism would push the belligerent to offer concessions in the form of more generous war termination offers intended to end the war quickly. Such concessions, of course, mean that the belligerent is giving up on pursuing absolute victory. However, severe commitment credibility fears mean that such a war-ending peace deal achieved through concessions would have little value, because the adversary is thought to be likely to break a peace deal. Such a fearful belligerent might reject an unattractive short-term peace deal and instead pursue absolute victory, even if discouraged by battlefield setbacks, knowing that absolute victory offers the only real solution to the problem of an untrustworthy adversary.

Consider Britain in the early phase of World War II in Europe. By late May 1940, things looked very bad for Britain. German forces had run up an impressive string of victories – having already conquered Poland, Denmark, Norway, Belgium, and the Netherlands – and were in the process of conquering France. The Soviet Union and Italy were essentially pro-German allies, and though President Roosevelt was sympathetic to Britain's cause, America was not close to entering the war. Many feared that after France fell, German forces would next invade and perhaps conquer Britain itself.

The highest levels of British leadership grimly discussed British war termination strategy in late May. Some advocated lowering Britain's war termination offer, making concessions to Germany to end the war, in the hopes of stopping the war before German forces landed on British shores. However, Prime Minister Winston Churchill spoke out vehemently against seeking any deal with Adolf Hitler. He agreed that Britain faced a dire threat, but feared that any peace deal with Hitler offered no long-term assurance of peace, because Hitler could not credibly commit to abide by the terms of a peace deal. Hitler had a record of violating international agreements. Further, Churchill feared, any peace deal with Hitler would require Britain to hand over the foundations of British power, including its colonies and the Royal Navy, further strengthening Hitler. An empowered Hitler would have no incentive to abide by a peace deal, and would likely demand even more from Britain, including perhaps that a Nazi puppet be installed as Britain's national leader. Further, without its navy to shield the home islands, Britain would be even more vulnerable to a Nazi invasion. Churchill persuaded the rest of the British government that negotiating with Hitler was not an option, and that Britain must fight on in the pursuit of complete victory, even in the wake of recent battlefield defeats. He famously declared in a public speech, "We shall go on to the end. We shall fight in France, we shall fight on the seas and oceans … we shall defend our island, whatever the cost may be. We shall fight on the beaches, we shall fight on the landing grounds, we shall fight in the fields and in the streets, we shall fight in the hills; we shall never surrender." He also declared, less publicly but more powerfully: "If this long island story of ours is to end at last, let it end only when each of us lies choking in his own blood upon the ground" (quoted in Reiter 2009, 99).

Bargaining and Civil Wars

Most of the discussion thus far has focused on wars between states. However, bargaining helps explain what happens before and during civil wars, as well. Before civil wars break out, the political dynamics are fundamentally similar, in that governments and sub-state actors negotiate over scarce goods. In Syria in 2011, opposition groups wanted democratic and other political reforms, and the dictator Hafez al-Assad did not want to make reforms; their failure to reach an agreement on the scarce good of reforms led to violence. In 1994, the Chechens, an ethnic group residing within Russia, wanted to declare independence and secede from Russia. The Russian government did not want to grant them independence, and the failure to reach a deal led to the outbreak of violence, the First Chechen War.

Also, as with conflicts between nations, sub-state actors in disputes over scarce goods sometimes reach an agreement that enables them to avoid civil war. National governments sometimes make concessions to restive minority groups, sufficient to dissuade those groups from turning to violence. For example, Québécois in the 1960s and 1970s began to demand greater independence from the rest of Canada. The national government made sufficient concessions to Québécois demands, including allowing two provincial elections on independence and granting concessions on language policy, to prevent these demands from escalating to violence.

Commitment credibility concerns are especially acute during civil wars, perhaps more so than during interstate wars. After interstate wars, states usually withdraw their armies back to their home territories, retaining them to provide security. But after civil wars, rebel groups usually are required to hand over their weapons, restoring the government's monopoly on the use of force. This creates tremendous commitment credibility problems, as the government might be sorely tempted to renege on the promises it made as part of the war-ending peace treaty, including promises to make internal political reforms, not to imprison or execute former rebel leaders, and so forth. After all, once the rebels have disbanded their army and handed over their weapons, they could not (easily) restart war in reaction to a government abandoning its commitments. This intense commitment credibility problem gives rebels a powerful incentive to seek the civil war equivalent of absolute victory, overthrowing the central government, or at least seceding from the rest of the country to form an independent state.

Scholars have observed that these severe commitment credibility problems may help explain why some civil wars last so long. The civil war in Colombia, for example, endured for more than half a century before finally ending in 2016. Absent commitment credibility problems, these civil wars should not have lasted so long, as surely it would not take years or decades for governments and rebels to learn enough about the true balance of power or resolve to permit bargaining space to appear. Rebels keep fighting because they often fear that the central government cannot credibly commit to a peace deal.

Fortunately, there are tools available to alleviate these credible commitment concerns sufficiently to help civil war belligerents sign a peace deal. Specifically, peace deals become more likely and stable when they provide for power sharing in the postwar political environment, and when international actors deploy peacekeepers to enforce the terms of the agreement. Power sharing means making formal, codified plans to guarantee that previously excluded groups, including former rebels and their supporters, receive political power, in forms such as allowing rebels to join the military, guaranteeing former rebels or members of an aggrieved group representation in parliament or the cabinet, and others. The logic is that if these individuals hold formal power in the new political system, it will help them ensure the implementation of the agreement.

Peacekeepers are another tool that can help reduce credible commitment problems (Fortna 2008). Troops and other personnel deployed by third-party actors like the United Nations often aim to monitor and enforce the implementation of civil war peace agreements. If peacekeepers make it more difficult or more costly for a government to break an agreement ending a civil war, then rebels will be more likely to settle a conflict and lay down their arms, more confident in the credibility of the government's commitment to peace (see Chapter 10).

Possible Critiques of the Bargaining Model

The bargaining model of war is a powerful tool for understanding war. That said, it has attracted scholarly debate. Some of the most salient critiques of the bargaining model contend that war is not costly, point out that actors do not always process information in the manner the bargaining model requires, refer to the illusion of indivisibility, and emphasize the effects of the evolution of fighting during war.

Fighting War Is Not Costly

A core assumption of the bargaining perspective is that the process of fighting war is always costly for both sides, in blood and treasure. However, what if this is not a valid assumption? What if the process of fighting wars (remember, the process of fighting wars is separate from the benefits one might receive from winning the war) is not only not costly, but might actually provide benefits? Then, even if there are no information, commitment, or issue indivisibility problems, war might break out anyway.

The most prominent argument that fighting wars is politically beneficial rather than costly focuses on the potential domestic political benefits of fighting war. Some have proposed that fighting war might trigger a "rally round the flag effect," a dynamic in which when a nation is at war, the population rallies around the national leadership, making the national leader more popular (see Chapters 3–5). A national leader who strongly desires to boost his or her popular support might see the domestic political benefits of fighting as outweighing its human and financial costs. Indeed, some have proposed that leaders under domestic political threat may be more likely to initiate war in order to boost their own support, a proposition termed the **diversionary hypothesis** (Miller 1995). If rally round the flag effects did provide important domestic political benefits to leaders, then we would expect wars to break out for reasons other than what the bargaining model forecasts. Wars might break out even when two sides agree about the balance of power and resolve, credible commitment problems are absent, and the disputed issue is divisible. Even with all this in place, wars would be more likely to break out when a leader perceived that she needed a boost in her domestic political support.

However, rallies round the flag are not always easily achieved, as they are most likely and largest when a country has been attacked, and when the international community supports the use of force (Chapman 2011). Leaders under domestic political threat who need a rally are not always in the right kind of international environment, when they can persuade their people that they have been attacked, and the international community supports a forceful defense.

Processing Information

The bargaining model presents belligerents as actors that observe signals and events, and then calmly and appropriately change their beliefs in reaction to signals and events. However, what if this is an overly optimistic portrayal of the ability of actors to process information? If actors do not process information in the manner described by the bargaining model, then perhaps the bargaining model might not provide a completely accurate view of how wars start and end.

There is a broad set of ideas from the field of behavioral economics describing how decision-makers might not process information in the manner described by the bargaining perspective. Specifically, actors sometimes do not pay enough attention to new information. **Confirmation bias**, for example, is a dynamic in which actors tend not to pay attention to information which appears to disconfirm their existing beliefs (Kahneman 2013). So, a national leader confident in military victory might slough off news of battlefield defeats, dismissing them as isolated or incorrect, rather than, as the bargaining perspective would forecast, using these reports to reduce their assessment of the likelihood of eventual victory. The confirmation bias proposition, then, would predict that new information will not change belligerents' beliefs and war termination offers as rapidly as the bargaining model might forecast.

Another information processing critique concerns the nature of military organizations. The bargaining model assumes that during war national leaders demand that their militaries provide information about how the war is going, so they can update their assessments about who is eventually going to win, those assessments in turn affecting the leaders' war termination offers. To assess how the war is going, militaries need to establish indicators of success, performance metrics that indicate how well they are doing. All organizations use such indicators, such as business firms focusing on net profits, police departments focusing on crime rates, and so forth.

The potential difficulty is that militaries sometimes focus on misleading indicators of success when evaluating how they are doing. As mentioned, during the Vietnam War the US military assessed its effectiveness on the basis of the number of enemy combatants it had killed, or body count. However, counterinsurgency experts now widely agree that this is the wrong way to think about how to defeat insurgencies; it is often much more important to secure the support of the population than to kill insurgents. As US Army General David Petraeus said in 2010 about the Afghanistan insurgency, counterinsurgent forces "cannot kill or capture their way to victory" (quoted in *Guardian* newspaper, 2010). That is, the focus of the US military during the Vietnam War on body count may have caused it to make inappropriately optimistic assessments of how the war was going. These overly optimistic assessments may have then given the United States a falsely encouraging sense of the progress of the war, discouraging it from lowering its war termination offer and causing the war to drag on for longer than the bargaining model might have predicted (Gartner 1997; Kirshner 2000).

The Illusion of Indivisibility

Though the issue indivisibility proposition fits neatly within the bargaining model, in reality most things that states are in dispute over, such as territory and natural resources like oil, are physically divisible. Some scholars have proposed that items which are physically divisible like Jerusalem might be politically indivisible, and such political indivisibility might make war more likely. However, it is important to keep in mind that sometimes such statements proclaiming indivisibility are bluffs, issued for political effect but not genuinely reflective of actors' beliefs. For example, in the 1944 war termination negotiations between Finland and the Soviet Union, there was discussion about whether Finland would be able to keep the Finnish territory of Karelia. A Finnish delegate attempted to improve Finland's bargaining leverage by arguing that Finland viewed Karelia as an indivisible issue, as this territory "constitutes in the economical as well as in the national sense so to speak an organic part of our nation's body, and it affects our total existence in a most decisive way ... the ceded part of Karelia belongs organically to Finland, and ... our people cannot conceive that this frontier will be a final one" (quoted in Reiter 2009, 49). But, this indivisibility claim was a bluff, as the Finns ended up ceding Karelia in the peace treaty with the Soviet Union.

Another limitation to the issue indivisibility argument is that even if an issue appears indivisible, actors can use what are called "side payments" to craft a mutually acceptable resolution to a dispute over an indivisible good (Powell 2006). One side might be willing to accept a deal in which it gets none of the disputed, indivisible good, if it receives something else in compensation. For example, if two sides are bargaining over a paper dollar that cannot be divided, they still might be able to reach a settlement if the side that received the paper dollar gave the other side something else worth about a dollar, such as a candy bar. This occurs frequently in international relations, as for example when Ukraine agreed in 1994 to give up its inherited nuclear arsenal in exchange for economic and diplomatic side payments.

The Evolution of Fighting during War

The bargaining model assumes that the balance of power between states does not change across the course of war. Regarding information dynamics, the core assumption is that the balance of power is fixed but unknown, and the process of fighting serves to clear the fog as belligerents get a progressively more accurate picture of the (unchanging) balance of power. The war ends once the states agree sufficiently on what the balance of power is and always has been.

However, the balance of power in actual wars may be more fluid than this account suggests. War starts with each side possessing a military of a certain size, fighting with certain strategies and technologies. As war endures, though, belligerents frequently take steps to change the balance of power by improving their fighting power, including building bigger armies, altering military strategies, and developing better weapons (Gartner 1997). During World War II, for example, Soviet tanks increased in size more than fivefold.

If belligerents are confident they can improve their chances of winning as the war endures, then this may make it more difficult for bargaining space to appear. Imagine if a belligerent observed its military performing poorly in battle at the outset of war. The bargaining model would propose that this ought to lower its estimated likelihood of eventually winning, in turn leading it to make concessions and lower its war termination offer. This would make it more likely that bargaining space would appear, making it possible for the war to end. Now, consider what might happen if the belligerent is confident that it might be able to improve its military effectiveness and therefore its chances of winning the war. Setbacks on the battlefield might not cause the state to lower its estimate of eventually winning, so initial battlefield setbacks would not cause the belligerent to lower its war termination offer, and war's end would not be any closer. The United States suffered early setbacks in World War II partly because it was using ineffective torpedoes, obsolete tanks (the early American Lee tank, carrying a crew of seven, was so awful it was termed by some a "coffin for seven brothers"), and inferior fighter aircraft, but fought on because it guessed accurately that its fighting effectiveness would rise as its weapons improved. The implication is that when belligerents think the balance of power might change across the course of the war, then the flow of information provided by battle outcomes might not change states' war termination offers and hasten the end of the war as quickly as the bargaining model might predict. Wars may endure longer than the bargaining model would forecast.

CASE STUDY

Bargaining and World War II in the Pacific

In 1931, Japan launched a war of empire in Asia. It was a terrible war, inflicting tremendous suffering on Chinese civilians, including instances of mass killing and sexual assault, perhaps most notoriously the 1937 "Rape of Nanking." By 1940, Japan was deeply enmeshed in an intense and genocidal war in China (see Figure 1.5).

Many Americans felt sympathy for China, and opposed Japan's war of empire. This was the scarce good that Japan and the USA held in dispute: Japan wished to engage in an unfettered pursuit of empire, and the USA wished for Japan to cease its war. The USA took a series of increasingly firm measures towards Japan in the late 1930s and early 1940s, both to signal its opposition to Japan's war, and to pressure Japan to end the war.

These efforts culminated in a major set of American economic sanctions on Japan in summer 1941. The most important action was an end to American oil and gasoline exports to Japan. Japan had very little oil production of its own, and at this stage had not yet captured territory that contained oil reserves. As a result, the cutoff of American oil exports threatened to cripple the Japanese army and navy, and the war effort in China more broadly.

The American sanctions sparked a serious debate within the Japanese leadership about whether to go to war with the United States. Japan saw itself as having essentially two choices: strike a deal with the United States over China that would get the sanctions lifted, or go to war with the United States. The goal of going to war would not be to conquer the United States, but rather to provide the conditions under which Japan could

Figure 1.5. This terrified infant may have been the only person still alive after the Japanese bombing of Shanghai's South Station in China, August 28, 1937. The extent of Japanese brutality in the wars across the 1931–1945 time period, especially against Chinese, Korean, and Southeast Asian civilians, is difficult to exaggerate, and rivals the brutality of the Nazi German regime. US National Archives and Records Administration.

(cont.)

achieve its imperial ambitions, by destroying the American Pacific fleet, and establishing a strong defensive line through the Pacific Ocean that would prevent US interference in Japan's war of empire.

Japan viewed striking a deal with the United States as an unattractive choice. Many actors in Japanese politics, especially the Japanese army and certain large Japanese corporations, were deeply committed to expanding Japan's empire through war. Further, even if a deal with the United States was acceptable to Japan on its merits, Japan was concerned about the credibility of an American commitment to such a deal. Japan saw the United States as growing stronger in relation to Japan, and feared this growth in power would tempt it to renege on any deal. A late 1941 official Japanese government report argued, "Even if we should make concessions to the United States by giving up part of our national policy for the sake of a temporary peace, the United States, its military position strengthened, is sure to demand more and more concessions on our part; and ultimately our empire will lie prostrate at the feet of the United States" (quoted in Ike 1967, 152). Relatedly, some Japanese leaders were concerned that America's growth in power would make Japan less likely to win a war in the future as compared with the present: "We might avoid war now, but go to war three years later; or we might go to war now and plan for what the situation will be three years hence. I think it would be easier to engage in a war now. The reason is that now we have the necessary foundation for it" (quoted in Ike 1967, 202).

In short, commitment credibility concerns made a war-avoiding peace deal less attractive to Japan. A second question about the option of war was, could Japan win? Here, there were elements about the course of a possible war upon which the United States and Japan agreed, and elements upon which they disagreed. They both agreed that the United States enjoyed a monumental advantage in raw power, in terms of size of economy, size of population, and natural resource endowments. Japan might be able to enjoy some initial military successes, but as time passed, the mobilization of the American Goliath would crush Japan. In 1940 the Japanese navy conducted a study of how a war with the United States might unfold, and concluded that, "Should the war continue beyond a year, our chances of winning would be nil" (quoted in Sagan 1988, 897). The Americans were similarly confident of their considerable military–industrial advantages. In view of American advantages, some viewed the Japanese attack on Pearl Harbor as pure folly. After the attack occurred, one Congressman declared, "The Japanese have gone stark, raving mad, and have, by their unprovoked attack committed military, naval, and national suicide" (*Congressional Record* 1941).

There was, however, one important area of disagreement between the United States and Japan: over American resolve to fight. The Japanese believed that the American people had low resolve and were unwilling to suffer significant costs in the course of fighting. Japanese leaders ascribed this low resolve to the spiritual emptiness of American liberal democracy,

(cont.)

a culture that emphasized the individual over the collective. The selfishness of American citizens would cause them to recoil from making the human and financial sacrifices a long war would require. Interestingly, this belief about American spiritual weakness affected Japan's beliefs about America's power as well as its resolve, specifically leading some Japanese leaders to conclude that US soldiers and sailors would not have the courage or stamina to fight well in modern combat conditions. The Japanese believed, for example, that they need not fear American submarines, because American sailors lacked the mental and physical toughness required for long-term submarine missions.

This belief in low American resolve was the key assumption underpinning the Japanese plan for victory over America. Japan would run up a string of victories in the first few months of war, establishing a strong defensive perimeter stretching across the Central Pacific from the Aleutian Islands off Alaska down to the Gilbert Islands to the northeast of Australia. America would realize that the struggle to defeat Japan would be long and costly, and low American resolve would push the United States to settle for peace rather than fight. A leading Japanese admiral compared Japanese forces attacking the United States to hornets attacking a large but lethargic farm animal: "If the hornets around it buzz loudly enough, even a hefty animal like a horse or a cow will get worried, at least. American public opinion has always been very changeable, so the only hope is to make them feel as soon as possible that it's no use tackling a swarm of lethal stingers" (quoted in Reiter and Stam 2002, 36).

The Japanese plan worked, but only up to a point. As envisioned, Japan assembled a string of impressive victories in the six months following the December 7, 1941 Pearl Harbor attack, conquering French Indochina (present-day Vietnam, Laos, and Cambodia), Singapore, Malaya (present-day Malaysia), the Philippines, the Dutch East Indies (present-day Indonesia), half of New Guinea, two islands in the Aleutian chain off of Alaska, and several small islands in the Pacific. However, the other part of Japan's strategy proved to be flawed, as the assessment of low American resolve was inaccurate. The attack on Pearl Harbor had the exact opposite of the hoped-for effect. Rather than demoralize the American public, the attack frightened and enraged Americans, leading them to fear an invasion of California and to demand revenge. The public became immediately and deeply committed to total victory over Japan, even if such a war had great costs and took years. Americans flocked to join the military and work in munitions factories. Some American boys lied about their ages to join up early, before finishing high school. Americans easily accepted restrictions on consumption to facilitate a titanic economic mobilization for war. Reports of Japanese war crimes like the Bataan Death March infuriated the American public further, and solidified the conviction that the Japanese were brutal killers who had to be destroyed, even at great cost.

In short, the bargaining model helps explain the causes of the Pacific War: Japan attacked because of disagreement between Japan and the United States over the balance

(cont.)

of resolve, and because of Japanese concerns over the credibility of American commitments. The bargaining model also sheds light on diplomacy during the Pacific War, specifically why the Allies decided to pursue Japan's unconditional surrender in May 1942, even after the Allies had just experienced a series of battle defeats at the hands of Japanese attackers. Just as Japan did not trust the United States to make credible commitments, the United States (and the other Allies) did not trust Japan. Roosevelt was haunted by the utter failure of the Versailles Treaty, the agreement that ended World War I. That treaty demanded concessions from Germany, but did not allow the Allies to occupy all of Germany, or to revamp Germany's political system. Like others, Roosevelt blamed the limited ambitions of the Versailles Treaty for the collapse of the interwar order and the outbreak of World War II.

Roosevelt above all else wanted to avoid repeating the Versailles nightmare, defeating Germany and Japan in World War II only to fight them again a few years later. He told the nation in his January 1943 State of the Union address,

> We have learned that if we do not pull the fangs of the predatory animals of the world, they will multiply and grow in strength – and they will be at our throats once more in a short generation. . . . It is clear that if Germany and Italy and Japan – or any one of them – remain armed at the end of this war, or are permitted to rearm, they will again, and inevitably, embark upon an ambitious career of world conquest. They must be disarmed and kept disarmed. (Roosevelt 1943)

Others shared his concern. One senator warned that the Japanese "don't seek real peace—only an armistice to give some years for preparing another attempt to dominate the entire Far East, and then the remainder of the world" (quoted in Reiter 2009, 114).

This concern about the credibility of Japanese commitment to peace pushed Roosevelt to reject consideration of peace talks, and instead to pursue Japan's unconditional surrender. Roosevelt and others saw that the taproot cause of the war lay in the political and economic system of Japan, and the only way to provide the basis of a durable peace would be to require Japan's unconditional surrender and then completely remake the Japanese political and economic order, replacing the old imperial order with democratic institutions. Such actions would prevent Japan from breaking its commitment to peace. The Japanese, not surprisingly, reacted in horror to the idea of dismantling their political system, and for years clung to the hope that they could inflict enough damage on American forces to convince them to agree to a peace deal that would allow Japan to keep its emperor and political system, even as Japanese forces lost battle after battle. The Allies refused to budge, and in August 1945 Japan finally agreed to virtually all of the Allied demands after suffering the twin blows of Soviet entry into the war and the nuclear annihilation of two Japanese cities. More than three and a half years after Pearl Harbor and some fourteen years after Japan started its war against China, the bloody horror of the Pacific War finally ground to a halt.

QUANTITATIVE STUDY

The Settlement of Civil Wars

This section illustrates the ideas of the bargaining model using quantitative empirical analysis. It applies insights from the bargaining model to answer a question of crucial policy significance: what causes civil wars to end in negotiated settlement, rather than drag on until one side achieves absolute victory? The bargaining model provides an answer to this question, and a policy solution to the problem: civil wars sometimes drag on because of credible commitment concerns, and these concerns can be overcome to help end the war if a third party can offer a security guarantee to the warring parties, such as with United Nations peacekeepers. This argument was originally made by Barbara F. Walter in her landmark book, *Committing to Peace: The Successful Settlement of Civil Wars* (2002). The Walter study both presents the theoretical argument, and conducts quantitative empirical analysis to see if it is supported by data.

Research Question

What causes a civil war to end in negotiated settlement?

Theory and Hypothesis

The bargaining model forecasts that belligerents fighting wars may be especially concerned about commitment credibility problems, the possibility that the adversary might not abide by a peace deal and either renege on the terms of the peace deal or reattack sometime in the future. These concerns are especially acute during civil wars, as civil war agreements often call on at least one of the sides, often the rebel side, to lay down its arms. Such demobilization could tempt the government to renege on its peace treaty commitments. Distrusting the government to abide by a peace deal, the rebels then have an incentive to eschew a negotiated settlement and seek absolute victory and the overthrow of the government, even if such a campaign takes years or decades and leads to the deaths of thousands, tens of thousands, or even millions.

It is possible that third-party security guarantees might reduce these credible commitment fears enough to make a negotiated settlement more likely. Actors outside the conflict, such as the United Nations or regional security organizations like the Organization of African Unity, sometimes attempt to end civil wars. One way they can accomplish this goal is by providing security guarantees for a peace deal – that is, helping ensure that the terms of a negotiated settlement are complied with, through monitoring, implementing, or enforcing compliance, often through the deployment of peacekeepers. If belligerents receive a third-party security guarantee, they become less fearful that the other side will break a peace deal, and in turn more likely to accept a negotiated settlement.

Hypothesis: Civil wars are more likely to end in negotiated settlement if, during the civil war, a third party offers a security guarantee.

Data

The data include all seventy-two civil wars that began between the years 1940 and 1992. A civil war is a conflict that occurs within an independent state, involves nonstate actors from within the country as belligerents, includes the government as a belligerent, experiences at least one thousand battle deaths per year, and includes nongovernment actors with fighting power (excluding instances of governments simply massacring their populations).

Dependent Variable

The dependent variable measures whether or not the civil war ended in negotiated settlement, the two sides signing a bargain that divides the disputed good. Civil wars that do not end with a signed bargain generally culminate in absolute victory for the government or rebels.

Independent Variable

The main independent variable is if a third party offered to provide a security guarantee for a negotiated settlement. Security guarantees come in the form of the deployment of peacekeepers to the conflict area, tasked with either monitoring compliance with the deal or enforcing the deal.

Control Variables

We want to know if any observed correlation between the independent and dependent variable is causal, the independent variable actually causing the dependent variable, or merely spurious (the observed correlation is coincidental, and does not indicate that the independent variable is actually causing the dependent variable). One way to do this is to include control variables, other phenomena that might also affect the dependent variable. If we include a variety of control variables and still observe that the independent variable is correlated with the dependent variable, we can be more confident that there is a causal relationship.

The study included several control variables that might also affect the likelihood that a war would end in negotiated settlement, including the goals of the two sides, whether a mediator was present, the political system of the country, whether the belligerents came from different ethnic groups, and others.

Results

The empirical results demonstrated that the presence of a third-party security guarantee made it significantly more likely that a civil war would end in negotiated settlement, even accounting for other factors. Specifically, without a third-party security guarantee there was only a 5 percent chance of a negotiated settlement, an unlikely prospect. Conversely, the presence of a negotiated settlement raised the likelihood of a negotiated settlement to 55 percent, not a sure thing but a much more likely outcome than if no security guarantee were present.

Conclusions

The bargaining model proposes that credible commitment concerns can cause civil wars to drag on for years as the fearful side seeks absolute victory. The study provides support for this proposition, demonstrating that the presence of third-party security guarantees in civil wars can reduce credible commitment concerns and significantly increase the likelihood of a negotiated settlement. This finding provides important encouragement for the international community. Though such guarantees are not silver bullets guaranteed to end conflicts, their use makes settlements more likely, giving peace a fighting chance.

SUMMARY

The bargaining model makes the following propositions:

- Adversaries fight over scarce goods like territory
- Because fighting wars is costly for both sides, adversaries prefer to divide goods peacefully
- Peaceful divisions of goods can be prevented by disagreement between the sides about who would win a war, the inability of one side to commit credibly to accept a peaceful division of the good, or the indivisibility of a disputed good
- Combat during wars provides information about the balance of power and/or resolve, the provision of this information causes belligerents to revise their assessments of the balance of power and/or resolve, these revisions reduce disagreement between the two sides, and when their disagreement has been sufficiently reduced, the war can end
- Credible commitment problems can be solved if the fearful side can inflict absolute defeat on the other side, or if it can capture goods that shift the balance of power in its favor
- The bargaining perspective can be applied to both interstate and civil wars

KEY TERMS

Bargaining
Scarce goods
Ideal point
Reservation point
Bargaining space
Reversion outcome
Resolve

Cheap talk
Commitment
Credible commitments
Issue indivisibility
War termination offer
Diversionary hypothesis
Confirmation bias

REVIEW QUESTIONS

1. What are scarce goods?
2. What is an "ideal point"? What is a "reservation point"?

3. What is the "bargaining space"?
4. Why is war unlikely to happen if both sides know what the outcome will be?
5. If the costs of war go up, why does that mitigate the possible effects of disagreement on the likelihood of war?
6. What are five sources of potential war-causing disagreement?
7. Why might credible commitment concerns cause war?
8. Why might war be more likely if the dispute is over an indivisible good?
9. How might the process of fighting the war reduce disagreement between the sides, permitting war termination?
10. How might the process of fighting the war reduce credible commitment concerns?
11. In World War II in the Pacific, what scarce good was the United States and Japan in dispute over? What credible commitment concerns did Japan have in 1941? How did Japan and the United States disagree about American resolve? Why did Roosevelt pursue unconditional surrender?

DISCUSSION QUESTIONS

1. If wars are caused by information, commitment, and/or indivisible good problems, what steps can the international community or individual nations take to reduce the likelihood of war?
2. After reading the World War II case study, if you could go back in time to 1941, what steps could have been taken to dissuade Japan from attacking the United States in 1941?

ADDITIONAL READING

Fearon, J. D. (2004). Why do some civil wars last so much longer than others? *Journal of Peace Research* **41**, 275–301.

Goddard, S. E. (2009). *Indivisible Territory and the Politics of Legitimacy: Jerusalem and Northern Ireland.* Cambridge: Cambridge University Press.

Goemans, H. E. (2000). *War and Punishment: The Causes of War Termination and First World War.* Princeton: Princeton University Press.

Heinrichs, W. (1988). *Threshold of War: Franklin D. Roosevelt and American Entry into World War II.* Oxford: Oxford University Press.

Kahneman, D. (2013). *Thinking, Fast and Slow.* New York: Farrar, Straus & Giroux.

Reiter, D. (2009). *How Wars End.* Princeton: Princeton University Press.

Sagan, S. D. (1988). The origins of the Pacific War. *Journal of Interdisciplinary History* **18**, 893–922.

Walter, B. F. (2002). *Committing to Peace: The Successful Settlement of Civil Wars.* Princeton: Princeton University Press.

REFERENCES

Beinart, P. (2017, April 21). How America shed the taboo against preventive war. *The Atlantic.* www.theatlantic.com/international/archive/2017/04/north-korea-preventive-war/523833

Brodie, B. (1973). *War and Politics.* New York: Macmillan.

Chapman, T. L. (2011). *Securing Approval: Domestic Politics and Multilateral Authorization for War*. Chicago: University of Chicago Press.

Churchill, W. (1955). Never despair. https://winstonchurchill.org/resources/speeches/1946-1963-elder-statesman

Congressional Record. (1941, December 8). 77th Congress, 1st session, vol. 87, part 9, 9521.

Dower, J. W. (1986). *War without Mercy: Race and Power in the Pacific War*. New York: Pantheon.

Fearon, J. D. (1995). Rationalist explanations for war. *International Organization* **49**, 379–414.

Fortna, V. P. (2008). *Does Peacekeeping Work? Shaping Belligerents' Choices after Civil War*. Princeton: Princeton University Press.

Gartner, S. S. (1997). *Strategic Assessment in War*. New Haven: Yale University Press.

Guderian, H. (1952). *Panzer Leader*. New York: E.P. Dutton & Co. Inc.

Hassner, R. (2009). *War on Sacred Grounds*. Ithaca, NY: Cornell University Press.

Ike, N. (1967). *Japan's Decision for War: Records of the 1941 Policy Conferences*. Stanford: Stanford University Press.

Kahneman, D. (2013). *Thinking Fast and Slow*. New York: Farrar, Straus & Giroux.

Kirshner, J. (2000). Rationalist explanations for war, *Security Studies*, **10**(1), 143–150.

Miller, R. A. (1995). Domestic structures and the diversionary use of force. *American Journal of Political Science* **39**(3), 760–785.

Powell, R. (2006). War as a commitment problem. *International Organization*, **60**(1), 169–203.

Reed, W. (2003). Information, power, and war. *American Political Science Review* **97**(4), 633–641.

Reiter, D. (2009). *How Wars End*. Princeton: Princeton University Press.

Reiter, D. and Stam, A. C. (2002). *Democracies at War*. Princeton: Princeton University Press.

Roosevelt, F. D. (1943). State of the Union Address. www.presidency.ucsb.edu/documents/state-the-union-address-0

Sagan, S. D. (1988). Origins of the Pacific War. *Journal of Interdisciplinary History,* **18**(4), 893–922.

Schelling, T. C. (1960). *The Strategy of Conflict*. Cambridge, MA: Harvard University Press.

Stein, J. G. (1992). Deterrence and compellence in the Gulf, 1990–1991: A failed or impossible task. *International Security* **17**(2), 147–179.

2 Sex, Gender, and Violence

VALERIE M. HUDSON AND DAN REITER

Introduction

One of the most important aspects of our lives is our sex, whether our bodies are male, female, or something else. How our sex gets expressed through gender roles and stereotypes has an outsized impact not only on our lives as individuals, but also on our societies. Your own sex and sense of your gender role is something that you yourself probably think about, whether you are more traditional or more modern in your values, more religious or less religious, are more certain about who you are, or feel like you are still figuring things out.

Unfortunately, these most essential elements of human identity are inextricably related to the ugliest of human behaviors, interpersonal violence. This chapter discusses the very complicated and often disturbing relationships between sex, gender, and violence. The goal of the chapter is to demonstrate some different ways of thinking about these relationships, to provide you with some new lenses which might help you see more and bring things into clearer focus. The chapter makes three central points:

- The ongoing problem of violence against women and girls is far, far worse than you are probably aware of.
- There are powerful and ubiquitous male power structures throughout human societies.
- Male power structures contribute to violence in general and violence against females in particular, in both direct and indirect ways.

Some of the ideas in this chapter may push back against some of your ways of thinking. But these patterns we describe are, perhaps unfortunately, well documented by a variety of kinds of evidence, including data that are archaeological, historical, from laboratory experiments, from analysis of public opinion surveys, and from statistics. Facts are stubborn things, even if they are inconvenient or make us uncomfortable.

The chapter may also suggest a broader conception of the word "war" than what you are used to, an issue broached in the Introduction to this book. You may equate war with conflict between the armies of states, troops in uniform fighting against each other, for their own countries, in fields of battle. One theme in this book is to think about war more broadly, not just wars between uniformed national armies, but also violence between governments and rebels, between ethnic and other subnational groups, and, as described in this chapter, wars against women and girls. A broader conception of war makes us aware of human suffering that we might otherwise not see. Further, as we demonstrate in this chapter, these different kinds of conflict do not exist in isolation from each other, as the oppression of women and girls makes interpersonal violence, terrorism, civil wars, and wars between states more likely, and violence against women and girls is sometimes a consequence of civil and traditional wars.

The questions this chapter will address include:

- What is "sex" and what is "gender"? How do they interact and affect conflict behavior?
- Are men more aggressive than women? How and why?
- What are male power structures? Why are they important?
- How do male power structures generate violence?
- What are realistic policy solutions we can implement to reduce the violence and subordination of women generated by male-dominated power structures?

The War against Women and Girls

Most of us do not realize there's a world war going on now. There are and have been some regional conflicts, such as the Syrian and Yemeni civil wars, a grey war in Ukraine, and so forth, but certainly most would say the world is not "at war." In one sense, however, the world *is* at war. The war we refer to is the war against women and girls. One recent estimate is that there are 142.6 million females missing in the world's population today, meaning that there are 142.6 million fewer girls and women on planet Earth compared to how many there should be if female fetuses were not aborted at higher rates than male fetuses and if infant girls weren't murdered at higher rates (United Nations Population Fund 2020). In comparison, about 75 million persons died in World War II ("World War II Casualties by Country" 2022). While the 1,021 fatal police shootings of 2020 in the United States have been discussed ("People Shot to Death by US Police" 2022), what about the estimated 1,500 domestic violence homicides of women per year in the United States (Friedel and Fox 2019; Holson 2019)? Or the estimated 137 women killed daily by intimate partners or relatives across the globe – a total of over 50,000 a year (Paul 2018)? Or the estimated 1.7 million future girls who are aborted each year because of preference for sons (Ritchie and Roser 2019)? Or the 295,000 women across the globe who die preventable deaths each year during pregnancy and childbirth ("Maternal Mortality" 2019)? There is a war ongoing, and it's not hidden. It's just that we've normalized it and so we do not see it for what it really is.

In addition to death, there are all sorts of sex-specific suffering imposed upon girls and women, such as sexual assault, sterilization, female genital cutting, forced childbearing, breast ironing, force-feeding for weight gain, and other practices. And even though men are also subject to domestic violence, incest, and child marriage, or are forcibly sterilized or raped, these crimes are overwhelmingly perpetrated against females.

But this war is not only fought with direct violence. The war against women is also fought with laws, customs, and norms. In some countries, a woman need not even be present for her marriage ceremony, as it is an exchange between her father and her husband-to-be. She may be "bought" with a brideprice, or "sold" with a dowry, have little to no right to end her marriage, and virtually no right to custody of children after a divorce. Her husband may take additional wives without her consent. She may have little to no right to inherit from her parents or her husband. She may not even be able to pass her citizenship to her own children. There may be customs of females eating last after males have eaten, or not being immunized while their brothers are, or of being pulled out of school prematurely just for being a girl. She may be killed if she is raped – or even if seen speaking with a man who is not a member of her family.

Even when good laws protecting women are present, they are often simply not enforced. India, which recently recorded the most lopsided birth sex ratio since achieving independence (Dhar 2011), has excellent laws on the books criminalizing fetal sex identification and sex-selective abortion. Despite strict rules forbidding sexual assault in the US military, lax enforcement and the prospect of retaliation have meant that women serving in the US military are at grave risk of being assaulted, and of being disbelieved, and threatened further, if they do report the assault.

Because of these realities, women may lead very different lives than men do, lives that involve lesser mobility, freedom, opportunities, and influence. This is reflected in the leadership of our world. Political, military, and business leaders across the globe are primarily males. The world average of women in parliament hovers around 25 percent (Inter-Parliamentary Union 2022); only 22 (Vogelstein and Bro 2021) of 193 countries have a female head of state; 29 percent ("Women in Management" 2022) of senior business executives are women.

While leadership and power are often male possessions in our societies, we often also normalize other things that are primarily male phenomena: violent crime, mass murder, harming women and girls. Overwhelmingly, mayhem, destruction, and violence are committed by men (Peterson and Wrangham 1997). While these male perpetrators may be a minority of all men, the devastation is usually not caused by females: it is male in origin.

In sum, a country may be "at peace" while there is a war raging within its borders. Consider the account "Ana" gives of her own country, Romania ("Nordic Model Now" 2020). She speaks of the horror of schoolgirls being ensnared by sex trafficking rings, with police unwilling to even investigate the disappearance of these children. She reflects,

Even though the total population of Romania is only about 19 million, there are thousands of Romanian women and children forced into street prostitution in Italy alone – and that's not counting those in strip clubs, brothels and 'escort' prostitution … Romania has haemorrhaged more than a million children (girls and boys) and women into the prostitution trade in these countries.

Meanwhile, our authorities complain about the decrease in fertility. The 2011 census showed that the number of women aged 15–55 was lower than the number of men of the same age. Since then, not a day goes by without at least one case on the news of a woman (of active fertile age) being stabbed, strangled, shot or otherwise murdered by her partner in domestic violence – this makes for an officially declared number of about 300 women killed per year (the real number is higher) since the 2011 census.

That is added to more than 1.5 million who have been annihilated by human trafficking in the past 15 years. That's about a quarter of the female population of reproductive age.

Who is supposed to make the babies to increase the fertility rate? Will we get to the point where we put the remaining fertile women into cages and forcefully impregnate them to keep the population up?

Because what we see in my country is borderline genocide. Female genocide. I think it's pretty safe to say that.

Did you think Romania is at peace? Do you think the women and girls of Romania feel secure?

Sex, Gender, and Aggression

To understand the relationships between sex, gender, and violence, we first need to know what we mean by the category of sex and the category of gender. The category of sex refers to an individual human's role or potential role in biological reproduction. The **sex** categories of female and male are distinguished by differences in chromosomes, the processes by which genes control body functions, hormone levels and function, and reproductive and sexual body parts. However, not all humans can be straightforwardly categorized as biologically either male or female. A small percentage of people are not only male or female at birth across all these anatomical categories, for example having atypical chromosomes or ambiguous genitalia. These are intersex individuals.

Gender roles and stereotypes refer to how our society customarily expresses sex. Gender roles and stereotypes are sometimes described as "socially constructed," which simply means that social interactions help us as individuals come to understand what it is to be a man, a woman, or something else, within a particular culture or society. This happens in many ways, such as boys being given toy weapons to play with and girls being given dolls to play with. Not everyone classifies themselves as male or female, their anatomy aside, and many cultures have additional categories into which individuals are socially placed.

We ask, what are the relationships between sex, gender, and violence? Are males more violent than females (a sex approach), and/or do certain identities and beliefs about what it means to be a man or to be a woman make violence more likely (a gender approach)? The big picture is there is evidence that males may have a greater proclivity to aggression and violence, but violence is also driven by beliefs about manhood and masculinity that can exacerbate biological patterns. Importantly, cultural factors can fuel violence and can mediate relationships between sex and violence, and sometimes sex and gender reinforce each other in a feedback loop breeding violence.

If men are more aggressive or violent than women, we might blame the hormone **testosterone**. All humans have testosterone, just as all humans have estrogen, a hormone more frequently associated with females. Testosterone serves a number of biological functions, especially related to sex drive and building muscle mass. Though testosterone levels vary significantly, especially over an individual's age, average adult males tend to have approximately fifteen times (Handelsman et al. 2018) the testosterone levels of average adult females.

Do higher levels of testosterone make aggressive or violent behavior more likely? The answer is: sort of. There is a very wide body of research on the testosterone–aggression connection, and it is a surprisingly complicated relationship. Some studies are more straightforwardly supportive of the testosterone–aggression relationship. One study found that college fraternities with members that exhibited higher testosterone levels were wilder and more unruly than fraternities with members with lower testosterone levels (Dabbs et al. 1996). Another found that prisoners with higher testosterone levels were more aggressive and violent (Dabbs et al. 1995). Some studies have also found that among women higher levels of testosterone are correlated with aggressive behaviors (Denson et al. 2018).

But look a little further and the picture quickly gets very complicated. The direct correlation between testosterone and aggression is actually relatively limited, meaning increased levels of testosterone only lead to small increases in aggressive behavior, including in laboratory studies in which subjects were directly injected with testosterone to see if such injections increased aggressive behavior. Put differently, the studies do not show that one individual with ten times the testosterone of another individual is ten times more violent or aggressive.

A more nuanced interpretation, based on newer studies, is that higher levels of testosterone cause individuals to seek higher status and dominance, sometimes without resorting to aggression or violence. Higher status and dominance means achieving control of a social network or organization, achieving physical control over others through threats or demonstrations of strength, succeeding in competitions such as getting better grades, earning a promotion, or winning in sports, and so forth. One study found even more nuanced patterns, that higher levels of testosterone increased dominance behavior among high-status males, but caused low-status males to be more acquiescent, pushing them to support more strongly the hierarchical male network (Inoue et al. 2017). This is a good example of biological and social factors working together, as higher levels of testosterone are causing different forms of social behavior, even cooperative behavior, rather than simply blind aggression. And if higher levels of testosterone push males or male networks to seek to achieve status and dominance within social, political, or economic organizations, they can create cultures of male repression, a gendered effect. As we describe later in the chapter, male networks are critical to understanding violence against women, and male-dominated power structures more broadly.

The behavior of sports fans demonstrates the complexity of the testosterone–aggression relationship. Men experience higher levels of testosterone when their sports teams win, and lower levels when they lose. But, studies also demonstrate a gigantic spike in violence against women and children, as much as 40 percent, when home sports teams play, whether the home team won or lost, perhaps because watching sports can involve heavy alcohol consumption and surges in feelings of violent tribalism (Pescud 2018). This surge in aggression from sports can escalate. One study found that when a country's national soccer team qualifies for the World Cup, the country becomes more likely to become involved in violent conflict with another country (Bertoli 2017).

There are other complicated relationships between sex, gender, and violence. Consider video games. Males are more likely than females to play violent video games, and some studies show that playing violent video games makes some forms of aggressive behavior more likely, such as making children more likely to play with guns and pull the trigger if they do (Carroll 2019). Anecdotally, several male mass shooters played violent video games, including the 1999 Columbine High School killers who played the first-person shooter game Doom. Before they murdered thirteen people, the killers made a video declaring that it would be "like [expletive] Doom," and they described the sawed-off shotgun they used as being out of the Doom game (Kenworthy 1999).

This phenomenon of males seeking out violent activities, stimuli, or professions which in turn make them more violent is a point that has also been made regarding war toys, gun ownership, viewing misogynist pornography, and joining police forces. That is, it may be the case that males are biologically inclined to seek out violent culture, and elements of violent culture in turn serve to fuel violent behavior. Maleness, masculinity, and violence can all synergistically feed off each other, sometimes creating cultures of **militarized masculinity**. These are warrior cultures that emphasize values such as aggressiveness, obedience, courage, stoicism, domination of others, and loyalty, over other, more feminine values. These images are frequently present in military recruitment posters, such as the 1900 US military recruitment poster in Figure 2.1.

A related question is the connection between sex, gender, cooperation, and competition. Are males less inclined to cooperate and more likely to compete as compared with females? As with many other areas of studying sex and gender, experimental studies provide mixed findings (it's a complicated world!). One examination of nearly 300 different scholarly experiments on sex and cooperation found that in experimental lab settings (think of subjects playing simple computer games where they have the opportunity to cooperate with other subjects), women were not significantly more likely than men to cooperate (Balliet et al. 2011). However, results were different when experimentalists looked at attitudes towards competition. In some lab experiments, scientists sometimes found that women were less inclined to compete against men, and less inclined to perform as well as they might otherwise as the competitiveness of the game increased. Some have speculated that females may be less inclined to compete against males because they realize the possible negative implications of doing so, for men compete with ferocity when they believe they are going to lose to a woman (Niederle and Vesterlund 2005). One way to urge women to compete, interestingly enough, is to have them compete on behalf of others, meaning that competitive success would provide benefits to others, especially others to whom they feel a duty of care. In such experiments, women increase their competitiveness significantly (Cassar and Rigdon 2021). In contrast, men are more likely to welcome competition for the opportunity to acquire status and dominate.

Before we move on to the next section, it's important to lay out one very important caveat to the discussion. The studies summarized above describe average effects, in that in a sample of 10,000 people, women might on average be less aggressive or violent than men. But these are average effects, and there is a lot of variance among women and among men. Some women are competitive, aggressive, and violent, and some men are cooperative and peaceful. Some women join state militaries, rebel groups, and terrorist groups, and proceed to kill civilians, torture, commit war crimes, and engage in sexual assault. And some men join peace movements, become nurses, embrace pacifism, mediate conflicts, and choose prison over military service.

Further, the effects of sex and gender on conflict can vary widely by culture, race, class, ethnicity, nationality, and political ideology. The interactions between different kinds of identity, like sex and race interacting such that European American men have different ideas about gender compared with African American men, is called intersectionality. There are many international examples of context shaping sex and gender. Though, as we note below,

Figure 2.1. Note the elements of militarized masculinity embodying duty and honor in this 1900 American recruitment poster. And note that the recruiter in the poster image is calling on the (male) reader to act to protect the helpless woman in the image. ©Bettmann / Contributor/Bettmann/ Getty Images.

American women are generally less supportive of the use of force compared with American men, public opinion surveys show that in both Arab countries and Israel there are no significant differences between men and women regarding support for peaceful solutions to the Arab–Israeli conflict (Tessler et al. 1998). The Taliban in Afghanistan generally disallow women from joining their militant ranks, whereas nearly one third of the fighters in the Tamil rebel group in Sri Lanka were women. Context matters.

The First Political Order

The previous section focused on the individual, how sex and gender tend to affect individual behavior, such as individual proclivity to aggression. In this section, we develop a broader argument thinking about how sex in particular has helped create political and social structures that in turn are the taproot sources of a variety of forms of violence, that is, we describe how sex helped form gender. These dynamics are so entrenched in our political systems that we describe them as the "first political order."

An important part of understanding where we are now concerns where we have come from, specifically the long course of human evolution. Whether we approve or not, human evolution has resulted in a legacy where there is on average a significant difference between the bodies of males and the bodies of females. This is most obvious in the vastly different physical involvement in reproduction; only females bear young, which involves nine or more months of intensive energy expenditure, as well as possible death, while male involvement in reproduction may be limited to a couple of minutes of low-cost energy expenditure. But there are other differences, as well. The most important physical difference relates to the use of physical force. We have previously noted the effect of testosterone on the predisposition to use physical force, but it is also true that men have bodies that are, on average, much more physically powerful than those of women, with an average 80 percent more muscle mass in their arms, and having significantly greater overall muscle mass, weight, and height (Barash 2016). A man's punching force, for example, is 162 percent that of a woman's, on average (Morris et al. 2020).

We can see from this evolutionary legacy an imprint of what our ancestors faced in order to reproduce. Our female ancestors were coerced into reproduction by more physically powerful males, who contributed little physical effort for reproduction but depended on females. Our male ancestors' hopes for reproduction were threatened by other men, specifically their murder at the hands of other males. We see echoes of this today: the overwhelming majority of women killed are killed by men, and not just any men, but men with whom they have been sexually involved. The overwhelming majority of men killed are murdered by other men, and these figures are particularly high for young adult men. Furthermore, the sheer number of men killed by other men utterly dwarfs the number of women killed by men (United Nations Office on Drugs and Crime 2019).

There are thus foundational sex-based security dilemmas in any human society. Women in every human society face predation by males who seek to control their sexual and reproductive behavior and are prepared to resort to violence to maintain that control. Men in every society face the threat of annihilative violence by other men. Indeed, one of the most interesting anthropological findings of recent years is the discovery of how often a given genetic group completely disappears in human history, indicating that whole **male kin groups** – networks of male family members – were slaughtered en masse by other male kin groups, with the women of the group spared to become the property of the victorious group (Zeng et al. 2018).

We are already hinting at the mechanism that has been used throughout human history by men to protect themselves: the male kin group. The key network within almost every human society has been the male fraternity, cemented by blood ties. The male kin group is the structure that allows males to feel secure in a world of a sex-based security dilemma created by constant threat from other males and male networks. The formation of a dominance hierarchy within the male kin group allows men to trust one other, and creates a leadership structure that dampens in-group rivalries and conflict between the men of the group. In human history, the larger and more powerful a male kin group, the more likely individual men had children and lived to see old age. Fraternity was a winning strategy for men over eons of human history and is reflected in the saga of human history and in the subordination of women worldwide.

Male kinship groups rest on male dominance structures within families. Especially important is **patrilineality**, the practice of tracing family membership through the father. Patrilineality can have a variety of manifestations and implications, including that children get the last name of the father, sons rather than daughters have primary inheritance rights, the father rather than the mother leads and speaks for the family, sons have more autonomy in choosing spouses than daughters, and others.

Male fraternity, and the creation of that fraternity through kinship, has been the default form of governance structure, and is often resorted to even in the twenty-first century when states become incompetent or fail. In modern times, these male kinship structures may be referred to as clans, tribes, gangs or other types of organizations (brigades, teams, factions, etc.). They resurge in times of exigency, and do not fully disappear when the exigency is past, for men have been molded by our evolutionary past to form male-bonded exclusionary groups easily and swiftly for security as well as capturing the resources of out-groups (David-Barrett et al. 2015). Remember those disappearing genetic groups in human history? They disappeared because one male-bonded group annihilated a smaller male-bonded group completely, and took all they possessed, including the women of the annihilated group of men. The purpose of the male-bonded kin group, first and foremost, is the protection of males in the group from threat by male-bonded out-groups; these groups are a security provision mechanism, if you will, and they provide primarily security for males.

At this point we can begin to see some application to the study of international relations and war. But before we proceed, let's recognize the limits of the evolutionary perspective. While evolution can speak pretty accurately to general trends among human beings, it can never determine individual choices or situations. To take a trivial example, some women are stronger and taller than some men. But more importantly, just because males may have been primed by evolution to swiftly form all-male exclusionary groups, to subordinate females, and to use their fraternal bonds to defend against and prey on others does not mean that any particular man will necessarily do this. It is even possible for whole societies to attempt to fight these patterns, introducing robust incentives and disincentives that militate against them. No one is helpless against our common evolutionary heritage – but no one is immune from it, either.

In human history, male-bonded kin groups are ubiquitous as power nodes within society. In the modern day such groups have an apparent rival: centralized states. Such powerful states would seem to subsume and eliminate male-bonded kin groups as a serious force in society. However, many modern states are weak, allowing male-bonded kin groups to be the de facto power within the state; this is not only true of openly clan-based societies such as Somalia and Afghanistan, or of openly tribal societies such as Nigeria, but also of societies that at first glance might seem merely autocratic, such as in the Caucasus or the Balkans.

Further, even strong states do not always displace male kinship dynamics. Governments, including in democracies, are frequently controlled by male networks that are sometimes hostile to conceding political power to women. Women politicians and staffers are unfortunately confronted with widespread sexual harassment, as was revealed in modern scandals in the UK and Australia. Women politicians are sometimes the target of threats and even violence, from inside and outside of government. One study found that 44 percent of women parliamentarians worldwide had been the subject of threats of rape, murder, beatings, or abduction (Inter-Parliamentary Union 2016). And sometimes these threats are carried out, as when Finnish and British members of parliament Anna Lindh and Jo Cox were murdered in 2003 and 2016, respectively, each time stabbed to death by a man. Perhaps needless to say, the grave risks of taking political office dissuade some women from even running for election.

The logic of the male-bonded kin group always rests on the subordination of female interests to the interests of males. In a sense, then, the very first political order is the order established between the two halves of human society who must together provide a future for the group. While one could imagine a first, sexual political order based on equity and egalitarianism between men and women, the long-standing privileging of male interests more often results in both direct and systemic subordination of females, and this is clearly seen in the severe inequality between men and women in open clan-based societies. Direct violence against women is commonplace; for example, in the clan-based society of Afghanistan, surveys have found about 87 percent of women have experienced domestic violence (Moylan 2015). There are several repressive, devaluing, and violent practices (some of which we discuss later in the chapter) against girls and women, such as low investment in girls' health and education, female genital mutilation, early marriage for girls, polygyny (one man taking several wives), brideprice and dowry (the groom's family paying the bride's family to "purchase" the bride, or the reverse), sex-selective abortion and infanticide, lack of property and inheritance rights for females, inability to marry whom one wishes or to marry at all, lack of access to family planning, and so forth.

Beyond these dire consequences for women and girls, the first political order deeply shapes the entire society. Reliance on extended male kin groups for security produces a dysfunctional, corrupt, violent destiny. The primary reason it does so is due to the character and structure of the first sexual political order. When that first order, encompassing as it does the two halves of the human race, is predicated on violence, predation, oppression, coercion, and exploitation experienced by one half at the hand of the other half (to which it has given birth, ironically enough), the die is cast.

We can be confident of the disastrous effects of the repression of women because the data do not lie. The US Department of Defense funded the largest-ever empirical examination (Hudson et al. 2020) of the proposition that nation states where women were highly subordinated were also those with the worst national outcomes across many dimensions of national security, stability, and resilience. The study examined the degree to which women are subordinated in society by examining eleven variables: overall level of violence against women; societal sanction for the murder of women; laws exonerating rapists if they offer to marry their victim; prevalence of patrilocal marriage (meaning, new brides move in with their new husbands' families); prevalence of cousin marriage; son preference and sex ratio abnormalities; age of first marriage for girls in law and in practice; overall inequity in family and personal status law favoring males; prevalence of brideprice and dowry; prevalence of polygyny in law and practice; property and inheritance rights of women in law and in practice. The study examined 161 national outcome variables, and in 74 percent of the statistical analyses performed, this index of the degree of subordination of women was significantly associated with worse outcomes. The study found that for every step worse on the index of women's subordination, there was 1.25 times the chance of being poor and experiencing economic decline; 1.6 times the chance of a high level of preventable deaths; 1.8 times the chance of having a worse score on the Global Hunger Index; 1.9 times the chance of having a higher fertility rate; 1.3 times the change of having worse environmental quality.

It would take an extraordinary assault on the components of that repressive first political order for society to escape its fate. What you do to your women, you do to your country, and if you curse your women, you curse your country. The choice of security provision mechanism determines, in large part, the horizon of possibility for things that the majority of human beings value deeply: democracy, human rights, rule of law, peace, and prosperity. The next three sections describe implications for the repression of women on violence.

Marriage Market Obstruction: Brideprice, Polygyny, and Sex-Selective Abortion/Infanticide

Especially if you are in your late teens or early twenties, you may be starting to develop your own views about marriage, whether or not getting married is something you (eventually) may find to be personally rewarding. But in some societies getting married is tremendously important for non-emotional reasons, including securing access to social and economic power. In patrilineal societies, men must marry in order to become a full member of that patriline and in turn the kin group. Without marriage and the birth of one or more sons, a man does not occupy a place of respect in the kin group, and will not merit mention in the patriline's genealogy (Hudson et al. 2020). Thus, unlike in what we might term post-marriage societies where marriage rates are in decline, the issue of marriage is a chief concern of young adult males in patrilineal societies emphasizing male kinship networks.

The problem is that the subordination of women may reduce marriage prospects for men in these societies. We refer to this dynamic as "**marriage market obstruction**," meaning that there is market imbalance if demand for wives is outstripping supply. Any circumstance that threatens to reduce marriage prospects for men will be viewed by these men as deeply threatening, even justifying a resort to violence. Marriage market obstruction for young men can quickly threaten social stability, and even national security.

The three practices most disruptive to marriage markets are brideprice inflation, polygyny, and sex-selection abortion/infanticide targeting daughters. Consider first brideprice (see Figure 2.2). In societies dominated by male kin groups, marriage often entails men exchanging women amongst themselves for a price. In most such societies, a brideprice is affixed, wherein the groom and his family pay the bride's family for the costs incurred in raising her. Because there is usually a "going rate" for a bride, young men from poorer families are already disadvantaged in the marriage market. A poor family may successfully raise the funds for a brideprice for the eldest son, but younger sons may be left to their own devices. However, as in many subjective pricing markets, brideprice is prone to sudden and swift inflation. It is not unheard of for brideprice to double, triple, or quintuple over the space of a few years. Such inflationary tendencies result in many more young men also being priced out of the market for brides.

Figure 2.2. This photo shows the many items used to pay the brideprice in 2016 in Nigeria. Brideprice is sometimes paid in items, such as farm animals, rather than money. Brideprice can be dauntingly high, especially in less wealthy areas.
REUTERS / Alamy Stock Photo.

In such circumstances, it is wealthy men who are most able to afford brides, and this provides a tie-in to the second structural factor leading to marriage market obstruction: **polygyny**, one man taking several wives. Almost all brideprice societies also practice polygyny, especially societies where women double as laborers, for there the more wives a man has, the richer he can become. Prevalent polygyny reduces bride availability in a straightforward fashion. If 10 percent of wealthy men have two wives, then 10 percent of poor men will not have any. The distortions increase with the number of wives. While four wives is officially the limit in some nations, in other countries there is no cap: one man in Zimbabwe was recorded as having sixteen wives and 151 children (Abrahams 2021). And, of course, there is a feedback loop with brideprice; the more polygyny is practiced, the scarcer brides are, and the higher a brideprice that can be demanded.

In societies with brideprice and polygyny, the market is obstructed despite the fact that enough brides are physically present in the society. But sometimes that is not the case. Because of the deep devaluation of female life in societies where male-bonded kin groups hold power, girls may go missing, in the sense that these societies do not have the number of girls (and women) we would expect to see if girls and boys were valued equally. Girls are often fed last and with poorer quality food, and families may also hesitate to take girls in for medical care, preferring to save money to spend on the needs of more valued sons. Thus, there may be abnormally high childhood mortality rates for girls. Child marriage and its associated very high rates of maternal mortality are another source of the disappearance of females from the population, as are female-targeted honor killings and honor "suicides."

However, the most egregious source of the physical disappearance of women from the population is sex-selective abortion/infanticide. Specifically, some parents prefer sons to daughters. When the wife becomes pregnant, the couple conducts an ultrasound test to determine the gender of the fetus, and if the ultrasound indicates that the fetus is female, in some societies the couple is much more likely to abort the fetus. Even worse, in some cases the couple observes the sex of the baby after it is born, and observing that it is a girl, murders her.

Estimates are that at least 142 million missing girls and women in the world today are missing because of these practices. Leaving aside for now how morally horrifying these practices are, this kind of sex selection has devastating impacts on society by creating a lopsided birth sex ratio, the ratio of boys born to girls born. (A normal birth sex ratio is close to even.) Birth sex ratios are abnormal in at least nineteen countries today, though China and India account for most of the missing girls and women. Birth sex ratios come to haunt a country for decades, as the birth sex ratio in one year affects the marriage market sex ratio about twenty years into the future. China, which has recently lifted punishments for having additional children, will still feel the effects of the one-child policy for decades to come. It's estimated that about 12 percent of female births are culled in India, and almost 15 percent in China, translating to 12 percent of Indian males and almost 15 percent of Chinese males who will have difficulty finding brides within their own nations. Brides may also be imported from neighboring countries, which in effect exports marriage market obstruction to other nations.

A sense of deep grievance among young men attends obstruction of marriage markets. Those who find themselves without realistic marriage prospects – we will call them by the Chinese term "**bare branches**" – are highly motivated to rectify the situation, sometimes by any means necessary. Thus, we find a variety of fairly predictable strategies being employed by bare branches to better their position, bolster their reputation, and establish their honor – none of which enhance the stability, security, or resilience of their society.

Unmarried young men are dangerous in part because of their comparative physical strength as young adult males and their willingness to use that strength, especially in male-bonded groups and even in illegal or sociopathic ways. They seek to gain what they need, especially more money to compete for scarce wives, including paying inflated brideprice rates. One study found that in China for every 1 percent alteration of the sex ratio in favor of males, there was a corresponding 3.7 percent increase in violent and property crime rates (Edlund et al. 2013). But imbalanced sex ratios also make non-economic crimes more likely, as humiliated men commit violent acts to assert their dominance and sense of power. Honor – with its laser-like focus on respect and disrespect – takes on heightened salience in cultures with a sizeable number of bare branches. And, as males become more focused on protecting their honor, they become more likely to engage in male-to-male dominance contests (Mazur and Booth 1998). One study of six Asian countries found that in areas with more imbalanced sex ratios, men were significantly more likely to have raped a woman or gotten into a fight with a weapon (Diamond-Smith and Rudolph 2018). Dominance contests can also catalyze risky behavior among groups of young men, as they become more willing to take greater risks collectively than individually. Such regard for honor may even come to color national politics: countries with highly masculinized sex ratios such as China and India exhibit potentially belligerent nationalism, especially with each other.

Governments cannot easily meet the demands of bare branches and provide enough wives for them, and though governments may turn a blind eye to predictable consequences such as the cross-border trafficking of women, they cannot ignore spikes in violence. Governments may find they have no choice but to turn to "hard" tactics of authoritarianism in response to bare branches violence, brutally suppressing violence internally. Instability, crime, authoritarianism, and even greater suppression of women attend the development of abnormal sex ratios favoring males, which adds to – and follows logically from – the dysfunctional predispositions created by the obstructive practices.

A similar chain of events attends societies that accept polygyny, because polygyny serves as the functional equivalent of an abnormal sex ratio. By marrying multiple women, elite men create an underclass of young adult men who are elbowed out of the marriage market because there are not enough women in that market: these women are alive – unlike societies with abnormal sex ratios – but they have been monopolized by men with far greater resources than these young men. The effects are sometimes significant; in 1950s West Africa, for example, a quarter of men were permanently excluded from the marriage market because of polygyny (Tucker 2014, 83). The marriage market distortions of polygyny can encourage groups of unmarried men to engage in violent activity to capture wealth enabling them to compete in the marriage market, or even to capture women to be their wives (Henrich et al. 2012, 660). One study found that in Africa, ethnic groups with higher rates of polygyny experienced higher rates of intergroup conflict, and unmarried men from polygynous groups were more likely to believe violence is an acceptable tool to resolve social grievances (Koos and Neupert-Wentz 2019).

Although these same marriage market obstruction patterns are present in polygynous societies as well as societies in which the sex ratio is altered as a result of culling female births and infants, the flavor of grievance in polygynous societies is somewhat different and perhaps more intense than in societies with abnormal sex ratios. When girls are culled from the birth population, it is difficult to blame specific individuals for the dislocations that result. Indeed, many families within the society – perhaps even one's own – may be practicing offspring sex selection. In polygynous societies, however, it is clear to everyone who has unfairly accumulated many wives: wealthy men. Thus, there is a more personal, more specific cause of the grievance in full view in polygynous societies than in abnormal sex ratio societies. One's chances of overcoming this obstruction seem significantly better than in those latter societies – if the collective action problem among one's similarly marginalized fellows could be solved.

No wonder, then, that some studies have shown greater ease of recruitment into rebel groups in polygynous societies. In Sierra Leone, a country wracked by civil war through the 1990s, obstructed marriage markets fueled rebel recruitment. Polygyny and brideprice practices made marriage at best a crippling economic burden for poorer men, and many joined rebel groups because the rebels promised to provide women or money to pay brideprice to afford getting married. Indeed, most rebel recruits came from regions with brideprice practices (Mokuwa et al. 2011). And this tactic paid off for the recruits in the sense that marriage became easier. In areas of Sierra Leone that experienced high conflict, though, the average age of male marriage dropped by seven to fifteen years (from twenty-five to thirty-five down to eighteen to twenty), and marriage markets cleared. Almost certainly, however, nothing changed for the better for the women (Nielsen 2017).

In addition to feeding social grievance and conflict, this lack of resilience in polygynous cultures may manifest in more rigid, and therefore more fragile, governance systems. Polygyny is a culture of hierarchy, and authoritarianism may emerge as a response to groups of marginalized and disaffected young men. Polygynous societies are more likely to be authoritarian, to have lower respect for political and civil liberties, and to have higher per capita arms expenditures (Betzig 2008; McDermott and Cowden 2015).

Brideprice, too, can destabilize nations. For example, an entire ethnic group in South Sudan was destabilized by rising brideprices among the group around the time of independence

(Richmond and Krause-Jackson 2011). Cattle theft rose precipitously as desperate would-be grooms sought additional livestock to meet the rising price of brides, and revenge attacks followed these thefts. Jada Tombe, a young man in South Sudan, noted, "We risk our lives to raid other communities so we can pay bride price" (Aleu and Mach 2016). A US Institute of Peace field study explained:

Emmanuel Gambiri said an educated wife in his cattle-herding Mundari tribe in South Sudan costs 50 cows, 60 goats and 30,000 Sudanese pounds ($12,000) in cash. "At that price, some men who otherwise can't afford a bride turn to stealing livestock in order to buy a wife and gain status," said Gambiri, citing a friend who is now a cattle rustler. A surge in "bride price" has fueled cattle raids in which more than 2,000 people are killed each year. (Richmond and Krause-Jackson 2011)

The effects of obstructed marriage markets on internal violence and instability have been demonstrated in North Africa, as well. When a journalist asked Libyan rebels what were their dreams, they replied, "Help us get married" (Shane and Becker 2016). In Egypt, during the 2011 protests that led to the downfall of autocratic leader Hosni Mubarak, male protesters, frustrated by the high price of marriage, chanted, "We want to get married." Young men there were forced to delay marriage into their early thirties, because the price of marriage was some thirteen times the average annual salary (Murdock 2011). The so-called "youth bulge," when a growing fraction of the population is young, may exacerbate societal tensions if it means there are more young men unable to find wives because of marriage market obstructions (Urdal 2006).

Furthermore, rebel and terrorist groups are attuned to this source of discontent, and they openly recruit by promising to solve the marriage asset problem for young men. It is fascinating to see just how many terrorist and rebel groups are so very concerned about the marriage prospects of the young men in their ranks. For example, in Syria the Islamic State was well known for providing its foreign jihadis with the opportunity to marry that they may not have had in their home country. In one such campaign, the Islamic State offered fighters a $1,500 bonus for a starter home and a free honeymoon (Baker 2015). These dynamics are not new, as historically, younger sons (whose families may not have been able to accumulate brideprice for more than one or two sons) were often agents of military expansion (Adams 2008). During the Middle Ages, European younger sons unable to find wives tended to join the Crusades, often flocking to younger princes, who themselves felt the same challenges (Boone 1983, 1986). States also sometimes step in, using brideprice to attract young men to their militaries. The Syrian government provides brideprices and weddings for its soldiers, including those who are wounded or who lost brothers in the civil war (Brennan 2017).

Even more disturbing, rebel groups such as Nigeria's Boko Haram sometimes use brideprice grievance to attract recruits through promises of facilitating marriage through the capture and trafficking of young women (Hudson and Matfess 2017). "In this crisis, these men can take a wife at no extra charge," explained Kaka, a young African woman orphaned, captured, and raped by Boko Haram. "Usually it is very expensive to take a wife, very hard to get married, but not now" (Matfess 2016).

In sum, in societies based on male kinship as the primary security provision mechanism, marriage markets obstructed by high marriage costs, prevalent polygyny, or abnormal sex ratios favoring males fuel violence and instability. The young men themselves engage in crime to pay brideprices. Rebel and terrorist groups exploit young adult men who are interested in redressing the injustice they feel on a personal level, by force if necessary, thereby seriously degrading the stability and security of the society. States react to these threats by expanding authoritarian control. "Sex" is essential to explaining and predicting instability, insecurity, and conflict.

Male Violence against Women (MVAW)

The dynamics described in the previous section generally described how the repression of women and girls generates a number of forms of violence and war. Unfortunately, the first political order of male oppression also fuels violence against women, including beatings, rape, and murder. For many women, the reality of violence is ubiquitous. Rebecca Katibo, married as a child in South Sudan, puts it simply, "In my husband's house everything is by force – there is no request. If I refuse there will be a problem. My husband will beat me" (Chamberlain 2017).

The tendency for males to attack females far, far more frequently than the reverse is very widely cross-cultural (Gat 2008, 79). The psychologist David Barash grimly noted that "the male–female difference in perpetrators of violent crime is about 10 to 1, consistent across every state in the United States, and true of every country for which such data are available . . . . The overwhelming maleness of violence is so pervasive in every human society that it is typically not even recognized as such; it is the ocean in which we swim" (Barash 2016, 27). When females are physically hurt, the overwhelming proportion of perpetrators are male, close to 100 percent (Catalano et al. 2009).

Even the form of entertainment men perhaps most consume – pornography – has been proposed to have a variety of disturbing connections to violence against women. Some pornography directly portrays violence against women, some pornography is the filming of actual rape, sex traffickers sometimes force their victims to participate in the production of pornography, and some scholars believe that pornography can play disturbing roles in intimate partner violence (Tyler and Tarzia 2021). Indeed, the popular pornography website "Pornhub" – in 2020 130 million people visited Pornhub each day – attracted so much negative attention around some of these issues that it inspired the creation of watchdog websites (Cry 2020).

Within virtually all societies, it seems, women's everyday physical insecurity is viewed as completely unremarkable, and in this way, given tacit sanction. Levels of domestic violence, rape, and even domestic murder remain high, even in states that have largely made their laws sex-equitable (Brysk 2018). Phumzile Mlambo-Ngcuka, executive director of UN Women, has stated that "Violence is the biggest challenge facing women around the world," and "even countries that have the highest indicators on gender equality like Iceland . . . still have to confront the issue of violence against women" (Wulfhorst).

Coercion for the sake of asserting masculinity is a prominent motivation for violence at the level of individual males, but it is also true that the logic holds at the kin group level, as well. The interests of the male kin group must dominate over female interests, but patrilines often find that women – even women born to the patriline – do not always share their interests. Mothers may object to child marriages of their daughters. Sisters may object to a lack of inheritance. Wives may object to male dominance in household decisionmaking, including decisions that bring a new wife into the family. Therefore, in addition to inequities in family law that keep male interests superordinate – such as arranged child marriage, polygyny, and patrilocality – the patriline is also prepared to use physical force to maintain the dominance of its interests over those of women. Thus, we expect that societies reliant on the male kin group as a security provision mechanism would tolerate the highest levels of violence against women (even though all societies tolerate a significant level of such violence), and that is indeed what the Department of Defense study found (Hudson et al. 2020). That is why even when new laws against violence against women are proposed, such as in Morocco, spousal abuse is often excepted, for the woman is the property, if you will, of the patrilineal kin group (ANSAmed 2018).

To uphold the patriline's interests in cases where childhood socialization is not effective, more coercive means will be unveiled. One study conducted thirty focus group interviews with 250 women in Pakistan. The authors found that

from childhood, girls are informed, taught and trained to believe that only men who are physically powerful and hence mentally competent to make decisions; *She is counseled, and if this does not work, she is forced through threats and violence to believe that she is an object that has to be operated by a male family member.* In cases where women challenge these patriarchal privileges and/or seek to enforce their rights, violence is used as a means to control them. (Rizvi et al. 2014)

Moreover, they explain that the types of violence experienced by the women in their study were quite varied: "It could be physical ranging from slapping to burning; verbal such as taunting, use of bad language; mental like threats of divorce and actual divorce; and sexual in the form of rape and incest." Indeed, one of the most appalling aspects of violence against women is the wide variety of forms it takes. The United Nations Population Fund recently released a report that identifies nineteen different violent cultural practices that harm women, aside from crimes such as murder and rape. These include accusations of witchcraft (often a prelude to murder); female genital cutting; brideprice and dowry-related assault and murder; child marriage; sex-selective abortion and infanticide; under-feeding of girls; virginity testing; widow inheriting and widow cleansing; breast ironing; honor crimes, and others (United Nations Population Fund 2020).

Indeed, one of the worst elements of MVAW is how often the violence is perpetrated not only with the consent of society, but with society's approbation or even its insistence. Especially in the case of so-called honor crimes, men may feel virtuous for harming women, including murdering them or forcing their suicides (misleadingly labelled "honor suicides"). Reasons of male honor are often invoked, and these crimes may have deep cultural resonance. This case in Ankara, Turkey plays out similarly in many places across the world: "Ignoring the pleas of his fourteen-year-old daughter to spare her life, Mehmet Halitogullari pulled on a wire wrapped around her neck and strangled her – supposedly to restore the family's honor after she was kidnapped and raped. Nuran Halitogullari, buried Thursday in a ceremony attended by women's rights advocates, is the latest victim in a long history of 'honor' killings" (World Datelines 2004). The crude saying "A man's honor lies between the legs of a woman" encapsulates the logic of why some men feel they must murder women and girls who have been violated.

Sanction for a female's killing may extend beyond a woman's sexual behavior to any type of "deviant" woman. As we have seen, if one is regarded as a "witch," one may be killed with impunity in certain cultures. Often perpetrators feel they are undertaking a heroic task. One of a mob who killed a "witch" in Papua New Guinea was quoted in Morris as saying, "I see myself as a guardian angel. We feel that we kill on good grounds and we're working for the good of the people in the village" (Morris 2017).

This idea that **honor killing** is a virtuous act is common. The brother who kills to cleanse the family honor after his sister has been raped may say, "Yes, she's my sister and I love her, but it is a duty" (Husseini n.d.). When this degree of societal sanction for killing women exists, it is clear the interests of the male kin group fraternity are paramount.

It is not only codes of honor that give cover to MVAW: the law enforcement establishment may tacitly give impunity to those who harm women. Crimes of honor may be punished with lesser sentences (The Penal Code 2021). In Syria, for example, the punishment for murder is twenty years in prison at hard labor. The minimum punishment for the killing of a woman for reasons of male honor is but two years, and after his release the murderer may be treated as a hero. Even in more developed countries with more equitable laws, there may be subcultures where male honor is inextricably tied up with female sexual behavior. In Texas, a man was given a four-month sentence for killing his ex-wife due to "sudden passion," while given fifteen years for wounding her male lover at the very same time.

More than this, though, sometimes laws against MVAW are simply not enforced. Consider the virtual "decriminalisation of rape" in the United Kingdom, in the words of one high British government official (Barr 2020). Only about 1.5 percent of rapes recorded by police in England and Wales result in a charge or a summons (Bowcott and Barr 2019). In 2020, 41 percent of reports were dropped as the complainant did not support actions called for by police or prosecutors to build a case or bring charges. Rape victims face an average wait of 98 days for a decision to charge or drop their case. The average wait for a charge is 395 days, the longest of any crime type. In other words, when the likelihood of facing actual criminal conviction for rape is so low, then rape has been de facto legalized (Home Office 2020).

One of the first things a Martian visiting planet Earth would notice is just how stunningly prevalent male-on-female violence is, the tremendous costs it imposes on society, women, and children, and how much MVAW is taken for granted, ignored, or even applauded among humankind. How can you call a society secure when half the population is so devastatingly insecure?

The Repression of Women, Civil Wars, and Wars between Nations

We can easily see how the repression of women can lead to violence on individual and social levels, to sex-selective abortion, infanticide, honor killings, sexual assault, property crimes, and others. But how might the repression of women translate into violence at broader levels, civil wars within countries and wars between countries? These connections may be a bit more difficult to see, but they are there. This section describes these connections.

Wars between Nations

Wars between nations start because a national government decides to use force rather than diplomacy or other means to achieve its national goals. The repression of women and the domination by men might make the national use of force more likely, through two different pathways.

First, broadly speaking men and women have on average different views about the use of force in foreign policy. One analysis of seventeen different public opinion studies found that in general 50 percent of men were likely to support the use of force in foreign policy, and only 38 percent of women, a significant difference (Barnhart et al. 2020). This difference may be driven in part by sex differences, men on average being more supportive of aggression and domination to achieve their goals as compared with women, and perhaps also experiencing less empathy with the individuals who experience the costs of war (Christov-Moore et al. 2014). The use of force also avoids the necessity of making concessions in diplomacy, an action men may oppose because of their desire to dominate. However, gender matters as well as sex. One study found that both men and women with more gender egalitarian attitudes were less likely to support the use of force in foreign policy (Wood and Ramirez 2019. That said, there is less of a gap between men and women on some uses of force, as women are more willing to use force in pursuit of humanitarian goals such as protecting civilians (Eichenberg 2019).

The next step in the argument asks, how does opinion about the use of force translate into the actual use of force? If men are more prone than women to use force, then empowering women means solidifying peace. The idea that empowering women bolsters peace has a long history. Women have formed their own peace movements since at least World War I. Today, the United Nations has formally recognized that "the active participation of women, on equal terms with men, at all levels of decision-making is essential to the achievement of equality, sustainable development, peace and democracy" (United Nations 2012). Governments of nations such as the United States have made similar declarations.

Let's dig even deeper. In democracies, political power comes through the vote. As discussed in Chapter 3, for centuries observers have proposed that democracies are less likely to fight each other, because the people hate war and in democracies leaders have to answer to the people. However, women have not always had equal voting rights with men. Up through the early twentieth century, women did not have voting rights in the United Kingdom, until eventually the Suffragette movement (see Figure 2.3), using tactics such as protests, political writings, hunger strikes, and even hundreds of nonlethal arson and bombing attacks, won for British women the right to vote.

This insight that men are more likely than women to support the use of force suggests an important limitation on the democratic peace: democracies are more peaceful with each other, but only when men as well as women are given the vote, for if only men get the vote, then the voters (all male) will not push their elected governments to peace. And this is exactly what we observe. One study looked at all countries in the world back to 1816. It found that even after controlling for other potential causes of conflict, such as military–industrial power, trade, and alliances, democracies that gave women the right to vote were nearly half as likely to get involved in violent interstate disputes as compared to either dictatorships or democracies that did not give women the right to vote (Barnhart et al. 2020). Other studies have shown that nations spend less on the military and are less likely to get involved in international crises when

Figure 2.3. Suffragettes in Britain, 1908. The Suffragette movement, made up mostly of women, demanded that women be given the equal right to vote. Though it took decades, the insistent demand for justice and equality eventually succeeded.
©Heritage Images / Contributor/ Hulton Archive/ Getty Images.

they have more women serving in the legislature (Koch and Fulton 2011). (Chapter 5 takes up the question of whether female national leaders are less likely to take their countries to war.)

Think about the United States in 1898. As a crisis brewed between the USA and Spain over the Spanish colony of Cuba, women's groups advocated for arbitration, but American women were not at this point guaranteed the right to vote, limiting their political power. Many American men saw the Cuba crisis as an opportunity to establish and strengthen American manhood and honor through war. One Congressman declared that "we fight because it has become necessary to fight if we would uphold our manhood," and another opined that the choice is to fight to defend American honor or "remain impotent" (quoted in Hoganson 2000, 70). The men of America got their war with Spain, and in victory built an empire that led immediately to a brutal counter-insurgency war in the Philippines, and decades of ongoing repression in Cuba.

A more gendered path between the repression of women and conflicts between states concerns cultures of **militarized masculinity**. Societies that repress women sometimes also embrace cultures of militarized masculinity, idolizing war as glorious for men, as the path men must take to earn their personal honor and place within society. Women, on the other hand, are not given the role of glorious warrior, and instead are tasked with tending to home and family. On the national level, cultures of militarized masculinity often seek out war. When societies idolize war as intrinsic to attaining honor, war becomes almost an end in itself, making the costs of war much more acceptable, meaning it is more difficult for two sides in conflict to

Figure 2.4. Russian President Vladimir Putin affirms his masculine virtues. The Russian government released a steady stream of official photographs such as this one, showing a shirtless, vigorous Putin in the wild with a hunting rifle.
©DMITRY ASTAKHOV / Stringer/ AFP/Getty Images.

find bargaining space and reach a war-avoiding peace deal (see Chapter 1). Further, militarized masculinity extols the urge to dominate others, for example acquiring needed natural resources through empire rather than through trade, and eliminating potential threats through conquest rather than conflict resolution.

Politicians or political systems sometimes bundle together repression of women and militarized masculinity into a single set of cultural norms and ideas, in preparation to launch wars of empire. It is no coincidence that two of the most war-prone regimes in history, World War II Germany and Japan, extolled the glory of war in cultures of militarized masculinity that kept women in strictly defined roles. In both these deeply racialized regimes, women did not serve in the military, had no political power, and were tasked primarily with procreating their race, expanding the population of the racially pure to dominate lesser races in other countries. After the Nazi German and Imperial Japanese regimes were destroyed in the war, the United States wrote into their new constitutions explicit recognition of the equal rights of women. Since 1945, both countries have enjoyed decades of peace.

In the twenty-first century, themes of masculine domination course through the foreign policy ideas of the world's more aggressive regimes. Vladimir Putin has carefully cultivated an image of manliness, distributing photos of himself shirtless while engaging in traditionally masculine activities such as hunting and fishing (see Figure 2.4, and online Ukraine War module).

Not coincidentally, Putin has entrenched male domination of women in Russia, for example in 2017 de facto decriminalizing domestic violence (Ferris-Rotman 2018). In taking aggressive actions such as the annexation of Crimea, support of separatist rebels in Ukraine, and the expansion of the Russian nuclear arsenal, Putin routinely espouses militarized masculine values of resolve, honor, and domination. Of Russian seizure of Crimea and aggression in Ukraine, Putin declared that "a bear doesn't ask permission of anyone." Of Putin's regional rival, the president of Georgia, he dismissively declared, "Saakashvili is far from having democratic values – not to speak of male ones – he doesn't have any of those at all" (quoted in Sperling 2016, 18, 16). The authoritarian tools of the Russian state under Putin make it relatively easy for Putin to squash Russian women's groups and women's protests denouncing repression and war, including the 2021 Chain of Solidarity and Love protest, the female punk rock group Pussy Riot, and others.

Civil Wars

Repression of women can also make civil wars more likely. As described, obstructed marriage markets can facilitate rebel recruitment of bare branches young men. The reverse can occur as well, as the oppression of women can cause women themselves to join rebel or terrorist groups. Tamil rebels in Sri Lanka successfully recruited women fighters in part by promising gender equality if they won their war and created an independent Tamil state.

There are other connections, as well. The repression of women does not occur in isolation, but is usually part of society-wide repression, that is, political cultures and institutions that repress women also lend themselves to repressing other groups. At the broadest level, the essence of the repression of women is the rejection of the belief that all people are created equal and deserve equal treatment. It is the rejection of Marie Shear's famous statement that, "Feminism is the radical notion that women are people." Denying the rights of one group creates the context for broader violations of rights. Male kinship groups, critical elements of the first political order, control women to maintain rather than share power, and this tendency to dominate rather than include easily spreads to the treatment of other groups.

A more sex-oriented account focuses on what happens when men hold political power. If men are more likely than women to seek dominance over others, and are more willing to use force to dominate, then political systems that are dominated by men are more likely to be willing to violate human rights, to deprive groups of equal rights, and to imprison, torture, and execute political opponents. When women have more political power, then political systems are more likely to respect the rights of individuals and groups, and political leaders are more likely to seek to resolve disputes through cooperation and the rule of law rather than brutal oppression.

Repressive societies are in turn more likely to experience civil war. Repression fuels discontent among angry minorities and other groups. Repressive governments are less likely to consider war-avoiding concessions to disaffected minorities, fearing that such concessions may encourage other groups to demand change, unraveling their hold on power (see Chapter 7).

It may be difficult to see these direct connections in action. But studies have consistently demonstrated broad empirical support for both steps in the argument. Several studies have shown that societies that repress or disempower women have consistently worse human rights records. Specifically, more gender-unequal states were five times more likely to experience civil war as compared with the most gender-equal states (Dahlum and Wig 2020). And, there are other pieces of evidence that demonstrate the importance of women for building peace. One study of all conflicts since 1975 found that when women sign peace agreements, the peace lasts longer (Krause et al. 2018). Another study found that when women are empowered after civil war, peace is likely to be more durable (Best et al. 2019).

Consider the unlikely success story of Rwanda. Rwanda was wracked by decades of internal conflict after independence, including the shocking 1995 genocide that killed hundreds of thousands of people. Since the genocide, Rwanda has been a remarkable success story, enjoying the fastest rate of economic growth in Africa, an increase in life expectancy of fifteen years, and most importantly internal peace and stability. Rwanda's post-genocide parliament also has the highest percentage of women in the world (Figure 2.5).

Figure 2.5. Rwanda has achieved a higher percentage of women in its parliament than any other country. Xinhua / Alamy Stock Photo.

Policy Solutions

While there may never be a complete solution to the problems of subordination of and violence against women, we are not helpless before our evolutionary legacy. A sizeable number of nations have moved past the frank subordination of women to more mitigated versions of it. Further, there remain several specific, feasible policies governments can implement to reduce oppression and violence. We list a few here, choosing some that might surprise you a bit.

One vitally important policy lever is ensuring that only adult women marry. Child marriage devastates not only the girls involved, but condemns the next generation to a lower quality of life as children of children. Impressively, since the turn of the century, fifty-two nations have increased their marriage age for females to at least eighteen, and other countries have attempted to close loopholes that allowed such marriages. Unfortunately, as can be imagined, laws on the books are not as powerful as practices on the ground, and child marriage is still prevalent in our world. If it were not, an important source of women's subordination and negative nation-state outcomes would vanish.

Old age pensions are another crucial lever in improving women's circumstances and reducing their vulnerability. In societies organized around male kin groups, it is sons who are tasked with providing economically for aged parents. As a result, in countries with no old age pensions, son preference is rife, with its attendant ills of lack of investment in daughters (including investment of food and medical care) and sex-selective abortion/infanticide. Providing a pension cuts the link between social security and sons and undercuts the rationale for devaluing daughters, especially as daughters are more willing to provide personalized care to elderly parents. Indeed, establishing a pension system played a key role in reversing the abnormal birth sex ratios of South Korea (Hudson and den Boer 2005). Ironically, daughters are now more valued than sons, because South Korea practices brideprice, and now a family must pay a brideprice on behalf of a son but cannot expect financial support from that son later on in life.

Establishing, protecting, and enforcing property and inheritance rights for women is a fourth policy with great potential to offset the subordination of women. The male kin group systematically precludes women from controlling anything valuable: land, money, livestock, housing, even their own children. Such control must be shaken for the subordination of women to be alleviated. This is a tough challenge, for male kin groups are prepared to fight to retain their rights of control. Even so, promising programs exist. In particular, progress has been made in putting married women's names on land titles. Organizations such as Landesa have field workers wielding computer tablets, who locate women in rural areas and apply online to have these women's names put on land titles (Giovarelli and Scalise 2013). Other organizations are fighting practices that evict widows from their husband's property. Such efforts are important in helping women have access to sources of wealth – which translates into sources of independence – within the society.

There are other worthwhile ways to push back against the subordination of women. One is to undercut the prevalence of polygyny within societies that still practice it. As we have seen, polygyny ties in with both child marriage and brideprice inflation, and if polygyny were less prevalent, these other practices would also become less prevalent. Another way is to address the often large gap between laws on the books and practice on the ground for women. Many countries have fairly equitable laws, but the lack of enforcement means that women still stand unequal to men under the law. Men are often given impunity or light sentences for horrible crimes against women and children, a phenomenon that some call "himpathy" (Manne 2017). These crimes should, however, be viewed as connected to the threats of domestic terrorism and mass killings and deserve to be treated with the utmost seriousness. After all, one of the best predictors of who will become a mass shooter or domestic terrorist in the United States is a prior run-in with the law over domestic violence (Anderson 2021). Governments can also work to cap brideprices and wedding costs in order to prevent inflationary bubbles, and many have made efforts on that front. Where laws are still highly inequitable towards women, such as in citizenship and nationality laws, legal action must be undertaken to try and have these declared unconstitutional. For example, only a few years ago, the Ugandan high court ruled that a woman could proceed with a divorce even if she did not repay her brideprice, and that the law that had mandated such a refund was unconstitutional (Library of Congress 2015).

Finally, of course, we must increase our investment in women: their education, their health, their access to credit and other means to produce economic autonomy, their access to justice. Women must also receive outreach so that they will know what their rights are, for often they do not, especially in rural areas. There is so much that can be done to hack at the roots of the subordination of women, and there is plenty of room for a wide variety of approaches.

CASE STUDY

India

More than one in six of all human beings live in India. India has enjoyed decades of democratic governance, and since the 1990s has experienced impressive reductions in its crushing poverty. However, India has had and still has tremendous sex inequality. Only about 12 percent of members of India's parliament are women. Women earn only about 75 percent as much as men, and male participation rates in the labor force are about triple the labor participation rates for females. The United Nations Gender Inequality Index rated India as being one of the more gender-unequal countries in the world, 123rd out of 162 countries ranked. This oppression of women and girls in India generates a number of different forms of violence.

Preference for Sons and Missing Females

There is an old saying in India, "A daughter is a burden on her father's head." Several factors encourage a preference for sons among many Indian families. India is a majority Hindu country, and within Hinduism a dead parent's soul can only reach heaven if the parent has a son to light the funeral pyre, and the parent's salvation requires that there be a son to worship the ancestors. There are also son preferences among other religious groups within India, including Sikhs and Muslims. Economic factors can encourage son preference within India. There are strong dowry norms in India, meaning that upon marriage the parents of the bride are required to make a substantial financial payment to the new couple, and cover the costs of the wedding. Dowry aside, another economic incentive to bear sons is the norm within India that sons take care of elderly parents, and the higher earning potential of men compared to women in the gender-discriminatory Indian economy contributes to a parental preference for sons.

The preference for sons manifests and reinforces sex inequality and violence against females in India in different ways. Families are more likely to invest in the education of sons, in part because their sons' economic success eventually will serve as a retirement pension for parents, and sons are expected to be the breadwinners when they have their own families. Boys sometimes get better healthcare and nutrition than girls after birth. One study found that among mixed sex twins in India (one boy, one girl), the girls were significantly more likely to die than the boys before age five (Kashyap and Behrman 2020). This finding is especially disturbing because comparing twins within families means that the difference in survival rates across sexes cannot be attributed to income, religion, education, or other factors.

More disturbingly, India has one of the worst missing female problems, and it is a problem that is not alleviated among wealthier Indian families. According to one government estimate, there are 63 million missing women in India, and some 21 million unwanted girls (Associated Press 2018). The missing females come from decades of sex-selective

(cont.)

abortion, female infanticide, gendered differences in healthcare and nutrition, and parents being more likely to stop having children after having sons compared with after having daughters.

Gender asymmetries in the population can create violent conflict in part because of the bare branches problem, men unable to find wives. Districts within India with higher ratios of men to women have higher rates of several categories of violent crime, including property crime, assault and murder (South et al. 2013). Young men in India unable to find wives roam around in groups, harassing and assaulting men and women; some villages hesitate to send their women to work in fields for fear that they will be raped (Kaur 2013).

There are other factors in India that may make the bare branches problem worse over time. Men tend to marry women younger in age, and because overall fertility rates in India are slowing, this means even fewer women available for men to marry. And, as Indian women become more educated, more of them are delaying marriage, or forgoing marriage entirely. The end result is that even if the sex ratio at birth were to be made completely even across the sexes today, the bare branches problem in India will get worse before it gets better, as by 2050 in India there may be only 100 women seeking marriage for every 164 men seeking marriage (*Economist* 2015).

Violence against Women and Girls

Modern India has been plagued by violence against girls and women since its founding. The 1947 partition of the colony of India into separate countries witnessed mass sexual assault, and several tens of thousands of Hindu, Sikh, and Muslim women were abducted, raped, forced into marriage, forced to convert, and/or murdered by Hindu, Sikh, and Muslim men. Some Sikh women were preemptively murdered by their own families to forestall the dishonor of being captured and converted. Some women's bodies were mutilated (Butalia 1993).

Women and girls across India are in grave danger of being the targets of violence, including murder and sexual assault. One 2018 expert survey rated India as the most dangerous country in the world for women, largely because of the threat of sexual assault and enslavement (Bellinger 2018). It is difficult to know the extent of sexual assault in India as there is likely significant underreporting because of widespread rape shaming, blaming the rape survivor (even if she is a child) for the attack, castigating her for bringing shame on her family, and declaring her unfit for marriage. In 2021, a sixteen-year-old rape survivor was tied with rope to her attacker and both were paraded through her village, where she and the attacker were kicked, punched, and spat on. Three years earlier, another sixteen-year-old rape survivor was set on fire and murdered.

Dowry, payments from the bride's family to the groom or groom's family, also endangers women in India, through the practice of "bride burning." Sometimes, after

(cont.)

marriage the groom or his family demand additional dowry payments from the bride's family, and if those payments are not made, the bride may be murdered, sometimes by burning. This is not an isolated phenomenon: in 2015 alone 7,634 Indian women were murdered over dowry issues (Kaur and Byard 2020). For context, this deaths figure (from only one year) is almost equal to the total number of Indian soldiers killed in the 1947, 1965, 1971, and 1999 wars with Pakistan, combined.

As in other countries, in India rape and other acts of violence against women and girls are both manifestations of male power, and tools for the maintenance of male power. Practices of patrilocality in India make married Indian women more vulnerable to attack. A preference for sons creates bare branches dynamics which make sexual assault and other forms of violence more likely. Male power structures in politics, including the underrepresentation of women in national and state legislatures, slow the passage and enforcement of laws that would protect girls and women; indeed, several male members of the ruling BJP party have been formally accused of sexual assault. One BJP lawmaker helped gang-rape a seventeen-year-old in 2017, offered her a job to buy her silence, and when finally jailed allegedly tried to arrange her murder from his prison cell (Vij 2019).

India's Civil Wars and Interstate Wars

India has, since independence, experienced extensive and frequent internal political violence and interstate wars. It has been afflicted by several major insurgencies, including in the northern border region of Kashmir; a Marxist insurgency in central India; and a third revolt in northeast India. It has seen shocking terrorist attacks, including assassinations of two of its national leaders (Mahatma and Indira Gandhi), an attack on the Indian parliament in 2001, and others. There has been less organized but sometimes quite deadly violence between religious groups, especially majority Hindu mobs attacking Muslims and Sikhs. And India has fought five wars with neighboring countries, four with Pakistan and one with China. India also has had ongoing, grinding border clashes with Pakistan and China that kill many soldiers each year, and is engaged in one of the world's deadliest nuclear arms races with Pakistan.

Oppression of women has played a role in sparking and fueling these conflicts in different ways. At a more general level, male political leadership has combined with cultures of militarized masculinity to eschew cooperation and embrace violence and subjugation. Consider the evolution of Hindu nationalism in India. Though India was founded as a secular nation, its politics over the years have evolved toward a masculine, dominating Hindu nationalism. Especially beginning in the 1990s, Hindu nationalists began to stress a warrior version of Hinduism. Hindu nationalist parties described themselves as protecting and advancing the Hindu nation, like a mythological Hindu warrior, from threats. Muslims, Sikhs, and others were excluded from this vision, and seen as outsiders to be expelled from the true Hindu nation. The founder of one leading

(cont.)

Hindu nationalist party, the RSS, declared that the central goal of the party would be "invincible physical strength. We have to be so strong that none in the world will be able to overawe and subdue us. ... Swami Vivekenanda used to say, 'I want men with muscles of iron and nerves of steel ... Don't sit down and weep like little girls'" (quoted in Banerjee 2003, 172).

The BJP Hindu nationalist party has been in power in India off and on since 1998, and represents an ideology that envisions subjugating non-Hindus, women, and non-Hindu women in particular. The BJP is infused with male domination. It is led by men, and only a fraction of BJP members who run for election are women. There were many masculinized elements of this new vision, beyond the general emphasis on power and domination of the perceived inferior. The Hindu god Ram was sometimes portrayed visually as displaying more traditionally feminine values such as compassion or even with androgynous body type (see Figure 2.6), but was reinvented in BJP political posters as a heavily muscled and masculine warrior (see Figure 2.7).

There has been in recent years growing Hindu mob violence against Muslims, and the BJP ignores and even condones this violence. Indian Hindu nationalists killed thousands of Muslims, displaced tens of thousands from their homes, and burned down Muslim temples. Some Muslims have been killed out of fear that they might seek to marry Hindu women. BJP leaders continue to make anti-Muslim remarks in public, and sometimes incite their supporters to attack Muslims. One BJP leader in the 2019 election campaign urged people to vote for the BJP to "destroy the breed of Muslims" (*The Wire* 2020). BJP supporters have eagerly taken these cues. Police in Indian states ruled by the BJP routinely attack Muslim protestors, sometimes killing them (Human Rights Watch 2020).

The BJP condones violence against non-Hindu women in particular. When an eight-year-old Muslim girl was gang raped and murdered, two BJP ministers attended a protest supporting the accused men. When a nineteen-year-old Dalit woman was gang raped and murdered in 2020, former and current BJP leaders held rallies in favor of the accused, blamed the dead victim, blamed the parent of the victim for not teaching her proper values, and declared the innocence of the accused (*The Wire* 2020). When thousands of Muslim women and others peacefully protested a national citizenship law reducing the rights of non-Muslims, some BJP politicians called for the protestors to be killed (*Economic Times* 2020).

The BJP and other Hindu nationalists have also been confrontational with Muslim-majority Pakistan, as part of their demonization of Muslims. The BJP ordered a round of nuclear tests in 1998, the first in a quarter century, prompting Pakistan to respond with its first nuclear test. Following the terrorist attack on the Indian parliament in 2001, India ignited military clashes with Pakistan that lasted through 2002, killing thousands and posing an outside risk of escalation to nuclear war. In the late 2010s, tensions continued to flare up, with a deadly Indian airstrike on Pakistani territory in 2019.

(cont.)

Figure 2.6. Traditional image of the Hindu god Ram as kind and compassionate. In this picture, the image of Ram (second from left in image) is somewhat androgynous, lacking defined musculature and having delicate features. History/Universal Images Group via Getty Images.

Figure 2.7. 2017 BJP political poster. Ram is portrayed as a warrior with more masculine features, such as more typically male musculature. DIBYANGSHU SARKAR/ AFP via Getty Images.

QUANTITATIVE STUDY

Gender, Peacekeeping Forces, and Peacekeeper Abuse

Peacekeepers from the United Nations and other international actors are tasked to build peace, order, justice, prosperity, and freedom after violent conflict. However, one of the dark sides of peacekeeping is that peacekeepers themselves sometimes engage in sexual exploitation and abuse (SEA), which is engaging in transactional sex (paying for sex with money, food, or assistance) with individuals in the country in which they are deployed, sexual abuse, and rape. Some view transactional sex as untroubling because it appears consensual, but keep in mind the context, of girls and women in shattered, war-torn societies perhaps having no choice but to agree to transactional sex with foreign men to secure essentials for themselves or their families, such as food, money for healthcare, desperately needed documents (such as work visas), or jobs.

This phenomenon is both disturbing and distressingly common. One study found that over one-fourth of all women aged eighteen to thirty in the Liberian capital city of Monrovia had engaged in transactional sex with a UN peacekeeper. Worse, there are also incidents involving peacekeepers in countries such as Congo and Haiti raping women and even girls under the age of fifteen, sometimes in refugee camps administered by the UN.

Needless to say, such acts are terrible crimes. Further, they cut against the larger goals of peacekeeping missions. Most peacekeeper goals require support of the population, as peacekeepers are trying to earn the trust of the population. If peacekeepers prey on girls and women, this can hardly fail to undermine popular faith in their motives and trustworthiness.

With this in mind, Sabrina Karim and Kyle Beardsley conducted a study to better understand the sources of peacekeeper SEA, focusing on military and police peacekeepers, as opposed to civilians deployed as part of a peacekeeping mission.

Research Question

What are the causes of peacekeeper SEA?

Theory and Hypotheses

Karim and Beardsley posited that one general cause of peacekeeper SEA might be cultures of militarized masculinity within peacekeeping contingents. Another cause of SEA might be patriarchy, society-wide beliefs in sexual inequality and the rights of men to dominate women. Other studies have demonstrated that patriarchal beliefs are an important reason why men sexually exploit and abuse girls and women.

The study puts these two general ideas together to predict which peacekeeper missions are more likely to engage in SEA against civilians. Though militarized masculinity is difficult to measure, we might expect that it would be reduced or less toxic if a peacekeeping mission contains more women. Note that this is a sex- and gender-based argument, as it argues that sex drives gender, in the sense that the presence of more women provides the opportunity to change the culture of the peacekeepers.

Hypothesis 1: The more women within a peacekeeping mission deployment, the less likely that deployment will engage in sexual exploitation and abuse.

Peacekeeping missions are usually composed of peacekeepers contributed from several countries, and peacekeepers are of course drawn from the various contributing countries. The individual beliefs of peacekeeping troops are likely formed in part by their home countries, from growing up and living in those societies. We might expect that societies that embrace gender inequality are in turn more likely to produce individuals who view women as sexual objects and engage in SEA.

Hypothesis 2: The more peacekeeping troops that a peacekeeping mission draws from countries with lower levels of gender equality, the more likely that mission will be to engage in SEA.

Data

The Karim and Beardsley study examined all years of all UN peacekeeping missions from the years 2009–2013. Each case in the data is a mission-year, such as the UN mission in Lebanon in the year 2010.

Dependent Variable
The dependent variable is the number of SEA allegations for each mission year, ranging from zero allegations to as high as forty. You might question the completeness of these data, as there are very likely a number of SEA events that go unreported. This problem is common to sexual assault and harassment data more broadly, including sexual assault on college campuses. But, as is often the case when we try to understand the world, we can only work with the data we have to try to make things at least somewhat more clear.

Independent Variables
The first independent variable, used to measure the militarized masculinity of the peacekeeping mission, is the percentage of women troops within any single peacekeeping mission within a particular year. For hypothesis 2, the study has three different measures of societal patriarchy: the proportion of women in the labor force, the proportion of girls in elementary school as a measure of gender equality in education, and the presence of legal protection of women within the society.

Control Variables
The paper also includes a number of control variables to address the possibility of spurious correlation, such as the level of economic development of the host country, and whether or not there was mass rape during the war that preceded the deployment of the peacekeeping mission.

Results

The statistical analysis shows some interesting patterns. The evidence provides some indication that peacekeeping missions with more women peacekeepers are less likely to engage in SEA. However, the evidence is stronger that peacekeeping missions that draw troops from more gender-equal societies are significantly less likely to engage in SEA. For example, an increase in the percentage of women in the labor force from 40 percent to 55 percent is correlated with a 50 percent decrease in SEA.

Conclusions

Peacekeeper SEA is a serious problem, and the findings of this study provide concrete policy recommendations. If peacekeeping missions can incorporate more women, this might reduce SEA. Fortunately, the UN has passed a formal resolution calling for more women peacekeepers. Further, the more that peacekeeping missions can be drawn from countries with higher gender equality, the more that peacekeeper SEA will be reduced.

SUMMARY

This chapter has made a number of points about the complex but important relationships among sex, gender, and violence:

- Girls and women around the world confront a tremendous amount of violence and oppression
- Sex is a biological category and gender is a social category
- Both sex and gender affect violence and violence against women, and they sometimes work in synergy
- Obstructed marriage markets, caused by polygyny, son preference, and brideprice, fuel a variety of forms of violence
- Male kin groups are an important structure that fosters the subordination of and violence against women
- Sex and gender affect a variety of forms of violence, including interpersonal violence, civil wars, interstate wars, and terrorism

KEY TERMS

Brideprice
Sex
Gender
Testosterone
Polygyny
Bare branches

Militarized masculinity
Male kin group
Patrilineal
Marriage market obstruction
Honor killings

REVIEW QUESTIONS

1. Describe the "war against women and girls," including the problem of the missing women and girls.
2. Are males more aggressive than women because men have higher levels of testosterone? Explain.
3. What are some differences in physical capabilities between the average male and the average female? How did these differences in physical capabilities create the foundations for societies that empower males over females?
4. In what ways do societies that experience higher levels of repression of females experience greater problems and lower quality of life for their citizens, in comparison with societies that experience lower levels of repression of females?
5. How do polygyny, brideprice inflation, and sex-selective abortion obstruct marriage markets? Why do obstructed marriage markets make violence more likely, and what kinds of violence are made more likely?
6. How do the following factors affect male violence against women: patrilineality, lax enforcement of laws, and attitudes towards female victims of sexual assault?
7. Are democracies that give women the right to vote more peaceful in their relations with other states? Why?
8. Why does the repression of women make civil wars more likely?
9. What are some policy solutions that might alleviate the repression of girls and women and in turn reduce conflict and violence?

DISCUSSION QUESTIONS

1. How does the case of India demonstrate some of the sex, gender, and violence dynamics described in the chapter?
2. In your own communities, what are some realistic steps that could be taken to reduce the repression of and/or violence against women and girls?
3. How hopeful are you that the human race can over the next twenty-five years or so reduce repression of and/or violence against girls and women? Are you more hopeful, somewhat hopeful, or less hopeful? Why?

ADDITIONAL READING

Bloom, M. (2012). *Bombshell: Women and Terrorism*. Philadelphia: University of Pennsylvania Press.
Cohen, D. K. (2016). *Rape during Civil War*. Ithaca, NY: Cornell University Press.
Enloe, C. (2000). *Bananas, Beaches, and Bases*. updated edn. Berkeley: University of California Press.
Goldstein, J. S. (2003). *War and Gender: How Gender Shapes the War System and Vice Versa*. Cambridge: Cambridge University Press.
Hudson, V., Ballif-Spanvill, B., Caprioli, M., and Emmett, C. (2012). *Sex and World Peace*. New York: Columbia University Press.
Hudson, V., D. L. Bowen, and P. L. Nielson. (2020). *The First Political Order: How Sex Shapes Governance and National Security Worldwide*. New York: Columbia University Press.

Potts, M. and T. Hayden. (2008). *Sex and War: How Biology Explains Warfare and Terrorism and Offers a Path to a Safer World*, Dallas: BenBella Books.

Sjoberg, L. (2013). *Gendering Global Conflict: Toward a Feminist Theory of War*. New York: Columbia University Press.

Tickner, J. A. (1992). *Gender in International Relations*. New York: Columbia University Press.

REFERENCES

Abrahams, K. W. (2021, May 20). This Zimbabwean man has 16 wives and 151 kids and he still wants more. www.news24.com/you/news/international

Adams, J. (2008). Politics, patriarchy and frontiers of historical sociological explanation. *Political Power and Social Theory* **19**, 289–294.

Aleu, P. T. and Mach, P. (2016, June 26). Bride-price tradition is destructive, but strong, in strife-torn South Sudan. www.dandc.eu/en/article

Anderson, C. (2021, July 25). Perpetrators of domestic abuse committed 2 of 3 mass shootings from 2014–2019, study finds. www.columbian.com/news/2021/jul/25

ANSAmed (2018, February 15). Morocco OKs law against violence on women, wives excluded – politics. www.ansamed.info/ansamed/en/news/sections/politics/2018/02/15

Associated Press (2018, January 30). More than 63 million women 'missing' in India, statistics show. *The Guardian*. www.theguardian.com/world/2018/jan/30

Baker, K. (2015, May 26). ISIS offers fighters $1,500 starter home bonus and free honeymoon. *Daily Mail*. www.dailymail.co.uk/news/article-3098235

Balliet, D., Li, N. P., Macfarlan, S. J., and Van Vugt, M. (2011). Sex differences in cooperation: a meta-analytic review of social dilemmas. *Psychological Bulletin* **137**(6), 881–909.

Banerjee, S. (2003). Gender and nationalism: The masculinization of Hinduism and female political participation in India. *Women's Studies International Forum* **26**(2), 167–179.

Barash, D. P. (2016). *Out of Eden: The Surprising Consequences of Polygamy*. Oxford: Oxford University Press.

Barnhart, J. N., Trager, R. F., Saunders, E. N., and Dafoe, A. (2020). The suffragist peace. *International Organization*, **74**(4), 633–670.

Barr, C. (2020, July 17). One in 70 recorded rapes in England and Wales led to charge last year. *The Guardian*. www.theguardian.com/society/2020/jul/17

Bellinger, N. (2018, January 20). India has a sexual assault problem that only women can fix. https://theconversation.com

Bertoli, A. D. (2017). Nationalism and conflict: Lessons from international sports. *International Studies Quarterly* **61**(4), 835–849.

Best, R. H., Shair-Rosenfield, S., and Wood, R. M. (2019). Legislative gender diversity and the resolution of civil conflict. *Political Research Quarterly* **72**(1), 215–228.

Betzig, L. L. (2008). *Despotism and Differential Reproduction: A Darwinian View of History*. London: Routledge.

Boone, J. L. (1983). Noble family structure and expansionist warfare in the late Middle Ages: A sociological approach. In R. Dyson-Hudson and M. A. Little, (eds.). *Rethinking Human Adaptation: Biological and Cultural Models*. London: Routledge, pp. 79–96.

Boone, J. L. (1986). Parental investment and elite family structure in preindustrial states: A case study of late medieval–early modern Portuguese genealogies. *American Anthropologist* **88**(4), 859–878.

Bowcott, O., and Barr, C. (2019, July 26). Just 1.5% of all rape cases lead to charge or summons, data reveals. *The Guardian*. www.theguardian.com/law/2019/jul/26

Brennan, S. (2017, February 6). Here come the brides! *Daily Mail*. www.dailymail.co.uk/femail/article-4197474

Brysk, A. (2018). *The Struggle for Freedom from Fear: Contesting Violence against Women at the Frontiers of Globalization*, New York: Oxford University Press.

Butalia, U. (1993). Community, state and gender: On women's agency during partition. *Economic and Political Weekly* **28**(17), WS12–WS21, WS24.

Carroll, L. (2019, May 31). Kids who play violent videogames may be more likely to pick up a gun and pull the trigger. *Reuters*.www.reuters.com/article

Cassar, A. and Rigdon, M. L. (2021). Option to cooperate increases women's competitiveness and closes the gender gap. *Evolution and Human Behavior* **42**(6), 556–572.

Catalano, S., Smith, E., Snyder, H. and Rand, M. (2009). *Female Victims of Violence*. US Department of Justice Office of Justice Programs.

Chamberlain, G. (2017, June 8). South Sudan's battle for cattle is forcing schoolgirls to become teenage brides. *The Guardian*. www.theguardian.com/global-development/2017/jun/08

Christov-Moore, L., Simpson, E. A., Coudé, G., Grigaityte, K., Iacoboni, M., and Ferrari, P. F. (2014). Empathy: Gender effects in brain and behavior. *Neuroscience & Biobehavioral Reviews* **46**(4), 604–627.

Cry, E. (2020, June 30). Viral trafficking hub campaign releases video exposing pornhub's alleged crimes. www.prnewswire.com/news-releases

Dabbs, J. M., Carr, T., Frady, R. L., and Riad, J. (1995). Testosterone, crime, and misbehavior among 692 male prison inmates, *Personality and Individual Differences* **18**(5), 627–633.

Dabbs, J. M., Hargrove, M. F., and Heusel, C. (1996). Testosterone differences among college fraternities: well-behaved vs. rambunctious. *Personality and Individual Differences*, **20**(2), 157–161.

Dahlum, S., and Wig, T. (2020). Peace above the glass ceiling: The historical relationship between female political empowerment and civil conflict. *International Studies Quarterly* **64**(4), 879–893.

David-Barrett, T., Rotkirch, A., Carney, J., Behncke Izquierdo, I., Krems, J. A., Townley, D., ... Dunbar, R. I. (2015). Women favour dyadic relationships, but men prefer clubs: Cross-cultural evidence from Social Networking. *PLOS ONE* **10**(3).

Denson, T. F., O'Dean, S. M., Blake, K. R., and Beames, J. R. (2018). Aggression in women: Behavior, brain and hormones. *Frontiers in Behavioral Neuroscience* **12**.

Dhar, A. (2011, April 1). At 914, child sex ratio is the lowest since independence. *The Hindu*. www.thehindu.com/news/national

Diamond-Smith, N. and Rudolph, K. (2018). The association between uneven sex ratios and violence: Evidence from Six Asian countries. *PLOS ONE* **13**(6).

Economic Times (2020, February 3). Hate speeches made by BJP leaders using 'fear of rape as campaign message': Women's groups to PM. economictimes.indiatimes.com/news/politics-and-nation

The Economist (2015, April 18). Bare branches, redundant males. www.economist.com/asia/2015/04/18/bare-branches-redundant-males

Edlund, L., Li, H., Yi, J., and Zhang, J. (2013). Sex ratios and crime: Evidence from China. *Review of Economics and Statistics* **95**(5), 1520–1534.

Eichenberg, R. C. (2019). *Gender, War, and World Order: A Study of Public Opinion*, Ithaca, NY: Cornell University Press.

Ferris-Rotman, A. (2018, April 9). Putin's war on women. *Foreign Policy*. https://foreignpolicy.com/2018/04/09/putins-war-on-women

Friedel, E. E. and Fox, J. A. (2019). Gender differences in patterns and trends in U.S. homicide, 1976–2017. *Violence and Gender* **6**(1), 27–36.

Gat, A. (2008). *War in Human Civilization*, Oxford: Oxford University Press.

Giovarelli, R., and Scalise, E. (2013). *Women's Land Tenure Framework for Analysis: Inheritance*. Seattle: Landesa. Available at www.landesa.org/wp-content/uploads/LandWise_Inheritance-Framework_2013JanVersion.pdf

Handelsman, D. J., Hirschberg, A. L. and Bermon, S. (2018). Circulating testosterone as the hormonal basis of sex differences in athletic performance. *Endocrine Reviews* **39**(5), 803–829.

Henrich, J., Boyd, R., and Richerson, P. J. (2012). The puzzle of monogamous marriage. *Philosophical Transactions of the Royal Society B: Biological Sciences* **367**(1589), 657–669.

Hoganson, K. L. (2000). *Fighting for American Manhood: How Gender Politics Provoked the Spanish–American and Philippine–American wars*. New Haven: Yale University Press.

Holson, L. M. (2019, April 12). Murders by intimate partners are on the rise, study finds. *New York Times*. www.nytimes.com/2019/04/12/us/domestic-violence-victims.html

Home Office (2020, July 17). Crime outcomes in England and Wales 2019 to 2020. www.gov.uk/government/statistics/crime-outcomes-in-england-and-wales-2019-to-2020

Hudson, V. M. and den Boer, A. M. (2005). *Bare Branches: The Security Implications of Asia's Surplus Male Population*, Cambridge, MA: MIT.

Hudson, V. M. and Matfess, H. (2017). In plain sight: The neglected linkage between brideprice and violent conflict. *International Security*, **42**(1), 7–40.

Hudson, V. M., Bowen, D. L., and Nielsen, P. L. (2020). *The First Political Order: How Sex Shapes Governance and National Security Worldwide*. New York: Columbia University Press.

Human Rights Watch (2020, June 16). "Shoot the traitors." www.hrw.org/report/2020/04/09

Husseini, R. (n.d). Speak truth to power – telling stories. *Public Broadcasting Service*. www.pbs.org/speaktruthtopower/rana.html

Inoue, Y., Takahashi, T., Burriss, R. P., Arai, S., Hasegawa, T., Yamagishi, T., and Kiyonari, T. (2017). Testosterone promotes either dominance or submissiveness in the ultimatum game depending on players' social rank. *Scientific Reports* **7**(1).

Inter-Parliamentary Union (2016). Sexism, harassment and violence against women parliamentarians. http://archive.ipu.org/pdf/publications/issuesbrief-e.pdf

Inter-Parliamentary Union (2022). Global and regional averages of women in national parliaments. https://data.ipu.org/women-averages

Kashyap, R. and Behrman, J. (2020). Gender discrimination and excess female under-5 mortality in India: A new perspective using mixed-sex twins. *Demography* **57**, 2143–2167.

Kaur, N. and Byard, R. W. (2020). Bride burning: A unique and ongoing form of gender-based violence. *Journal of Forensic and Legal Medicine* **75**.

Kaur, R. (2013). Mapping the adverse consequences of sex selection and gender imbalance in India and China. *Economic and Political Weekly* **48**(35), 37–44.

Kenworthy, T. (1999, December 13). Columbine Killers Wanted to 'Kick-Start a Revolution.' *Washington Post*. www.washingtonpost.com/wp-srv/WPcap/1999-12/13

Koch, M. T. and Fulton, S. A. (2011). In the defense of women: Gender, office holding, and national security policy in established democracies. *Journal of Politics* **73**(1), 1–16.

Koos, C. and Neupert-Wentz, C. (2019). Polygynous neighbors, excess men, and intergroup conflict in Rural Africa. *Journal of Conflict Resolution*, **64**(2–3), 402–431.

Krause, J., Krause, W., and Bränfors, P. (2018). Women's participation in peace negotiations and the durability of peace. *International Interactions*, **44**(6), 985–1016.

Library of Congress. (2015, August 12). Uganda: Court declares refund of bride-price under customary law unconstitutional. www.loc.gov/item/global-legal-monitor/2015-08-12

Manne, K. (2017). *Down Girl: The Logic of Misogyny*, New York: Oxford University Press.

"Maternal Mortality" (2019). Organisation for Economic Cooperation and Development. www.oecd-ilibrary.org/sites/12a2742f-en/index.html?itemId=/content/component

Matfess, H. (2016, December 7). Here's why so many people join Boko Haram, despite its notorious violence. *Washington Post*.

Mazur, A. and Booth, A. (1998). Testosterone and dominance in men. *Behavioral and Brain Sciences* **21** (3), 353–363.

McDermott, R. and Cowden, J. (2015). Polygyny and violence against women. *Emory Law Journal* **64**(6), 1767–1814.

Mokuwa, E., Voors, M., Bulte, E., and Richards, P. (2011). Peasant grievance and insurgency in Sierra Leone: judicial serfdom as a driver of conflict. *African Affairs* **110**(440), 339–366.

Morris, J. S., Link, J., Martin, J. C., and Carrier, D. R. (2020). Sexual dimorphism in human arm power and force: implications for sexual selection on fighting ability. *Journal of Experimental Biology*, **223**(2).

Morris, L. (2017, April 12). Witch hunting in Papua New Guinea. *National Geographic*. www.nationalgeographic.com.au/people

Moylan, D. (2015, May 1). Afghanistan is failing to help abused women. *Foreign Policy*. https://foreignpolicy.com/2015/05/01

Murdock, H. (2011, February 23). 'Delayed' marriage frustrates Middle East Youth. www.voanews.com/a

Niederle, M. and Vesterlund, L. (2005). Do women shy away from competition? Do men compete too much? *Quarterly Journal of Economics* **122**(3), 1067–1101.

Nielsen, R. (2017, July 10). Presentation on Sierra Leone Research. WomanStats co-PI meeting.

Nordic Model Now (2020, March 2). The cost of Western Europe's rampant prostitution: the genocide of Romanian women. https://nordicmodelnow.org/2020/03/02

Paul, D. (2018, November 26). U.N. Finds Deadliest Place for Women Is in Their Home. *Washington Post*. www.washingtonpost.com/world/2018/11/26

The Penal Code (2021, November 5). www.equalitynow.org/discriminatory_law/syria_the_penal_code

People Shot to Death by US Police. (2022). Statista Research Department, www.statista.com/statistics/585152/people-shot-to-death-by-us-police-by-race

Pescud, M. (2018, July 7). Whether teams win or lose, sporting events lead to spikes in violence against women and children. https://theconversation.com

Peterson, D. and Wrangham, R. (1997). *Demonic Males: Apes and the Origins of Human Violence*, Boston: Mariner Books.

Richmond, M. and Krause-Jackson, F. (2011, July 25). Cows-for-brides inflation spurs cattle theft in South Sudan. www.bloomberg.com/news/articles/2011-07-26

Ritchie, H. and Roser, M. (2019). Gender ratio. https://ourworldindata.org/gender-ratio

Rizvi, N. S., Khan, K., and Shaikh, B. T. (2014). Gender: Shaping personality, lives and health of women in Pakistan. *BMC Women's Health*, **14**(1).

Shane, S. and Becker, J. (2016, February 28). A new Libya, with "very little time left." *New York Times*. www.nytimes.com/2016/02/28/us/politics/libya-isis-hillary-clinton.html

South, S. J., Trent, K., and Bose, S. (2013). Skewed sex ratios and criminal victimization in India. *Demography* **51**(3), 1019–1040.

Sperling, V. (2016). Putin's macho personality cult. *Communist and Post-Communist Studies* **49**(1), 13–23.

Tessler, M., Nachtwey, J., and Grant, A. (1998). The gender and pacifism hypothesis: Opinion research from Israel and the Arab world. *Israel Affairs* **5**(2–3), 265–278.

Tucker, W. (2014). *Marriage and Civilization: How Monogamy Made Us Human*. New York: Regnery Publishing.

Tyler, M. and Tarzia, L. (2021, May 3). We need to talk about pornography. https://pursuit.unimelb.edu.au/articles

United Nations (2012, March 19). Women and political participation. www.un.org/ga/search/view_doc .asp?symbol=A/RES/66

United Nations Office on Drugs and Crime (2019). Global study on homicide. www.unodc.org/unodc/en/ data-and-analysis/global-study-on-homicide.html

United Nations Population Fund.(2020). *State of World Population*. www.unfpa.org/sites/default/files/ pub-pdf/UNFPA_PUB_2020_EN_State_of_World_Population.pdf

Urdal, H. (2006). A clash of generations? Youth bulges and political violence. *International Studies Quarterly* **50**(3), 607–629.

Vij, S. (2019, September 25). India's ruling Bharatiya Janata Party has a rape problem. https://qz.com/ india/1715615/kathua-unnao-up-cases-show-modis-bjp-has-a-rape-problem

Vogelstein, R. B. and Bro, A. (2021). Women's Power Index. *Council on Foreign Relations*. www.cfr.org/ article/womens-power-index

The Wire (2020, October 7). Hathras: BJP leader implies woman was victim of honour killing, says accused are innocent. https://thewire.in/politics

Women in Management (2022). Workplaces that work for women. www.catalyst.org/research/women-in-management

Wood, R., and Ramirez, M. D. (2019). Exploring the microfoundations of the gender equality peace hypothesis. *International Studies Review* **20**(3), 345–367.

World Datelines (2004, April 30). *Deseret News*. www.deseret.com/2004/4/30/19826086/world-datelines

"World War II Casualties by Country" (2022). *World Population Review*. https://worldpopulationreview .com/country-rankings/world-war-two-casualties-by-country

Wulfhorst, E. (2017, March 6). Violence is the biggest challenge facing women – UN women chief. https:// news.trust.org/item/20170306050632-czatd

Zeng, T. C., Aw, A. J., and Feldman, M. W. (2018). Cultural hitchhiking and competition between patrilineal kin groups explain the post-neolithic Y-chromosome bottleneck. *Nature Communications*, **9**(1).

Part II

Domestic Politics and War

3 Domestic Political Institutions and War

JESSICA L. P. WEEKS

Introduction

In April 1982, the leader of Argentina's military junta, General Leopoldo Galtieri, sent the Argentine military to occupy the British-governed Falkland/Malvinas Islands, a lonely, sheep-studded piece of territory in the South Atlantic that had long inspired conflict between the UK and Argentina. Within days, British Prime Minister Margaret Thatcher had started to dispatch a large task force to the region. Argentina's forces proved no match for the British ones, and by June, Argentina had surrendered control of the islands back to Britain. Within days of the surrender, Galtieri's colleagues in the junta met and removed him from power. Across the ocean, buoyed in part by her victory in the Falklands, Thatcher remained Prime Minister for another eight years, becoming Britain's longest-serving modern leader.

Eight years after that war, in the scorching desert heat of the summer of 1990, Iraqi dictator Saddam Hussein ordered an invasion of Iraq's neighbor Kuwait, announcing that his country was finally reclaiming its "nineteenth province." The United States and a large coalition of allies soon intervened on Kuwait's behalf, driving Iraqi forces out of Kuwaiti territory in a matter of weeks. Despite this humiliating defeat, Saddam remained in power for more than another decade. In ironic contrast, President George H. W. Bush, who led the United States to victory, was voted out of office in the fall of 1992.

In this chapter, we focus on the role that **domestic political institutions** play in military conflicts – the wars that leaders choose to fight, the outcomes of those conflicts, and the domestic political fates of the leaders who are responsible. We define domestic political institutions as the rules, structures, and organizations that determine how a country is governed. Domestic political institutions therefore include phenomena such as whether and how elections are conducted; whether a legislature exists and if so, how powerful it is; procedures for removing and replacing the national leader; and so on. Around the world, countries organize their domestic political systems in many different ways, including democratic systems in which leaders answer to the public, autocratic systems in which a single dictator wields absolute power, regimes in which military officers or members of a dominant party share decisionmaking authority with each other, and other variations. This chapter explores how these different kinds of domestic political institutions influence decisions about war and peace. Why do some countries fight wars even when victory seems unlikely, while others are much more cautious in their decisions about military conflict? Why do some leaders remain in power long after a military defeat, but others lose office within days of an unfavorable war outcome? These kinds of questions have fascinated scholars of international relations for decades, centuries, and even millennia.

In foreign policy, more so even than in domestic policy, state leaders play a crucial role. Even in democracies, the fact that governments often need to react quickly to external events means that individual leaders often have significant leeway when it comes to foreign policy, particularly in the early stages of military conflict. Therefore, we will first explore how domestic political institutions affect the kinds of leaders that come to office in the first place.

We then turn to how political institutions shape policies once leaders have come to power, asking how domestic political institutions shape domestic accountability for foreign policy and how expectations about accountability influence leaders' decisions about war and peace. For example, how do institutions influence what governments want to achieve in international politics, what kinds of risks they are willing to take, and what kinds of policies they think are normatively acceptable? How do institutions affect what happens to leaders after they lose power? In a related vein, we explore how institutions influence the kind of information that leaders have at their disposal when making decisions: can they obtain accurate intelligence and advice that allows them to gain a clear picture of the domestic and international situation, or do domestic political incentives systematically distort the kinds of information that reaches leaders? Similarly, we will examine how institutions influence the kinds of resources that leaders have at their disposal: how do institutions influence countries' ability to generate military power and attract foreign allies?

In order to explain patterns of war and peace, however, we cannot just study decisionmaking *inside* individual countries. War only breaks out when *two* countries disagree with each other and are unable to resolve their disputes through peaceful means (see Chapter 1). Therefore, the chapter concludes by investigating how domestic political institutions influence interactions *between* countries, or more specifically, their ability to reach peaceful agreements that avoid war. One major impediment to peace is that countries often find it difficult to communicate with each other. For example, leaders have reasons to say things that are not true, because this could help them get a better bargain. We therefore explore how institutions affect countries' ability to bargain more effectively. We will consider the possibility that some kinds of institutions allow leaders to convey information more convincingly than other kinds of institutions, and that this helps some countries avoid war.

Together, these insights will help us to get a handle on longstanding questions in international relations. Is democracy, as some have argued, a force for peace, and will the world become a more peaceful place if democracy spreads? On the other hand, are all nondemocratic regimes equally war-prone, or are there some kinds of nondemocracies that are more cautious than others when it comes to making foreign policy? The rest of the chapter will explore these questions in detail.

How Politics within States Affects Conflict between States

Types of Domestic Political Institutions

Countries organize their domestic politics in many different ways. For a long time, people studying how domestic political institutions influence international relations focused primarily on the difference between democracies and nondemocracies. In **democracies**, ordinary people choose their leaders and representatives in competitive elections. In an ideal democracy, every adult citizen has the right to vote, and political institutions are designed so that real political power roughly reflects the wishes of the population as a whole. Moreover, in ideal democracies there are relatively few restrictions on who can compete for office, and formal rules are enforced for everyone. Of course, few democracies live up to all of these ideals all of the time, but a hallmark of democracies is that political institutions encourage leaders to pay attention to what ordinary people think. Thus, many have argued, democratic leaders have reason to pay attention to what the public wants when making decisions about war and peace.

In **nondemocracies,** in contrast, institutions do not allow ordinary citizens to choose their own leaders or replace them if they don't like their policies. Instead, leaders come to power in other ways, such as by overthrowing the incumbent government through brute force, inheriting office from a family member, or manipulating institutions to make it seem like they were elected democratically when really the electoral rules were rigged in their favor. For example, many modern nondemocracies have rigged elections that make it seem like the leader or parliament was democratically elected, when in fact the rules were designed to predetermine the outcome. North Korea, for example, holds regular sham elections for its parliament in which only one name appears on each ballot and votes are not secret (Figure 3.1). In fact, however, North Korea is a dictatorship in which political power is highly concentrated in the hands of the central leader. A crucial difference between democracies and nondemocracies is that because of these institutional differences, leaders of nondemocracies have less reason to worry about what the public thinks when making decisions about war and peace.

Figure 3.1. Inside the sham parliament of North Korea's personalist regime. Like any Potemkin village, looks can be deceiving, as no political power resides in this apparently modern and well-kept room and building. ©btrenkel/iStock/Getty Images

However, there are important distinctions between different kinds of nondemocracies (see Geddes et al. 2018). On the face of it, Russia under Vladimir Putin, Myanmar led by its national military, and China led by Xi Jinping are lookalike repressive regimes, but the closer one looks, the more differences among these nondemocracies can be noted. These differences show up not only in day-to-day life for their citizens, but also when it comes to foreign policy and war-making. One way to think about differences among authoritarian regimes is to focus on two dimensions: how much power is concentrated in the hands of the individual leader, and whether the leadership consists of military officers versus civilians.

The first dimension – the degree to which the individual leader personally controls the levers of state power – is often referred to as **personalism**. In personalistic regimes such as Iraq under Saddam Hussein or North Korea under the Kim dynasty, political institutions exist largely to serve the leader, rather than representing independent sources of political power. The leader personally chooses who holds important government and military positions, typically picking individuals who are especially unlikely to challenge the power structure. For example, in Iraq, Saddam Hussein handpicked the men who would hold key political and military positions, often installing family members (such as his own sons) in particularly important roles. Likewise, in the Soviet Union, Josef Stalin had often elevated individuals to key positions based on their personal loyalty, rather than other attributes such as competence or seniority. Vyacheslav Molotov was one of Stalin's most trusted advisers, in part because their friendship went back decades. They first met when Molotov's aunt rented a room to Stalin back in 1912, and the two served together through the Bolshevik Revolution and Russian Civil War. Personal loyalty to himself was prized by Stalin above all other qualities a subordinate might have. Some personalist leaders value loyalty so highly that they choose patently incompetent advisers as long as they are loyal; Idi Amin of Uganda, for example, was known for choosing aides who were illiterate.

In less personalistic regimes, in contrast, in which institutions such as political parties and military hierarchies are stronger, elites can work together to constrain the leader. Moreover, individuals are more likely to work their way up through less personalistic regimes based in part on seniority, merit, and competence rather than purely through loyalty. When individuals who have worked their way up from inside the system on the basis of merit hold high government or military positions, they are not personally beholden to the leader in a way that a handpicked crony is. Thus, in nonpersonalistic regimes, regime insiders can provide a significant counterweight to the leaders. For example, in the Soviet Union under Khrushchev and Brezhnev as well as China under Hu Jintao (see Figure 3.2), institutions such as the Communist Party allowed elite politicians inside the regime to work together to place constraints on the leader's rule. Likewise, in some military dictatorships, such as Argentina's military junta from 1976 to 1983, there is a very clear hierarchical structure, often with (as in Argentina's case) formal rules about how power will be shared and rotated across leaders. Thus, in nonpersonalistic dictatorships, rule may not be "by the people and for the people," but power is at least shared among regime elites.

A second key dimension along which nondemocracies vary is whether the leadership consists primarily of military officers, versus primarily of civilians (see Table 3.1). In civilian-led regimes, the role of the military is primarily restricted to military affairs, while civilians make

Table 3.1. Nondemocratic regime types

	Personalistic	Non-personalistic
Led by military officers	Strongman	Junta
Led by civilians	Boss	Machine

Figure 3.2. Chinese President Hu Jintao and the Politburo Standing Committee, 2007. Though powerful, the Chinese leader was not unconstrained, and paid attention to the politics and preferences of his inner circle to avoid being overthrown.
©Guang Niu / Staff/Getty Images News/Getty Images.

most of the political decisions, including, ultimately, those about national security. In **military regimes**, in contrast, military officers hold the reins of power and are responsible for decisions not only about military matters, but about domestic and foreign policy more broadly. Military regimes are less common today than they have been in the past, but military rule persists: military officers continue to rule in Myanmar, the military has carried out successful coups d'état (overthrows of civilian leaders) in countries such as Sudan and Mali in recent years, and the military continues to play a key role in politics in Egypt.

These two dimensions of militarism and personalism combine to form different kinds of authoritarian regimes (Table 3.1). Some regimes, such as Uganda under Idi Amin, are both personalistic and led by a military officer ("strongman" regimes). Other regimes, like Argentina in the late 1970s and early 1980s, are nonpersonalistic military regimes (military "juntas") in which military officers share power with each other. The Soviet Union under Stalin, North Korea under the Kim dynasty, and Iraq under Saddam Hussein are all examples of personalist regimes with civilian leaders ("boss" regimes), while the Soviet Union under Khrushchev and Brezhnev and China under Hu Jintao were nonpersonalist regimes led by civilians ("machines").

Political Mechanisms Determining War and Peace

Above, we introduced the concept of domestic political institutions, and explained the differences between democracies and various types of nondemocratic regimes. We now explore how exactly these different kinds of institutions can influence decisions about war and peace.

There are three key pathways through which domestic institutions shape patterns of military conflict. First, domestic political institutions can influence *who comes to power*. As Chapter 5 on leaders explains in more detail, the identity of the national leader can have important effects on foreign policy decisions. As we will see below, some kinds of institutions make it more likely that the individuals who come to power see military force as a useful and legitimate tool of foreign policy. To put it differently, some institutions "select for" more warlike and bellicose leaders than others. Thus, to the extent that individual leaders influence foreign policy, institutions influence who comes to power in the first place.

Second, institutions shape *what leaders do once they are in office*. Here, institutions can matter in several different ways. One way is that institutions affect whether the leader is accountable to any domestic groups, as well as which domestic actors, specifically, have the ability to constrain the leader from making certain kinds of policy decisions. Also, institutions can affect the resources that leaders have at their disposal, in several ways. Institutions affect whether leaders have access to high-quality information and advice about potential military conflicts and the alternatives. Institutions also influence whether countries are able to harness their human and economic resources to build effective military power, and whether they can recruit foreign allies to fight on their behalf.

Finally, institutions can influence *negotiations and communication between countries*. War does not always break out when countries disagree about important issues. Sometimes, countries can resolve even serious disagreements peacefully. War only breaks out when countries fail to find a peaceful *alternative* to war. To find solutions that both sides are happy with, however, countries need to be able to communicate with each other. This is often difficult in international politics because leaders have strong incentives to bluff about how powerful they are and how willing they are to use military force. Domestic political institutions, as we will see, can influence that process.

Below, we will discuss each of these pathways in detail, explaining how particular domestic institutions influence when and under what conditions states fight wars. Of course, in the real world, multiple pathways are usually at work: thus, these mechanisms are complementary rather than mutually exclusive.

How Institutions Shape Who Leads

The first pathway through which institutions influence decisions about war is by shaping who comes to power in the first place. As we discussed above, leaders are particularly important when it comes to decisions about foreign policy. Even in democracies, leaders often have wide latitude in their ability to wage war, especially in the short term. If different kinds of individuals have different preferences about war and peace – whether due to personal experiences, ideology, age, health, or other factors (as Chapter 5 explores in greater detail) – then one way that domestic political institutions can matter is by influencing what kinds of leaders come to power in the first place.

In democracies, leaders come to power through regular, free and fair elections, though to be sure there is variance among democratic systems, such as whether it is a presidential or parliamentary system, how much power the legislature has over the executive, the extent to which the entire adult population is allowed to vote, and so on. Foreign policy can play an important role in electoral campaigns. Some candidates advocate for more "hawkish" foreign policies, such as being tough on terrorism and building up the military. Other candidates campaign on more "dovish" platforms, such as strengthening global institutions and using diplomacy and economic relations, rather than military might, to resolve conflicts. But despite these differences, it is relatively rare for voters in democracies to choose extremely bellicose leaders (see Chapter 4). War is very expensive, from the standpoint of both blood and treasure. Moreover, some voters find it morally objectionable to use force under certain kinds of circumstances. For these reasons, in democracies, the kinds of leaders who are the most appealing to the largest number of voters, and who thus have the best shot at winning elections, tend to be relatively moderate when it comes to matters of war and peace, willing to use diplomacy whenever possible and only resort to war when it is absolutely necessary. Moreover, in democracies, voters often tend to prefer candidates with proven political experience. Successfully navigating the domestic political landscape in democracies tends to require a willingness to compromise and resolve disagreements peacefully. Therefore, the kinds of leaders who tend to emerge on the national landscape in democracies are inclined to value compromise and diplomacy – or at least are more likely to do so than leaders in some other kinds of political systems.

In nondemocracies, the path to power varies greatly depending on the type of regime. In nonpersonalistic regimes, leaders tend to rise to power by working their way up through the ranks of a political party or the military. However, in personalist regimes, leaders tend to come to power through force or treachery – what Chapter 5 refers to as irregular succession – or to inherit power from an ancestor who came to power in such a way. For example, consider how Saddam Hussein of Iraq cemented his grip on power. In the early days of his rule, in July 1979, he called top members of his Ba'ath Party into an auditorium in Baghdad. As video cameras looked on, he revealed that he had foiled a plot to remove him from power. One by one, the names of fifty alleged co-conspirators were read out and each man was led out of the room by armed guards. The panicked audience began shouting out its allegiance to Saddam as party leaders handed the survivors guns and ordered them to execute those who had been named.

While this display of violence was particularly shocking, leaders of personalist regimes commonly use violence both as a way to come to power, and as a way to stay in power, purging political rivals rather than seeking compromise with them or competing with them in fair elections. For example, Muammar Gaddafi of Libya, Mao Zedong of China, and Idi Amin all came to power through means such as revolution, civil war, or a violent coup. In the process, these leaders learned that force can be an effective means of resolving disputes. Other person-alist leaders, like Kim Jong-il and Kim Jong-un, inherited power rather than seizing it themselves. But they grew up inside regimes where violence was clearly "politics as usual."

Personalist regimes are not the only kinds of regimes to "select for" leaders who are accustomed to violence. Military regimes, likewise, often come to power through the threat or actual use of violence, for example through military coups in which power is seized at the point of a gun. Even when military regimes manage to avoid violence when seizing power, they tend to produce leaders who see military force as a normal part of foreign policy. After all, officers who have devoted their careers to military service are likely to think that military power should play an important role in managing international disputes. Evidence shows that they are, on average, more likely than civilians to be skeptical of diplomacy and to perceive military force as necessary for solving international disputes. As discussed in Chapter 5, military leaders without combat experience and/or who are former rebels are especially likely to favor using force.

In sum, political institutions can influence how leaders come to power. In democracies and civilian, nonpersonalistic dictatorships, leaders tend to rise through the ranks of established institutions. Because these kinds of leaders rise to power only if they enjoy broad support from voters or, in nondemocracies, other regime elites, they tend to have views about when and how to use military power that are relatively moderate. In contrast, in personalist regimes and military regimes, the individuals who come to power are more likely to see violence as an effective and legitimate policy tool. These views, in turn, can increase their likelihood of using military force once in office.

How Institutions Shape Leaders' Behavior Once They Are in Office

Institutions not only determine who comes to power, they also shape the behavior of leaders once they take office. Below, we discuss three main ways in which domestic political institutions shape the policies that leaders pursue. First, institutions determine who, if anyone, can hold the leader accountable, which in turn shapes leaders' incentives to choose more versus less bellicose policies. Second, institutions shape the ability to get quality information about policy. When leaders get poor-quality information, this can reduce their ability to assess the likelihood that a war will be successful, reducing their rate of victory in war. Third, institutions can affect the capacity to generate effective military power, including whether or not the country can attract foreign countries as military allies, multiplying their homegrown military power. Military power, like high-quality information, affects whether leaders tend to win the wars that they do get involved in.

How Institutions Shape Domestic Accountability for Foreign Policy

Above, we described how domestic political institutions influence who comes to power. The identity of leaders matters because leaders typically have sincere policy preferences that, all else equal, they would like to see enacted. But regardless of their private policy views, leaders typically want to *stay* in power. Thus, in order to understand leaders' decisions about foreign policy, we need to understand who, if anyone, they need to please with their policy decisions in order to stay in power. In other words, does the leader face a politically powerful **domestic audience**, and if so, how does that audience think about war and peace (Hyde and Saunders 2020)? The concept of a domestic audience is closely related to that of the selectorate, the set of people who determine who is the leader, a concept described in Chapter 5.

In democracies, ordinary citizens choose their leaders in free and fair elections. The key domestic audience for democratic leaders is therefore voters: leaders need to keep voters happy in order to get reelected. However, the opinions of voters matter even when leaders face term limits. Leaders typically want to ensure that they do not exit office prematurely, and democracies typically feature provisions to remove leaders early for egregious performance. Moreover, leaders usually want to ensure that they have the political support necessary to pursue other elements of their policy agenda. Given that leaders find it easier to pass legislation when they are domestically popular, they have reason to keep voters happy even when an election is not looming. Thus, for all of these reasons, leaders of democracies have strong incentives to choose foreign policies that voters find acceptable.

This raises the question, what kinds of policies do voters tend to favor? Or more specifically, in what kinds of situations are democratic voters willing to wage war? Of course, the specific answer depends on the context, such as the country's geopolitical situation and the threats that voters perceive from abroad. But in general, scholars agree that democratic voters are relatively prudent. On average, particularly in the long term, they tend to see military force as a tool of last resort to be used only when there is no other way to keep their country safe or achieve other "legitimate" objectives.

For example, voters may approve of wars that they believe are important for removing important security threats, such as the 2001 and 2003 American-led invasions of Afghanistan and Iraq, which were justified in the name of fighting terrorism, preventing the proliferation of weapons of mass destruction, and spreading democracy. Voters in democracies have also, at times, supported wars with humanitarian objectives such as removing a regime that abuses its own citizens. In contrast, voters are likely to disapprove of fighting wars for some other kinds of motives, such as seizing another country's territory for glory or economic gain.

Voters also tend to be sensitive to the costs of wars, both for themselves and, in some circumstances, for the target country. Ordinary citizens tend to favor minimizing casualties among their own soldiers, for example, and they tend to approve more strongly of wars that are more cost-effective. (On the economic costs of war, see Chapter 6.) The mounting toll of casualties was an important factor turning Americans against the Vietnam War, for instance. Voters also tend to disapprove strongly when their country loses a war: when democratic leaders lose wars, they are frequently removed from office – much more often than personalistic dictators are. At the same time, voters often care about the consequences of war for citizens in the target country. All else equal, they tend to disapprove of indiscriminate violence against foreign civilians and the abuse of foreign prisoners, and they tend to disapprove of using certain kinds of weapons, such as nuclear weapons – though under some circumstances, they may tolerate even these seemingly "taboo" behaviors. Democratic voters also tend to frown upon behavior that they think would violate international law; for example, as discussed in Chapter 12, they are less likely to support drone strikes when they are told that the strike violates international law. (Though again, public disapproval of law violations is not absolute.)

Put together, the potential for ordinary citizens to punish and even remove leaders for their decisions about war generally creates incentives for democratic leaders to be "selective" about wars. This selectivity results in a variety of outcomes. First, leaders of democracies have incentives to avoid unnecessary wars or wars with low chances of victory. Historical evidence backs this up: on average, democracies win a high proportion of wars that they fight, and tend to be very cautious about getting involved in wars unless the national interest is clearly at stake (Reiter and Stam 2002). Moreover, given that voters are averse to casualties, leaders of democracies also have incentives to keep casualties to a minimum and to avoid taking actions that voters would see as immoral, such as using certain kinds of weapons or abusing prisoners of war. While the historical record here is somewhat more mixed (see Downes 2008), evidence suggests that, at a minimum, leaders think about how the public will respond to "immoral" behavior in war, and mainly resort to normatively objectionable behavior when it can either be kept secret or when it is seen as necessary for protecting the national interest. In summary, the preferences of voters influence not only which wars democratic leaders fight, but how they fight them.

While our discussion so far has focused primarily on the foreign policies of individual states, some have speculated that the constraints that voters can place on leaders of democracies have a particularly strong effect on relations *between* democracies. A large literature has explored the phenomenon of the **democratic peace**, or the fact that even though democracies frequently fight wars against nondemocracies, they almost never fight wars against fellow democracies (Russett and Oneal 2001). For example, many people think that the spread of democracy across Western Europe after 1945 helped cure it of centuries of conflict: as democracy spread across the region, conflict between states vanished, even though this was a region that had witnessed world wars that killed tens of millions of people.

What are the mechanisms behind the democratic peace phenomenon? Scholars have proposed many explanations. One important possibility has to do with the political constraints democratic leaders face. As we discussed above, voters tend to disapprove of using force unless it is absolutely necessary. When two democracies have a conflict of interest, both sides know that the other side's leader would be unlikely to fight a war that the public does not support. This fact makes it unlikely that minor disputes will escalate into serious conflict due to fears of surprise attack. But more subtly, democratic institutions can influence whether states ever reach a point of disagreement in the first place. Given that voters in democracies tend to share similar goals, such as peace and economic growth, and share similar values, such as the belief that disputes should be worked out peacefully, democracies are less likely to have policy disagreements in the first place (Russett and Oneal 2001). In sum, by empowering voters, domestic institutions in democracies influence foreign policies in general, and have a particularly profound effect on relations *between* democracies.

The idea of the democratic peace has had profound political consequences, with policymakers using it as a motivation for a variety of policy initiatives and foreign policies, from the Versailles Treaty in the aftermath of World War I, to the expansion of organizations such as NATO and the European Union after the Cold War, to attempts to democratize Afghanistan and Iraq. During the 1990s and 2000s, US politicians from both major political parties invoked the ideas behind the democratic peace to advocate spreading and strengthening democratic institutions around the world. Democratic President Bill Clinton said in his 1994 State of the Union address that "the best strategy to ensure our security and to build a durable peace is to support the advance of democracy elsewhere. Democracies don't attack each other. They make better trading partners and partners in diplomacy" (Clinton 1994). Likewise, Republican President George W. Bush said in his own State of the Union address eleven years later that "Our aim is to build and preserve a community of free and independent nations, with governments that answer to their citizens, and reflect their own cultures. And because democracies respect their own people and their neighbors, the advance of freedom will lead to peace" (Bush 2005). Similar sentiments have been articulated by leaders around the world; in 2017, former UN Secretary General Kofi Annan said that "I have been a tireless defender of democracy all my life because I am convinced it is the political system most conducive to peace" (Annan 2017). In sum, the phenomenon of the democratic peace is both widely accepted by scholars and invoked by politicians to justify their own foreign policies.

The previous discussion paints a relatively rosy picture of how democracy influences leaders' incentives to get involved in wars, suggesting that democratic institutions should generally make leaders reluctant to wage war except in extreme circumstances. At the same time, though, the potential for accountability could create some perverse incentives for democratic leaders. As described in Chapter 4, voters sometimes respond to perceived foreign threats with a rally effect: a temporary increase in approval of leaders or governments at the outset of international wars or other serious crises. For example, in the aftermath of the September 11 terrorist attacks that killed thousands of American civilians, US President George W. Bush saw his popularity skyrocket. Likewise, during the Cuban Missile Crisis standoff with the Soviet Union in 1962, public support for President John F. Kennedy experienced an appreciable if temporary bump.

Some scholars have speculated that the existence of rally effects gives leaders incentives to initiate crises or even wars in order to distract attention from domestic problems, such as poor economic performance or domestic unrest. These kinds of conflicts are known as **diversionary wars**: conflicts initiated, at least in part, with the purpose of diverting public attention from unfavorable domestic political situations. For example, some have accused US President Bill Clinton of using airstrikes on Afghanistan, Sudan, and Iraq in 1998 to distract attention from the Monica Lewinsky scandal and subsequent impeachment hearings. However, scholars remain unsure whether diversionary conflict is really a common phenomenon, and whether it is limited to democracies; many have argued that the 1904–1905 Russo-Japanese War, for instance, and the 1982 invasion of the Falkland/Malvinas Islands involved diversionary motives. On balance, the evidence seems to suggest that democratic institutions tend to constrain the use of military force because voters are prudent, rather than encourage the use of force because voters rally to the side of a leader during conflict (Oneal and Tir 2006).

Thus far our discussion has focused on democracies, but citizens in many countries in the world do not live under democratic rule. How do domestic institutions influence foreign policies in nondemocracies? As we saw above, nondemocratic governments come in many different shapes. These differences, in turn, influence whether a leader faces a domestic audience that can constrain their foreign policy decisions, and if so, what the identity of that audience is.

In nonpersonalist regimes that are led by civilians, i.e. machine regimes such as the Soviet Union after Stalin and China under Deng Xiaopeng and Hu Jintao, leaders face a domestic audience of other regime elites. In such regimes, leaders can face a real threat of punishment if the key regime insiders agree to replace them with someone new. The potential punishment comes from powerful elites, rather than voters, but the leader still must conduct foreign policy in the knowledge that domestic punishment could follow a misstep. Thus, some have argued, leaders of nonpersonalist civilian autocracies behave much like leaders of democracies: they are choosy about when to use military force, avoiding conflicts that are likely to be costly or that will result in defeat.

In nonpersonalist regimes led by military officers, aka juntas, the situation is mixed. On the one hand, the leader faces the prospect of domestic punishment for fighting unnecessary, costly,

Figure 3.3. Celebrating Saddam Hussein on the anniversary of Iraq's 1991 Gulf War defeat. Even one of the most decisive military defeats in history did not push Iraqi leader Saddam Hussein from power. Whether genuine or staged, demonstrations like this one bear witness to his grip on power. ©Robert Nickelsberg / Contributor/ The Chronicle Collection/Getty Images.

or unsuccessful wars. For example, the military junta in Argentina ousted Leopoldo Galtieri after Argentina's ill-fated invasion of the Falkland (Malvinas) Islands. On the other hand, the audience with the capacity to impose punishment consists of military officers. As we argued above, these kinds of individuals may be more likely than their civilian counterparts to see military force as a prudent approach. Thus, we might expect these kinds of nonpersonalist regimes to be slightly less selective about conflict than their civilian-led counterparts.

In contrast, in personalist regimes – i.e., boss and strongman regimes – dictators face few constraints on their policies and have almost total leeway when it comes to decisions about war. In these kinds of regimes, leaders do not need to be nearly as careful about avoiding casualties or economic costs, because there is no easy way for ordinary citizens *or* domestic elites to punish or constrain the leader . For example, as the case study below explains in more detail, Saddam Hussein of Iraq could plan the 1990 invasion of Kuwait largely without worrying about domestic blowback. Even when his invasion triggered US intervention, resulting in a humiliating defeat of the Iraqi Army, Saddam remained in power (see Figure 3.3). The 2022 Russian invasion of Ukraine was likely facilitated because Vladimir Putin leads a boss regime in Russia. (See the online Ukraine War module for further discussion.) These issues can be compounded when the individual dictator has a military or rebel background that further encourages the use of military force as a policy option, i.e., in strongman regimes. Thus, due to the absence of a domestic audience to discourage risky or ill-advised military adventures, we would expect personalist regimes to be the most conflict-prone of all.

How Institutions Affect Information that Leaders Receive

Next, institutions can shape the information that leaders have at their disposal when making and implementing decisions about war. Leaders' ability to obtain high-quality information and advice is not only crucial to their ability to make decisions that further their intended foreign policy objectives: it could also influence the likelihood of war more broadly. Above, we saw that leaders in democracies and nonpersonalistic authoritarian regimes may have stronger incentives to weigh the consequences of their decisions about military conflict than leaders of personalistic regimes. Since leaders of the former of these kinds of regimes know that they can be punished for foreign policy failures such as defeat in war, they have strong incentives to seek out information about the costs and benefits of using military force. But crucially, domestic political institutions can affect whether leaders actually get honest information and feedback when they ask for it. In order to make well-informed decisions about foreign policy, leaders need substantial intelligence and expert advice. For example, they need to know how powerful their own military is, how powerful potential opponents are, and they need to make projections about how third parties – other foreign countries – are likely to react. How do domestic political institutions affect the ability of leaders to elicit quality intelligence and advice?

In democracies and nonpersonalist dictatorships, institutions are more likely to encourage the flow of information. In democracies, for example, a robust **marketplace of ideas** allows for open debate about the wisdom of fighting versus choosing other techniques of dispute resolution (Reiter and Stam 2002). Political opponents, newspapers, and voters all have the freedom to weigh in on debates, which can make it more likely that high-quality information and the soundest ideas prevail. The same can be true of nonpersonalistic autocracies. For example, in the Soviet Union under Brezhnev, political elites engaged in heated debate about the wisdom of using military force in Czechoslovakia, with the Politburo only reaching a consensus after carefully weighing the costs and benefits of military intervention. Likewise, the collective North Vietnamese leadership vigorously debated the wisdom of each escalatory move in the war against South Vietnam (and later, the United States). In both cases, the military intervention was successful.

The situation is quite different in personalist regimes, in which promotion to high office depends primarily on the personal preferences of the dictator. In these regimes, leaders typically surround themselves with trusted sycophants and use ruthless strategies to discourage defection. When high-level officials depend on the personal whims of the dictator in order to stay in power, and fear for their lives if they upset the leader, this can discourage them from providing information that the leader does not want to hear, such as sharing disappointing information about the state of the country's military readiness or offering a criticism of the leader's preferred strategy.

For example, in the Soviet Union from 1936 to 1938, Stalin carried out ruthless purges of rivals inside the Communist Party leadership and Red Army. The terrified survivors learned that there was "a clear etiquette: it was deadly to disagree too much. . . . Silence was often a virtue and veterans advised neophytes on how to behave and survive" (quoted in Montefiore 2004, 341). Stalin's subordinates learned to be so obsequious that when Stalin mispronounced a word in a speech, later speakers would repeat the mistake rather than being accused of "correcting" him. Even Stalin's inner circle feared to offer opinions that might contradict his; instead they often did their best to guess Stalin's opinion ahead of time and tailor their comments to what they thought he would agree with. This atmosphere of fear contributed to terrible foreign policy miscalculations such as the Soviet invasion of Finland in 1939: the Soviet Army, ill-prepared for fighting in the cold, lost 125,000 soldiers in a humiliating fiasco that failed to achieve its primary objectives and drove Finland into the arms of Germany.

Figure 3.4. Finnish officers inspect captured Soviet propaganda during the Russo-Finnish War. Propaganda, purges, secret police, and a climate of fear, all tools for making a personalist leader more powerful internally, can have pernicious effects on a state's foreign policy and military capabilities. ©Keystone / Stringer/Hulton Archive/ Getty Images.

Machinery that strengthened Stalin's power within his country undermined Soviet power when fighting other countries (see Figure 3.4).

These kinds of dynamics not only produce erratic and faulty assessments about foreign policy: the pressure to please the dictator may systematically result in overoptimism. For example, officers in Saddam Hussein's Iraq were reluctant to deliver anything other than exaggeratedly positive reports about Iraq's military effectiveness because it would reflect poorly on their own competence and leave them vulnerable to Saddam's frustration. Thus, personalist dictators are particularly likely to have a distorted, overoptimistic picture of their own relative military capabilities as well as other factors that could influence the wisdom of initiating military conflict.

Building this discussion on previous themes, the combination of overoptimism and lack of domestic political accountability for war outcomes could make personalist dictators both particularly likely to initiate war, and particularly likely to lose the wars that they fight. Earlier, we saw that personalist leaders need to worry less than other kinds of leaders – both democratic and nondemocratic – about being punished for poor war outcomes, which could make them willing to initiate a broader range of conflicts than more accountable leaders would.

The fact that they tend to have more inflated ideas about the likelihood of victory could produce a similar pattern. Thus, personalist leaders seem more likely to initiate conflict, all else equal, than other kinds of leaders. At the same time, personalist leaders are more likely to lose the wars that they start. Again, both the lack of accountability and overoptimism produce this effect. Lack of domestic accountability means that personalists are *willing* to accept a lower likelihood of victory; problems with the "marketplace of ideas" mean that they tend to overestimate the likelihood of victory in the first place. Thus, personalist leaders are more willing to fight risky wars that more accountable, and less biased, leaders would systematically try to avoid, driving down the rate of victory by personalist leaders.

How Institutions Affect Military Power and the Ability to Attract Allies

Finally, institutions can influence the kinds of military resources that leaders are able to amass, both domestically and internationally. More specifically, domestic political institutions can influence the level of military power that leaders are able to generate domestically as well as the extent to which countries can attract foreign allies who will help them in military conflicts.

First, institutions can affect leaders' ability to harness their country's military capacity. One possibility is that different kinds of political institutions produce different kinds of soldiers. Scholars have argued, for example, that democracies produce soldiers who show more leadership and initiative on the battlefield, because individuals' experiences as democratic citizens teach them how to be resourceful and proactive in their professional lives (Reiter and Stam 2002).

A different set of arguments focuses on the challenges that leaders face in holding on to power, and what this means for the tradeoffs they have to make when it comes to organizing their militaries. Ideally, countries design military institutions with a focus on deterring and fighting external threats, such as threats of military invasion. To do this, they try to create competent and professional military organizations that are optimized for projecting military power toward foreign foes. These kinds of military organizations emphasize, for example, extensive training of troops, promotion on the basis of merit, decentralized command arrangements that allow commanders to operate based on local conditions, clear chains of command, and the free flow of information both up and down the chain of command and between military units.

However, when leaders fear certain kinds of *internal* threats, such as coups, then these very same institutionalized military practices can actually prove to be a liability, because political rivals could use a competent and well-organized military to pose a domestic challenge to the incumbent leader. Instead, when leaders believe that they face a high risk of a coup, they engage in **coup-proofing**: measures designed to reduce the risk that political rivals, including military officers, could use the military against the leader (Talmadge 2015). When leaders fear coups, they design militaries in which information and communication are compartmentalized, they promote officers on the basis of loyalty rather than merit, they restrict training opportunities, and they centralize the chain of command in the individual person of the leader. These measures, however, make it much more difficult for the country to project power against conventional foreign adversaries. Thus, militaries organized in this way are less likely to prevail in foreign wars. In sum, the domestic threat environment influences whether the military is built

Figure 3.5. Egyptian soldiers surrendering to Israeli forces during the Six Day War, 1967. Israel achieved a decisive and shocking defeat of Jordan, Egypt, and Syria, in part because coup-proofing in those states had substantially undermined their military effectiveness.
©Hulton Deutsch / Contributor/Corbis Historical/Getty Images.

for internal coup prevention or external war-fighting. To the extent that different domestic political institutions, such as personalistic rule, make coups a salient risk, personalistic leaders may find it more difficult to amass military power. Coup-proofing helps explain why some nondemocratic militaries fight surprisingly poorly, including Arab states in their wars against Israel (see Figure 3.5), Iraq in its wars against Iran and the US, and South Vietnam during the Vietnam War.

At the same time, a strong domestic military is not the only way to build military power. Leaders can also recruit foreign allies to fight on their behalf, as discussed in Chapter 9. Here, domestic political institutions could also play a role. Countries are much more willing to sign alliances with countries that they perceive to be credible and trustworthy. Moreover, countries have reasons to avoid forming alliances with countries that they fear will entrap them in unnecessary wars. On both of these grounds, democratic countries, and to a lesser extent nonpersonalistic autocracies, could have an advantage over personalistic dictatorships. Leaders of democracies and nonpersonalist autocracies could face serious domestic consequences if they abandoned allies: their voters and/or regime insiders could punish them for sullying the country's reputation. Thus foreign countries might see them as more reliable allies who are more likely to stick to an agreement, and would be more willing to form alliances with them in the first place. Fears of entrapment could also motivate countries to pursue alliances with democracies and nonpersonalist autocracies. If the above arguments are correct, these kinds of regimes are less likely to provoke military conflict than personalist regimes who face fewer constraints on conflict initiation. Prospective allies might therefore be wary of forming an alliance with a personalist regime because they expect to be drawn into the country's belligerent foreign policies. Thus, domestic political institutions could not only influence a country's ability to generate military power domestically: it could also affect the country's ability to recruit powerful friends abroad.

It is also possible that similar regimes are more likely to ally with each other because they perceive shared interests. States tend to prefer to ally with countries that they think share their security interests, because countries are more likely to uphold promises to defend their allies when military conflict is in their own national security interest, independent of the alliance. When states share similar political systems, in turn, it is possible that they could perceive each other to share ideological and political goals and to share similar interests more generally, such as democracies allying with other democracies, and Communist states allying together during the Cold War. Thus, we might expect to see pairs of regimes with similar institutions allying with each other more frequently than mixed pairs of countries.

How Institutions Affect Bargaining and Communications between Countries

Above, we focused mainly on how domestic political institutions influence the decisions of individual countries and their leaders, including questions such as what kind of goals countries hope to achieve through war, what kinds of policies governments believe are normatively acceptable, how important it is to them that their military interventions are successful, and what resources they have to achieve their goals. However, "it takes two to tango" – not only on the dance floor, but in international politics as well: war only occurs when two (or more) countries fail to reach a peaceful agreement about an important international issue. We therefore investigate how domestic political institutions influence interactions *between* countries, or more specifically, their ability to reach peaceful agreements that avoid war.

One major obstacle to peace is that countries often find it difficult to communicate with each other. Reaching a peaceful agreement that both countries prefer to war requires leaders to make estimates about issues such as how resolved the opponent is: how willing it is to bear the costs of fighting in order to achieve the benefits of victory. The problem is that the desire to gain an advantage during the bargaining process gives leaders reasons to say things that are not true, such as exaggerating their own military capacities or embellishing how important the issue is to their country and thus how willing they are to fight. More broadly, leaders sometimes have incentives to make empty threats: to say that they will use military force to resolve an issue in the hope of persuading the other side to compromise, when in reality they do not intend to fight. The fact that leaders sometimes have incentives to bluff, in turn, means that countries never know whether an opponent's threat is credible or not: does the opponent really intend to go to war if no agreement is reached, or is it just blustering in the hope of getting a better deal?

Perhaps counterintuitively, scholars have argued that all else being equal, the more persuasive or credible a sender's threat is, the less likely war becomes. The reason is that credible threats make it more likely that the target will be motivated to make a deal that will resolve the dispute peacefully. The reason is that the opponent has a more accurate estimate of whether the sender genuinely intends to fight, and therefore is more likely to offer a peaceful bargain that the sender will accept.

This leads us to ask whether domestic political institutions allow some kinds of regimes to issue more credible threats than others. A large body of research has argued that democracies, and to some extent, nonpersonalist autocracies, have advantages when it comes to conveying their willingness to fight: they find it easier to make persuasive threats and more generally to convince the other side that they are serious about their foreign policy objectives. Thus, foreign countries know when these kinds of regimes are serious that a peaceful deal is needed to avert war.

Figure 3.6. Watching President John F. Kennedy's televised address during the Cuban Missile Crisis. By publicizing his threats as widely as possible – on national, live TV – Kennedy ran the risk of being politically crucified if he failed to follow through on his threat. Ironically, making himself more vulnerable in that way made the threat more credible in the eyes of Moscow.
©Bettmann / Contributor/Bettmann / Contributor/ Getty Images.

One potential reason that democracies and nonpersonalist autocracies can make more credible threats has to do with the strength of the domestic audience, a concept we introduced above. We saw above that in democracies and nonpersonalist autocracies, leaders face a powerful domestic audience, such as voters or regime insiders. Leaders of these kinds of regimes have reason to believe that if they make a threat and then back down from it, they will suffer **audience costs**, defined as the penalty a leader pays for making a threat and backing down, relative to never having made a threat at all. The reason that voters and regime insiders have a tendency to punish leaders who make empty threats – to impose audience costs – is both that threats tarnish the national honor and reputation and that threats can seem overly belligerent. The fact that democratic (and nonpersonalist) leaders expect they will be punished for empty threats, in turn, gives them incentives to avoid bluffing. They tend to only issue threats when they really intend to follow through. For example, in 1967, Israel launched a war against Egypt when Egypt failed to heed its warning that closing the Straits of Tiran would be considered an act of war. The knowledge that democratic leaders tend not to bluff makes their threats more persuasive. For example, when President John F. Kennedy went on national television in October 1962 to demand that the Soviet Union remove its nuclear missiles from Cuba, observers had reasons to believe that he would follow through with his demands or face a firestorm of criticism at home (Figure 3.6). This arguably contributed to the Soviet decision to remove its missiles.

Personalist leaders, in contrast, have fewer incentives to refrain from bluffing. Even if they are forced to back down from an empty threat, there is no domestic group that will punish them. For example, North Korea's leaders have a long and colorful history of making empty threats without any domestic consequences. Knowing this, targets have fewer reasons to believe personalistic autocracies when they make threats, and they are therefore more likely to underestimate the resolve of such regimes and stumble into war against them by failing to make an appealing peaceful bargain.

Even when autocracies lack a powerful domestic audience of elites, they sometimes have another tool at their disposal to signal their intentions: allowing public nationalist protest. Of course, in autocracies, ordinary people cannot use elections to vote leaders out of office. Citizens can, however, rebel against the leader, by joining with other citizens, flooding the streets, and refusing to comply with government orders. Rebellions, however, do not usually emerge out of nowhere: they typically begin as a peaceful demonstration that has somehow escalated to the point that it poses a real threat to the regime. One type of public demonstration that has a particularly strong possibility to inspire public passion, and thus to potentially escalate in a way that is dangerous to the incumbent regime, is nationalist protest, such as citizens gathering to criticize the country's treatment at the hands of a foreign rival. Thus, any time a regime allows a public anti-foreign demonstration to go forward, it raises the risk that the demonstration will blossom into a fully fledged rebellion that would threaten the regime if the dispute is not resolved in a favorable manner. What this means is that autocracies can decide to strategically *allow* demonstrations to show other countries that they mean business in the context of an international dispute. Scholars have shown that China, for example, uses this strategy to signal its resolve even though voters cannot punish leaders at the ballot box. For example, when US airstrikes accidentally hit the Chinese embassy in Belgrade in 1999, killing three Chinese nationals, the Chinese government permitted anti-American public demonstrations. By doing so, the Chinese government created a risk that the protests would escalate and threaten Beijing's rule, which in turn communicated convincingly to the United States that China would not tolerate US provocations in the future.

Thus, countries can use domestic politics and particular domestic political institutions in order to convey their resolve to foreign opponents, which can have the counterintuitive effect of reducing the probability of unnecessary war. Some scholars have argued that this mechanism could contribute to the democratic peace, or absence of war between democracies, laid out earlier. The fact that, in pairs of democracies (or, by extension, perhaps pairs of other kinds of nonpersonalistic regimes), both sides are able to communicate their resolve means that these pairs of states are particularly likely to avoid the kinds of costly and unnecessary conflicts that plague other state-to-state interactions.

CASE STUDY

Saddam Hussein and the 1990 Invasion of Kuwait

This chapter has investigated how domestic political institutions influence decisions about war and peace. One recurring theme was the idea that although personalistic leaders are particularly likely to initiate wars, and particularly likely to lose the wars that they do initiate, they are relatively unlikely to face domestic punishment compared to other kinds of leaders. This case study explores these issues in the context of Iraqi leader Saddam Hussein's 1990 decision to invade Kuwait.

Iraq under Saddam Hussein: A Personalistic "Boss" Regime

Iraq under Saddam Hussein clearly fits the characterization of a *boss* regime – a personalist regime in which institutions are too weak to allow domestic actors to constrain the leader and in which the majority of key decisionmakers are civilians rather than professional military officers.

   Saddam Hussein came to power in July 1979, after working his way up through the ranks of the Ba'ath Party. From the year he took power until the United States toppled him in April 2003, Saddam's Iraq was one of the most autocratic countries in the world. Of course, the regime lacked competitive elections and freedom of the press, so ordinary citizens did not have a way to influence government policy. But the regime also lacked the kinds of strong institutions that can allow elite regime insiders to constrain the leader, either directly or indirectly. The regime nominally featured some of the trappings of elite power-sharing, such as a cabinet and a national parliament. But in reality, the cabinet was personally selected by Saddam and those elections were a sham. Instead, Iraq was dominated by one man. Saddam formally held all of the key offices, including prime minister and commander-in-chief of the armed forces. Just as importantly, he controlled political appointments, allowing him to put cronies and family members into key positions, such as promoting his sons Uday and Qusay to high military positions. He built an extensive internal security apparatus, with overlapping internal intelligence agencies reporting directly to him about citizens, elites, and even the other intelligence agencies. Saddam also tampered with the military hierarchy to make it hard to launch a military coup, taking measures like creating parallel hierarchies and competing security forces, rotating top commanders so that they could not build their own loyal power bases, and even going so far as to require extensive background checks of potential brides before officers married. All the while, he heaped rewards on those who remained loyal. Both inside and outside the military, elites knew that the best path to safety – and riches – was to stay completely loyal.

Saddam As an Individual: Attracted to Violence and Extremely Ambitious

On their own, a lack of constraints and a low likelihood of being punished could encourage personalist bosses to be more war-prone than leaders of other kinds of regimes. However,

(cont.)

this chapter argued that the kinds of individuals who come to power in personalist regimes – or who deliberately create this type of political regime – share certain traits and worldviews that make them unusually disposed to using violence. These leaders tend to be highly ambitious – even more so than other political leaders – and also tend to believe that violence is an effective tool for solving conflicts. Thus, personalist bosses not only pay fewer costs for using violence internationally but also tend to be uncommonly motivated to change the status quo to fulfil their ambitions.

Saddam's personal characteristics certainly fit this description. From very early in his life, Saddam was highly ambitious and attracted to violence. Saddam grew up in a village outside the northern city of Tikrit. After his father died, he worked as a thug carrying out dirty work for his uncle, and he is even said to have assassinated one of his uncle's rivals. Saddam soon moved into politics, participating in a Ba'athist assassination attempt in 1959. He was forced to flee abroad, where he got to know prominent Arab nationalists. After a few years, he returned to Iraq and soon acquired a seat on the influential Ba'ath Party intelligence committee. Not long after, he was arrested for suspected involvement in a coup attempt and spent several years in jail. Soon after leaving prison, Saddam helped bring about the 1968 coup that carried the Ba'ath Party to power. Saddam became deputy chairman of the Revolutionary Command Council (RCC), a key organization inside the Ba'ath Party. This position allowed him to stealthily stack key governing bodies with cronies and family members and to start to build a cult of personality.

Saddam formally seized power in 1979. Having been involved in political violence since his teenage years, later that year he engaged in the dramatic display of violence described above, commanding half his inner circle to slaughter the other half. Thus, by that time it was apparent that violence was his preferred strategy rather than a tool of last resort.

Like his willingness to use force, Saddam's *ambitions* were also more extreme than those of other leaders. While most state leaders are ambitious, Saddam's goal was nothing less than leadership of the Middle East. Saddam considered himself the successor to Nebuchadnezzar, the Babylonian leader who ruled Egypt and conquered Jerusalem, and Saladin, who recaptured Jerusalem from the Crusaders in the twelfth century. Drawing on these role models, Saddam believed that it was Iraq's destiny to be the most powerful country in the region, with himself as leader of the Arab world. Combined with his willingness to use violence, and a political system with few constraints, this ambition was an added ingredient in a powerful recipe for international conflict.

The Decision to Invade Kuwait

We now explore how these factors help explain the course of events in 1990. First, what did Saddam hope to gain from invading Kuwait? There were several motivations. Kuwait's resources provided a possible way to close the gap between Iraq's economic situation and Saddam's regional ambitions. The Iran–Iraq War had left Iraq with huge

(cont.)

debts and an economy in shambles. In early 1990, Iraq was further devastated by a sharp drop in the price of oil; Saddam blamed this on the Organization of Petroleum Exporting Countries (OPEC), of which Kuwait was a member. Saddam also accused Kuwait of illegally tapping into Iraqi oilfields near their border. Moreover, Iraq had only limited port access to the Gulf, and one of those ports was effectively surrounded by Kuwaiti territory. Thus, invading Kuwait could potentially alleviate some of Iraq's economic and strategic problems while also providing a major boost to Iraq's – and therefore Saddam's – prestige.

An important question is whether an Iraqi leader with different perceptions, ambitions, and constraints would also have wanted to invade Kuwait. The evidence suggests that Saddam's personal ambitions and his beliefs in the necessity and effectiveness of war played an important role in the decision to invade. Moreover, for a leader with a more tenuous grip on power, the domestic political downsides of an unsuccessful invasion would have been daunting. Saddam, however, was unusually insulated from the domestic downsides of war, and it seemed unlikely that a foreign army would come all the way to Baghdad. He had elaborate security measures already in place to protect himself against domestic threats; access to numerous underground bunkers in the event of an air assault; and a network of safe houses. Thus, Saddam was free to focus on the upsides of winning – power, glory, influence, and freedom from economic constraints – without worrying too much about possible negative consequences.

Consistent with this perspective, there is little evidence that Saddam undertook serious assessment of the costs or consequences of invading Kuwait. It seems that he made the decision in isolation, possibly after consulting only with his son-in-law. The Republican Guard was not asked to plan for a military operation until June, an assignment that was carried out by a small and secretive group. As for a strategic assessment of the likelihood of victory or the responses of other countries, the little evaluation that Saddam did request appears to have come in a series of five reports produced only weeks before the invasion. Only one of these reports offered anything close to a strategic assessment – and it arrived only seven days before the invasion. Moreover, the few individuals who were consulted had little incentive to speak out against the plan, out of fear that criticism could be taken as a sign of disloyalty. According to interviews and documents recovered after the US-led invasion of Iraq in 2003, many government officials were completely in the dark about war preparations until the last minute. One advisor has suggested that before August 1, 1990, only six individuals knew that Iraq would soon invade Kuwait.

This raises two questions: Did Saddam believe that the United States would respond militarily, and if so, why did he proceed with the invasion? The evidence is mixed on the first question. Saddam consistently dismissed the possibility that the United States would enter the conflict, in part because few of his yes-men tried to disabuse him of this belief. On the other hand, the report that arrived on the eve of the war indicates that Iraqi intelligence believed there was a strong chance of a Western response. Thus it is unlikely

(cont.)

that Saddam was completely unaware of the chance of a US response. Then, why did he invade Kuwait if the United States might intervene? The answer appears to be that Saddam thought he could weather a US intervention and perhaps even benefit from it. Saddam doubted that US forces would venture all the way to Baghdad and depose him, an expectation that turned out to be right. Instead, Saddam appears to have thought he could gain personal prestige by standing up to the West. For Saddam personally, even a moderate chance of US intervention was unlikely to be prohibitively costly.

Defeat – and Domestic Political Survival

Saddam mobilized the Iraqi Republican Guard in July 1990. On August 2, 100,000 Iraqi troops started their invasion of Kuwait, quickly conquering the tiny country and its minuscule army. The United Nations Security Council (UNSC) immediately passed a resolution demanding that Iraq withdraw, and the United States, which already had troops in Saudi Arabia, asked the UN for authorization to use force to liberate Kuwait. The UN granted the authorization and gave Saddam a deadline. The UN deadline passed, and the aerial phase of the Gulf War began on January 17, 1991. A few weeks later, it took coalition ground forces only 100 hours to crush the Iraqi military and liberate Kuwait (see Map 3.1). On March 2, the UNSC passed Resolution 686, outlining the conditions Iraq had to meet in order for a ceasefire to take place. Iraq accepted the terms, and a week later the coalition forces withdrew.

Despite this crushing defeat, Saddam survived in power. How did he do it? Iraqi people understood that Iraq had been defeated, even though Saddam tried to use his control over the press to frame the war as a strategic victory for Iraq. Public unrest began at the end of the war when an Iraqi tank commander fired a shell at a large mural of Saddam in Basra. This was followed by more widespread vandalism and targeting of government personnel, and uprisings soon spread through several areas of the country. The uprisings were doomed, however. In about one month, regime loyalists, headed by the Republican Guard, had restored order, although over 100,000 Shi'a and Kurdish civilians lost their lives in the violence.

The regime's ability to quash the rebellion can be attributed to several factors, including lack of foreign support for the rebels. But most importantly, the vast majority of the Iraqi political and military elite remained loyal to Saddam. Although some demoralized soldiers did turn against the regime, most of the elites stuck by their boss. The structure of punishment and reward that Saddam had so carefully crafted helped ensure that officers in the various military organizations remained loyal. This was partly because, unlike in democracies and nonpersonalist machines and juntas, so much of the leadership was composed of relatives and other cronies who would have sunk with Saddam had he lost power. It was also partly because of Saddam's ability to monitor his subordinates and their fear that they would face serious punishment for defecting; indeed, Saddam foiled apparent plots in the summer of 1992 and arrested and/or executed the culprits. Saddam,

(cont.)

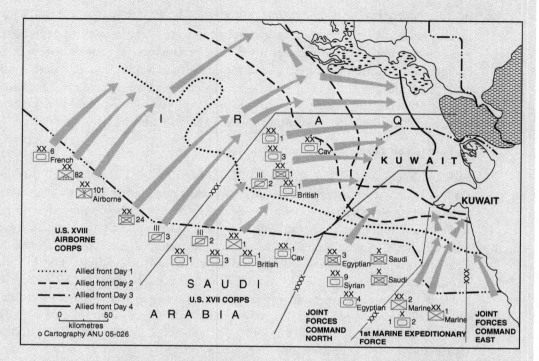

Map 3.1. The massive, multinational effort led by the United States to liberate Kuwait from Iraqi capture, 1991. A United Nations force of nearly a million soldiers needed only 100 hours, suffering less than 150 combat deaths, to achieve its mission and utterly crush the Iraqi military. Even after such a gigantic foreign policy failure, Saddam Hussein still held on to power in Iraq. D. M. Horner, Australia and the 'New World Order': From *Peacekeeping to Peace Enforcement*: 1988–1991.

not only because of the fear that his brutal regime instilled in the masses but also through the support and fear he had encouraged within the ruling elite, was able to survive a terrible military mistake.

In sum, the Iraqi case illustrates important implications of the argument about how personalism fosters international conflict. First, Saddam was even more ambitious than the kinds of leaders who usually end up ruling nonpersonalist regimes. He believed it was his destiny to lead the Middle East, and thought that invading Kuwait was a step toward that goal. Second, Saddam consistently believed that violence was the key to realizing his political goals, whether domestic or international. Force, rather than diplomacy, was usually his tool of choice. Third, because there were few domestic actors with the will and ability to restrain or punish him, Saddam was free to enact his plans with little fear of the repercussions. The result was a poorly planned war, an embarrassing defeat, and yet more than another decade of power for Saddam.

QUANTITATIVE STUDY

Domestic Political Institutions and War Outcomes

Why are some kinds of political regimes so much more successful in war than others? This chapter reviewed the idea that domestic political pressures force democracies and some kinds of authoritarian regimes to be highly selective about resorting to military force, while leaders of other kinds of regimes are either freer to indulge in riskier behavior or, because of their military backgrounds, more likely to see force as preferable to diplomacy. The case study in the previous section applied this question to the case study of Iraq and Saddam Hussein. In her book *Dictators at War and Peace*, Jessica Weeks analyzes historical data to explore whether these arguments explain success and failure in war in the last century.

Research Question

What is the effect of regime type – democracy, junta, machine, boss, and strongman regimes – on the rate of defeat in war?

Theory and Hypotheses

How wars are won is strongly affected by how wars start. If a state only starts wars when it is very confident that it will win, then that state will win most of the wars it fights, because it avoids losing battles. Conversely, if a state is riskier and willing to start wars when it has a lower chance of winning, or makes bad guesses about the chances of victory and sometimes starts wars with a misplaced sense of confidence, then it will lose more of its wars.

Domestic political institutions have a strong effect on how wars are started, and in turn who wins wars. Democracies, in which leaders are accountable to voters, and "machines," in which leaders are accountable to civilian regime elites, should be the most careful about using military force and therefore should be the least likely to lose the wars they get involved in.

In juntas, leaders are also accountable to a domestic audience for failure in war, but war outcomes should be slightly more mixed because the domestic audience in juntas – military officers – are more likely than civilians to feel that it is necessary to take on risky wars. They should therefore lose wars at a moderate rate.

Finally, personalist boss and strongman regimes, in which the leader is not constrained by a powerful domestic audience, should be the least selective about war and should lose their wars at the highest rate. This theory generates the hypotheses:

Hypothesis 1: Democracies and machines win more of their wars than other kinds of regimes.

Hypothesis 2: Juntas win fewer of their wars than democracies and machines, but more of their wars than personalist boss and strongman regimes.

Data

This study evaluates the relationship between regime type and war outcomes for all major participants of interstate wars initiated between 1921 and 2007. A country enters the data set if it was a sovereign country that was a "major" participant in a war fought in that time period, meaning that it contributed at least 10 percent of the maximum troop strength deployed by all countries fighting on its side during the conflict.

Dependent Variable

The dependent variable is the outcome of the interstate war, whether a participant won, lost, or drew (tied) the war. Outcomes are considered victories if a significant portion of the war aims were achieved, draws if the objectives were not achieved and the status quo did not worsen, and losses if the status quo deteriorated. This implies that the outcomes are not always zero-sum: a victory for one side does not automatically imply defeat for the opponent. Of the 120 war participants in the sample, 47 of the war participants won, 20 drew, and 53 lost.

Independent Variable

The independent variable is authoritarian regime type. Weeks collected information about the regime type of every authoritarian war participant. She and a team of research assistants classified the regime type of each war participant to assess whether the leader was effectively constrained by a domestic audience. If the leader was constrained by a domestic audience, she assessed whether that audience was composed primarily of civilians (machines) or stemmed from the military ranks (juntas). If the regime was not constrained by a domestic audience, she determined whether the leader had a civilian background (bosses) or military background (strongmen). She coded regimes as "new/ unstable" if they underwent significant institutional change up to two years before the initiation of the war. In these new regimes, it is too difficult to establish a clear record of the leader's power to reach a reliable coding of the constraints on the leader.

Control Variables

Control variables include the characteristics of the target states, terrain, relative capabilities, and others.

Results

The study found that there is significant variation in war outcomes among authoritarian regimes, and that some kinds of nondemocracies lose a similar proportion of wars as democracies. Elite-constrained civilian machines lost 25 percent of their 20 wars, similar to democracies' 28 percent out of 29. Juntas lost 38 percent of their 8 wars, a proportion that is higher than that of democracies and machines, though not significantly so in a statistical sense, perhaps due to the small number of observations. Personalist civilian

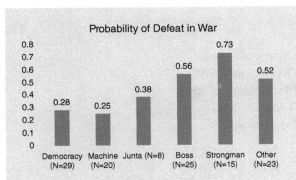

Figure 3.7. Probability of defeat in war, by regime type, 1921–2007.

bosses in contrast lost 56 percent of their 25 wars, and strongmen lost an abysmal 73 percent of 15 wars. These results were confirmed in more sophisticated statistical analyses that included control variables. Figure 3.7 displays these patterns graphically.

In sum, unconstrained personalists fared very poorly in war, while elite-constrained civilian machines did nearly as well as democracies. Juntas did slightly worse than machines. This supports the theory that domestic political institutions affect war outcomes, and that there are important differences among nondemocracies as well as between democracies and (most) nondemocracies.

SUMMARY

As we have seen, domestic political institutions can have profound effects on leaders' decisions about war and peace. Some of the most important conclusions from this chapter are as follows:

- There are many different kinds of political regimes, including democracies, nonpersonalist autocracies including civilian machines and military juntas, and personalist autocracies including civilian bosses and military strongmen.
- Institutions influence decisions about military conflict through many different mechanisms.
- Institutions shape who leads: different kinds of institutions make it more versus less likely that individuals with belligerent policy preferences come to power.
- Institutions shape leaders' behavior once they are in office, because institutions determine the identity of the domestic audience – if there is one – that can constrain the leader. The identity of the domestic audience affects the policy preferences of that domestic audience and therefore the leader's foreign policy incentives.
- Institutions affect leaders' ability to get high-quality information about issues such as relative military capabilities
- Institutions affect the ability of states to generate military power and to attract powerful allies.
- Institutions affect states' ability to communicate information to each other by generating audience costs, which can make it easier to avoid unnecessary wars.
- Through a combination of these mechanisms, democracies are particularly unlikely to fight wars against fellow democracies.

KEY TERMS

Domestic political institutions
Democracies
Nondemocracies
Personalism
Military regimes
Domestic audience

Democratic peace
Diversionary war
Marketplace of ideas
Audience costs
Coup-proofing

REVIEW QUESTIONS

1. Why do personalist dictators fight so many military conflicts, and why do they lose such a high proportion of the wars that they fight?
2. What are the similarities between democracies and machines when it comes to foreign policy decisionmaking? What are the differences?
3. What is the democratic "marketplace of ideas"?
4. Why do leaders coup-proof their militaries? What are the possible consequences of doing so?
5. Why is it difficult for leaders to communicate their intentions in international relations? How do audience costs help with that? What kinds of regimes find it easiest, and most difficult, to generate audience costs?
6. What is the "democratic peace", and what are some possible explanations for it?
7. The case study of Saddam Hussein's decisionmaking in 1990 shows how personal rule can increase the risk of military conflict, because personalist regimes lack constraints and often have leaders who are particularly attracted to violence and are particularly ambitious. How might Iraq's decisionmaking have looked if it were a "machine" regime rather than a personalist one? How might the situation have looked if Iraq had been led by a military junta?
8. Machines initiate and win wars at similar rates as democracies. Are there other areas of foreign policy where you would expect the decisions of democracies and machines to *differ* from each other? Why?
9. Explain how a junta regime works. How do military officers think about military conflict? How does this affect leaders' decisions to initiate military force, even though the leaders are accountable to an elite audience?

DISCUSSION QUESTIONS

1. Which regime types will have the most effective foreign policies? That is, what domestic political institution arrangements help a state best accomplish its foreign policy goals?
2. How did Iraqi domestic political institutions under Saddam Hussein Iraqi foreign policies?

ADDITIONAL READING

Chiozza, G. and Goemans, H. E. (2011). *Leaders and International Conflict*. New York: Cambridge University Press.

Sassoon, J. (2011). *Saddam Hussein's Ba'th Party: Inside an Authoritarian Regime*. Cambridge: Cambridge University Press.

Weeks, J. (2014). *Dictators at War and Peace*. Ithaca, NY: Cornell University Press.

Weiss, J. C. (2014). *Powerful Patriots: Nationalist Protest in China's Foreign Relations*. New York: Oxford University Press.

Woods, K. M., Pease, M. R., Stout, M. E., Murray, W. and Lacey, J. G. (2006). *Iraqi Perspectives Project: A View of Operation Iraqi Freedom from Saddam's Senior Leadership,* Norfolk, VA: United States Joint Forces Command, Joint Center for Operational Analysis.

REFERENCES

Annan, K. (2017, September 13). The Crisis of Democracy. *Kofi Annan Foundation.* www.kofiannanfoundation.org

Bush, G. W. (2005, February 2). State of the Union Address. https://georgewbush-whitehouse.archives.gov/news/releases/2005/02/20050202-11.html

Clinton, W. J. (1994. January 25). Address before a Joint Session of the Congress on the State of the Union. www.presidency.ucsb.edu/documents/address-before-joint-session-the-congress-the-state-the-union-12

Downes, A. B. (2008). *Targeting Civilians in War*. Ithaca, NY: Cornell University Press.

Geddes, B., Wright, J., and Frantz., E. (2018). *How Dictatorships Work: Power, Personalization, and Collapse*. Cambridge: Cambridge University Press.

Hyde, S. D. and Saunders, E. N. (2020). Recapturing regime type in international relations. *International Organization* **74**(2), 363–395.

Montefiore, S. S. (2004). *Stalin: The Court of the Red Tsar*. New York: Knopf.

Oneal, J. R. and J. Tir. (2006). Does the diversionary use of force threaten the democratic peace? Assessing the effect of economic growth on interstate conflict, 1921–2001. *International Studies Quarterly* **50**(4), 755–779.

Reiter, D. and Stam, A. C. (2002). *Democracies at War*. Princeton: Princeton University Press.

Russett, B. M. and J. R. Oneal. (2001). *Triangulating Peace: Democracy, Interdependence, and International Organizations*. New York: Norton.

Talmadge, C. (2015). *The Dictator's Army: Battlefield Effectiveness in Authoritarian Regimes,* Ithaca, NY: Cornell University Press.

4 Public Opinion and the Conduct of Foreign Policy
CHRISTOPHER GELPI

Introduction

The spread of democratic political systems has been among the largest and most consequential changes in the international system over the past century. In the midst of World War II, less than a dozen nations were considered democratic according to the most widely used social science measure (Herre and Roser 2013). But by 2009 that number had grown to nearly ninety democratic states around the world. Similarly, as late as the 1940s less than a quarter of the world's population was governed by democratically elected leadership, but by 2015 that proportion had risen to more than 50 percent.

International diplomacy has long been known as the realm of "high politics." Many classic theories of international relations explicitly assumed that national leaders are immune from the influence of domestic politics when making foreign policy. But the rise of democratic governance created the possibility that ordinary citizens might influence foreign policy. Moreover, to the extent that we share the democratic belief that government policy ought to represent the will of its citizens, we should also believe that public opinion ought to "matter" for the foreign policy behavior of democratic states. Sending soldiers to fight, kill, and die on the battlefield is one of the most consequential decisions that a government can make on behalf of its citizens. Are there pathways through which the opinions of ordinary citizens regarding such actions can influence their government's behavior? More recent social science theories about the foreign policy behavior of democratic states depend on the constraining effects of public opinion on their leaders. For example, most theories explaining the relative lack of military conflict between democratic states – known as the democratic peace – rely on public opinion to explain this pattern. But what does the evidence show? Can citizens fulfill their democratic duty and constrain the behavior of their leaders by expressing their collective will? We will address this question with a particularly strong eye toward understanding American foreign policy behavior, though the ideas should apply to public opinion anywhere. We focus on the United States both because it continues to be the most heavily polled public in the world, and because America's outsized influence on world affairs, for better or worse, makes the extent of public constraint on the exercise of American power an important issue for citizens around the world.

Our discussion will begin by investigating whether public opinion is actually capable of influencing foreign policy in a democracy. Current research suggests that the answer to this question depends on three conditions. First, citizens must actually have foreign policy attitudes. Second, these foreign policy attitudes must be important to citizens relative to their attitudes on other issues. And third, political party platforms must differ from one another on foreign policy issues so that citizens can translate their foreign policy attitudes into political behavior – such as voting or protests – that can influence national leaders.

Even if the public is capable of influencing foreign policy in a democracy, however, it is not necessarily clear that this influence will be a good thing. Both policymakers like Henry Kissinger and journalists like Walter Lippmann, for example, have famously bemoaned the influence of public opinion on American foreign policy as ill-informed, impulsive, and open to manipulation. Once again, current research suggests that three conditions must be met in order for public opinion to reflect the informed judgment of the popular will rather than the demands of an impetuous mob. First, citizens must have some order and coherence to their foreign policy beliefs. Second, these attitudes must be resistant to influence or manipulation by political leaders. And finally, citizens must be able to obtain information about foreign policy issues in order to reach reasoned judgments and update their beliefs in response to new information.

Throughout the remainder of this chapter we will explore whether public opinion can influence foreign policy behavior and whether that influence makes democratic foreign policy an informed reflection of the popular will. To preview our conclusions, public opinion can matter for foreign policy in important ways and on important issues. Moreover, the public appears surprisingly capable of expressing coherent and reasonably informed views on foreign policy – at least when viewed in the aggregate. Finally, the biggest threats to public constraint on foreign policy come from elite institutions including the news media and political parties. Public access to reliable information from the media and politicians' willingness to take clear and divergent stands on foreign policy issues are the greatest hurdles that democratic citizens face in constraining the international behavior of their leaders.

Can Public Opinion Influence Foreign Policy in Democracies?

Three key factors are necessary for the public to be capable of influencing foreign policy behavior in a democracy: (1) the public must have opinions; (2) the public must care about these opinions; and (3) politicians must differ on foreign policy issues to allow the public to act on these opinions. We will review the evidence regarding each of these conditions in order to determine whether and when the public can matter for foreign policy.

Does the Public Have Opinions?

One of the most robust findings in survey research is that the average citizen is able to express factual knowledge about very few things that relate to politics. In the United States, for example, a 2014 Study by the Annenberg Public Policy Center found that only 36 percent of their respondents could name all three branches of the American government (legislative, executive, and judicial), and nearly as many could not name a single one of the branches (Annenberg Public Policy Center 2014). Similarly, a cross-national study found that the public's factual knowledge of international affairs was generally quite spotty across nearly a dozen democratic states. For example, less than a third of citizens polled in Britain, the United States, Japan, and Australia could correctly identify the secretary general of the United Nations (Aalberg et al. 2013). If citizens are unaware of such basic aspects of the political system, how can we expect them to form and retain any coherent attitudes about much more complex questions of foreign policy?

The key to unlocking this paradox is understanding the way in which individuals form and maintain attitudes and beliefs. Research on attitude formation outlines two distinct processes by which individuals may make and retain judgments: memory-based processing and online processing. **Memory-based processing** involves the construction of attitudes through the simultaneous recall and evaluation of multiple pieces of information in order to form an overall judgment. For example, forming a memory-based judgment about a political candidate would involve recalling the candidate's political party, her stances on all relevant policy issues, and any other factors that might be relevant as well. Then you would combine all of those pieces of information – weighted by their relative importance – into an overall attitude of support for or opposition to the candidate. As new information about the candidate became available, a memory-based process of updating your attitudes would involve recalling all of this old information, adding the new information, and then combining the new and old information based on the weighted relative importance of each piece of information. Memory-based processing ensures that we are considering and comparing all the relevant information when forming judgments, but it requires a large capacity to retain and recall specific information. As noted above, public opinion research suggests that individuals often do not display the capacity to retain and recall this kind of information about politics.

Online processing, on the other hand, involves serially incorporating each new piece of information into an existing attitude or belief. After the new information has been integrated into an overall attitude, the specific piece of information is discarded and only the updated overall judgment is retained. This process serves as a kind of mental shortcut that allows people to form attitudes that reflect lots of information without actually having to remember all that information. Returning to our example of attitudes toward a political candidate, an online attitude formation process would involve making an initial judgment about a candidate based on the first pieces of information that one obtains about her, such as her political party and a few of her stances on important issues. After you formed an attitude of support or opposition, you would then forget the specifics of the issue positions that led you to that judgment. As new information about the candidate became available during the campaign, such as new issues or candidate characteristics, you would evaluate each of those pieces of information and adjust your attitude toward the candidate in a positive or negative direction depending on your views of the new information. Once again, after making a new summary judgment about the candidate, you would not bother to retain the specific information that led you to change your views. Online summary judgments can be easily and quickly stored for future recall without requiring you to retain any of the information that led you to this complex assessment.

Of course, individuals sometimes use memory-based processing and other times use online processing. But the online model is especially prevalent regarding issues such as public opinion on foreign policy, where most individuals will not spend large amounts of effort gathering and retaining factual details. Interestingly, however, research suggests that attitudes constructed through online processing may become more strongly held and more quickly recalled than those formed with memory-based processing. This pattern seems to explain how new pieces of information about a foreign policy issue – such as casualties in a military conflict – can cause people to update their attitudes about the conflict even if they do not remember how many casualties have occurred, or remember that they received new information about casualties at all. However, another important consequence of online processing is that since individuals forget the information that they used to form their summary judgments, attitudes based on incorrect information may become difficult to alter even if the individual is presented with new correct information. The effects of falsehoods on attitudes may linger precisely because they have been forgotten.

Online processing helps us to understand how individuals who appear to be uninformed may nonetheless hold attitudes and beliefs that are shaped by facts about the real world. When people use online processing to form their opinions, they do receive new information and use it to update their beliefs. But if a public opinion pollster contacted them later and asked about that same information, they would no longer be able to recall it despite the fact that they retain the resulting attitude.

Moreover, public opinion – meaning the collective attitudes of all of the citizens together – may be more well-informed than any individual opinion. The reason for this pattern is what is known as the **wisdom of crowds**. An individual may be poorly informed about a particular issue, but as we combine the attitudes of many citizens the individual errors that people make tend to cancel one another out. As a result, the average opinion within the group tends to reflect a more informed viewpoint even if many members of the group are uninformed. For example, in 2004 a survey asked Americans how many US soldiers had been killed in the Iraq War (Berinsky 2007). Estimates given by survey participants varied widely, indicating that the public was uninformed. But the median estimate, the estimate exactly in the middle if you ranked all the estimates from highest to lowest, was almost exactly correct. Specifically, the median response was 900 soldiers killed, while the actual number of American battle deaths during the period that the survey was in the field ranged from 901 to 915. So while many Americans may not have known the death toll in Iraq, the average American voter had a pretty good guess.

Does the Public Think Foreign Affairs Are Important?

Citizens' energy and attention is limited in terms of which issues can determine their votes or their willingness to influence their leaders in other ways such as letters, phone calls, or protest activities. In order for public opinion toward foreign policy to put pressure on elected leaders to change or adopt policies, foreign affairs need to be influential in the public mind relative to other issues. Many polling organizations have kept track of the salience of foreign affairs and other issues over the decades by asking the public the open-ended question, "What do you think is the most important problem facing the country today?"

In the United States, the most common answers have historically related to the economy. The prevalence of these responses helps to explain why economic performance plays such an important role in determining American presidential election results. The American public's references to foreign affairs in response to this question, on the other hand, are more varied and episodic in the wake of international events. But the salience of foreign affairs can still be very intense. World War II and the wars in Korea, Vietnam, Iraq, and Afghanistan dominated the "most important" problem responses for extended periods of time. And during the Cold War concerns over a range of different issues related to war and peace – including nuclear weapons, the spread of Communism, and various military crises – were collectively more salient than domestic issues. Similarly, ISIS-inspired terrorist attacks within the United States from 2014 through 2016 also peaked as the nation's "most important problem" (Riffkin 2015).

Of course, the public salience of foreign policy issues varies substantially across the globe. For some citizens, such as those in Israel and South Korea, foreign affairs are consistently front and center. But a focus on the United States provides us a challenging test for the claim that foreign affairs can shape popular political behavior. The relative security and isolation of the United States has made it possible for the American public to ignore foreign affairs when it prefers to do so.

That said, responses to an open-ended question about the most important problem may not necessarily be the best measure of what people truly think is important. The open-ended format of the question encourages a "top-of-the-head" response where survey respondents are likely to select the issue that first comes to mind. Quick and easy recall may be partly determined by their assessment of its importance, but it is also likely driven by news coverage of current events rather than their own assessment of what will determine their voting behavior or other political participation.

A more important question is whether foreign policy issues can actually determine the outcomes of elections. Studies of American voting behavior over the past four or five decades indicate that foreign policy issues can be a powerful determinant of vote choice, and are often as influential as economic issues. For example, one prominent study of foreign policy voting concluded that in the five American presidential elections between 1968 and 1984, only in the 1976 contest between Jimmy Carter and Gerald Ford were foreign policy issues not important to voters (Aldrich et al. 1989). Another important study directly compared the impact of foreign and domestic issues on the perceptions of presidential candidates in the 1980 and 1984 elections, and found that the two sets of issues were roughly equal in their impact on voters (Nincic and Hinckley 1991). More recently, numerous studies demonstrate that attitudes toward Iraq dominated presidential voting behavior in 2004 and 2008, and even shaped the outcome of the midterm elections of 2006. In countries like Israel, foreign affairs have played an even more prominent electoral role. For example, one study found that attitudes toward the Intifada were more impactful than any other set of issues in the 1988 election (Barzilai 1990). Thus the impact of foreign policy issues on voting behavior appears to be the rule rather than the exception.

Importantly, however, not all foreign policy issues influence public political participation equally. Nearly all of the factors shaping voting behavior discussed above related to international security and issues of war and peace. Though the domestic performance of the economy has been important to voters, international economic issues have not generally received the same level of attention – in the US context, the 2016 campaign of Donald Trump is a notable exception to this pattern. One possible reason for the lower levels of attention to these issues – as we will discuss below – is that the Democratic and Republican parties have not generally differed much on their international trade policies. In this sense, Trump's campaign truly confronted the political establishment in both parties. And yet prior to the Vietnam War, Democrats and Republicans did not generally differ in their approach to American security either – yet those issues remained salient and important in the public mind. Thus the persistent salience of international security in American elections is more likely due to the fact that these issues are demonstrably threatening to the American public. The deaths or potential deaths of Americans – due to participation in war or foreign or foreign-inspired attacks – are self-evidently important. But it can be very difficult for citizens, and even for experts, to understand what the overall impact of trade agreements will be.

Differences in Party Platforms

Even if citizens develop informed attitudes and care deeply about foreign policy issues, they will be unable to affect the behavior of their leaders if political parties do not give citizens a real choice. Citizens in a democracy may try to influence their leaders in various ways, including voting, contacting their representatives to express their views, donating money, or participating in protest demonstrations. But politicians will not feel pressured by any of this behavior without the existence of a competing politician behind whom dissatisfied citizens can rally.

In the US context, since the end of World War II, a bipartisan consensus has underpinned certain important foundations of American grand strategy, including the Cold War strategy of containment, the promotion of trade and open markets, and the prevention of nuclear proliferation. However, even within this consensus – which peaked during the early part of the Cold War – we find important party differences over how this grand strategy should be translated into policy. Dwight Eisenhower, for example, rose to the presidency in 1952 in large part because of his criticism of the Truman administration's handling of the Korean War. Similarly, Lyndon Johnson's 1964 "Daisy Girl" television commercial claimed that the Republican challenger, Barry Goldwater, was likely to entangle America in a nuclear war.

Since 1968 the Democratic and Republican parties have come to differ more frequently and sharply on foreign policy issues, and some issues – such as the war in Iraq – became highly partisan. Even when a foreign policy issue is controversial or unpopular, however, party platforms may not always diverge. In some cases, politicians may have incentives to obscure their differences with opposing candidates on some issues in order to focus voters' attention on other issues. For example, in the 1968 presidential campaign Republican candidate Richard Nixon and Democratic candidate Hubert Humphrey deliberately obfuscated their policy differences over the Vietnam War. As a result, while much of the public was very dissatisfied with the conduct of the war, Vietnam had little impact on voting behavior since voters were not offered a clear choice on this issue. More recently, in 2012, Barack Obama appears to have benefitted from a similar circumstance regarding the war in Afghanistan. More than 1,500 US soldiers were killed in Afghanistan during the first Obama administration, and the war had become deeply unpopular. However, Republican candidate Mitt Romney did not challenge Obama's policies in Afghanistan, nor did he offer any strategic alternatives. Consequently, Obama was able to sideline the costly failures of his Afghanistan policy throughout the 2012 campaign, and many voters were left with no way to express their dissatisfaction with the war. During the Cold War era, by contrast, although there had been broad consensus on American grand strategy, substantive foreign policy differences could usually be seen between the Democratic and Republican platforms. The end of the Cold War appeared to mute partisan differences over foreign policy, but the attacks of September 11, 2001 brought international terrorism and foreign policy to the very center of political debate, where it has largely remained. As we discussed earlier, attitudes toward Iraq played a critical role in the 2004 and 2008 elections, and the 2016 clash between Hillary Clinton and Donald Trump included sharp differences over a wide range of foreign policy issues, including international trade and environmental agreements, nuclear proliferation, and the use of military force against the Islamic State.

Partisan differences in foreign policy platforms are equally prevalent – though not ubiquitous – across other prominent democracies as well. In Britain, for example, the Conservative Party has generally been more hawkish on international security issues than its main rival, the Labour Party. Yet Labour's criticism of the 2003 Iraq War was muted by internal party divisions, and the Liberal Democrats were the party that voiced the strongest dissent before the war. The issue of British withdrawal from the European Union – known popularly as Brexit – was similarly marked by oscillation between consensus and partisan division. Prior to the 2016 referendum, both Labour and Conservatives sought to remain in the EU, but after the "leave" position prevailed in the referendum the two parties divided as the Conservatives shifted to strong support of Brexit.

Should Public Opinion Influence Foreign Policy in Democracies?

The potential ability of public opinion to influence foreign policy raises the question of whether this impact would be a good thing. Of course, the guiding principle of democratic governance is that policy should reflect the will of the governed. But this principle is founded on the assumption that the popular will reflects some reasoned judgment rather than an impetuous mob sentiment. Current research suggests that three conditions are necessary for public opinion on foreign policy to reflect a reasoned judgment of the citizenry: (1) public opinion on foreign policy issues must have a coherent structure; (2) the public must be independent of manipulation or control by politicians; and (3) the public must be able to stay informed about foreign policy events in order to update and revise their beliefs (even if only in an online manner).

Are Attitudes Coherently Organized?

If public opinion is to shape government policy, then we would like to know if it has some internal coherence and structure. That is, we would like to know if an individual's attitude toward one issue is linked to their attitudes on other issues. Otherwise, the public will impose a more disjointed foreign policy agenda on its leaders. Moreover, public opinion seems more likely to shape foreign policy consistently and systematically if leaders have a broad sense of what their constituents want them to do. Developing any sense of a general public orientation to foreign policy will be impossible if the public has no such structure to its thinking.

In the American context, individuals' attitudes on many domestic political issues line up along a liberal/conservative spectrum. But early research on foreign policy attitudes uncovered no such single dimension to foreign policy views. However, this result does not mean that American public attitudes on foreign policy are without structure. Instead of a single liberal/conservative dimension, foreign policy attitudes appear to be structured along two key dimensions: cooperative internationalism (CI) and militant internationalism (MI) (Holsti 1979; Wittkopf 1990). Individuals who support either form of internationalism are generally supportive of American engagement in international affairs. However, CI supporters prefer an accommodative diplomatic approach, while MI supporters prefer resolute military responses to international issues. Those who do not support either militant or cooperative internationalism are isolationists.

This two-dimensional structure meant that many foreign policy issues did not align closely with differences between the Democratic and Republican parties in the United States. To be sure, foreign policy issues sometimes become extremely partisan. American attitudes toward the Iraq War, for example, were very strongly associated with party identification. Moreover, since the end of the Vietnam War the Democratic Party has been more closely associated with cooperative internationalism, including an emphasis on diplomacy and multilateralism; while the Republican Party has been more closely associated with militant internationalism, including an emphasis on military strength and reliance on coercive force.

But similarities in foreign policy views across party lines – as well as differences within parties – generally outweigh partisan divides over American foreign policy. Despite all of their stark differences on domestic issues, for example, 2016 American Republican presidential candidate Donald Trump and candidate for the Democratic nomination Bernie Sanders were much more similar to one another in their views on international trade than they were to other candidates in their own parties. Both of these candidates harkened back to traditions of isolationism that have long histories in both major American political parties. Perhaps the unusual nature of the 2016 American presidential campaign was not the fact that isolationist candidates sought the highest office, but rather that one of them was actually successful in doing so.

On the other hand, 2016 Democratic candidate Hillary Clinton's views on American military intervention in Syria, Libya, and elsewhere were much closer to those of former President George W. Bush than they were to Bernie Sanders, further indicating the important ways in which American foreign policy views may not be taken as read from party labels. In fact, one prominent study of American foreign policy attitudes found that the starkest divide regarding the use of force is not between Democrats and Republicans, but rather between those who have and have not served in the military (Feaver and Gelpi 2005). Veterans and those who are currently serving tend to be reluctant to use force, perhaps because they are more vividly aware of both the limits of military capability and the costs of war (see Chapter 5). Those who have not served are more likely to support sending troops abroad to address a wide variety of problems and conflicts.

One of the most remarkably constant aspects of American attitudes toward foreign policy has been the stability of the isolationist/internationalist divide. For many decades now, the Chicago Council on Foreign Affairs has been asking Americans, "Do you think it will be best for the future of our country if America takes an active role in world affairs or if we stay out of world affairs?" In 1947, 68 percent of Americans felt that the United States should take an active role. In 2010, that number was 67 percent, and for the most part there has been remarkably little change in the intervening years (Chicago Council Survey n.d.). The only exception to this pattern has been when periods of sustained economic stress have led to an increase in isolationist sentiment. For example, between 1974 and 1982, years of inflation and unemployment followed by outright recession reduced support for internationalism from 66 percent to 54 percent. Similarly, the Great Recession of 2009 and the very sluggish recovery that followed drove internationalism down from 67 percent to 58 percent.

Since 2001, Gallup has asked a related but distinct question about whether America should "take the leading role in world affairs, take a major role, but not the leading role, take a minor role (or) take no role at all in world affairs?" These data show a great deal of stability in American internationalism, with 70–75 percent of the public supporting a "major" or "leading" role (U.S. Position in the World, n.d,). Most of the variation in internationalism in the Gallup data consists of changes in the proportion of the public that feels that America should take a "leading" rather than a "major" role. Support for a "leading" role hit low points in 2007 – perhaps in response to the deterioration of American military efforts in Iraq – and again in 2011 – perhaps in response to the Great Recession. But by 2017, support for a "leading" American role had recovered to pre-recession levels, and President Trump's vocal "America First" stance and his disdain for multilateral organizations only modestly reduces American internationalism.

While data on the structure of foreign policy attitudes in other democracies is less extensively available, there too we do see evidence of relatively stable internationalism combined with significant partisan policy differences. A 2015 British study of public attitudes toward foreign affairs, for example, found little evidence of any erosion in the stable public support for international involvement – even as the referendum on Brexit loomed (Raines 2015). Much like the United States, however, as the survey focused on specific questions about how to engage internationally – including support for Brexit – the public became more sharply divided. As noted above, we also see sharp differences within Britain's parties, suggesting that domestic and international issues may not be organized around the same dimensions.

Are Public Attitudes Manipulated By Political Spin?

One of the most common objections to the claim that public opinion constrains policymaking is the argument that public attitudes are simply a function of what politicians tell people to think. Some view this as a situation of "rational ignorance" of a public that has little time or energy to think about politics. Others contend that politicians sometimes evade or manipulate the public will. The practice of political "spin" is as old as politics itself, but politicians in democratic societies have developed increasingly sophisticated methods of shaping their communications in an effort to influence public opinion. Frank Luntz, for example, famously built a career helping Republican candidates wordsmith their way into office by reframing issues for the public. Luntz played a critical role in the formulation of the 1994 "Contract with America" that fundamentally reshaped control of the House of Representatives, and arguably ushered in a renewed era of partisan polarization in America. Luntz was also influential in transforming the "estate tax" into a "death tax," and turning "drilling for oil" into "energy exploration" (Luntz 2007).

So how malleable are public attitudes about foreign affairs? The discussion of this question has been dominated by a debate between two schools of thought: (1) the **elite rhetoric model** and (2) the **rational expectations model**. The elite rhetoric model argues that public attitudes are primarily shaped by the way that political leaders talk about issues. The rational expectations model, on the other hand, contends that the public is capable of forming attitudes that are a function of "real-world" events at least partly independent of political spin.

The elite rhetoric model is founded on a very large and longstanding literature on **framing** that bridges the disciplines of political science, psychology, and communications. This literature clearly demonstrates that the way that people talk about issues can shape their attitudes and beliefs. An issue frame tells individuals how to give meaning to new information. We are constantly being confronted with information about a complex world, and as our discussion of online processing suggests, our limited brains are constantly looking for ways to simplify this information processing. Issue frames tell people how they should connect new information to their existing attitudes. For example, if a politician is proposing a regulation regarding access to abortion services, should one think about this regulation as being about an individual's right to privacy, or is it a question of the government's right to regulate medical procedures? Our adoption of one frame or the other will determine which set of attitudes we bring to bear in evaluating this new policy.

The public opinion literature on question wording effects suggests that framing effects can matter a lot. For example, one 2004 survey asked a representative sample of Americans about their support for a possible military intervention in Yemen. The researchers randomly varied the wording of the question to describe the reasons for the intervention as relating to access to oil, protecting local citizens from human rights violations, and fighting terrorism. As displayed in Figure 4.1, when the mission was framed in terms of oil, only 47 percent supported the intervention. When it was framed in terms of fighting terrorism, on the other hand, the same operation received 70 percent support. Interestingly, humanitarianism garnered more support than oil but less than terrorism, at 61 percent.

Politics can often be understood as a competition to frame issues. In late 2006, for example, as Iraq was descending into its worst depths of violence against civilians, American journalists extensively debated whether to use the term "civil war" to describe the conflict. By this time the large numbers of casualties on both the Sunni and Shia sides of the conflict made it abundantly clear from a social science perspective that the conflict had long since become a civil war (Sambanis 2006). But the Bush administration put extensive pressure on journalists not to use this label, out of fear that it would further erode support for the war. Pressure from the administration was so strong that NBC decided to make a formal announcement that it would use the term, and made an extensive defense of its applicability.

Figure 4.1. Percent strongly or somewhat strongly supporting intervention in Yemen, 2004. Note that merely changing the framing of the question, mentioning different justifications for intervening, can substantially change levels of support. Gallup.

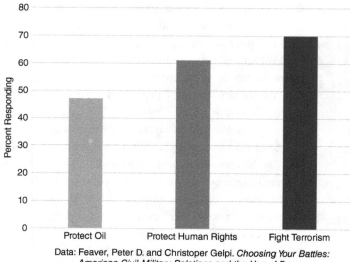

Data: Feaver, Peter D. and Christoper Gelpi. *Choosing Your Battles: American Civil-Military Relations and the Use of Force*, (Princeton: Princeton University Press, 2009)

Of course, military missions are often complex, and the reality is that many missions – including Iraq and Afghanistan – consist of a mixture of civil and international conflict. However, research indicates that the dominant political narrative surrounding a military operation can affect the public's response. In the case of the Iraq War, public support did erode following the use of the term "civil war" to describe the conflict, but since support for the war had been declining for some time already, it is difficult to say precisely how much difference the use of that term made.

Framing and narrative clearly matter for the formation of public opinion, but is there a limit to their effects? Is public opinion simply political spin all the way down? The rational expectations model of public opinion contends that there is a limit to the influence of spin, and that the public can form independent judgments about foreign policy issues. To determine the limits of political spin we need to understand the reasons that framing and spin are effective. The central problem lies in two differences between the mass public and their elected representatives: (1) political leaders have more information than the public, and (2) political leaders care more about the policy outcome on most issues than does the public. These two gaps between citizens and their government determine what has been termed the **elasticity of reality**. The term "elasticity" here refers to the extent to which political leaders can influence public perceptions of an issue. When perceptions of reality are highly elastic, leaders have great leeway in shaping public opinion. When the elasticity of reality declines, on the other hand, public opinion becomes more strongly rooted in objective sources of information that are beyond the control of politicians. The greater the gap in both information and motivation between political leaders and the public, the greater the elasticity of reality. Thus the elasticity of reality will vary across different foreign policy issues, and it will also change over time.

For example, during a military crisis but prior to the onset of war, political leaders will have much more information than the public about the threat facing their country and the likelihood that a military operation will be successful. At this time, leaders have wide leeway in communicating to the public what the potential war is about and what is likely to happen. In January 2003, for example, as the Bush administration made the case for war with Iraq, National Security Advisor Condoleezza Rice argued against waiting for further evidence of an Iraqi nuclear weapons program because "we don't want the smoking gun to be a mushroom cloud" (CNN 2002). This argument for war vividly combines concerns about nuclear weapons and terrorism, but it was very difficult for the public to assess the veracity of the claim. As national security advisor, Rice potentially had access to information about the Iraqi nuclear program and Iraqi support for terrorists that was not available to the public. Consequently, in the absence of an independent basis for assessing her claim, many Americans were inclined to accept Rice's assessment of the Iraqi nuclear and terrorist threat. This information gap between citizens and leaders at the outset of many military conflicts means that leaders are initially given a wide berth to justify the use of force.

This informational advantage and the power it gives leaders to justify war also helps to explain the so-called "**rally 'round the flag**" effect, where public support for the use of military force and the national leader her- or himself sometimes sharply increases immediately after the conflict begins. The size and length of these rallies vary substantially depending on various factors including the extent of media coverage of the conflict. For example, the rally effects enjoyed by Margaret Thatcher after launching the Falklands/Malvinas War were both larger and longer-lasting than the boost that John Major received from the 1991 Gulf War (Lai and Reiter 2005). But in general the informational advantages that leaders have over their publics in justifying a conflict provide a permissive condition that allows rallies to operate across a variety of conflicts.

As a military conflict continues, however, the information gap between leaders and the public will narrow. Under these conditions, the rational expectations model contends that the public will be able to form independent judgments about foreign policy issues based on international events rather than elite rhetoric. For example, while reasonable observers could differ on the likelihood of an Iraqi nuclear weapons program prior to the US invasion in 2003, by 2004 it was clear to all that no such program existed. Perhaps even more importantly, while leaders often have private information that can support various arguments regarding the justification for war, assessments of the success or failure of the operation are more difficult to manipulate. For example, the lack of an Iraqi weapons of mass destruction (WMD) program led the Bush administration to refocus on the democratization of the Middle East as a justification for an ongoing American military presence in Iraq. Eventually, the public largely accepted this new justification for the war because citizens lacked the information to make an independent assessment of the importance of a democratic Iraq for American foreign policy. But the persistent, costly, and escalating civil war in Iraq made it clear to any reasonable observer that whatever the possible merits of a victory in Iraq, the mission was unequivocally failing.

The inelasticity of perceptions of military success and military casualties may be why these factors play a central role in the rational expectations model's explanation of continuing support for ongoing military operations. For example, one prominent study of American foreign policy examined public support for Korea, Vietnam, Iraq and several other conflicts across the second half of the twentieth century. While the sources of public support are complex and can be shaped by many factors, one consistent result that emerged from the study was that perceptions of the success of the mission matter most in determining the public's willingness to continue prosecuting a war in the face of American casualties (Gelpi et al. 2009).

The elasticity of reality may vary over time within a single issue and it can also vary across issues, especially as a function of the level of public interest and attention. Military conflicts that cause American casualties, for example, are likely to attract a great deal of public interest and concern. Public demand for news coverage of these events will be high, and citizens will be motivated to collect information and form beliefs about the conflict. Other issues, however, have more difficulty attracting sustained public interest. The disbursement of foreign aid, for example, is largely invisible to most Americans, and its goals and effectiveness are difficult to assess. Thus it should not be surprising that the American public persistently misperceives (and exaggerates) the level of federal spending on foreign aid.

Can the Public Stay Informed about Foreign Policy?

If public opinion is going to reflect an informed judgment, then citizens must be able to gather information about international events and must update their views based on these events. As we discussed above, public access to independent information about foreign events is critical for limiting the "elasticity of reality" and the potential impact of political spin. Since most citizens have little or no direct experience with foreign events, the news media play an absolutely critical role in helping the public learn about such events. But can the news media be a reliable source of unbiased information, or do they simply amplify political spin? The answer to this question depends centrally on the structure and incentives of the news media. The importance of these effects can be illustrated through a brief review of the history of the news media in America.

For the first century-and-a-half of American history, the news media were notoriously partisan and editorial in their coverage of events. This emphasis on sensationalism and editorial slant over factual reporting peaked in the late nineteenth century with the "yellow journalism" battles between newspaper magnates Joseph Pulitzer and William Randolph Hearst. Hearst is famously credited (or blamed) for manufacturing political pressure that culminated in the Spanish–American War. While we do not have polls that measure public opinion at the time, President McKinley was clearly reluctant to declare war on Spain in 1898. He felt pressure for war, however, from the public, which had been agitated by the sensationalistic coverage of the situation in Cuba. The sinking of the USS *Maine* and the subsequent news coverage made this pressure irresistible and led McKinley to declare war.

The advent of radio and eventually television as news media led to a dramatic transformation of the news environment in the United States. In response to the cluttering of the radio airwaves Congress passed the Radio Act of 1927 and the Communications Act of 1934 that established the **public interest standard** to justify the use of public airwaves. These pieces of legislation explicitly argued that the state had the right to regulate the use of airwaves for news and other broadcasts in order to maintain "public trust." Congress created the Federal Radio Commission (FRC), which became the Federal Communications Commission (FCC), to monitor the use of this public asset. While the FCC did ban certain specific kinds of content – such as obscenity – its most profound effects shaped the way that broadcasters began to deliver the news. The FCC's application of the "public interest" standard required distribution of programming on news and public affairs, the presentation of diverse views, and equal access to the airwaves for political candidates. The application of this standard placed significant constraints on the editorial excesses of the "yellow journalism" era, and as television took over from radio as the primary medium for news, the "public interest" standard ushered in the "network era" of television news from the mid 1950s to the early 1990s.

Scientific methods of survey research came of age alongside broadcast news on radio and especially television. For example, George Gallup's surprisingly accurate prediction of the 1936 election based on scientific sampling immediately followed the Communications Act, and the central survey for the study of American voting behavior, the American National Election Study, was first fielded in 1952, the same year that the Democratic and Republican campaign conventions were covered on television. By 1960, nearly 90 percent of American households owned a television, and TV news – as presented by the three major broadcast networks, CBS, NBC, and ABC – became the primary way that Americans got their political information. Journalists like John Chancellor and Walter Cronkite became trusted sources of information for large segments of the American public during the network era of television news.

The Cable News Network (CNN) was launched in 1980, but it remained a minor news market player until the Gulf War of 1990. When President George H. W. Bush spoke to the nation announcing the American attack on Iraq in January 1991, television viewership reached its highest point since the funeral of John F. Kennedy, and viewership of CNN rivaled that of the broadcast networks (Carter 1991). In fact, CNN's ability to provide round-the-clock coverage established it as the leading news source for the Gulf War. The success of CNN demonstrated that there was a market for networks that cover news twenty-four hours a day. But a more profound change in the news environment occurred in 1996 with the creation of the Fox News Channel.

Because Fox News broadcasts on cable rather than public airwaves, the FCC did not have authority to regulate its content. Consequently, Fox owner and global media mogul Rupert Murdoch hired a Republican political consultant, Roger Ailes, to create a conservative news organization with a strong editorial perspective that was distinct from the broadcast networks. While the network's slogan was "fair and balanced," the network explicitly blended coverage of news events with a strongly conservative editorial tone. The network was anchored by prime-time news commentary shows hosted by outspoken conservatives like Bill O'Reilly and Sean Hannity. The format quickly attracted viewers, and by 2002 it had surpassed CNN as the most popular cable news network. The success of Fox News encouraged other cable news channels, such as MSNBC, to develop a similarly partisan blend of news and editorial content, with outspoken liberal hosts such as Keith Olbermann and Rachel Maddow.

As with the change from newspapers to radio, the shift from broadcast to cable TV had a profound impact on the information that citizens obtained about politics. During the era of network news, one could choose from only three major sources, and the sources did not vary significantly in their editorial tone. Due in large part to their "public interest" obligations, news across the broadcast networks remains quite similar even in the age of cable and internet news.

During the 2016 election, for example, the Shorenstein Center measured the tone of news coverage toward the major party candidates. The tone of network coverage of Hillary Clinton was nearly uniform, with stories taking a negative tone 61 percent, 63 percent, and 63 percent of the time on CBS, NBC, and ABC respectively. However, the Shorenstein Center coded more than 80 percent of the stories on Fox News regarding Hillary Clinton as negative (Patterson 2016). Coverage of Donald Trump was generally negative across all major outlets, but once again little difference in editorial tone was observed across the broadcast networks, while Fox News was substantially more favorable to Trump than broadcast news. The variation in editorial slant becomes even wider as we shift our attention from cable news to the Internet, as online sources are also not subject to FCC regulation or the "public interest" standard (Baum and Groeling 2008).

The shift in news media away from broadcast networks and toward cable news and internet sources has the potential to return the American media environment to the characteristics of the nineteenth century. Just like the "yellow journalism" newspapers of that era, news organizations in the twenty-first century are increasingly blending factual and editorial content and competing for viewership with increasingly sensational – and sometimes even nonfactual – reporting. And newspapers continue to vary widely in editorial tone, just as they have always done. As the 2016 presidential campaign began, the Pew Center found that 59 percent of those who consumed news about the election found cable news, online sources, or newspapers to be the most helpful source of information. Only 35 percent of respondents identified television or radio broadcasts as most helpful (Gottfried et al. 2016).

President Donald Trump's reliance on direct communication with the public and the media through social media only served to accelerate the prominence of partisan news sources. President Trump's ability to change the news cycle with his own "tweet" on Twitter, and the ability of his supporters to "retweet" and disseminate partisan, hateful, and even outright false information created grave concern about a crisis of misinformation crippling the ability of the public to construct reasoned attitudes and beliefs. One study even found that exposure to President Trump's Twitter feed caused increases in xenophobic tweets and hate crime behavior.

This shift in news consumption toward cable and online sources is important for the impact of public opinion on foreign policy because much of the evidence suggesting that the public does a reasonably good job in updating its attitudes and opinions in response to real-world events is drawn from the network news era, when editorial tone was decidedly muted. One famous and comprehensive study of public attitudes from 1935 to 1979 found that changes in public opinion "were not random or inexplicable; they were usually related to important changes in citizens' lives and in their social and economic environments. Abrupt shifts in preferences generally coincided with major events in international affairs or the economy" (Page and Shapiro 1982).

But what about in the era of cable and internet news? The Iraq War became an important testing ground of this new media environment, and a number of studies suggested that the rise of Fox News tracked with certain notable trends in public opinion. For example, one study found that in the summer of 2003, 67 percent of Fox News viewers believed that the United States had discovered "clear evidence in Iraq that Saddam Hussein was working closely with the al-Qaeda terrorist organization," when no such evidence had been found (Kull et al. 2003).

Only about 50 percent of broadcast network viewers held this mistaken belief. A similar study demonstrated that Fox News viewers made significantly lower estimates of the number of American casualties suffered in the Iraq War (Morris 2005).

It is more difficult to say whether these differing perceptions of the Iraq War are caused by the consumption of Fox News or are simply a function of the fact that viewers with those beliefs are more likely to watch Fox News. But regardless of the persuasive effects of editorial news coverage, the splintering of the media environment, and increasingly blurred distinction between the reporting of fact and opinion, the shift toward more partisan news sources has at least two effects that raise questions about the ability of the public to update its views in response to international events. First, the more politically polarized news environment has reduced trust in the news media as a whole. According to Gallup, in the late 1990s – as partisan news coverage began to return to cable television – a majority of Americans expressed "a great deal" or "a fair amount" of confidence in the news media. By 2016 that proportion had dropped to less than one-third. Moreover, the percentage of Americans stating that they had no confidence at all in the news media had nearly tripled, from around 10 percent to nearly 30 percent. Interestingly, the presidency of Donald Trump is associated with a modest increase in confidence in the media despite – or perhaps even because of – his persistent attacks on journalists and journalism. But the American public's expression of confidence began to decline again in 2021 (Brenan 2022).

Second, the division of the media environment along partisan lines allows citizens to select news coverage that reinforces their existing beliefs rather than allowing them to update and revise their views in response to real-world events. Experimental research suggests that individuals can and often do update their beliefs and attitudes when presented with surprising new information (Einstein and Glick 2014). People can update in this way even on issues that are highly partisan and emotional, and even when they have well-established views on the issue. For example, one study of attitudes toward the Iraq War, in 2008, found that exposing a Democrat to a "good news" story about progress in Iraq increased the likelihood that he would expect the war in Iraq to be a success from 18 percent to 28 percent. Conversely, exposing a Republican to a bad news story about stalemate and continued violence in Iraq reduced the likelihood that she would evaluate President Bush's "surge" strategy in Iraq as successful from 81 percent to 68 percent (Gelpi 2010). Even amidst the extreme concerns regarding the spread of misinformation during the Trump presidency, numerous studies documented the consistent ability of the public to correct its beliefs when presented with accurate information.

This kind of updating of beliefs can only occur if citizens are actually exposed to surprising information in the real world as opposed to in an experimental laboratory. If people only consume information from media outlets that reinforce their existing views, then they are unlikely to be exposed to the kind of surprising information that shapes deliberative debate. Thus the partisan splintering of the news media presents an important potential threat to the impact of public opinion on government policy – foreign or otherwise. Increased sharing of news information on social media platforms may also have important effects on public opinion. On the one hand, the posting and sharing of false news stories on Facebook, Twitter, and elsewhere raised questions about the integrity of the 2016 election. On the other hand, research indicates that Facebook friend networks – while partisan and biased – are more open and diverse than most of the other real-world networks through which people get their news. Consequently, shared news stories on Facebook tended to increase rather than decrease the likelihood that individuals would encounter perspectives on the news with which they disagreed (Bakshy et al. 2015).

How Does Public Opinion Affect Policy?

Finally, even if public opinion can be reasoned and deliberative, and even if it has the potential to influence the outcome of elections, how exactly should we expect these attitudes to influence or constrain foreign policy behavior? When seeking to alter domestic policy, democratically elected heads of state generally face many bureaucratic and legislative hurdles. However, chief executives – regardless of whether they are in presidential or parliamentary systems – usually have very wide authority to conduct foreign policy as they wish. Moreover, the informational advantage that leaders have at the outset of an international conflict makes it unlikely that citizens will preemptively restrain their leaders' foreign policy options. As a result, public opinion must shape international behavior primarily in one of two ways: (1) leaders may anticipate that certain actions will be highly unpopular, or (2) the public may punish leaders after they take unpopular actions.

President George W. Bush's decision to go to war in Iraq in 2003 illustrates the flexibility that leaders have to do as they wish in foreign policy, as well as the two types of constraints that the public can place on their elected representatives. Clearly, President Bush was free to use military force against Iraq at the time and place of his choosing, regardless of the opinions of the American people, not to mention foreign governments, foreign publics, and international institutions. He did so without the authorization of the United Nations, without the support of major US allies, and with a very bare majority of Americans supporting his actions prior to the attack. But public opinion did shape American policy toward Iraq in significant ways both at the outset and in the final resolution of the conflict.

First, President Bush's anticipation of the public's response to war with Iraq significantly affected the timing of the conflict. Immediately after the attacks of September 11, 2001, several members of the Bush administration – including Secretary of Defense Donald Rumsfeld and Vice President Dick Cheney – began to press the president to attack Saddam Hussein in Iraq. While any direct connection between Hussein and 9/11 was dubious at best, a number of members of the administration had sought to topple Hussein since the end of the 1991 Gulf War and they saw 9/11 as an opportunity to justify that attack as part of a broader war on terror. Secretary of State Colin Powell, on the other hand, argued that the immediate focus should be on Afghanistan and al-Qaeda. "Any action needs public support," he contended. "It's not just what the international coalition supports; it's what the American people want to support. The American people want us to do something about al-Qaeda" (quoted in Foyle 2004, 275). Powell won the day as Bush decided that the public would first need to be persuaded of the importance of seeing war with Iraq as part of a larger war on terror.

Shortly after the tide had turned against al-Qaeda and the Taliban leadership in Afghanistan, President Bush turned his attention to making the case to the public for war with Iraq. The effort began with the 2002 State of the Union Address – also known as the "axis of evil" speech – in which Bush identified the regimes governing Iraq, Iran, and North Korea as threatening to the United States because they allegedly brought regime-sponsored terrorism together with WMD. From January 2002 through March 2003, the Bush administration conducted a sustained public relations effort to persuade the public to support an attack on Iraq, but this effort was largely unsuccessful. In February 2001, prior to the 9/11 attacks, a slim 52 percent majority of Americans supported using American troops to remove Saddam Hussein from power in Iraq. By November 2001 that number had spiked to 74 percent, but support for an attack steadily eroded from that point despite the Bush administration's considerable efforts. Just prior to the eventual attack, public support for toppling Hussein by force had declined to 59 percent. Moreover, each wave of public discussion and debate seemed to reduce support rather than increase it (Foyle 2004, 273).

Once again, the Bush administration was not preemptively constrained from doing as it pleased in Iraq, and so the president ordered the attack in March 2003. The public initially rallied to support the president after the attack, as his approval rating quickly spiked from 58 percent to 70 percent (The American Presidency Project n.d). Nonetheless, Bush's failure to persuade the public on the merits of the mission prior to the attack, combined with his failure to persuade the United Nations and some of America's NATO allies, had significant consequences as the war wore on. The public rallied to support the president immediately after the attack, but as the initial combat mission ended and an insurgency against the American occupation began to take hold, support quickly fell back to prewar levels. By September 2003, the president's approval rating had fallen back to 50 percent. In particular, Democrats and Independents quickly turned against the president and against the war because they had never been persuaded of the importance of the mission. Early success led them to be permissively supportive, but the looming prospect of failure in a civil war quagmire quickly undercut their support.

The stalemated, costly, and controversial war in Iraq led the public to begin pressuring President Bush during his 2004 bid for reelection. Specifically, casualties from the war cost Bush votes, especially outside of Southern states, which tend to lean Republican (Karol and Miguel 2007). But the president was able to rally support for the war in Republican-leaning states by arguing that some progress was being made in Iraq and by linking the war to the broader war on terror, which remained relatively popular (Gelpi et al. 2007). On balance, in October 2004 a slim majority of Americans continued to think that the Iraq War was not a mistake, and the president retained the White House by nearly that same slim margin.

Bush survived his 2004 reelection bid, but the war in Iraq proved costly in other ways. As is often the case, the unpopularity of his overseas military engagements stalled his domestic political agenda (Gelpi and Grieco 2015). For example, Bush's ambitious plans for revising Social Security in his second term were essentially dead on arrival on Capitol Hill. Significant erosion of the security situation from the spring of 2005 through the fall of 2006 further undermined public support for the president and the war. By October 2006, Bush's approval rating had fallen below 40 percent, and nearly 60 percent of Americans had come to the conclusion that the Iraq War was a mistake. The public's dissatisfaction with Iraq led it to inflict massive losses on the Republican Party in the 2006 midterm election, when it lost control of the House of Representatives, the Senate, and a majority of the state governorships for the first time since 1994.

The 2006 midterm elections clearly delivered a message to the president, but even this rebuke could not directly force him to end the war. In fact, in the wake of this stinging defeat President Bush chose to double down on the Iraq War by escalating the American troop presence in what came to be known as "the surge." The escalation in American military presence, combined with a shift in American counterinsurgency strategy and the "Sunni awakening," whereby local Sunni leaders largely in Anbar province broke their alliance with al-Qaeda and agreed to work with US forces, initially led to higher rates of violence and casualties for US forces. However, by the fall of 2007, rates of violence and US casualties had begun to decline. The success of the surge in reducing violence and US casualties also succeeded in reducing public political pressure to withdraw immediately from Iraq. To be sure, the lack of progress in constructing a stable political, economic, and social environment in Iraq led most Americans to continue feeling that the Iraq War was a mistake. However, the military stability brought a dramatic reduction in media coverage of combat in Iraq, which reduced the pressure for an immediate withdrawal.

Despite the president's insistence on staying the course in Iraq, and the respite that the surge eventually gave him on this issue, the public's disapproval of the war continued to shape the political process throughout 2007 and 2008 in ways that would eventually bring an end to the conflict. Hillary Clinton was the prohibitive favorite to win the Democratic nomination for president in 2008. Clinton, however, was known as a hawk on Iraq who had voted to grant President Bush the authority to go to war in the fall of 2002. Her weakness on this issue with the progressive base of the Democratic Party provided an opportunity to a little known first-term senator from Illinois named Barack Obama. In October 2002, just as Clinton was voting to authorize war, Obama gave a prominent speech denouncing the war as "dumb" and "rash."

Obama's defeat of Clinton in the 2008 primary elections was a function of various factors, including his skillful use of the caucusing process and his strong appeal to African American voters. But Clinton's support for Iraq was the key issue position that Obama exploited to batter her in debates and rally progressive white voters. Analyses of the 2008 general election also demonstrate that opposition to Iraq played a pivotal role in Obama's defeat of Republican John McCain (Hill et al. 2010). In short, Obama swept both the nomination and the White House on a promise to end the war in Iraq. And while it took some time to complete, he fulfilled his campaign promise in August 2010 when he announced the end of American combat operations in Iraq.

It is difficult to say with certainty, of course, whether Hillary Clinton or John McCain would have ended American participation in the conflict at a similar time had they been in the White

House. However, both Clinton and McCain were vocally opposed to the kind of explicit timetable for withdrawal that the Obama administration announced. Clinton became a late convert to the timetable policy as it became clear that her opposition was damaging her among Democrats, but Republicans – McCain among others – remained staunchly opposed to timetables. Thus it seems likely that Obama's early, vocal, and consistent opposition to the Iraq War helped him win the White House and helped – after some delay – to end the war.

The Iraq War illustrates both the limitations and the potential impact of public opinion as a determinant of foreign policy. Moreover, it shows how public opinion matters both through leaders' anticipation of public opposition and through the public's punishment of unpopular policies after the fact. Prior to the conflict, President Bush understood that he needed to build public support for the war, so he waited until after attacking Afghanistan to turn toward Iraq. Of course, even when Bush was largely unable to move the public to support the war, he was nonetheless able – as commander-in-chief – to invade Iraq. But while Bush was able to launch the war with impunity, its unpopularity hijacked the domestic political agenda of his second term, cost his party control of Congress in 2006, and ultimately lost the Republican Party the White House in 2008. Moreover, despite the president's resolute insistence on prosecuting the war even when it was unpopular, the public was able to end the conflict earlier than Bush and his Republican colleagues would have preferred.

CASE STUDY

Casualties and Support in the Iraq War

Military casualties represent the kind of political issue where the public should be most capable of influencing the behavior of its leaders. The coverage of casualties by the media is widespread, factual, and generally relatively free of editorial content. Even in a highly politically polarized media environment such as the United States during the early twenty-first century, news outlets on both sides of the partisan divide felt an obligation to report the number of American soldiers killed in combat. Moreover, even when other aspects of news reporting were highly editorialized, a bipartisan respect for the military and for the sacrifices of the soldiers killed meant that the reporting of casualties was largely free of editorial content. Reporting on casualties is especially widespread and nonpartisan because local news sources – including TV, radio, and newspapers – generally reported on casualties in their communities, and these stories had a "human interest" rather than political slant to them.

Second, casualties are relatively easy to understand as a political issue. It is clear that the loss of an American soldier is a cost to the United States. Moreover, it is a cost that is felt widely across the country because of the esteem in which most Americans hold the military, and because their status as soldiers and representatives of the state means that these men died on behalf of the national community. Members of the public can and do differ, of course, on the meaning that they attach to these deaths, and these different interpretations may lead to different policy responses. But casualties clearly represent an important cost to the public that merits a response.

Finally, perceptions of casualties will be relatively hard to "spin" as a political issue. Politicians can provide the public with reasons why they should tolerate the deaths of Americans, but the fact of the deaths provides fairly unambiguous indication that a foreign policy mission is costly. In this sense, the information gap between leaders and citizens that allows for the prospect of manipulation and spin is quite narrow in this case.

We focus our attention on the dynamics of casualties and public opinion in the 2000s war in Iraq as one of the most prominent examples of how citizens respond to the human costs of war. The case identifies both the capacity and the limitations of the public as a factor that can influence foreign policy. In particular, the American public's response to casualties in Iraq illustrates three key elements of the dynamics of public opinion during war. First, the public is open to guidance and persuasion from its leaders regarding the reasons to go to war. Second, the level of support for war after the conflict has begun is strongly determined by the perceived success of the military operation. And finally, unlike the justifications for fighting a war, public perceptions of success and failure are relatively insensitive to spin from political leaders. Thus while the formation of public opinion about the initiation of war may be a "top down" process, public opinion on the progress of war after it has begun is largely a "bottom up" process.

(cont.)

Framing the Justification for the Iraq War

Even prior to the terrorist attacks of September 11, 2001, the American public was permissively supportive of attacking Iraq for any number of reasons. The public supported attacks on Iraq in 1990 after its invasion of Kuwait, and the public supported military strikes at various times since the end of that war over conflicts regarding international inspections to ensure that it did not develop nuclear, chemical, or biological weapons. So when President Bush began to argue in January 2002 that the United States should consider attacking Iraq because he thought that they may have restarted their nuclear weapons program and were collaborating with terrorists, he was pushing on an open door with the American public. Several months after the war began, however, it became clear to all observers that the initial justification for war – an Iraqi WMD program – was mistaken. David Kay's testimony to the Senate in January 2004 profoundly undermined more than a year's worth of claims by the Bush administration regarding the reasons for war. The report was briefly damaging to public support for the conflict, but the Bush administration quickly moved to redefine the goals of the Iraq War. Instead of WMD, the administration focused on democracy and economic development in Iraq as a method for building a more peaceful and stable Middle East. Even more importantly, the Bush administration linked Iraq to the popular issue of terrorism, and argued that the war was the "central front" in a global war on terror.

This rebranding effort was largely successful with the American public despite the fact that the terrorists the United States were fighting in Iraq were able to operate there precisely because of the American invasion. For example, one study found that only a month after the release of the Kay Report on WMD, more than three-quarters of the American public described the goals of the Iraq War as constructing a democratically elected Iraqi government that provided stability for the Iraqi people and was capable of providing for its own security (Gelpi et al. 2009). This framing of the policy objectives closely mirrored Bush administration rhetoric on the issue. Only about 10 percent of respondents mentioned combating terrorism, and only about 5 percent mentioned preventing future WMD programs. Similarly, about 50 percent of the public agreed with the Bush administration's claim that Iraq had become the "central front" in the war on terror. And over 75 percent of those who linked Iraq with the war on terror stated that President Bush had done the "right thing" when he initially decided to attack Iraq (Gelpi et al. 2009). Thus the Bush administration was able to shape and then reshape public understandings of the reasons for the war.

Perceptions of Success and the Willingness to Sustain a Costly Fight

Despite Bush's reframing of the reasons to stay in Iraq, the public's willingness to tolerate military casualties was more heavily determined by public perceptions of the success of the mission. The initial attack on Iraq in March that led to the toppling of Saddam

(cont.)

Hussein in April resulted in about 200 American soldiers being killed in action. Despite these costs, the public rallied to support the war because of the dramatic success of the military operation, which was punctuated by the famous toppling of Saddam Hussein's massive statue in Baghdad (see Figure 4.2).

As the glowing success of April 2003 faded into the persistent anti-American insurgency of June and July, however, public support for the president and for the war began to decline steeply. The first year of American occupation, from May 2003 until June 2004, was punctuated by persistent attacks and American deaths, and support for the war declined steadily. The only respite came when American forces captured Saddam Hussein in December 2003, raising the prospect that the insurgency might collapse. When success remained elusive, public support eroded once again.

The transfer of sovereignty to a transitional Iraqi government in June 2004 altered the trajectory of public support. As we discussed above, the Bush administration had successfully reframed its justification for the war as the construction of democracy in Iraq. Accordingly, the transfer of power and the prospects of elections renewed the American public's willingness to sustain the fight. Between June 2003 and June 2004, the United States suffered more than 600 casualties, and approval of President Bush's job performance dropped from nearly 65 percent to about 50 percent. Between June 2004 and the first "ink finger" election in Iraq in January 2005, the United States suffered an additional 600 casualties, but in this case Bush's approval rating remained unchanged. As the spring of 2005 arrived, however, it became clear that holding elections had not solved Iraq's problems. Violence persisted, and the newly elected representatives remained stalemated and unable to form an effective government. Consequently, public optimism about progress in Iraq evaporated, and casualties began to erode support once again. Between

Figure 4.2. Saddam Hussein statue toppling, Baghdad, March 2003. ©*Daily Mirror* Gulf coverage / Stringer/ 3rd Party – Misc/Getty Images.

(cont.)

January and November 2005, the United States suffered another 600 soldiers killed in action, and President Bush's approval rating declined from near 50 percent to below 40 percent.

The Inelasticity of Success

Frustrated with the public's mounting pessimism regarding the war, the Bush administration launched a major series of speeches and public events in an attempt to reframe the success of the war, much as they had reframed the justification for the war a year earlier. The president began this effort on November 30, 2005, and concluded it with a prime-time televised address from the Oval Office on December 18, 2005 in which he reflected upon the success of a second set of Iraqi elections. Prior to these speeches, public approval of the Bush administration was at a low point. ABC News found that approval of Bush's handling of the Iraq War was at 36 percent on November 2, and his overall presidential approval rating was at 39 percent. By December 18, approval of Bush's handling of Iraq jumped to 46 percent and his overall approval moved up to 47 percent.

But by March 2006 President Bush found his approval numbers sagging again and he gave another series of speeches on March 13, 20, and 29 emphasizing the progress he saw in Iraq. The president also held a press conference on March 21 that focused largely on Iraq. This time, however, the president lacked a "real-world" successful event to which he could anchor his speeches, and presidential rhetoric had no measurable impact on public attitudes toward the war. In early March the president's approval ratings – both on Iraq and overall – were at approximately 35 percent, and they remained unchanged throughout early April.

This pair of Bush administration efforts to bolster public perceptions of success in Iraq illustrates the limits of political spin and the elasticity of reality regarding perceptions of success in military conflicts. When events on the ground in Iraq plausibly justified some optimism about the result of the operation, the Bush administration was able to draw attention to these events and bolster public support for the president and the war. Absent a real-world anchor, on the other hand, the Bush administration claims of success did not move public opinion at all.

The dynamics of the political primary process among Democrats in both 2004 and 2008 provide further evidence of the "bottom up" nature of public opposition to the war. In October 2002, President Bush requested authority from Congress to use force against Iraq, and the leaders of the Democratic Party establishment – including eventual nominee John Kerry – voted to give the president this authority.

Opposition to the war was muted at best among Democratic Party leaders throughout 2003, despite the increasing frustration with the war among the base of Democratic primary voters. Popular opposition to the war among rank-and-file Democrats fueled the campaign of political outsider Howard Dean, who had been a vocal opponent of the

(cont.)

war from the outset. Dean's campaign was ultimately unsuccessful, but the energy and momentum that he received from rank-and-file Democrats due to his opposition to the war began to pull other Democratic leaders like Kerry steadily – if somewhat tepidly – toward opposition to the war.

By the beginning of the 2008 presidential primary campaigns, Democrats were even more deeply opposed to the war. Once again, however, party establishment figures like Hillary Clinton found it difficult to carry the anti-war banner because they had voted to authorize the war. Clinton's ambivalent stance on Iraq opened the door to another political outsider – Barack Obama – who unlike Dean was able to topple the party establishment and take the nomination, in part because of the increasingly popular appeal of his anti-war message. Eventually, Obama made good on his promise to end the war in Iraq. It seems unlikely that either McCain or Clinton would have been as explicit about setting a finite timeline for withdrawal. Moreover, rather than cajoling the masses into opposing the president, in each of these instances, we find that party leaders were scrambling to keep up with changes in mass opinion on the war.

Conclusion

The public's response to military casualties in war is one of the most important dimensions of public engagement with foreign policy. The American public's response to casualties in the war in Iraq illustrates at least three key results about the public's power to constrain its elected leaders. First, leaders generally have wide leeway to justify the use of military force, and the public is relatively uncritical in its evaluation of presidents' justifications. This implies that the formation of attitudes about a conflict prior to the outbreak of hostilities is likely to be a largely "top down" process. Second, once a conflict has begun, perceptions of the efficiency and success of the conduct of the crisis begin to dominate the formation of public attitudes. Finally, perceptions of success are relatively inelastic and insensitive to political spin because the public is more capable of assessing success as opposed to more abstract arguments about the justifications for a conflict. Consequently, the most critical aspects of public opinion after a war has begun tend to be "bottom up" influences of the mass public on their leaders rather than the other way around.

QUANTITATIVE STUDY

Battlefield Events, Leadership Rhetoric, and Support for the Iraq War

Research Question

Do citizens form their attitudes about international issues in response to real-world events, or in response to the rhetoric of their political leaders?

Theory and Hypotheses

The "rational expectations" model (discussed above) predicts that individuals will change their opinions about a foreign policy issue when they are presented with surprising news events that cause them to question and reevaluate their existing beliefs on the issue. The "elite rhetoric" model (also discussed above) predicts that individuals will change their opinions to match the positions expressed by the leaders of their political party. In the spring of 2008, Christopher Gelpi (2010) conducted a survey experiment to test these arguments against one another.

Since Democrats and Independents were generally opposed to the Iraq War in 2008, the "rational expectations" model predicts that Democrats and Independents who are exposed to positive news events about conditions in Iraq will be surprised by this information and will become more optimistic about the war.

Hypothesis 1: Democrats and Independents who are exposed to positive news events about conditions in Iraq will become more optimistic about the war.

Since Republicans were already optimistic about the war in 2008, the "rational expectations" model predicts that Republicans who are exposed to negative news events about Iraq will become more pessimistic about the war.

Hypothesis 2: Republicans who are exposed to negative news events about Iraq will become more pessimistic about the war.

The "elite rhetoric" model, on the other hand, predicts that Republicans who are exposed to President George Bush saying optimistic things about Iraq will become more optimistic, while Republicans who are exposed to the president saying cautious things about the war will become more pessimistic.

Hypothesis 3: Republicans who are exposed to President George W. Bush saying optimistic things about Iraq will become more optimistic.

Hypothesis 4: Republicans who are exposed to President George W. Bush saying cautious things about the war will become more pessimistic.

Data

The data for the study came from an experiment. Participants in the experiment were asked to read different news stories and political commentaries from major newspapers, and then were asked their opinion. The hypotheses predict that the content of the news material that the participants read would affect their stated opinions.

Dependent Variable

The experiment measured the dependent variable of optimism about the Iraq War by asking the participants, "As you may know, last year President Bush sent approximately 30 thousand additional U.S. military forces to try to restore civil order in parts of Iraq. Do you think this increase in U.S. forces has made the situation in Iraq better, worse, or hasn't made much difference?" The study then identified participants who stated that the situation had gotten better as optimistic, and those who thought it had not changed or had gotten worse as pessimistic.

Independent Variables

There were different types of stories and commentaries, some of which provided information about events (positive or negative), and some of which provided comments from the president (positive or cautious). The experiment also asked participants for their partisan affiliations.

Results

Figure 4.3 displays the effects of the news story treatments on Democrats, Independents, and Republicans. The responses of Democrats are identified by the light grey columns, Independents are identified by the mid-grey columns, and Republicans are identified by the dark grey columns. The vertical axis represents the percentage of participants in each group that expressed an optimistic opinion about Iraq.

Figure 4.3. News events and optimism about Iraq.

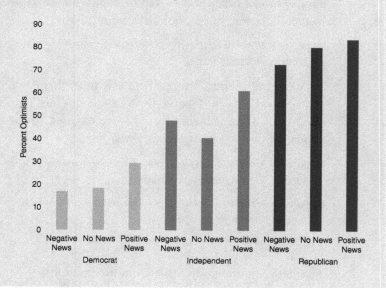

As we would expect, Democrats were generally the most pessimistic about Iraq, with only an average of 21 percent stating that conditions were improving. On the other hand, an average of 79 percent of Republicans saw improvement in Iraq. Independents were somewhere in between, but their views were closer to Democrats than Republicans.

More importantly for our theories, as predicted by the rational expectations model, Democrats and Independents exposed to a "good news" story were more optimistic than those who read a story with no news events. Specifically, 19 percent of Democrats who did not read about any news events were optimistic, as compared to 30 percent who read a "good news" story. Similarly, 61 percent of Independents were optimistic after reading a "good news" story, as compared to 41 percent who read no news events. Exposure to "bad news" events did not significantly change the attitudes of either Democrats or Republicans because both of these groups were already relatively pessimistic, and so the "bad news" event was not surprising to them. These changes in opinion in response to the "good news" stories are statistically significant, meaning that they are unlikely to have occurred by chance.

Also consistent with the "rational expectations" model, Republican participants became more pessimistic about Iraq when exposed to a "bad news" story, but exposure to a "good news" story did not change their opinions because they were already generally optimistic about Iraq. In this instance, the change in Republican opinion is in the direction expected by the "rational expectations" model, but the change was not quite large enough to meet standard levels of statistical significance. Specifically, 73 percent of Republicans who read a bad news story were optimistic about Iraq, as compared to 80 percent of those who read no news events. The effect of a variable is generally considered "statistically significant" if there is less than a 5 percent probability that the association occurred by chance. In this instance, the probability of a chance association was 6 percent. Nonetheless, the data are generally supportive of the "rational expectations" model, especially when viewed in combination with the results for Democrats and Independents.

Figure 4.4 displays the effects of the political rhetoric treatments from President George W. Bush. Once again, the responses of Democrats are displayed in Blue, Independents are in purple, and Republicans are in red. The vertical axis reflects the percentage of optimists.

Consistent with the expectations of the elite rhetoric model, we find that Democrats and Independents ignored statements by the Republican president. About 20 percent of Democrats and 30–40 percent of Independents expressed optimism regardless of what kind of statement from the president – if any – they read. Contrary to the predictions of this model, however, we find that Republicans ignored the president as well. Specifically, 81 percent of Republicans who read a positive statement from President Bush were optimistic about progress in Iraq. But this did not differ from the 80 percent of Republicans who read no statement from the president. Perhaps most importantly, 83 percent of Republicans who read a cautious statement from President Bush also remained optimistic, despite the fact that such a statement from the president would have been rare and surprising.

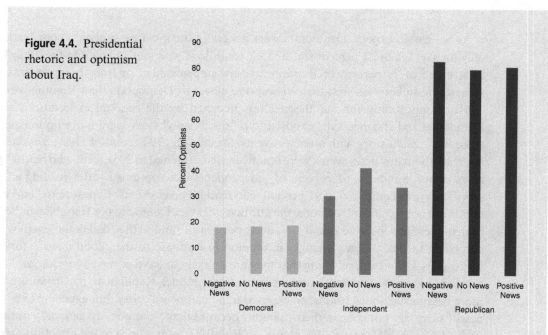

Figure 4.4. Presidential rhetoric and optimism about Iraq.

Conclusions

The results of this experiment support the "rational expectations" model of public opinion about foreign policy at the expense of the elite rhetoric model. This result has important implications for the possibility that public opinion could shape foreign policy behavior because it suggests that the public's views are a reflection of real-world events and not just a reflection of what their political leaders want them to hear. This result is particularly important because it shows that citizens can alter their views on important policy issues even when the issues are contentious and sharply divided along partisan lines.

SUMMARY

This chapter has made a number of central points about foreign policy, including that:

- Three conditions are necessary for public opinion to be capable of influencing foreign policy:
  - The public must actually have foreign policy attitudes
  - The public must care about those attitudes relative to other political issues
  - Political party platforms must differ from one another on foreign policy issues
- Three more conditions are necessary in order for public attitudes toward foreign policy to represent a reasoned collective judgment of citizens rather than an impulsive or manipulated passion of the masses:
  - The public's foreign policy attitudes must have a coherent structure
  - Public attitudes must be at least partially insulated from political leaders

- The public must gather unbiased information about foreign policy events
- When public opinion is able to influence foreign policy behavior in democratic states, we should see this influence through two distinct political mechanisms:
  - Politicians may avoid policies that they expect to be unpopular
  - Politicians may be punished after the fact for policies that become highly unpopular
- The news media and political parties can prevent the public from realizing its ability to form reasonable foreign policy attitudes

KEY TERMS

Memory-based processing
Online processing
Wisdom of crowds
Elite rhetoric model
Rational expectations model

Framing
Elasticity of reality
"Rally 'round the flag" effect
Public interest standard

REVIEW QUESTIONS

1. What does America's experience in the war in Iraq teach us about the influence of public opinion on foreign policy?
2. What are the differences between memory-based processing and online processing?
3. What three conditions are necessary for public opinion to affect foreign policy in a democracy?
4. What three conditions are necessary for public opinion to reflect reasoned judgment?
5. What are the differences between the elite rhetoric and rational expectations models?
6. If public opinion is able to influence foreign policy in a democracy, by what two mechanisms is this influence demonstrated?

DISCUSSION QUESTIONS

1. Which would help a democratically elected government make better foreign policy choices, if public opinion were formed by elite rhetoric, or by actual events?
2. If public opinion is formed by elite rhetoric, how does that undermine achievement of democratic norms and values?

ADDITIONAL READING

Baum, M. A. and Potter, P. B. K. (2015). *War and Democratic Constraint: How the Public Influences Foreign Policy*. Princeton: Princeton University Press.

Berinsky, A. J. (2009). *In Time of War: Understanding American Public Opinion from World War II to Iraq*. Chicago: University of Chicago Press.

Croco, S. E. (2015). *Peace at What Price? Leader Culpability and the Domestic Politics of War Termination*. Cambridge: Cambridge University Press.

Gelpi, C., Feaver, P. D., and Reifler, J. (2009). *Paying the Human Costs of War: American Public Opinion and Casualties in Military Conflicts*. Princeton: Princeton University Press.

Mueller, J. (1994). *Policy and Opinion in the Gulf War*. Chicago: University of Chicago Press.

Saunders, E. N. (2011). *Leaders at War: How Leaders Shape Military Interventions*. Ithaca, NY: Cornell University Press.

REFERENCES

Aalberg, T., Papathanassopoulos, S., Soroka, S., Curran, J., Hayashi, K., Iyengar, S., . . . Tiffen, R. (2013). International TV news, foreign affairs interest and public knowledge. *Journalism Studies* **14**(3), 387–406.

Aldrich, J. H., Sullivan, J. L., and Borgida, E. (1989). Foreign affairs and issue voting: Do presidential candidates "waltz before a blind audience"? *American Political Science Review* **83**(1), 123–141.

The American Presidency Project (n.d.). Presidential job approval. www.presidency.ucsb.edu

Annenberg Public Policy Center (2014, September 17). Americans know surprisingly little about their government, survey finds. www.annenbergpublicpolicycenter.org

Bakshy, E., Messing, S., and Adamic, L. A. (2015). Exposure to ideologically diverse news and opinion on Facebook. *Science* **348**(6239), 1130–1132.

Barzilai, G. (1990). National security crises and voting behavior: The Intifada and the 1988 elections 1. In A. Arian and M. Shamir (eds.). *The Elections in Israel – 1988*. Boulder, CO: Westview, 65–76.

Baum, M. A. and Groeling, T. (2008). New media and the polarization of American political discourse. *Political Communication* **25**(4), 345–365.

Berinsky, A. J. (2007). Assuming the costs of war: Events, elites, and American public support for military conflict. *Journal of Politics* **69**(4), 975–997.

Brenan, M. (2022, October 18). Americans' trust in media remains near record low. *Gallup*. https://news .gallup.com/poll/403166/americans-trust-media-remains-near-record-low.aspx

Carter, B. (1991, January 18). War in the Gulf: The networks; giant TV audience for Bush's speech. *New York Times*. www.nytimes.com/1991/01/18/us

Chicago Council Survey (n.d.). *Chicago Council on Global Affairs*. www.thechicagocouncil.org/research/ lester-crown-center-us-foreign-policy

CNN (2002, September 8). Top Bush officials push case against Saddam. www.cnn.com/2002/ ALLPOLITICS/09/08/iraq.debate

Einstein, K. L. and Glick, D. M. (2014). Do I think BLS data are bs? The consequences of conspiracy theories. *Political Behavior* **37**(3), 679–701.

Feaver, P. D. and Gelpi, C. (2005). *Choosing Your Battles: American CivilMilitary Relations and the Use of Force*. Princeton: Princeton University Press.

Foyle, D. C. (2004). Leading the public to war? The influence of American public opinion on the Bush administration's decision to go to war in Iraq. *International Journal of Public Opinion Research* **16**(3), 269–294.

Gelpi, C. (2010). Performing on cue? The formation of public opinion toward war. *Journal of Conflict Resolution* **54**(1), 88–116.

Gelpi, C., Feaver, P., and Reifler, J. A. (2009). *Paying the Human Costs of War: American Public Opinion and Casualties in Military Conflicts*. Princeton: Princeton University Press.

Gelpi, C. and Grieco, J. M. (2015). Competency costs in foreign affairs: presidential performance in international conflicts and domestic legislative success, 1953–2001. *American Journal of Political Science* **59**(2), 440–456.

Gelpi, C., Reifler, J., and Feaver, P. (2007). Iraq the vote: Retrospective and prospective foreign policy judgments on candidate choice and casualty tolerance. *Political Behavior* **29**(2), 151–174.

Herre, B. and Roser, M. (2013). Democracy. *OurWorldInData.org*. https://ourworldindata.org/democracy

Hill, S. J., Herron, M. C., and Lewis, J. B. (2010). Economic crisis, Iraq, and race: A study of the 2008 presidential election. *Election Law Journal: Rules, Politics, and Policy* **9**(1), 41–62.

Holsti, O. R. (1979). The three-headed eagle: The United States and system change. *International Studies Quarterly* **23**(3), 339–359.

Karol, D. and Miguel, E. (2007). The electoral cost of war: Iraq casualties and the 2004 U.S. presidential election. *Journal of Politics* **69**(3), 633–648.

Kull, S., Ramsay, C., and Lewis, E. (2003). Misperceptions, the media, and the Iraq War. *Political Science Quarterly* **118**(4), 569–598.

Lai, B. and Reiter, D. (2005). Rally 'round the Union Jack? Public opinion and the use of force in the United Kingdom, 1948–2001. *International Studies Quarterly* **49**(2), 255–272.

Luntz, F. I. (2007). *Words That Work: It's Not What You Say, It's What People Hear*. New York: Hachette Books.

Morris, J. S. (2005). The Fox News factor. *Harvard International Journal of Press/Politics* **10**(3), 56–79.

Nincic, M. and Hinckley, B. (1991). Foreign policy and the evaluation of Presidential candidates. *Journal of Conflict Resolution* **35**(2), 333–355.

Page, B. I, and Shapiro, R. Y. (1982). Changes in Americans' policy preferences, 1935–1979. *Public Opinion Quarterly* **46**(1), 24–42.

Patterson, T. E. (2016, December 16). News coverage of the 2016 general election: how the press failed the voters. *Shorenstein Center of Media, Politics and Public Policy, Harvard University*. https://shorensteincenter.org/news-coverage-2016-general-election

Raines, T. (2015, January 30). Internationalism or isolationism? The Chatham House–Yougov survey. *Chatham House*. www.chathamhouse.org/2015/01

Riffkin, R. (2015, December 14). Americans name terrorism as no. 1 U.S. problem. https://news.gallup.com/poll/187655

Sambanis, N. (2006, July 22). It's official: There is now a civil war in Iraq. *New York Times*. www.nytimes.com/2006/07/23/opinion/23sambanis.html

U.S, Position in the World. (n.d.). *Gallup*. https://news.gallup.com/poll/116350/position-world.aspx

Wittkopf, E. R. (1990). *Faces of Internationalism: Public Opinion and American Foreign Policy*. Durham, NC: Duke University Press.

5   Leaders, Decisions, and Foreign Policy

MICHAEL C. HOROWITZ

Introduction

The election of Donald Trump as president of the United States in November 2016 represented a potentially significant moment for American foreign policy, as well as for global politics. Trump, the Republican nominee, emerged victorious in a hard-fought campaign over the Democratic nominee, Hillary Clinton. A political outsider who campaigned on "draining the swamp" of Washington, DC, Trump promised a foreign policy different from those of his predecessors, both Democrats such as Barack Obama and Republicans such as George W. Bush.

On trade policy, Trump promised to withdraw from the Trans Pacific Partnership (TPP), a free trade agreement negotiated by the Obama administration that was designed to solidify US trade leadership in Asia. Trump also stated that he would renegotiate the North American Free Trade Agreement (NAFTA), a free trade agreement between the United States, Canada, and Mexico designed to decrease barriers to commerce after the Cold War. On security policy, Trump questioned the value of US security alliances in Europe, such as the North Atlantic Treaty Organization (NATO), and US partnerships in Asia with countries such as Japan and South Korea.

Clinton promised more continuity with what many observers would characterize as a traditional post–World War II US foreign policy approach, having previously been Secretary of State during the Obama administration. While Trump's rhetoric on those alliances became more restrained during his presidency, he did withdraw from the TPP and renegotiated NAFTA. Foreign ambassadors in late 2017 suggested that, when meeting President Trump, "He wanted to know how much their countries were spending on defense and the size of their trade deficit with the United States" (Birnbaum and Jaffe 2017).

Even without the benefit of detailed historical documentation, the 2016 US presidential election seems like an important moment. The election of Joe Biden in 2020, and the shift in US foreign policy that followed, further illustrates the importance of leaders. Both the 2016 and 2020 elections were extremely close – determined by a small number of voters in a smaller number of states – and moreover, foreign policy is rarely, if ever, a deciding factor in elections.

Voters generally make decisions based on economic policy, social issues, and other factors, with the classic case being Franklin Roosevelt's election in 1932 in the midst of the Great Depression. Thus, an election outcome that could have easily gone the other way, and that was not decided on the basis of foreign policy, potentially had significant consequences for foreign policy.

Leaders clearly matter, at some points, for the making of foreign and defense policy. Leaders make decisions about whether to take their countries to war, and their own personal experiences can shape these decisions. One of the clearest historical cases of the role leaders play comes from a war that most Americans have never heard of – the López War, named after Francisco Solano López, the president of Paraguay from 1862 to 1870. Placed into a position of power by his father, the previous ruler, López's desire for glory led Paraguay into a disastrous war with Brazil, Argentina, and Uruguay that killed 90 percent of the men in the country before it ended with López's death. Commentators have noted that, without López's specific interests and preferences, the war likely would not have occurred.

However, leaders do not operate in a vacuum, but rather make choices as parts of institutions. Government agencies and officials have voices in national security decisions beyond that of the leader, though the specific role the leader and the rest of the government plays can vary across different types of political institutions, such as democracies and autocracies (autocracies are more repressive regimes like dictatorships). In general, leaders in autocracies are less constrained by domestic political institutions than those in democracies, but these constraints can change from regime to regime.

This chapter answers several important questions about leaders. First, what role should we expect leaders to play in foreign policy? Second, how are leaders selected, and how do cross-national differences in the selection of leaders matter for understanding the foreign policy decisions that countries make? Third, where do the beliefs and attitudes of leaders come from, and what role do the background experiences of leaders play? Finally, how do the domestic political incentives of leaders influence their foreign policy choices?

Leaders and International Relations Theory: A Missing Dimension?

Leaders are absent from major international relations theories such as realism, institutionalism, and constructivism. In Kenneth Waltz's levels of analysis, the leader level was the one he sought to theorize beyond, introducing the state and the system as more important (Waltz 1959). This is a reversal from the beginnings of the fields of history and political science. History and political science used to focus on leaders such as Abraham Lincoln, Frederick the Great, and Napoleon Bonaparte, whose decisions shaped the world we live in today. The historian Thomas Carlyle wrote in the nineteenth century that "the history of the world is but the biography of great men" (Carlyle 1968). This "**great man history**" paradigm used to be very influential.

Traditional studies of diplomacy examined leaders, such as Prussian Chancellors Otto von Bismarck and Klemens von Metternich, who rose in the aftermath of the Napoleonic Wars and negotiated the diplomatic agreements and alliances that defined European power politics before World War I. This emphasis on the importance of leaders occurred despite hesitation on the part of some of the subjects themselves. Bismarck, for example, famously said that "Man cannot create the current of events. He can only float with it and steer" (quoted in Lee 1988, 89). American President Abraham Lincoln agreed: "I claim not to have controlled events, but confess plainly that events have controlled me" (quoted in Donald 1995, 514). They were describing the constraints that leaders face – the idea that they are prisoners of the structural conditions they inherit, such as the balance of military power.

Post–World War II schools of thought about international politics incorporated this skepticism about the significance of leaders. Waltz, one of the most important international relations theorists of the twentieth century, argued that there were three "levels" to international politics: the individual or leader, the state, and the system (Waltz 1959). Waltz argued that leader behavior was difficult to explain systematically, because leaders were too idiosyncratic. He also argued that leaders were too constrained by the state and the system for their individual attitudes and preferences to make a difference much of the time.

The state level of politics is that of the individual country, such as the United States of America or Brazil. Individual states have particular attributes that are relevant for international politics, such as whether they are a democracy or an autocracy, and whether their economy depends on foreign trade or domestic production. Individual countries also have different-sized militaries and diplomatic corps.

The system level of politics is the constellation of states, and how states interact. The bipolar system that characterized the Cold War, where the United States and the Soviet Union were the two most powerful countries in the world, is one example of an international system. Another is the multipolar world order prior to World War I, where countries such as Germany, France, and the United Kingdom all had relatively similar levels of power and competed for influence and status.

Waltz and other realists argued that the system plays a primary role in determining how countries behave. After the system affects state behavior, states have a little bit of flexibility left to make choices, but those choices are severely constrained by the international system. Only at that point does the leader matter – and generally wields the smallest amount of influence. Liberal institutionalists, in contrast, focus on the state level, arguing that it is the domestic politics of countries that influence their foreign policy choices. Neither realists nor liberal institutionalists believe that individual leaders are crucial for the international security environment.

The realist and liberal perspectives notwithstanding, there are several areas of international politics where leaders might play a defining role. First, and most important, it is leaders who make the fundamental choices about whether their countries go to war or stay at peace. Leaders make the final decision about the initiation and escalation of military conflicts. How leaders make those choices is a critical question.

Second, leaders make choices about foreign policy strategy short of war. For example, in 2017, the United States embarked on a more confrontational policy towards North Korea than at any time since the end of the Korean War in 1953. Rather than responding to North Korean provocations by viewing North Korean rhetoric as "cheap talk," as it had for decades, the United States began fighting rhetorical fire with rhetorical fire. What explains this policy shift?

Figure 5.1. The racist, brutal apartheid regime in South Africa ended in the early 1990s in large part because of decisions made by apartheid's last leader, F. W. de Klerk (left). De Klerk handed power over peacefully to Nelson Mandela (right), the leader of the African National Congress. Mandela was a political prisoner for twenty-six years before gaining power in a free, fair, and peaceful election in 1994. World Economic Forum (www.weforum.org).

It is most likely the preference of President Trump, whose political instincts pushed him to respond to provocations with threats of his own, rather than back down.

Third, leaders make consequential decisions about investments in military technologies that can shape national security, such as whether their country should arm itself with nuclear, biological, or chemical weapons. Those types of large-scale decisions generally come from the head of state and can lead countries to pursue weapons of mass destruction or, equally, to give them up. For example, South African Prime Minister B. J. Vorster approved the development of a nuclear arsenal in 1974, and as the South African apartheid regime came to an end around 1990, South African President F. W. de Klerk made a decision that no country has made before or since – to give up South Africa's nuclear arsenal and unilaterally disarm (Figure 5.1).

Finally, leaders are the driving force when it comes to how their countries bargain with the world. Through public and private statements, leaders communicate with the leaders of other countries, the international community, and their own publics about the international security environment. A key role leaders play is in issuing statements during international crises that explain what a country is doing, and why. For example, in a 1948 dispute known as the Berlin Crisis, the Soviet Union blockaded the part of Berlin controlled by the United States and its allies (the Soviet Union controlled the other part of Berlin), preventing the entry of supplies by land routes. Josef Stalin, the leader of the Soviet Union, was trying to demonstrate the ability of the Soviet Union to control West Berlin, in the hope that the United States and its allies would give the Soviet Union control over all of eastern Germany. Instead, US President Harry S. Truman issued what is called a **statement of resolve**, a declaration of willingness to defend a national interest rather than back down, even at risk of war (on leaders and resolve, see Lupton 2020). He publicly announced, "We shall stay, period."

There are three perspectives, essentially, on the role of leaders in international politics. First, in combination with domestic political institutions and the international system, who leads a country can make a difference in foreign policy decisionmaking, in ways that we can forecast and understand. Second, while leaders may matter, they are only relevant in random ways that are too difficult to understand to incorporate into how we study international politics. Third, leaders do not matter, because the power of the international system and domestic institutions over countries is such that leaders are too constrained to make a difference in foreign policy most of the time. How can we navigate between these perspectives? The place to start is by unpacking how leaders are chosen in the first place. The next section addresses this critical question.

The Selection of Leaders

Leaders come to power in the context of their domestic political environments. Whether they do so through a revolution and civil war, as Mao Zedong did in China in 1949, through hereditary succession, as Kim Jong Un did in North Korea in 2011, or through a democratic election, as President Trump did in the United States in 2016, there is a domestic pathway to power. Generally, it makes sense to think about the ways that leaders come to power as falling into two categories: **irregular succession and regular succession** (Chiozza and Goemans 2011).

Irregular successions occur when leaders come to power through means other than planned elections or clear rules of succession from one ruler to the next. Coups d'état and mass revolutions are examples of irregular successions. For example, Muammar Gaddafi came to power in Libya in 1969 in a military coup. Trained at the Royal Military Academy in Benghazi, Gaddafi formed what was called the Free Officers Movement. The movement plotted against the Libyan government, which it regarded as too pro-Israel, as well as corrupt. On September 1, 1969, Gaddafi's forces launched a coup, occupying airports, media such as radio and television stations, and government offices. Coups aside, leaders sometimes take power through irregular succession following revolutions and civil wars, such as Vladimir Lenin, who came to power in Russia in the October Revolution of 1917, an event that led to the founding of the Soviet Union.

In contrast, regular successions follow prescribed rules that determine who selects the leader, the rules used to select the leader, and, if there is a vote (as in a democracy), how that vote occurs and is tallied. The individuals described by formal rules as having the power to choose the leader are called the **selectorate** (Bueno de Mesquita et al. 2004). The US Constitution, for example, lays out the basic requirements for the election of the president of the United States. Subsequent federal and state laws then further narrow down how the election occurs. The US presidential election occurs on the first Tuesday after the first Monday in November, every four years, due to a law passed by Congress in 1845. Similarly, when a US president dies in office, as in the case of John F. Kennedy's assassination in 1963, the US Constitution states that the vice president assumes the presidency. Authoritarian political systems also have selectorates, but their selectorates tend to be much smaller groups – elites and leaders rather than all citizens.

Some might argue that if we understand how leaders are chosen, we do not really need to focus on who is actually in office. For example, if the majority will in a democracy determines who is elected president, and we really want to understand a democracy's foreign policy choices, we need to focus on understanding the majority will, not the actual person who is chosen. Even in nondemocracies, if shifts in the political environment determine who is chosen to be leader, we need to focus on that environment, and need not worry about who is actually chosen.

For those who think leaders generally do not matter, the selection process in every country means that leaders almost by definition are not unique. Leaders reflect the political environment and particular time period in which they come to power. Thus, to attribute importance to the leader is to miss the fact that, if a particular leader did not exist, the same circumstances that led to the rise of that leader would likely lead to the rise of another with similar preferences.

Moreover, those who think leaders are not important can argue that it is not simply that leaders reflect the political time in which they rise to power. The set of people who are in contention to be leaders could, in theory, have similar backgrounds and life experiences in ways that might make the individual who rises to power less relevant. For example, a generation of people that experience the same war or economic conditions might come to have similar views due to those shared experiences. All of those who survived the Great Depression in the United States, for example, might as a cohort be more favorably inclined towards social programs such as welfare.

These arguments about how leader succession makes leaders less important, from the perspective of understanding foreign policy, might be overstated. First, leaders are rarely selected primarily on the basis of their views about foreign policy. Economic and other domestic policy issues generally play the most prominent role in any campaign or a selection process. Whether they are part of an interest group in an autocracy or voters in a democracy, what motivates most people is what a leader will mean for their economic wellbeing, and the economic wellbeing of their community.

Second, leaders who gain power through irregular succession are by definition, not selected through a regular process on the basis of their foreign policy attitudes. In addition, they often take power despite the will of the people, not because of that will. In the Qaddafi example mentioned above, his movement did not have the mass support of the population, or even most Libyan elites at the time he took power.

Third, even in societies where one might imagine that the set of possible leaders have all had similar experiences, there are potentially consequential differences. In 2000, Republican nominee George W. Bush won a very closely contested election against Democratic nominee Al Gore. Both were of the Vietnam generation, and while George W. Bush served in the Air National Guard, Al Gore deployed to Vietnam, though only for a short period of time and not on the front line. Less than a year after Bush entered office, the September 11, 2001, attacks occurred, claiming several thousand lives as the Twin Towers fell in New York and the Pentagon was damaged in Washington, DC. The American-led invasion of Afghanistan that followed shortly after would almost certainly have happened no matter who won the 2000 election, but the US-led invasion of Iraq in 2003 might not have. In what was described as a war of choice even by advocates, in March 2003 US military forces rolled into Iraq to end the brutal regime of Iraqi dictator Saddam Hussein. Would that invasion have happened if Gore had won, instead of Bush? It is hard to say. While both political parties believed that Saddam Hussein's regime represented a threat to the region, some of the strongest advocates for military action were so-called neoconservatives and others close to the George W. Bush administration. Bush's victory in what was a coin toss of an election thus had significant consequences.

Figure 5.2. Adolf Hitler, the eager face of the new Germany, and Paul von Hindenburg, the tired face of the old Germany, 1933. No other political transition has had a bigger effect on world history.
© Culture Club/Contributor/Hulton Archive/Getty Images.

The argument that leaders simply reflect the political environment also does not hold up at the extreme, e.g. the sorts of close elections described above, for leaders who are extremely effective or, potentially, for leaders who have extreme viewpoints. The argument would suggest that even a leader such as Adolf Hitler in Germany was not consequential; he simply reflected the political and economic context in Germany in the 1930s. In reality, Hitler's rise was idiosyncratic. He rose to power after the Nazi party earned 33 percent of the popular vote in the 1932 election and, once appointed Chancellor by a reluctant president Paul von Hindenburg, quickly amassed power through intimidation, law-breaking, and violence, including orchestrating (or exploiting) the burning-down of the German parliamentary building (the Reichstag) in 1933 (Figure 5.2). Moreover, once Hitler took power, it became clear that his personality and preferences would have a unique impact on Germany's national security strategy. Sir Horace Rumbold, the British ambassador to Germany, infamously stated in the early 1930s that "Hitler may be no statesman, but he is an uncommonly clever and audacious demagogue" (quoted in Ford 1953, 445).

The Policy Preferences of Leaders: Where Preferences Come from and Why They Can Matter

Leaders do not enter office as blank slates. Instead, they have their own pre-formed views about the world: from general views about the types of strategies and approaches that will bring them success to specific views about foreign policy. Leader beliefs are thought to stem from a combination of nature (biological factors) and nurture (environmental factors).

The beliefs of leaders can shape how they react to the world, and how they negotiate, both domestically and internationally. As leaders come of age, they develop beliefs about what causes conflicts (Saunders 2011). These beliefs reflect, in part, what are called **efficacy beliefs** – or views about the types of strategies likely to lead to success or failure. In the foreign policy realm, this relates to how leaders view the security environment. Some leaders view threats as emanating from external conditions. They see threatening moves by other countries, such as troop movements, arms buildups, or demands for concessions, as the result of the foreign policies of those states. In this view, national foreign policy choices are the result of leaders having flexibility and discretion in their choices. In contrast, others view threats as mostly arising from countries being driven into policy choices by domestic politics. Some research suggests that leaders then connect their theory of where threats come from to the necessary strategy for confronting threats. When leaders view threats as being externally driven – by opposing leaders and countries that have discretion – that ironically makes them easier to manage. In contrast, threats that come from deep-rooted domestic political or related situations are much more difficult to solve, and thus need to be confronted with more transformational strategies. Essentially, the causal beliefs that leaders have about the source of threats can lead them to different policy proposals for how to address those threats.

One way to contextualize how different leaders think about threats is to compare US Presidents Kennedy and Johnson and the contrasting ways they viewed Vietnam in the 1960s (Saunders 2011). President Kennedy viewed the threat in Vietnam as coming from domestic political instability in Vietnam and he viewed South Vietnam's leader, Ngo Dinh Diem, as part of the problem. He was thus attracted to US military efforts designed to fundamentally change South Vietnam. The Strategic Hamlets Program, for example, authorized by the Kennedy administration, attempted to rebuild Vietnam village by village, and thereby reshape Vietnamese politics. President Johnson, in contrast, was less persuaded of the link between Vietnam's domestic politics and the challenge the United States faced in Vietnam. Thus, rather than supporting US military operations designed to promote local stability, Johnson favored more traditional military operations that would not depend on transforming South Vietnamese politics.

Leader Background Experiences

Thinking about the role of leader beliefs in shaping how leaders make foreign policy choices raises the question, of course, of where those leader beliefs come from. One answer to that question is the background life experiences of leaders, the personal and professional histories that influence their worldviews. Humans often reason by analogy, as we know from behavioral psychology (Khong 1992). In the Korean War, for example, when evaluating what North Korea's 1950 invasion of South Korea meant for the broader Cold War, US and British leaders were influenced by the experience of German aggression in the 1930s.

At a meeting in Munich in 1938, the leaders of Britain and France agreed to give Hitler the Czech territory of the Sudetenland, hoping that these territorial acquisitions would satisfy Hitler and discourage him from further aggression (Figure 5.3). Those beliefs were sadly mistaken, of course, as appeasement merely emboldened Hitler to demand more. Less than two decades later, faced with a North Korean invasion backed by Soviet leader Josef Stalin, Western leaders such as Harry Truman drew heavily on the Munich case when considering how to respond. Believing that the lesson of Munich was that giving the dictator, in this case Stalin, an inch meant he would take a mile, the United States, the United Kingdom, and their allies decided to defend South Korea in full.

Figure 5.3. Neville Chamberlain celebrated the 1938 Agreement handing over a large slice of Czechoslovakia to Hitler as "Peace for Our Time." The willingness of Chamberlain and the French leadership to appease Hitler rather than fight reflected their own background experiences, the recalled horrors of World War I, and shaped the background experiences of future leaders, as to this day leaders recoil at the thought of committing another "Munich." Imperial War Museum.

Events much less foundational than Munich can also shape how leaders evaluate the world before they enter office, and the more personal the experience, the more it tends to influence their future attitudes. Background experiences are a a pool of lessons learned that help drive the development of efficacy beliefs.

Consider, for example, an activity that the average person might view as risky, such as bungee jumping. Here, we can see the way that nature and nurture interact to produce people with different risk profiles. Some people are more inclined than others, based on biology, to go bungee jumping, despite the nonzero risk of an accident that could lead to injury or even death. Others might not necessarily be more likely to go bungee jumping, but having gone bungee jumping successfully, might view that kind of behavior – behavior others view as risky – as something that they can engage in safely and can continue doing. In this way, participation in the activity can generate efficacy beliefs that make future bungee jumping – as well as other risk-taking behavior – more likely.

More generally, poignant life experiences during childhood, adolescence, and early adulthood can have a formative and long-term impact on leader behavior (Horowitz et al. 2015). Understanding the background characteristics of leaders can therefore help explain why leaders have the preferences they have about war and peace, in turn shedding light on what types of leaders make war and peace more or less likely (there are always exceptions, of course).

Research demonstrates that two background characteristics of leaders make them particularly prone to develop efficacy beliefs that make international conflict more likely. An obvious reference point when trying to predict how a leader will think about the use of military force is whether that leader served in the military. Decades ago, political scientist Samuel Huntington wrote about the "military mind" and contrasted it with civilian perceptions of the world. Huntington argued that those with the military mind were more likely to see the world as threatening and support military arms buildups, among other policies. Yet there are many differences in types of military service; one might serve for a brief or extended time, in the army or the navy, as an officer or enlisted personnel. A key distinction is whether that person participated in combat operations while in the military.

Those who experience combat tend to have two characteristics: confidence in their level of knowledge about the military and military operations, relative to the general population; and an understanding of the danger and costs of war, from facing the risk of death themselves and potentially seeing their friends killed or wounded. While the first characteristic might make someone more inclined to support the use of force, the second characteristic might make them less inclined to do so. Thus, combat experience, on average, does not necessarily make a leader with military service more or less likely to support the use of military force.

In contrast, those who have prior national military service but no combat experience appear significantly more likely to support the use of force if they become a national leader. Like Kaiser Wilhelm II, who led Germany into World War I, as described below, those with military service but no combat experience view themselves as having military expertise and tend to glorify the military – but without understanding the potential costs of war. This makes them, on balance, more conflict-prone when they enter office.

A second key characteristic of leaders that is associated with a greater propensity to start wars is prior rebel experience. The image of the rebel is often that of Che Guevara in Cuba or Mao Zedong in China, but the list of leaders with prior rebel experience is much longer. Participating in a rebellion is a dangerous activity. Rebels take up arms against the existing government of a territory, and that existing government is generally better armed, and has more support in the local population, than the rebels. Most rebellions end in defeat – and being a rebel means facing a constant threat of being killed or captured.

It is therefore risky and dangerous to be a rebel. Those who become rebels and survive and go on to become leaders are shaped by the experience. They are more likely to view themselves as capable of engaging in risky gambits, and less trusting of the world. Former rebels who enter office, whether their initial agenda is revolutionary or not, tend to start and escalate more military conflicts than those who do not have rebel experience. For example, Saddam Hussein, previously a rebel, entered the government of Iraq in 1968, a decade before he took power in a 1979 coup.

These characteristics, however, are mediated by domestic political institutions, meaning the types of leaders with these experiences that one sees in a democratic country may be different than those in an autocratic country (see also Chapter 3). In a democracy, running for higher office generally means getting the approval of a political party and appealing to a broad segment of the population. This means those with extreme risk-taking propensities are less likely to get elected, unless those propensities reflect the attitudes of the population.

On the other hand, autocratic regimes with irregular selection processes (to return to a concept introduced in the previous section) sometimes select for the opposite traits in their leaders. Research shows that the selection process in autocratic regimes more often requires risk-taking, such as participating in a rebellion or a coup. Thus, because risk takers are more likely to try to take power in autocracies, risk takers are more likely to become leaders in autocratic regimes.

What about Sex and Gender?

Does it matter, from a foreign policy perspective, whether a leader is male or female? (See Chapter 2.) One theory would suggest that the answer is yes. Essentialist perspectives on sex, gender, and behavior, viewing women as intrinsically more nurturing and supportive than men, have traditionally thought about women as, on average, less militaristic than men as well. Thus, one would imagine women as peacemakers more than warriors when it comes to making decisions as leaders. Another theory, however, would suggest the opposite. Given the varieties of discrimination against women in almost every country, women are less likely than men to become heads of state in the first place. Those women who do rise to higher office are thus more likely to be those who, on average, demonstrate behavioral characteristics more like the average man, since that helps them get selected. If this alternative theory is true, one would imagine female heads of state behaving very similarly to male heads of state when it comes to foreign policy, especially in the use of force.

Evidence is quite limited due to the small number of female heads of state, overall, in modern political history, even though female leaders such as Angela Merkel of Germany have had great prominence in international politics in the first part of the twenty-first century. The evidence that does exist, however, from analyzing over 100 years of military dispute initiations by every country around the world, suggests that there are not systematic differences in the behavior of men and women when it comes to the propensity to start military conflicts (Horowitz et al. 2015). While the most dangerous leaders in history, such as Hitler and Stalin, have all been men, it is possible that that is a matter of chance more than anything else, due to the much larger pool of male leaders.

It is also possible that gender matters for leaders in ways relevant for the international security environment, but beyond the question of which leaders are more likely to start military conflicts. Female leaders, for example, might be more likely to be underestimated due to sexism. Opponents evaluating female leaders might be less likely to take their threats seriously, and thus less likely to back down when facing a militarized challenge from a female leader. One example comes from the tenure of Margaret Thatcher, who was prime minister of the United Kingdom. During Thatcher's first term in office, in 1982, a British territory in the South Atlantic, the Falkland Islands, was invaded by Argentina, which at that time was run by a military regime. It is hard to know for certain, but it is possible that Argentina's leaders underestimated Thatcher's resolve. Known now for her iron will, Thatcher's global reputation for determination and steadfastness grew out of her resolve and determination to retake the Falkland Islands from Argentina. She ordered the British military to fight, and they defeated the Argentine military. Thatcher reinforced her reputation in standing tough against the Irish Republican Army (IRA) terrorist group. In 1984, the IRA detonated a bomb in a hotel where Thatcher was staying, narrowly missing killing her (the bathroom in Thatcher's suite was destroyed; she was in the sitting room at the time). Six other hotel guests, including a Member of Parliament, died; another thirty-one were injured. Six hours later, Thatcher delivered a scheduled political speech to the Conservative Party conference, defiantly declaring that "all attempts to destroy democracy by terrorism will fail" (Figure 5.4).

Figure 5.4. Unscathed and unruffled, British Prime Minister Margaret Thatcher refused to back down in the face of Argentine aggression or IRA terrorism; here she is seen speaking publicly just hours after barely escaping an assassination attempt in October 1984. Keep calm and carry on, indeed.
©Bettmann / Contributor/Bettmann/ Getty Images.

Ideology

The ideology of leaders can also be critical in understanding their foreign policy preferences. **Ideology** refers to systems of beliefs and ideas that coherently connect to policy preferences. Ideology can be, but is not necessarily, linked to life experience. Leaders normally enter office as representatives of political parties with programs for government. As explained above, leaders rarely, if ever, operate without constraints. As the head of a political party, leaders run for office (especially in democracies) on political platforms that make promises about the policies that will be enacted if the leader wins. Those platforms often reflect ideological beliefs about the world.

For example, the 1980 US presidential election saw sitting President Jimmy Carter, a Democrat, take on Republican nominee Ronald Reagan. Carter was a graduate of the US Naval Academy who, though he did not participate in combat operations while in the Navy, served on some of the first US nuclear submarines. In contrast, Reagan's military experience was mostly confined to a sound stage in California in World War II helping promote the Allied war effort against Germany and Japan.

Yet, in the 1980 election, it was Reagan who was the hawk, favoring a massive defense buildup in response to the Soviet invasion of Afghanistan and the revolution in Iran. The 1980 Republican platform reflected Reagan's staunch anti-communist ideology. Carter, rightly or wrongly, is now considered arguably the most dovish US president elected since World War II. He was skeptical about the use of military force as a means to achieve positive outcomes, and supported more conciliatory policies, such as continued arms control negotiations. This example highlights the way that leader background experiences, while important for predicting leader behavior, are not necessarily destiny. The example also showcases the importance of ideology.

Health

Another factor that shapes the worldviews of leaders is their health (McDermott 2008). A fair number of leaders become ill while in office, or enter office with chronic health problems. For example, think of the large number of heads of state that contracted COVID-19 during the pandemic, such as then US President Donald Trump. Health-stricken leaders were especially common prior to the advent of modern medicine. Even today, however, people with substantial health problems end up as head of state, especially in less democratic countries where leaders can rule for decades. But this is not just an issue for nondemocracies. Due to advanced age, chronic health conditions, or accidents, health concerns can limit the cognitive capacity and decisionmaking of democratic leaders as well. Some US presidents have dealt with issues of addiction, such as President Kennedy's addiction to painkilling medication. Most famously, President Woodrow Wilson's stroke in 1919 severely compromised his ability to secure Senate passage of the Treaty of Versailles. With a restricted physical ability to lobby and declining judgment due to his mounting health concerns, Wilson could only watch as one of his signature foreign policy accomplishments, the creation of the League of Nations, was voted down by the United States Senate.

Age

A final factor that can influence the behavior of leaders is age. Younger leaders, almost by definition, have less life experience than older leaders, and potentially a different relationship with government institutions. This can shape foreign policy decisions. As people age, their level of testosterone decreases. Research in psychology and criminology shows that, on average, higher levels of testosterone are correlated with more aggressive behavior. Thus, one might imagine that younger leaders, with higher levels of testosterone (again on average), would be more prone to aggression in international politics. Older leaders may have more political power, however, if they come to power after a career that gives them a good sense of how government works. They may also have shorter time horizons, leading them to contemplate more aggressive behavior as they attempt to make a difference before their time passes. The 2020 election in the United States featured two of the oldest candidates ever for the presidency – Donald Trump (seventy-three) and Joe Biden (seventy-seven). Improvements in healthcare have extended life expectancy, meaning that potential candidates for leadership can spend longer in contention for leadership and/or leading once in power (especially in an autocracy). Thus, if the average age of world leaders increases in the coming years, the consequences for international politics will be interesting to track. Empirical studies have shed some useful light, showing that older leaders, especially in democratic settings, are more likely to initiate international conflicts as compared with younger leaders (Horowitz et al. 2015).

Leaders and Domestic Politics

Even given the ways leaders can make a difference in driving their nations' foreign policies, leaders operate within domestic political institutions (see Chapter 3). With rare exceptions, such as revolutions that sweep away the entirety of the previous government, these institutions, including the political parties that leaders direct and the governmental agencies they inherit, can influence how the attitudes and views of a leader are (or are not) translated into policy.

Most broadly, there are differences between more democratic and more autocratic regimes that influence the average relative impact of a new leader on foreign policy. In the most autocratic regimes, such as Stalin's Soviet Union, leaders have personalistic control over the levers of power. Personalist leaders are those that rely on only a very small selectorate to stay in power, meaning they are less constrained in making policy than other leaders. In the most autocratic, personalist regimes, then, the preferences of the leader most directly translate into policy.

In other autocracies, while the leader often has flexibility, they are still responsible to some set of interest groups whose support is necessary to keep them in power. These interest groups could be the military, trade organizations, natural resource companies (if the country is rich in natural resources), or other groups. In these types of regimes, the leader often has greater foreign policy flexibility than in democracies. However, leaders need to avoid pursuing foreign policies that would alienate their core constituencies, which can cut both ways when it comes to the potential for war or peace. For example, core constituencies that favor military buildups and war can push leaders toward more aggressive foreign policies, as was arguably the case with Japan prior to World War II.

Elected leaders are more constrained than unelected leaders. Elected leaders need to maintain public support to be reelected. That said, elected leaders are not completely constrained in choosing whether or not to use force. Leaders have an informational advantage at the beginning of a crisis, for example, given their access to classified information. This gives leaders the ability to shape the narrative and pursue their preferred policy outcome at the outset. Over time, as information spreads and other political elites develop policy preferences, the flexibility of the leader can decline (see Chapter 4). Leaders are also sometimes elected or take office in part because of specific policy actions they say they will take that are different than those of their predecessors, and they can feel bound by those expectations.

Beyond these overall differences, there are specific aspects of domestic institutions and a leader's tenure in office that influence how leaders make foreign policy. These aspects are described in the sections that follow.

Political Parties

From Angela Merkel's Christian Democratic Union in Germany to Saddam Hussein's Ba'ath Party in Iraq, both democratic and non-democratic leaders often enter office at the head of a political party. At the point when leaders enter office, it is generally on platforms that involve, at least in part, rejecting the legacies of their predecessors. The Donald Trump administration in the United States, for example, spent much of 2017 attempting to roll back the legacy of the Obama administration, such as rejecting the TPP deal that the Obama administration negotiated. When Republican George W. Bush became president of the United States in 2001, the perceived rejection of the Democratic Clinton administration was so strong that Bush's policy direction was labeled as "Anything but Clinton."

Leaders also often feel beholden to those who helped them enter office – their selectorate – and wish to implement specific promises that they campaigned on. For example, while exit polling suggested it played a small role in his election, Barack Obama campaigned in 2008 in part on withdrawing the United States military from Iraq. Once he entered office in January 2009, President Obama felt compelled to follow through, at least in part, on that campaign promise, and his administration planned for eventual US withdrawal from Iraq. Another example, referenced above, is President Trump withdrawing the United States from the TPP, one of his campaign promises.

Bureaucracy

The bureaucracy of a government is generally defined as unelected officials that serve in the executive branch of a government. Leader attitudes are sometimes socialized in office by more permanent government officials. Whether a country is a democracy or an autocracy, unless a leader takes power by completely sweeping away the prior government, he or she generally inherits a foreign policy, intelligence, and defense bureaucracy that has its own preferences, from experience and self-interest, about the world. Besides a few trusted advisers brought in by an administration, most of the people that are assessing threats, devising policy proposals, and suggesting defense policies are long-serving policy experts and civil servants. They have the ability, in many cases, to shape not just the overall options presented to the head of state, but the information the head of state receives. This information function of the bureaucracy can limit and constrain even a leader who seeks to implement significant change in a policy area.

The interaction between the bureaucracy and the leader can depend on two factors in particular. First, leaders may be perceived to have a personal mandate due to the strength of an electoral victory, or because they are leading an autocracy with few checks and balances. Leaders with a mandate may be positioned to ignore or overcome the bureaucracy more easily. Second, on issues where the bureaucracy brings special expertise, such as long-running foreign policy challenges where classified information differs from publicly available information, bureaucratic actors may be more successful at influencing leaders.

One example of this comes from the 1961 Bay of Pigs incident. After Fidel Castro seized power in the Cuban Revolution of 1959, Cuba and the United States became adversaries. The United States government began working on ways to displace Castro and either restore the old regime or replace Castro with other leaders who might be more pro-American. Throughout the last year of the Eisenhower administration, the White House and the Central Intelligence Agency (CIA) worked together on a plan that involved the United States deploying over 1,000 armed Cuban expatriates who would take back the country. When he entered office in 1961, President Kennedy was presented with the plan, which the Eisenhower White House had approved but not begun work on. Kennedy authorized the invasion, which occurred in April 1961 and became a debacle – the US-backed forces were quickly defeated, and it became an enormous embarrassment for the CIA and the United States. In the aftermath, President Kennedy and his advisors argued that their lack of knowledge had led them to approve the operation without sufficient investigation and oversight on their own part. Essentially, the bureaucracy had convinced them to do something they did not want to do. While a convenient explanation for the Kennedy administration, attempting to minimize its accountability, the example does show the ability of the bureaucracy to leverage leaders into policy choices at times.

Timing

Time in office can matter for leaders in several ways. Leaders age in office, both physically and mentally. The weight of decisionmaking can be tiring, even for an autocrat. However, there is no experience like being the head of state. As one commentator noted in the wake of the September 11, 2001, attacks against the United States, "Nothing in Mr. Bush's previous career has remotely prepared him for these vast challenges" (Fletcher 2001). The assumption made here was that US President George W. Bush was new in office and thus, by definition, unprepared.

Heads of state are often surprised by the diversity of the challenges they confront in office, and how difficult those challenges are to handle. After all, if a challenge was obvious and there was an easy answer, chances are that the previous leader would have already solved the problem. (This is one reason why, when new leaders of major powers take office, often the only challenges on the table at the beginning of an administration are the hardest problems that the last administration had to grapple with, e.g., North Korea for the Trump administration.)

It is also not simply that new leaders enter office inexperienced. New leaders also usually lack the detailed knowledge of potential adversaries, as well as of present and previous adversaries, that their more experienced counterparts have. New leaders also do not usually have long-running personal relationships with other foreign leaders (sometimes this is not the case, such as when a previous vice president or other political elite takes office, but it is true most of the time, especially in democracies). All of these things generate instability, which is one reason why, in the United States, for example, international crises are significantly more likely in the first year, and especially the first two years, of a presidential term. For example, Soviet leader Nikita Khrushchev sensed in 1961 that the new, young President Kennedy might be weak and ineffective, encouraging Khrushchev to challenge Kennedy verbally at their June 1961 summit in Vienna, and later that summer to initiate against the United States one of the most dangerous crises of the Cold War, over the political status of West Berlin. Kennedy's failure at the Bay of Pigs and his acquiescence in the building of the Berlin Wall were both vital pieces of information that Khrushchev used to evaluate JFK and conclude that he was a weak leader. In the United States, at least, research shows that the probability of a new crisis declines significantly after the midterm elections.

Job Security

The political power of the chief executive often waxes and wanes, especially in a democracy. While US President George H.W. Bush had an approval rating over 90 percent in early 1991 in the wake of Operation Desert Storm against Iraq, he lost his campaign for reelection in 1992 to Democratic nominee Bill Clinton.

The job security of the leader, something inherently related to domestic political institutions (see Chapter 3), can also influence the way leaders behave in the international realm, including the probability that leaders will start new military conflicts and the way they act when military conflicts are ongoing. The top priority of a leader, in general, is staying in power. The significance of staying in power, and what makes a leader more likely to stay there, can vary a great deal across domestic political regimes. Autocratic leaders do not have to worry about reprisal at the ballot box if they start a war and lose, but they do have to worry about the possibility of a popular uprising or other elites removing them from office in the event of military disaster, as Argentina's junta discovered after they lost the Falklands War against the United Kingdom in 1982.

Fear of the consequences of losing office, and the likelihood of losing it, can influence how leaders behave while in office. In democracies, power transitions are generally peaceful, and leaders who have lost power do not have to worry about reprisals such as jail time or death. In autocracies, outcomes for leaders who leave office vary much more – and the risk that leaving office will lead to your death is a strong incentive for a leader to hold on to power for as long as possible, at any cost. These dynamics can influence leader behavior. First, if leaders fear that policy concessions, such as backing down in an international crisis, will make it more likely that they lose power (either through a future election or a coup), they will logically become less likely to back down. This is especially true if the consequence of losing power might be imprisonment or death. Second, leaders in the midst of a war often have to decide whether to keep fighting or try to settle the conflict. Autocrats who fear they will lose power if they settle the conflict – and that losing power could carry severe personal consequences – are less likely to settle and more likely to keep fighting.

Note that these consequences from losing power can come either from internal forces – i.e., other domestic actors that will punish a former leader – or from the international community. Some argue that this is one reason why Syrian leader Bashir al-Assad did not step down at the start of the Syrian Civil War, despite severe pressure from the international community. Having fought a brutal civil war, used chemical weapons, and committed war crimes, if Assad left office he would have faced punishment either from the next government of Syria or an institution like the International Criminal Court. Thus, fear of severe consequences for himself pushed Assad to reject any end to the civil war that would require him to step down from power.

Fears about job security have different effects on the decision to start a war. Scholars have argued for decades about whether and when diversionary wars occur. **Diversionary wars** are those initiated by a national leader to shift political attention away from domestic problems toward an external enemy (see Chapters 3 and 4). The hope is that an international conflict can cause a "rally 'round the flag" effect and bolster the leader. A truly diversionary war would exemplify a leader-driven conflict, since it would be a leader starting a conflict purely to stay in office. The challenge is that wars happen for complicated and multifaceted reasons, meaning true cases of diversionary war are rare, at best. Moreover, some political science research suggests that leaders with unstable political coalitions, or who are nearing the ends of their terms – i.e., leaders with less political capital – are less likely to engage in dangerous endeavors such as starting wars. Debate remains, however, over when and whether this is true.

Whose Reputation?

A final question for understanding leaders and the international conflict process has to do with the reputations that countries and leaders have for being willing to use force – and how those reputations influence behavior. Many believe that actions build reputations, and that standing firm builds a reputation for toughness, whereas backing down builds a reputation for weakness (Schelling 1966). This was the logic behind the domino theory during the Cold War. The United States worried that if it allowed communism to expand, especially against an American ally, it would undermine the belief of allies that the United States would defend them. This would make it harder for the United States to sustain its alliances in Europe and Asia, and thus undermine the ability of the United States to confront the Soviet Union.

There is an ongoing debate about the importance and nature of reputation in international relations (Kertzer 2018). Those who believe in reputation point to evidence that countries do, indeed, cite the past behavior of others when making decisions about the future. Osama bin Laden, for example, reportedly argued that US withdrawal from Somalia in 1993 proved that the United States would withdraw if attacked, meaning al-Qaeda had no need to worry about an overwhelming US military response to the September 11, 2001, attacks. (Bin Laden was wrong, of course.)

Reputation skeptics argue that countries make policy choices based on their perceptions of the immediate costs and benefits, and evaluate the probable behavior of other countries on the same basis, and pay little attention to past actions. According to this logic, for example, US defeat in the Vietnam War did not undermine the credibility of the US commitment to defend Japan, a critical US ally during the Cold War. Japan was a much more important country than South Vietnam. Japan knew that, and thus would not have worried about a lack of US resolve in defending Japan even if the United States had never defended South Vietnam from communist incursions in the first place.

If reputations exist, do they reside with a country or a leader? Does a country have a reputation for toughness that travels from leader to leader, or does reputation "reset" every time a new leader takes power (Wolford 2007)? The paragraphs above are notable for the way that they assume that reputations are specific to countries. Bin Laden, for example, viewed the

Somalia example as instructive about US behavior even though Bill Clinton was president during the Somalia crisis, and George W. Bush was president in 2001. The loss of personal relationships when new leaders enter office can lead to foreign policy instability because new leaders lack a track record, so leaders around the world are not sure how they will act, and vice versa. Thus, changes in political regimes such as democratization or changes in leadership can generate uncertainty on the part of both allies and adversaries. And since uncertainty is generally thought to make conflict more likely, it is during periods of leadership turnover or political institutional change that reputations are in flux, creating instability.

Over time, leaders develop reputations for how they behave. The leader-specific effects of reputation are strongest, potentially, when a leader takes power after a revolution that upends the political institutions of a country. For example, after the Chinese Civil War concluded in 1949 with the victory of the Communists, China's foreign policy shifted dramatically, and countries had to calibrate their expectations of Chinese behavior anew. No one expected Mao to fulfill the previous foreign policy commitments of Chiang Kai-Shek.

Even in more democratic regimes, however, leader-specific reputations can matter – or at least leaders behave as if they matter. Following the George W. Bush administration, Barack Obama entered office promising a more open, friendlier US foreign policy than before, reaching out to the Arab world and envisioning a world without nuclear weapons. He hoped that this would show he was different and thus give him a fresh start in his relationships with countries around the world. The debatable success of this initiative – highly questioned by his successor, President Trump – shows that these goals of leaders do not always translate into reality.

Thinking about reputation also generates the logical question of which leaders care about reputation, and which do not. Some research shows that leaders who are higher self-monitors, essentially those who care the most, personally, about the impressions they convey to others, are more likely to act on the basis of reputation (Yarhi-Milo 2018). In contrast, lower self-monitors are less tied to how others perceive them, so are therefore less likely to act to reinforce or change a reputation. This, of course, also ties into work on individual personality and decisionmaking. For example, leaders that are more narcissistic might be more likely to centralize power and rely on themselves when making decisions, while leaders with higher degrees of openness might be more likely to listen to the opinions of others, including their advisors. The question of leader psychology connects to how cognitive biases shape everyone's behavior, including the behavior of leaders. For example, individuals can suffer from anchoring bias, where the first piece of evidence they receive about information shapes their attitudes even if future information contradicts that initial information. For leaders, this can have potentially serious consequences if they get anchored to information that turns out to be incorrect in the context of a crisis. Confirmation bias is when people interpret information, no matter what it is, as reinforcing their prior beliefs. For example, a leader that believes another country is inherently threatening is likely to interpret any information about that country as evidence of a threat.

CASE STUDY

World War I

As this chapter demonstrates, leaders play a large role in international politics at some times, but they are also constrained by the international system, as well as their own domestic political environments. The onset of World War I is a hard case for thinking about the role of leaders in international politics. The chain of events set in motion by the assassination of the Austrian Archduke Ferdinand on June 28, 1914, is considered a prototypical example of a spiral to war driven by offensive military doctrine and distrust that flowed from political institutions, rather than people. A close look at some of the key leaders making decisions in World War I, however, reveals the ways that they influenced, or did not influence, the outbreak of the war and how it was fought.

This case study looks at four leaders: Kaiser Wilhelm II of Germany, Prime Minister H. H. Asquith of the United Kingdom, Prime Minister David Lloyd George of the United Kingdom, and President Woodrow Wilson of the United States. The discussion of each leader illustrates two things. First, the interaction of leaders, domestic political institutions, and the international system shape the relative importance of leaders in a given situation. Second, in situations where leaders can make a difference, their individual beliefs matter a great deal in determining policy outcomes.

To start, consider Kaiser Wilhelm II, who led Germany throughout World War I. He came to the throne at the age of twenty-nine, in 1888, and two years after that he forced the resignation of Bismarck, the architect of German unification. Wilhelm II fits the profile of a leader predisposed to aggression, which played out in his decision to mobilize the German army (a key step in escalating the July crisis preceding the outbreak of war). From the start of his reign, Wilhelm II was insecure about Germany's position in the international system and his own position among European monarchs, especially relative to established leaders such as the United Kingdom's Queen Victoria. He believed that Germany had to strive to assume its "place in the sun." Queen Victoria was Wilhelm II's grandmother, and Wilhelm II attempted to build German power to match that of the United Kingdom. Some argue that this attitude played a role in his approval of Admiral Tirpitz's ambitious plan to expand the German navy prior to World War I, which touched off the Anglo–German arms race. The United Kingdom possessed the world's most capable navy, and Kaiser Wilhelm II wanted Germany to catch up, competing first with Victoria, then her successor King Edward VII (1901–1910), then his successor King George V (1910–1936) (Figure 5.5).

Wilhelm, while prince, had entered the military as a captain in 1880 and was promoted quickly due to his royal heritage, reaching the rank of colonel by 1885. Yet Wilhelm did not seem to recognize that his heritage drove his rapid ascent, instead viewing it as evidence of his military talent. He saw his military experience as giving him strategic expertise. According to one biographer, Wilhelm II had an "exaggerated opinion of his

(cont.)

Figure 5.5. Kaiser Wilhelm's frenetic rivalry with British leaders such as King George V fueled the Anglo–German naval race and a broader antagonism that helped pave the way for World War I. George, Wilhelm's uncle, is seen here (left) with Wilhelm in 1913, on the eve of the most terrible war in human history.
©Print Collector / Contributor/Hulton Archive/ Getty Images.

own military competence," and "his presumption that he was endowed with the qualities of a military leader had disastrous consequences" (Rohl 1998, 441). While in the army, Wilhelm II never saw combat. He therefore had precisely the type of military experience that some research on leaders suggests makes future aggression more likely – national military service, but without combat experience.

In the July crisis, Wilhelm II demonstrated a view of deterrence and war consistent with his prior military experience. He consistently encouraged the Austro-Hungarian Empire to get tough with the Serbs, believing that the Serbs would eventually back down, and that if they did not, German military might would allow Germany to emerge triumphant in any war that did occur.

Finally, Wilhelm II had lifelong medical issues that shaped his perspective on the world. Due to a complicated birth, some of the nerves leading to his left arm were severed, leaving his arm partly paralyzed. The arm never recovered, and a childhood spent enduring attempts to fix it, including electroshock applications, left him embittered about his physical condition. Some argue that this led Wilhelm II to accentuate military power, in particular, at the national level. Research also suggests that Wilhelm II may have suffered from a personality disorder. As a leader in an autocratic regime, he faced

(cont.)

some constraints, but had much independence, in shaping Germany's trajectory, and he arguably played a decisive role in the march of Germany towards World War I.

In contrast to the role played by Wilhelm II was that played by the leader of the United Kingdom, Germany's most powerful counterpart at the outset of the war. Britain's decision, made by Prime Minister Asquith, to get involved in World War I arguably had more to do with structural and domestic political conditions. Asquith became prime minister in 1908 and supported an expansion of the British Navy to counteract Germany's rapid naval construction program. However, most commentators believe that it was the British commitment to Belgium, more than anything else, that brought England into the war. Germany's invasion of Belgium as part of its Schlieffen Plan strategy for conquering France forced Britain's hand. This would have occurred regardless of who was prime minister.

Wilhelm II and Asquith are discussed above for their roles in the outbreak of war. As this chapter discusses, the relevance of leaders can go beyond the outbreak of war to cover decisions during wars. And the interaction between leaders and bureaucratic institutions such as the military can be critical. Yet this does not always happen in easily predictable ways, reflecting the fact that the impact of leaders, while real, can be hard to forecast at times.

The British prime minister who replaced Asquith in 1916, Lloyd George, had a consequential impact on the trajectory of the war despite structural and domestic political constraints facing Great Britain. Like Asquith, Lloyd George had no military experience. In fact, he had opposed British involvement in the Boer War in the late nineteenth century and also viewed the British naval buildup in the early twentieth century with suspicion. Once World War I started, however, Lloyd George supported British engagement, and he led efforts to replace Asquith in 1916. On becoming prime minister, Lloyd George initiated a critical policy change that involved taking on the powerful leadership of the British navy.

Germany was engaged in unrestricted submarine warfare against commercial shipping headed for Great Britain, and German U-boats were sinking so much commercial shipping that Great Britain's ability to continue fighting the war was in doubt. After reading British assessments of the impact of the U-boat war, Lloyd George decided that "'if Allied shipping continued steadily to disappear at this *accelerating rate* the end was not distant'" (Gartner 1997, 62).

At the time, the British Admiralty, leaders of the British navy, were deploying British naval ships throughout the Atlantic in an attempt to find and sink German U-boats. Like President Lincoln, who despite his lack of military experience challenged the expertise of General McClellan in the US Civil War, Lloyd George concluded that an alternative strategy was necessary. Instead of deploying the British Navy to search for and destroy U-boats, he would deploy them to protect commercial shipping in convoys. Since

(cont.)

commercial shipping was the center of gravity providing the supplies necessary to keep Britain in the war, it had to be protected above all else.

The British naval leaders protested bitterly, arguing that it was their job to fight, not to protect commercial ships. Lloyd George insisted, however, overriding their objections and ordering the implementation of the convoy system in April 1917. It turned out that Lloyd George was correct – and not only did implementation of the convoy system help protect commercial shipping, it also helped the British Navy sink more U-boats. While the British Navy only sank nineteen U-boats in 1915, before the convoy system was even considered, they sank sixty-nine in 1918, following the complete implementation of the convoy system.

It was Lloyd George's advocacy, in particular, that ensured the implementation of the convoy system, in the teeth of military opposition. This illustrates the way that individual leaders can make a difference even in a large-scale conflict such as World War I.

President Wilson was the architect of both America's initial decision to stay out of the war and its eventual entry. Wilson rose to the presidency as the Democratic Party nominee in 1912, following experiences as the governor of New Jersey, the president of Princeton University, and a professor at Princeton University. An intellectual at heart, one of Wilson's defining characteristics was his belief in himself and the moral correctness of his views.

Believing in the moral superiority of the United States relative to the feuding European powers, Wilson initially focused on ways to keep the United States out of the war. Wilson's reelection campaign in 1916 even focused, in part, on the success of his efforts to avoid US entanglement in World War I. Germany's January 1917 declaration of unrestricted submarine warfare did not just lead to strategic challenges for the British; it influenced the United States as well. As a traditionally neutral power, the United States, where there was already much public sympathy for Great Britain and the Entente powers, reacted strongly and negatively to Germany's announcement that US commercial vessels headed for the United Kingdom would now be subject to attack. This helped trigger American involvement in the war. It is probably fair to say that almost any US president, not just Wilson, would have gotten the United States involved at that point.

What was unique about Wilson, however, was the way he took the moment as an opportunity to assert the universal values at stake in the conflict and place himself at the center of the story. As historian Walter McDougall (1997, 132) writes, "He did it because he believed that remaining above the battle was the only way that he, Wilson, could exert the moral authority needed to end the war on terms that would make for a lasting peace." From the moment of the US decision to intervene, Wilson wanted to play a decisive role in the end of the war. This desire did help lead to the creation of the League of Nations, but it also led to disappointment for Wilson when, at the Versailles negotiations, he found the British and the French much more interested in punitive measures against the Germans than he thought was reasonable.

(cont.)

When Wilson refused to compromise, especially after his stroke, this reflected a key part of his personality that his political opponents at the time believed limited his effectiveness. After Wilson passed away, Republican Senator Henry Cabot Lodge discussed this explicitly. He stated that "Mr. Wilson in dealing with every great question thought first of himself. He may have thought of the country next, but there was a long interval . . . . Mr. Wilson was devoured by the desire for power" (quoted in McDougall 1997, 145). It was that desire for power that made him unable to compromise, because it was not just that he wanted power, but he wanted it on his own terms.

Thus, across World War I, a war where one might imagine leaders not playing a significant role, we see large variation in the relevance of leaders. In Germany, Kaiser Wilhelm II helped accelerate the process of escalation, whereas British Prime Minister Asquith played a less definitive role. During the war, British Prime Minister Lloyd George, through his willingness to challenge military leaders, drove changes in British naval strategy that proved crucial. After the war, US President Woodrow Wilson pursued a negotiation strategy that was likely unique to him and a function of his personality, but broader structural forces made his efforts unsuccessful.

QUANTITATIVE STUDY

Rebel Experience of Leaders and Nuclear Proliferation

The previous section used the concepts discussed in the chapter to explore the case of World War I, showing the way the life experiences and personalities of several national leaders in World War I did, or did not, influence the war. This section turns to another aspect of leaders and international politics: the way that a particular background experience of a leader, participating in a rebellion prior to entering office, can make that leader more likely to pursue nuclear weapons.

Nuclear weapons are one of the most important military technologies in world history. Political scientists have explored what makes countries more or less likely to pursue a nuclear weapons program. Most research on nuclear proliferation focuses on security threats that make countries feel that they need nuclear weapons, the way alliances shape whether countries pursue nuclear weapons, and how domestic political institutions influence how countries calculate the costs and benefits of nuclear weapons.

Political scientists Matthew Fuhrmann and Michael Horowitz (2015) investigated this question in 2015 with a new area of emphasis – the leader.

Research Question

What is the impact of having a former rebel become head of state on the probability that a country pursues nuclear weapons?

Theory and Hypothesis

Former rebels tend to place a higher emphasis on ensuring national independence, since they understand all too well the potential for rebellions. This makes them more likely to discount the possibility of using external alliances to provide for their security. Due to their efficacy beliefs from their experience as rebels, former rebels who become leaders are also more likely to underestimate the financial and political challenges associated with pursuing nuclear weapons.

Hypothesis: Countries with former rebels as heads of state are more likely than states with nonrebel leaders, on average, to pursue nuclear weapons programs.

Data

The data set includes all leader years in the international system from 1945 to 2000, meaning one observation per leader, per year. This is different from a country-year setup because there can be more than one observation in a given country year if there was more than one leader in a country in a given year. For example, if the data set extended to 2017, in the United States there would be an observation for Barack Obama, who was president until January 20, 2017, as well as an observation for Donald Trump, who took office on January 20. The data set contains 1,342 leaders covering 6,980 leader-year observations.

Dependent Variable

The dependent variable is a dichotomous variable, nuclear weapons pursuit, that is coded 1 if a leader is actively trying to build nuclear weapons in year t and 0 if not. Hypothesis 1 predicts that leaders with prior rebel experience will be more likely to pursue nuclear weapons. The article also uses alternative dependent variables, including whether a country begins a nuclear weapons program in a given year, as opposed to continuing a nuclear weapons program.

Independent Variable

The main independent variable is a dichotomous variable that measures whether a leader had rebel prior rebel experience. It is coded 1 if a leader was a member of a group that attempted to overthrow the government of a state, prior to entering office, and 0 otherwise. This includes individuals who participate in civil wars, such as Mao, individuals who participate in coups, such as Qaddafi, and individuals who fight in wars of national liberation, such as former Israeli Prime Minister David Ben-Gurion.

Control Variables

The model accounts for other potential factors that might influence the probability that a country pursues nuclear weapons. Some of these factors are irregular entry into office, prior civil war, regime type, the security threats a country faces, and whether a country has an alliance with a superpower.

Results

The quantitative analysis shows that prior rebel experience is strongly correlated with whether a country pursues nuclear weapons. There is less than a 0.01 percent chance that the results are due to chance alone. Substantively, rebel experience increases the probability of nuclear weapons pursuit by almost 415 percent (a fourfold increase). Former rebels have a 23 percent probability of pursuing nuclear weapons in a given year, as opposed to 4 percent for leaders who did not have rebel experience.

Conclusions

The results demonstrate that former rebels, from Ben-Gurion in Israel to Qaddafi in Libya to Hussein in Iraq, are significantly more likely to pursue nuclear weapons than leaders without rebel experience. This finding indicates the importance that individual leaders have in determining the course of international relations.

SUMMARY

The topic of leaders, domestic political institutions, and foreign policy decisionmaking is an important one for international politics. The relevance of leaders in some aspects of foreign policy decisionmaking is clear, but systematically analyzing interaction between leaders and domestic political institutions is complicated. This chapter makes a number of critical points on this topic, including:

- Leaders play a vital role in national security decisions, especially choices about war and peace.
- Leaders often face constraints when attempting to conduct foreign policy, including limits imposed by the international system and domestic political institutions.
- Leaders enter office through regular and irregular means, and those leaders who enter through irregular means are often more conflict-prone.
- Key life experiences that predict which leaders are more likely to start military conflicts include national military service but no combat experience, and prior rebel experience.
- Gender does not appear to impact whether leaders are more or less likely to start wars, but the jury is still out.
- Leaders in more autocratic countries, and especially personalist regimes, face fewer limitations on their power than in democracies, meaning leader preferences translate more directly into policy.
- Political parties, bureaucratic politics, the timing of elections, and fears about job security can also shape the way leaders behave.

KEY TERMS

"Great man history"	Efficacy beliefs
Statement of resolve	Ideology
Irregular and regular succession	Diversionary war
Selectorate	

REVIEW QUESTIONS

1. What are Kenneth Waltz's three levels of international politics? Which two of those levels prevent a leader from simply implementing the foreign policy of her choice at all times?
2. What kinds of leaders are more likely to take more risks? Does it matter what type of government (i.e. autocracy or democracy) they are governing?
3. What is the difference between regular entry into office and irregular entry into office for a leader?
4. How might the gender of a national leader influence foreign policy and international conflict?
5. What prior life experiences of leaders play the most important role in shaping their propensity to use military force once they become a leader?

6. What are the risks to a country of having a leader with chronic physical or mental health issues?
7. How do political parties, bureaucracies, and civil servants influence the way that leaders behave, especially in democracies?
8. What are examples of leaders who affected the onset and course of World War I?
9. What affects leaders' international reputations, once in office?

DISCUSSION QUESTIONS

1. How do you think world history might have been different if the following failed assassination attempts had succeeded: Franklin Roosevelt (1932); Adolf Hitler (1932); Ronald Reagan (1981)?
2. Let's say you are an evil genius, and want to create in your laboratory the most aggressive, pro-war leader possible. What kind of background a or personal characteristics would that leader have?
3. Are you confident that the domestic political institutions of your country, including its political parties, bureaucracies, civil servants, election system, legislature, courts, and other constraints on the national leader, would prevent a truly dangerous national leader from dragging your nation into a disastrous war?

ADDITIONAL READING

Byman, D. L. and Pollack., K. M. (2001). Let us now praise great men: bringing the statesman back in. *International Security* **25**(4), 107–146.
Carlyle, T. (1935). *On Heroes, Hero-Worship, and the Heroic in History*. London: Oxford University Press.
George, A. L. and George, J. L. (1964). *Woodrow Wilson and Colonel House: A Personality Study*. Mineola, NY: Dover Publications.
Johnson, D. D. P. and D. Tierney. (2011). The Rubicon theory of war: How the path to conflict reaches the point of no return. *International Security* **36**(1), 7–40.
Kahneman, D. (2011). *Thinking, Fast and Slow*, New York: Farrar, Straus, and Giroux.
Kennedy, A. B. (2011). *The International Ambitions of Mao and Nehru: National Efficacy Beliefs and the Making of Foreign Policy*, Cambridge: Cambridge University Press.
Lee, S. J. (1988). *Aspects of European History 1789–1980*, London: Routledge.
McDougall, W. (1997). *Promised Land, Crusader State: The American Encounter with the World since 1776*, New York: Houghton Mifflin.

REFERENCES

Birnbaum, M. and Jaffe, G. (2017, November 18). Frustrated foreign leaders bypass Washington in search of blue-state allies. *Washington Post*. www.washingtonpost.com/world/national-security
Bueno de Mesquita, B., Smith, A., Siverson, R. M. and Morrow, J. D. (2004). *The Logic of Political Survival*. Cambridge, MA: MIT Press.
Carlyle, T. (1968). *Carlyle on Heroes, Hero-Worship, and the Heroic in History*. London: Oxford University Press.

Chiozza, G. and Goemans, H. E. (2011). *Leaders and International Conflict*. New York: Cambridge University Press.

Donald, D. H. (1995). *Lincoln*, New York: Simon and Schuster.

Fletcher, M. (2001, September 22). Attack on America: Challenge like no other. *The Times* (London).

Ford, F. L. (1953). Three observers in Berlin: Rumbold, Dodd, and François-Poncet. In G. A. Craig and F. Gilbert (eds.). *The Diplomats, 1919–1939*. Princeton: Princeton University Press.

Fuhrmann, M. and Horowitz, M. C. (2015). When leaders matter: Rebel experience and nuclear proliferation. *Journal of Politics* **77**(1), 72–87.

Gartner, S. S. (1997). *Strategic Assessment in War*. New Haven: Yale University Press.

Horowitz, M. C., Stam, A. C., and Ellis, C. (2015). *Why Leaders Fight*. New York: Cambridge University Press.

Kertzer, J. (2018). *Resolve in International Politics*. Princeton: Princeton University Press.

Khong, Y. F. (1992). *Analogies at War: Korea, Munich, Dien Bien Phu, and the Vietnam Decisions of 1965*. Princeton: Princeton University Press.

Lee, S. J. (1988). *Aspects of European History 1789–1980*. London: Routledge.

Lupton, D. L. (2020). *Reputation for Resolve: How Leaders Signal Determination in International Politics*. Ithaca, NY: Cornell University Press.

McDermott, R. (2008). *Presidential Leadership, Illness, and Decision Making*. New York: Cambridge University Press.

McDougall, W. A. (1997). *Promised Land, Crusader State: The American Encounter with the World since 1776*. New York: Houghton Mifflin.

Rohl, J. C. G. (1998). *Young Wilhelm: The Kaiser's Early Life, 1859–1888*. New York: Cambridge University Press.

Saunders, E. N. (2011). *Leaders at War: How Presidents Shape Military Interventions*. Ithaca, NY: Cornell University Press.

Schelling, T. C. (1966). *Arms and Influence*. New Haven: Yale University Press.

Waltz, K. N. (1959). *Man, the State and War: A Theoretical Analysis*. New York: Columbia University Press.

Wolford, M. S. (2007). The turnover trap: New leaders, reputation, and international conflict. *American Journal of Political Science* **51**(4), 771–781.

Yarhi-Milo, K. (2018). *Who Fights for Reputation: The Psychology of Leaders in International Conflict*. Princeton: Princeton University Press.

6   Economics and War

PAUL POAST

Introduction

When thinking of war, what comes to mind? Perhaps you lament war's destruction and devastation. Or maybe you think of famous battles, influential weapons, or notable commanders and generals. But what about money and markets? The brute reality is that fighting a war requires resources and acquiring those resources requires money and markets. The father of modern economics, Adam Smith, recognized this point back in 1776. In *The Wealth of Nations*, Smith wrote, "the wealth of a neighboring nation [is] dangerous in war and politics . . . [because] in a state of hostility it may enable our enemies to maintain fleets and armies superior to our own" (Smith 1952, paragraph 40). At the same time, the use of force has economic consequences. War can wreak economic devastation, which is why some have declared that asking who won a war is like asking who won the San Francisco earthquake (Waltz 1959, 1). Such devastation is heightened if it is fought on a nation's territory. Moreover, if two countries become dependent on one another economically, perhaps through trade, this can further raise the costs associated with war (since, presumably, the international commerce between the two nations would cease or be severely reduced by war). War's potential to wipe out trade is why another famous economist, John Stuart Mill (1884, paragraph 14), remarked in the mid nineteenth century that "It is commerce which is rapidly rendering war obsolete."

When discussing the economic aspects of military power, a useful starting point is a classic idea familiar to students who have taken an introductory economics course: the "guns versus butter" tradeoff. According to this concept, a national economy has a set endowment of resources – capital, labor, and land – that determine all that the economy can produce at a given moment in time. Overall, the goods that can be produced from these resources fit into one of two categories: "guns" or "butter."

"Guns" are all means of arming to secure a state: soldiers, sailors, pilots, support personnel, guns, tanks, military aircraft, warships, missiles, submarines, etc. At the end of the day, a primary function of government is to provide external protection, which is facilitated by possessing such "guns." But a government should not focus solely on providing guns.

The Nobel-winning economist James Tobin, along with the esteemed economist William Nordhaus, once referred to military spending as a "regrettable expense." This is because "No reasonable country buys 'national defense' for its own sake... if there were no war or risk of war, there would be no need for defense expenditures and no one would be the worse without them" (Tobin and Nordhaus 1972, 8). For example, while an infrastructure project can immediately enhance private business productivity, the purchase of arms does not directly lead to further productive enhancements in the economy.

"Butter" generally refers to the government's provision of a host of goods aimed at enhancing social welfare (beyond the welfare gained by protection from foreign aggression). "Butter" could literally refer to the provision of butter to citizens (and real butter would definitely be preferable to margarine), but it usually means the provision of items such as roads, hospitals, and schools. For instance, in discussing how spending on arms can reduce the funds available for spending on social programs, US President Dwight D. Eisenhower (1953) famously remarked:

Every gun that is made, every warship launched, every rocket fired signifies, in the final sense, a theft from those who hunger and are not fed, those who are cold and are not clothed. This world in arms is not spending money alone. It is spending the sweat of its laborers, the genius of its scientists, the hopes of its children.

Eisenhower then made the tradeoffs explicit:

The cost of one modern heavy bomber is this: a modern brick school in more than 30 cities. It is two electric power plants, each serving a town of 60,000 population. It is two fine, fully equipped hospitals. It is some 50 miles of concrete highway. We pay for a single fighter plane with a half million bushels of wheat. We pay for a single destroyer with new homes that could have housed more than 8,000 people.

Cognizance of the guns-versus-butter tradeoff contributes to the regular complaints by officials in the United States that its European allies in the North Atlantic Treaty Organization (NATO) spend an insufficient amount on guns. As former US President Donald Trump declared while campaigning in 2016: "We pay so much disproportionately more for NATO. We are getting ripped off by every country in NATO, where they pay virtually nothing, most of them. And we're paying the majority of the costs" (quoted in Kessler 2016).

Overall, the guns-versus-butter tradeoff provides a useful foundation for discussing the means and methods that governments use to acquire arms. It shows that the production of "guns" must come from a nation's resources. Consequently, it also shows that there are, as the saying goes, "no free lunches" in the economy: acquiring more "guns" means giving up, all things being equal, more "butter." Nations address this tradeoff in a range of ways, from North Korea literally starving its population to prop up a massive military and nuclear weapons program (Neuman 2021), to a country like Luxembourg that spends less than 1 percent of the country's Gross Domestic Product (GDP) on defense.

Studying the economics of war is about taking seriously the guns-versus-butter tradeoff. And, you, the average college student, should take this seriously, because it affects you in the most direct way: more rifles can mean fewer teachers or higher tuition. How should you think about this tradeoff? This chapter explores the economics of war, focusing in particular on how interstate wars are funded, the economic consequences of interstate wars, and how economic factors affect the onset of interstate wars (on economic dimensions of substate conflict, see Chapters 2, 7, 8, and 13). The first part of this chapter explores how *consuming* guns influences butter consumption by understanding how arms are acquired via markets and money. The second part of this chapter explores how *using* guns influences butter consumption by unpacking how the "butter" acquired via international commerce can make countries wary of using guns.

Guns and Butter

Perhaps the most important function of the state is to protect its citizens, and the most important task of the state when it comes to accomplishing this goal is to muster the resources necessary to fight wars. Indeed, some have proposed that the European state was created for just such a function; the sociologist Charles Tilly (1975, 42) once remarked, "War made the state, and the state made war."

The critical importance of economic mobilization for war was emphasized in the two world wars of the twentieth century. In particular, America's industrial power was described as the "arsenal of democracy" (the phrase coined by the Frenchman Jean Monnet and used by President Franklin Roosevelt). The idea of using economic power for wartime production is so powerful that it is used even outside the context of war. In early 2021, US President Joe Biden (2021) referred to the US economy as being on a "war footing" when it came to producing the equipment and vaccines necessary to "combat" the virus causing the COVID-19 global pandemic. Indeed, the strong link between economic strength and military might is why formative books in the study of international politics stress the war–economy link. In his *Theory of International Politics*, Kenneth Waltz (1979, 94) wrote that "economic capabilities cannot be separated from the other capabilities of states," a point that Robert Gilpin (1981) reinforced in *War and Change in World Politics*. States may not always choose to convert all their wealth into military power. But states must possess a sufficient level of economic and financial wherewithal to equip a military capable of providing for the country's defense.

This section focuses on how economic resources enable states to acquire arms. To explain how economic power underpins military power, this section explores how governments work with markets to acquire military capabilities and how governments obtain the money to finance the purchase of these capabilities. Hence, this section will be divided into two parts: military power through markets, and military power via money.

Note that this section focuses on the tradeoffs a government faces when it relies on *its own* economic resources to provide for its own security. States can acquire security through an ally, meaning another state agrees to use its own arms or troops to secure the state. Allies offer the state a means of acquiring military power that circumvents the internal guns-versus-butter tradeoff. Indeed, as suggested by the above citations of US leaders complaining about NATO, sometimes a state can feel that it is enabling its allies in consuming *too much* butter. Though we will not be able to say more in this chapter about the role of allies in the guns-versus-butter tradeoff, this idea is discussed more in Chapter 9.

Markets and Military Power

A government requires "guns" to provide for its own security and to fight a war. The notion of "guns" captured in the guns-versus-butter tradeoff is not intended to be fully literal. Of course a military requires actual guns in the form of rifles and handguns of various types. But the word "guns" is instead intended to capture the broader notion of "actual" military capacity. (This is in contrast to "latent" military capacity, meaning the overall economic power of the economy that could *potentially* be translated into military power.) Active military capacity includes *weapons*, meaning the equipment used by a state's military to engage in conflict, and *warriors*, meaning the people who comprise a state's military and use the military equipment acquired by the state.

In either case – weapons or warriors – military capacity is acquired through markets. The word "market" need not (and does not) refer to a "perfectly competitive market" filled with numerous buyers and sellers adjusting and haggling over prices until sales are made and a "market-clearing" price is found. The markets in which military capacity is acquired are a far cry from perfectly competitive markets. As economist Brad De Long (1993, 247), in reference to the United States during World War II, argues, "I have never thought that economists should try to account for the World War II experience using a market-clearing, competitive model." Indeed, there are times when a government's acquisition policies are of such a draconian nature, as with the implementation of mandatory universal conscription to recruit military personnel (discussed below), that one would find little to resemble a market transaction. To be clear, when discussing government acquisition of military capacity, the word "market" is used in its most basic sense: a place where a buyer acquires a good from a seller at an agreed-upon price. The market might have only a handful of buyers (in fact, there might well just be a single buyer), only a small number of sellers (in reality, depending on the item, there might only be one entity capable of selling it), and heavy government intervention (in actuality, there might be a command economy whereby the government directly controls production and consumption). While all of these are deviations from the perfectly competitive market frequently studied in introductory economics texts, military capacity is nevertheless acquired through "markets" in the broadest and most basic sense: a place where suppliers provide a good to a consumer. We will now explore the two markets for military capacity: the market for weapons and the market for warriors.

The Markets for Weapons

The notion of "weapons" is used broadly in this chapter. It stands for three types of military material: support systems, small arms, and major weapons systems. We will now look at each type of military material and discuss the market for each type.

We begin with support systems. It has long been recognized that militaries rely on logistics, as conveyed by the phrase frequently attributed to Napoleon that "an army marches on its stomach." Everything from barracks to mess halls to pay services plays an essential role in the smooth operation of a military, either at war or during peace. In military parlance, supply equipment is referred to as the "tail" needed to support the "tooth" equipment and personnel (i.e., those actually carrying out the fighting).

Indeed, in an effort to focus more military assets on actual "tooth" activities, the modern United States military has sought to allocate an increasing number of "tail" activities to "Private Military Contractors" (PMCs). Much attention is given to PMCs such as Blackwater or Executive Outcomes. The former provided security detail in Iraq for US forces in the early to mid 2000s, while the latter conducted full-scale military operations on behalf of the Sierra Leone government in the mid 1990s. But the reality is that PMCs are primarily used to fulfill the logistical needs associated with "tail" activities (Erbel and Kinsey 2016, 71). While many of these PMCs perform basic tasks (e.g., cooking, cleaning, barracks maintenance, transportation services), more frequently they are relied upon to provide maintenance for ever more technologically sophisticated weapons systems (which are developed in the private sector, where some of the relevant intellectual property is retained by the firm) (Erbel and Kinsey 2016, 73). This may well explain why, for instance, in 2008 the nearly 72,000 PMCs in Afghanistan far outnumbered the approximately 32,000 US troops. Indeed, the ratio of PMCs to regular US military personnel has gradually increased over time, from 1:20 in World War I, to 1:6 during Vietnam, to a complete reversal of the ratio in current wars.

While the "tail" is critical to military success, a military's hallmark is the personnel and weapons in its "tooth." Small arms comprise the first component of "tooth" weapons. Small arms are, quite simply, the weapons directly carried by military personnel. These range from rifles and machine guns to long swords and machetes. These are the smallest and least expensive of the three types of military material. This is why the small-arms sector best approximates the ideal market economy: there are a number of firms that can produce arms and a number of entities with the financial and economic capacity to purchase such arms. But even then, while the price in a competitive market should be relatively stable, the price for a given small arm can in actuality vary widely, depending on how it was produced, to whom it was sold (e.g., to a state or a nonstate actor) and the demand for the item locally (e.g., if it is in or near an active combat zone). This is best illustrated by perhaps the most widely distributed small arm in history: the Kalashnikov rifle, also known as the AK-47. It was initially produced by the Soviet Union in the late 1940s and early 1950s, but the production capacity eventually spread to numerous other countries, ranging from Iran to China to Greece. The AK-47 proliferated to combat zones around the world because it was sold and resold in both resale markets and markets for smuggled goods (black markets) (Poast 2006, 138). Given the number of firms in various nations willing to produce and supply Kalashnikov rifles, the price of the rifle should be comparatively low and relatively uniform. But this is not the case. According to a 2017 report by *Global Financial Integrity*, the price in US dollars for an AK-47 can vary from as low as $148 (when produced by a small-scale local producer in Pakistan) to as high as $3,600 (when purchased through the "Dark Web" illegal online market) (Mavrellis 2017).

Major weapons systems are the other component of "tooth" weapons. These are the weapons that cannot be carried by an individual soldier but are in many ways the primary instruments of state military power: cannons, tanks, warships, and so forth. A critical

Figure 6.1. Willow Run B-24 bomber factory during World War II. Each plane had about 1.5 million parts, and by 1944 Willow Run was producing a plane every sixty-three minutes, twenty-four hours per day, seven days per week. With good reason President Franklin Roosevelt referred to the United States in 1940 as the "arsenal of democracy."
United States Library of Congress.

difference between how major weapons systems and small arms are produced is resource intensity. Constructing a major weapons system of any form is substantially more resource-intensive than constructing a small arm. As a simple illustration of the resource intensity that can go into major weapons systems, consider that the Ford plant to build the B-24 bomber in Willow Run, Michigan, during World War II had an area of 3,500,000 square feet, making it the largest factory under one roof anywhere in the world (Figure 6.1). The assembly line to produce the B-24 was more than a mile (1.6 kilometres) long. Operating and maintaining a major weapon system also requires more personnel than operating and maintaining a small arm. A single soldier can operate and maintain a rifle. In contrast, a single major weapon system, such as a fighter jet, requires a large number of individuals to operate and maintain. Even if a single fighter jet is flown by a single pilot, there is a sizable crew of mechanics and technicians required to prep and repair the vehicle, along with a radio tower crew required to assist the pilot in flight.

This resource intensity means that major weapons systems tend to be highly client-specific, as the systems are "made to order" and typically unique to the needs of a particular government. Consequently, unlike the competitive markets for small arms, the markets for major weapons systems become what economists call a **dual monopoly**: a market with a single buyer for a good (called a **monopsony**) and one supplier for the good (called a **monopoly**). Indeed, it is an understatement to say that a dual monopoly market is "unlike" a competitive market; it is the *exact* opposite of a competitive market with many buyers and sellers. When a government seeks to acquire a major weapons system, there might be an initial step whereby the government requests proposals for creating the weapons system. This can result in major weapons systems being quite expensive (or at least more expensive than they would be in a more competitive market) (Augustine 1983, 105, 107).

Perhaps the main driver of increases in the cost of major weapons systems is the advancement in technology. This is most evident in aircraft production, which led then Chairman of the

Defense Science Board (and eventual CEO of defense contractor Lockheed Martin) Norman Augustine to remark in 1983 (in only a half-jest) that, "In the year 2054, the entire defense budget will purchase just one aircraft. This aircraft will have to be shared by the Air Force and Navy 3-1/2 days each per week except for leap year, when it will be made available to the Marines for the extra day" (Augustine 1983, 107).

Interestingly, governments have historically seemed more than willing to accept the high costs of major weapons systems. This can be largely attributed to politics: at both the international and domestic levels, political pressures push governments to ignore the price being paid for a major weapons system.

Internationally, a government could seek a weapons system of a particular "value" in order to acquire a weapon already in the possession of a rival or to gain an advantage over a rival. In other words, a classic arms-race dynamic compels the government to seek a weapon without paying attention to cost. For example, arms race competition is a well-studied component of the lead-up to World War I, with total defense spending for the major European states rising nearly 40 percent between 1908 and 1913 (the fastest rate since 1870) (Stevenson 2007, 132). The historian David Stevenson (2007, 133) wrote that "the suddenness, accelerating pace, and simultaneity that characterized the growth of the Continental armies strongly suggest a competitive process, driven by a deteriorating external environment that every country viewed as menacing." While some of the additional arms, as suggested by Stevenson's quote, were additional rifles and soldiers, a significant portion was driven by the acquisition of major naval weapons systems. Between 1898 and 1903 alone, the pursuit of naval expansion led the German government to increase its debt by 672 million marks (D'Lugo and Rogowski 1993, 81). This was matched by the British raising their naval expenditure estimate for 1903–1904 to £2.5 million; in actuality, the 1903–1904 naval estimate came in at £4 million (D'Lugo and Rogowski 1993, 85). Such ratcheting of military expenditures has consequences, as governments cannot indefinitely trade "butter" for more "guns."

Domestically, a government can become impervious to the price of producing a major weapons system because the funding of such a system is a form of political patronage. This lies at the heart of President Dwight D. Eisenhower's warning regarding the "military industrial complex," meaning the entrenched relationship between government and military firms (Poast 2006, 50). In his 1961 farewell address, Eisenhower (1961) warned of the corrupting influence of special interests in seeking to maintain a high military expenditure level:

In the councils of government, we must guard against the acquisition of unwarranted influence, whether sought or unsought, by the military-industrial complex. The potential for the disastrous rise of misplaced power exists and will persist. We must never let the weight of this combination endanger our liberties or democratic processes. We should take nothing for granted. Only an alert and knowledgeable citizenry can compel the proper meshing of the huge industrial and military machinery of defense with our peaceful methods and goals, so that security and liberty may prosper together.

One way these dynamics play out is that munitions manufacturers are able to secure Congressional support for their weapons by spreading out the economic benefits to a high percentage of senators and congresspeople through subcontractors. Any individual senator or congressperson is more likely to vote to purchase a weapon if that contract translates into jobs

Figure 6.2. The B-2 Spirit bomber. With spreading of production across the vast majority of states and congressional districts, congressional support becomes more likely. The military-industrial complex manipulates the incentives of congresspeople in order to get the bomber that the Air Force and the weapons manufacturers want. But is the public interest served?
©Stocktrek/Photodisc/Getty Images.

in her state or district. For example, the components of the B-2 Spirit bomber (Figure 6.2) are produced or assembled in 46 out of 50 different states, and 383 of 435 congressional districts (Silverstein and Moag 2000). When the Congress authorizes purchasing the B-2, the manufacturers get increased profits, the US Air Force gets more bombers, and sitting members of Congress boost their odds of reelection. But do these dynamics of the military-industrial complex undermine the ability to have open debate about whether purchasing these bombers on balance serves the national interest, and merits the guns–butter tradeoff?

The Markets for Warriors

While the acquisition of weapons can be quite expensive, warriors are also a major expense of most militaries. The term "warriors" refers to military labor, meaning all persons employed in a government's armed forces. This includes soldiers, sailors, pilots, and support personnel (ranging from technicians to cooks). Prior to the industrialization of military power following the industrial revolution, labor was the primary military instrument of states. But even with the increased mechanization of military power, labor remains a major military expense for governments. Consider the US military, the most technologically advanced military that has ever existed. The reliance on personnel can be seen in the United States defense budget. In 2021, the total defense budget for the United States military was approximately $750 billion. While a sizable portion of the budget goes towards equipment (in the form of procurement, research and development, and maintenance), approximately one-third of the budget is focused on pay and benefits for military personnel (Harrison and Daniels 2021). This does not include "off-budget" expenditures, such as expenses for veteran care. Once such additional expenses are accounted for, nearly half of US defense spending is dedicated to personnel.

In one key respect, the market for military labor is similar to the market for weapons: it is a monopsony. On the one hand, it is true that there are mercenaries who would sell their services to the highest bidder, such as those who comprised the bulk of the Brandenburg-Prussian army during the Thirty Years War (Nolan 2008, 378). In such a case, there are multiple "buyers" of the labor. On the other hand, since the French Revolutionary and Napoleonic Wars, soldiers have largely come from the population under control of the government: the proverbial "citizen-soldier" (Avant 2000). The result was that there was now a sole buyer of military labor within a market. (E.g., for the pool of French citizens, the only buyer of their military services was the French government.)

In another respect, the market for warriors is much different than the market for weapons: there are *many* suppliers of warriors. Essentially, the entire population of a country serves as a pool for military personnel. This should mean that the government can acquire military labor at a low price. However, we are talking about people joining an occupation where violent death is a real and imminent possibility. Hence, citizens of a country may be reluctant to join the military. Indeed, compelling the citizenry to fight on behalf of the state has been a perennial challenge of governments. For example, when improvements in firearms increased the lethality of artillery in the 1700s, this created a problem described well by political scientist Barry Posen (1993, 84), of "how to keep these dispersed, scared, lonely individuals risking their own lives, and cooperating to take the lives of others."

While compelling an assembled army to fight is a challenge, bringing the army together in the first place is also not a trivial task. Governments have largely relied on two systems for recruiting military labor: **volunteerism** and conscription.

The phrase "volunteer" does not mean that the soldiers freely give of their time and effort (and possibly lives) to the state. Compensation is still required. While the government can make appeals to nationalism, patriotism, and civic duty, these may prove inadequate to entice a sufficient number of volunteers. Monetary compensation or material compensation (also called "in-kind payments") must be offered. The positive of using monetary and material compensation to incentivize volunteerism is that the government is, at least in theory, only attracting people who are willing to join and fight. From the standpoint of societal wellbeing, it is most efficient to allow people to choose whether their labor time is best allocated to military service or elsewhere. However, depending on the incentives that must be offered, this could prove quite expensive from a budgetary perspective.

The potentially budgetary high cost of volunteers is why governments have, from time to time, turned to conscription. In a **conscription** system, the government mandates military service for all (universal conscription) or a portion (selective conscription) of the population. Rather than offering positive inducements to join the military, the government relies on the threat of punishment for not complying with an order to participate. Punishments could range from fines to imprisonment. While this can lower the budgetary cost for a given size military, it has a cost: potentially high inefficiencies. If the conscription system is universal, then the requirement of military service will compel people to forgo employment and life opportunities that may have produced greater individual and societal benefits. Consider Henry Moseley, a British physicist and likely Nobel Laureate who was conscripted into service and then died during World War I.

In short, the central issue for governments in acquiring military labor is the tradeoff between conscription and an all-volunteer force. And as has been already suggested, the choice of recruitment system is as much a political decision as an economic one. Just as the need of governments to acquire major weapons systems was a function of both international and domestic political considerations, the same goes for the choice of recruitment system.

Domestically, conscription can be more politically contentious than an all-volunteer force. Conscription is generally politically unpopular. Enacting conscription raises potential political costs for the leader and even risks protests – an example is Israel, where serious consideration is being given to ending compulsory military service due to growing discontent among younger Israeli citizens over the issue (Berger 2019). Enacting conscription generates a guns-versus-butter tradeoff that may be politically risky.

Internationally, a country's choice of recruitment system might be compelled by arms-racing dynamics. If a country's neighbors are building up larger militaries via conscription, then that country might itself adopt conscription to build up its own military. Additionally, the choice of recruitment system conveys information to other countries. Because conscription is politically costly domestically, adopting such a system conveys a government's resolve to take measures necessary to achieve security. From the perspective of other states, such a signal suggests that the state would be more likely to make the hard choices necessary to fight a war. Such a signal could deter a threatening state or reassure potential allies that the government will be less likely to "free-ride" on the contributions of others. This is important, as a major issue in alliance politics is how states can avoid the issue of free-riding, meaning they contribute their fair share to a joint military effort. Hence, adopting conscription could be politically useful by making the state more likely to attract allies (Horowitz et al. 2017).

Money and Military Power

Acquiring the instruments of military power is expensive. In 43 BCE, during his fifth oration to the Senate pleading for opposition to Mark Antony, Cicero famously remarked that the "sinew of war" was "a limitless supply of money." Cicero was echoing an even earlier assessment by Thucydides in his history of the Peloponnesian War: "war is a matter not so much of arms as of expenditure." Indeed, so critical is money for the conduct of war that central banks, the institutions of government responsible for managing an economy's money supply, were developed largely out of a need to facilitate war finance. For example, the Bank of England was formed by the British government in 1694 to ease the expense of its wars against Louis XIV of France, while the Banque de France was instituted by Napoleon as a means of financially supporting his military campaigns.

Allocating money towards arms can be conceptualized as sacrificing "butter" for "guns." This is because the monies used on "guns" are no longer available to use for other government programs, whether infrastructure projects or social policies (the proverbial butter offered by governments). Acquiring the monies for "guns" can be done in a host of ways, ranging from forced labor to receiving reparation payments from the defeated side. But by and large, governments have three primary ways of taking money from "butter" and allocating it towards "guns": tax, print money, or borrow (or some combination of the three) (Capella-Zielinski 2016, 14).

Taxation is the most direct, and oldest, means of acquiring military power. So tight is the link between taxation and military power, that many scholars who study the creation of states argue that state institutions and bureaucracies were created expressly for the purpose of taxing citizens in order to finance a military (Fukuyama 2011, 111–114). The taxes can range from standard income taxes (see the case study below) to taxes on inherited wealth (Scheve and Stasavage 2012). Indeed, some scholars have shown a link between major war and increases in the top rate of inheritance taxes. A government could also rely on taxing goods entering the country – imports. But this source of tax revenue can be unreliable during an actual war. As US Congressman Cordell Hull remarked in 1910 (during congressional debates over the implementation of an income tax), "We cannot expect always to be at peace. If this nation were tomorrow plunged into a war with a great commercial country from which we now receive a large portion of our imports, our customs revenues would inevitably decline and we would be helpless to prosecute that war or any other war of great magnitude without taxing the wealth of this country in the form of incomes" (quoted in Poast 2006, 20). One benefit of taxation is that the total budgetary cost of the war is kept low because, by paying for the war with current revenues, the state avoids the interest payments associated with borrowing. The other benefit is fairness: assuming the soldiers themselves are not taxed as heavily as the rest of the populace, those citizens who do not fight pay for those who do fight. But taxation has notable disadvantages. First, there is a hard limit on the extent to which a government can tax, namely 100 percent of citizen income (and likely lower than that rate). Second, taxes can heighten citizen discontent with the military and, if the country is engaged in a war, make the war unpopular. As a *Washington Post* editorial remarked in 1919 in response to the passage of a tax bill related to US expenses in prosecuting World War I, "The average citizen feels the effect of the war tax when he arises in the morning . . . he is reminded of it the last thing at night when he puts on his tax-assessed pajamas" (quoted in Flores-Macias and Kreps 2013, 836).

Printing currency entails putting new money in circulation in order to cover military expenditures. In this case, the government leverages its monopoly control of the creation of currency by forcing military personnel and suppliers of military equipment to accept government currency as payment. The consequence of overproducing currency is inflation. The famous economist Milton Friedman (1963, 17) observed that "inflation is always and everywhere a monetary phenomenon." The reason is simple: if the number of goods available for purchase stays the same but there is now more currency available for purchases, then consumers have more money to use to pay for those goods. The result is a "bidding up" of the price. If such a bidding up is expected and steady, then the consequences can be minimal. However, rapid monetary growth can cause sudden increases in prices. For instance, the massive money supply growth in the Southern Confederacy induced price increases that were dramatic and debilitating. Within a few years, prices rose for wheat by 1,700 percent, for bacon by 2,500 percent, and for flour by 2,800 percent (Fulghum 1979). Inflation and its more dire consequences are not uncommon during war. Far from it, as it is perhaps one of the oldest economic consequences of war. While he did not explicitly discuss debasement or the printing of money, Sun Tzu in *The Art of War* (1963, 74) observed that "Where the army is, prices are high; when prices rise the wealth of the people is exhausted." It is for this reason that governments have implemented wartime rationing as a means of limiting the ability of the civilian populace to "bid up" the price of goods. During World War II, for example, the British government immediately implemented rationing programs. This contrasted with World War I, in which the British government never instituted rationing. One measure of the price level in Britain, the *Labour Gazette*'s cost-of-living index, rose by 43 percent during World War II.

While still a notable increase in prices, this was less than half of the increase observed in World War I (Braun and McGrattan 1993, 214).

Borrowing is an alternative to taxation and printing money. In fact, as the means of war became increasingly expensive, especially after the year 1500 or so, governments increasingly have relied on borrowing to pay for the acquisition of military equipment and labor. For instance, governments in World War I ran campaigns to encourage the public to lend them money through the purchase of bonds, as famously captured by war bond posters. Posters for the United States, Britain, and Germany are shown in Figure 6.3. The German poster is of particular note, as it is very explicit in linking the money raised from the bond purchase to the acquisition of military equipment: "This is how your money helps you fight! Turned into submarines, it keeps enemy shells away! That's why you should subscribe to war bonds!"

Borrowing has advantages and disadvantages. The advantages to borrowing are obvious. Unlike taxation, borrowing through the issuance of bonds enables a government to delay incurring the budgetary costs of acquiring military power. Another advantage of borrowing is that, compared to taxation, it grants governments access to a substantially larger pool of funds. Taxes have an upper bound of 100 percent and public resistance will likely keep taxes well below that level.

Borrowing's advantages are directly tied to its disadvantages. A key drawback to borrowing is that it requires a government to find a willing lender. This can be difficult as it runs into what is known as the **fundamental problem of sovereign finance**: the inability of lenders to compel governments to repay debt. Governments are sovereign, meaning there is no higher political authority above them. Hence, while an individual could be taken to bankruptcy court in order to compel the repayment of debts, this is not the case with sovereign governments. If a sovereign government chooses to default on its debts, there is no legal recourse that can be pursued by the lenders. The uncertainty of debt repayment can make lenders highly reluctant to allow a government to borrow funds. To compensate for the possibility of default, the lender could ask for a higher interest rate. This means the government will have to pay back in the future the borrowed amount *plus* an additional quantity of money. Hence, while borrowing funds can be advantageous to a government, as it allows a government to acquire the funds required to finance its arms acquisition, it has the drawback of placing the government in a situation where it must make a larger repayment in the future.

A deceptive property of borrowing is that, in the short run, one could think of borrowing money to finance the military as a way of acquiring funds for arms that does not require reducing the funds allocated to "butter." In the long run, however, the bonds used to borrow funds must be paid when the bonds reach their maturity date. If the bond repayment is accomplished via taxes, then the government will have fewer funds at that point to allocate to social programs. Hence, while the government might avoid the "guns-versus-butter" tradeoff in the short run, the tradeoff will be realized in the long run. Of course, the government could just issue new bonds in order to raise funds to pay off the maturing bonds. This is the sovereign equivalent of paying off one credit card with another credit card. The problem with this strategy is that lenders may well request a slightly higher interest rate in order to purchase the new debt. This is because, as with an individual who continually rotates through credit cards in order to make payments to creditors, lenders could become wary of lending to a

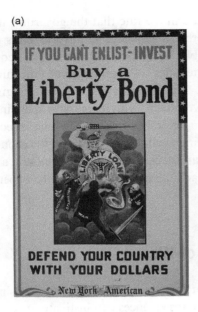

Figure 6.3. World War I bond posters: (a) United States, (b) Germany, and (c) Great Britain. When governments issue war bonds to finance war efforts, they are marketing a product, just like any business, leveraging calls to patriotism to persuade citizens to buy the bonds.

United States Library of Congress (a, b); (c) is from Wikipedia, which in turn indicates the source is the United Kingdom government.

government that continually issues new debt to pay off old debt. The increase in interest rates charged to the government by lenders means the government must now set aside additional funds to make the interest payments. Given the prominence of government involvement in many sectors of an economy, an increase in the rate that the government must pay to borrow could also raise the interest rates offered to others. The government's continued borrowing could also reduce the pool of loanable funds available to other economic actors. These consequences are the classic characteristics of **crowding-out**, meaning that government borrowing impedes private borrowing. This happens because, at any given time, banks only have so much money to lend. If the government, with its massive spending needs, begins using these funds, there is less available for other borrowers. The end effect is that, in essence, borrowing for arms reduces the borrowing available for butter in the economy. This is partially why some scholars have found that states lacking adequate economic and financial capacity will seek to avoid war (as they simply lack the means to finance the expenses needed to fight a war) (Shea and Poast 2017).

The Economic Consequences of War

Beyond the necessity of economic might to acquire the means of exercising military force, war has economic consequences, and those consequences can instigate or restrain the use of force. With respect to instigating the use of force, states have used military power as a way to acquire economic resources. From Iraq's 1990 invasion of Kuwait as a response to a dispute over a shared oilfield, to the use of "gunboat diplomacy" in the nineteenth century to compel trade openness and foreign debt repayments, there is a long history of commercial interests serving as motivation to engage in militarized violence. Moreover, a state may have an incentive to enter a war in order to protect a key trade partner from military aggression, such as the United States leading the coalition in 1990–1991 to protect Saudi Arabia from invasion by Iraq.

With respect to economic considerations having a pacifying effect, there is the possibility that going to war could devastate one's economy. While it was discussed above that countries require a certain level of "economic wherewithal" to equip a military and fight, the desire to avoid disrupting butter consumption can hold a country back from going to war. One source of disruption is physical destruction: people will be killed and portions of a country's economic wealth could be destroyed by war. Another source of disruption is **opportunity costs**: what one could have done with the resources now allocated to the war effort. The quote from Eisenhower's speech perfectly captures the idea of opportunity costs, as he is directly listing items that were *not* purchased because the money instead went towards military items. Some of these costs were discussed above, from the alternative employment of soldiers conscripted to fight, to the income taxed for the purpose of funding a war effort. Of course, the idea of opportunity costs presumes that the resources – both labor and financial – could have been productively employed absent the war. A line of thinking, called **militaristic Keynesianism**, holds that war can be economically beneficial in those instances where a country's resources are unemployed (meaning the individual is not working and is not seeking work) or under-employed (meaning the individual is working, but in a job that fails to utilize that individual's skills and training).

Figure 6.4. Should the spread of McDonald's restaurants to China reassure us that common commercial interests might reduce the likelihood of war between China and the United States?
©Danny Lehman/The Image Bank Unreleased/Getty Images.

The Commercial Peace

In the study of international politics and war, perhaps no source of opportunity cost has been more widely studied than the loss of economic interaction between the belligerents. Scholars have long explored the "**commercial peace**": the notion that economic interdependence between nations can prevent war. This idea can be traced to such thinkers as Montesquieu (1949, book XX, ch. 2) – "The natural effect of commerce is to bring peace'" – and Immanuel Kant (1795) – "the spirit of commerce ... cannot tolerate war" – and John Stuart Mill (1884, book 3, ch. 17, para. 14) – "It is commerce which is rapidly rendering war obsolete." More popularly, this idea is captured in Thomas Friedman's (1999, ch. 12) "Golden Arches Theory," which maintains that no two countries that both have McDonald's franchises have ever gone to war with one another *after* acquiring those franchises. The claim is not that eating two all-beef patties with special sauce, lettuce, and cheese pacifies humans. Instead, the claim is that the presence of a McDonald's serves as a *proxy* – or indicator – of a country being open to the global economy (see Figure 6.4).

Related to having long intellectual lineage, the commercial peace is one of the most empirically evaluated claims in international relations, even in the social sciences, perhaps second only to the related idea of a democratic peace (see Chapter 4). Scholars create large data sets of trade flows between countries and then use statistical tools to see how strongly such flows are correlated with the presence (or, more specifically, the absence) of conflict (Barbieri 2002; McDonald 2009). Even when the data show that trade flows are related to less conflict between two (or sometimes more) states, scholars debate the direction of the relationship (is trade leading to peace or is peace creating conditions that foster trade?) or whether something else is explaining *both* the presence of peace and the expansion of trade (perhaps the hegemonic influence of the United States following World War II).

Regardless of what scholars say about the relationship between commerce and peace, one can see the logic of trade fostering peace in the actions and words of policymakers. After Israel signed the "Abraham Accords" with the United Arab Emirates (UAE) in 2020, the deputy mayor of Jerusalem and cofounder of the UAE–Israel Business Council remarked, "Business is one of the best forums to create a warm peace" (Stub 2021). A key motivation for South Korea pursuing its "sunshine policy" with North Korea was the notion that expanding economic ties would contribute to settling the longstanding military rivalry on the Korean peninsula (Kahler and Kastner 2006). An important step in the improvement of relations between Argentina and Brazil was the creation of the Integration and Economics Cooperation Program and the Treaty of Integration, Cooperation, and Development in the late 1980s, followed by the formation of the MERCUSOR regional free-trade agreement in the early 1990s (Poast and Urpelainen 2018, 170). Such sentiments and actions embrace the remarks made by Cordell Hull (1948, 81), shortly after serving as US Secretary of State during most of World War II, that "unhampered trade dovetailed with peace; high tariffs, trade barriers, and unfair competition, with war."

But how exactly do economic ties foster peace? There are two mechanisms underlying the commercial peace. One mechanism is opportunity costs. Under this mechanism, a state is reluctant to use military force against another state because doing so could result in the loss of trade. If trade will continue in the absence of military force, then this incentivizes the parties to avoid military force. Consider the US reaction during the Suez Crisis of 1956. When Egyptian President Nasser nationalized the Suez Canal in July 1956, the United States chose to not respond with military force. According to Eisenhower in his memoirs,

the main issue at stake, therefore, was whether or not Nasser would and could keep the waterway open for the traffic of all nations … As it [turned] out, not only were the Egyptian officials and workmen competent to operate the Canal, but they [demonstrated] that they could do so under conditions of increased traffic and with increased efficiency. … *any thought of using force, under these circumstances, was almost ridiculous.* (quoted in Copeland 2015, 285–288; emphasis added)

In other words, while nationalizing the Canal Zone could have been grounds for the United States to join Britain, France, and Israel in using force against Egypt, the fact that Egypt would continue to allow open trade – and that attacking Egypt could jeopardize that trade – led Eisenhower to take the use of militarized force off the table.

Another mechanism is signaling. According to this mechanism, the point is not that countries that trade with one another fear taking coercive measures against one another, but rather that states linked through trade have more tools, beyond the military, to coerce one another into changing policies. Specifically, a government can use costly economic sanctions as a means of "signaling" that it is displeased with a policy pursued by its counterpart and that it is willing to enact a costly action in order to change that policy. In other words, trade provides a nonviolent means for states to punish one another. This is why the authorization of economic sanctions is a widely used instrument of the United Nations Security Council: it enables the Council to authorize coercive measures to punish unacceptable behavior – such as genocidal policies or attempted acquisition of nuclear weapons – without having to authorize the use of military force.

While these mechanisms are plausible, there are also reasons to think that economic cooperation does not stop the potential use of force. Most notable are Marxist claims that commercial competition can feed imperialism and then war. While Marxism has fallen out of fashion, there remain other arguments for questioning the pacifying effect of trade.

First, there remains the possibility of low-level conflict. If states believe that economic interdependence will incentivize both parties to keep a dispute from escalating to war, then the parties might be more willing to make threats or even engage in lower-level militarized disputes, such as mobilizing forces or having forces encroach on airspace. For example, strong US–Chinese trade ties could explain why China is willing to engage in more provocative actions against Japan in the South China Sea: China suspects that the United States government is unwilling, in order to avoid disrupting trade in the region and with the United States, to encourage Japan to push back against Chinese actions. Of course, given that the United States and China are both nuclear powers, it is possible that it is the fear of a conflict escalating to nuclear war that is driving US restraint, not the fear of losing trade.

Second, there is the notion that when core strategic interests are at stake, commercial interdependence will have no effect on state behavior. Consider the crisis between the United States and North Korea in August 2017, in which there appeared to be the real potential for the United States to go to war over North Korea's pursuit of a nuclear weapons program. North Korea threatened to launch missiles towards the US territory of Guam, with the United States threatening to use military force to eliminate North Korea's nuclear program. The Chinese government responded to the escalating threats by saying that while it would remain neutral if North Korea first attacked the United States, it would support North Korea if the United States preemptively struck North Korea. Hence, the massive levels of trade between the United States and China did not prevent the Chinese government from declaring its intent to go to war to protect a core strategic interest – in this case, the sovereignty of North Korea (Reuters 2017).

Third and perhaps most problematic for those who claim that economic cooperation can restrain the use of force, many countries have continued to trade while at war. Even if war disrupts trade and reduces the level of trade between adversaries, some trade frequently continues between the belligerents. Some of this trade is illicit smuggling, but not all. Most notably, the German government signed the Maltese agreement with Denmark in October 1939. This allowed Danish ships to deliver food to Britain (meaning the Danish ships would not be sunk by German submarines) despite Germany and Britain being officially at war. A primary motivation for allowing this trade was that the German Foreign Ministry anticipated a long war and, therefore, wanted to maintain Denmark as a potential source of trade with the rest of the world (including to adversaries of Germany) (Barbieri and Levy 2004, 27).

Fourth, the commercial peace's opportunity cost mechanism might work *too* well: economic interdependence could undermine peace by making actors unwilling to make deterrent threats or even prevent a state from intervening. Indirect evidence suggests that the German government might have tried to use economic leverage to prevent British intervention during the July crisis of 1914. British trade with Germany was substantial, nearly equal to its trade with France and Belgium *combined* (Barbieri et al. 2009). Financiers in the City of London, fearing the disruptions of a major war, urged British officials to abstain from intervening against Germany. For instance, Sir Eyre Crowe reported to the British Foreign Minister Grey on July 31, 1914 how "'[t]he panic in the City has been largely influenced by the deliberate acts of German financial houses, who are in at least as close touch with the German as with the British Government" (quoted in Albertini 1952, 375). Such considerations may have led Britain to not make a firm deterrent threat against a German invasion of Belgium (Levy 2003, 139). Of course, it must be recognized that concerns about disrupting this interdependence did not outweigh Britain's strategic considerations in favor of intervention: once Germany invaded Belgium, Britain perceived Germany as a direct threat to its strategic interests (Albertini 1952, 386–392).

CASE STUDY

American Income Taxes and World War

As mentioned above, war financing via taxation epitomizes the guns-versus-butter trade-off. Taxation represents a direct redistribution of goods away from private consumption and investment (butter) and toward military purchases (guns). Studying war taxes in the context of the US economy is particularly useful, as the modern US taxation system is directly the product of war taxation. While the United States has not implemented war taxes during its three most recent wars (the 1991 Persian Gulf War, the war in Afghanistan that began in 2001, and the 2003–2011 Iraq War), the United States implemented war taxes during the Revolutionary War, the "Quasi-War" with France from 1798 to 1800, the War of 1812, the Mexican–American War, the American Civil War, the Spanish–American War, World War I, World War II, the Korean War, and the Vietnam War (Flores-Macias and Kreps 2013). In the last case, the Vietnam War, taxation contributed to the war's unpopularity with the US public, a consequence President Lyndon Johnson had tried to avoid (Capella Zielinski 2016, 53).

But the US experience during World War I and World War II is different from earlier and later experiences with war taxation. With the needs to raise, equip, and transport millions of soldiers, sailors, and pilots in a short period of time, the financial scale of these two wars is almost beyond comparison. In just under two years of actual war involvement (and one year of postwar demobilization), World War I participation cost the United States government approximately $32 billion (almost $600 billion at 2020 prices) (Rockoff 2012). The budgetary cost of World War II far surpassed that amount, $320 billion ($5.5 trillion in 2020 prices) in just four years. While debt played the primary role in covering these costs, the money collected through taxes was not trivial. Thirty percent of World War I's budgetary cost was covered by taxes, while nearly half of the cost of World War II was paid for through taxes (Rockoff 2012, 171).

As a result, the wars led to permanent changes in the US tax system. Earlier wars were funded by temporary surcharges or short-term income taxes. But while it has long been acknowledged that taxes (along with death) are the only certainties in life, in the United States this was not necessarily the case for taxes on income, though income taxes were imposed elsewhere at least as far back as ancient Egypt, Rome, and China. In the United States, a permanent annual tax on income only came into existence with the passage of the Sixteenth Amendment in 1909 (ratified in 1913). The income tax was not adopted during a time when the United States was at war, and a host of political economic considerations contributed to the adoption of the income tax. But the needs of war finance played a notable role in its adoption. Cordell Hull, then a Tennessee representative in the House of Representatives (and later Secretary of State), remarked in 1910, "During the great strain of national emergencies, an income tax is absolutely

(cont.)

Table 6.1. US income tax brackets (in current year prices) from 1913 to 1920. The 1917 War Revenue Act raided the paychecks of America's richest citizens. If your annual income was $2 million in 1917, then for every dollar you earned above that threshold you only took home 33 cents, after federal taxes. The rest went to buy uniforms, bullets, rifles, and everything else demanded for the war effort

Year	End of Lowest Bracket	Tax Rate	Start of Highest Bracket	Tax Rate
1913	$20,000	1%	$500,000	7%
1914	$20,000	1%	$500,000	7%
1915	$20,000	1%	$500,000	7%
1916	$20,000	2%	$2,000,000	15%
1917	$2,000	2%	$2,000,000	67%
1918	$4,000	6%	$1,000,000	77%
1919	$4,000	4%	$1,000,000	73%
1920	$4,000	4%	$1,000,000	73%

without rival as a relief measure. Many governments in time of war have invoked its prompt and certain aid" (quoted in Poast 2006, 21).

Prior to the Sixteenth Amendment, the primary source of revenue for the US government was taxes derived from foreign trade. For example, in 1902, $243 million of $653 million in government revenue came from tariffs. (The second largest source was revenue from the taxes on the sale of alcoholic beverages.) Tariff revenue comprised $310 million of $962 million in government revenue in 1913 (with, again, the second largest source of revenue coming from taxes on the sale of alcoholic beverages) (US Department of Commerce 1975, 1122).

Though war finance was one among many considerations leading to the implementation of an income tax, it was the core factor leading to the widespread application of that tax on the US population. Consider Table 6.1, which shows data from the US Internal Revenue Service on marginal tax brackets (US Internal Revenue Service n.d.). A marginal tax bracket means that every dollar a person earns above a set level (say $10,000) is charged the rate associated with that bracket (say 5 percent) until that person's income reaches the next level. For example, suppose the tax brackets are a 1 percent tax for each dollar between $10,000 and $20,000 earned by an individual, 5 percent for each dollar between $20,000 and $40,000 earned by an individual, and 10 percent for each dollar earned above $40,000. If a person makes $50,000 per year, then she will pay $0 tax on her income between 0 and $10,000, $100 tax for her income between $10,000 and $20,000, $1,000 on her income between $20,000 and $40,000, and $1,000 for her income between $40,000 and $50,000. Hence, her total tax bill will be $2,100 for the year.

(cont.)

Table 6.2. US income tax brackets (in current year prices) from 1939 to 1946. In 1944, if you were lucky to enough to earn $200,000, for every dollar you earned above $200,000, you only took home 6 cents, after federal taxes.

Year	End of Lowest Bracket	Tax Rate	Start of Highest Bracket	Tax Rate
1939	$4,000	4%	$5,000,000	79%
1940	$4,000	4.4%	$5,000,000	81%
1941	$2,000	10%	$5,000,000	81%
1942	$2,000	19%	$200,000	88%
1943	$2,000	19%	$200,000	88%
1944	$2,000	23%	$200,000	94%
1945	$2,000	23%	$200,000	94%
1946	$2,000	19%	$200,000	86%

Table 6.1 shows that when the income tax was implemented in 1913, an individual only paid a 1 percent tax on income up to $20,000. This level of income sounds modest, but one must adjust this for inflation (the gradual rise in the overall prices of goods and services). Doing so, using the US Bureau of Labor Statistics CPI Inflation Calculator (www.bls.gov/data/inflation_calculator.htm), reveals that $20,000 in 1913 is equivalent to nearly $500,000 in 2017 prices! In other words, most Americans paid very modest taxes. The highest tax bracket when the income tax was implemented in 1913 began at $500,000 in 1913 prices (the equivalent of nearly $12.5 million in 2017 prices).

Things changed dramatically in 1917 with the US entry into the war and the passage of the War Revenue Act. This Act lowered the lowest tax bracket to just $2,000. Adjusted for inflation, this was the modern equivalent of approximately $50,000 a year. Hence, a lot more households were now paying higher taxes. While the highest rate was increased to $2 million (the inflation-adjusted equivalent of nearly $500 million), the rate eventually rose to a staggering 77 percent! Who paid that high of a tax? John D. Rockefeller was estimated to be the richest American in 1918, with an annual income of $60 million (at 1918 dollars). Indeed, the year 1918 was the first year that *Forbes* produced a list of the thirty richest Americans, with the thirtieth person on the list (Henry Phillips) making just over the threshold for the highest tax bracket ($2.5 million) (Hesseldahl 2002).

World War II again witnessed substantial changes in the marginal income tax rates (Table 6.2). In 1939, the year war broke out in Europe, the end of the lowest income bracket was only $4,000 (where it had stood since 1918). In 1939, this was the equivalent of approximately $70,000 a year. The bracket cutoff dropped to just $2,000 in 1941, but the most notable change was the increase in the tax rate. The rate more than doubled from 1939 to 1941 – rising from 4 percent, where it had stood for most of the 1930s, to 10 percent – and then more than doubled again in 1944 (to 23 percent). These changes were due to passage of the Revenue Acts of 1942 and 1943. The latter is politically notable as it

(cont.)

marked the first time in US history that a revenue law was passed by overriding a presidential veto. (President Franklin D. Roosevelt had vetoed the bill, but both the US House and Senate voted to override the veto.)

What is most striking is the change brought about at the high end of the tax bracket. The marginal tax rate for the highest bracket, at 79 percent, was already quite high in 1939. By 1944, the rate was a staggering 94 percent, meaning nearly every dollar earned in that bracket went to the government in the form of a tax. Moreover, the cutoff for the bracket had plummeted from $5 million in 1941 (the equivalent of nearly $87 million in 2017 prices) to just $200,000 in 1942. In 1942, $200,000 was the equivalent of $3.5 million in 2017. While this is still a high income, it targeted a substantially wider swath of the US population, as only two Americans in 1941 had incomes above $5 million: John D. Rockefeller ($5.28 million) and Clarence Dillon ($5.23 million) (Brandes 1983).

Another major change was the implementation of tax withholding. When we receive a paycheck (whether weekly, biweekly, or monthly), we see that a portion of our pay went towards federal taxes. This gives each of us an incentive to file our tax returns each spring, as we hope that the federal government withheld too much money (and we receive a federal income tax refund). But such a system only started in 1943 with the Current Tax Payment Act. (Tax withholding had existed for only three years from 1913 to 1916.) Prior to that time, individuals paid taxes in quarterly installments. But the expansion of the tax base due to the above-mentioned changes in the tax brackets meant more people would have to remember to pay their taxes. Tax withholding eased the ability of people with lower incomes to pay taxes. Moreover, it gave people an incentive to actually file their taxes. As a Treasury Department official testified in early 1943:

Up until 1941 we never received as many as 8,000,000 individual income-tax returns in a year. In 1941 that number increased to 15,000,000; in 1942 it increased to 16,000,000. This year we expect 35,000,000 taxable individual income-tax returns. (Twilight 1995, 370)

The reality is that many Americans were now being asked to pay income taxes for the first time. The US government responded by initiating advertising campaigns aimed at reminding Americans to file their tax returns (such as the poster shown in Figure 6.5). *Time* magazine included an article in March 1943 (65–66) observing that "This week the U.S. citizen faces a hard and stubborn fact of wartime living ... The U.S. Treasury on March 15 will demand and get more money from more people that at any time in the history of the republic." Following the war, the expanded tax brackets and policy of tax withholding were retained.

Income taxes directly took money out of the pockets of American families that might have been spent on consumer goods, redirecting it to buying weapons, converting butter

(cont.)

Figure 6.5. A 1945 poster reminding Americans to file their 1944 income tax returns.
United States National Archives.

into guns. And there were other manifestations of the guns–butter tradeoff during World War II, as well. During the war, production of automobiles for civilian use plunged 95 percent, so that factories could focus on building tanks, jeeps, bombers, and other military equipment. Gasoline and tires for civilian use were heavily restricted, to provide adequate supplies to the armed forces. Even the production of children's toys was affected, as the US government passed laws strictly limiting the use of strategic materials such as iron, zinc, steel, and rayon in toy manufacturing.

In both World Wars, such policies funded a substantial portion of the war's cost. One can clearly see that while Americans are now very used to paying income taxes and having a portion of each paycheck withheld in the form of federal taxes, both were introduced to the United States in the twentieth century, brought about primarily by the costs of war.

QUANTITATIVE STUDY

Does Cheaper Debt Help You Win a War?

A fundamental (if not *the* fundamental) question left unaddressed by the above work is whether cheaper finance, the ability for a government to take out war loans at lower interest rates, actually helps a country win its wars. Cheaper finance might be critical to helping a state win if it allows the state to build the larger army it needs for victory. But in reality, does cheaper finance actually translate into victory? The political scientist Dr. Patrick Shea (2014) published a quantitative study that attempted to answer this very question.

Research Question

Is a state more likely to lose a war if it is unable to acquire affordable credit?

Theory and Hypotheses

Dr. Shea's answer is, "it depends." Specifically, access to loans and the cost of loans, specifically the interest rate the government must pay on loans, have a much more important effect on the ability of democratic belligerents to build military power and win wars as compared with nondemocratic belligerents. Shea argues that democracies are more sensitive to the societal pressures that emerge as wars drag on and impose escalating costs, and these pressures can push a government to exit the war sooner, even accepting defeat. However, affordable financing can mitigate these pressures. Of course, affordable financing can help all states, but it is particularly valuable for democracies. More precisely, since raising taxes runs the risk of making a war unpopular and democratic leaders require widespread public support to stay in office, democracies will benefit more from the ability of placing the financial burden on debt rather than taxation. Hence, Dr. Shea proposes that cheaper finance will help democracies win wars, but will not help nondemocracies win wars, as cheaper debt helps solve a problem faced by democratic belligerents but not nondemocratic belligerents.

Hypothesis: The price of credit is more important for democratic states in determining war outcomes.

Data

The data begins with the full set of interstate wars in the Correlates of War (COW) data set. This data set covers the participants of all interstate wars from 1823 to 2007. In COW, a war is a conflict between two or more sovereign states that resulted in at least 1,000 battle deaths. An observation in this study is a state in a war: such as the United States in World War II. Overall, Shea has a data set of 237 country-war observations.

Dependent Variable

The dependent variable codes whether a state is on the winning side of a war. The COW data set codes whether a state was victorious in war (meaning the other side surrendered and the war concluded), lost the war (meaning the state surrendered to the other party and this concluded the war), surrendered (meaning the state surrendered but other parties continued the war), or experienced a war-ending stalemate (meaning the parties agree to a truce). Since Shea is interested in identifying the determinants of victory, the dependent variable classifies whether a state was victorious.

Independent Variable

The main independent variable is the interest rate on a government's debt in the year that the war began. Interest rates are a commonly used indicator of creditworthiness and the cost of borrowing. All things being equal, raising money is more expensive the higher the interest rate. When the debt comes due, the government will have to pay back the borrowed amount and any interest accumulated. Higher interest rates mean a larger repayment. Since tax revenue is a source of the funds used to repay the debt, higher interest rates will eventually lead to higher taxes (in order to repay the debt).

But keep in mind that the hypothesis is *conditional*. The effect of the interest rate will depend on the regime type of the state. This requires coding whether the state was a democracy or nondemocracy. Shea does so by drawing on the Polity data set. This data set assigns each country a *polity* score on a scale from −10 to 10. The score is determined by considering a variety of features of a state's governing institutions, such as whether the leader must gain approval of a legislature. It is standard in much political science scholarship to consider countries with a *polity* score of 6 or higher as democracies. Shea follows this practice. Shea then uses this democracy variable to create a variable that allows him to see the effect of the interest rate when a country is a democracy and the effect when the country is a nondemocracy.

Control Variables

Many factors determine the outcomes of war. Borrowing costs are important, but their effect might be trivial compared to other factors. Indeed, after accounting for these other factors, it might be the case that interest rates play little role at all. Shea accounted for several such factors. These included whether the state initiated the war, the state's available military capabilities entering the war, and whether the state had the support of allies. The last variable is especially important, since a state might be victorious in a war largely (perhaps even completely) because of allied support. Moreover, as discussed above, allied support can enable a state to avoid the need to draw on its own resources to acquire the arms of war.

Results

Shea finds that a higher interest rate lowers the probability of a country being victorious, regardless of its regime type. Indeed, depending on the magnitude of the interest rate increase, the probability of victory can be reduced by almost 70 percentage points (from a nearly 70 percent probability of victory down to 0). However, this is the effect across both regime types. If he considers how the effect differs from democracies to nondemocracies, he finds that for countries with the lowest *polity* scores (near −10) a lower interest rate has virtually no effect on the probability of victory. Most of the benefit of a lower interest rate on the probability of war victory is found in the middle to high values of *polity*.

Conclusion

The study provides evidence that higher borrowing costs can influence the war-fighting ability of a state, though the benefit is more notable for democracies than for nondemocracies.

SUMMARY

This chapter has made a number of points about the relationship between economics and war. They include:

- Economic power is the foundation of military power.
- War is expensive and finding ways to cover these costs has long been recognized as a critical component of war fighting.
- The cost of arming a military compels governments (and the economies they oversee) to trade off between military consumption – arms – and private consumption – butter.
- Governments interact with firms to acquire weapons, whether small arms or major weapons systems.
- The markets for arms are not perfectly competitive. They are commonly characterized as dual monopolies, meaning a single buyer (a monopsony) and a single supplier (a monopoly).
- The market for military labor is also not perfectly competitive. The government is a single buyer.
- Governments can compete in the open market for military labor (through a volunteer recruitment system) or compel individuals to serve (through conscription).
- For governments to acquire weapons and warriors via markets, the government needs money. This money can be acquired via borrowing and taxation.
- Economic linkages between countries can restrain states in the use of military force, but there are exceptions.

KEY TERMS

Dual monopoly
Monopsony
Monopoly
Volunteerism
Conscription

Fundamental problem of sovereign finance
Crowding-out
Opportunity costs
Military Keynesianism
Commercial peace

REVIEW QUESTIONS

1. In what way does government acquisition of "guns" capture the adage that "there is no such thing as a free lunch?" What is the guns vs. butter tradeoff?
2. In what ways does a dual monopoly market differ from a perfectly competitive market? Use an example from the defense sector to illustrate your answer.
3. What are the advantages and disadvantages of using conscription rather than a volunteer military recruitment system?
4. Why should lenders be wary of making a loan to a government, especially one at war?
5. What are the advantages and disadvantages of using taxation, rather than borrowing, to finance a war?
6. What mechanisms can explain why countries being economically interconnected gives governments an incentive to abstain from using military force against one another?
7. How might countries being economically interconnected *not* compel governments to refrain from using military force? Could it even possibly make the use of force more likely?
8. How did the United States use income taxes to fund military expenditures during the World Wars?

DISCUSSION QUESTIONS

1. The guns–butter tradeoff affects us all, whether we think about it or not. Would you personally be willing to pay an extra $100 in taxes per year to reduce the likelihood of a deadly terrorist attack on the territory of our country by 20 percent?
2. Do you think your national government should spend more on defense, more on social priorities, or is the balance about right?
3. Under what national security circumstances, if any, could you see yourself volunteering to serve in your nation's military?

ADDITIONAL READING

Cappella Zielinski, R. (2016). *How States Pay for War*. Ithaca, NY: Cornell University Press.

Fordham, B. (1998). *Building the Cold War Consensus: The Political Economy of U.S. National Security Policy, 1949–1951*. Ann Arbor: University of Michigan Press.

Kirshner, J. (2005). *Appeasing Bankers: Financial Caution on the Road to War*. Princeton: Princeton University Press.

Kreps, S. E. (2018). *Taxing Wars: The American Way of War Finance and the Decline of Democracy*. New York: Oxford University Press.

McDonald, P. J. (2009). *The Invisible Hand of Peace: Capitalism, the War Machine, and International Relations Theory*. New York: Cambridge University Press.

Poast, P. (2006). *The Economics of War*. New York: McGraw Hill-Irwin.

Rockoff, H. (2012). *America's Economic Way of War*. Cambridge: Cambridge University Press.

Tooze, A. (2006). *Wages of Destruction*. New York: Penguin Press.

REFERENCES

Albertini, L. (1952). *The Origins of the War of 1914*. London: Oxford University Press.

Augustine, N. R. (1983). *Augustine's Laws and Major System Development Programs*. New York: American Institute of Aeronautics and Astronautics.

Avant, D. (2000). From mercenary to citizen armies: Explaining change in the practice of war. *International Organization* **54**(1), 41–72.

Barbieri, K. (2002). *The Liberal Illusion: Does Trade Promote Peace?* Ann Arbor: University of Michigan Press.

Barbieri, K. and Levy, J. S. (2004). Trading with the enemy during wartime. *Security Studies* **13**(3), 1–47.

Barbieri, K., Keshk, O. M. G., and Pollins, B. M. (2009). Trading data. *Conflict Management and Peace Science* **26**(5), 471–491.

Berger, M. (2019, June 1). How anger over taxes and conscription is widening split among Israel's Jews. *The Guardian*. www.theguardian.com/world/2019/jun/01

Biden, J. (2021, March 11). Remarks by President Biden on the anniversary of the COVID-19 shutdown. www.whitehouse.gov/briefing-room/speeches-remarks/2021/03/11

Brandes, S. D. (1983). America's super rich, 1941. *The Historian* **45**(3), 307–323.

Braun, R. A. and McGrattan, E. R. (1993). The macroeconomics of war and peace. *NBER Macroeconomics Annual* **8**, 257–258.

Capella-Zielinski, R. (2016). *How States Pay for War*. Ithaca, NY: Cornell University Press.

Copeland, D. C. (2015). *Economic Interdependence and War*. Princeton: Princeton University Press.

De Long, J. B. (1993). [The Macroeconomics of War and Peace]: Comment. *NBER Macroeconomics Annual* **8**, 247–250.

D'Lugo, D. and Rogowski, R. (1993). The Anglo-German naval race and comparative constitutional "fitness". In R. N. Rosecrance and A. A. Stein (eds.). *The Domestic Bases of Grand Strategy*. Ithaca, NY: Cornell University Press.

Eisenhower, D. D. (1953, April 16). The chance for peace. www.eisenhower.archives.gov/all_about_ike/speeches/chance_for_peace.pdf

Eisenhower, D. D. (1961, January 17). President Dwight D. Eisenhower's Farewell Address. www.archives.gov/milestone-documents/president-dwight-d-eisenhowers-farewell-address

Erbel, M and Kinsey, C. (2016). Privatizing military logistics. In R. Abrahamsen and A. Leander (eds.). *Routledge Handbook of Private Security Studies*. New York: Routledge, Taylor & Francis Group.

Flores-Macias, G. A. and Kreps, S. E. (2013). Political parties at war: A study of American war finance, 1789–2010. *American Political Science Review* **107**(4), 833–848.

Friedman, M. (1963). *Inflation: Causes and Consequences*, Bombay: Asia Publishing House.

Friedman, T. L. (1999). *The Lexus and the Olive Tree: Understanding Globalization*. New York: Farrar, Straus & Giroux.

Fukuyama, F. (2011). *The Origins of Political Order*, New York: Farrar, Straus & Giroux.

Fulghum, N. (1979). Moneys for the Southern Cause. *Documenting the American South*. https://docsouth.unc.edu/imls/currency/index.html

Gilpin, R. (1981). *War and Change in World Politics*, Princeton: Princeton University Press.

Harrison, T. and Daniels, S. (2021). *Analysis of the FY 2022 Defense Budget: Funding Trends and Issues for the Next National Defense Strategy*. Washington, DC: CSIS International Security Program's Defense Outlook Series.

Hesseldahl, A. (2002, September 27). The first rich list. *Forbes*.www.forbes.com/2002/09/27/0927richestphotos.html

Horowitz, M. C., Poast, P., and Stam, A. C. (2017). Domestic signaling of commitment credibility. *Journal of Conflict Resolution* **61**(8), 1682–1710.

Hull, C. (1948). *The Memoirs of Cordell Hull*. New York: Macmillan.

Kahler, M. and Kastner, S. L. (2006). Strategic uses of economic interdependence: Engagement policies on the Korean peninsula and across the Taiwan Strait. *Journal of Peace Research* **43**(5), 523–541.

Kant, I. (1795). Perpetual peace. *Project Gutenberg*. www.gutenberg.org/files/50922/50922-h/50922-h.htm

Kessler, G. (2016, March 30). Trump's claim that the U.S. pays the 'Lion's Share' for NATO. *Washington Post*. www.washingtonpost.com/news/fact-checker/wp/2016/03/30

Levy, J. S. (2003). Economic interdependence, opportunity costs, and peace. In E. D. Mansfield and B. Pollins (eds.). *Economic Interdependence and International Conflict: New Perspectives on an Enduring Debate*. Ann Arbor: The University of Michigan Press.

Mavrellis, C. (2017, March 27). Transnational crime and the developing world. https://gfintegrity.org/report/transnational-crime-and-the-developing-world

McDonald, P. J. (2009). *The Invisible Hand of Peace: Capitalism, the War Machine, and International Relations Theory*. New York: Cambridge University Press.

Mill, J. S. (1884). *Principles of Political Economy*. New York: Appleton.

Montesquieu, B. D. (1949). *The Spirit of the Laws*. New York: Haffner Press.

Neuman, S. (2021, April 9). North Korea's Kim alludes to 1990s famine, warns of 'difficulties ahead of us.' www.npr.org/2021/04/09/985743058

Nolan, C. J. (2008). *Wars of the Age of Louis XIV, 1650–1715: An Encyclopedia of Global Warfare and Civilization*. Westport, CT: Greenwood Press.

Nordhaus, W. D. and Tobin, J. (1972). *Is Growth Obsolete?* Cambridge: National Bureau of Economic Research.

Poast, P. (2006). *The Economics of War*. New York: McGraw-Hill Irwin.

Poast, P. and Urpelainen, J. (2018). *Organizing Democracy: How International Organizations Assist New Democracies*. Chicago: University of Chicago.

Posen, B. R. (1993). Nationalism, the mass army, and military power. *International Security* **18**(2), 80–124.

Reuters (2017, August 10). Chinese paper says China should stay neutral if North Korea attacks first. www.reuters.com/article/us-northkorea-missiles-china-media

Rockoff, H. (2012). *America's Economic Way of War and the US Economy from the Spanish–American War to the First Gulf War*. Cambridge: Cambridge University Press.

Scheve, K. and Stasavage, D. (2012). Democracy, war, and wealth: lessons from two centuries of inheritance taxation. *American Political Science Review* **106**(1), 81–102.

Shea, P. E. (2014). Financing victory: Sovereign credit, democracy, and war. *Journal of Conflict Resolution* **58**(5), 771–795.

Shea, P. E. and Poast, P. (2017). War and default. *Journal of Conflict Resolution* **62**(9), 1876–1904.

Silverstein, K., and Moag, J. (2000, January 1). The Pentagon's 300-billion-dollar bomb. *Mother Jones*. www.motherjones.com/politics/2000/01

Smith, A. (1952). *The Wealth of Nations*. Chicago: Encyclopedia Britannica.

Stevenson, D. (2007). Was a peaceful outcome thinkable? The European land arms race before 1914. In H. Afflerbach and D. Stevenson (eds.). *An Improbable War? The Outbreak of World War I and European Political Culture before 1914*. New York: Berghahn Books.

Stub, Z. (2021, August 8). One year into Abraham Accords, Israel's trade with UAE tops $570M. *Jerusalem Post*. www.jpost.com/middle-east

Tilly, C. (1975). Reflections on the history of European state making. In C. Tilly (ed.). *The Formation of National States in Western Europe*. Princeton: Princeton University Press.

Time (1943, March 15). Ides of March. 63–66.

Twilight, C. (1995). Evolution of federal income tax withholding: The machinery of institutional change. *Cato Journal* **14**(3), 359–395.

Tzu, S. (1963). *The Art of War*, trans. S. B. Griffith. London: Oxford University Press.

US Internal Revenue Service (n.d.). IRS tax bracket data from United States Internal Revenue Service. www.irs.gov/statistics/soi-tax-stats-historical-table-23

US Department of Commerce (1975). *Historical Statistics of the United States: Colonial Times to 1970*. Washington, DC: US Department of Commerce.

Waltz, K. N. (1959). *Man, the State, and War: A Theoretical Analysis*. New York: Columbia.

Part III

Conflict within States

7 Civil Wars

KATHLEEN GALLAGHER CUNNINGHAM

Introduction

Civil wars are armed conflicts involving the government that occur within existing countries. While American readers will probably be familiar with the American Civil War, both large- and small-scale armed internal conflicts have taken place around the world in all types of countries and over many different issues. Civil wars within countries are the most common kind of armed conflict around the globe, and over 250 internal armed conflicts have occurred since 1945. Into the 2020s, civil wars raged in Syria, India, Yemen, Afghanistan, and elsewhere around the world.

These violent conflicts, where organized groups of individuals challenge their government militarily, have led to millions of deaths since World War II. Figure 7.1 demonstrates the staggering human cost of civil wars since the end of the Cold War. Moreover, civil wars often spread across borders, leading to massive flows of refugees and internally displaced persons, as well as economic and humanitarian crises. A great deal of international attention is now focused on resolving ongoing civil wars, and preventing new ones. Despite this, civil wars remain intractable in many ways.

This chapter explores civil wars. It will first describe civil wars in general terms. Next, it will explore the causes of civil wars. Then, it will unpack the dynamics that occur during civil wars. It will then describe how and why civil wars end, and the long-term effects of civil wars. The quantitative case study examines whether peacekeeping works, and the case study of the Syrian Civil War (see also Chapter 13) highlights the many challenges of resolving civil wars, and the many negative consequences of them.

What Is a Civil War?

Defining the term "civil war" is not a purely rhetorical exercise. There has been a great deal of public debate about whether and when Iraq was experiencing civil war after the invasion by the

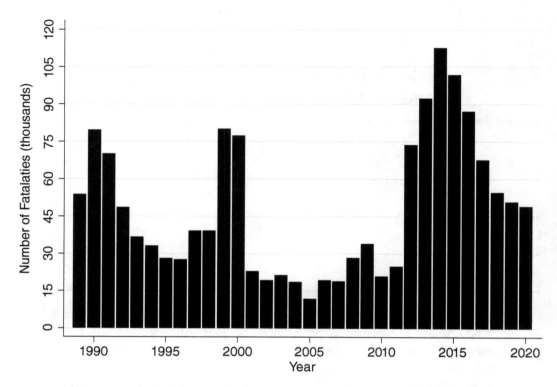

Figure 7.1. The staggering human costs: fatalities from civil wars, 1989–2016. PRIO.org.

United States in 2003. But for students of politics and political violence, there are clear criteria that armed disputes must meet to be considered a civil war. First, one of the actors in the conflict must be the government (also called the state, such as "Iraqi state"). Outbreaks of even sustained violence among civilians or between different groups in society are not considered civil wars if the government is not involved. Second, the opposition (or "rebels") must be organized. That means that we would not consider spontaneous riots or demonstrations that led to violence to be "civil wars." Third, civil wars must lead to a sufficiently high number of fatalities before we consider them to be wars. While there is a great deal of variation in how intense different civil wars are, a dispute that leads to very few instances of combatant deaths, such as clashes between government forces and protesters leading to only a few people killed, is not considered a civil war. Last, civil wars exclude instances of one-sided violence, as when a government commits genocide or other human rights abuses against its own people but there is no organized rebel movement.

As a general framework, we can approach the occurrence of civil war as a product of two actors making the decision to fight. These actors are the country's government and whatever set of insurgent organizations comes together to challenge that government. If people do not act together to challenge the government, there is no organized insurgency. If the government does not respond with force in the face of a challenge, we might see a relatively low-level conflict or no conflict leading to regime change, government change, or secession.

Figure 7.2. Children displaced by the Lord's Resistance Army, 2005. The human suffering caused by civil wars goes beyond those who are killed or wounded in fighting. Chip Somodevilla/Getty Images.

In the many disputes that would qualify as civil wars, there are several key issues over which war is usually fought. First, many wars are fought for control of the government. For example, in the early 1990s the government of Ethiopia was overthrown in a war where multiple groups coordinated to attack the state and overthrow the existing regime. Historically, we can see the revolution in Russia that led to the creation of the Soviet Union as a civil war for control of the government, but also as a conflict aimed at fundamentally changing the way that government worked.

Other wars are fought with **secessionist** aims in mind (Griffiths 2017). Secession is the complete political separation of a territory from an existing country. The American Civil War was of course fought over the issue of slavery, but it can also be seen as one of many conflicts about what constitutes a legitimate government, and who has the right to be their own country. In many instances, secessionist aims are linked to a specific **nationalist** group, where a set of people lay claim to a homeland and identify as a cohesive "nation." In 2011, South Sudan became an independent country through a secessionist civil war that was fought on and off across a number of decades. In 2005, a peace agreement was reached which allowed the people of South Sudan to vote in a referendum on whether they should have an independent country. A similar process occurred in East Timor in the late 1990s. After a long civil war against Indonesia, and after intervention by the international community, the East Timorese were allowed to vote on whether or not they would stay unified with Indonesia or separate to become an independent country.

In addition to or in place of taking control of the government, or seceding (i.e. fighting to become your own country), rebel groups and the broader political movements to which they are linked have other aims. Some of these are easy to categorize, because they are essentially **predatory** (Weinstein 2006). For example, the Lord's Resistance Army (LRA) in Uganda does not appear to have any clear political aims with respect to seizing control of government or seceding. Instead, the LRA operates more as a personal power fiefdom with the goal of maintaining Joseph Kony's power base. Such rebels may be classified more aptly as protecting local warlords than as vanguards of political movements. The actions of some rebel groups can affect the entire range of society, not just those who are politically engaged; Figure 7.2 shows children displaced by the LRA.

Figure 7.3. A publicity photo from ISIS, of a masked ISIS fighter holding an ISIS flag, somewhere in Iraq or Syria in 2015. The words on the flag mean, "There is no god but Allah. Muhammad is the messenger of Allah," and emphasize the religious motivation of ISIS.
©Pictures from History / Contributor/ Universal Images Group/ Getty Images.

The Islamic State of Iraq and Syria (ISIS) demonstrates another somewhat unique agenda for a rebel movement. ISIS seeks to create a caliphate, which would be a global Islamic authority. While not necessarily secessionist or seeking to control a single existing country, the aims of ISIS do relate to governance more broadly. While it is religiously inspired and motivated, ISIS is not unique in that. There are many rebel groups that draw on religious texts or beliefs to support their claims. Figure 7.3 shows the flag used by ISIS to symbolize their claim. The references to Allah and Muhammad in the flag both demonstrate ISIS's deep religious foundations, and make it sacrilegious to desecrate it.

Why Do Civil Wars Occur?

Civil wars occur for a variety of reasons and we can examine motivations for insurgents or opposition movements to use violence, as well as motivations for states to respond to citizens with violence.

Grievance

Beginning with insurgents, we can think about civil war requiring both grievance and opportunity. What is **grievance**? All individuals have some level of grievance, as very few people experience a completely frictionless life with no unaddressed needs. But recall, to get to civil war, a number of people must come together to challenge the government. Thus, when we are talking about grievance and civil war, the questions we are really asking is, "Are there collective grievances?" and "Are people willing to mobilize, or put their lives at risk, in pursuit of addressing these grievances?"

History helps to inform our understanding of the role of grievance and the political processes that lead to mobilization for civil war. Many of the most prominent historical civil wars have been studied as "revolutions." For example, the Shining Path insurgency in Peru started as a grassroots movement to change the fundamental nature of governance within the country, eventually evolving into a Communist revolutionary movement. Mobilization began in the late

1960s, led by Abimael Guzmán. At the start, insurgents worked throughout the countryside and in small villages to recruit peasants to their way of thinking about governance, and about how the country would benefit from a Communist regime. They made appeals based on class differences, and encouraged individuals to support the cause in any way they could. Shining Path was able to successfully recruit foot soldiers this way, but it was also able to create a durable network of people who were willing to support the movement through a variety of means, such as providing resources and sheltering soldiers when needed. The ideological struggles related to Communism were common grievances in Cold War–era civil wars, but declined when the Soviet Union collapsed in 1991.

Other forms of grievance have taken a more central role in wartime mobilization in recent decades. Ideology based on the distinction between Communism and the West has given way to collective grievances related to government neglect and abuse that take many forms including economic and cultural grievance. A number of wars have been linked to the ideas of "**deprivation**" and "**relative deprivation.**" Conceptually, deprivation is an idea that draws from psychologist Abraham Maslow's hierarchy of needs. The idea is that all individuals (and, of course, groups of individuals) have basic needs, and when these are not met, there is a greater risk of social disruption. Further, even if their basic needs are being met, individuals or groups of people may be dissatisfied with their lot compared to others, contributing to a feeling of deprivation vis-à-vis another group in society. This type of grievance is more likely to arise when there are stark disparities among the population, such as economic inequality. Empirically, we see collective action and mobilization leading to civil war in situations where such inequality lines up with other differences in society (such as linguistic groups) and when individuals or groups feel that they cannot move beyond their social stratum (Cederman et al. 2013).

Identity

Another key dimension on which wars have been increasingly fought since the late 1980s concerns what we can broadly call **identity issues**, which encompasses a number of ways that individuals identify with different groups in society (such as ethnicity or religion). "Ethnicity" is a multifaceted concept, which can include elements of race, language, or religious belief, and many wars can be classified as "ethnic" in nature. Civil wars sometimes erupt across ethnic lines, though violence in these cases is frequently caused by political and economic as well as ethnic factors. It is important to note that while ethnicity is often the identity around which conflict occurs, it is not itself a "direct cause" of violence. In many instances multiethnic communities exist in peace. Moreover, ethnicity is a social construct that is shaped, in part, by conflict.

Many of the conflicts in the 1990s centered on ethnic identification. For example, the conflict culminating in the Rwandan genocide emerged from a long-running dispute between Hutus and Tutsis. The Hutu/Tutsi ethnic distinction developed as part of Belgian colonial rule. Tutsis were favored by the Belgians, creating a long-lasting and very politicized distinction between the two groups. After decades of intermittent fighting, Hutu and Tutsi forces came to the table and in 1993 made an agreement to end conflict which is known as the Arusha Accords. The 1994 Rwandan genocide signaled the failure of those accords. In the genocide, members of the Rwandan Hutu political and military elite organized the systematic killing of hundreds of

Figure 7.4. We must never forget the horrors: Genocide Memorial Center, Kigali, Rwanda. Nearly a million people, mostly civilians, were murdered in the mid-1990s Rwandan genocide.
Dave Proffer, CC BY 2.0, via Wikimedia Commons.

thousands of Tutsis. This was an explicit attempt to exterminate a group of people based on their ethnic identity. Figure 7.4 shows the main genocide memorial in Kigali, the capital of Rwanda. However, a close look at the process of the genocide reveals that the architects of the genocide first worked to eliminate moderate Hutu politicians who might try to stop it or who were political opponents (Straus 2015). This would suggest that, while the conflict played out along ethnic identity lines, it was not solely motivated by ethnic hatred.

A second prominent case of ethnic war in the 1990s involves the breakup of the former Yugoslavia. For decades, this country was ruled by a Communist regime that included a number of different ethnic and religious groups, and these distinctions were successfully suppressed as meaningful political identities. Yugoslav President Josip Tito was able to maintain a unified and stable Yugoslavia, but after his death in 1980, the divisions among groups within society began to play a bigger role in political and social identification. During the 1980s, Kosovars, Croats, Slovenes, Bosnians, Serbs, and Macedonians all began to mobilize for greater group rights. A combination of greater ethnic mobilization, political manipulation, and repression by the Serb leader Slobodan Milosevic led to large-scale war, and eventually international intervention. As with Rwanda, the fighting and atrocities (including mass killings) mainly occurred along ethnic and religious identity lines, and political motivations fused with ethnic divisions to cause conflict.

"Ethnic" motivation or divisions in war sometimes line up with secessionist motivations. When this occurs (and part of a territory attempts to break off and form its own country), the

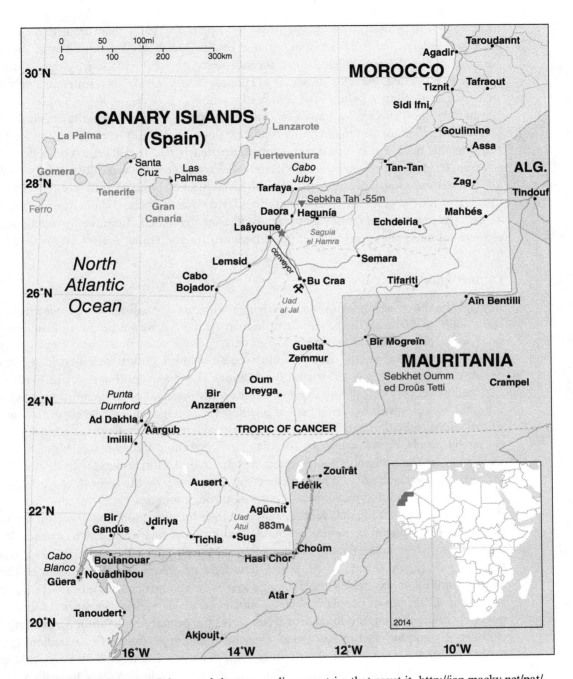

Map 7.1. Western Sahara and the surrounding countries that covet it. http://ian.macky.net/pat/map/eh/eh.html

conflicts are often referred to as secessionist. While these secessionist aims may match up with ethnic identity, they are always linked to the concept of nationalism. Nationalist claims are usually based in cultural distinction and/or a historical right to a homeland. For example, when Spanish Sahara was decolonized by Spain in 1975, Morocco and Mauritania each grabbed part of the homeland claimed by the people of Western Sahara, the Western Saharawis. The Western Saharawi call for independence, led by the rebel group POLISARIO (Frente Popular de Liberación de Saguía el Hamra y Río de Oro), has resulted in a fight for self-rule since then. Map 7.1 shows the contested territory.

Similarly, the Tamils in Sri Lanka lay claim to the territory of Eelam in the country's northern coastal areas. Tamils and the majority Sinhalese population differ in ethnicity and religion, but the demands made by Tamil organizations (particularly the Tamil Tigers) have been for self-governance in their own legitimate homeland. Nationalist conflicts typically feature strong claims about the connection of people to their land. This connection is often based on direct links, such as claims that their ancestors are buried in the land. However, homeland claims are also the product of historical myths and stories that help to develop the nation. Empirically, many wars have elements of nationalist sentiment, ethnic difference, and sometimes religious difference.

Opportunity

Beyond grievance, which forms the underlying motivation for insurgency, people must have the **opportunity** to challenge the government. In many instances, we see people with similar degrees or types of grievance, but civil war occurs only in some cases or at some points in time. In addition to motivation, the creation and success of rebel groups depends on the resources people can muster, as well as structural conditions that make fighting easier or harder.

A number of factors feed into the opportunity structures that potential rebel groups face. For example, societies with high numbers of unemployed young men have larger sets of people for whom joining rebellion may be relatively costless. When there are few economic opportunities for young people, they lose little by forgoing participation in the economy. Moreover, without a clear role in the economy, many young men are left adrift in society, with limited prospects for marriage and stability. These factors can contribute to the appeal of participating in rebellion if they can find meaning and purpose through joining.

Another factor that impacts rebel resources is their location. Some rebel groups are based in territories with mineral or natural resource wealth that is relatively easy to extract. We have seen a set of rebel actors emerge under such conditions, and effectively fuel their rebellions through looting goods such as oil, blood diamonds, or opium and selling them on the black market. In this context, rebels are often able to sustain insurgency without broad support from any particular group of people in society, which can make ending war more difficult because political concessions are no longer (or never were) the primary motivation for fighting.

Other geographic factors can also play into the opportunity for rebellion to occur. Returning to the example of the Shining Path (Sendero Luminoso) in Peru, that group's ability to base in mountainous territory played a large role in its power to sustain itself and resist government counterinsurgency efforts over a number of years. In general, rough terrain (such as mountains or heavy forests) favors insurgents, allowing them respite from government troops when they can effectively use these territories as a base of operations. Similarly, rebel groups at times are based outside the borders of the country to avoid being attacked by government troops that will not cross the border. Map 7.2 show the geographic evolution of

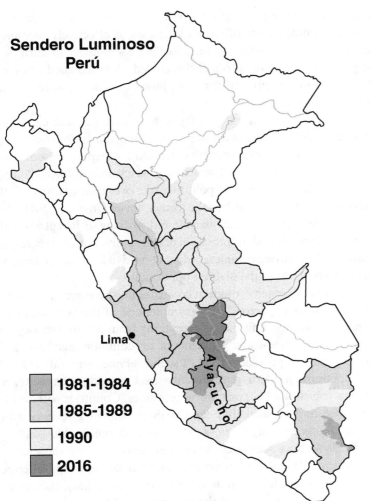

**Sendero Luminoso
Perú**

Lima

Ayacucho

■ 1981-1984
□ 1985-1989
□ 1990
■ 2016

Map 7.2. The spread of Shining Path operations from the mountains to the rest of Peru from 1981 to 1990. The protection of the mountains helped Shining Path to first emerge, and as it grew in strength, it spread to other areas, including areas without mountains Wikipedia.

operations by the Shining Path, beginning in the early 1980s in the highlands of the Ayachuco province before spreading to other mountainous regions in late 1980s, and then to other lowland areas.

State Capacity

Thus far, we have focused our attention on the conditions under which groups of people will be motivated, and have the chance, to engage in civil war with the government. The nature of the government they face will also affect the likelihood of conflict. Governments vary quite a bit in the extent to which they are willing to both repress and fight civilian populations. Some governments have weak political and military institutions that make them vulnerable. One of the challenges for countries in political transition (that is, countries that are becoming more democratic) is that the government often wants to exercise restraint in dealing with the civilian population. In such situations, space opens up for political dissent to be voiced because of liberalization policies, but governments are often not prepared to effectively manage dissent through policy change. At times, this leads to large-scale dissent that, in turn, leads the government (or specific government leaders) to feel threatened. A heightened sense of threat can lead governments to crack down on protests (or other forms of dissent), which in turn leads to an escalation of violence and to civil war.

In addition to willingness to repress, governments vary widely in their overall capacity. This is often referred to as **state capacity**, and the concept includes a number of dimensions (see Chapter 13). At its most basic, it is the capacity of the government to deter, limit, or repress dissent through the provision of order. At one extreme we see countries like Somalia, which are considered "failed states" in large part because they are unable to provide any political order over their territory. At the other end of the spectrum are totalitarian countries, such as the former Soviet Union (USSR). The USSR was able to control and direct nearly every part of civilian life and, in doing so, it kept a very tight rein on political behavior. The role of capacity and the provision of strict political order is tightly linked to grievance as well. Governments that provide complete order but no civil liberties can foment broad-based grievance that erupts into civil war at the slightest opportunity.

Beyond direct control or military capacity, modern countries must engage in a whole host of other functions that comprise "state capacity." For example, one of the key tasks of modern governments is to manage the economy. This means everything from printing money and fiscal policy to making decisions about free-trade agreements or common markets. Relatedly, modern governments are expected to provide a level of social services unparalleled in history. In order to fulfill these functions, modern governments need extractive capacity, and this typically comes from either a robust tax base or natural resources. Countries with low capacity perform poorly in these tasks, and as such they tend both to foment grievance among the population and to be unable to successfully address problems with policy changes.

One of the interesting trends we have seen over the last few decades is that the source of state revenue appears to play a critical role in the state capacity/civil war relationship. When countries rely primarily on natural resource wealth (such as from oil or natural gas), they often fail to develop strong links between the population and the government. Ideally, the population will form a viable tax base, and demand and receive services from the state. This is the way countries develop high capacity over time. But when leaders of governments can rely solely on natural resource wealth, they often ignore the general population. This creates situations of high-intensity grievance over time, increasing the chance of civil war. This has been characterized as the "oil curse" or "resource curse." It represents a paradox, in that countries that are endowed with natural resources should be best placed for strong economic and political development. Instead, they tend to lag behind in both of these areas because leaders in these countries fall prey to incentives to exploit natural resources in lieu of creating a robust economic infrastructure (including investments in health and education, as well as a functioning taxation system).

When Governments and Opposition Fail to Compromise

Governments and opposition (or rebel) groups are both necessary to bring about civil war. We identified conditions leading to both high motivation and high opportunity for war to occur.

Figure 7.5. An indivisible holy of holies? Temple Mount/Haram esh-Sharif in Jerusalem. Both Judaism and Islam hold this site to have great religious value, making it difficult for either side to accept proposals to share it and making conflict over the site more likely.
Atlantide Phototravel/Corbis Documentary/Getty Images.

But what these factors do not account for is why state governments and rebel groups (or potential rebel groups) cannot resolve their differences before fighting starts. In almost all cases, opposition actors attempt to elicit concessions from the government before the outbreak of war. Insurgency does not develop in a vacuum, and many governments try to make political changes to avoid violent conflict with citizens. Why do these efforts fail?

Governments and potential rebels fail to compromise, and thus avoid conflict, for three key reasons (see Chapter 1). First, in some situations compromise may not be possible. These are what we call **indivisible conflicts.** This is relatively uncommon, and these disputes tend to center on specific flashpoints such as religious sites (Hassner 2013). While many things can be negotiated or split across groups in society, there are some territories, or even buildings, that multiple actors lay claim to and that are seen as fundamentally indivisible (i.e. they do not lend themselves to compromise). One example is the Temple Mount/Haram esh-Sharif in Jerusalem (see Figure 7.5).

Second, a common reason that governments and potential rebels fail to make a deal before fighting starts is that they are uncertain about what agreement would avoid conflict. This is similar to many bargaining situations in everyday life. Given the opportunity to negotiate over something you want, people are willing to compromise but would like to get the best deal possible. The same is true for governments and rebel groups. These actors have strong incentives to bluff in an effort to get the best deal they can. Bargaining fails when both sides have incentives to bluff and are unsure about the capabilities and resolve of their opponents. This problem can be particularly difficult before civil war starts, as there is often a lot of uncertainty about opposition capabilities, as opposition actors must often conceal themselves from government for self-protection. This difficulty can contribute to bargaining failure and lead to armed conflict.

A third key reason that civil wars do not get resolved before they start is that these actors often have difficulty trusting one another (often referred to as a **commitment problem**). Specifically, it is very difficult for rebels or potential rebels who are mobilizing against the state to believe government promises about the future. Nearly all governments have much more power at their disposal than groups within society. Thus, it would be relatively easy and low-cost for governments to renege on promises they make to resolve group grievances. Even when governments are earnest in their desire to avoid conflict, societal groups are wary of putting themselves in more vulnerable positions. Similarly, governments have reason to mistrust the promises of these opposition groups at times, as such groups may renege on promises to eschew violence or lay down their arms. Many civil wars are actually conflicts that stop and start over time. **Recurrent civil war** suggests that one or both parties to the dispute failed to keep up their end of the bargain. Thus, it is difficult to resolve underlying disputes and avoid civil war when there are acute problems of trust and uncertainty about what possible settlement or political chance would avoid war.

Conflict Dynamics in Civil Wars

Civil wars are not single, simple events, but rather relatively complex political processes. As such, they are dynamic in many respects. Here, we address several important dynamics, including the fragmentation of conflicts and actors and the transnational dynamics of civil war.

Fragmentation

For many years, salient civil wars – such as the American Civil War and the Greek Civil War – led us to characterize civil wars as fights between an existing state government and a unified opposition. However, the more recent trend is towards recognition of what we call "fragmented" civil wars (Cunningham 2006). Fragmented civil conflicts are more complex than "state versus rebels" or "north versus south." Instead, these conflicts often have multiple rebel groups fighting the same state. Individual actors themselves can be fragmented, such as when the opposition or the state has multiple internal factions that impact conflict dynamics. There are two primary ways that conflicts are **fragmented**: (1) there are many actors, and/or (2) actors have multiple factions within them.

We can think of the Catholic self-determination movement in Northern Ireland as a fragmented opposition. It included a number of actors that were all fighting (or using other tactics) in pursuit of the same goal (a unified Ireland). The Irish Republican Army (IRA) was a paramilitary organization closely connected to Sinn Fein, which primarily operated (and still operates) as a political party. This connection persisted for many decades, with Sinn Fein considered by some to be the "political wing" of the IRA. The Irish movement was always internally complex and became more so as factions of the IRA proliferated over time. Figure 7.6 shows a mural in support of one such organization – the Provisional IRA (PIRA). The mural depicts Kieran Nugent, a PIRA volunteer who after being convicted of hijacking a bus declared himself a political prisoner and not a criminal, and refused to wear prisoner uniform, instead wearing a blanket (hence being a "blanketman"). In other situations, a single organization divides into multiple components with often complex relationships over time between them. For example, in the mid 1960s, the rebel group FROLINAT challenged the government of Chad. By the early 1970s, the initial rebel group had splintered into multiple groups.

In some cases, we see a rebel group maintain unity over time. The Kurdish Democratic Party of Iran (KDPI) has represented Kurds in Iran since 1946, and has remained fairly cohesive. Yet

Figure 7.6. Mural in support of the Provisional IRA in Belfast, Northern Ireland. Kieran Nugent is the first "Blanketman," as when jailed he refused to wear the same prison uniform as individuals convicted of nonpolitical crimes like robbery. He called himself a political prisoner, and instead wore a blanket as a protest. Symbolism of all kinds can be tremendously important in civil wars.
Keith Ruffles, CC BY 3.0, via Wikimedia Commons.

other oppositions see rampant splintering. Among the most fragmented oppositions is that representing Muslim Kashmiris. The Kashmiri territory is spread across India and Pakistan, and is home to a large Muslim population as well as Hindu and Buddhist Kashmiris. The fight for greater local control has included dozens of organizations active over the decades-long course of the conflict.

In some wars, the opposition actors are fundamentally divided in terms of what they want out of the conflict. This can lead to a situation of **multiparty civil war**, in which rebel groups fight both the government and each other. Civil wars in Afghanistan, Cambodia, Iraq, Lebanon, Syria, and Somalia, for example, all involved a number of actors battling across the country. In these wars, rebel groups may try to work together, but often change their allegiances in the midst of war (Christia 2012).

As well as the number of rebel groups in a conflict, there are two other dynamic processes that contribute to our understanding of how fragmented a dispute is. First, when there are many opposition actors, their connection to one another matters. We conceptualize this as the degree of **institutionalization** among organizations in a single opposition (Bakke et al 2012). As with the IRA and Sinn Fein, political and military wings are often linked formally. The two organizations may work together on strategy and policy, but then specific tasks are undertaken by the different wings. "Umbrella groups" often link multiple rebels together as a way to coordinate during conflict, particularly during negotiations with the state.

The degree of institutionalization captures the strength of ties between rebel groups (or political/military wings). When these ties are strong, the opposition is more unified, less fragmented. This is distinct from situations in which there are multiple opposition actors in the conflict that are not connected – such as the war in the Democratic Republic of the Congo in the late 1990s. In that war, the Rally for Congolese Democracy (RCD) and Movement for the Liberation of Congo (MLC) formed independently, had unconnected leaderships, and fought against the government separately. These two opposition actors did not have ties to each other or a clear shared goal.

Second, the balance of power varies across rebels even when they are explicitly linked together and pursue the same end goal. Sometimes there is a dominant organization that holds the majority of power. The Tamil Tigers (LTTE), for example, were the militarily strongest power (and often enjoyed the most societal support) among Tamil organizations in Sri Lanka. In stark contrast, there have been major shifts in power and local dominance among organizations within the Palestinian movement challenging Israel. Fatah, Hamas and Palestinian Islamic Jihad have all vied to lead this movement. When there is **centralized power**, we can think of opposition movements as less fragmented. In such cases, one rebel group has the majority of power and influences the behavior of other rebel groups. We can think of these oppositions as hegemonic rather than fragmented.

Each of these dimensions is dynamic: organizations splinter or coalesce; umbrella groups disintegrate and form; power shifts over the course of conflict. Because of these dynamic changes, it can be difficult to decide with whom to engage in dialogue once the dispute becomes violent. The current civil war in Syria illustrates all of these elements. It includes fragmented actors and is a multiparty conflict. The conflict has seen a proliferation of opposition groups of different types, and even identifying which actors carried out which attack or who may control what territory is challenging. There have been numerous efforts to encourage organizations to ally or coalesce but these have generally been unsuccessful. The case study below delves into this case in more detail.

Why are some conflicts fragmented? Some countries have structural preconditions that make it particularly likely that conflicts will involve multiple actors. This is often true in ethnically divided societies, especially where there is a history of economic discrimination and political exclusion. For example, the Ethiopian civil war included Tigrayan, Eritrean, Oromo, and Somali armed groups. While they allied to fight together against the Communist government, many of the rebel groups continued to fight after the war was won because they perceived the new administration as too dominated by the Tigray group.

Repression by the government affects fragmentation and can either break apart or fuel the opposition. Repression nearly always increases the costs of participation for individuals. As the costs and risks associated with rebellion increase, individuals or factions respond in a variety of ways. Different responses to the costs of repression can lead to dissent within the original group. For example, increasing stress on the Tamil Tigers in Sri Lanka led to the splintering of the group. The leader of the breakaway Karuna faction claimed that the LTTE leadership no longer had the interests of its people in mind, and that the negative consequences of the war were being unevenly borne across the Tamil population.

Another way that repression fragments oppositions is by prompting defection or **side switching**. This refers to a rebel group joining the government side and fighting against other opposition organizations. For example, in 1992, part of the Southern Sudanese Liberation Movement broke off of the main organization (to form the SPLM/A-Nasir) and began to fight for the government rather than against it. Some defections are motivated by intense state pressure on rebels that makes rebel leaders fear for their own survival and induces them to turn on their brethren. Side switching can also happen for more opportunistic reasons. In order to stay in power, rebel leaders often have to fight against local rivals. When their survival is at stake, some rebel leaders would rather defect than risk annihilation.

While repression does splinter oppositions in some cases, it galvanizes support and actually increases cohesion in others. Crackdowns by government forces can generate new supporters, and can reinvigorate fighters by turning their attention to perceived injustices. For example, Iraqi repression of the Kurdish population has been argued to provide a rallying point for the group. Whether repression fragments the opposition or increases unity depends, in part, on the stability of the leadership structures at the outset. Repression puts stress on opposition movements, and those with already deep internal divisions are likely to break under pressure.

Transnational Dimensions

Extending beyond the boundaries of a single country, there are a number of transnational dimensions of civil war. Historically, there have been individuals that fight in foreign wars, and we see a number of **foreign fighters** moving across borders to join conflict today. Countries that are external to the civil war also get involved, sometimes on the side of the government and sometimes on the side of the opposition. The participation of foreign actors (individuals or other countries) has a number of implications for civil war. On the whole, **intervention** by another country that includes military support (i.e. troops on the ground, or weapons being sent to the conflict) tends to create longer wars. In some instances, competing interventions on different sides of the civil war lead to intractable conflicts. For example, the civil war in Angola against UNITA rebels included substantial support from both South Africa and Cuba to opposing sides in the war. The war was only brought to an end when the external countries intervening in the civil war were willing to pull back.

Intervention is also linked to the ways that wars end. When an external country intervenes in a dispute, it lengthens the time to a negotiated settlement. However, such interventions are also associated with faster military victory. The impact of the intervention depends on how much it changes the balance of power in the war (i.e. can it help get one side to a quick victory?). When the intervention is balanced by support going to both (or all) sides, conflict will drag on even longer as a result of the external support.

Foreign fighters have had substantial impacts on civil wars. For example, the long-running conflict between Chechen secessionists and Russia fundamentally changed after foreign fighters began to participate. These fighters (often from Saudi Arabia) brought new ideas and expertise to the Chechen forces. Over time, interaction between foreign and domestic fighters shaped the degree to which Chechen soldiers focused on religious identity over nationalist appeals.

Early mobilization by Chechens centered on their homeland and self-rule claims. This changed to an increasing focus on the dispute with Russia as an Islamic struggle. This change can be attributed to foreign influence on the leaders of the Chechen movement, as well as the impact foreign-sponsored training camps had on soldiers. The changes in soldier training impacted both how the local soldiers perceived opposition movement goals and the degree to which they saw certain tactics (especially violence against other Chechens) as legitimate and productive. Soldiers became more aligned with the Islamist goals of the movement, and began to accept more radical and violent tactics being used in the dispute. The integration of foreign fighters led to divergence in movement goals and tactics, which created a foundation for splintering, as some members embraced Islamic ideology while others held strong to Chechen nationalism, and further disagreements arose over tactics.

More recently, people from all over the world have been drawn to the Middle East to fight on behalf of ISIS. International recruits are typically young and untrained until they reach ISIS-controlled areas. Unlike the Chechen case, they are not bringing new ideas or expertise to the dispute. It is not yet clear what the overall impact of foreign fighters will be in ISIS's multifront war, though in the past foreign fighters have not been able to sustain ISIS's initial territorial gains, especially in Iraq.

The ease with which rebels can reach audiences beyond their territory, including potential recruits and the broader international community, is a recently changing dynamic in contemporary civil wars. The Internet has played a key role in this. Between 2003 and 2009, the number of websites maintained by terrorist-related actors more than doubled. The ability to easily access traditional and social media allows small, newly formed, insurgent organizations to develop a base of support and to market their views and ideals to a large number of people. While rebels have long sought support outside their borders, the means through which this happens has changed and expanded the number and variety of people they can reach.

Contemporary civil wars are also complex and dynamic in the ways in which they are financed, often drawing from a number of external sources. Actors outside civil wars contribute to the fight, including countries such as the United States, other rebel groups around the world, and organizations that represent the interests of specific religious or ethnic communities. As well as governments, opposition and rebel movements provide support (such as that given by al Qaeda to expand its affiliate network), as do diaspora groups. These actors provide a variety of types of external support, including money, weapons, intelligence, training, and troops that participate directly in conflict. Changes in the global financial industry now facilitate supporters transferring funds without necessarily having any direct contact with opposition actors they support.

A final transnational dimension of civil war worth noting is the spatial contagion of conflict. Empirically, we see that civil wars cluster in places around the world. This is sometimes referred to as a **neighborhood effect**. That is, some areas have been identified as "bad neighborhoods" in terms of conflict potential, such as the Middle East/North Africa in the past few decades. There are several reasons that we see clustering of civil wars. First, some of the underlying conditions that we know make civil war more likely also tend to be clustered. For example, wars are more common in relatively impoverished countries. If we look at global trends in economic development, we see poorer countries clustered in the same regions. Similarly, the outbreak of civil war has been associated with political regimes that are transitioning toward or away from democratic government. "Regime types" (democracy, nondemocracy, transitioning countries) also tend to cluster spatially.

A second explanation for spatial clustering of civil wars is direct **contagion.** Contagion means that the war moves from one country to another. For example, in places with porous borders, we see arms and weapons moving across borders. This can make rebellion easier. Similarly, there are often substantial flows of people across borders during civil war. Refugee crises can foment dissent, increasing the motivation for conflict. Negative effects (both political and economic) associated with population flows can impact the local population and lower the opportunity costs for conflict in the country receiving these refugees. An **opportunity cost** is what is forgone in lieu of participating in conflict. For example, if a person has to give up a lucrative job in order to join the rebellion, she has a high opportunity cost. Finally, connections between populations in conflict can increase the chance of conflict nearby. Potential rebels can learn from conflicts nearby, adopting similar tactics. These conflicts can also inspire similar groups (such as those with a shared ethnic identity across the border) to have a heightened sense of insecurity and lead to conflict.

It is difficult for countries to completely control the spillover effects of civil war. This is especially true if there are preexisting ties between the populations. However, one factor found to help countries resist the contagion of conflict is high state capacity. States of this type are best able to manage the challenges of wars on their borders and influxes of displaced people because they have more robust infrastructure and the capacity to adjust policies as needed.

How Civil Wars End

Civil wars end in one of three ways. First, a great number of wars essentially "peter out" with no formal peace settlement and no decisive victory by one side. This happens for several reasons. In some cases, the opposition can no longer sustain the fight against the state, but their grievances remain and there is high potential for remobilization. This turn of events could happen because external support ended, or the rebel group splintered. Alternatively, some wars peter out because rebels are able to achieve enough of what they want such that large-scale mobilization against the government is no longer supported. In these cases, there is no formal war-ending settlement, but the government has ameliorated some of the rebels' grievances through policy changes. For example, the Front for Islamic Salvation (FIS) fought the Algerian government in the 1990s, but eventually ceased military activity against government forces. The Algerian government did negotiate and make some concessions (mainly related to language), but there was no formal agreement that defined terms for ending the war.

Some wars peter out because the government is no longer willing to fight, and this leads to "de facto states" where the status quo is opposition control over a territory within the country. This has happened in a number of wars, resulting in the establishment of de facto states such as Nagorno-Karabakh in Azerbaijan and South Ossetia in Georgia. Wars that end in this way often recur because the opposition is not entirely defeated and the fundamental dispute is not resolved.

Wars can also, of course, end in victory. Historically, victory was a more common way for civil wars to end. For example, there was a clear victor in the American Civil War, the Spanish Civil War, and the Greek Civil War. Particularly before the end of the Cold War, civil wars that did end decisively (as opposed to petering out) typically had a clear victor. In practice, this outcome looks like either the annihilation of the opposition forces (or their complete surrender as in the American Civil War), or the complete overthrow of the country's government.

Peace Processes

The third, and increasingly common, way that wars end is for the parties to the conflict to sign a **negotiated settlement**. In these situations, existing governments and some set of rebels negotiate to determine what the post-conflict government will look like or for some degree of self-rule for the territory in dispute. These negotiations typically involve other actors as well. The United Nations, for example, participates in a number of conflict resolution processes. Regional organizations, such as the African Union, also participate and promote multiparty negotiations in which many countries or other actors are brought in to assist the warring parties in coming to a compromise and ending the war.

These peace processes vary quite a bit in terms of how long they take, who is involved, and the degree to which they are successful (see Chapter 10). The post–Cold War period has seen several successful negotiation processes, such as those leading to an end of war in El Salvador, Guatemala, and Mozambique. Other processes have been less successful. A number of outside countries and international agencies have attempted to help negotiate a settlement between the Palestinians and Israelis over contested status and territory. The Oslo-based peace processes (referred to as Oslo I and Oslo II) brought together a wide set of actors including the European Union, the United States, and Norway in an attempt to resolve this dispute. This process led to the creation of the "Roadmap to Peace" wherein all the negotiating parties agreed to a plan moving toward resolution of the conflict. That dispute, however, has not been successfully ended.

The peace process that led to the creation of South Sudan, which seceded from Sudan based on an agreement made in 2005, also included a number of international actors, including the Intergovernmental Authority on Development, an African organization that promotes trade. Not only did this civil war settlement see the creation of two separate political entities (now Sudan and South Sudan), it addressed one of the key dimensions of the conflict, oil revenues. As with many countries in civil war, Sudan had an extensive natural resource industry. The oilfields, however, were primarily located in the south, while the center of political power was in the Sudanese capital of Khartoum in the north. Thus, the government in Khartoum had very strong incentives not to allow the south to secede. The war between northern Sudan and southern Sudan raged on and off for decades before a negotiated settlement was reached.

Negotiated settlement is now the most common way that civil wars end. Yet there are substantial barriers to successful peacemaking through negotiations. First, when there are many parties to the war, they bring a diversity of preferences that can make finding a compromise more difficult. Second, as noted in Section 7.4, these wars are quite dynamic. In practice, this means that who matters for civil war settlement is not always obvious. When the government side or the opposition side is changing (either becoming more unified or more fragmented), neither the combatants nor outsiders attempting to help end the conflict can easily see which rebels or which parts of the government must be a part of the deal to make it work. Even when the actors are relatively stable, we can see shifting alliances among groups in multiparty conflicts that make durable agreements much more difficult. For example, in the Afghan Civil War, a number of alliances were made and broken and sometimes remade among the different rebel groups representing the various ethnic groups. As a result, because alliances are continually shifting, it is never clear how much power any particular set of actors will continue to hold relative to the others. When governments, rebels, or another actor outside the conflict (such as the United Nations or a major power like the United States) do not have a good idea of how strong the different sides of the conflict will be over the long term, it is very difficult to know what kind of negotiated settlement will bring lasting peace.

Credible Commitments: Problems and Solutions

Another major challenge to ending wars is the acute commitment problem that develops during the conflict. The central problem is that both governments and rebels may have incentives to renege on a conflict settlement later on. For example, rebels may have pressed the state to make political concessions to end the war that involve greater autonomy or self-government. But what is to stop the government from reversing these concessions once the rebels have disarmed, particularly if new people come into power in government? Post-conflict, the state maintains its coercive forces, but the rebels do not generally maintain an independent army. Thus, it is often very difficult for rebels to believe government promises, even those made in good faith.

Several solutions are used to mitigate the problems of credible commitments. First, some civil war settlements involve what are called **third-party guarantors**. These are external countries or international organizations that make a commitment to help the former combatants stick to the deal that has been made. This "guarantee" goes beyond the immediate end of the conflict, and is often linked to specific postwar institutions (such as power-sharing arrangements that specify which groups get a say in governance, or territorial autonomy arrangements). An enduring guarantee could include peacekeeping forces, but typically does not.

Second, peace agreements often entail complex designs for power sharing among the former combatants as a way to institutionalize (and make less changeable) the concessions that were made. The exact power-sharing institutions vary across different war settlements and often reflect the deep divisions in society (especially ethnic and religious divisions). However, all of these arrangements include a clear specification of which groups will be represented in government, autonomy for these groups to conduct their own affairs to some extent, and veto power over major decisions. For example, the power-sharing government in Lebanon mandated a ratio of Christians to Muslims in the legislature and in top positions in government to create a stable balance of power among the groups.

Third, the integration of military and security forces has been used specifically to help post-conflict societies develop greater trust in the military and prevent rapid remobilization along the lines of the conflict. This process typically entails the integration of opposition forces into the country's military apparatus. The most successful type of integration, some argue, is one where former opposition soldiers are dispersed throughout the military (i.e. they do not have their own units) and are included in the hierarchy of the military.

Not all peace agreements are designed to fully end civil wars. In some cases, we see both governments and external mediators respond to multiparty conflicts by pursuing "**partial peace**" agreements in which some, but not all, of the rebels participate. In Chad, for example, the government has signed peace agreements with a series of rebel groups, although the conflict has continued as new groups have emerged. An examination of these partial peace agreements from the past few decades shows that they can work for getting some groups to agree to stop fighting. However, they rarely end multiparty wars completely. Rebel groups that do not sign the peace deal may eventually follow suit, but they have incentives to hold out for a better deal if they can continue the fighting unilaterally.

Other key actors in durable ends to civil war are **peacekeepers**. The United Nations (UN), regional organizations such as the African Union or the North Atlantic Treaty Organization, and individual countries (such as India) sometimes provide ground troops to help maintain a peace settlement. Traditionally, the role of United Nations peacekeepers was to observe compliance with ceasefires and peace agreements, and to form a barrier between formerly combating armies. The goal in doing so was to avoid a failed peace process due to concerns that the other side was not carrying through on its commitments or to skirmishes among soldiers, rather than deliberative decisions by the leaders in the civil war.

Since the 1990s, there has been a fundamental change in the nature of peacekeeping. Peacekeepers now engage in a number of different kinds of peace operations. The soldiers still engage in traditional peacekeeping, but peacekeeping forces have also engaged in diplomacy, institution building, and peace enforcement. One of the key differences between traditional peacekeeping and new peace operations is that the traditional peacekeeping forces were invited in by all parties to the conflict to help the resolution process. Now, United Nations peacekeepers sometimes enter into conflicts without the consent of all the warring parties, and try to play a more active role in the resolution process. These "enforcement missions" are authorized under UN Charter chapter VII (see Chapter 10).

A study of these different missions shows that peacekeeping can play a positive role in resolving conflicts. Civil wars that end with peacekeeper involvement are less likely to recur. Even so, the dynamic nature of civil wars impacts the effectiveness of peacekeeping as well. A study of twenty-five international "peacebuilding" missions led by the UN to countries in a state of civil war shows that the UN was successful in about half of them. Yet, if we look at civil wars with more than two sides, we see that the success rate of UN peacekeeping is only about 25 percent.

Long-Term Effects of Civil War

Civil wars themselves of course impose direct, immediate, and horrifying costs on civilians. For example, in the decades-long Colombian Civil War, the number of civilians killed, more than 214,000, was nearly five times as high as as the number of fighters killed (Colombia: armed conflict fatalities 1958–2018, by category 2021). Beyond the direct costs of civil war in terms of lives lost and infrastructure destroyed, there are long-term implications for societies that have been afflicted by these conflicts. Substantial evidence has been gathered in the areas of health, economic development, and education in the wake of civil wars. A central conclusion from research in these areas is that the effects of civil war are quite long-term. Even once the fighting is over, it takes decades for societies to rebuild.

Research into health crises in civil war suggests multiple paths through which conflict impacts the civilian population long after fighting stops. Most straightforwardly, disruption of government service means poorer sanitation conditions and blocked access to medical care, two reasons why the recent civil war in Yemen contributed to nearly a million cases of cholera, a preventable and sometimes fatal disease. Further, large-scale displacement of civilians increases disease and disability among the population. Even in areas with no direct fighting, we see an increase in mortality rates, including from malaria and the spread of HIV. Some of this is thought to be a product of refugees fleeing their homes and ending up in desperate living conditions. There are also substantial effects on long-term mental health. Sexual violence, including rape, is used both by state governments and rebel groups as a tool of warfare: one study found that rates of sexual violence were fifty-five times higher in areas of the Democratic Republic of Congo directly affected by civil war violence, as compared to areas not directly affected (Kalonda-Kayama 2010; see also Chapter 2). This violence and the recruitment of child soldiers are two processes of war that have very long-term implications both for individuals who suffer from mental trauma and for societies that struggle to deal with the aftermath of these practices.

We have also seen that there are long-term economic implications of civil war, as both human and physical capital are damaged during conflict. During civil war, economic growth typically comes to a standstill, or declines. Violence in civil war destroys houses, livestock, and infrastructure such as roads and bridges. Even after war, these resources take time to rebuild and renew. Relatedly, infrastructure for education is typically damaged. Schools are destroyed, and teachers cannot be found for many classrooms even after conflict has ended. During wartime, children lose the opportunity to continue their education. This leads to high illiteracy rates after conflict, and a general decline in the education of the population. Thus, countries afflicted by civil war face long-running challenges in rebuilding, including populations with limited access to education, poor health, and few economic opportunities. In this light, it is easy to see why conflict recurs in so many places.

Refugee flows set off by civil war also have longer-term consequences for both communities of refugees and countries that receive them. Refugees often face significant hardship as they flee, and often their circumstances remain dire during long stays in refugee camps. The resettlement of refugees abroad is at times met with resistance – sometimes violent – in the receiving country. Refugee flows have also been associated with increased risk of conflict in the receiving country, contributing conflict contagion.

Another long-term though less well-understood impact of civil conflict is on the environment (see Chapter 13). Rebels and other armed groups have been responsible for environmental degradation in places like Senegal and Brazil. The use of land mines in particular creates sustained environmental challenges. Yet, the relationship between conflict and the environment is not always clear-cut. For example, rebels in the Democratic Republic of Congo have both adversarial and cooperative relationships with conservation efforts there. The interplay between civil war, rebel actors, and the environment will continue to be a global concern as climate change alters the environmental stressors in many conflict-affected areas.

CASE STUDY

The Syrian Civil War

The civil war in Syria, which began in 2011, illustrates many of the dynamics described in this chapter (see also Chapter 13). It has been a very destructive conflict, in which more than 500,000 people have been killed, creating about five million refugees and an additional six million internally displaced people out of a prewar population of about 23 million. The Syrian conflict has been very fractionalized and has involved a high level of external involvement on all sides. The war has had profound effects on Syria's neighbors and the region as a whole, and efforts by international actors to facilitate a negotiated settlement have proven ineffective. Map 7.3 shows a map of Syria with the distribution of different ethnic and religious groups.

The conflict in Syria followed in the wake of a period of political protest and change in the Middle East/North Africa. In late 2010 and early 2011, large-scale nonviolent protests in Tunisia and Egypt led to the removal of long-established autocrats. Protests swept across much of the rest of region as well and came to Syria in 2011. A key goal of the initially nonviolent protest movement was political liberalization.

At the time protest broke out, Syria shared many features in common with other countries in the region. It had an autocratic government, which for four decades had been led by the Assad family: Hafiz al-Assad until his death in 2000 and then his son Bashar al-Assad. In 2011, Syria's economy was stagnant and unemployment was high. Additionally, the Syrian government was very repressive toward civilians.

Syria's population is religiously and ethnically diverse. The majority population is Muslim, but there are significant religious minorities including Maronite Christians and Druze. The majority of Syria's Muslims are Sunni, but the Alawi group, a minority Shia sect, comprises about 11 percent of the country's population. For much of the time since Syria became an independent country, the Alawi have had a privileged political and economic position. The Assads are Alawi and have appointed Alawi to key posts in their governments and militaries. Syria's Sunni population is largely Arab, but there is also a significant Kurdish minority. These ethnic and religious differences have been important factors in the armed conflict.

The Syrian Civil War started as a nonviolent movement for regime change, and the government responded to protests with massive repression. Rather than ending the protests, this repression intensified them. The effects of repression can be uncertain, and in this case, the extreme response of the Assad regime to largely peaceful protest inspired greater commitment by many individuals to challenge the regime. In July 2011, a group of Syrian military officers defected and formed the Free Syrian Army, the first named rebel group in the conflict. Defection of military personnel can spell the imminent total collapse of a government, and it appears that many observers outside the conflict saw this as a turning point that would lead to the end of the Assad government. Instead the Assad forces began fighting opposition forces, and for the rest of 2011 and into 2012 the conflict became more violent until the country was in full-scale civil war.

We can think of the civil war in Syria as having four broad "sides": the government and its supporters, and three main opposition groups. There are internal divisions within each

(cont.)

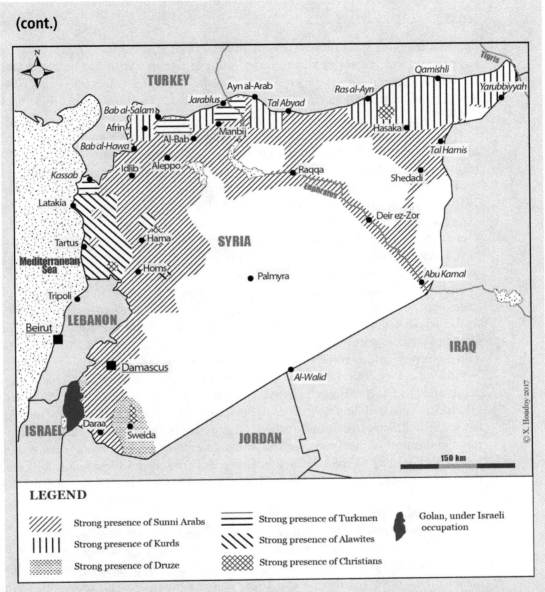

Map 7.3. Demographic map of Syria, before the civil war. Some but not all conflict occurred across ethnoreligious lines, with the government being mostly Alawite and some groups being Kurdish. Baczko, Dorronsoro and Quesnay, *Civil War in Syria: Mobilization and Competing World Orders* (Cambridge: Cambridge University Press).

side, and external actors have played a role by supporting or directly participating in the fighting. The Assad regime received support from Iran, the Lebanese rebel group Hizbullah, and (since 2015) Russia.

Of the three opposition sides, the first is a set of rebel groups that are fighting primarily on behalf of the Kurdish population and seek greater autonomy (or potentially

(cont.)

independence) for Syrian Kurds. The Kurdish groups have achieved military success and have carved out control of significant portions of Syrian territory. The Kurdish ethnic/ nationalist group is spread out across territory in Turkey, Iraq, and Iran as well. This has led to significant differences among international actors about supporting the Kurds in Syria.

The second opposition side is a set of groups, primarily made up of Sunni Arabs, that calls for a greater role of Islam in Syrian society. The most prominent of these groups is ISIS, which started in Iraq and has declared an Islamic caliphate. At its peak, ISIS controlled territory in Syria and Iraq in which ten million people lived, though since 2015 the group has lost control over substantial areas of territory. Another prominent "Islamist" group is the al-Qaeda affiliate in Syria, Jabhat-al-Nusra, which has an agenda similar to ISIS's but has had direct clashes with the group over strategy. These groups have received funding from countries and rich individuals in the region. Map 7.4 shows the territory that ISIS controlled at one point in the conflict.

The third opposition side is often referred to as the "moderate" or "secular" opposition and comprises a large number of rebel groups primarily made up of Sunni Arabs opposed to the Assad regime. There have been efforts to coordinate the political and military activities of these groups but they have been largely unsuccessful. The United States and Turkey have provided some support to these groups in the conflict.

While these opposition groups generally seek regime change in Syria, they differ substantially in their visions of what a postwar Syria would look like. At times these groups have clashed directly with each other and the extreme degree of fractionalization can make it difficult to determine who the key actors in the conflict even are at times. The fractionalization of the Syrian conflict and high level of external involvement have been key factors leading to the conflict's intensity and resistance to resolution. Not only are there diverse preferences among opposition actors, but they compete for external support. This creates strong incentives for opposition militias to stake out their own territory in the dispute, rather than cooperate with one another.

The Syrian conflict has continued for many years despite high-profile international efforts at mediation. Early in the conflict, former United Nations Secretary General Kofi Annan was appointed the joint United Nations/Arab League Envoy for the conflict, and he sought to bring the combatants together to negotiate an end to the war. Annan's efforts were unsuccessful and he was followed by Algerian diplomat Lakhdar Brahimi, who also attempted to facilitate a settlement. Throughout the war there have been frequent international conferences bringing together regional leaders and some opposition groups, but it has been impossible to get all of the key actors to sit down at the table together. In addition, while there has been some success in negotiating limited ceasefires, there has been no progress toward getting a cessation of hostilities along the main battle lines and between the largest combatants.

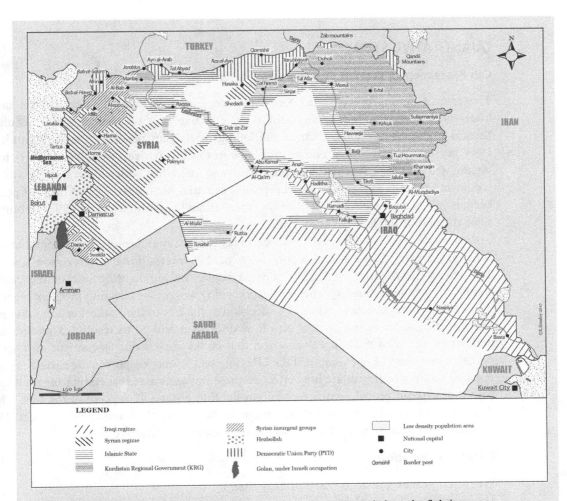

Map 7.4. ISIS-controlled territory, 2014. Note how ISIS carried out its fighting across national borders, as part of its campaign to establish an Islamic caliphate, a single, new country across the Muslim world that it would govern according to its interpretation of strict Sharia Islamic law. Baczko, Dorronsoro and Quesnay, *Civil War in Syria: Mobilization and Competing World Orders* (Cambridge: Cambridge University Press)

The Syrian Civil War demonstrates a number of key issues for civil war resolution. The opposition forces have no reason to trust any promises made by the government; i.e., there is a credible commitment problem. This is especially true because of the extent of human rights abuse by the Assad government. There remains uncertainty about what kind of settlement might be agreed to by the government or opposition forces. Among the opposition, it is unclear which factions can work together in a conflict resolution process. Finally, external support for the competing sides in the war makes it harder to bring to an end. There does not seem to be an easy path forward for getting these external actors out of the conflict.

QUANTITATIVE STUDY

Can Peacekeeping Prevent Civil War from Recurring?

The role of peacekeeping forces has expanded over time, and it is critical for us to understand whether their deployment is an effective way to prevent further conflict. Several high-profile events, such as the killing of Belgian peacekeepers in Rwanda in 1994 and UN peacekeepers' committing rape in Central African Republic in 2016, have highlighted the fact that peacekeeping can pose risks for both soldiers and civilians. Understanding the efficacy of peacekeeping is essential because the deployment of peacekeepers has been the primary tool of the international community for conflict resolution since the end of the Cold War in 1989.

Page Fortna tackled the question of peacekeeper efficacy at its most fundamental level in her 2004 article "Does peacekeeping keep peace? International intervention and the duration of peace after civil war." Fortna begins by highlighting one of the central challenges for understanding whether peacekeeping works: the selection problem inherent in deciding where peacekeepers go. The decision of the UN to send peacekeepers takes into account the nature of the conflict and how difficult it will be to resolve. This decision-making process is a meaningful selection that could impact our assessment of whether peacekeepers work. For example, if the UN only sends peacekeepers to the easiest cases to resolve, we may overestimate how effective these missions are. Just comparing civil wars with and without peacekeepers, we see that fighting restarts 42 percent of the time when there were no peacekeepers and 39 percent of the time when there were peacekeepers. That difference does not suggest that peacekeeping is especially effective.

Research Questions

Where do peacekeepers go (hard or easy cases)?
Does peacekeeping work?

Theory and Hypotheses

The central argument in Fortna's article is that we cannot assess the efficacy of peacekeepers until we know what type of cases they are sent to, and without making appropriate comparisons that account for different lengths of time before fighting reerupts. The simple comparison, above, that motivates the study (between war recurrence after wars that end with peacekeepers and those that do not) fails to account for two important facts. The first is that war settlements break down at different intervals. The 1990 war in Rwanda was preceded by twenty-six years of peace, but the next settlement failed and saw new fighting in about a year. A second fact missed by this comparison is the role that the selection process that determines where peacekeepers are sent (discussed above) might have in biasing the study. It could be that peacekeepers only go to wars that are very hard to resolve, so peacekeepers look less effective than they are. Or, they could go primarily to easy-to-solve wars, and thus the effect of peacekeepers looks greater than it is.

Fortna evaluates two potential hypotheses:

Hypothesis 1: Peacekeepers are more likely to go to hard cases.

Hypothesis 2: Peacekeepers decrease the chance of recurrent war.

Data

To evaluate these hypotheses, Fortna creates a data set of 115 "spells of peace." A spell of peace is the length of time from when a civil war ends to when fighting restarts. To examine the two hypotheses, Fortna uses two types of tests. First, she uses analysis to predict where peacekeepers go. Second, she analyzes the duration of peace spells.

Dependent Variable

In the first test, the dependent variable is whether peacekeepers were deployed. Some international personnel were sent to keep the peace after forty-one civil wars. The UN sent missions in thirty of these cases.

In the second test, the dependent variable is the duration of peace. This is the length of time between when fighting ends and (if it erupts again) a new war between the same two parties starts, a civil war being defined as a substate conflict in which there are at least 1,000 total battle deaths (Fortna 2004). Fighting restarted in about 40 percent of the wars in the data.

Independent Variable

In the first test, the independent variables are designed to capture how difficult a civil war is to resolve. These include whether the war ended in victory or a treaty, the type of war (ethnic, religious, and identity conflicts versus ideological, revolutionary, or other wars), the cost of the war measured by combatant and civilian deaths, how long the war was, and whether there were more than two factions fighting.

In the second test, the independent variable is deployment of a peacekeeping mission to the war.

Control Variables

Both tests control for the country's level of primary commodity exports, its level of economic development, whether it had a history of democracy, and the size of the government army.

Results

There are two central findings. First, Fortna (2004, 282) provides a number of tests to explore which wars get peacekeepers when they end, but ultimately suggests that "It depends on whether we are talking about UN peacekeeping or missions by other actors, and it depends on what type of peacekeeping we are interested in." She does find that peacekeepers tend to go to harder cases when we look at deployments that were "consent-based," meaning all warring parties wanted peacekeepers there.

The second finding is much more robust – peacekeepers help keep the peace. After the Cold War, peacekeepers reduce the risk of another war by 84 percent. All types of peacekeeping missions appear to have a positive effect on stopping the return of war.

Conclusions

This study addressed key challenges in understanding whether or not peacekeeping works. It provides a novel statistical analysis and reveals two important findings. First, peacekeepers tend to be sent to conflicts that are harder to resolve. Second, post-1990, peacekeepers play a role in maintaining peace after civil war: i.e., peacekeeping works.

SUMMARY

This chapter demonstrated several points, including:

- Civil wars are armed conflicts between a government and some set of opposition rebel groups taking place primarily within one recognized country.
- Civil war is the most common kind of violence in the international system today.
- Contemporary civil wars are complex, often with multiple rebel groups that are complex and often fragmented.
- Civil wars often have underlying causes related to the economic or political status of groups of people.
- Civil wars end in any of three different ways: petering out, victory, or negotiated settlement.
- Negotiated settlement is the most common way for wars to end now, and peacekeepers have a positive effect on long-term stability and peace.

KEY TERMS

Secessionist
Nationalist
Predatory rebel groups
Grievance
Deprivation
Relative deprivation
Identity issues
Opportunity
State capacity
Indivisible conflicts
Commitment problem

Recurrent civil war
Fragmented actors
Multiparty civil war
Institutionalization
Centralized power
Side switching
Foreign fighters
Intervention
Neighborhood effect
Contagion
Opportunity cost

Negotiated settlement   Partial peace
Third-party guarantors   Peacekeepers

REVIEW QUESTIONS

1. What are the key components in a definition of civil war?
2. What is the "commitment problem" for rebels and governments? What strategies are used to address this problem in civil war settlements?
3. What is "deprivation"? How is this different from "relative deprivation"?
4. What is a multiparty civil war? How does this differ from a conflict with a "fragmented actor"?
5. In general, what is the effect of external support on civil war duration? What causes that effect?
6. What are the major challenges to ending the Syrian Civil War?
7. How can power sharing help to prevent recurrent civil war?
8. What are the ways that civil war can be "transnational"?
9. What are the main challenges to determining whether peacekeepers work?
10. What is a "predatory" rebel group?

DISCUSSION QUESTIONS

1. Did the international community make a mistake in not sending peacekeepers to Syria during the 2010s?
2. Identity can sometimes be a factor causing civil wars, though everyone whether at war or peace has their own personal identity. What four words would you use to describe your own identity, whether it be your religion, gender, ethnicity, race, nationality, political beliefs, socioeconomic class, or anything else?
3. Imagine a hypothetical country, let's call it "Fredonia." Let's say you are an evil genius, and want to design Fredonia to be at as high a risk of experiencing a civil war as possible. What would Fredonia look like?

ADDITIONAL READING

Cunningham, D. E. (2011). *Barriers to Peace in Civil War*. Cambridge: Cambridge University Press.
Cunningham, K. G. (2014). *Inside the Politics of Self-determination*. Oxford: Oxford University Press.
Fortna, V. P. (2004). *Peace Time: Cease-fire Agreements and the Durability of Peace*. Princeton: Princeton University Press.
Kalyvas, S. N. (2006). *The Logic of Violence in Civil War*. Cambridge: Cambridge University Press.
Mason, T. D. and S. M. Mitchell (2016). *What Do We Know about Civil Wars?* Lanham, MD: Rowman and Littlefield.
Walter, B. F. (2002). *Committing to Peace: The Successful Settlement of Civil Wars*. Princeton: Princeton University Press.
Walter, B. F. (2022). *How Civil Wars Start and How to Stop Them*. New York: Penguin.
Wood, E. J. (2003). *Insurgent Collective Action and Civil War in El Salvador*. Cambridge: Cambridge University Press.

REFERENCES

Bakke, K. M., Cunningham, K. G., Seymour, L. J. M., (2012). A plague of initials: Fragmentation, cohesion, and infighting in civil wars." *Perspectives on Politics* **10**(2), 265–283.

Cederman, L., Gleditsch, K. S., and Buhaug, H. (2013). *Inequality, Grievances, and Civil War.* Cambridge: Cambridge University Press.

Christia, F. (20120). *Alliance formation in civil wars.* Cambridge: Cambridge University Press.

Colombia: Armed conflict fatalities 1958–2018, by category (2021, July 5). *Statista.* Available at www .statista.com/statistics/987115.

Cunningham, D. E., (2006). Veto players and civil war duration. American Journal of Political Science. **50**(4), 875–892.

Fortna, V. P. (2004). Does peacekeeping keep peace? International intervention and the duration of peace after civil war. *International Studies Quarterly* **48**(2), 269–292.

Griffiths, R. (2017). *Age of Secession: The International and Domestic Determinants of State Birth.* Cambridge: Cambridge University Press.

Hassner, R. E. (2013). *War on Sacred Grounds.* Ithaca, NY: Cornell University Press.

Kalonda-Kayama, I. (2010). Civil war, sexual violence, and HIV infections: Evidence from the Democratic Republic of Congo. *Journal of African Development* **12**(2), 47–60.

Straus, S. (2015). *Making and Unmaking Nations: War, Leadership, and Genocide in Modern Africa.* Ithaca, NY: Cornell University Press.

Weinstein, J. M. (2006). *Inside Rebellion: The Politics of Insurgent Violence.* Cambridge: Cambridge University Press.

8   Terrorism

PHILIP B. K. POTTER

Introduction

Terrorism and counterterrorism have defined global politics and US foreign policy for much of the twenty-first century. Scholars estimate that over the last twenty years terrorism has cost the world over $600 billion and directly caused almost a quarter-million deaths. Terrorism also has had far-ranging consequences for development, global and domestic stability, and migration. The Middle East, South Asia, and Africa have been particularly afflicted, but terrorism is global as is apparent in Map 8.1.

The attacks on the United States on September 11, 2001 ushered in an era of heightened global attentiveness to terrorism and the issues that surround it (see Figure 8.1). They were the deadliest terrorist attacks in history and arguably the most sophisticated. The attacks are estimated to have cost between $400,000 and $500,000 and killed nearly 3,000 people. By way of comparison, a typical suicide vest costs about $1,200 and the modal terrorist attack kills only a few people. While most terrorism is conducted locally by individuals or small groups, al-Qaeda successfully funded and coordinated four separate assaults by nineteen hijackers thousands of miles away from its base of operations in Afghanistan.

Following the 9/11 attacks on the United States, President George W. Bush declared a "war on terrorism" in a speech on September 16, 2001. The label of "war" is often applied metaphorically to indicate the seriousness of a policy (for example, the "war on poverty" or the "war on drugs"). That was the case here. Terrorism should be understood as a tactic to be countered, rather than an adversary to be combated. While the war on terrorism entrenched norms against violence targeting civilian noncombatants by nonstate actors it did not reduce the actual violence; terrorist attacks against civilians have actually increased since 2001.

Despite the scale, sophistication, and human cost of the 9/11 attacks, it is still surprising that a nonstate actor like al-Qaeda could shape global politics for a generation. The response from the United States, the lone superpower in the international system in that period, resulted in wars in Afghanistan and Iraq that deposed regimes and killed more than 6,000 US service

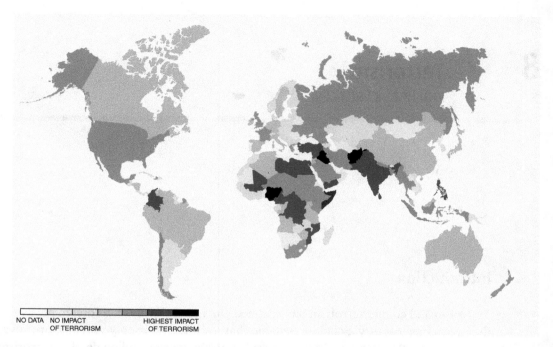

Map 8.1. The impact of terrorism by country. The index contains four indicators, each a five-year weighted average: incidents, fatalities, injuries, and property damage.
© 2022 Institute for Economics & Peace.

Figure 8.1. The skyline of Manhattan after the September 11th terrorist attack on the World Trade Center.
US Library of Congress.

members, with many more wounded. More than 600,000 died in the conflicts and insurgencies overall. The total cost to the United States was nearly $3 trillion.

The difference in scale between the 9/11 attacks and the United States' response is a hallmark of terrorism. Terrorism is a tool of asymmetric conflict, commonly employed by weaker nonstate actors to provoke an overreaction from the target. In the case of the 9/11 attacks, al-Qaeda successfully triggered an outsized response that damaged the strength and credibility of the United States. This, however, came at a high cost to the organization itself, which went into decline and failed to achieve its larger political objectives.

This chapter will explore the characteristics and evolution of modern terrorist organizations and tactics. It will clarify what terrorism is and describe the scale and political effectiveness of this kind of violence. It will also explore why groups resort to terrorism, investigate why individuals join terrorist groups, and discuss what can be done about it.

What Is Terrorism?

The term "terror" was first applied to violence by the *state* against its population, typically in revolutionary and autocratic regimes. It rose to prominence as a description of mass executions and massacres during the French Revolution (1789–1799). The young revolutionary government leveraged violence, and even more so the *fear* of violence, to reorient French society. Accusations of "terror" were also broadly applied to authoritarian regimes in the 1930s that sought to intimidate minorities and suppress dissent – for example, Stalin's Great Terror and the Nazi terror. Over time, however, the term evolved to describe illegitimate violence perpetrated by *nonstate* actors against civilian targets.

Precisely defining terrorism is challenging because the term serves multiple purposes that are sometimes at odds. Governments designate individuals or organizations as "terrorists" based on their sporadic use of a tactic (terrorism). The term analytically categorizes acts of violence while also carrying a normative connotation that delegitimizes those labeled with it. These usages can sometimes conflict with one another and lead to confusion. The terrorist label tends to be reserved for ideas and organizations that we do not like or support, but that instinct makes it difficult to capture the analytical concept consistently.

The competing objectives that drive the use of "terrorism" as a label are on full display in the various definitions that exist among scholars and practitioners. Notably, these definitions shift according to the analytical, political, or contextual needs of those doing the defining.

Definitions of terrorism vary between countries. The US Code of Federal Regulations, for example, defines terrorism as an act that "includes the unlawful use of force and violence against persons or property to intimidate or coerce a government, the civilian population, or any segment thereof, in furtherance of political or social objectives" (Legal Information Institute, n.d.). The United Kingdom holds that terrorism includes acts "directed towards the overthrowing or influencing ... of her Majesty's government ... or any other government." France, on the other hand, defines terrorism much more broadly, with no distinction between "attacks" or "terrorist acts" (OECD, n.d.).

Definitions of terrorism tend to converge on three defining characteristics. Terrorism is violence that is: (1) perpetrated by nonstate actors; (2) against civilian targets; and (3) committed for political ends.

The first of these elements points to an important parameter for terrorism. While states commit all manner of repressive, inhumane, and illegal acts, terrorism is the domain of nonstate actors. Sovereign states possess a legitimate monopoly over the means of violence– domestically when enforcing the law and internationally in armed conflict. When nonstate actors employ force against civilians, they violate this monopoly on the use of force. This delegitimizes the activity and sets it apart from the use of force by states. Put differently, states can, under some circumstances, lawfully coerce civilians with violence; nonstate actors cannot. While human rights violations by states are sometimes described as "state terrorism," most analysts draw a firm distinction between state repression and war crimes (regardless of how objectionable) and terrorism.

The second definitional element places civilian targets at the center of modern terrorism. Terrorists target civilians to magnify the impact of their actions. Indiscriminately targeting civilians generates broad fear within society. This mechanism is central to the effectiveness of terrorism as a tactic of asymmetric conflict because it allows a comparatively small and weak organization to drive the behavior of a much larger group of people.

Limiting the concept of terrorism to civilian targets also clarifies how the tactic relates to the concepts of insurgency and rebellion. Terrorism can be challenging to define and identify in societies on the cusp of civil war. When violence is endemic, state control can erode to a point where it becomes unclear who holds authority and the monopoly on legitimate violence. In these contexts of insurgency and rebellion, violence against civilian targets is described as terrorism while attacks on military or security forces are not. That said, terrorist attacks are, unfortunately, often carried out by rebel groups (on civil wars, see Chapter 7).

The third and final component of the definition, a political motive, distinguishes terrorism from crime. Nonstate actors perpetrate violence against civilians for a wide range of reasons that, while objectionable and illegal, are not ideological or political. For example, governments have at various points in time sought to label the violence perpetrated by drug cartels as "narco-terrorism." Similarly, some have applied the terrorism label to mass shootings in the United States, to emphasize their gravity. Such labels can drive attention and official action. Still, they muddy the waters analytically because the motivations that drive cartel violence and mass shootings are distinct both from each other and from those that drive political violence.

Consequently, the actions that governments can take in response are distinct. For example, policies that increase the costs of violence, such as longer prison sentences, are more likely to change the behavior of a drug cartel than an ideologically motivated terrorist organization. Mental health services or gun control measures that could be appropriate responses to mass shootings would likely be ineffective as a counterterrorism strategy.

Additionally, terrorist attacks are usually designed to have psychological or policy consequences beyond the immediate target. In many cases, the specific target of a terrorist attack – for example, a market, bus, or police station – seems to have been chosen at random. These are also often **soft targets**, meaning that they are lightly defended or not defended at all. These targets are easy for terrorists to inflict damage on, and doing so underscores the vulnerability of all kinds of potential targets central to a population's day-to-day life.

Figure 8.2. A fence installed for security became a site for citizens' impromptu tributes at the Oklahoma City National Memorial after the April 19, 1995, bombing of the Alfred P. Murrah Federal Building by antigovernment, white supremacist domestic terrorists. There are toys in the picture because 19 of the 168 people killed in the attack were children.
US Library of Congress.

Individuals typically overestimate their own chances of falling victim to this violence, and this provokes fear and demands for a governmental response. Through this process, terrorists magnify the effect of small-scale violence, transforming it into a potent tool of asymmetric conflict.

Terrorists and terrorist organizations also have varying geographic reach and motivations that can be broadly classified as "international" or "domestic." This distinction matters because it is associated with differences in motivation and capability. International terrorist organizations, for example, have broader networks and, therefore, access to more capabilities than organizations that only operate within one country.

Perpetrators of international terrorist attacks cross national borders to conduct violence. These attacks can be state-sponsored or otherwise inspired by or associated with states or foreign terrorist organizations. In contrast, domestic terrorists do not cross borders and are often motivated by hatred of a racial or ethnic group within a country, hatred or mistrust of governmental authorities, or are motivated by extremist stances on single issues including abortion, animal rights, the environment, or misogyny. Prominent examples of domestic terrorist incidents include the 1995 Oklahoma City bombing (see Figure 8.2) and the 2011 attacks on a Norwegian summer camp.

The Historical Evolution of Terrorism

Modern terrorism evolved in four waves (Rapoport 2004).

1. **The anarchist wave** (1880–1920) first emerged in Russia but rapidly spread to much of the world, including Europe and the United States, through communication and collaboration among anarchist organizations. Waves of terrorism are commonly associated with particular; in the anarchist wave this was assassination. Political leaders across the globe came

under fire. To take a prominent example, the assassination of Archduke Franz Ferdinand in 1914 at the hands of Bosnian nationalists played a role in the outbreak of World War I. United States President William McKinley was also slain in 1900 by an anarchist's bullet.

2. **The anti-colonial wave** (1920–1960) filled the gap as anarchism began to fade as a political ideology. In the wake of World War I, movements and ideologies committed to national liberation and self-determination bubbled up worldwide. A prominent example is the rise of the Irish Republican Army (IRA), which emerged to contest British rule in Ireland, often by brutally targeting civilian loyalists. While the IRA waged a much longer struggle, the wave faded as decolonization allowed most movements to achieve their aspirations after World War II.

3. **The "New Left" wave** (1960–1980) emerged in the United States but rapidly spread to encompass "red" organizations across the globe, particularly in Europe. In many cases, these organizations appeared on or around college campuses and were animated by anti-war sentiments. The Weather Underground, for example, emerged in the United States at the University of Michigan as a violent offshoot of student protests against the Vietnam War. In Germany, the Red Army Faction, driven by far-left aspirations and funded at times by East German security services, engaged in a series of bombings, shootings, and kidnappings over three decades. In the context of the Cold War, the "New Left" wave inevitably became another dimension of the proxy conflict between the United States and the Soviet Union, with the USSR in some cases funneling support to these organizations. Airline hijacking was the signature tactic of this period, rapidly rising to prominence before receding in the face of counterterrorism measures. These measures included metal detectors, universal screening, and more direct responses from states such as the Israeli storming of a hijacked airliner at Entebbe, Uganda in 1976.

4. **The "religious" wave** (1980–) is commonly traced to the Iranian Revolution in 1979 and the subsequent upheavals that rocked the broader Middle East in the years that followed. This wave was dominated by Islam. However, religiously motivated violence emerged globally in forms as varied as Aum Shinrikyo's sarin gas attack on the Tokyo subway system that killed 14 and injured more than 1,000 and the Lord's Resistance Army, which emerged from the Ugandan Civil War to plague Uganda, South Sudan, the Central African Republic, and the Democratic Republic of the Congo. Most prominent, however, were the organizations that emerged under the broad banner of Salafi jihadism. While the wave began twenty years prior, the attacks of September 11, 2001, solidified a shift in attention to jihadist extremists as a primary terrorist threat to global security. Unlike prior waves that fit relatively neatly into twenty-year bins, the religious wave has had double that lifespan and only now, with the relative decline of the Islamic State, shows indications of ebbing.

What comes next? Scholars and law enforcement have become increasingly concerned about the emergence of a "fifth wave" that is authoritarian, racially oriented, and driven by right-wing radicalization. For example, data collected by the Center for Strategic and International Studies shows that acts of domestic terrorism have increased annually in the United States since 2006, particularly by white supremacist and far-right militia groups (Jones et al. 2021). These patterns are replicated across much of the Western world.

The "wave" model is a stylized way of thinking about the evolution of terrorism in the last 150 years. In reality, many organizations and incidents contain elements from one or more of these waves. For example, in the period in which leftist terrorist ideologies were ascendant, many movements contained this element but also harbored longstanding anti-colonial or **ethnonationalist** grievances. Similarly, many organizations that could be categorized as religious are now also motivated by an underlying desire for self-determination. A good example of this dynamic is the various Palestinian organizations that have, at points, resorted to terrorist tactics. During the Cold War, some of these organizations defined themselves according to leftist ideologies, but are now increasingly religious in their rhetoric. The commitment to Palestinian grievances against Israel, however, has remained constant.

The Logic of Terrorism

For decades, specialists have noted that terrorism rarely results in political success. In the 1970s, Walter Laqueur published "The futility of terrorism," claiming that practitioners seldom achieve their strategic demands. In the 1980s and 1990s, researchers continued to find that terrorist organizations rarely attained their long-term political objectives.

More recently, empirical studies confirmed that only a handful of terrorist groups in modern history have managed to accomplish their political objectives. The latest wave of scholarship finds that violence against civilians hinders nonstate actors from obtaining their demands. It may seem counterintuitive, but groups are significantly more likely to induce government compliance when they direct violence against military targets instead of civilian ones. It's almost a punchline at this point: "Never negotiate with terrorists."

How do terrorists choose their tactics? Some scholars draw on terrorism's poor track record of ultimate success to argue that the use of the tactic fails to be consistently strategic. Consequently, this school of thought sees terrorism as largely irrational and immune to deterrence. Others see terrorism as tactically ineffective but posit that individuals join these organizations for other, perfectly rational reasons. For example, militant groups might attract sympathizers through the social services they provide. In extremist groups, otherwise alienated individuals have a sense of community, shared purpose, significance, power, and control. Finally, others see terrorism as rational – in that it does successfully send signals to the state and population about grievances and political instability – but still highly costly. The tactic can alter the political status quo even if the organization's ultimate aims never come to pass. In this telling, the overall rate at which terrorist organizations achieve their political objectives is the result of their underlying weakness. It is that weakness that drives them to terrorism as a tool of asymmetric conflict, rather than terrorism, that precludes their success.

Who Becomes a Terrorist?

No single factor determines who becomes radicalized into terrorism and who does not. Violent extremists come from diverse socioeconomic classes, educational backgrounds, and cultural groups. Political grievances – including state repression of minority groups, perceptions of inequality, or racism and xenophobia – and social instability can cause groups and individuals to turn to terrorism. In interviews, former extremists cite various factors contributing to their radicalization, including financial instability and feelings of stigmatization or marginalization, with no one predominant cause. Online propaganda, social bonds, and direct recruitment efforts play an essential role in radicalization, capitalizing on individuals' grievances and vulnerabilities. In many instances, the defining component of recruitment is social: alienated individuals are susceptible to the community and purpose offered by militant organizations.

Terrorist organizations can also step in where governments or other community organizations fail to provide social services and local stability. Hezbollah, for example, has built and run schools and hospitals in Lebanon. This attracts individuals to the organization and legitimizes it in local communities, generating a broader support base than an organization might with violence alone. Mechanisms like these allow organizations like Hezbollah and Hamas to become both terrorist groups and political parties with representation in official government bodies.

Contrary to popular belief, terrorism is not directly correlated with poverty. Globally, terrorism is comparatively rare in the poorest countries and among the poorest individuals. Political engagement of any kind is a luxury when immediate physical needs are not met. However, there may be more complex relationships between economic factors and terrorism, as under some conditions individuals with less to lose economically may be more likely to join terrorist groups (Lee 2011).

Evidence indicates that people are more commonly radicalized by the perception that they are unjustifiably disadvantaged in comparison to another group that they perceive to have undue status or resources. For example, white-nationalist and right-wing extremism can be a reaction to material conditions seen as threats to the social and economic position of a white majority, but this is only part of the story. Very few people actually base their political positions on objective readings of their social and economic conditions. Rather, they tend to react mainly to their prejudices and the ideas promulgated by media outlets, "influencers," and other ideological leaders. The emergence of the conservative and "alt-right" media system has fueled a cycle of mistrust, xenophobia, and anger. White nationalist militants are then prone to violence in part because alt-right media outlets have tapped into their feelings of disenfranchisement, positioning "mainstream" society and minorities as the beneficiaries, even though there is no evidence to support such claims. The anger and resentment they may harbor can make them more sympathetic to extremist ideologies and more vulnerable to recruitment by terrorist groups.

Feelings of disenfranchisement and the drive for belonging and meaning have also led to an upsurge in **foreign fighters** who travel to join militant organizations. Foreign fighters are individuals who join terrorist organizations, insurgencies, or other military groups outside their home countries. These fighters tend to be young men, though not exclusively, and often are radicalized through online propaganda. According to the International Centre for Counter-Terrorism, the majority of foreign fighters from Western countries are single, under thirty, and came from Muslim émigré families (Dawson 2021). Figure 8.3 provides some descriptive data about foreign fighters traveling from the United States. Foreign fighters were very prominent in the conflict with Islamic State in Syria. According to the United Nations Office on Drugs and

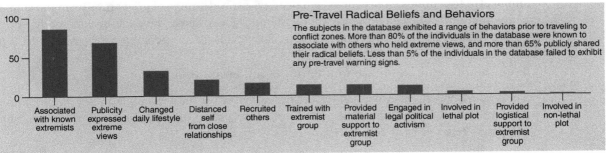

Figure 8.3. These data support some dynamics we might have suspected, including that the Internet and social media are important contributors encouraging people in the United States to travel abroad as foreign fighters.
US Department of Homeland Security.

Crime (n.d.), by 2015, more than 40,000 individuals had traveled from their home countries to join organizations in Iraq and Syria alone. However, foreign fighters have been a prominent feature of terrorism for decades and will likely continue to be so.

Not all individuals who turn to terrorism join organizations. **"Lone wolf" terrorism** is violence committed by an individual who may be driven by a particular organization's ideology but is not directly associated with that organization. Although they may have been radicalized by propaganda, they act without the direct influence of a leader or hierarchy. They may learn from online or printed resources, but their choice of tactics and target is their own, subject to no direct command or direction. Lone wolf terrorists are almost always domestic terrorists; very few travel outside of their home country to commit attacks. According to a US Department of Justice report, while there is no one description that encompasses every attack, lone wolf terrorists are predominately unemployed men with previous criminal histories who tend to be older and less educated than the typical member of a terrorist organization (Hamm and Spaaj 2015).

Lone wolves are responsible for an increasingly large share of terrorist violence. According to the Global Terrorism Database, lone wolf attacks have risen from under 5 percent of all terror attacks in the mid 1970s to more than 70 percent of the attacks that took place between 2014 and 2018. Today, lone wolf attacks are far more likely to be associated with far-right or Islamist extremist groups than far-left, separatist, or environmentally motivated terrorist attacks (Global Terrorism Database 2021).

Lone wolf attacks over the last two decades have been increasingly tied to online radicalization. Perpetrators find community in conspiracy theories, racism, and other radicalizing beliefs on sites like Reddit, 8chan, and even Facebook. They often "self-radicalize" by following these entry points toward further fringe beliefs and violent action.

While the lethality of lone wolf attacks is not on the rise – in fact, it peaked in the 1990s – the motivations and methods by which attacks are carried out have evolved over time. Today's attacks still include the use of bombs, knives, and firearms, but attackers' arsenals have expanded to include the use of biological agents automobiles, airplanes, and even construction equipment. Motivations have evolved to encompass a wide range of grievances from those that are jihadist and al-Qaeda–inspired to racist, anti-government, anti-establishment, or anti-abortion views. At the same time, targets have evolved to encompass places of worship and schools.

Well-known examples of lone wolf terrorists and incidents include:

- Timothy McVeigh, an American terrorist responsible for the 1995 Oklahoma City bombing
- The anti-industrialist Unabomber, Theodore Kaczynski, who engaged in a mail bombing campaign between 1978 and 1995
- Anders Behring Breivik, a Norwegian terrorist who killed seventy-seven people in 2011 after writing a manifesto decrying the "cultural suicide" of Europe
- Dzhokhar and Tamerlan Tsarnaev, American domestic terrorists who set off bombs at the 2013 Boston Marathon
- The 2014 Isla Vista killings by Elliot Rodger, an "involuntary celibate" terrorist who killed six people after publishing a misogynistic manifesto
- The 2019 Poway synagogue shooting by John Timothy Earnest, who published online an antisemitic and racist manifesto before the attack during Passover that killed one and wounded three.

Regime Type and Terrorism

The political institutions that govern a country have a meaningful impact on susceptibility to terrorism in the long and short term (Chenoweth 2013). As a general rule, democracies are more susceptible to terrorism in the short term because they lack the capacity for harsh repression that can forcibly suppress organizations and those who might support them. Democracy requires an independent civil society, but this creates spaces in which militancy can emerge. At the same time, democracies also lack the mechanisms for information control required to prevent terrorists from communicating their message to the broader society through violence. An independent and vibrant media is nearly synonymous with democracy.

Terrorist violence typically instills fear beyond the immediate target of the attack. To instill this fear and panic in a broader audience or society, terrorists need publicity and media coverage to reach their intended political audience. Publicity can also help terrorist groups recruit potential supporters and contribute to the spread of successful terrorist tactics elsewhere. However, these outcomes can only prevail under certain information conditions that, in turn, tend to be associated with certain regime types.

The spread of this fear, and its impact on the relationship between citizens and the government, gives terrorism its power as a tool of asymmetric conflict. This process works best when information flows freely. Democracies, for their part, find it hard to control information, even when doing so might be in the best interests of their citizens. United Kingdom Prime Minister Margaret Thatcher recognized the amplifying role that media could play in the cycle of political violence and called on the British media to stop providing Irish Republican Army terrorists with the "oxygen of publicity." Her requests, however, were hopeless in a democracy with a free and competitive media market. In most countries, the public has a voracious appetite for this information along with a fundamental right to it. Of course, no such right is acknowledged in an autocracy.

Not only is it nearly impossible to control information in democracies, but the privatized and commercialized news industry also develops a symbiotic relationship with terrorism. Violence attracts attention and helps media outlets compete for readers and viewers, while terrorist groups crave publicity. As the adage goes, "If it bleeds, it leads."

In contrast, autocracies are generally intolerant of independent civil society, capable of substantial extrajudicial repression against individuals and organizations, and are willing and able to control media and other routes by which information can spread. In the long term, however, autocratic tendencies feed the underlying grievances that fuel violence, while the lack of democratic outlets removes alternative mechanisms for political contestation.

Because authoritarian regimes are capable of controlling, censoring, and manipulating information, many believe that such regimes enjoy a strategic advantage in combating terrorism in that they can order state media to deprive terrorists of this "oxygen" and crack down on commercial media that refuses to play along. Autocracies can also be more effective than democracies in countering terrorism because they have more power to stamp out dissent by force. One problem inherent in counterterrorism, however, is that, although heavy-handed repression of militant groups may stave off terrorism by raising the costs of participation and choking off the publicity that feeds would-be terrorists the illusion of success, repressive tactics are also more likely to provoke the grievances that stoke terrorism in the first place. In general, autocracies also tend to stop dissidents from engaging in nonviolent opposition, limiting further any other methods of expression.

Variations in autocratic regime types influence the level of repression and other conditions that make states more or less conducive to terrorism. More information on the different types of autocratic regimes can be found in Chapter 3. The information picture becomes more mixed in more institutionalized autocracies such as single-party states like China.

Institutionalized autocracies have slightly less control of the information flow in their countries, tending to still control the official media outlets but being unable to stem social media and other unauthorized sources. In these countries, public opinion matters more, meaning that information control cannot be as absolute and repression must be more discriminating. As technology proliferates, autocrats have attempted to clamp down on new media that are central to day-to-day life for their citizens, but with mixed results.

While blocking news coverage of terrorist attacks can discourage militants from adopting a violent strategy, tighter social media censorship comes with other risks for the regime. If the state keeps too tight a grip on information, it may exacerbate the grievances that motivate terrorist violence in the first place. Rather than discouraging violence, such strict information control may just push terrorists to amplify their voices by killing more people, projecting violence against highly visible soft or symbolic targets, and adopting more sophisticated tactics.

Transitional governments, sometimes called **anocracies**, fall prey to the worst of both types of regimes and are often the least adept at dealing with terrorism in both the short and long term. Anocracies are governments that combine some democratic and some autocratic features. They are typically transitional between one type of regime and another, such as when an autocracy has collapsed in the wake of civil war and democracy is struggling to emerge as a replacement. Political institutions in anocracies, such as voting rules, independent courts, separation of powers between branches of government, and protections of individual rights, are often ineffective because they are new, poorly developed, and weakly enforced.

Because anocracies are poorly institutionalized and maintain some authoritarian characteristics, their citizens typically have as many grievances as those in democracies. Like dictatorships, the anocracy will offer few to no avenues for peaceful expression. Some autocratic features often remain in anocracies, as interim governments, at least in theory, work to shift from what may have been decades of dictatorship. At the same time, the new political systems set up by transitional governments frequently do not have the legitimacy or the capability to address citizens' concerns. While in this environment anocratic governments have less repressive power, they also have less control over information and the citizenry, limiting their ability to quash militant rhetoric and activity.

Such transitional governments are short-lived, by definition. Compared to stable democracies, they have shorter windows of opportunity – or "time horizons" – to accommodate the public's grievances. The newness of their institutions often makes them unable to handle domestic pressure from their populations. As they labor to establish legitimacy on the world stage, they are also operating under political and economic pressure – perhaps from the media, the United Nations, their neighbors, and their own citizens – while attempting to create the processes and capabilities to wield actual power. From both their frequent reliance on international support and the fragility of their attempts to build a new government, anocratic regimes lack the complete repressive power that autocracies wield to subdue terrorist violence.

Additionally, transitional governments must negotiate the basic foundations of a new state – the drafting of constitutions, the distribution of public goods, mapmaking, and conflict stabilization. With all that in mind, they may lack the bandwidth effectively to address evolving terror threats. These inherently unstable anocracies are fertile ground for terrorism, as citizens may turn to other organizations to provide local stability and social services, and they may seek out other avenues to express their anger and frustration.

Libya provides an illustrative example of this precarious situation. After forty-two years in power, Muammar Gaddafi was deposed and the country went through a brief civil war in 2011, followed by the installation of the National Transitional Government that same year. The transitional government was met with destabilizing militia violence, including an attack on the American diplomatic compound in Benghazi on September 11, 2012. The next day, an interim prime minister, Mustafa A. G. Abushagur, was elected by the new General National Congress. Less than a month later, he was ousted before ever being officially sworn in, after parochial squabbling over representation culminated in a mob storming the national assembly while it considered Abushagur's cabinet nominations.

The infighting in the wake of Abushagur's dismissal left a power vacuum that, among other things, made room for extremists to seize territory in Libya for the Islamic State. After several more years of tumult and coup attempts, an interim government was again established in April 2021, although elections scheduled for December 2021 were indefinitely postponed.

In the past decade, this pattern has been noted in states where coups have toppled the existing governments. After a year of constitutional crisis, Nigerian soldiers overthrew President Mamadou Tandja and unveiled a "Supreme Council for the Restoration of Democracy." The council reigned for a year before holding elections in 2011. Terrorist attacks skyrocketed in Nigeria following the coup, jumping from fewer than 100 per year from 1970 to 2010 to at one point more than 700 per year – even after the controversial 2011 presidential election. Similar spikes in terrorist attacks occurred in Mali following the 2012 coup that overthrew the second democratically elected president, Amadou Toumani Touré, in Egypt after the 2013 overthrow of Mohamed Morsi, and in the Central African Republic after the 2012–2013 uprising.

Terrorist Tactics

Terrorism encompasses a wide and ever-expanding set of tactics. Nonstate actors that target civilians for political ends have done so with bombings, shootings, kidnappings, and myriad other approaches to violence. **Tactical innovation** is a hallmark of terrorism because it allows perpetrators to evade counterterrorists.

Terrorist organizations are responsive to the risks and rewards of their actions, adopting specific tactics that yield rewards and spurning those that do not. Selection of tactics is therefore a largely rational response to the perception of their efficacy. Terrorist organizations are more likely to achieve their goals when they quickly adopt tactics that prove to be successful and shed those that authorities have grown accustomed to. The Popular Front for the Liberation of Palestine (PFLP), for example, bedeviled Israeli counterterrorism efforts for decades by expanding its tactical portfolio. By altering its mix and style of hijackings, assassinations, and bombings, the PFLP complicated the Israeli response while simultaneously crafting new appeals to its public constituency and keeping its rivals guessing. Failed attacks can be public relations windfalls for the state because they make the group look ineffective and the government competent. Consequently, organizations have a strong incentive to move away from tactics that authorities have "figured out" such that they no longer impose political costs on governments or offer the possibility of eliciting concessions from them.

An excellent example of the evolving nature of terrorist tactics is airline hijacking. The first recorded case of modern airline hijacking occurred in 1961 during the third, or "New Left," wave of terrorist violence when a group of Cubans took over a National Airlines plane flying from Miami to Key West. In subsequent years, hijacking grew into a preeminent terrorist tactic, including one noteworthy period between 1968 and 1969 when seventy-five successful hijackings occurred. The bellwether incident occurred in 1968 when the Popular Front for the Liberation of Palestine (PFLP) gained control of an El Al Boeing 707 in transit to Tel Aviv. Three PFLP members aboard demanded that the plane fly to Algeria where they sought the release of Arab prisoners in Israel in exchange for the safe return of the crew and passengers. The attack was a substantial success for the hijackers: all three escaped after securing the release of sixteen convicted compatriots. Media coverage of this event turned it into a crucially important signal for other militant groups about the utility of hijacking.

Rapid diffusion quickly followed the infamous National Airlines hijacking. Hijacking became the go-to tactic for groups seeking to gain attention for their cause while demonstrating competence and sophistication. Throughout the period, the PFLP remained a key innovator and model for other groups. For example, after extensive media coverage of the PFLP's simultaneous hijackings in September 1970, hijackings of Iranian, Costa Rican, and Indian planes immediately followed. When the PFLP hijacked a German plane and held it for ransom in 1972, at least eight other aircraft were hijacked for ransom by other organizations the same year.

In response to this wave of successful hijackings, in 1973 the United States introduced metal detectors in all airports and required the screening of passengers and their carry-on luggage. During this same period, governments developed profiles of suspected hijackers, upgraded airport perimeter security, and trained flight crews to thwart the demands of hijackers. These measures played a vital role in rapidly reducing the number of hijackings (see Figure 8.4).

The most famous airline hijacking in modern history – the September 11, 2001 attacks when hijackers seized and then crashed four passenger aircraft killing all on board – represented the last gasp of the airline hijacking tactic rather than its apex. The 9/11 attacks broke the implicit contract that made the traditional model of hijacking work: the perception that acquiescence with the hijackers would minimize the loss of life, that hijackers would not kill the passengers if their demands were met. By making the death of the passengers integral to the attack, the 9/11 attackers merged hijacking with suicide bombing and ensured that passengers would be less compliant in future hijacking incidents.

Passengers adapted at once. Having learned the fates of the other hijacked flights that same morning, passengers on the fourth plane, United Flight 93, stormed the cockpit and prevented what would have been a more catastrophic attack, though during the struggle for control the plane crashed in a Pennsylvania field. Subsequent incidents on aircraft have been met with near-immediate passenger retaliation. In two such cases, passengers quickly subdued airline attackers Richard Reid (the shoe bomber) and Umar Farouk Abdulmutallab (the underwear bomber) because they assumed (correctly) that they would be killed if they did not resist. By making death seem inescapable, the 9/11 hijackers changed the payoffs for future hijackers and passengers in a way that resolved the collective action problem that previously enabled one or a few lightly armed hijackers to pacify dozens or hundreds of passengers.

This rapid rise and fall of a terrorist tactic is typical. One organization typically identifies an effective tactic while followers adopt and refine it. Counterterrorists are initially challenged by the

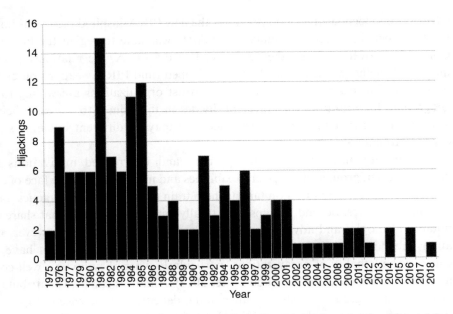

Figure 8.4. Airline hijackings by year. Attacks declined steadily after the introduction of metal detectors and passenger screenings. Horowitz, Perkoski and Potter, "Tactical Diversity in Militant Violence," *International Organization* 72 (Winter 2018).

innovation, but over time catch up. As they do, the tactic declines in effectiveness and presents vulnerabilities to those who utilize it. Organizations therefore begin to abandon it in favor of new innovations, and the cycle begins again. That full cycle is evident in the story of airline hijacking.

More recently, suicide bombing has been the most challenging terrorist tactic worldwide. We may, however, be seeing the beginning stages of its decline. For example, some argue that the indiscriminate suicide attacks that occurred during the Iraq insurgency discredited the tactic among elite practitioners and the public alike.

Cooperation among Violent Groups

Another variable determining the capability of terrorist organizations, and therefore how dangerous they are, is the extent to which they cooperate effectively with other militant organizations. Cooperation can be important because it can lead to terrorist groups sharing tactical knowledge, intelligence, and weapons.

An example of the deadly effect of **terrorist alliances** comes from links between the Provisional Irish Republican Army (PIRA) and the Revolutionary Armed Forces of Colombia (FARC). The PIRA–FARC relationship translated into increased effectiveness for both organizations. During one raid on a FARC outpost, the Colombian army found mortars with designs similar to those used by the PIRA in Northern Ireland. A 2002 committee report from the US House of Representatives noted that, after interacting with the PIRA, the FARC began to employ new techniques in urban terrorism, specifically car bombings targeting first responders. The tactic was startlingly effective: the Colombian police lost more than 10 percent of their bomb technicians in the year after the new PIRA-inspired tactic was implemented. As a result of their increased capability, the FARC was able to regain the initiative and put the Colombian government on the defensive. For the PIRA, the relationship yielded primarily financial benefits. Money from the FARC helped fund PIRA weapons purchases and pay for personnel. This example illustrates that terrorist organizations are willing to bridge extreme geographical, cultural, and ideological divides in their quest to increase their capabilities. It also underlines that the rewards for each side may be different but may still increase their capacity to kill.

Militant organizations have two primary and interrelated motivations for cooperative behavior. First, groups ally to pool capabilities and information in the face of common threats. They may share information on targets, help train each other in new tactics, or share weapons or other resources. Second, groups tend to ally with organizations that share attributes, most notably ideologies and adversaries. Regardless of the motivation, however, militant cooperation enhances allied groups' capabilities. For instance, alliance ties have been shown to enhance the lethality of organizations, particularly when they involve well-connected "hubs" in alliance networks (Horowitz and Potter 2013). Alliances can also contribute to the diffusion of tactics, help groups manage organizational deficits, and increase groups' longevity. Given these benefits, many analysts prioritize degrading militant cooperation.

Forming and maintaining such relationships, however, is not always easy for these organizations. Militant groups interested in cooperation face a commitment problem. State repression puts pressure on groups to scale back their operations, and thus potentially renege on agreements made with other terrorist groups. Intelligence on havens may be shared in exchange for training on bombing tactics, or money in exchange for weapons, but those goods may never be received because of pressures from states, deception, or lack of actual capability. Militancy is an inherently risky enterprise, so armed groups tend to discount the future for concerns in the present. While more legitimate organizations can solve commitment challenges through institutions, militant groups have few means to ensure that agreements are upheld or to punish defectors, as what little institutionalization and monitoring are possible tends to increase security risks.

While rarer conditions like shared state sponsorship can help enforce cooperation, terrorist organizations most commonly sustain partnerships through the bond forged by shared, ethnicity, ideology, or shared adversaries. When trust exists between groups, shared interests and identity coalesce in a self-reinforcing cycle, making substantive cooperation likely.

Militant groups can also compete with each other. Given their illicit nature, the most immediate threat to the survival of militant organizations comes from the state. But over the longer term, success is only achieved by also outcompeting rival organizations to win the hearts and minds of a target population. When constrained to the same geographic space, groups have to compete for money, civilian support, and recruits. As the number of active organizations increases in a discrete region, groups become ever more violent in an attempt to "outbid" competitors for notice and popular support. This "outbidding" process leads to an overall escalation of violence. Successful, spectacular attacks demonstrate to the population that an organization is capable of confronting the state and leading the movement, and is therefore worthy of their support.

State Sponsorship of Terrorism

Rather than relying on other nonstate armed groups, militants can use state patrons to increase their capabilities and mobilize resources. States, for their part, can benefit from sponsoring militants by essentially outsourcing a portion of their military pursuits, achieving cost savings or efficiency gains, while keeping their distance from illicit activities. The United States Department of State maintains a list of state sponsors of terrorism, sanctioning countries cited for repeatedly supporting international terrorism. These sanctions include restricting foreign assistance, banning exports of dual-use and defense items, and other financial limitations. The number of countries listed has dwindled in recent years and is now reduced to Cuba, North Korea, Iran, and Syria.

Local armed militants can provide a state sponsor with operational capabilities that regular armed troops do not have. In asymmetric conflicts, locally recruited and locally managed militant organizations can have information advantages regarding local terrain and populations. In addition, states that sponsor militants to do their "dirty work" may maintain plausible deniability over negative fallout. By delegating to nonstate armed actors, the government distances itself from the direct use of force even when the relationship between the state and the militant group is more or less known.

While state sponsors are able to save money and increase efficiency, militants increase their capabilities and mobilize resources more quickly. Political violence requires human resources, money, training, and armaments; thus, states are well situated to provide militants with the necessary assets to combat a shared rival. States may also provide militant organizations safe havens from external rivals (or foreign intelligence agencies) with the space to rest, train, and prepare for combat. Militants may also receive more specific incentives from state sponsors, such as increased autonomy over territory or implicit permission to extract resources from their victims.

This arrangement, however, comes with risks for both sides. Militant organizations might still deviate from the state's preferences, partially due to the information asymmetries that exist between the state and militant agents. Militants may have better information than their state sponsors, and states do not have complete control over militant groups' actions. States may also miscalculate the capability of their agent groups, and militant groups may mislead states about their true intentions or otherwise back out of agreements made with the state. For their part, militant groups also incur risks when cooperating with a state. They might lose autonomy over their operations, they might lose their support base, and they might be asked to waste time engaging in activities that do not further their primary objective. In addition, militant organizations may face abandonment by the state; state sponsors can shift their funding priorities and policies at any time. In these cases, the militant organization may find itself unable to carry out its mission if it had become dependent on sponsorship.

One of the best-known modern examples of **state-sponsored terrorism** is the Iranian support of Hezbollah (Kreps and Byman 2010). Opposing Israel and Western powers in the Middle East, Hezbollah functions in some respects as a proxy for Iran. Since its founding in the 1970s, Hezbollah has received training and funding from Iran. According to the US Department of State, in recent years Iran has supported Hezbollah with more than $700 million each year in addition to supplying weapons and training. In return, Hezbollah has conducted bombing campaigns and other attacks against US and Israeli forces and Westerners around the world and supported the Assad regime during the Syrian Civil War.

In many instances, there is an inherent tradeoff between state sponsorship and inter-organizational relationships. States already face substantial trust issues when it comes to nonstate proxies, and these are worsened when these organizations have independent relationships and resources. As a consequence, states tend to be jealous partners and make their support conditional on relative exclusivity. At the same time, militant organizations are suspicious of potential organizational partners that themselves have state relationships. Such organizations may not be truly independent and the political compromises intrinsic to their relationship with a state actor may render them insufficiently committed to the shared political cause.

Counterterrorism and Deradicalization

Counterterrorism programs around the globe differ in their scope, goals, and capabilities. In the United States alone, there are multiple agencies at all levels of government engaged alongside international bodies.

Nations combat, investigate, and prosecute international and domestic terrorism in different ways. In the United States, for example, the line between domestic and international governs the jurisdictions of the various organizations charged with investigating and countering terrorists and potential terrorists. International terrorists are subject to the full capability of the US Department of Defense and the intelligence community. US law, however, prohibits these entities from operating domestically. Inside the United States, responsibility for investigating and prosecuting acts of domestic terrorism falls to the Federal Bureau of Investigation, Department of Justice, and local law enforcement.

These jurisdictional divisions can introduce gaps and vulnerabilities. The 9/11 Commission, which prepared a complete accounting of the attacks to diagnose what went wrong and improve preparedness, identified the divide between international and domestic jurisdictions as a gap that led authorities to fail to "connect the dots" as planning and preparation for the attacks unfolded. In response, the United States now has entities like the National Counterterrorism Center that are charged with maintaining coordination domestically and internationally and across levels of government (federal, state, and local). Other "fusion centers," including at sub-national levels, also seek to facilitate coordination across agencies and jurisdictions.

At an international level, countries frequently partner to conduct military joint counterterrorism exercises, running mock drills, sharing training strategies, and equipping states that may be particularly susceptible to militant groups. Nations also cooperate to ensure that sensitive technologies and weaponry do not fall into the hands of terrorist groups, and they share intelligence about the movement of known or suspected militant groups. The United Nations has developed infrastructure that enables countries to share information to detect,

Figure 8.5. Military raid for arms in Jaffa, Jerusalem on July 13, 1938, a counterterrorism measure taken after attacks targeting Arabs by the militant Zionist group Irgun. Precisely the same counterterrorism tactic, of heavily armed government troops traveling by motorized vehicle to capture weapons in a city, has been used off and on for nearly a century. Has it worked?
US Library of Congress

track, and thwart known terrorists' travel. Counterterrorists also sometimes use force, whether dispatching ground forces to raid a building suspected of holding terrorists or their arms (see Figure 8.5) or launching aerial or drone strikes against ground targets (see Chapter 12).

National governments frequently work with local authorities to coordinate efforts to address threats of international and domestic terrorism. In the United States, the Central Intelligence Agency, the Federal Bureau of Investigation, the Nuclear Regulatory Commission, and the Departments of State, Defense, Homeland Security, Energy, Treasury, Agriculture, Transportation, and Health and Human Services all play roles in the detection of and fight against terrorism. Some of these agencies have more specialized mandates than others; the Department of Energy, for example, monitors the nation's nuclear stockpile to ensure that fissile materials do not fall into the hands of bad actors. Local law enforcement agencies tend to tackle cases of domestic terrorism. These organizations work independently or partner with federal agencies to investigate threats of terrorism within their jurisdiction and defend their communities' critical infrastructure from threats.

Counterterrorism measures also attempt to tackle the root causes of individual radicalization and to rehabilitate those who have been radicalized. **Deradicalization** programs aim to help radicalized individuals leave terrorist movements and become functioning members of society. The programs also attempt to counter the endemic social problems – including a lack of education or employment opportunities, racism, or other perceived inequality – that would make certain segments of populations susceptible to radicalization in the first place.

Concerns also arise about the return of foreign fighters. Absent effective deradicalization, their return can increase radicalization in their home communities. Individuals who joined militant groups abroad may have become further radicalized while also being trained in violence, posing a risk. Returnees are also sometimes venerated for their dedication to the cause and the training they gained while operating abroad. Two of the deadliest terrorist attacks in Tunisia's modern history, for example, were carried out by returned foreign fighters. The Bardo National Museum attack and the Sousse beach attacks killed sixty-three people, including the perpetrators, who all had been trained in Libya by al-Qaeda.

Defining radical behavior is highly subjective, which makes defining deradicalization techniques equally challenging. Some countries define radical acts and their corresponding sentences by law, while others determine this on a case-by-case basis through more subjective administrative or legal procedures. While the practice of deradicalization is broad and typically involves police work, it is not punitive. Though some deradicalization programs may be imposed on the unwilling, they are not designed to punish. People who abandon their radical beliefs do so, most often, due to their own sense of disillusionment, while punitive measures may encourage them to double down on their radical beliefs.

Generally, deradicalization efforts are broad in scope and encompass both individual rehabilitation and community engagement strategies. Individual rehabilitation strategies work after the fact to disengage terrorists from their violent networks and ideologies and to provide them with alternative sources of stability, community, and purpose. Rehabilitation usually involves providing psychological support in addition to education and vocational training. These strategies also ensure that people in the rehabilitation program have access to housing and employment.

Families and other social groups have been shown to be good environments in which to monitor and mitigate early signs of extremism and to establish relationships useful in reintroducing radicalized people into society. Almost all deradicalization programs – from those of Saudi Arabia to Denmark – focus heavily on integrating family and community members into the process. Community engagement strategies look to tackle the root causes of radicalization to prevent extremism before it takes hold in individuals. Key engagement strategies include:

- ensuring at-risk families and communities can recognize signs of radicalization and have a safe way to report it
- providing broader access to social and mental health services
- making mentors and community support groups available to individuals who are vulnerable to extremist movements, or to those who have left them.

In recent years, social media and other digital technologies have been integral to radicalization. Online propaganda and misinformation are breeding extremism and political violence. In 2016, for example, Edgar Maddison Welch drove from North Carolina to Washington, DC and shot into Comet Ping Pong – a popular family pizza restaurant – to free trafficked children that he believed were in the basement. There was no basement and no trafficked children, but Welch had been exposed repeatedly to social media conspiracy theories.

The ability to recognize false information and propaganda is becoming ever more important as bad actors increasingly weaponize misinformation. In this environment, media literacy and access to reputable sources of information are vital to deradicalization efforts.

Deradicalization efforts are not without their challenges. Compulsory participation in these types of programs is legally fraught, and it can be difficult to compel individuals as yet unconvicted of crimes to enroll in deradicalization programs.

Deradicalization programs target populations in a variety of ways. Some programs, like those in Denmark, are entirely voluntary and primarily rely on parents enrolling their children. Others, like those of Saudi Arabia or Israel, are compulsory – though Saudi Arabia restricts eligibility to those convicted of low-level terrorist activity. A middle ground, taken by countries such as the United Kingdom, relies on referrals made by frontline agencies such as social workers, schools, local police, and immigration agencies. Other programs rely heavily on military intelligence to identify those in need of deradicalization, and because they tend to be in some type of detention already, participation is mandatory and easy to enforce.

When considering deradicalization programs, we must also be cognizant of societal biases, to ensure programs are set up to target all types of extremism, rather than profiling specific groups. Deradicalization efforts also run the risk of feeding back into extremism by increasing feelings of repression and marginalization. In other instances, repression may be labeled as deradicalization in order to make it more acceptable. China, for example, has attempted to subdue Muslim Uyghurs in detention facilities and by quartering members of mainstream Chinese society in Uyghur homes under the guise of deradicalization. Yet prisons, by their very nature, have been found to be breeding grounds for radicalization.

In other words, deradicalization may be perceived as just another form of repression, and repression magnifies a militant group's desire to retaliate against the state. This is especially true when the repression is indiscriminate in nature – China, for instance, monitors all Uyghur ethnic minorities. Broad-brush repression can anger the local population, drive recruitment, and create additional grievances.

CASE STUDY

Al-Qaeda and Its Network

As this chapter demonstrates, terrorists can magnify their capabilities by developing organizations. These organizations, in turn, can benefit from relationships with other terrorist organizations. Al-Qaeda, as one of the most capable terrorist organizations of the last two decades, offers important insights into terrorist organizations and their networks.

Al-Qaeda (AQ) emerged in the context of the anti-Soviet "jihad," in which Muslims from around the world flocked to Afghanistan to wage war against the Soviets and drive them from the country. It drew its ideological inspirations in part from the 1950s and 1960s radical writings of Sayyid Qutb, an imprisoned leader of the Egyptian Muslim Brotherhood movement. However, by the time AQ was coalescing as an independent organization in the 1990s, the fight against the Soviets was over and no longer served as the primary organizing principle for that Salafi jihadist terrorist network. AQ came to the forefront of this network because it was able to manage that transition.

The early precursors of AQ grew out of Osama bin Laden's efforts to assist Arabs who sought to travel to Afghanistan to fight against the Soviets. By 1985, these efforts had produced training camps in Afghanistan and Pakistan for jihadists coming from all over the globe to fight. While this was an important role, it was one of support – the organization provided training and logistics rather than strategy and ideology. This organizational and physical infrastructure, however, proved important and adaptable. After the Soviet withdrawal in 1989, bin Laden transformed AQ into an independent, ideologically driven organization, establishing a centralized leadership and providing financing and training for terrorist attacks after moving to Sudan in 1990.

Osama bin Laden had the necessary funding but lacked the manpower and ideological credibility required to wage this global struggle and attract followers to the cause. To rectify this, he formed a partnership with Ayman al-Zawahiri and his organization Tanzim al-Jihad. Zawahiri drew his fellow Egyptian jihadists into the AQ fold. Together, these individuals came to form the core of the AQ leadership. Building on finances from bin Laden and ideological credibility from Zawahiri and his followers, the group established itself as the leading global jihadist organization and launched a series of attacks against Western targets during the second half of the 1990s.

As a result of its global orientation and origin as a foreign fighter organization, AQ lacked the natural local constituencies enjoyed by ethnonationalist militant organizations. To compensate, the organization utilized its global brand and clout within the jihadi community and international ties with other militant organizations to ensure a steady stream of recruits to its training camps and perpetuate the ideological credibility the bin Laden–Zawahiri "marriage" had produced. More important, however, was the network of affiliates that AQ was able to build, in part based on relationships formed in the camps. This network gave AQ global operational reach and made the movement durable against external attack, as it leveraged its ideological credibility to wage a global jihad.

Building these transnational ties was relatively straightforward in the 1990s. During this period, AQ was able to maintain its physical infrastructure and centralized leadership and

(cont.)

therefore could develop relationships and centrality in the global network by leveraging its training camps in Sudan and Afghanistan to maintain its prominent position and relevance. AQ established international relationships by both opening its camps to individuals from around the world and providing financial support for affiliates' operations.

After moving AQ back to Afghanistan in 1996, bin Laden made a decisive strategic decision to wage global jihad. Breaking from the traditional jihadist emphasis on the local struggle against pro-Western Arab regimes such as Egypt and Jordan that had been the norm since the 1970s, AQ instead espoused a transnational agenda that called for concerted attacks against the "far enemy" (i.e. the United States). This culminated in the attacks of September 11, 2001, described at the start of this chapter.

With the US invasion of Afghanistan in 2001 in response to the 9/11 attacks came the loss of the group's safe haven and significant damage to its operational capability. In response, AQ leveraged its international networks. Rather than imploding and disintegrating after the 2001 setback, AQ leveraged its network of affiliates across regions to carry out attacks inspired by or in the name of the original group. The group's increasingly valuable global "brand" allowed AQ to pursue its goals through the growth of affiliates such as al-Qaeda in the Arabian Peninsula (AQAP), the Islamic Movement of Uzbekistan, Jabhat al-Nusra in Syria, and al-Qaeda in the Islamic Maghreb, operating in North Africa. Though what is left of the original AQ organization played relatively little role in these affiliates' function and operations, they perpetuated the group's continued relevance in the context of the global jihadi movement by providing the means through which AQ's operational credibility is secured.

An important organization in this network was al-Qaeda in Iraq (AQI), the precursor organization to Islamic State, which played a central role in the Iraqi insurgency that developed in response to the US invasion in 2003. Osama bin Laden was wary of AQI's indiscriminate targeting of civilians (particularly Muslims) and the organization's goal of stoking the flames of a sectarian conflict between Sunni and Shia. But despite such suspicions and disapproval, AQ developed the relationship in order to maintain its relevance by playing a role in the insurgency in Iraq.

Al-Qaeda has faced challenges over time. Al-Zawihiri, the decade-long leader of al-Qaeda, was killed in a US drone strike in July 2022. Al-Qaeda competes with the Islamic State terrorist group across the Middle East and Africa. More generally, many years have passed since al-Qaeda's last major terrorist attack on a target in the United States or Europe, the 2005 London bombings, despite its ongoing emphasis on attacking the West.

That said, in Iraq and elsewhere, AQ has been able to adapt to changing circumstances by leveraging its international networks to maintain flows of recruits, resources, and weapons to its global jihadist cause and brand. This ability has played an important role in the organization's remarkable resilience. Even with the death of Osama bin Laden in 2011, the loss of a host of top commanders, the retreat from Afghanistan, and the rise of Islamic State, AQ's global network allows it to continue to pose a threat and remain central to transnational terrorism.

QUANTITATIVE STUDY

Leadership Removal and Terrorist Alliances

Terrorist groups make decisions on when and how to cooperate. Leaders of these organizations cultivate capabilities, control group behavior, and maintain trust between organizations, roles that are key to preserving intergroup alliances. Given the role that leaders have in supporting these relationships, we might suspect that their removal can weaken the groups they lead and degrade cooperation and trust between militant groups, causing their alliances to break down. Christopher W. Blair and his colleagues conducted a study to examine whether removing a terrorist leader helps undermine cooperation between violent groups (Blair et al. 2022).

Research Question

Does removing the leadership of a terrorist organization lead to the breakdown of cooperative relationships with other terrorist organizations?

Theory and Hypothesis

The primary motivations driving militant group alliance behavior are the desire to pool capabilities in the face of common threats and the tendency to ally with organizations that have common ideologies and adversaries. This cooperation enhances allied group capabilities, contributes to the diffusion of tactics, aids in managing organizational deficits, and increases groups' longevity. Despite these benefits, the incentive to renege on alliance obligations in the face of repression, militant groups' tendency to discount the future, and the difficulty of enforcing alliance obligations can make forming and maintaining alliances difficult.

Leaders play a significant role in ideology and recruitment, propaganda, internal security, and organizational longevity while motivating sacrifice, organizing collective action, and providing the operational direction necessary for a militant group's success and survival. Leaders strengthen intergroup cohesion and alliance durability by promoting goodwill, better enabling the screening of potential partners, and facilitating coordination of beliefs, tactics, and strategies among allied groups. Leaders are also critical for maintaining cooperation between militant groups, leveraging their expertise, reputations, and personal relationships to form and sustain inter-organizational trust.

The importance of leaders in militant alliance formation and maintenance means that unplanned leadership turnover can degrade the capabilities and trust these leaders sustain and subsequently disrupt cooperation between allied groups. Leadership targeting significantly increases the likelihood of alliance termination.

Because of their integral role in creating groups, founders disproportionately influence groups' strategies, tactics, and ideologies and are thus uniquely important in militant group cooperation. Founders are more likely to have personal ties to other group leaders and to have accrued attractive reputations. Their significance to intra- and intergroup dynamics means that the effect of leadership targeting on militant alliance termination is strongest when directed at founding leaders.

Leadership targeting drives alliance termination via four primary mechanisms: it weakens, and in some cases even collapses, groups, making cooperation with other groups impossible; it raises fears about operational security, making intergroup cooperation riskier for allied groups; it makes collaboration more difficult to sustain by eliminating personal ties between leaders; and it induces command-and-control problems, driving preference divergence between allied groups over strategy and tactics and making cooperation with the targeted group less appealing.

Leadership targeting can induce alliance termination by severely degrading the targeted group, reducing its capabilities, and, in extreme cases, causing the targeted group and its alliances to cease to exist. Even when targeted groups survive decapitation, the subsequent reduction in their capabilities makes them less attractive alliance partners.

Leadership decapitation can increase operational security risks, especially for a targeted group's allies, and alliance termination can result. Decapitation compounds allied groups' concerns about operational security practices in the targeted group, diminishing the former's trust that the latter will continue to protect the details of the partnership and risking the allied group's discovery by counterterrorist intelligence measures against the targeted group. When the targeted group is decapitated, the allied group may become the counterterrorist state's next target. This risk is highest when allied groups occupy the same theater.

Leadership targeting can also catalyze the breakdown of militant alliances by dissolving intergroup personal ties. Personal relationships between militant group leaders foster mutual trust between groups and create reputational bases for cooperation but leave alliances vulnerable to dissolving when one group is decapitated.

Alliance breakdown can also happen when leadership targeting drives preference divergence between a targeted group and its allies. Lower-level members in a militant group tend to prefer higher levels of civilian victimization and more radical strategies than leaders. When leadership decapitation occurs, these lower-ranking members gain greater tactical control, causing the group to engage in more civilian victimization, anti-conciliation actions, and other behaviors opposed by allies, resulting in alliance termination.

Hypothesis: Leadership targeting increases the probability of militant group alliance termination.

Data

The data examine militant group alliances from 1971 to 2009. A group is included if it has committed at least four attacks, inflicting at least one fatality. Two (or more) groups have an alliance if a least one of the following is exchanged between the groups: operational, material, territorial, training, and/or financial support.

Dependent Variable

Across hundreds of alliances, there were 429 alliance terminations, 50 from group collapse, and 279 from inter-organizational splits.

Independent Variable

There were 272 instances of leader decapitation, of a militant group leader being arrested or killed.

Control Variables

To improve confidence that any observed correlation between leadership targeting and alliance termination is causal rather than spurious, the study included a number of control variables that might be correlated with alliance termination. They include the age of each militant group in the alliance, the difference between group ages, group capabilities, shared ideology, shared state sponsor, the number of new alliances each group formed in the prior year, the distance between the two countries in which militant groups are based, and the population and gross domestic product of countries in which groups are based.

Results

Analysis shows that leadership decapitation has a statistically significant, positive effect on militant alliance termination, with the targeting of a founding leader and the targeting of a nonfounding leader associated with a 39 percent and 32 percent increase in the probability of alliance termination, respectively. This supports the argument that, by removing leaders serving in key alliance management roles, decapitation increases the probability of alliance breakdown.

Further analysis shows that shared ideology and increased age of allied groups strengthens ties between groups even in the face of decapitations, decreasing the likelihood of alliance termination. However, larger age differences and distances between allied groups make alliance termination more likely.

Looking at how decapitation causes alliance termination, the study differentiates between alliance termination resulting from the collapse of the group targeted by decapitation and that resulting from a split between allied groups. The authors find a strong positive relationship between decapitation and alliance breakdown via inter-organizational split, demonstrating that this mechanism is primarily responsible for alliance termination.

Conclusions

The study's analyses support its initial argument, indicating that decapitation disrupts inter-organizational cohesion and trust. More importantly, they demonstrate that focusing on the effect of leadership targeting on targeted groups' longevity and operations alone can conceal the ability to terminate alliances by inducing splits between groups that result from heightened inter-organizational mistrust.

SUMMARY

These are some of the central points from this chapter:

- Although many different definitions of terrorism exist they tend to share three essential attributes. Terrorism is (1) perpetrated by nonstate actors; (2) against civilian targets; and (3) committed for political ends.
- There is no one character sketch of a terrorist. Rather, individuals are often radicalized by societal and environmental factors that prey on vulnerabilities including feelings of marginalization or discrimination.
- There are many distinctions that can be made between different types of terrorism. Attacks perpetrated within a terrorist's home country are most often considered "domestic" terrorism, while attacks undertaken by a foreign group or individual are "international." International terrorists are most often part of a larger organization, many housed across several national boundaries and occasionally state-sponsored. Domestic terrorists, in contrast, are more likely to be "lone wolf" terrorists, sometimes "self-radicalized" and often motivated by hatred of a racial or ethnic group within a country, hatred or mistrust of authority in general, or an extremist stance on a single issue, such as abortion, animal rights, the environment, or misogyny related to involuntary celibacy.
- All regime types face terrorist threats, but for different reasons. Autocracies are adept at repressing terrorist activity in the short term, but their lack of strategies for the legitimate, peaceful airing of grievances allows the threat of violence to go unaddressed in the long term. Democracies, conversely, do not have many legal mechanisms to crack down on political violence, but open societies offer many more avenues to air grievances and avoid the resort to violence. Anocracies, generally transitional states, comprise the worst of both regime types, often lacking autocracies' power to stamp out terrorist activity but without the democratic means for an aggrieved population to express their concerns.
- Terrorist organizations and lone wolves draw on a diverse range of tactics to achieve their political objectives, depending on their level of sophistication and their goals.
- Terrorist organizations do not operate in a vacuum. There is competition and collaboration among groups, particularly those operating in the same geographic or ideological space. Some terrorist organizations are sponsored by states. Cooperation is associated with increased resources and capability. It is not without its risks, however, both for militant organizations and for any states that may sponsor them.
- Counterterrorism efforts occur at many levels, from international organizations down to local law enforcement and social organizations. These efforts focus on prosecution of terrorist activities, rehabilitation of radicalized individuals, and addressing the societal factors that may make people more likely to become radicalized toward terrorism.

KEY TERMS

Terrorism

Anarchism

Ethno nationalism

New Left

Religious wave   Tactical innovation
Foreign fighters   Terrorist alliances
Lone wolf   State-sponsored terrorism
Soft targets   Deradicalization
Anocracy

REVIEW QUESTIONS

1. How did the 9/11 attacks affect the national security policies pursued by the United States and the jurisdictions of organizations charged with investigating and countering potential terrorists?
2. What are the difficulties associated with defining terrorism? Do countries share the same definition of terrorism? What are the three essential characteristics of terrorism?
3. What are some factors that may lead to individuals becoming radicalized into terrorism?
4. What are the four waves of modern terrorism?
5. How have the motivations and methods by which attacks are carried out evolved over time?
6. Are democratic regimes more susceptible to terrorism in the short term or in the long run? What about authoritarian regimes? What factors contribute to these time horizons?
7. Why are anocracies such fertile ground for terrorism?
8. What tactics are used by terrorists to target civilians?
9. How has airline hijacking, as a terrorism tactical innovation, evolved over time?
10. Why is the cooperation of terrorists with other military organizations and state patrons crucial to achieving their objectives? How do these groups sustain their partnerships and are there any risks involved?
11. What is the purpose of deradicalization and what types of programs can it involve?
12. What is the effect of leadership targeting on militant group alliance termination?

DISCUSSION QUESTIONS

1. In the face of a serious domestic terrorist threat, would you support your government restricting individual freedoms, through actions such as permitting torture as a means of interrogating suspects, reducing individual privacy including regarding personal information, making it easier for the government to monitor phone calls and place wiretaps in homes, permitting the unlimited detention of terrorism suspects without trial, and so forth?
2. How has al-Qaeda's network structure impacted its effectiveness and durability?
3. Are terrorist tactics ever justified, in pursuit of a political goal?

ADDITIONAL READING

Bergen, P. L. (2013). *Manhunt: The Ten-Year Search for Bin Laden from 9/11 to Abbottabad*. New York: Crown.

Bloom, M. (2011). *Bombshell: Women and Terrorism*. Philadelphia: University of Pennsylvania Press.

Cronin, A. K. (2011). *How Terrorism Ends: Understanding the Decline and Demise of Terrorist Campaigns*. Princeton: Princeton University Press.

Jordan, J. (2019). *Strategic Targeting of Terrorist Organizations*. Stanford: Stanford University Press.

Kroeger, A. B. (2018). *What Makes a Terrorist: Economics and the Roots of Terrorism*, 10th anniversary edn. Princeton: Princeton University Press.

Pape, R. A. (2006). *Dying to Win: The Strategic Logic of Suicide Terrorism*. New York: Random House.

Sageman, M. (2017). *Turning to Political Violence: The Emergence of Terrorism*. Philadelphia: University of Pennsylvania Press.

Shapiro, J. N. (2013). *The Terrorist's Dilemma: Managing Violent Covert Organizations*. Princeton: Princeton University Press.

REFERENCES

Blair, C. W., Horowitz, M. C., and Potter, P. B. (2022). Leadership targeting and militant alliance breakdown. *The Journal of Politics* **84**(2), 923–943.

Chenoweth, E. (2013). Terrorism and democracy. *Annual Review of Political Science* **16**, 355–378.

Dawson, L. L. (2021). *A Comparative Analysis of the Data on Western Foreign Fighters in Syria and Iraq: Who Went and Why?* The Hague: International Centre for Counter-Terrorism.

Global Terrorism Database (2021). University of Maryland. www.start.umd.edu/gtd

Hamm, M. and Spaaj, R. (2015, February). Lone wolf terrorism in America: Using knowledge of radicalization pathways to forge prevention strategies. https://nij.ojp.gov/library/publications

Horowitz, M. C. and Potter, P. (2013). Allying to kill: Terrorist intergroup cooperation and the consequences for lethality. *Journal of Conflict Resolution* **58**(2), 199–225.

Jones, S. G., Doxsee, C., Hwang, G., and Thompson, J. (2021, April 12). The military, police, and the rise of terrorism in the United States. www.csis.org/analysis/military-police-and-rise-terrorism-united-states

Kreps, S. and Byman, D. (2010). Agents of destruction? Applying principal–agent analysis to state sponsorship of terrorism. *International Studies Perspectives* **11**(1), 1–18.

Lee, A. (2011). Who becomes a terrorist? Poverty, education, and the origins of political violence. *World Politics* **63**(2), 203–245.

Legal Information Institute. (n.d.). Cornell University. law.cornell.edu/cfr/text/28/0.85

Organization for Economic Cooperation and Development (OECD) (n.d.) Definition of terrorism by country in OECD countries. www.oecd.org/daf/fin/insurance/TerrorismDefinition-Table.pdf

Rapoport, D. (2004). "The Four Waves of Modern Terrorism," in Audrey Cronin and James Ludes eds., Attacking Terrorism (Washington, DC: Georgetown University Press) pp 46–73.

United Nations Office on Drugs and Crime (n.d.). Foreign terrorist fighters. www.unodc.org/unodc/en/terrorism/expertise

Part IV

Diplomacy and Conflict

9 International Alliances

DAN REITER

Introduction

International alliances are formal agreements between states. They describe how the signatories agree to cooperate to advance their security interests. Alliances are essential elements of international politics, and have determined the course of world history. Ancient Greece was shaped by the Athenian and Spartan alliances during the Peloponnesian Wars. The last 700 years of European politics have been dominated by alliances squaring off against each other. Napoleon Bonaparte's nearly successful bid for a French empire across Europe was defeated in 1815 because of the opposition of a Grand Alliance of virtually all the other major powers of Europe. Germany and its Austro-Hungarian and Ottoman allies almost won World War I when Russia abandoned its British, Italian, and French allies, but ultimately lost after the United States declared war on Germany and took Russia's place. The powerful World War II alliance of Germany, Japan, and Italy was ultimately defeated by the even more powerful alliance of the United States, Britain, the Soviet Union, and China. The Cold War was largely a confrontation between one alliance system dominated by the United States and another dominated by the Soviet Union.

Alliances remain a critical part of international politics in the twenty-first century. North Korea has been held at bay largely because of the American alliance with South Korea. The North Atlantic Treaty Organization (NATO) alliance is a cornerstone of Western security and helped protect persecuted Balkan minorities in the 1990s, overthrow the Taliban government in Afghanistan in 2001, and remove the Libyan dictator Muammar Qaddafi in 2011. Russia has supported aggression against Ukraine, a country that is not a member of NATO, but has generally left alone NATO members located near Ukraine such as Estonia, Latvia, Lithuania, and Poland (see online Ukraine War module). The foundation of Japan's security is its alliance with the United States. Russia has bolstered security cooperation among former Soviet republics by forming and supporting the Commonwealth of Independent States alliance.

This chapter describes international alliances. It answers a series of questions about alliances. What are alliances, and what different forms do alliances take? Why do states join alliances?

Why do states comply with alliance agreements? How do states choose alliance members? How do alliances shape international relations?

Why Do States Form Alliances?

The world can be a dangerous place for states. It is filled with potential adversaries. One way to survive in a threatening world is to arm oneself to the teeth, building a national military powerful enough to fend off any foe. However, it is difficult for smaller countries such as Taiwan or Estonia individually to amass enough power to match up with giant potential adversaries like China or Russia. Further, relying solely on oneself for security can be expensive, as high levels of military spending can undermine economic growth and investment in social priorities. As economists have long put it, more guns means less butter (see Chapter 6)

For states who believe that relying solely on oneself for security is not feasible or desirable, a common approach to dealing with a threatening international environment is to enter an international alliance. **International alliances** are examples of problem-solving international cooperation, in that two or more states draw up formal agreements describing actions the signatories commit to take to address international problems. States also draw up other kinds of formal agreements, taking actions such as lowering barriers to international trade and reducing greenhouse gas emissions.

Many alliances include a **security guarantee**, treaty language that indicates that if one of the signatories finds itself at war, the other signatories are obligated to intervene on behalf of that embattled ally. Sometimes, an alliance security guarantee will be limited, such that signatories are required to go to war only if an ally is attacked first; these kinds of guarantees are called **defense pacts**. Conversely, if an alliance security guarantee requires that a signatory go to war only if an ally *starts* a war, then it is termed an **offense pact**. Two states might sign an offense pact not only to address a threat, but also to coordinate capturing territory from a third country, as Germany and the Soviet Union did with their 1939 offense pact alliance aimed at Poland.

States hesitant about committing to intervene in the event of war but still motivated to improve security cooperation might sign other forms of alliances. Instead of committing to go to war if one signatory is attacked, they may commit merely to consult with each other in the event of crisis or war, a relatively painless action to take. These kinds of alliance are called **consultation pacts** (or, sometimes, ententes). Or, two states unwilling to commit to go to war on each other's behalf might instead make the lesser commitment of agreeing not to attack each other. These kinds of alliances are called **nonaggression pacts**. Relatedly, an alliance agreement may commit the member states not to join any other state fighting another signatory. These agreements are called **neutrality pacts**.

Alliances are *formal* commitments to cooperate to address common security threats, meaning that they are written down in treaties and sometimes managed by international organizations such as NATO. If states work together on security matters without the basis of a formal agreement, such as cooperation between the United States and Israel, this is described as **alignment** rather than alliance.

Note that a formal alliance agreement is not necessary for one state to go to war on behalf of another state; sometimes alignment is sufficient. One state may simply have an interest in protecting another state from being conquered, even if the two have not signed a formal agreement, and that interest may be enough to push that state to intervene in the event of war. The United States intervened on behalf of South Korea in 1950, some three years before the US–South Korea alliance was signed, and later that year China intervened in the Korean War on behalf of North Korea, though there was at that point no alliance between China and North Korea. Similarly, the United States went to war to liberate Kuwait in 1991 though the United States and Kuwait were not allied.

Alliances are an integral part of the **balance of power**, a dynamic in which states attempt to maintain world order by dissuading aggressors from launching wars. It is called a "balance" of power in the sense that the international system maintains its equilibrium if the power of a potential aggressor state is balanced sufficiently by the combined power of states seeking to keep peace. States sometimes form alliances to create powerful counterweights to potential aggressor states, demonstrating that aggressors would face powerful defensive coalitions if they did resort to war. Great Britain in particular has used alliances to maintain the balance of power for centuries. It built alliances to contain the French monarchy in the eighteenth century, to fend off the French dictator Napoleon Bonaparte in the early nineteenth century, to defeat Wilhelmine Germany and then Nazi Germany in the first half of the twentieth century, and then to deter the Soviet Union in the second half of the twentieth century (Snyder 1997).

That said, alliances are more likely to contribute to peace if they are publicly known. This is not always the case, as some alliances are secret, known only to the signatories. When alliances are secret, this can contribute to disagreement between two sides as to the likely outcome of war, if one side underestimates the other side's power because the other side's alliance is not known. This can make it more difficult for the two sides to find a bargain both prefer to war, making war more likely (see Chapter 2).

The United States has over its history had shifting attitudes about alliances. In its first century and a half, it viewed alliances with great disdain. Its first president, George Washington, warned in his farewell address that America must "steer clear of permanent alliances with any portion of the foreign world" (Washington, 1796). In 1917 America joined the Allies fighting in World War I, but returned to relative diplomatic and military isolation after war's end. World War II demonstrated that the great oceans no longer served to ensure American security, and US foreign policy made an enduring shift away from isolation and towards international engagement.

A central element of America's new post-1945 internationalism was an eager embrace of alliances, signing a series of alliance agreements with dozens of countries around the world including South Korea, West Germany, Taiwan, Britain, and others, to deter possible Communist aggression. Indeed, in the 1950s the Eisenhower administration embraced such agreements so enthusiastically, its attitude was described by some as "pactomania." The Soviet Union also formed a series of alliances during the Cold War, most notably the Warsaw Treaty Organization (or Warsaw Pact) which had several Communist, East European states as signatories. When the Cold War ended, the Warsaw Pact collapsed, but American alliances such as NATO endured. Into the twenty-first century, alliances remain an essential element of American foreign policy in particular and international relations more broadly.

The Problem of Compliance

So far, this all seems pretty straightforward: states sign alliances to balance against potential aggressors, and if the alliance is big enough the potential aggressor is deterred and war is averted. However, this simple story is complicated by a problem that plagues all international agreements: compliance. Why would states comply with an alliance or any other international agreement, given that there is no world government to force them to comply? If an alliance requires a signatory to go to war to aid an ally, and that signatory does not want to go to war, what is to prevent the signatory from remaining neutral, in violation of the alliance? As citizens, we usually comply with unpopular national laws, like speed limits, because we know that violators of the law will be punished if caught. But in the international system, there is no formal mechanism for punishing violators of international agreements like alliances, no world government to impose fines, no world police force to haul the offending government off to jail. So why would a state comply with an alliance agreement if it did not want to?

The compliance problem is especially critical for alliances, as complying with an alliance can mean taking the tremendously risky and costly step of going to war. A state might be strongly motivated to violate an alliance agreement if the agreement requires the state to enter a war it would rather stay out of. In today's world, consider what the US response might be if Russia attacked the small European state of Latvia, an American ally and member of NATO. Latvia is not terribly important to American interests, and most Americans would probably have difficulty finding Latvia on a map. It is a small state, about the size of West Virginia. It is not a major US trading partner and exports no important natural resources like oil. One can see how if Russia invaded Latvia, the United States might prefer to stay out of the conflict rather than intervene and risk major war – even nuclear war – with Russia. Indeed, one 2014 poll found that only 21 percent of Americans would support using military force in reaction to a Russian invasion of Latvia (Calabria 2014). The February 2022 Russian invasion of Ukraine only partly overcame this hesitance: a poll taken only days after the invasion revealed that just 35 percent of Americans would be willing to use military force if Russia attacked Latvia (Daily Survey: Russia and Ukraine 2022).

The compliance problem strikes at the very heart of what many alliances aim to do: deter aggression, and defeat aggressors if deterrence fails. If states are unlikely to comply with an alliance agreement, then aggressors know they can effectively isolate potential targets and defeat them in war. This knowledge in turn makes such aggressors more likely to launch attacks, and those attacks are more likely to succeed if states are abandoned by their allies. Alliances then become worthless scraps of paper, background noise in the din of world politics.

However, states do join alliances and at least sometimes comply with them. What might cause states to comply with alliances, even if they do not have to? There are three main reasons why states comply with their alliance agreements: first, when alliances increase fighting power, treaty signatories are more likely to comply and intervene because the likelihood of victory is higher; second, states want to maintain political capital and not lose face on the world stage; and third, more subtly, states only join the alliances they are willing to comply with.

Alliances Can Help States Fight Wars More Effectively

Alliance compliance is fundamentally about deciding to go to war, specifically to enter a war that has already started. A primary reason that a state might not want to enter war is if it thought it would be joining a losing cause. No state wants to join a war it will go on to lose, as losing a war means sacrifice of life and economic resources without accomplishing one's war aims. In November 1956, the Soviet Union invaded Hungary, and the United States and other Western states elected not to intervene on Hungary's behalf, in part because there was little the West could do to save Hungary, short of perhaps launching an all-out nuclear war.

How does this pertain to alliances? Consider if state A is attacked, and state B has to choose whether or not to intervene on behalf of state A. The more confident state B is that its intervention will succeed, the more likely it is to intervene. If the presence of an alliance might make such an intervention more likely to succeed, that is, if an alliance in some way boosts the joint fighting power of the two states, then that would make state B more willing to intervene, compared to if the two sides did not have such a power-boosting alliance.

This raises the question, how can alliance agreements make groups of states more militarily powerful? One might suspect that alliances ought not to matter much in affecting the military power of a group of states, as the collective military power of a group of states is determined simply by how big the states' armies are. If two countries each have an army of 500,000 soldiers, then if they fight together, they should have the same combined fighting power as a single country fielding an army of a million soldiers, whether or not they have an alliance. That is, a set of states fighting without an alliance agreement ought to be as powerful as a set of states fighting with an alliance agreement.

But things are not quite so simple. When multiple states fight alongside each other in a wartime coalition (a coalition is a group of states that are fighting together during war, whether or not they have signed an alliance agreement), problems can appear that undermine their combined fighting power. Coalition members might have different ideas about how to prepare for or conduct war, leading them to pull in opposite and perhaps counterproductive directions. The coalition members might be unable to agree on who should be the supreme commander of the coalition, a potentially critical problem if the lack of a single commander causes the coalition to react sluggishly, plan poorly, or fight without a unified mission. And coalition members need to sort out a number of other questions central to a coordinated fighting effort, such as designing an integrated supply system across the coalition, standardizing weaponry and communications, and other facets of what military experts call "interoperability."

Sometimes coalitions fail to solve these problems and fight less effectively, either because they are fighting without an alliance agreement or because the alliance agreement they do have does not take the necessary steps to address these problems. Italy and Germany were allies in World War II, and did not coordinate major decisions about launching offensives. Irritated by German dictator Adolf Hitler, Italian dictator Benito Mussolini in October 1940 rashly decided to invade Greece, without consulting his German ally (Map 9.1). The campaign turned into a catastrophe

Map 9.1. Italy's failed 1940 invasion of Greece, launched from the Italian-controlled nation of Albania. When Greek forces threw the invaders back across the border, Germany was forced to intervene, diverting critically needed troops from North Africa. Wikipedia.

for Italy over the winter, requiring German intervention to help save the Italian force and defeat the Greeks. Though German efforts to defeat Greece were easily successful, the Greece campaign doomed the Italian North African offensive against British forces, both because Italian troops were being directed to Greece rather than to North Africa and because German forces that could have aided the North Africa campaign were instead sent to Greece. In 1940 and 1941, the Axis powers had an opportunity to sweep Britain from North Africa and capture from Britain Egypt's critical Suez Canal, a much higher priority than the conquest of Greece. Mussolini's unwillingness to coordinate with Hitler helped cause the Axis to miss this golden opportunity to seize the Suez and sever the jugular vein of Britain's global economic empire.

The Allies in World War II also experienced problems in coalition warfare. Though Britain and France were committed to defend Belgium against German attack, Belgium refused to coordinate war planning efforts with those two countries as late as a month prior to Germany's May 1940 invasion. Belgium's refusal to coordinate with Britain and France on matters such as predeploying Anglo-French forces onto Belgian soil undermined the ability of Britain and France to parry Germany's attack. Partly as a result, Germany quickly conquered Belgium before moving on to defeat France.

Prewar alliance agreements can alleviate these coalition coordination problems (Poast 2019). They can make the coalition a more effective fighting force, in turn making allies more willing to intervene in the event of war because they are more confident they will win. As potential adversaries observe that states are more likely to comply with their alliance agreements, they in turn become less likely to attack.

Alliances can alleviate coordination problems in several ways. Some alliances include specific provisions for how military forces are to be commanded during war. The 1955 Warsaw Pact between the Soviet Union and several East European communist countries established the principle of joint command among the signatories. Other alliances describe specific provisions for troop contributions in the event of war. The 1892 Franco–Russian alliance declared that in the event of war with Germany, France would field 1.3 million soldiers, and Russia would field between 700,000 and 800,000 soldiers.

An alliance agreement can also allow for the peacetime deployment of one ally's forces on the territory of another. Such plans can be critically important in maximizing the fighting power of an alliance. If one of the members of the alliance is especially likely to be the target of an attack, then the peacetime deployment of allied troops onto that member's territory can reduce the likelihood that an attacker might be tempted to launch a surprise attack and overrun that alliance member before allied forces can arrive to assist. This is especially important when allied countries are thousands of miles distant, as there would be substantial delay in the arrival of friendly forces to the area of combat. For example, in the presence of an escalating Russian threat in the mid 2010s, more American, German, and British forces were deployed in peacetime to the territories of NATO allies bordering Russia such as Norway and the Baltic states.

Peacetime deployment of troops was a critical part of US alliance planning during and after the Cold War. American defense planners feared that the armies of key US allies like West Germany and South Korea might be swiftly overwhelmed by attacking Communist forces, conquering these countries before substantial numbers of US troops could be transported across the oceans from North America. To reduce this vulnerability, the United States prepositioned tens of thousands of American troops and needed supplies to the territories of distant American allies.

Besides reducing transportation problems, the peacetime deployment of allied forces also facilitates effective preparation for war. Permanent military bases provide a logistical infrastructure to support allied troops during war. Being physically present helps allied commanders learn the terrain and plan for an effective defense, improving inter-allied cooperation and planning. In particular, peacetime troop deployments facilitate war games that allow allied militaries to practice fighting together. The United States and South Korea frequently engage in war games on South Korean territory, such as the 2016 Ulchi Freedom Guardian Wargames involving 75,000 American and South Korean troops, to prepare for the possibility of a North Korean invasion and to signal to North Korea the American commitment to its South Korean ally.

NATO is the gold standard of an alliance engaging in extensive peacetime planning, designed to maximize the combined military power of member states. After the United States and other countries signed the North Atlantic Treaty in 1949, they began to use NATO as a means to coordinate their militaries and plan for war. NATO members knew that such peacetime efforts would be critical, as the most likely event in which the North Atlantic Treaty would be invoked would be a Soviet invasion of Western Europe, and given Soviet military superiority and the long distance between American military-industrial power and the heartland of Europe, NATO defenses of Europe would need to be well planned and efficient. NATO established a permanent military planning headquarters in Brussels and worked to hash out several critical issues the coalition would face in the event of World War III, such as how many troops each NATO member would contribute, where in Europe each nation's troops would actually fight, predeployment of American and other forces onto NATO territory, appointment of a Supreme Allied Commander of Europe to lead NATO forces, agreement on a unified military strategy, standardization of logistics, and so on. This coordination continued after the Cold War. NATO has become a large peacetime bureaucracy to accomplish these missions, employing some 6,000 civilians in addition to the military officers involved.

In summary, peacetime planning, often carried out through a formal military alliance, can bolster the joint military power of states fighting together during war, improving their chances of winning the war. This reduces the compliance problem because as the likelihood of winning the war goes up, allies become more willing to intervene on behalf of an embattled ally, and potential aggressors become more hesitant to attack an alliance member. The historical record offers some support for this perspective. Specifically, no aggressor states saw fit to challenge the Cold War alliances that enjoyed the highest levels of peacetime coordination, such as NATO, the US–South Korea alliance, the Australia–New Zealand–US alliance, and the US–Japan alliance – perhaps because aggressors knew that these alliances had helped transcend many of the problems of coalition warfare and increased the likelihood that signatories would comply with the alliance agreements.

The Political Costs of Violating Alliances

Though an alliance signatory would not face legal sanctions if it violated an alliance, it might face political costs of breaking its word and abandoning an ally. The fear of paying these political costs in turn provides an incentive for states to abide by their alliance commitments, making compliance more likely.

What kinds of political costs might alliance violators pay? Breaking an alliance would be costly for a state because it would negatively affect the reputation of the state on the international stage, and perhaps also the reputation of the state's leader in the domestic political arena (Crescenzi 2018). Put differently, failure to comply would lower the reputation of the state in the eyes of third-party actors or "audiences," such as other countries around the world or a country's domestic population, and these audiences would reply by imposing "costs" on the state or the leader. These costs are sometimes called "**audience costs**." Making it costly to break an agreement increases the likelihood that a state will comply with an agreement, to avoid those costs. Ironically, creating audience costs for breaking an alliance makes the alliance more powerful by reducing the signatories' freedom of choice, a dynamic sometimes described as **tying hands** (as in, "Because it is too costly to break my word, I will be forced to follow through on my promise; my hands are tied").

Let's break this down. Consider international audience costs, the political costs that international actors would impose on a state that violated an alliance agreement. These costs come in the form of a damaged reputation for the alliance violator. This begs the question, what kinds of international reputations do most states like to have? Most states like to have reputations for being willing to fight, and for honoring their agreements. If others believe a state is willing to fight to defend its interests, then they will come to believe that they cannot bully that state into abandoning its commitments and retreating, and they will be less likely to threaten or attack the state or its interests. Conversely, if a state is not seen as tough, others believe the state may abandon its commitments and will not go to war to defend its interests, and thus it can be bullied into retreating, making threats and attacks against it more likely.

To break it down further, having a reputation for being tough and honorable affects the beliefs and behavior of three categories of international actors. First, it affects potential aggressors. As potential aggressors come to believe that a state will comply with its alliance agreements and go to war to protect its allies, those aggressors become less likely to attack those allies. Second, it affects current allies. States belong to alliances by choice, and can exit by choice. When a state is more confident in its ally's reputation for being tough and honorable, that state is more likely to stay in its alliance. If it comes to doubt the reputation of its allies, it will be more likely to leave. Third, it affects potential allies. States that are currently neutral are more likely to form an alliance with a state that has a reputation for being tough and reliable.

For centuries, states have been obsessed with building and maintaining their reputations for being tough, honorable allies. This was certainly the case for the United States during the Cold War. American presidents such as Harry S. Truman were haunted by the belief that Nazi Germany started World War II because it came to regard Britain and France as not being tough or willing to stand by their commitments in the face of German aggression. Most infamously, in 1938 Germany demanded that Czechoslovakia hand over the Sudetenland, a strategically critical portion of Czech territory. Even though Czechoslovakia was a French ally, at a meeting in Munich, Germany, Britain, and France acceded to German demands, vainly hoping that appeasing Germany would provide peace and security (see Map 9.2). Truman and other post-1945 presidents vowed not to repeat their mistake, believing that acceding to initial aggressive acts would undermine America's reputation for toughness, encouraging further aggression.

The United States during the Cold War believed that Communist states were considering aggression against American interests around the globe, and concluded that the best way to prevent such aggression was to form alliances with threatened states and to convince Communist states that the USA was tough and willing to honor these alliance commitments. The United States was also fearful that damage to its reputation as an ally would convince allied states to exit the US camp, and neutral states to lean towards Communism. During the Vietnam War, the Johnson administration described the possibility of a "domino effect" if the United States abandoned South Vietnam. If South Vietnam went Communist, a chain reaction would occur with other Asian states, such as Laos, Cambodia, Thailand, Burma, and India, succumbing to Communism like falling dominoes.

Bolstering this kind of reputation does not come cheaply. The United States came to believe it had to run significant risks and fight bloody wars to convince Communist states that it was tough and honorable. Several American presidents feared that a failure to stand by an ally risked

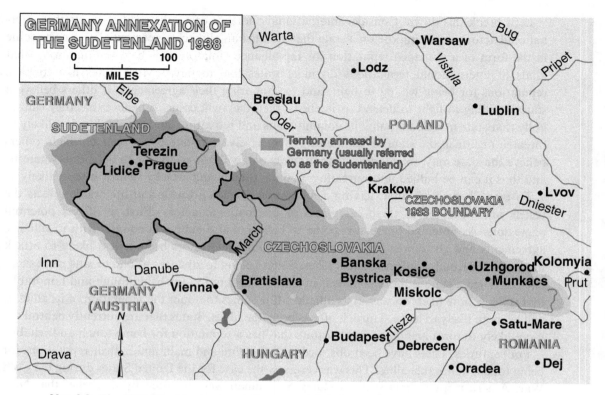

Map 9.2. The 1938 Munich agreement: France and Britain attempted to appease Hitler by giving him the Sudetenland, a strategically important portion of Czechoslovakia. France and Britain hoped the deal would provide peace and security. It gave them neither. The United States Holocaust Memorial Museum.

sowing the seeds of doubt about America's reputation, emboldening aggressors to challenge American interests in Western Europe, East Asia, and elsewhere, and inspiring America's own allies to doubt American reliability. The United States risked nuclear war and lost nearly 40,000 lives in fighting the Korean War, protecting South Korea against Communist aggression. President Dwight Eisenhower stood by US ally Taiwan in the 1950s against Chinese aggression, twice threatening China with nuclear war in support of Taiwan. Presidents Eisenhower and John F. Kennedy risked nuclear war against the Soviet Union when the Soviets threatened aggression against West Berlin, then part of the territory of West Germany, an American ally. By far the most important reason that Presidents Kennedy and Lyndon Johnson became embroiled in the Vietnam War, a conflict that cost more than 50,000 American lives, was not to spread democracy in Southeast Asia or some other lofty goal, but rather to maintain America's reputation by standing by the American ally South Vietnam. President Richard Nixon was obsessed with American reputation, and he was convinced that any American withdrawal from Vietnam must occur slowly so as to minimize any damage to American credibility.

Beyond international ramifications, a leader might also be concerned that breaking an alliance agreement would invoke domestic audience costs. Leaders, especially elected leaders, want to avoid becoming unpopular, because unpopular leaders are less likely to stay in power. Foreign policy mistakes are one good way for a leader to lose popularity and risk being voted out of office. If a leader were to violate an alliance commitment and fail to rescue an ally at war, this might risk public ire and encourage the public to replace the leader, as the public would fear that abandoning an ally would undermine the nation's global reputation for being tough and reliable. A legislature might also be less willing to support the policy agenda of a national leader with plummeting popularity ratings. Seeking to avoid these kinds of political consequences, leaders are motivated to abide by their alliance commitments and maintain public support.

Let's take a closer look at the Vietnam War, a good example of an elected leader reluctantly going to war out of fear of the domestic political and international audience costs of abandoning an ally. The United States was a signatory of the 1954 Manila Pact, the treaty which formed the basis of the Southeast Asian Treaty Organization (SEATO). In that treaty, signatories agree to "act to meet the common danger" of aggression in Southeast Asia. The Communist government of North Vietnam had by the early 1960s been actively destabilizing the non-Communist government of South Vietnam, and the United States had been providing increasing levels of military aid and other support to shore up South Vietnam.

By 1964, it was becoming evident that these low levels of American support for South Vietnam were not sufficient, and President Johnson needed to decide whether to escalate American support on behalf of South Vietnam, or to abandon it to Communist aggression. The audience costs of reneging on the alliance commitment weighed heavily on the minds of the American leadership. Johnson feared that failure to stand by America's alliance commitment would damage America's reputation as a tough and reliable ally, encouraging America's allies to exit their treaties and Communist countries to launch attacks. As Johnson explained to Senator Birch Bayh in June 1965, "If we walked out of [Vietnam], we would bust every treaty we got. Forty-four nations would say that [the] United States couldn't be depended on for anything" (quoted in Beschloss 2001, 354–355). Indeed, in one internal 1965 memo, a high-level US official wrote that 70 percent of the reason the United States was fighting for South Vietnam was "To avoid a humiliating US defeat (to our reputation as a guarantor)," and only 10 percent was to improve the quality of life of the people of South Vietnam (McNaughton 1965).

Relatedly, Johnson was also concerned that failure to stand by South Vietnam would cause him to suffer domestic political costs. In the early 1960s, there was broad bipartisan consensus in America about the importance of fighting the Cold War and standing up to Communism. Johnson feared that failure to stand by South Vietnam as it faced Communist aggression would give powerful ammunition to his Republican Party enemies, especially to Senator Barry Goldwater, his Republican opponent in the November 1964 presidential election. In surveying his Vietnam options in February of that year, Johnson remarked that one choice would be to "run and let the dominoes start falling over. And God Almighty, what they said about us leaving China [in 1949] would just be warming up, compared to what they'd say now. I see [Republican former Vice President Richard] Nixon is raising hell about it today. Goldwater too" (quoted in Beschloss 1997, 213). Johnson was also concerned about political attacks from within his own Democratic Party, and specifically the threat that abandoning South Vietnam would undercut the willingness of some Democrats to support his anti-poverty Great Society legislation.

All that said, there are limits to the effects of audience costs on alliance compliance behavior (Snyder and Borghard 2011). Fear of the audience costs of breaking an agreement might not be enough to pull an ally into an unwanted war – or keep an ally from continuing to fight – if the costs of war exceed the reputational costs of abandoning the ally. A nation's public sometimes prefers peace with a damaged reputation over war with an intact reputation; certainly, French and British leaders presumed correctly in 1938 that their publics preferred conceding the Sudetenland to Germany over starting another war. When French President Édouard Daladier returned to France from the 1938 Munich meeting, crowds lined the streets of Paris to cheer him and support the Sudetenland settlement that kept the peace at the expense of abandoning a French ally, shouting "*Vive Daladier! Vive la Paix!*" (Hucker 2011, 54–55). The French parliament approved the infamous agreement in a landslide vote of 535 to 75, validating Daladier's guess that the French body politic preferred a dented alliance reputation to war with Germany.

And, though reputation concerns pulled the United States deeper into the Vietnam War in 1964 and 1965, the American public's will to save South Vietnam from Communism eventually became exhausted. After the January 1973 Paris Peace Accords ended the Vietnam War, North Vietnam invaded South Vietnam, and the American public preferred that Presidents Nixon and Ford not intervene to save South Vietnam, notwithstanding any potential damage to America's global reputation. America declined to intervene, and in April 1975 North Vietnam conquered South Vietnam, creating the unified, Communist Vietnam that has endured to the present day.

So far, the discussion has focused on how the prospect of paying audience costs, either domestic or international, might push a state to comply with an alliance agreement. The assumption is that the mere existence of the alliance treaty is enough to create audience costs, encouraging signatory compliance. However, some states wish to go further, taking steps to increase the audience costs of violating an alliance, the logic being that the costlier they can make a violation of an alliance ahead of time, the more tightly they can tie their hands, and the more successful they will be at convincing potential aggressors that they will comply with the alliance, thereby reducing the likelihood that the aggressor will challenge the alliance and attack.

Sometimes allies can do this verbally, publicly proclaiming their commitment, the idea being that the more publicly known is the commitment domestically and internationally, the higher the audience costs to be paid if the commitment is broken.

For example, in the late 1950s and early 1960s, the United States was concerned about Soviet threats against West Berlin, then an "island" of territory formally part of the NATO ally West Germany, but located completely within the territory of Communist East Germany. Presidents Eisenhower and Kennedy signaled that the United States viewed the NATO treaty as committing the United States to come to the defense of West Berlin. In 1963, Kennedy traveled to West Berlin and gave a speech publicly binding the United States to its defense, proclaiming, "*Ich bin ein Berliner*" ("I am a Berliner"). Given such an unequivocal commitment to Berlin, Kennedy and the United States would have paid spectacular audience costs had the United States abandoned West Berlin in the face of a Soviet attack.

More recently, the United States became concerned about escalating China–Japan tensions over a territorial dispute regarding the uninhabited Senkaku Islands, located in the East China Sea (see Map 9.3).

China claims sovereignty over these islands (China calls them the Diaoyu Islands), and there is the lingering possibility of military conflict. The United States has a defense pact with Japan committing the USA to intervene if Japan is attacked, but the Senkaku Islands are located several hundred miles from the main Japanese islands. If China were to consider invading the islands, it might conclude that the United States would argue that the US–Japan alliance does not extend over the Senkakus, given their detached remoteness, and therefore the United States

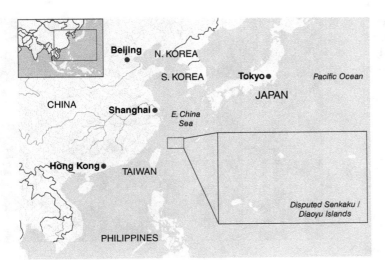

Map 9.3. Senkaku/Diaoyu Islands, claimed by both Japan and China. Voice of America News.

would not be required to intervene on Japan's behalf in a China–Japan war over the Senkakus. That is, China might conclude that the United States believed that it (the United States) would not suffer audience costs if it did not intervene in a Senkakus war. If China thought the United States might not intervene in such circumstances, then China might be encouraged to attack. To reduce the possibility that China would doubt US willingness to intervene, the Obama, Trump, and Biden administrations publicly declared that the US–Japan alliance does cover the Senkaku Islands. Now the United States cannot argue that the alliance does not require US intervention over the Senkakus, and the United States would be more likely to suffer audience costs if it did not intervene, with the result that it is more likely to intervene in the event of a Senkakus conflict, and in turn China is less likely to start such a conflict.

Beyond making commitments more public, alliance signatories can take other steps to amplify the audience costs of breaking an alliance agreement. One approach to increase the audience costs for abandoning an ally would be for a state to predeploy its troops to the territory of an ally that might get attacked. The logic is that if war starts, the state's predeployed troops will immediately get involved in fighting, forcing the ally's government to declare war to support its own embattled troops. That is, if an ally's troops were immediately involved in combat and the ally elected to withdraw from fighting under fire, this would impose an especially heavy set of international reputational audience costs on the state, and domestic audiences would be outraged that their own troops had been abandoned. Fear of these severe audience costs ensures that the state will follow through with its alliance commitments. This is sometimes called a "tripwire" strategy, in the sense that the troops act as a tripwire, immediately triggering allied involvement in the event of war.

The United States frequently deployed its troops in peacetime to the territory of its allies for just this reason. Even if the deployed troops were not powerful enough to fight off an invasion, their very presence and involvement in early combat would tie the American president's hands if war occurred, forcing the United States to intervene. Perhaps the most salient Cold War example was the predeployment of American troops to the city of West Berlin. The 7,000 or so American troops deployed to West Berlin would not be powerful enough to fend off a Soviet invasion of the city, but their immediate involvement in combat would force American

Figure 9.1. Demonstrating American resolve to fight: President John F. Kennedy reviewing American troops in West Berlin, 1961.
United States National Archives.

intervention (see Figure 9.1). As the Nobel Prize–winning economist and strategist Thomas Schelling once colorfully described the goal of the deployment of a small number of US troops to West Berlin, "What can 7,000 American troops do, or 12,000 Allied troops? Bluntly, they can die. They can die heroically, dramatically, and in a manner that guarantees that the action cannot stop there" (Schelling 1966, 47). That said, some have disputed whether tripwire deployments actually make alliance commitments more credible (Reiter and Poast 2021).

The United States continues this policy today, predeploying troops to NATO members like Poland, which is at risk of attack by Russia, and South Korea, at risk of attack by North Korea. Indeed, as of 2021 there were more than 28,000 US troops deployed to South Korea. Not coincidentally, several American military bases in South Korea are located near the border with North Korea, ensuring that American forces would be immediately involved in combat in the event of a North Korean invasion.

Join and Design Alliance Treaties Carefully

Our central question is, why do states comply with alliance treaties, when there is no international government to enforce compliance? So far, we've developed two answers to this question: alliances can make compliance more likely by improving the chances that a coalition can win a potential war, and by increasing the audience costs a state would suffer from abandoning an ally. A third answer to this question is a bit more subtle. States comply with the alliance treaties they sign because they are careful about what alliance treaties they sign in the first place (Poast 2019). Specifically, states avoid signing alliances they think they might not wish to comply with in the future. Further, if states do sign alliances, they try to make sure that the alliance agreements contain only those compliance requirements they are likely to abide by. Put simply, states agree in the alliance to take actions they think they would be willing to take, and they avoid agreeing to take actions they might be unwilling to take. This is of course a common dynamic among all types of treaties, with countries tending to sign a treaty if they plan on complying, and tending not to sign if they do not plan on complying. This is why, for example, countries without nuclear weapons ambitions such as Botswana, Canada, and Costa Rica have signed the Nuclear Non-Proliferation

Treaty, an agreement requiring its signatories to forgo the acquisition of nuclear weapons, whereas states with nuclear ambitions such as Israel, India, and Pakistan have refused to sign the treaty.

The historical record provides examples of states electing not to join alliances because they feared that a compliance problem might emerge. A growing unwillingness to become embroiled in other states' wars was the primary reason that the United States Senate declined to approve American entry into the alliance-like League of Nations in 1920. After World War II, Sweden wished to stay out of any war between the United States and the Soviet Union and accordingly declined to enter NATO, despite a fervent US invitation that was coupled with vague threats that the United States might bomb Sweden if it did not join.

Relatedly, alliances sometimes bar a prospective member from joining because the signatories do not want to commit to going to war to defend that prospective member. Spain and Israel both requested to join NATO in the early 1950s, but were turned down (Spain was eventually allowed to enter in 1982). Decades later, in the 1990s and 2000s, NATO also declined Ukraine's request to join NATO, in part because of fear that the likelihood of a Russia–Ukraine war was too great, and NATO would not want to become involved in such a conflict.

There are also examples of a state signing an alliance, but skirting the compliance problem by ensuring that the text of the alliance does not require the state to do something it might prefer to avoid (Benson 2012). For example, a state considering allying with a second state might be willing to go to war if the second state were attacked, but not if the second state started a war. Such a state might be willing to sign a defense pact, but not a security guarantee requiring intervention if an ally started a war. Many contemporary alliances, including NATO and bilateral American alliances, are defense pacts.

States that fear getting dragged into wars of aggression incorporate defense pact language into alliance treaties, and then sometimes use defense pact language to justify nonintervention if an ally is the aggressor. In the 1950s the United States was willing to commit to the defense of Taiwan if it was attacked by China, but it did not want to get involved in a war started by a Taiwanese attack on China, and certainly didn't want to sign an alliance that might encourage a Taiwanese attack on China with a promise of American assistance. As a result, the 1954 Taiwan–US alliance indicates that the signatories need to assist each other in the event that there is an armed attack "against the territories of either of the parties," specifically excluding a requirement to assist each other if one side initiated a war.

More rarely, states limit their compliance requirements by signing offense pacts rather than broader security guarantees. Prussia and Italy signed an offense pact alliance in 1866, in which Italy agreed to declare war if Prussia attacked Austria. Later that year Prussia initiated the Seven Weeks War against Austria, and Italy intervened on Prussia's behalf, an action which helped Prussia win the war.

Alliances include other kinds of language that limit the compliance requirements of the treaty. Some alliances require intervention only if war occurs with a specific aggressor. For example, the Soviet Union and China signed an alliance in 1950 requiring action only in the event of war with Japan or an ally of Japan. Relatedly, some alliances are restricted to a specific region. The 1954 Manila Pact, an eight-nation alliance that served as the basis of SEATO, is restricted to the region of Southeast Asia. When the North Atlantic Treaty was being negotiated in the late 1940s, the United States was concerned about the possibility of getting dragged into conflicts involving the colonial possessions of its prospective NATO allies in Africa, Latin America, and Asia.

Accordingly, the United States demanded that the North Atlantic Treaty include language limiting its scope essentially to North America and Europe. This allowed the United States to stay out of French colonial conflicts in Southeast Asia in the 1950s; conflicts between France, Britain, and Egypt over the Suez Canal in 1956; and the 1982 Falklands War between Argentina and Britain, without violating the North Atlantic Treaty.

States hesitant about committing to intervene in the event of war but still motivated to improve security cooperation might sign less committing forms of alliance. Instead of committing to go to war if one signatory is attacked, they may sign a consultation pact, committing them only to consult with each other in the event of crisis or war, a relatively safe action. Or, two states unwilling to commit to go to war on each other's behalf might instead make the lesser commitment of agreeing not to attack each other, signing a nonaggression pact, or perhaps a neutrality pact.

Choosing Alliance Partners

An important part of alliance politics is choosing your alliance partner. If in general threatened states are more likely to seek to join an alliance, a next question is, with whom should a threatened state ally itself? Specifically, should a threatened state ally against the source of threat or, perhaps paradoxically, ally with the source of threat? As discussed earlier, allying against an external threat is the core dynamic of the balance of power, and accordingly is labeled **balancing** behavior.

The opposite strategy, allying *with* the threatening state so that state does not attack you, is a dynamic termed **bandwagoning**, as in, jumping on the bandwagon of a threatening or aggressive state (on balancing and bandwagoning, see Walt 1987). There are a couple of possible motives for bandwagoning. The first is strictly protection, as joining with an aggressive state might reduce the likelihood that that aggressor would attack. After World War II, Finland remained fearful of its Soviet neighbor, having lost two wars with the Soviet Union in the previous decade. To reduce the possibility of a third war, Finland signed an alliance treaty with the Soviet Union in 1948, bandwagoning with Moscow.

Another motivation for bandwagoning is greed. A state joins with a powerful, aggressive state hoping that it can share in the spoils. Italy was neutral when World War II broke out in 1939. However, by June 1940 it became clear that Germany was enjoying great success, especially as it was on the brink of conquering France. Italy joined the war on Germany's side, enabling it to capture a piece of French territory once Paris surrendered to the German invaders.

One intriguing question is whether states with common political ideologies are especially likely to ally with each other, an example perhaps of birds of a feather flocking together. There is some evidence that in general democracies may be more likely to ally with each other, especially in the period since 1945. However, this tendency seems to depend on the security environment. Intense security considerations can push democracies to cooperate with nondemocracies, perhaps overwhelming a disinclination to partner with tyrants. During World War II, the United States and Britain allied with the Soviet Union after Germany invaded that country, despite Stalin's deserved reputation as a genocidal dictator. Both US President Franklin Roosevelt and British Prime Minister Winston Churchill recognized in the most explicit terms that they were choosing the lesser of two evils, allying with a brutal Soviet Union to defeat the even more frightening Nazi Germany. Roosevelt remarked, "I can't take Communism nor can you, but to cross this bridge I would hold hands with the Devil." Churchill saw things similarly: "If Hitler invaded Hell, I should at least make a favourable reference to the Devil in the House of Commons" (quoted in Reiter and Stam 2002, 84). During the Cold War, the United States allied with several undemocratic regimes, such as Portugal, Greece, Turkey, the Philippines, South Korea, Taiwan, and others. In the twenty-first century, especially to fight terrorism and insurgent violence, the United States has proven willing to cooperate with nondemocracies such as Pakistan under military rule, Egypt, Saudi Arabia, and Uzbekistan.

Other Advantages of Alliances

So far, the discussion of alliances has revolved around how they can help states defend each other, and perhaps help states promise not to attack each other. There are other potential advantages of alliances (Kim 2016). They can be used as instruments of control, especially by larger states to manage – or even interfere with the domestic politics and policies of – smaller states. For example, they can be used to encourage smaller allies to make concessions in trade or other negotiations.

However, these efforts do not always work, especially when trying to get allies to improve their human rights records. In the 1970s, for example, President Jimmy Carter threatened to withdraw American troops from South Korea because of Seoul's repression of political opposition, and when South Korea counter-threatened to acquire nuclear weapons if the United States withdrew its support, the United States backed off. After the 9/11 attacks, the United States established a security relationship with Uzbekistan, using Uzbek territory for basing and logistical transit to facilitate military operations in Afghanistan and elsewhere in Central Asia. The George W. Bush administration tried in the early 2000s to put pressure on Uzbekistan to improve its human rights record, and the Uzbek dictator responded in 2005 by revoking US access to military bases on Uzbek territory, after which the United States relaxed its pressure. In both of these cases, part of the reason the humans rights pressure failed is that when push came to shove the United States prioritized security interests above human rights concerns.

States can also use alliances in more heavy-handed ways, for example if an alliance permits a larger ally to station troops on the territory of a smaller ally and then uses those troops to keep in power a particular leader or government of the smaller ally (Lake 2009). In the 1950s, the Soviet Union formed the Warsaw Pact alliance with several Communist East European states, an alliance that permitted the Soviet Union to permanently station Red Army troops in those countries, in turn helping keep Communist governments in power. Soviet troops were needed, as they helped crush anti-Communist movements in Eastern Europe several times, including in Hungary in 1956 and Czechoslovakia in 1968. They also served as a backstop when Polish government troops stamped out anti-Communist uprisings in Poland in 1956 and 1981. On the American side, the United States deployed more than a half-million troops to South Vietnam in the 1960s in an ultimately unsuccessful effort to prop up the authoritarian and corrupt government in Saigon.

Peacetime deployment of troops onto an ally's soil can advance other goals, as well. Peacetime deployments sometimes enable states to project power in the larger region, beyond the more limited mission of using those troops to protect their ally. The Soviet Union's alliance with Cuba during the Cold War enabled it to establish a strong military foothold just 90 miles (about 150 kilometers) from Florida. The Soviet alliance with Vietnam facilitated Soviet use of the Cam Ranh Bay naval base there. America's Cold War alliances enabled it to establish bases and project military and naval power around the world.

The deployment advantages of alliances have endured after the Cold War. The US alliance with Bahrain allows the United States to maintain a major naval base there, which in turn facilitates the projection of American naval power in the Persian Gulf, protecting the flow of international oil traffic and containing Iranian aggression. After the 9/11 attacks, the United States deployed its forces around the world to bases in friendly countries, using these bases to help prosecute the ongoing war on terror, including launching airstrikes, drone strikes, and special forces operations against a wide variety of targets in Afghanistan, Pakistan, Yemen, Iraq, and elsewhere. America launched airstrikes in 2011 in support of anti-government rebels in Libya largely from the territory of NATO allies like Italy. China made waves in 2014 by announcing a security agreement with the tiny northeastern African state of Djibouti allowing China to establish a military base there, serving a variety of Chinese foreign policy interests. Russia ratified a treaty with Syria in October 2016 providing Russia with enduring basing rights in Syria, facilitating its power projection in the region.

That said, not all smaller allies consent to larger allies' requests for predeployment and basing rights. American allies such as Japan and New Zealand have refused to allow the United States to station nuclear weapons on their territories. During the Cold War, Norway refused to allow the United States to permanently station troops on Norwegian territory. In 1966, France severed its military ties with the rest of NATO and demanded the evacuation of American troops from its territory. When the United States launched airstrikes against Libya in 1986 in an attempt to assassinate Libyan leader Muammar Qadaffi, though the planes launched from bases in Britain, American allies Spain, Italy, and France refused to allow those planes to fly through their airspace en route to Libya, forcing them to take the longer route and fly over Portugal and the Straits of Gibraltar. In 1992, the Philippines demanded that the United States close its massive naval base there. And most dramatically, when Communist governments fell from power in Eastern Europe in 1989, their non-Communist successors demanded the evacuation of Soviet forces from their territories.

Beyond power projection, alliances also serve the interests of larger states by helping dissuade smaller states from acquiring nuclear weapons. A security guarantee, the peacetime deployment of the large state's nuclear weapons on the small state's soil, and/or other levers provided by an alliance relationship can help a large state dissuade a small state from acquiring nuclear weapons. Germany, Japan, South Korea, and Taiwan all have had the technical capability to build nuclear weapons, and each may have gone nuclear without their alliances with the United States. Conversely, in the early 1970s Pakistan sought to create an alliance with security guarantees from the United States to address the threat posed by India, and when the United States demurred, Pakistan began to pursue its own nuclear arsenal. Nonaggression pacts might also be able to help contain nuclear proliferation. A state is often motivated to acquire nuclear weapons because it perceives a second state to be a threat. If those two states sign a nonaggression pact, this might reduce the first state's sense of insecurity enough to persuade it to forgo nuclear weapons. Russia signed a nonaggression pact with Ukraine in 1994, persuading the latter to abandon its inherited Soviet nuclear arsenal. The United States in 2013 offered to sign a nonaggression pact with North Korea on the condition of North Korean denuclearization. North Korea declined.

Perhaps surprisingly, alliances sometimes provide opportunities for small states to exploit large states. Consider, for example, an alliance such as NATO that contains a large state and one or more small states. Each alliance member needs to decide how much to spend on defense. However, everyone recognizes that the small states ultimately cannot contribute much to the collective defense, as only the large state has the capability to build a large enough army to deter the threat. This provides an incentive for the small states to engage in what economists call **free riding**, enjoying the protection offered by the alliance without contributing their fair share. This dynamic occurred within NATO during the Cold War. The United States devoted a higher percentage of its economy to defense spending as compared with smaller NATO members like Belgium or Luxembourg. Then Republican presidential candidate Donald J. Trump made this a political issue during the 2016 campaign, proclaiming that he would demand that American allies contribute their fair share to the common defense, and suggesting he would not intervene on behalf of any ally that did not contribute its fair share. He declared during the campaign that he would "call up all of those countries . . . and say 'fellas you haven't paid for years, give us the money or get the hell out.' I'd say you've gotta pay us or get out. You're out, out, out . . . Maybe NATO will dissolve, and that's OK, not the worst thing in the world" (quoted in Tomkiw 2016). Relatedly, small powers are sometimes paid handsomely for agreeing to ally with great powers, with large amounts of economic or military aid. During the Cold War, for example, the Soviet Union channeled vast economic resources to many of its allies, such as Cuba and Communist states in Eastern Europe.

Another way in which the small can exploit the large is by playing great powers off against each other in the hopes of extracting economic, military, or political benefits. Large states need small states, and when a small state has the opportunity to ally with more than one large state, it can demand more from a large state by threatening to switch alliances or actually doing so. In the 1970s, Egypt switched allegiance from the Soviet Union to the United States, in the process securing vast amounts of American military and economic aid. The Philippines under the rule of President Rodrigo Duterte adopted this strategy in 2016. Though the Philippines has long been a staunch ally of the United States, Duterte resented American protests against the brutal tactics used by his government as part of its domestic war on drugs. Duterte pushed back by publicly tilting towards China in October and November 2016, even though China and the Philippines were locked in a contentious conflict over territorial rights in the South China Sea, perhaps hoping that the threat of a Filipino defection to China would persuade the United States to relax its pressure on the Philippines over its anti-drug policies (see Figure 9.2).

Figure 9.2. Philippines President Rodrigo Duterte and Chinese President Xi Jinping, October 2016. King Rodriguez of Philippine Presidential Department, Public domain, via Wikimedia Commons.

CASE STUDY

Alliances and the Onset of World War I

World War I (1914–1918) was so unimaginably destructive that it was initially called the War to End All Wars, a conflict so horrific that many (incorrectly) assumed that humanity would never again consider picking up arms. More people were killed in World War I than in any previous war, including some 8.6 million soldiers. The war also had far-reaching political consequences that echo to the present day. The war destroyed the Russian, Ottoman, and Austro-Hungarian empires, and sowed the seeds for the fragmenting of the British and French empires. It led to the emergence of the world's first Communist state. It caused the redrawing of boundaries and borders in the Middle East, setting the stage for the birth of nations like Israel, Egypt, Jordan, Syria, Turkey, and Iraq, as well as many of the deadliest conflicts the world faces in the twenty-first century, including the Israeli–Palestinian conflict, ethnic conflict within Iraq, the Syrian Civil War, and others. Recognizing the brutality and political significance of World War I demands that we ask the crucial question: How did it start? Answering that question requires accounting for alliances. (On the onset of World War I, see Tuchman 1976.)

Alliances before the War

Prior to World War I, European politics were deeply driven by balance of power dynamics, as states balanced against each other using international alliances. Europe was a checkerboard of ambitious and powerful states, and many states sought safety in numbers through alliances. On the eve of war in 1914, Germany, Italy, and Austria-Hungary were members of a defense pact called the Triple Alliance. Those three powers also had a separate, secret defense pact with Romania. In opposition, France and Russia had signed a defense pact in 1892. Britain and France had signed a series of treaties in 1904 and 1912 that improved bilateral relations, and Britain and Russia signed an agreement in 1907 settling some of their disputes. This web of treaties among Britain, France, and Russia came to be referred to as the Triple Entente (see Map 9.4).

Britain, France, and Germany had separately signed an alliance agreement agreeing to respect and defend Belgian territorial borders and sovereignty, a sort of one-sided defense pact. (The agreement did not call on Belgium to go to war to protect the other signatories.) Globally, Britain signed an alliance with Japan in 1902, calling on each to offer support if its ally became involved in war with at least two other powers.

The alliance system in Europe at the time had its limits. Though states welcomed the protection that alliances offered, they also recognized that their alliance partners often were embroiled in conflicts that threatened to escalate to war, and they feared being dragged into wars they would otherwise wish to avoid. This is why the Triple Alliance was a defense pact, obligating signatories to intervene only if another signatory was attacked, not if a signatory launched a war. The Franco–Russian alliance was also a defense pact. Russia in particular worried that an alliance requiring intervention in any war might pull Russia into a war initiated by France, and might even encourage France to launch a war.

(cont.)

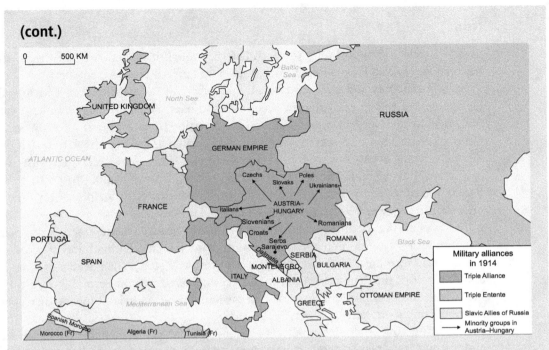

Map 9.4. Triple Alliance and Triple Entente, 1914. Wikipedia.

The absence of a formal alliance between Britain and France was also no accident, as each country was only slowly shedding a centuries-long enmity for and suspicion of the other. British hesitance to come to France's aid in the event of war was revealed in 1910, when a British general brazenly asked a French general that in the event of war with Germany, "What is the smallest British military force that would be of any practical assistance to you?" To which the Frenchman sharply replied, "A single British soldier – and we will see to it that he is killed" (quoted in Tuchman 1976, 68).

Some states were sufficiently fearful of entanglement that they avoided alliances altogether. The Netherlands, Norway, Sweden, Switzerland, Spain, and Denmark had neither alignments nor alliances with any European great powers, and no interests in getting dragged into war. The United States had followed George Washington's warning against foreign entanglements, and belonged to no alliances in 1914.

Conversely, there were strong ties between some states despite the absence of any formal alliance agreement. Though Russia and Serbia shared no alliance, Serbia's sovereignty and safety were deeply important to Russia. Russia was involved in an ongoing diplomatic rivalry with the Ottoman Empire in the Balkans, and regarded Serbia as a critical asset in this competition. Russia needed to protect Serbia to advance its ambitions.

The Summer 1914 Crisis

On June 28, 1914, a terrorist spark lit the fuse that led to World War I. A Serbian nationalist assassinated Archduke Ferdinand, the heir to the Austro-Hungarian throne, leading to an immediate and severe crisis between Serbia and Austria-Hungary. Austria-Hungary saw

(cont.)

this as a welcome opportunity to crush Serbia, though it recognized that the alignment between Serbia and Russia might bring Russia into an Austro–Serb conflict.

Austria-Hungary did not want to face Russia and Serbia alone. It had an ally in Germany, but the Triple Alliance was a defense pact, meaning that Germany was not obligated to intervene in a war initiated by Austria-Hungary. Soon after the assassination, Austria-Hungary secretly approached Germany, asking the latter if it would intervene in the event of war with Russia. Germany for its part needed its Austrian ally to survive, but beyond Austria-Hungary, Germany also was willing to go to war with Russia, because of its fears of the long-term growth in Russian power. It offered to intervene in any war between Austria-Hungary and Russia.

This was all the encouragement Austria-Hungary needed. It presented Serbia with an ultimatum, a set of ten demands that essentially demanded Serbia hand over its sovereignty; refusal to meet all ten demands would result in war. When Serbia met only nine and one half of the demands, Austria-Hungary declared war on Serbia. Russia was now faced with the possibility of Serbia being dismantled by Austria-Hungary. It responded by mobilizing its military, preparing for war.

Escalation now proceeded rapidly. Germany knew that Russia and France were allies, and assumed that war with one meant war with both. Germany's rigid war plan required that in the event of war with either France or Russia, Germany would invade France first, conquer Paris, and then invade Russia. Germany's plan for war was predicated on the assumption that it could complete the mobilization of its forces before Russia could mobilize its forces. If Germany did not mobilize its forces before Russia, then Germany would not have the luxury of ignoring Russia while fighting France, as Russian forces could attack Germany before France could be finished off. Germany ordered the mobilization of its forces in response to Russian mobilization, a process that would culminate in the initiation of war.

German military strategy contained another key piece linking alliances to the outbreak and escalation of war. The Franco-German border is relatively mountainous, difficult to move armies through. However, Belgium, located in between Germany and France, is by comparison relatively flat. Accordingly, Germany planned to invade Belgium en route to crossing into France, making use of its more forgiving terrain. This military strategy pushed Germany to declare war on Russia on August 1, and France on August 3.

German war plans presented Britain with a difficult choice. If Germany were to invade Belgium, Britain's alliance commitment would require it to go to war on Belgium's behalf. Britain's national interests would be damaged if Belgium were conquered by an outside power, in particular because of the strategic importance of the Belgian port of Antwerp for British commerce. The British government also recognized that it risked paying audience costs if it did not defend Belgium – both international audience costs, because abandoning Belgium would heavily damage Britain's reputation, and domestic

(cont.)

audience costs, because British public opinion would demand that its government abide by its commitment to Belgium.

But what if Germany were to invade France but *not* Belgium? Britain had no treaty commitment to go to war on behalf of France, as its 1912 alliance was a consultation pact with no security guarantees. Britain accordingly felt no treaty obligation to intervene automatically to defend France. This was a point that British Foreign Secretary Edward Grey made to a French representative at the height of the crisis: "As to the question of our obligation to help France, I pointed out that we had no obligation. France... was obliged to join in [the war], because of her alliance [with Russsia]. We had purposely kept clear of all alliances, in order that we might not be involved in difficulties in this way" (quoted in Albertini 1957, 394). As it happened, however, the German invasion of Belgium pushed Britain to declare war on Germany, bringing it into war alongside France.

What of Italy? Despite its Triple Alliance commitment to Germany and Austria-Hungary, Italy stayed out of the war in 1914. Germany and Austria-Hungary naturally sought Italian entry into the war, as the Serb assassination crisis escalated. However, Italy preferred to remain neutral, in part because Austria-Hungary was unwilling to offer Italy desired territorial concessions in return for Italy's entry into war. Italy justified its nonintervention by arguing that the Triple Alliance was a defensive pact, requiring intervention if a signatory had been attacked, whereas this was a war of German and Austro-Hungarian aggression, releasing Italy from its requirement to attack. Germany raged against Italy's neutrality, but Rome wouldn't budge. Worse, in 1915 Italy entered the fray on behalf of the Allies, declaring war on Germany and Austria-Hungary, a coalition that came to be known as the Central Powers (Italy was a member of the Allies and not the Central Powers). Italy's decision to enter the war is a good example of bandwagoning behavior, in that it entered the war not to balance against a threat, but rather in pursuit of territorial gains, in this case territory from Austria-Hungary.

Romania followed a similar course. Like Italy, it had a defense pact with Austria-Hungary and Germany in 1914, preferred to avoid entering the war, and justified its nonintervention on the grounds that it was a war of German and Austro-Hungarian aggression, meaning that its defense pact alliance had not been invoked. And like Italy, Romania eventually entered the war on the side of the Allies in 1916, also hoping to capture territory from Austria-Hungary.

Alliances and Planning for War

How did alliances affect planning for the war? The alliance between France and Russia delineated specific troop contributions each would make in war against the Triple Alliance. It also declared that in the event of war, Russian and French "forces shall engage to the full with such speed that Germany will have to fight simultaneously on the East and on the West." This provision proved to be of critical importance once war broke out. Russia kept its promise and attacked German forces soon after the German attack

(cont.)

on Belgium and France. Though the Russian attack ended in calamitous defeat, it did force Germany to transfer thousands of its troops from West to East, giving France just enough margin to stop the German advance at the critical battle of the Marne in September 1914, probably saving Paris from being conquered and France from falling.

The Belgian alliance failed to provide such prewar planning benefits. That alliance required several states, including Germany, to defend Belgian frontiers and neutrality. However, the alliance did not provide for prewar planning for common defenses, and not surprisingly, little such planning took place. Because Belgium viewed itself as not favoring any other European state and obliged to defend itself against any possible attack, it felt compelled to prepare for an invasion from any corner, including from British or French forces. Belgium did not allow Britain or France to predeploy their forces onto its territory prior to war, and Belgium dispersed its small army to cover attacks from all possible directions, sending some troops to its coastline (defending against possible British invasion), some to the French border, and some to the German border. As a result, only a portion of the Belgian military was optimally stationed to parry the impending German invasion, and the Belgian army was little more than a speed bump when the German army crossed the frontier, racing to Paris.

In contrast, the 1912 Britain–France consultation pact provided for important prewar coordination. Britain's greatest military asset was its Royal Navy, by far the world's most powerful. In negotiations from 1912 to 1914, France and Britain agreed that in the event of war, the Royal Navy would be deployed to protect France's English Channel and Atlantic coasts, permitting France to deploy its navy to the Mediterranean. Britain followed through on this plan, mobilizing its fleet on August 1, protecting the French coasts from possible German attacks.

That said, the 1912 pact fell short of some planning that might have persuaded Germany of Britain's commitment to defend Belgium and perhaps France. The German leadership saw a path to defeating France if it could overrun Belgium quickly, and hoped that British forces would arrive too late to rescue Belgium. But, if British forces had been predeployed to Belgium, they could have substantially slowed, if not stopped, the German advance, severely disrupting Germany's plans for victory. This might have been enough to deter Germany from escalating the crisis in summer 1914, avoiding the War to End All Wars.

The Evolution of Alliances across the War

Two last pieces remained. Japan complied with its alliance obligations with Britain, declaring war on Germany on August 23, 1914. Like Italy and Romania, Japan entered the war out of bandwagoning motives, hoping to capture German colonial possessions in the Pacific. The Ottoman Empire, known as the Sick Man of Europe because of its centuries-long decline, had no alliances with European powers when the summer crisis began in June. However, Britain, and especially Secretary of the Navy Winston Churchill,

(cont.)

mishandled the Ottomans, especially by commandeering two new warships built for the Ottoman government in British shipyards. The Ottomans were predictably insulted, and Berlin was able to persuade the Ottomans to join the Central Powers that fall. Mere weeks after an isolated terrorist incident in a dusty corner of Europe, most of the continent was in flames.

Table 9.1 recapitulates how and when several countries entered World War I.

Table 9.1. Alliances and countries' entries into World War I

	When did this country enter the war?	How did this country enter the war?	What role did alliances play in this country's entry into war?
Serbia	July 28, 1914	Attacked by Austria-Hungary	None, Serbia had no alliances
Austria-Hungary	July 28, 1914	Attacked Serbia	None directly, though German alliance encouraged Austria-Hungary to attack
Russia	August 1, 1914	Attacked by Germany	None, as Russia had no alliance with Serbia
Germany	August 1, 1914	Attacked Russia	Entered war to aid ally Austria-Hungary
France	August 3, 1914	Germany declares war on France	None; Germany attacked France before France had to choose whether or not to rescue its Russian ally
Belgium	August 4, 1914	Attacked by Germany	Belgium's alliance with Britain failed to deter Germany
Britain	August 4, 1914	Declares war on Germany	Entered war to aid ally Belgium
Japan	August 23, 1914	Declares war on Germany	Entered war to aid ally Britain
Ottoman Empire	October 29, 1914	Attacks Russia	None
Italy	May 23, 1915	Declares war on Austria-Hungary	Did not intervene to aid allies Austria-Hungary and Germany in 1914
Romania	August 27, 1916	Attacks Austria-Hungary	Did not intervene to aid allies Austria-Hungary and Germany in 1914
United States	April 6, 1917	Declares war on Germany	None

QUANTITATIVE STUDY

Do Alliances Bring States into Wars?

Analyzing quantitative data, this study explores perhaps the most fundamental alliances proposition, that if a state is involved in war, other states are more likely to intervene in the war on that state's side if they share a security guarantee alliance with the embattled state. Though this effect might seem sufficiently obvious that we should take it for granted, it is important to remember that like other international agreements, alliance treaties function in an environment of international anarchy, meaning that there is no world government or police to force compliance. At the moment of truth, an ally can decide to break an alliance, and not aid an embattled ally, as France abandoned its Czechoslovak ally in 1938. That said, we would like to know if systematically accounting for all the evidence encourages the conclusion that the presence of an alliance at least makes it more *likely* that a state will go to war on behalf of another state, any counter-examples notwithstanding. By evaluating a large set of opportunities to intervene, a quantitative test can assess whether alliances make it more likely that a state will intervene, even if there are some instances of a state breaking an alliance. The political scientist Dr. Jesse Johnson (2016) published a quantitative study in 2016 that tested this hypothesis.

Research Question

Is one state more likely to go to war on behalf of another state if the two states share an alliance with security guarantees?

Theory and Hypotheses

This study looks at two of the main reasons why an existing alliance will make a state more likely to intervene in the event of war. The third reason discussed above proposes that states only join those alliances they are likely to comply with, a dynamic that is not explored in the Johnson study. First, alliances often facilitate the kinds of prewar planning, including actions such as the coordination and predeployment of troops, that increase the likelihood of victory. As a state becomes more confident that it will be on the winning side of a prospective war, it becomes more willing to intervene. Second, a state that is a member of an alliance will pay political audience costs if it elects not to abide by its alliance obligations. It will pay international audience costs if it violates its alliance obligations, as allies, potential allies, and potential aggressors will all come to doubt the state's toughness and reliability. Governments, especially elected governments, might also pay domestic political audience costs, as governments that break alliance agreements might be thrown from power by a disgruntled public.

The study identifies the terms of alliance treaties, distinguishing between the requirements of offense pacts and defense pacts. The study tested two hypotheses, the first focusing on offense pacts and the second on defense pacts:

(cont.)

Hypothesis 1: A state will be more likely to intervene on behalf of the initiator of a war if it has an alliance with an offensive obligation to the initiator.

Hypothesis 2: A state will be more likely to intervene on behalf of the target of a war it if has an alliance with a defensive obligation to the target.

Data

The data begin with a comprehensive list of ninety-five interstate wars from 1816 to 2007. For a conflict to be included in the list, it must be a conflict between two states (as opposed to a civil war, which is a conflict between actors within a state), and there must be at least 1,000 soldiers killed in battle (excluding more minor conflicts such as the 1989 American invasion of Panama). A state is included as participant in a war if it contributes at least 1,000 troops or suffers at least 100 soldiers killed (excluding states that make minor contributions to a coalition, such as Luxembourg's contribution of eighty-five soldiers to the UN Coalition during the Korean War). In each of those ninety-five wars, the study assumes that all countries in the world have an opportunity to intervene in the war, some of which intervene and some of which do not. For example, during the 1967 Six Day War, initially involving Israel, Egypt, and Syria, Jordan decided to intervene after the war started, and Saudi Arabia decided not to intervene. The research design creates a list of a total of 7,829 intervention opportunities. That is, across these ninety-five wars, individual countries made 7,829 intervention decisions, such as Britain's decision to intervene in World War I, Switzerland's decision not to intervene in World War I, Britain's decision not to intervene in the Vietnam War, and so on.

Dependent Variable

The dependent variable codes the choice that the potential intervener makes, providing for three possible categories of action. Specifically, a state's choices are not to intervene in the war, to intervene on the side of the initiator (the country that started the war), or to intervene on the side of the target (the country that was attacked).

Independent Variable

The main independent variable is the presence of an alliance between the potential intervener and either the initiator or the target in the war. A potential intervener had an offense pact with the initiator in 15 percent of the 7,829 intervention opportunities, and a defense pact with the target in 1.6 percent of the 7,829 intervention opportunities.

Control Variables

It is certainly possible that other factors might affect a state's decision to intervene in a war, and we are going to get a better sense of the true effect of alliances on decisions to intervene if we control for these other factors.

(cont.)

The study incorporated control variables that might also affect a state's decision to intervene in a war. They include: the geographical distance between the state and the location of the war (states are more likely to intervene if they are closer); the potential contribution the state might be able to make to one side or the other (states might be more willing to intervene if they are large enough to tip the scales to victory); the initiator's likelihood of winning (states might be less likely to intervene if one side is likely to win decisively); and the similarities in political system between the intervener and the belligerents (a state might be more willing to intervene on behalf of a state with a similar political system).

Results

The statistical analysis of the data provides support for the two hypotheses. If there is an offense pact between the potential intervener (the state choosing whether or not to intervene) and the initiator, then the potential intervener is 150 percent more likely to intervene on the side of the initiator than if there is no such pact. Further, if there is a defense pact between the potential intervener and the target, then the potential intervener is 24 percent more likely to intervene on the side of the target than if there is no such pact. The analysis indicates that these observed effects are statistically significant, meaning we can be very confident that there is an effect of alliances on intervention.

Conclusions

The study provides evidence that alliances shape behavior, that a state is more likely to intervene in a war if it shares an alliance with one of the belligerents, and that offensive alliances push states to intervene on behalf of war initiators, and defensive alliances push states to intervene on behalf of war targets.

SUMMARY

Thus far, this chapter has made a number of points about alliances. They include:

- Joining alliances is one prominent way that states address international threats.
- Alliances can be a manifestation of the balance of power.
- States are more likely to comply with alliances if the alliance agreement improves prewar military planning, increasing the chances of victory.
- The prospect of paying international and/or domestic audience costs encourages compliance. Some alliances create higher audience costs for noncompliance.
- States carefully design alliance treaties, avoiding alliance commitments they are unlikely to want to comply with.
- Alliance agreements can include different kinds of commitments, including two kinds of security guarantees (defense pacts and/or offense pacts), consultation pacts, nonaggression pacts, and neutrality agreements.

- States sometimes ally against the source of threat (balancing behavior), and sometimes with the source of threat (bandwagoning behavior).
- States use alliances to serve a variety of functions, including protecting trading partners, projecting power around the world, controlling the domestic politics of other states, and preventing nuclear proliferation, sometimes with mixed success.

KEY TERMS

International alliances	Alignment
Security guarantee	Balance of power
Defense pacts	Audience costs
Offense pacts	Tying hands
Consultation pacts	Balancing
Nonaggression pacts	Bandwagoning
Neutrality pacts	Free riding

REVIEW QUESTIONS

1. What are security guarantees, defense pacts, offense pacts, consultation pacts, neutrality pacts, and nonaggression pacts?
2. What is the "compliance problem" for alliances? How might audience costs help solve the compliance problem? What are different kinds of audience costs?
3. What is the difference between "alliance" and "alignment"?
4. How do alliances relate to the balance of power? What is balancing? What is bandwagoning?
5. If alliances help states fight more effectively, why does this reduce the compliance problem?
6. If states are careful to sign only those alliance agreements they support, why might this make it less likely that we would observe alliances being violated?
7. How can alliance agreements help a state project its power?
8. Which of the following states entered World War I in 1914: Germany, Austria-Hungary, Russia, Romania, Italy, Britain, France, the United States? Of those eight states, who was allied with whom in 1914? What was the nature of those alliances; that is, which were defense pacts, which were consultation agreements, etc.?
9. What does "tying hands" refer to?

DISCUSSION QUESTIONS

1. Would you be willing to support your country going to war on behalf of an embattled ally? Under what conditions?
2. Would you personally be willing to fight in combat, in your country's military, on behalf of an embattled ally? Under what conditions? (Note: this is exactly the decision young American men had to make during the Vietnam War.)

3. On balance, do you think international alliances help make the world a safer place? If so, should more countries be allowed to join alliances such as NATO?

ADDITIONAL READING

Leeds, B. A. (2003). Alliance reliability in times of war: Explaining state decisions to violate treaties. *International Organization* **57**(4), 801–827.

Reiter, D. (1996). *Crucible of Beliefs: Learning, Alliances, and World Wars.* Ithaca, NY: Cornell University Press.

Schelling, T. C. (1966). *Arms and Influence.* New Haven: Yale University Press.

REFERENCES

Albertini, L. (1957). *The Origins of the War of 1914* (Vol. 3). London: Oxford University Press.

Benson, B. V. (2012). *Constructing International Security: Alliances, Deterrence, and Moral Hazard.* Cambridge: Cambridge University Press.

Beschloss, M. R. (ed.) (1997). *Taking Charge: The Johnson White House Tapes, 1963–1964.* New York: Simon & Schuster.

Beschloss, M. R. (ed.) (2001). *Reaching for Glory: Lyndon Johnson's Secret White House Tapes, 1964–1965.* New York: Simon & Schuster.

Calabria, S. (2014, April 1). Americans unsure about which countries they'd defend from Russia. *Huffington Post.* www.huffingtonpost.com/2014/04/01

Crescenzi, M. J. C. (2018). *Of Friends and Foes: Reputation and Learning in International Politics.* Oxford: Oxford University Press.

Daily Survey: Russia and Ukraine (2022). *YouGov.* https://docs.cdn.yougov.com/e1pqcsj7ov/tabs_ Russia_and_Ukraine_20220224.pdf

Hucker, D. (2011). *Public Opinion and the End of Appeasement in Britain and France.* New York: Routledge.

Johnson, J. C. (2016). Alliance treaty obligations and war intervention. *Conflict Management and Peace Science* **33**(5), 451–468.

Kim, T. (2016). *The Supply Side of Security: A Market Theory of Military Alliances.* Stanford: Stanford University Press.

Lake, D. A. (2009). *Hierarchy in International Relations.* Ithaca, NY: Cornell University Press.

McNaughton, J. T. (1965, March 24). Draft memorandum from McNaughton to Robert McNamara. www.mtholyoke.edu/acad/intrel/pentagon3/doc253.htm

Poast, P. (2019). *Arguing about Alliances: The Art of Agreement in Military-Pact Negotiations.* Ithaca, NY: Cornell University Press.

Reiter, D. and Poast, P. (2021). The truth about tripwires: Why small force deployments do not deter aggression. *Texas National Security Review* **44**(3), 33–53.

Reiter, D. and Stam, A. C. (2002). *Democracies at War.* Princeton: Princeton University Press.

Schelling, T. C. (1966). *Arms and Influence.* New Haven: Yale University Press.

Snyder, G. H. (1997). *Alliance Politics.* Ithaca, NY: Cornell University Press.

Snyder, J. L. and Borghard, E. D. (2011). The cost of empty threats: A penny, not a pound. *American Political Science Review* **105**(3): 437–456.

Tomkiw, L. (2016, July 21). Quotes from Donald Trump on NATO: What Republican candidate said about North Atlantic Treaty Organization and US obligations. *International Business Times*. www .ibtimes.com/quotes-donald-trump-nato-what-republican-candidate-said-about-north-atlantic-treaty-2393661

Tuchman, B. W. (1976). *The Guns of August*. New York: Bantam.

Walt, S. M. (1987). *Origins of Alliances*. Ithaca, NY: Cornell University Press.

Washington, G. (1796). Washington's Farewell Address 1796. https://avalon.law.yale.edu/18th_century/washing.asp

10 Third-Party Peacemaking and Peacekeeping

KYLE BEARDSLEY

Introduction

If we were to ask scholars and students of international politics what an ideal international order would look like, peace would likely be mentioned by most if not all respondents. Universally, peace tends to be desirable as both a normative virtue and a long-run policy objective. While it is common to believe that war can be a necessary means to various ends, few would consider war as a desirable end in itself.

So, when armed conflict erupts periodically around the world, a common cry is for someone to do something about it. Where are the peacemakers to end the bloodshed? And where are the peacekeepers to prevent a return to violence?

These cries are often met with action, even if the efficacy of the action leaves much to be desired. Few wars, either interstate or intrastate, occur in a pristine state of noninterference by "third parties." Indeed, 61 percent of the armed conflicts in Africa between 1993 and 2007 saw at least one instance of a third-party attempt to manage the conflict and attenuate the violence. In 50 percent of the African armed conflicts there was at least one third-party attempt to keep peace while terms of settlement were implemented (Croicu et al. 2013).

As policy tools, third-party attempts to make and keep peace are both appealing and frustrating. They sometimes score spectacular successes, like the resolution of the bloody, decades-long conflict between Egypt and Israel in the late 1970s. But they also sometimes fail to avoid catastrophic failures, one example being the inability of such efforts to prevent the genocide of nearly a million Rwandans in the mid 1990s.

In this chapter, we will explore the potential influence of mediation, peacekeeping, and other forms of third-party attempts to shape conflict and peace processes worldwide. We will consider these third-party efforts in both interstate and intrastate conflicts. After starting with some definitions of various types of third-party peace efforts, we will turn to the mechanisms by which third parties could improve the prospects of peace, focusing on how they affect the costs of failing to settle a dispute, how they improve the information environment, and how they soften political opposition to settlement. We will also assess the limitations of third-party involvement: even if third-party assistance on average improves the chances of making and keeping peace, it is not always effective and in some cases may even worsen the peace and security environments.

Definitions of Third-Party Efforts to Nurture Peace

Conventionally, a third party is any actor that is not fighting in the dispute in question. Even when there are more than two belligerents, as in World War II between the Axis powers and the Allied powers, or the Syrian Civil War between the Assad government and a variety of nonstate actors, "third parties" would still be used to refer to actors that are not active participants or stakeholders in the conflict. As we will see later, this does not mean that the third parties must be impartial – third parties often do support one side of a conflict more than others.

"Third-party involvement" can mean many different types of involvement. The term is so broad that it is not useful without specific reference to what the third party is doing. In what follows, we see the menu of ways in which third parties attempt to make and keep peace.

Peacemaking

The activity of many third parties can be understood as forms of **peacemaking**. Peacemakers are third parties that become involved during a violent conflict and try to help the actors move toward conflict de-escalation and resolution. While many third parties focus on peace as the absence of violence – a "negative" definition because the concept is defined by what it is not – other third parties focus on peace as the transformation of the relationship between the disputing parties so that it strengthens in attributes such as reconciliation, trust and justice – a "positive" definition of peace.

Mediation

One common form of peacemaking is **mediation**, defined as when third parties are in active discussions with both sides of a conflict and are not themselves participants in the armed hostilities. The participation of a mediator requires the consent of the combatants, and there is no expectation that the mediator's decisions are binding. This makes mediation distinct from arbitration or adjudication, discussed below. Mediation offers belligerents an opportunity to overcome barriers to settlement and an increased potential for a peace process to bear fruit. The roles that mediators play include facilitating discussion, proposing agreements, informing the parties about the interests of the adversaries, providing incentives to settle, offering assistance in implementing agreements, and helping the parties make concessions without losing face.

Mediation can take on a number of looks. A mediated process might occur during a single round of negotiations, as when representatives from Japan and Russia met under the auspices of US President Theodore Roosevelt in 1905 to negotiate the Portsmouth Accords which terminated the Russo–Japanese War (Figure 10.1). Or it might unfold over a series of negotiations, as when negotiators from Israel and the Palestinian Liberation Organization met in a

Figure 10.1. Teddy Roosevelt, with the Japanese and Russian delegations at Portsmouth, New Hampshire, 1905. ©Photos.com/PHOTOS.com>>/ Getty Images.

series of secret meetings in Oslo, Norway, before talks were concluded in Washington, DC with the 1993 signing of the Declaration of Principles (Oslo Accords).

Mediation might involve a single third party; Roosevelt's mediation of the Portsmouth Accords is again a clear example. Or it might involve multiple third parties who may or may not be coordinated in their peace efforts, as when the African Union, France, the USA, and Tanzania all helped mediate the 1993 Arusha Accords that ended the Rwandan Civil War and set the stage for the Rwandan Genocide (see the case study, page 323).

Mediation might involve direct talks in which representatives of the disputing parties meet with the third party at the same time, as when US President Jimmy Carter brokered the Camp David Accords between Israel and Egypt in 1978. Or it might involve shuttle diplomacy in which the third party travels from disputing party to disputing party, attempting to secure support for a peace plan, as when Henry Kissinger flew dozens of times among Jerusalem, Cairo and Damascus to mediate a series of disengagement plans in 1974 and 1975 to stabilize peace in the wake of the 1973 Yom Kippur War.

There is also considerable variability in the types of actors that serve as mediators. Representatives of global or regional international organizations such as the United Nations, European Union, and African Union are often mediators. These representatives might be

Figure 10.2. Kofi Annan, center, mediating a power-sharing agreement in Kenya, 2008. ©SIMON MAINA / Stringer/AFP/ Getty Images.

high-profile individuals such as the secretaries-general or presidents of the respective organizations, or they might be international civil servants, such as staff from the UN's Department of Political Affairs (DPA). Mediators might also represent third-party state governments. Presidents, prime ministers, foreign ministers, ambassadors and other members of the diplomatic corps frequently serve as mediators as they represent their country's interests in a peaceful settlement.

Aside from representatives of international organizations or states, mediators can also be nongovernmental organizations (NGOs) or private citizens. As private citizens, high-profile former leaders have mediated conflicts, such as when Nelson Mandela helped broker a promising but short-lived ceasefire in Burundi in 2000. As another example, Kofi Annan (former UN secretary-general) mediated a power-sharing accord in Kenya between political rivals Mwai Kibaki and Raila Odinga, de-escalating the political violence in 2008 (Figure 10.2). Moreover, NGO groups, often with humanitarian interests such as the Red Cross/Red Crescent, have a history of trying to broker ends to violence. Sometimes prominent individuals are involved as representatives of their NGOs, such as when Martti Ahtisaari, former president of Finland, mediated as part of his Crisis Management Initiative the end to an insurgency by the Free Aceh Movement in Indonesia.

Arbitration

In addition to mediation, peacemaking might involve **arbitration** or **adjudication**. Both arbitration and adjudication involve a third party hearing a case and issuing a resolution that the third party intends to be *binding*. Adjudication is distinguished from arbitration in that the third party is a standing court that has claimed jurisdiction over a dispute.

Cases of arbitration and adjudication often involve interstate disputes and originate from formal state obligations under treaties or from membership in international organizations. As a prominent example, in 2013 the Philippines challenged China's claims in the South China Sea

Figure 10.3. The International Court of Justice, 2004, which operates in a courthouse, hears arguments from lawyers, and produces decisions rendered by a panel of judges. Note the European-style clothes for the judges and British-style wigs for two of the lawyers, demonstrating the international nature of the court.
©CONTINENTAL / Staff/AFP/Getty Images.

and brought the arbitration case to a tribunal under the auspices of the UN Convention on the Law of the Sea (UNCLOS). In this case, while both the Philippines and China are parties to UNCLOS, China rejected the legitimacy of the case and ultimately rejected the ruling of the tribunal in favor of the Philippines. This case demonstrates a key challenge of arbitration and adjudication between states, which is that there is no standing enforcement entity in the international system to hold the parties to an arbitrated or adjudicated ruling. The extent to which a binding settlement is actually binding depends on the willingness of the disputants to see the arbitration or adjudication process as legitimate and the extent to which other actors, such as the UN Security Council or relatively powerful states, are willing to enforce a settlement that a disputing party rejects.

As another, more successful example of arbitration, Bangladesh filed a claim against India in 2009 regarding their maritime boundary in the Bay of Bengal. This was a longstanding dispute that had been the subject of multiple bilateral attempts at resolution. Both states are parties to UNCLOS, and this case was decided by a tribunal under the auspices of the Permanent Court of Arbitration in The Hague, Netherlands. The tribunal's 2014 ruling, which preserved India's claim to New Moore Island but also greatly expanded Bangladesh's exclusive economic zone, has been accepted by both sides.

The most noteworthy adjudicating body in international disputes is the **International Court of Justice (ICJ).** The ICJ was formed along with the other organs of the UN when the UN Charter was adopted in 1945. The ICJ is a standing body also located in The Hague. It is a court just like you might see in a domestic legal setting, in that each side presents evidence and argues a case, and a panel of judges renders decisions (Figure 10.3). The ICJ issues two types of decisions: binding decisions on contentious cases between states and advisory decisions used by other UN organs such as the UN General Assembly. It will only issue binding decisions if the states have consented to the ICJ's jurisdiction. States might accept jurisdiction explicitly over particular cases.

Alternatively, ICJ jurisdiction might originate from obligations from other treaties that the states have signed or from any precommitments by the states to compulsory jurisdiction. For example, when Nicaragua sued the United States in the ICJ over US support for the Contra rebels seeking to overthrow the Nicaraguan government, at the time the USA had committed to compulsory jurisdiction and, consequently, the ICJ ruled that the USA did not need to give explicit consent to this case for jurisdiction to apply. As the case went forward, the United States eventually denied that the ICJ had jurisdiction, and did not accept the 1986 ruling in favor of Nicaragua. In response to these events, the United States no longer grants compulsory jurisdiction to the ICJ. This case illustrates again that in the absence of an enforcement mechanism, states, especially superpowers such as the United States or China, occasionally do not comply with their precommitments to abide by a binding peace process.

Third-Party Consultation

Another type of third-party action used to foster peacemaking involves **third-party consultations** – when a third party is in direct discussions with a disputing party but is not involved as an intermediary between the disputing parties. Third-party consultants attempt to influence the trajectory of a conflict process but are not involved in brokering an agreement between the sides. For example, in the crises over North Korea's nuclear weapons, China has played the role of a third-party consultant in attempting to admonish the North Korean regime and ease tensions; indeed, disputing parties such as the United States have demanded that China play a more active role in this regard. China has also consulted with the United States and urged restraint, which is, again, a consulting role rather than that of a mediator facilitating agreement between Washington and Pyongyang.

Third parties might also try to make peace by providing **good offices** – when a high-profile actor such as the UN secretary-general provides legitimacy to a peace process. In many cases, the offer of good offices turns into a mediation relationship, once the disputing parties negotiate under the auspices of the third party. For example, in the early stages of Theodore Roosevelt's hosting of talks to end the Russo–Japanese War, his role was more symbolic than substantive; after ceremonially opening the talks, he retired to a vacation home and monitored the developments at a distance. Only when talks between the Japanese and Russian delegations stalled did he finally become actively involved as a mediator. In other cases, the offer of good offices remains a symbolic gesture in which the third party is merely recognizing the salience of the dispute and the desire to see a peaceful settlement reached.

Still another type of third-party peacemaking effort involves the formation of a **fact-finding mission** or **panel of experts**. These activities occur when independent actors are tasked with delivering a report to establish a set of facts and culpability that often serve as the basis for negotiations. The third parties in these situations serve a function of reducing uncertainty, trying to mitigate the potential for misinformation campaigns to spread "fake news" and other untruths, and otherwise gaining the trust of the disputing parties for potentially deeper involvement.

In a discussion of the mechanisms by which third parties contribute to peacemaking, later sections of this chapter focus on mediation. While all of these other functions of third-party involvement merit attention, mediation attempts are especially salient in explaining the evolution of conflict and peace in many contentious disputes.

Peacekeeping and Peacebuilding

Peacekeeping

The third-party involvement discussed thus far has been in the form of peacemaking: getting conflict to stop. **Peacekeeping** is when actors seek to sustain an already established peace. In the aftermath of war, disputants are prone to mistrust one another and feel vulnerable to the possibility that their adversaries might fail to uphold their ends of a deal. The sense of vulnerability is especially high when armed groups have to disarm or demobilize as part of the terms of settlement. Many conflicts relapse when actors take advantage of the vulnerability of an adversary during the implementation of a peace plan. Other conflicts relapse when actors choose not to comply with the terms of settlement because they do not want to become vulnerable.

Peacekeeping operations attempt to reduce perceptions of vulnerability during the implementation of peace plans through the participation of military personnel from one or more third parties acting with the consent of the disputing parties. Peacekeeping operations may have mandates to simply monitor and report on the security environment, or they may be given mandates to use force to maintain ceasefires and to protect civilian populations. Peacekeepers may also be used to train and assist domestic security institutions such as the national military or police forces. Most peacekeeping operations are carried out in the aftermath of civil wars, after which the existing security sector is typically in need of repair and reform (see Chapter 7).

In some deployments, the "peacekeeping" nomenclature is a bit misleading, for when a ceasefire does break down the peacekeepers may take on more responsibility as *peacemakers* in an active conflict zone. For example, the UN operation in the Democratic Republic of the Congo (DRC) was authorized in 1999 after the Lusaka Ceasefire Agreement was signed by the key belligerents; the ceasefire ultimately failed and war raged for three more years before there was actually peace to be kept. The UN "peacekeeping" operation in this case served an important peacemaking role in trying to de-escalate hostilities, establish order, and work with the belligerents in conjunction with other third parties to reach a more lasting political settlement from 1999 until the cessation of hostilities in 2002.

Peacekeepers are typically provided by member states of intergovernmental organizations such as the UN and African Union. Most peacekeepers worldwide deploy as part of UN operations, and as a result much of the research and policy attention has focused on UN peacekeeping. But it is worth noting that regional organizations such as the African Union, the Economic Organization of West African States, and the European Union have also played important roles in leading peacekeeping missions and in supporting UN missions. As of July 2021, twelve UN peacekeeping operations were in operation around the world, with about 88,000 peacekeeping personnel deployed (UN Peacekeeping 2022). The annual UN peacekeeping budget, which is separate from the general UN budget, for the 2021–2022 fiscal year was $6.4 billion.

All UN peacekeeping operations have mandates that are approved by the UN Security Council, which is a fifteen-member body with five veto-holding permanent members (USA, Russia, China, UK, and France) and ten rotating members. Since the UN Charter, the founding document of the UN, demands that all states respect the territorial integrity of other

Figure 10.4. Indian soldiers joining a UN peacekeeping mission in Angola, 1995. Over time, India has contributed 170,000 troops to UN peacekeeping missions, more than any other country (Asthana 2014). ©Robert Nickelsberg / Contributor/ The Chronicle Collection/Getty Images.

states and only gives the UN Security Council the ability to authorize military force against international threats to peace and security (Chapter VII, Article 42 of the UN Charter), even non-UN peacekeeping operations typically have authorization from a Security Council resolution.

Although most peacekeeping operations now have use-of-force mandates rooted in Chapter VII of the UN Charter, peacekeeping operations typically only deploy when they have consent from the host state to which they are deploying. It is even rare for a peacekeeping operation not to have the consent of nonstate rebel and militia groups that had been parties to recent armed conflict. Generally, the parties to a ceasefire or peace agreement explicitly consent to assistance from peacekeepers in the implementation of the peace plans. One example of a peacekeeping operation engaging in military action against the forces of the host state – notable because it is so exceptional – occurred in the West African nation of Côte d'Ivoire after incumbent President Laurent Gbagbo refused to concede a 2010 election that he had lost. Along with French forces, the UN operation assisted in taking action against Gbagbo's forces and ultimately arresting him.

There are no standing UN peacekeeping forces that are preformed and waiting for deployment. All UN peacekeeping operations involve the ad hoc combination of forces from different states, which typically send entire contingents of their military forces to serve alongside contingents of other states, all under the leadership of an appointed force commander. The UN secretary-general's office oversees the process of soliciting personnel contributions to peace operations, but it is up to the member states to decide whether and how to contribute.

Member states with large economies finance the bulk of the UN peacekeeping budget, but UN peacekeeping personnel typically come from developing countries with sizable militaries but low costs of living, such as Pakistan, Bangladesh, India, and Ethiopia (see Figure 10.4). Since the UN compensates countries which contribute personnel based on a fixed per-person rate, developed countries actually pay their personnel more than the countries receive in reimbursement and are, consequently, more hesitant to contribute peacekeeping personnel (Bove and Elia 2011). Moreover, personnel from developed countries are not always perceived as desirable, because of the role that developed countries tend to play in geopolitical meddling. At the same time, many developed European countries do contribute peacekeepers to European Union operations around the world.

The scope of UN peacekeeping is remarkable when considering that "peacekeeping" is not mentioned in the UN Charter. Yet early in the history of the UN, by 1948, peacekeeping was seen as a means to monitor and observe ceasefires, truces and peace agreements, such as those between Israel and its Arab neighbors, and between India and Pakistan. These peacekeeping operations only serve an observational role, but now most operations have **Chapter VII mandates**, which give them more leeway to use force against threats to peace and to engage in a broad range of activities to strengthen security. The turn to more robust peacekeeping mandates followed a series of catastrophes in the 1990s, including in Rwanda and Bosnia, in which UN peacekeeping operations failed to enhance the security environment and proved powerless to hinder the mass murder of civilians. In 2013, a UN Security Council resolution gave an unprecedented mandate to a United Nations Force Intervention Brigade as part of the UN mission in the DRC, authorizing the brigade to take offensive military action against the M23 militia group. While the resolution explicitly stated that this intervention brigade was not supposed to be precedent-setting, it fits a pattern of UN peacekeeping mandates giving missions more and more leeway in the types of activities they are expected to undertake in order to secure peace and stability.

Peacebuilding

Related to the broad range of activities that many peacekeeping operations are mandated to perform, peacekeeping takes its place in an even broader category of involvement, **peacebuilding.** Peacebuilding is intended to help states that have experienced civil war to move beyond merely an absence of conflict and create the societal, economic, and political conditions for long-term, stable peace. Peacebuilding thus includes nonmilitary forms of securing peace after episodes of violence, in addition to militarized peacekeeping. Again, most peacekeeping operations need to restore order in states ravaged by civil war, in which many political, legal, social, and economic institutions have collapsed or are dysfunctional. Peacebuilding activities that focus on the development of the political, legal, social, and economic infrastructure thus occur in parallel with the peacekeeping activities that attempt to stabilize the immediate security situation. For example, many UN peacekeeping operations, including the operation in the DRC, have mandates to assist in the implementation of local elections. As another example, the Organization for Security and Co-operation in Europe (OSCE) has a mission in Bosnia-Herzegovina that has focused on implementing rule of law, human rights and security sector reforms.

Increasingly, a broad array of peacebuilding efforts augment the role of peacekeeping troops in providing physical security. Specifically, it is now common for police forces to be part of the deployments of UN peacekeeping operations (see Figure 10.5). The UN Police forces can help provide basic law and order while also training and assisting local police forces. Local forces often need to undergo major reform after divisive civil wars in which it is common for abuse of power by law enforcement to be either a cause or a symptom of the breakdown of order.

Figure 10.5. United Nations Police searching for contraband in a displaced persons camp in South Sudan, 2016. Sometimes peacekeeping forces engage in everyday policing, as well as combat and monitoring activities. ©*The Washington Post* / Contributor/ The Washington Post/Getty Images.

Actors involved in peacebuilding are frequently intergovernmental organizations, but increasingly they consist of participants from private organizations and NGOs involved in the disbursement of development aid. While peacekeeping tends to focus on separating armed actors and providing a space for actors to demobilize with minimal vulnerability, general peacebuilding focuses on developing robust state institutions that can contribute to the provision of legitimate governance. These activities include assisting in constitutional reforms, election monitoring, provision of humanitarian aid, and the development of critical infrastructure like roads and water systems. To be effective in these functions, local knowledge is necessary, and NGOs and private organizations can partner with other international actors to assist in implementing policy.

The combination of peacekeeping and peacebuilding efforts, and the combination of international and local actors, are especially important in addressing issues of reintegration of displaced persons and armed actors. With regard to displaced persons, many conflicts uproot communities and cause massive numbers of refugees and internally displaced persons. As the security situation stabilizes, resettlement of those who were displaced needs to occur without creating disruptive economic and political dynamics. Failure to resettle promptly can lead to humanitarian crises and instability in the areas hosting the migrants fleeing conflict. At the same time, resettling in a haphazard manner can worsen the sense of insecurity felt by both the formerly displaced and the communities to which they are resettling. As a result, it has been important for peacekeeping operations to work with the UN Refugee Agency (UNHCR) and with local actors to effectively reintegrate refugees and internally displaced persons.

With regard to the reintegration of armed actors, most civil wars involve the need for some armed groups to demobilize and for their members to lay down their weapons. Doing so may risk vulnerability to retaliation. As a result, efforts to disarm, demobilize and reintegrate (DDR) are some of the most important functions of peacekeeping and peacebuilding operations. If armed actors do not have a viable exit strategy, they are likely to want to remain armed and mobilized. More fundamentally, communities might be rendered permanently divided if members of the community were recently at war with one another. Again, it is important for peacekeeping operations to work with local and international organizations that can assist with the reintegration of the combatants. This often involves developing a transitional justice process – which could include prosecution of war crimes, blanket amnesty, truth and reconciliation commissions, or some combination of these options – that is appropriate to the local context and geared toward making communities whole.

Mechanisms for Enhancing Peace

So, do third parties actually improve the prospects for peacemaking and peacekeeping? The most direct answer to this question, but not the most complete answer, is that, yes, many studies have found that on average the involvement of third-party peacemakers is associated with higher chances of reaching an agreement (Beardsley et al. 2006; Walter et al. 2021). Further, peacekeeping is associated with reductions in violence and longer durations of peace (Fortna 2008; Hultman et al. 2014). Even though it is easy to point to catastrophic failures of third-party involvement, such as that which preceded the Rwandan genocide, more often than not third parties do well in achieving their objectives of making and keeping peace.

A better answer would move beyond mere "on-average" correlations and speak to the specific mechanisms by which third parties can improve the prospects of peace. Simply knowing that third parties are associated with an outcome does not imply that third-party peacemaking and peacekeeping offer a panacea for conflict resolution. Moreover, such on-average associations only get us so far in developing policy solutions to apparently intractable conflicts. The set of cases in which third parties have helped make and keep peace are cases in which the disputing parties and the third parties agreed that intervention would be desirable. These cases do not shed light on how third parties are likely to fare in situations in which the disputing parties have not yet reached a consensus on whether it would be desirable to bring in a third party. So, from a policy perspective, a blunt approach to trying to increase the amount of third-party peacemaking and peacekeeping across the board might not actually produce significant dividends.

Policy relevance improves when we focus on the mechanisms by which third parties might help make and keep peace. In this vein, Jacob Bercovitch and Karl DeRouen emphasized a contingency approach in which we would understand the conditions that are most opportune – or ripe – for effective involvement (Bercovitch and DeRouen 2005). With a contingency approach, we are more interested in *when* third parties are likely to be effective than *whether* they are. Not only do we need to apply the right tool, but we also need to apply it at the right time. As we will consider below, misapplying third-party involvement can lead to, at best, wasted effort or, at worst, major setbacks in the peace process.

Toward the end of uncovering the mechanisms by which third parties can best succeed in making and keeping peace, it is crucial to understand the different functions that third parties serve. This chapter focuses on how they affect the costs of failing to settle a dispute, how they improve the information environment, and how they soften political opposition to settlement. With these functions in mind, advocates of peace can better work out what manner of third-party engagement is most needed for a particular situation, choosing the best tool for the job.

Leveraging Costs

The most direct mechanism by which third parties can improve the prospects of peace is to make conflict costlier and thereby less attractive than peace. William Zartman has introduced and developed the concept of "mutually hurting stalemate" to refer to phases of a conflict that are "ripe" for resolution (Zartman 1985, 2000). These are time periods in which the alternatives to negotiated agreement are perceived by the disputing parties to be unattractive because conflict is so costly. Third parties can cultivate perceptions of a mutually hurting stalemate by enhancing the perceived costs of nonagreement.

Peacekeeping forces directly pertain to this mechanism (Howard 2019). When third-party military forces deploy, they make it more difficult (costlier) for the disputing parties to use violence as a means to fulfill their objectives. If the peacekeepers are positioned between the parties, this presents a larger set of armed actors that the adversaries must battle in order to attack their opponents. Moreover, even a pure monitoring role that **traditional peacekeepers** play can make combat less appealing, as the third parties can make it harder for one side to launch a successful surprise attack and can otherwise help the actors secure defensive positions, reducing their vulnerability. For example, one crucial provision in the disengagement agreement between Israel and Syria in 1974 was the deployment of a UN mission to the Golan Heights, where a demilitarized zone could be maintained. This action made it less appealing for either Israel or Syria to break the peace and restart hostilities.

Even actors in peacemaking capacities, such as mediators and third-party consultants, can manipulate the costs that disputants face if they continue to fight. Third parties can threaten to punish intransigent actors. While such threats could take the form of military intervention, more commonly the third parties threaten to withhold aid, cut diplomatic or economic ties, or assist the other side. Third-party peacemakers can also offer positive incentives to the conflict parties if they reduce hostilities. These inducements – for example, promises of aid, trade or closer diplomatic relations – make non-agreement relatively costly in the sense that the actors would be forgoing potential gains by not settling. An example of positive and negative inducements can be seen in President Jimmy Carter's mediation of the Camp David Accords in 1978 and the Egypt–Israel Peace Treaty in 1979. In his role as mediator, Carter threatened both sides with the possibility that he might publicly blame an intransigent side and also promised to offer billions of dollars in annual military aid to the sides if they reached a settlement.

Leveraging costs pertains to both the immediate and future costs of fighting if the deployed forces, threats of punishment, and/or positive inducements extend into future periods. As discussed above, one major potential source of endemic conflict is the mistrust between adversaries who fear that their opponents will cheat on any agreement that is reached. In such situations, actors might prefer to fight toward complete victory rather than reach a settlement that might be temporary and may even leave them vulnerable if implemented. For instance, many peace agreements involve forms of disarmament or demobilization, but implementation is difficult: actors that comply with implementation by laying down their weapons and withdrawing from defensive positions will be at a significant disadvantage as against those that do not. Peacekeepers and other third parties that are able to maintain high costs for fighting can mitigate these concerns over the reliability of an opponent's commitment to the implementation of settlements. Barbara Walter has asserted that third-party enforcement is often necessary to remove the "critical barrier" to peace, which is the potential for noncompliance during the implementation of civil war settlement agreements (Walter 2002; see summary of quantitative study in chapter 1). Third parties can help the actors find settlement attractive immediately, and potentially into the future.

Information Environment

In addition to inflating the costs of fighting, third parties can influence the information environment. Uncertainty can be a key source of conflict in two ways. First, if actors do not know what offers their opponents will accept – because of the strong incentives to claim that they will walk away unless any given offer is higher – it is possible that the disputants will underestimate the willingness of their opponents to reject an offer. The actors might then fight because they cannot find a mutually satisfying deal. The actors would have not fought had they actually known one another's willingness to accept some offers and not others. Second, if actors do not know whether their opponents will comply with a peace arrangement or not – they mistrust their opponents' commitment to implementation – they may choose to fight so as to avoid agreeing to a deal that would leave them vulnerable to implementation failure. Even when an actor is trustworthy, its opponent may not know that to be the case and ultimately walk away from an agreement because of uncertainty over the feasibility of implementation.

Third parties can help reduce the problem of uncertainty in a few ways. First, mediators and other types of peacemakers, such as fact-finding missions and panels of experts, can provide their own assessments of the capabilities and resolve of the disputants and help the parties identify agreements that are mutually preferable to fighting. For example, American intelligence officials helped convince Pakistan to back down in a 2001 crisis with India by providing new evidence about the strength of India's military position. While such direct information provision does occur on occasion, it likely occurs infrequently because it is not often that a third party would have better intelligence than the disputing party itself.

A second means by which third-party peacemakers can reduce uncertainty is to make it easier for the disputing parties to negotiate. If the actors have difficulty even making and responding to offers, there will be persistent uncertainty about what a mutually satisfying agreement could be. Third parties can facilitate the exchange of offers by serving as a medium of communication between adversaries that lack direct diplomatic ties. It also might mean hosting talks away from the battlefield and behind closed doors so that the disputing parties can hear the demands of their adversaries, offer counter proposals and eventually narrow in on a set of mutually acceptable agreements. An extreme example of this is the Portsmouth mediation by Roosevelt between Russia and Japan, which involved the Japanese and Russian negotiators traveling for weeks to reach the negotiations on the other side of the world from the theater of combat. Although the negotiators were far removed from the fighting, they still had quick access to the key decisionmakers in St. Petersburg and Tokyo via telegraph communications, which prevented other sources of misinformation from disrupting the negotiations.

A third way in which third parties can improve the information environment is through monitoring. When compliance with the implementation process is in question, third-party actors can provide assurance about the mutual compliance of the disputing parties, which can allow them to take further steps in implementation. And, prior to agreement, the disputing parties will be more willing to settle if they know that their opponent will be less able to get away with cheating undetected and that they themselves will be less likely to be accused of cheating when in fact they have been fully compliant. For example, a critical provision of the 1975 Sinai II disengagement agreement between Israel and Egypt was UN monitoring and the construction of an early-warning system in a key mountain range in the Sinai Peninsula, which allowed both sides to perceive less vulnerability to a surprise attack. Perhaps not coincidentally, Israel and Egypt have since then enjoyed more than forty years of peace.

Political Environment

Still another mechanism by which third parties can improve the prospects for peace is by softening the political environment, making it more conducive to peace. Leaders will be reluctant to reach settlements that are unpopular with key constituencies. This is especially the case when leaders had publicly promised not to concede and then find that making concessions is in their side's best interest after all. Even when concessions are prudent, leaders might find themselves locked into conflict and unwilling to make concessions because they face enormous political or personal costs if they strike a deal. If concessions are likely to be extremely unpopular among key constituencies, leaders might prefer to fight rather than risk the loss of political power, or even exile, imprisonment or death, after a successful uprising against them.

Third parties might offer political cover for concessions – helping leaders save face and freeing them up to make prudent compromises – in a few ways. Binding third-party involvement such as arbitration and adjudication can take the decision to concede out of the leaders' hands, which reduces the culpability of the leaders for an unpopular agreement (Allee and Huth 2006). When an arbitrator or court hands down a decision, the leader can always decry the ruling as unfair and thereby deflect criticism. Although legal dispute resolution (arbitration and adjudication) does do well to produce arrangements that help resolve conflict, we should not expect this mechanism to completely shield leaders. Opponents of the leadership could still criticize the regime's willingness to let such an important issue be decided by a third party in a binding settlement. Moreover, as we saw above, there is a precedent for states to successfully flout so-called binding decisions from arbitration and adjudication processes. Critics of a deal might then still blame a leader for not similarly trying to abandon an unpopular decision. The effectiveness of legal dispute resolution in providing political cover thus depends on how legitimate the key constituents perceive the third party or court to be.

In addition, mediators and third-party consultants can signal the prudence of any concessions and legitimize a deal as being mutually beneficial (Beardsley and Lo 2014). The key constituents might learn about whether a deal is ultimately a good one or a rotten one through what a third party recommends. When the third party has better expertise and information than an individual, a strong endorsement by a mediator or third-party consultant can soften the

Figure 10.6. Yitzhak Rabin, Bill Clinton, and Yasser Arafat, signing the Oslo Accords, 1993. ©J. DAVID AKE / Stringer/AFP/ Getty Images.

uproar that would otherwise follow concessions made at the bargaining table. Again, the standing of the third parties in the eyes of the key constituents matters here. When the third parties are believed to have overlapping interests with constituents, their recommendations to concede are likely to sway more skeptics of the administration than third parties that lack such shared interests.

For example, for years the possibility of making a deal with Yasser Arafat and the Palestinians had been anathema in Israel, just as the possibility of making a deal with Israel had been in the occupied territories and throughout the Arab world. In this context, US President Bill Clinton's personal and public overseeing of the signing of the Declaration of Principles (1993) between Israel and the Arafat-led Palestinian Liberation Organization (PLO) was necessary even though the terms had already been agreed upon prior to Clinton's involvement. Clinton's personal involvement and hosting of a landmark handshake on the White House lawn helped bolster support among many Palestinians and Israelis who understood the importance of currying favor with – or at least avoiding the ire of – the most powerful state in the system (see Figure 10.6). Even so, Israeli Prime Minister Yitzhak Rabin was assassinated soon after by a radical Israeli who could not stand for Israel to have made such a peace with the Palestinians. And radical groups such as Hamas gained traction among Palestinians who became less inclined to support the PLO after it recognized the legitimacy of the state of Israel. This suggests that third parties might be able to provide just enough political cover to free up leaders to make needed compromises, even if they are not likely to sway the most ardent skeptics.

Limitations

Although third parties have the potential to improve the prospects of peacemaking and peacekeeping, they often struggle, for a variety of reasons, to achieve such peaceful outcomes. In discussing these limitations, we should bear in mind that third-party peacemaking and peacekeeping attempts tend to do better than noninvolvement on average. Understanding the limitations should not lead to general skepticism of third-party involvement but rather to a greater ability to get the most out of that involvement.

Long-Term Challenges

First, some of the struggles that third parties face relate to difficulties in fostering long-term peace. Durable peace requires that the negotiating parties continue to find peace more acceptable than war after the third parties withdraw. Even when third parties do well to encourage a cessation of hostilities in the short run, it is more difficult for them to help the parties reach a point at which they put off fighting indefinitely (Beardsley 2011; Werner and Yuen 2005).

When third parties provide incentives for the parties to settle, what happens when the flow of incentives declines? It is not common for third parties to be able to apply a permanent flow of inducements that make conflict costly and peace attractive. Such inducements are often costly for the third party; resource constraints and priorities elsewhere will lead to a lessening of the external incentives over time. If and when that occurs, the disputing parties may no longer find the terms of settlement attractive. Perhaps they settled because the third party pressured them into it or offered some form of positive side payment. After the pressure or payments abate, such efforts will struggle to establish an enduring cooperative arrangement. Perhaps they settled because the third party provided some sort of security guarantee in the form of peacekeeping forces or monitors. Such efforts also will struggle to establish a lasting peace when the peacekeepers and monitors go home and leave one or both of the hostile parties vulnerable to, and untrusting of, the former adversary.

Aside from often being unable to commit to indefinite inducements, third-party peacemaking interventions might interrupt the learning process that normally occurs in the midst of fighting. While fighting, actors can learn hard but important lessons about their potential to win militarily and about the resolve of their opponent to fight rather than concede. The eventual reduction of uncertainty through grinding combat can, ironically, provide the basis for long-term peace. If third parties quickly separate the sides as tensions rise, the actors may remain uncertain about what types of agreements would indeed be mutually preferable to conflict. Agreements reached in the absence of third-party involvement have a higher potential to rest on a foundation of strong mutual understanding of opponents' capabilities and resolve, and they may as a result be more stable.

Approaches to conflict resolution that view conflict as socially constructed – that conflict is a misalignment of meaning and values and not just a misalignment of preferences – offer additional critiques of third-party involvement that focuses too much on the manipulation of incentives to reach a "negative" peace. For example, work by John Paul Lederach points to the importance of *transforming* the relationship between the parties so that the parties move toward a "positive" peace and begin to recognize common values and develop mutual esteem for one another (Lederach 1996; see also Galtung 1969). From this perspective, peacemaking approaches that focus on short-term incentives for agreement will struggle to cultivate a transformative peace that can endure in the third party's absence.

This is not to say that third-party interventions are definitely not worthwhile even when they struggle to achieve a long-term peace. Sometimes short-term peace, and the preservation of blood and treasure that comes with it, is worth the long-term uncertainty. Sometimes it is mutually beneficial to kick the proverbial can continually down the road, to settle for short-term fixes to crises instead of pushing for a full resolution. Sometimes, stopping the killing is enough. By buying time, third parties can help prepare for further negotiations on more sticky issues, to build trust and to begin the process of conflict transformation (Ruhe and Volg 2021). Moreover, third parties can in some cases have sufficient vested interest in a peace process that they remain involved indefinitely. For example, the United States maintained and expanded its aid to Israel and Egypt in the decades following the Egypt–Israel Peace Treaty (Arena and Pechenkina 2016).

Peacekeeping Undercutting Peacemaking

A second limitation to third-party peace efforts relates to a problem in which the involvement of peacekeepers sometimes undercuts the efforts of bilateral or third-party efforts to negotiate a peace agreement (Greig and Diehl 2005). In a sense, peacekeeping can take the pressure off for the disputing parties to compromise and reach a permanent arrangement. If full resolution of the dispute is not desired because the lack of a resolution is not costly, the disputants might choose not to settle.

Scholars have found that bilateral negotiation and mediation attempts are much less common once peacekeepers are in place. Consequently, the likelihood of reaching a comprehensive agreement declines in the presence of peacekeepers. When peacekeeping operations deploy to a situation that is not fully settled, it potentially locks into a stalemate.

Again, this is not to say that it is misguided to deploy peacekeeping operations to conflict situations that are not fully settled. In the absence of peacekeeping, it is likely that violent conflict – between armed groups and also against civilian populations – would continue. For humanitarian reasons, peacekeeping operations can be worthwhile even if they impede the potential for a political settlement to be reached.

Missing the Local Context

A third issue that often limits the efficacy of mediation and peacekeeping efforts relates to pushes for reform that are not appropriate for the local context. This is especially problematic for peacebuilding efforts that attempt to address some of the underlying breakdowns in political, economic and social institutions that are at the root of the armed conflict. Yet such efforts have the potential to worsen the sense of insecurity in societies and decrease stability in the post-conflict period (Paris 2004).

In the wake of civil wars, international actors tend to push for reforms to bring institutions in line with those observed in well-functioning states, often associated with economically developed Western countries. For example, international actors might push for democratic reforms that involve the holding of regular elections. Or they might push for economic liberalization that increases the role of free markets and decreases state control of production.

While the successful adoption of such reforms would be symptomatic of a well-functioning state that has recovered well from civil war, the process of trying to attain them might actually make things worse in the short term.

For example, the holding of elections and the formation of political parties involves a competition between political groups that results in a set of winners and a set of losers. Immediately after a civil war, in which competing factions were actively trying to kill one another, it may be prudent to avoid high-stakes competition and the creation of losing groups that might return to violence as a means to achieve their desired policies. Similarly, market-based economic institutions rely on competition and the creation of winners and losers. Groups that are disadvantaged in the marketplace – whether from an imbalance in resource endowments or some other reasons – may again become aggrieved and turn to violence as a way to maintain access to state resources. If adequate institutional safety nets are not already in place to find legitimate political and economic options for losers, liberalization might actually hasten a return to civil war. As an example, the Hutu militias that perpetrated genocide in Rwanda in 1994 drew from political parties that had been excluded from power in the early 1990s as Rwanda experimented with multiparty politics, as well as many individuals who were unemployed and faced economic insecurity in the wake of the civil war.

The potential for swift liberalization to undermine peacebuilding success relates to a more general problem of international actors missing the local context. Intergovernmental organizations, aid donors, and NGOs tend to be dominated by actors – and money – from the developed West, and what has worked in the United States or Germany or the UK might not work well in the DRC or Nepal or Iraq. The problem of missing the local context is not just an issue in big reforms related to elections and economic competition, but also in more mundane interactions between local citizens and international peacekeepers. Indeed, peace-keeping operations can be rather tone-deaf in understanding what is best needed for local groups to feel secure and to make the best use of the assistance being provided (Autesserre 2014). As a result, many peacebuilding reforms struggle to get traction.

Peacekeeper Abuse

One pernicious side of peacekeeping is entirely preventable. Too often, we see peacekeeping operations make headlines for abuses of civilian populations. Of course, the abuses that make the headlines are only the tips of the icebergs, as so many victims in conflict zones are not able to come forward to report the injustice being done by the armed international actors purporting to be agents of justice.

While peacekeepers might abuse their power in many possible ways, sexual exploitation and abuse has received the most attention. Although there is a zero-tolerance policy for sexual relations between UN peacekeepers and civilians, the sex industry in geographic proximity to peacekeeping bases typically thrives, and stories abound of women having "boyfriend" peace-keepers. One study in Liberia in 2012 found that about a third of the women in a representative sample of eighteen- to thirty-year old women in Monrovia had engaged in transactional sex (prostitution) with a peacekeeper (Beber et al. 2017; Karim and Beardsley 2017). Although not necessarily a form of sexual violence, rampant transactional sex involving peacekeepers is associated with exploitation because of the potential abuse of power in which the promise of greater security can be perceived as part of the transaction for sex, and because of the strong association between prostitution and sex trafficking among vulnerable populations.

Especially worrying are the allegations of sexual violence that are frequently brought against peacekeeping personnel. In 2015, a formal Review by the High-Level Independent Panel on Peace Operations pointed to sexual violence as a serious concern to be addressed going forward. One of the issues has to do with the difficulty in bringing offenders to book. Although the UN Department of Peacekeeping Operations (DPKO) has formal procedures for investigating any allegations of sexual exploitation and abuse, it is still difficult for victims to bring perpetrators to justice. Local law enforcement has little recourse against peacekeepers, which means that victims have to bring their allegations to the attention of a peacekeeping operation associated with the perpetrator. The UN leaders of the peacekeeping operations also do not have much recourse available other than reassigning or sending home peacekeepers who have engaged in misconduct. It is the responsibility of the contributing countries to prosecute misconduct of their personnel, but it is difficult to try a case so far removed from the offense and there are so many steps along the way where misconduct can be covered up or dismissed out of hand – by the personnel in the field, by the mission leadership, by the host country, or by the contributing country.

One prominent example demonstrates the difficulty of holding peacekeepers accountable. In 2013 and 2014, dozens of French peacekeeping troops were implicated in the sexual abuse of children between the ages of nine and thirteen in the Central African Republic. The UN began a secret investigation, and France only discovered the allegations after a report leaked. France then opened a formal investigation, and a decision was reached in 2017. The decision was actually to close the case without charges being brought against the alleged perpetrators because of the difficulty in finding evidence beyond the word of the accusers. Whether the allegations were true or not, this case points to possible structural barriers in addressing peacekeeper abuse. The efforts of the UN and the efforts of a contributing country to investigate allegations of abuse are often in tension with one another and, even when aligned, have the potential to be biased in favor of giving the peacekeepers the benefit of the doubt. More fundamentally, it is difficult to expect that victims of abuse will want to come forward so as to endure a multi-year process of answering questions from multiple investigative teams employed by international actors who need to find definitive evidence of crimes of such a sensitive nature.

Feigned Interest in Peace As a Stalling Tactic

Another challenge that mediators and peacekeepers confront is the potential for disputing parties to use participation in peace processes as a means to improve their military position rather than to genuinely seek peace. Disputing parties might go along with a mediation or peacekeeping initiative if they expect to be in a stronger military position after the initiative has concluded. One of the sides might be losing ground, for example, and want time to regroup before renewing hostilities as well as delaying the further advance of the adversary. In these situations, the disputing parties might feign an interest in a peace process so that they can have more time to shore up their military positions before renewing hostilities. Parties might also try to make their opponents relax their defenses and even move toward disarmament with the hopes of taking advantage of that window of opportunity for a decisive blow.

Often it is a third party – which is either in on the incentive to stall or otherwise focused solely on a short-term abatement in hostilities – that allows the disputing parties to succeed in using a peace process insincerely. For example, Russia helped "mediate" a series of ceasefires in the Syrian Civil War that broke out in 2014, and this ultimately gave the Assad regime opportunities to regroup and plan an offensive against rebel positions. Russia had an interest in helping its ally; meanwhile, the rebels and their international supporters were unwilling to avoid the peace process for fear of provoking greater Russian military intervention. In a related example, North Korea was able to consolidate its nuclear program and extract substantial aid after 2002 during the six-party talks, which certainly China and Russia – and maybe even South Korea, Japan and the United States – strongly preferred to a potential for crisis escalation on the Korean peninsula even if none of the parties believed that North Korea was negotiating in good faith.

Dilemmas

The above discussion on limitations points to some dilemmas about whether mediation, peacekeeping or peacebuilding missions are sometimes worth the effort, especially when they carry a risk of making things worse. In many cases the dilemma is easy to resolve, as when a short-term reprieve from violence is unquestionably better than the alternative of letting violence rage. In this section, we see a few other dilemmas that relate to how third-party peacemaking and peacekeeping are executed.

Mediator Bias

Scholars have identified various strengths and weaknesses related to involving biased mediators (Beber 2012; Carnevale and Arad 1996; Kydd 2006; Rauchhaus 2006; Savun 2008; Svensson 2009). While it is commonly assumed that mediators should be unbiased, there are a number of benefits that may arise from the inclusion of a mediator who actually favors one of the disputing parties.

One benefit is that biased third parties try harder. In conflicts in which a third party needs to provide inducements for a settlement, biased third parties might be more willing than those without any skin in the game to offer side payments or to hold the parties accountable for any intransigence. For example, Arab states and Palestinian leaders have frequently called for American mediation in the various stages of the Arab–Israeli conflict precisely because the United States has a special relationship with Israel and can better leverage and hold Israel accountable than other actors. Indeed, one of the key ingredients for successfully reaching the Egypt–Israel peace treaty was the promise of billions of dollars of US military aid – to both actors, but more going to Israel – that has continued even until today.

A separate benefit to bias relates to the credibility of the third party's claims. If a mediator only values peace and has no preference regarding the terms of settlement, then any admonitions by the third party for the combatants to stop fighting will be seen as nothing but cheap talk. All such third parties have an incentive to claim that it is in everyone's interest for violence to end – that further fighting is futile, that the other side has the upper hand in the conflict. Such claims will not be seen as credible. In contrast, a third party that prefers a settlement to favor its protégé is capable of being heeded when it recommends to the protégé that it is prudent to settle. The protégé knows the mediator has overlapping interests and will only recommend settlement when in fact that is the prudent course of action.

Despite these potential benefits of including a biased mediator, other situations are best suited for impartial third-party involvement – especially when a lack of trust is at the root of the conflict. When the disputing parties do not believe that their opponents will abide by the terms of the commitment and will instead seize upon opportunities to exploit vulnerabilities, a biased mediator will not reduce the sense of insecurity perceived by one of the sides. The opponent of a mediator's protégé will suspect that the third party is not being equitable in the monitoring or enforcement of the deal and otherwise not interested in holding the protégé accountable, while the mediator will be suspected of unjustly assigning culpability to the nonfavored side.

For related reasons, it is generally expected that peacekeepers should be unbiased. Their task primarily focuses on monitoring and enforcement, and all parties to the settlement need to feel confident that violations will be treated equitably. Perceptions of imbalanced treatment may open up windows of vulnerability such that one of the actors would rather renew the state of armed hostilities than allow for an opponent to gain ground under the auspices of a favorable third party.

Moreover, some forms of third-party peacemaking such as adjudication and arbitration require the third party to be impartial (Gent and Shannon 2010). In cases when the third party is in a position to issue a binding resolution, the disputing parties must believe that the third party weighs the different claims fairly. Disputants that believe a judicial process will be biased against them will not recognize the legitimacy of the third party to issue a binding decision.

Leverage

The use of heavy-handed inducements also presents a dilemma for the practice of mediation. As we saw above, third-party inducements often cannot be sustained indefinitely. The challenge of reaching an agreement that can be durable in the absence of a third party is proportional to the strength of any promises of benefits for settlement (or punishments for intransigence). As the inducements become stronger, so too does the difficulty in securing a peace that can be weaned off the third party's involvement. When third parties provide a lighter touch and do not offer much by way of positive or negative inducements, the long-term viability of the settlement will depend less on the continued involvement of the third party.

Yet lighter mediation might not do much to help bring about a settlement in the most difficult conflicts to resolve. Especially in the midst of severe violence, a strong third-party approach may be needed to convince the actors to reach a ceasefire and to make progress at the negotiation table. Moreover, third parties who can credibly threaten military intervention in the event of peace breakdown can increase the incentives for further negotiations rather than a return to the battlefield (Pechenkina 2020). For humanitarian reasons, strong third-party involvement may be justified even if it risks putting off a full agreement that does not require the prodding of an external actor (Reid 2017; Ruhe and Volg 2021; Sisk 2009; Smith and Stam 2003).

Multiparty Involvement

Another dilemma relates to the inclusion of multiple third parties into a mediation, peacekeeping, or peacebuilding initiative (Böhmelt 2011; Crocker et al. 1999; Menninga 2015). In mediation, the presence of multiple third parties could increase the amount of leverage placed on the disputants, but of course that takes us back to the dilemma about the right balance of leverage. Multiple third parties are better able to provide inducements for peace, but a reliance on inducements can interfere with the ability to reach a sustainable agreement. Aside from leverage, multiparty mediation could strive for the best of both worlds when it comes to bias and impartiality. If third parties that are each biased toward one or other of the disputants are included in a peace process, then they might be able to bring the benefits of having a biased perspective without opening up the potential perception of vulnerability because each disputing party has a patron that could come to their aid in case an opponent or an opponent's patron tries to cheat.

Despite these potential benefits for multiparty mediation efforts, one important downside is that the coordination of the peacemaking efforts becomes more difficult when there are too many stakeholders involved. Coordination over the scope of a peace process, and much more the terms of the ultimate settlement, can be rather difficult when there are so many parties involved in a peace process. Chester Crocker and his coauthors have likened multiparty mediation to the problem of "herding cats" (Crocker et al. 1999). Such coordination problems can particularly cause practical problems in enforcement. When there are so many third parties, especially when no particular third party has taken ownership of the process, enforcement might fall through the cracks as each third party would like to free-ride off the efforts of another. In the end, enforcement might not be provided at all, and agreements might collapse in the absence of expectations of consequences for cheating.

For related reasons, peacekeeping and peacebuilding missions often struggle under the pressures of having many third parties involved. Almost all UN peacekeeping operations involve personnel contributions from a wide array of states; moreover, the force commanders and civilian leadership positions of the missions are typically staffed by individuals from different states. Each of the contributing countries has its own interests, and this can create dysfunctional breakdown as was seen in the mission to Rwanda. As contributing countries withdrew their forces, the mission weakened and violence increased, setting the stage for the 1994 genocide. As another example, competition between the leadership and forces of the large contributors, as with India, Pakistan and Bangladesh, could hamper the adoption of best peacekeeping practices.

The multiparty problem can be especially severe in the peacebuilding context. During a UN peacebuilding mission, not only is there interest divergence in the UN mission – again, security and civilian personnel are contributed by many different countries – but there is typically additional involvement of regional governmental organizations, aid donors, nongovernmental advocates, and even other UN agencies. Coordination can be an impediment to successful resolution. For example, the recent civil war in South Sudan has caused a substantial humanitarian crisis with over two million refugees and asylum seekers, and a number of actors – including the deployed UN peacekeeping operation, the UN Refugee Agency, the European Commission, the African Union, and other state-based and nongovernmental organizations – are involved in trying to address the problem. While it is good news that so many organizations are interested in addressing the plight of the South Sudanese people, the coordination difficulty is real, as enforcement responsibilities fall through the cracks.

CASE STUDY

The Value and Limitations of Third-Party Involvement in the Great Lakes Region of Africa

The roles of third-party peacemakers and peacekeepers are often an important part of the narratives of armed conflicts around the world. For example, the massive amounts of violence in the Great Lakes Region of Africa – specifically, Rwanda, Burundi, and the Democratic Republic of the Congo (DRC, previously Zaire) – from the 1990s to the early 2000s reveal the relevance of third parties for better and for worse (Map 10.1).

Sequence of Violence and Intervention

We'll start in Rwanda, where a civil war between the Hutu-dominated Rwandan government and the Tutsi-dominated Rwandan Patriotic Front (RPF) started in 1990. Over the almost three-year armed struggle, a number of attempts were made by third parties to bring the violence to an end. Mediators from the United Nations, the African Union, the European Union, and other regional states all tried at various times to broker a peace deal. A small peacekeeping operation, the UN Observer Mission Uganda–Rwanda (UNOMUR), was established to secure the border between Rwanda and Uganda, where

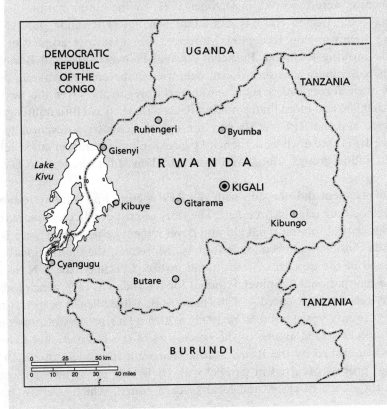

Map 10.1. Rwanda and its neighbors, location of massive levels of violence especially in the 1990s and 2000s. King, *From Classrooms to Conflict in Rwanda* (Cambridge: Cambridge University Press), p. xii.

(cont.)

Figure 10.7. The unimaginable but all too real horror: remains of some of the 800,000 genocide victims in Rwanda, 1994. How can we begin to grasp the scope of this tragedy?
©Alan Gignoux/Corbis Documentary/Getty Images.

the RPF had bases. Eventually, in August 1993, the African Union, France and the USA organized a peace process in Arusha, Tanzania, which ended the civil war.

The Arusha Accords were followed, in October 1993, by the authorization of a UN peacekeeping force – the United Nations Assistance Mission in Rwanda (UNAMIR). This peacekeeping force was slow to deploy. Moreover, when violence erupted in April 1994 after a plane carrying Rwandan President Juvénal Habyarimana and Burundian President Cyprien Ntaryamira was shot down, countries that were contributing peace-keepers withdrew their forces rather than sending reinforcements. Over the next few months, between 500,000 and more than a million Rwandans died as Hutu militia groups engaged in genocide and the RPF cut its way through the country to eventually take control (see Figure 10.7). Meanwhile, a French "peacekeeping" operation stood idly by and allowed Hutu militia groups, along with over a million Hutu refugees, to flee into eastern Zaire.

International involvement did not stop with the RPF victory and ultimate establishment of Paul Kagame's long reign as president. The story of post-conflict relative stability in Rwanda includes critical international aid and development projects that were necessary to put Rwanda onto a sound economic footing. Moreover, the international community was involved in the process of transitional justice. Crucially, the UN Security Council set up the International Criminal Tribunal for Rwanda (ICTR), which indicted ninety-three – sixty-one were sentenced – of the most responsible alleged perpetrators of the genocide over a twenty-year period from 1995 to 2015. (This process of prosecuting offenders for war crimes served as one of the precursors of the International Criminal Court, which was established by the Rome Statute and went into effect in 2002.) The ICTR international process occurred in parallel with trials held in the national courts, which prosecuted thousands of cases, and local Gacaca courts, which oversaw over a

(cont.)

million cases. The Gacaca courts focused on restoring perpetrators of violence, who could receive lenient sentences for confessing crimes, expressing remorse, and desiring reintegration with the local community.

The Hutu–Tutsi violence was not limited to Rwanda, as Burundi had previously experienced large-scale ethnic violence and was in the midst of a civil war that broke out after another assassination in 1993. The 1994 assassination of the Rwandan and Burundian presidents, both Hutus, precipitated violence not only in Rwanda but in Burundi, which had a tenuous power-sharing agreement between the Tutsi and Hutu factions in place. Although the violence was not as extreme as that in Rwanda, interethnic violence and political instability characterized Burundi until 2006. Nelson Mandela had tried to mediate a peace plan, again in Arusha, Tanzania, in 2000, but the plan ultimately collapsed. South Africa's Deputy President Jacob Zuma replaced Mandela as mediator.

In 2003, an African Union (AU) peacekeeping force was deployed to try and stabilize tensions after a 2002 ceasefire agreement with a key rebel group. The AU mission was replaced by a UN peacekeeping operation in 2004. The peacekeeping operation oversaw a 2005 round of elections and was replaced by a purely political mission (without armed personnel) in 2007, which was then replaced by a subsequent political mission in 2011.

Meanwhile, in the aftermath of the Rwandan genocide, violence shifted to the Kivu region of eastern Zaire. Motivated, in part, by a desire to continue the fight against the Hutu militias which had fled, Rwanda and Uganda supported a rebellion in eastern Zaire. The rebellion, led by Laurent Kabila against the Zaire government led by President Mobutu Sese Seko, ultimately succeeded and resulted in Kabila being installed as president. Zaire was renamed the Democratic Republic of the Congo (DRC).

More violence followed, as Rwanda and Uganda supported another rebellion in Kivu, this time against Kabila's forces. A number of other states in the region – Angola, Chad, Namibia, and Zimbabwe – joined the fight in support of the Kabila government. The internationalized civil war unfolded over a brutal four years in which more than 2.5 million people died.

During the conflict, a number of third-party mediators tried to stop the killing and facilitate a resolution. Most notably, Zambia hosted talks early in the conflict that yielded a ceasefire agreement. As a result of that ceasefire – the Lusaka Ceasefire Agreement – the UN Security Council authorized the establishment of a UN peacekeeping operation (United Nations Organization Mission in the Democratic Republic of the Congo, or MONUC). The MONUC mission was active throughout the conflict, even after the Lusaka agreement broke down, and served both mediating and security-providing capacities. Later in the war, South Africa was active as a mediator and helped produce both the short-lived Sun City agreement in April 2002 and the final Pretoria agreement that did hold in July 2002.

MONUC remained deployed to help oversee the landmark 2006 elections in the DRC, as well as to help manage periodic flare-ups of violence in the eastern part of the country.

(cont.)

In 2010, MONUC became the United Nations Organization Stabilization Mission in the DRC (MONUSCO), a relatively large mission (nearly 20,000 troops) that ultimately received an unprecedented mandate to form a combat brigade to fight against the M23 rebel group much as a national security force would.

Implications

These sequences of events in Rwanda, Burundi, and DRC (Zaire) illustrate some of the ways in which third parties are often active as peacemakers and peacekeepers in the deadliest conflicts around the world. It is difficult to describe the paths toward settlement in each of these conflicts without discussing the role of third-party actors that were active in the peace processes. In these cases, we saw a wide variety of mediators, including intergovernmental organizations such as the UN and African Union, states such as Tanzania, the United States, France and South Africa, and individuals such as Nelson Mandela. A fuller treatment of these cases would also reveal that NGOs were quite active in each of these peace processes.

It is also difficult to describe the implementation of peace after settlement without discussing the role of third-party peacekeepers. Peacekeeping operations featured prominently in these narratives. Multiple missions with different mandates in Rwanda, the DRC and Burundi all played important roles in providing third-party military support to try to stabilize the security environments. Each of these missions was deployed after some form of ceasefire or agreement, and each ended up deployed during periods of major hostilities after peace broke down at various points. These examples show that peacemaking and peacekeeping initiatives often overlap, and there is rarely a clean handoff from one to the other.

Moreover, we see the role of third-party efforts to help build peace in these cases. The missions in the DRC have had multidimensional mandates that incorporate political assistance in helping the state institute democratic reforms including the holding of free and fair elections. In Burundi, two political missions helped nurture the fragile political institutions after peace finally held. Moreover, the UN peacekeeping operation that preceded those missions oversaw the holding of elections at a critical juncture in 2005. In Rwanda, the ICTR prosecutions serve as an example of international efforts to help build the foundations of peace by addressing injustices committed during previous episodes of violence.

These instances of peacebuilding demonstrate that third-party assistance during the implementation phase of a peace process does not solely involve the deployment of military personnel who can monitor and intervene in the security situation. Overseeing elections and advising on the implementation of reforms related to the rule of law, the security sector, and economic policy are also crucial roles that third parties play in helping to secure peace.

(cont.)

While the third-party peacemakers were active, their level of success in helping to resolve the conflicts left much to be desired. The Arusha Accords in Rwanda ultimately broke down into genocide, and order was not restored in Rwanda until the RPF ultimately won military victory. A number of mediated peace attempts in the DRC failed to hold. Moreover, although much of the DRC has been free of major violence since 2002, still today the Kivu region experiences periodic flare-ups in political violence, requiring a continual peacekeeping presence. In Burundi, Mandela's efforts to broker a ceasefire, while at first promising, ultimately broke down, and peace was not fully secured until about five years later.

Even worse than simply failing to achieve the desired peaceful objectives is for third-party involvement to undermine the potential for peace to hold. As we saw in Rwanda, the combination of a third-party push for a premature agreement and the fumbling of third parties in following through on their commitments to guarantee the implementation of peace can lead to catastrophic violence. The delayed and weaker-than-expected deployment of the UNAMIR peacekeeping operation opened up a window of opportunity for Hutu militia groups to arm and spearhead violence against a vulnerable population. The Tutsi were without sufficient armed protection, given that the RPF had withdrawn to Uganda after the previous episode of civil war had ended. Once the violence started, the UNAMIR force only weakened. Together with French forces, UNAMIR was complicit in allowing armed Hutu militias to escape to eastern Zaire as the RPF fought southward.

It is likely that less devastation would have occurred had the third parties not pushed for the Arusha Accords with the promise of UN peacekeeping. The violence that followed the collapse of peace was much more extreme than the violence that preceded it. This is not to say that military victory is clearly the best way to resolve a conflict. Even though the RPF victory and establishment of rule by the Kagame government ultimately brought stability and order that has helped nurture robust economic growth, Rwanda has become increasingly authoritarian and it is not clear what the long-term promise of good governance looks like.

Finally, this case also illustrates the role of other types of third parties. Some third parties serve as joiners. States such as Angola, Chad, Namibia, and Zimbabwe entered into the DRC civil war from 1998 to 2002 on the side of Kabila's government. Some might term their involvement as peacemaking through armed participation – they were fighting against the aggression of the insurgents, Rwanda and Uganda, in an attempt to restore the status quo – but their armed-conflict participation should be kept distinct from the forms of third-party peacemaking considered in this chapter. Understanding the role of peacemaking through the use of force is a separate topic worthy of further exploration.

QUANTITATIVE STUDY

Mediation and Peace between Nations

Research Question

In their study, Kyle Beardsley and his coauthors explore the role of mediation in international crises from 1918 to 2015 (Beardsley et al. 2006). They ask, under what conditions does mediation improve the prospects for peace? More specifically, the analyses address whether mediation helps crisis actors reach major settlements and tension reduction in the short run, and which forms of mediation are most effective in achieving these outcomes. While earlier sections of this chapter explored a number of different third-party peacemaking and peacekeeping roles, this quantitative module will focus only on mediation in interstate crises.

Theory and Hypotheses

Mediators can perform a number of functions to help disputing parties reach an agreement. With the assistance of a third party, belligerents can find ways to reach a mutual accord rather than fighting for complete victory or leaving the dispute unsettled in a stalemate. One expectation is that mediated crises will be more likely than unmediated crises to terminate in a formal agreement, and also more likely to experience tension reduction in the immediate aftermath of a crisis.

One way in which mediators help to make peace is by changing the incentives – leveraging the costs – of the disputing parties. But providing incentives to avoid conflict creates a potential tradeoff in which durable peace might become more difficult because the settlement depends on the third-party leverage. As a result, we should expect mediation, especially manipulative mediation in which third parties provide larger incentives for peace, to do very well in helping actors reach formal terms of agreement, while the same type of manipulative mediation should do less well in helping the actors avoid a return to violence later on.

Hypothesis 1: Crises with mediation are more likely to end in a formal agreement than crises without mediation.

Hypothesis 2: Crises with mediation are especially likely to end in a formal agreement when the mediator manipulates the incentives for reaching a deal and stopping aggression.

Hypothesis 3: Mediation that relies on the manipulation of incentives will be less likely to increase the durability of peace after a crisis has terminated.

Data

The data come from the International Crisis Behavior (ICB) data project (version 14), which codes incidences of international crises since 1918 (Brecher et al. 2021). An ICB crisis is a crisis in which one state perceives another state to be a threat, there is a finite time to respond to the threat, and there is a heightened perception of military escalation. Although all crises involve the possibility of escalation to violence, some crises terminate prior to the use of force between the adversaries. There have been 487 crises in the period from 1918 to 2017. Some ICB crises are intra-war crises, which are characterized by distinct periods of crisis in the midst of major wars. For the sake of the analysis here, we drop those crises, which leaves 401 cases.

Dependent Variables

This module considers two potential outcome variables to see what effect the occurrence of mediation has on them. The first outcome variable is a measure of whether the parties reached a formal agreement as a means to terminate the crisis. Of the 401 cases in the analysis, 85 (21 percent) terminated in a formal agreement.

   The second outcome variable is a measure of whether the five-year period after a crisis terminated was characterized as having reduced tensions. Of the 395 cases that are not too recent, 224 (57 percent) were considered to have been followed by a period of reduced tensions between the adversaries.

Independent Variables

An indicator of whether mediation occurred during the crisis serves as the key explanatory variable. Of the 401 cases in the analysis, 122 (30 percent) experienced mediation. Figure 10.8 depicts the counts of all crises and mediated crises over time. We see that international crises have become less common since the Cold War. The proportion of mediated crises also appears to be moderately higher in the post–Cold War period than during many periods of the Cold War.

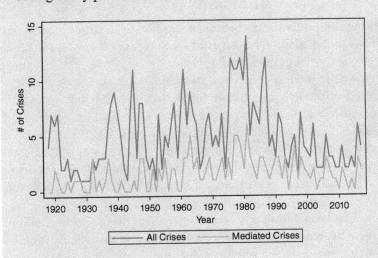

Figure 10.8. Trends in crises and mediated crises across the twentieth century. Mediation becomes somewhat more frequent during crises after 1945. International Crisis Behavior (ICB) data project.

Mediation comes in a variety of forms, and one key dimension in which mediation varies is the extent to which the third parties are manipulative in incentivizing the belligerents to settle. Manipulative mediation with leverage involves direct attempts by the third party to change the incentives for ending the crisis – by making peace more attractive and violent hostilities less attractive. Manipulative mediation contrasts with other forms of mediation, such as the mere hosting of talks (facilitation) or the mere involvement in the proposing of ideas (formulation). For the purposes of this brief analysis, the ICB variables that code for manipulation, formulation, or facilitation are used to create two categories of mediated crises: manipulative mediation or nonmanipulative (light) mediation.

Control Variables

For the purposes of this study, it is worth including control variables for the underlying complexity and intensity of the crises, which are potentially related to whether mediation occurs, the form of mediation that does occur, and the level of violence experienced in the crises. In addition, complexity and intensity are also likely related to the propensity for agreements to be reached and for tensions to be reduced after a crisis terminates. The statistical models therefore all control for the gravity of threat, the number of involved actors, and whether the crisis is a protracted conflict, which is a relationship between adversaries characterized by relatively frequent crises over similar underlying issues. In addition, the statistical models control for the level of violence in the crises. In the ICB data, the level of violence can take on the values of "no violence," "minor clashes," "major clashes," or "war."

Results

A regression of formal agreement termination on mediation and the control variables described above shows that mediation has an estimated positive effect on the likelihood of a crisis terminating in a formal agreement. Moreover, a similar regression with tension reduction as the outcome of interest shows that mediation also increases the potential for tensions to be reduced in the five-year post-crisis period. Figures 10.9 and 10.10 show expected probabilities (between 0 and 1) of each respective outcome for unmediated crises and mediated crises. The center points are the expected values, and the dashed lines give the 95 percent confidence intervals; that is, the data suggest we can be 95 percent certain that the actual effect is within the range described by dotted lines. These results confirm that mediation tends to have strong short-term effects in the attenuation of hostilities in interstate crises.

Mediation makes crisis termination in a formal agreement more than three times more likely. Mediation also increases, less starkly but still by a meaningful amount, the expected chance that a crisis results in tension reduction.

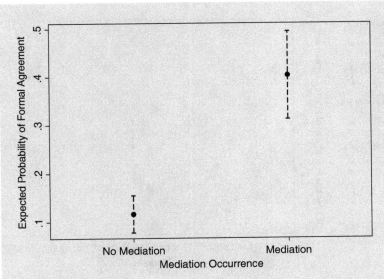

Figure 10.9. Mediation and formal agreements. The presence of mediation is nearly four times more likely to be associated with a formal agreement than if there is no mediation. International Crisis Behavior (ICB) data project.

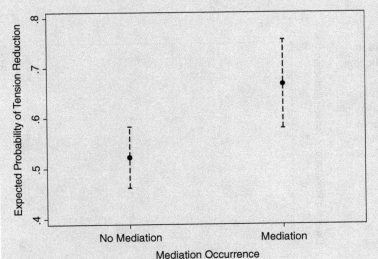

Figure 10.10. Mediation and tension reduction. Mediation is associated with a roughly one-third increase in the likelihood of tension reduction. International Crisis Behavior (ICB) data project.

What about the different effects of distinct styles of mediation? The regression model with mediation separated out by manipulative mediation and light mediation show that manipulation has a much stronger effect on the potential for a formal agreement than light mediation, which still improves the potential for a formal agreement over no mediation at all. As we see in Figure 10.11, the heavy-handedness of the mediation does shape the willingness of the actors to reach a formal compromise.

At the same time, there is not much of a difference between the mediation styles in the effect on tension reduction. As we see in Figure 10.12, both types of mediation are associated with a higher propensity for tension reduction. The lack of additional

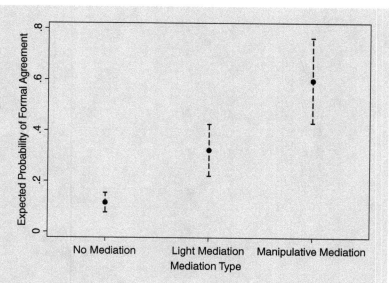

Figure 10.11. Mediation type and formal agreements. Formal agreements are more likely with manipulative or heavy-handed mediation as compared with light mediation. International Crisis Behavior (ICB) data project

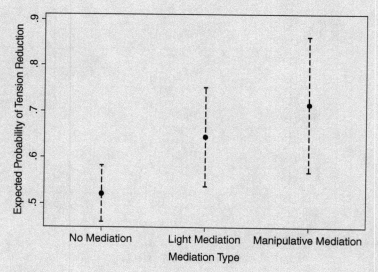

Figure 10.12. Mediation type and tension reduction. Both light and manipulative mediation reduce tension, but there is not a significant difference in the effect across the two. International Crisis Behavior (ICB) data project.

improvements in tension reduction when comparing manipulative mediation to light mediation is consistent with H3. It is striking that manipulative mediation does so well in helping disputants reach a formal agreement but the increase in potential for a formal agreement does not lead to much of an increase in tension reduction after the crises. Manipulative mediation potentially involves tradeoffs in that it can greatly incentivize peaceful settlement but does not sufficiently help the parties reach a durable peace that does not require constant third-party involvement.

Conclusions

This case study considers some basic relationships between mediation and short-term outcomes related to being able to reach a formal agreement and the reduction of tensions in the five-year post-crisis period. The results showed that mediation, especially manipulative mediation, does greatly increase the propensity for formal agreements.

Moreover, mediation does increase the propensity for medium-run tension reduction. Since manipulation does not appear to be especially conducive toward tension reduction we see some evidence that mediators who use substantial leverage face challenges in moving the parties toward sustainable peace. As mediators increase the incentives for the parties to settle, and as mediators become more concerned with the management of the violence rather than resolving the underlying sources of conflict, the third parties in some cases might only be promoting short-term fixes. This is not to say that mediation is not worth attempting when there are substantial challenges to reaching a more long-term settlement. Reducing bloodshed in many cases is a priority goal and can be an end in itself. Kicking the can down the road is often superior to idly watching a humanitarian catastrophe unfold.

SUMMARY

This chapter has considered a number of key points about third-party peacemaking and peacekeeping:

- Third-party involvement in peace processes is quite common.
- Mediation is a key form of peacemaking.
- Peacekeeping involves the deployment of military personnel and often occurs along with other peacebuilding efforts.
- On average, third-party participation in mediation and peacekeeping tends to improve the prospects of peace.
- Third parties often seek to increase the perceived costs of conflict, reduce levels of uncertainty, and reduce political barriers to peace.
- Third parties often struggle to help belligerents reach a sustainable peace, to maintain momentum toward full resolution while peacekeepers are deployed, to account sufficiently for the local context, to prevent abuse by both peacekeepers and belligerents, and to curtail the use of a use peace process to stall for time.
- There are a number of pros and cons around the questions of whether mediators should be unbiased, whether third parties should use leverage to make peace more attractive, and whether multiple third parties should be involved in peace processes.

KEY TERMS

Peacemaking
Mediation

Arbitration
Adjudication

International Court of Justice   Peacekeeping
Third-party consultations   Traditional peacekeeping
Good offices   Chapter VII mandates
Fact finding   Peacebuilding
Panel of experts

REVIEW QUESTIONS

1. Describe third-party efforts in the series of conflicts in the Great Lakes region of Africa.
2. What are some of the benefits and tradeoffs from the use of manipulative mediation tactics?
3. Why might a biased mediator be in some cases more desirable than an unbiased mediator?
4. Why might belligerents pursue mediation for insincere reasons?
5. Why might peacekeeping reduce the potential for belligerents to reach a full resolution of their dispute?
6. What types of actors can serve as third parties, and how might the type of actor affect how they are involved in a dispute?
7. What are the implications of an anarchic international system for how mediation, peacekeeping, arbitration and adjudication are carried out?

DISCUSSION QUESTIONS

1. Have third-party efforts in the Great Lakes conflict helped achieve and/or sustain peace?
2. Think about your own country. Given what you now know about the effectiveness of peacekeeping and peacebuilding, would you want your government to participate in peacekeeping and peacebuilding efforts, knowing that such efforts incur for your country both financial costs (spending on these missions) and potentially human costs (loss of life of your nation's soldiers while serving in such missions)?

ADDITIONAL READING

Diehl, P. F. and Druckman, D. (2010). *Evaluating Peace Operations*. Boulder, CO: Lynne Rienner.
Greig, J. M. and Diehl, P. F. (2012). *International Mediation*. Malden, MA: Polity.
Greig, J. M., Owsiak, A. P., and Diehl, P. F. (2019). *International Conflict Management*. Medford, MA: Polity Press.
Howard, L. M. (2008). *UN Peacekeeping in Civil Wars*. New York: Cambridge University Press.
Princen, T. (1992). *Intermediaries in International Conflict*. Princeton: Princeton University Press.
Wilkenfeld, J., Young, K., Quinn, D., and Asal., V. (2007). *Mediating International Crises*. New York: Routledge.

REFERENCES

Allee, T. L. and Huth, P. K. (2006). Legitimizing dispute settlement: International legal rulings as domestic political cover. *American Political Science Review* **100**(2), 219–234.

Arena, P. and Pechenkina, A. O. (2016). External subsidies and lasting peace. *Journal of Conflict Resolution* **60**(7), 1278–1311.

Asthana, S. B. (2014). UN peacekeeping operations: Relevance and Indian contribution? *United Service Institution of India.* https://usiofindia.org/publication

Autesserre, S. (2010). *The Trouble with the Congo: Local Violence and the Failure of International Peacebuilding.* Cambridge: Cambridge University Press.

Autesserre, S. (2014). *Peaceland: Conflict Resolution and the Everyday Politics of International Intervention.* New York: Cambridge University Press.

Beardsley, K. (2011). *The Mediation Dilemma.* Ithaca, NY: Cornell University Press.

Beardsley, K., and Lo, N. (2014). Third-party conflict management and the willingness to make concessions. *Journal of Conflict Resolution* **58**(2), 363–392.

Beardsley, K. C., Quinn, D. M., Biswas, B., and Wilkenfeld, J. (2006). Mediation style and crisis outcomes. *Journal of Conflict Resolution* **50**(1), 58–86.

Beber, B. (2012). International mediation, selection effects, and the question of bias. *Conflict Management and Peace Science* **29**(4), 397–424.

Beber, B., Gilligan, M. J., Guardado, J., and Karim, S. (2017). Peacekeeping, compliance with international norms, and transactional sex in Monrovia, Liberia. *International Organization* **71**(1), 1–30.

Bercovitch, J. and DeRouen, K. (2005). Managing ethnic civil wars: Assessing the determinants of successful mediation. *Civil Wars* **7**(1), 98–116.

Böhmelt, T. (2011). Disaggregating mediations: The impact of multiparty mediation. *British Journal of Political Science* **41**(4), 859–881.

Bove, V. and Elia, L. (2011). Supplying peace: Participation in and troop contribution to peacekeeping missions. *Journal of Peace Research* **48**(6), 699–714.

Brecher, M., Wilkenfeld, J., Beardsley, K., James, P. and Quinn, D. (2021). International Crisis Behavior data codebook, version 14. *International Crisis Behavior Project.* http://sites.duke.edu/icbdata/data-collections

Carnevale, P. J. and Arad, S. (1996). Bias and impartiality in international mediation. In J. Bercovitch (ed.). *Resolving International Conflicts: The Theory and Practice of Mediation.* Boulder, CO: Lynne Rienner, 39–53.

Crocker, C. A., Hampson, F. O. and Aall, P. (1999). *Herding Cats: Multiparty Mediation in a Complex World.* Washington, DC: United States Institute of Peace.

Croicu, M., Melander, E., Nilsson, M., and Wallensteen, P. (2013). Mediation and violence: Searching for third party intervention that matters. Paper presented at the Annual Meeting of the International Studies Association, April 3–6, San Francisco, USA.

Fortna, V. P. (2008). *Does Peacekeeping Work? Shaping Belligerents' Choices after Civil War.* Princeton: Princeton University Press.

Galtung, J. (1969). Violence, peace, and peace research. *Journal of Peace Research* **6**(3), 167–191.

Gent, S. E. and Shannon, M. (2010). The effectiveness of international arbitration and adjudication: Getting into a bind. *Journal of Politics* **72**(2), 366–380.

Greig, J. M. and Diehl, P. F. (2005). The peacekeeping–peacemaking dilemma. *International Studies Quarterly* **49**(4), 621–646.

Howard, L. M. (2019). *Power in Peacekeeping.* Cambridge: Cambridge University Press.

Hultman, L., Kathman, J., and Shannon, M. (2014). Beyond keeping peace: United Nations effectiveness in the midst of fighting. *American Political Science Review* **108**(4), 737–753.

Karim, S. and Beardsley, K. (2017). *Equal Opportunity Peacekeeping: Women, Peace, and Security in Post-conflict States.* New York: Oxford University Press.

Kydd, A. H. (2006). When can mediators build trust? *American Political Science Review* **100**(3), 449–462.

Lederach, J. P. (1996). *Preparing for Peace: Conflict Transformation across Cultures*. Syracuse, NY: Syracuse University Press.

Menninga, E. J. (2015). Multiparty mediation: Identifying characteristics of the mediation dream team. Unpublished Ph.D. thesis, University of North Carolina.

Paris, R. (2004). *At War's End: Building Peace after Civil Conflict*, Cambridge: Cambridge University Press.

Pechenkina, A. O. (2020). Third-party pressure for peace. *International Interactions* **46**(1), 82–110.

Rauchhaus, R. W. (2006). Asymmetric information, mediation, and conflict management. *World Politics* **58**(2), 207–241.

Reid, L. (2017). Finding a peace that lasts. *Journal of Conflict Resolution* **61**(7), 1401–1431.

Ruhe, C. and Volg, I. (2021). Sticks and carrots for peace: The effect of manipulative mediation strategies on post-conflict stability. *Research & Politics* **8**(2).

Savun, B. (2008). Information, bias, and mediation success. *International Studies Quarterly* **52**(1), 25–47.

Sisk, T. D. (2009). *International Mediation in Civil Wars: Bargaining with Bullets*. London: Routledge.

Smith, A. and Stam, A. (2003). Mediation and peacekeeping in a random walk model of civil and interstate war. *International Studies Review* **5**(4), 115–135.

Svensson, I. (2009). Who brings which peace? *Journal of Conflict Resolution* **53**(3), 446–469.

UN Peacekeeping (2022). Global peacekeeping data. https://peacekeeping.un.org/en/data

Walter, B. F. (2002). *Committing to Peace: The Successful Settlement of Civil Wars*. Princeton: Princeton University Press.

Walter, B. F., L. M. Howard, and V. P. Fortna. (2021). The extraordinary relationship between peacekeeping and peace. *British Journal of Political Science* **51**(4), 1705–1722.

Werner, S. and Yuen, A. (2005). Making and keeping peace. *International Organization* **59**(2), 261–292.

Zartman, I. W. (1985). *Ripe for Resolution: Conflict and Intervention in Africa*. New York: Oxford University Press.

Zartman, I. W. (2000). Ripeness: the hurting stalemate and beyond. In P. C. Stern and D. Druckman (eds.). *International Conflict Resolution after the Cold War*. Washington, DC: National Academy Press, 225–250.

Part V

Special Topics in Conflict

11 Nuclear Weapons

MICHAEL C. HOROWITZ

Introduction

Nuclear weapons are explosive devices that use nuclear energy, in the form of fission or fusion, to generate destructive force. Invented by the United States in 1945 as part of the World War II–era Manhattan Project, nuclear weapons have been used in war only once: by the United States in the bombings of the Japanese cities of Hiroshima and Nagasaki at the end of World War II. Nuclear weapons are the most powerful weapons in world history. "Little Boy," the nuclear weapon used in the bombing of Hiroshima, had an explosive yield of about 15 kilotons (1 kiloton is the same as 1,000 tons) and generated a destructive effect equivalent to an entire fleet of bombers armed with conventional bombs. During the Cold War, the United States, Soviet Union, and others built even larger nuclear weapons, including thermonuclear bombs with explosive yields ranging up to 50 megatons (1 megaton is the same as 1,000,000 tons) of TNT equivalent. (TNT refers to trinitrotoluene, a conventional explosive often used as a reference point for other types of explosives).

Nuclear weapons are the only weapons in military history where even the oldest and most rudimentary forms of the weapons have significant consequences for global politics. Old machine guns, tanks, aircraft carriers, and other weapons might make for good museum pieces, but they do not transform the way the world thinks about a country. In contrast, just replicating the Manhattan Project, something the United States completed more than seventy years ago, is enough to make front-page news. Think about North Korea. North Korea's prominence on the world stage is mostly due to its development of nuclear weapons. This would be true even if their nuclear weapons were as simple as those dropped on Japan in 1945.

How should we make sense of nuclear weapons? In this chapter we will look at how to think about these incredibly destructive arms. This chapter introduces what nuclear weapons are and why scholars and policymakers believe they are important. It then addresses four main questions. First, why do countries attempt to build nuclear weapons, and why haven't more countries acquired them? Second, what are nuclear weapons good for, and should the world fear North Korea's nuclear arsenal, or is it possible to deter North Korea's use of nuclear weapons? Third, does nuclear proliferation increase or decrease international stability? And fourth, how can arms control, or agreements between two or more states restricting the development, transfer, and/or use of nuclear weapons, reduce the risk of nuclear war?

Nuclear Weapons and How They Are Delivered

Nuclear weapons are explosives that harness the power of the atom to generate far greater destructive force than is possible from a comparably sized conventional explosive. There are two main types of nuclear weapons: atomic bombs and thermonuclear bombs. Atomic bombs work by generating a nuclear, fission chain reaction of either enriched uranium or plutonium. A heavy nucleus is split into two smaller nuclei, releasing energy. Thermonuclear bombs, also called hydrogen bombs, are even more powerful. They use an atomic bomb to create a fusion reaction of hydrogen nuclei. Two lighter nuclei fuse together, generating even greater energy than in a fission reaction. Nuclear weapons create mass physical destruction and release radiation into the atmosphere and soil at levels that are life-threatening to people, plants, and animals within range of the fallout.

From the first test of a nuclear weapon, in July 1945, it was clear that something was different about these weapons. Robert Oppenheimer was one of the leading scientists who developed the atomic bomb. Upon witnessing that first test, he paraphrased the Hindu text *Bhagavad Gita* and said, "Now I am become Death, the destroyer of worlds" (quoted in Rhodes 1986, 676). After the use of nuclear weapons against Hiroshima and Nagasaki, world leaders and strategists soon reached a similar judgment: there was something different about nuclear weapons compared to weapons that came before.

Bernard Brodie was one of the most prominent strategists of the early nuclear age. He compared the invention of nuclear weapons to gunpowder, an invention that caused a huge shift in warfare in its own right. He wrote, "People often speak of atomic explosives as the most portentous military invention 'since gunpowder.' But such a comparison inflates the import-ance of even so epoch-making an event as the introduction of gunpowder" (Brodie 1965, 147).

It is difficult to overestimate how shockingly powerful nuclear weapons are. Figure 11.1 is a photo of Hiroshima, taken just after a single atomic bomb was dropped on the city in 1945. Paul Tibbets is the pilot of the *Enola Gay*, the B-29 bomber that dropped the atomic bomb on the city.

Figure 11.2 is a photograph of a real atomic bomb test in the Pacific Ocean in 1946. Those are real, life-sized battleships in the photo, dwarfed by the scale of the blast.

What makes nuclear weapons so different? The sheer destructive power of one nuclear weapon, compared to other weapons, meant any country or actor with a nuclear weapon had the ability, with a handful of bombs, to level any city. The ability to destroy a city in a day – or a country, depending on how many nuclear weapons were used – was something people had never previously imagined. A country facing a nuclear-armed adversary might never feel safe, because it would be almost impossible to stop a determined country from launching nuclear weapons and destroying your country. Frederick S. Dunn (1946), writing in the aftermath of World War II, argued that the relative size and speed of destruction possible in the nuclear age "was a revolutionary development which altered the basic character of war itself." Most policymakers and scholars in the ensuing years have agreed with this assessment.

Figure 11.1. A destructive force like no other: the atomic bombing of Hiroshima, Japan, August 6, 1945.
U.S. Navy Public Affairs Resources.

Figure 11.2. A man-made tsunami? Nuclear test explosion, Bikini Atoll, Pacific Ocean, 1946.
United States Department of Defense.

A smaller number of strategists argue that the miniaturization of nuclear weapons, combined with precise weapons guided by satellite and other sensing tools, could make the use of nuclear weapons more normal and plausible without risking dramatic escalation (Lieber and Press 2017).

Once a country develops a nuclear weapon, it raises the question of how it would use that weapon against an adversary, In World War II, the United States Army Air Force used B-29 bombers to deliver nuclear strikes against Hiroshima and Nagasaki. After World War II, the United States, the Soviet Union, and other early adopters of nuclear weapons began working on building more nuclear weapons and developing other ways to launch a nuclear attack.

First Strike, Second Strike, and Mutually Assured Destruction

What happens when two rival states are both nuclear-armed? Imagine a country (call it Country A) would deliver its nuclear weapons through airborne bombers against its rival (call it Country B). If Country B began to fear that A might be preparing to launch a nuclear attack, then B might wish to destroy A's bombers on the ground at the beginning of the war, to eliminate the threat. The ability to destroy an adversary's nuclear arsenal in a first strike is referred to as **first strike capability**.

First strike capability might sound like something a country would like to have, but it actually can be quite dangerous. Country B has an incentive to use its first strike capability and attack A as soon as it fears A might attack. Conversely, think about how things look from A's perspective. Concerned about the potential for Country B to knock out its bombers at the beginning of a war, and thus eliminate its potential to launch nuclear weapons, Country A might decide it is in a "use it or lose it" position with regard to its nuclear weapons. Country A might then strike first, with nuclear weapons, because it is afraid that its nuclear weapons could not survive an attack by Country B. This is the problem of **first strike instability**: that first strike capability can make war more likely, in particular a war driven by fear and misperception of the other side's intentions, if one side falsely imagines the other side is about to attack.

To overcome first strike instability, countries with nuclear weapons often work on ways of delivering nuclear weapons that are very difficult for an adversary to destroy. The goal is to develop a secure **second strike capability** whereby a country has the ability to absorb a nuclear attack and still strike back with its nuclear weapons. The security of knowing that your weapons can survive an initial attack is thought to be stabilizing and to make war less likely. It reduces the incentive for the adversary to attack first (as attacking first will not rescue it from being destroyed in nuclear retaliation) and it removes "use it or lose it" incentives, because the state knows that its nuclear arsenal will survive a first strike. Two countries with secure second-strike capabilities that are facing each other are said to be in a position of **mutually assured destruction** (MAD), as the United States and Soviet Union were during the Cold War, since each side can assure the destruction of the other side. The advent of thermonuclear weapons, with their massive increase in destructive power compared to atomic bombs, helped illustrate the potential consequences of war and create a shared perception of risk that led to MAD between the United States and the Soviet Union.

Into the 2020s, China continues to increase the size of its nuclear arsenal, developing mobile missile forces that will be challenging to target, and, according to open source satellite information, building new ground-based launch locations for its nuclear missiles. China's expansion of its nuclear arsenal and efforts to make its nuclear weapons harder to target relate to its desire to create a relationship of MAD with the United States. Given ongoing US–China great power competition, China fears that, if a war with the United States occurs, the United States could use its precise conventional weapons to wipe out China's nuclear capabilities. China wants to ensure that, if a war occurs, no matter what happens, it has nuclear weapons to potentially attack the United States, thus generating MAD (or, even better from China's perspective, using the threat of nuclear escalation to deter American involvement in a conflict in the Asia-Pacific region in the first place).

Developing Second Strike Capacity

How do countries develop secure second-strike capabilities, which can both deter an attack by an adversary and reduce pressure to launch first if a crisis does occur? One way is by developing more ways to deliver nuclear weapons. Due to advances in missile technology during the Cold War, nuclear powers quickly moved beyond delivering nuclear weapons with bombers, adding the ability to launch missiles with nuclear warheads. By 1960, both the United States and the Soviet Union possessed intercontinental ballistic missiles (ICBMs), or missiles capable of flying thousands of kilometers to strike the Soviet Union from the United States, and vice versa. ICBMs are missiles with a minimum range of 3,400 miles (5,500 kilometers).

In addition to the ability to launch nuclear weapons from land-based ICBMs, nuclear-armed states then added the ability to launch nuclear missiles from submarines. Hard to track and deployable in secret around the world, submarines armed with nuclear missiles (these missiles are called submarine-launched ballistic missiles, or SLBMs) are designed to further increase the confidence of a country in its ability to strike back if it is ever attacked.

For the most advanced nuclear-armed states, the combination of nuclear-armed bombers, land-based ICBMs, and sea-based SLBMs forms a **nuclear triad**. Similar to the way investing in several companies as opposed to just one reduces risk to one's financial portfolio, the triad approach also reduces risk, maximizing the second-strike capability of adopters. For example, even if a country with a nuclear triad absorbed a surprise nuclear attack, a so-called "bolt from the blue" that knocked out its bombers and land-based ICBMs, it could still strike back with its nuclear-armed submarines.

There are options for increasing the security of a nuclear arsenal beyond the triad approach. One way is by making your nuclear weapons very hard to find. For example, during the Cold War, the Soviet Union developed what are called mobile transporter erector launcher (TEL) platforms for their nuclear missiles. By dispersing its nuclear missiles with TEL platforms along train lines and roadways in a crisis, the Soviet Union believed the United States would be unable to find the Soviet Union's missile launchers, and thus the United States could never be confident in its ability to destroy the Soviet Union's nuclear weapons in a first strike.

Another way to make your nuclear weapons more secure is by making your launch facilities hard to destroy. As of 2021, the United States has 400 active land-based ICBMs, including the Minuteman III missile (see Figure 11.3). These missiles are deployed in silos in Montana, North Dakota, and Wyoming. A silo is dug deep into the earth and covered with steel and reinforced concrete, making it very difficult to destroy unless it absorbs a direct hit from a nuclear weapon.

Consider one final distinction. The discussion above focuses on one type of nuclear weapon, **strategic nuclear weapons**, designed for use against an adversary's military command sites, bomber bases, ICBM silos, or cities, and delivered by the platforms described above – missiles or bombers. **Tactical nuclear weapons**, in contrast, are designed for use on the battlefield against an adversary's regular military forces and are often delivered by conventional military means, such as multirole fighter aircraft or artillery. Indeed, some have proposed that tactical nuclear weapons could be used to fight and win a limited nuclear war, a "war-fighting" perspective, though others, firm believers in the inevitability of mutual assured destruction, have been skeptical that any nuclear war could be kept limited. Strategic nuclear weapons generally have higher explosive yields than tactical nuclear weapons, though countries have developed tactical nuclear weapons with yields in the low tens of kilotons.

Figure 11.3. Minuteman III ICBM test launch; note the telephone poles in the photo to get a sense of scale. The missile is about sixty feet (twenty meters) tall, with a range of 8,700 miles (14,000 kilometers). It carries a nuclear warhead about twenty times as powerful as the bomb used to destroy Hiroshima (see Figure 11.1).
US National Parks Service.

Tactical nuclear weapons help illustrate the sheer size differential between nuclear weapons and conventional weapons. One of the smallest nuclear weapons ever built, a tactical nuclear weapon, was the M-388 produced by the United States. Designed for launch by the "Davy Crockett" tripod gun (Figure 11.4), it weighed less than 100 pounds and had an explosive yield of 0.01–0.02 kilotons, or 10-20 tons, of TNT. Compare this to the US-built GBU-43/Massive Ordinance Air Blast (MOAB) conventional bomb, also known as the "mother of all bombs." Weighing 21,600 pounds, the MOAB produces an explosive yield of 11 tons of TNT. The fact that the smallest nuclear weapon has an explosive yield equivalent to one of the largest conventional weapons, despite weighing over 200 times less, demonstrates the power of nuclear weapons.

Who Builds Nuclear Weapons?

As of 2021, there are nine countries thought to have nuclear weapons: the United States (acquired in 1945), the Soviet Union/Russia (1949), the United Kingdom (1952), France (1960), the People's Republic of China (1964), Israel (1967), India (1974), Pakistan (1990), and North Korea (2006). South Africa is believed to have tested a nuclear device in 1979 and acquired a rudimentary nuclear capability by 1982, but it dismantled its program in 1990. South Africa is the only country ever to voluntarily give up a homegrown nuclear arsenal. When the Soviet Union dissolved, the former Soviet republics of Belarus, Kazakhstan, and

Figure 11.4. Davy Crockett nuclear weapon/launch system. The bomb dropped on Hiroshima was much larger, about ten feet (three meters) long. Developing smaller nuclear weapons like the one shown here makes possible more widespread military uses, and makes terrorist use more feasible. United States Department of Defense.

Ukraine inherited Soviet nuclear weapons on their territory, but all returned them to Russia and so are not thought of as ever possessing nuclear weapons.

Basic nuclear weapons technology is now over seventy years old, which in the history of technology, if one thinks about other weapons such as fighters and tanks, means we would generally expect nuclear weapons to have spread to many more states. Why wouldn't all countries want to possess the most destructive weapon in military history? In the Cold War, world leaders thought the widespread proliferation of nuclear weapons was not just possible, but likely. In March 1963, while discussing issues surrounding nuclear weapons, US President John F. Kennedy stated, "I am haunted by the feeling that by 1970, unless we are successful, there may be ten nuclear powers instead of four, and by 1975, fifteen or twenty" (quoted in Gavin 2012, 7).

Kennedy was not wrong to think countries around the world were interested in acquiring nuclear weapons. After all, nuclear weapons function as a form of "invasion insurance" because nuclear-armed states can credibly threaten to destroy any country that might attack. A nuclear arsenal is therefore a tremendous deterrent against attack. Thus, an interesting question is not just why states pursue nuclear weapons, but why so many fewer states have nuclear weapons today than one might imagine. Understanding this requires thinking through three questions: Why pursue nuclear weapons, why *not* pursue nuclear weapons, and what are the barriers to acquiring nuclear weapons?

Why Countries Pursue Nuclear Weapons

The most common reason to pursue nuclear weapons is the most obvious: because a country believes it needs to acquire such weapons for national security (see Sagan 1996/1997). Countries facing significant external military threats often seek nuclear weapons because they believe in

nuclear deterrence – the idea that having nuclear weapons means that they will not face attack, what we described earlier as invasion insurance. In particular, states with rivals that are pursuing nuclear weapons or have acquired them may be much more likely to seek nuclear weapons. For example, one factor that motivated Pakistan to pursue nuclear weapons technology in the 1970s was fear of India's pursuit of nuclear weapons (China's nuclear arsenal may have also motivated India). States may also believe that having the ability to annihilate an adversary makes them more likely to win disputes, and shorten crises, against nonnuclear states.

Particular attributes of the domestic political regimes of countries might also make them more likely to seek nuclear weapons. For example, countries with personalist dictators as leaders, such as Iraq under Saddam Hussein, are often distrustful of the international community and have extremely high threat perceptions, meaning they think that everyone is plotting against them. Greater levels of perceived threat in turn make such leaders more likely to desire nuclear weapons. Personalist leaders also face fewer domestic political roadblocks to pursuing nuclear weapons, such as powerful interest groups that might prefer that a country invest its money elsewhere, in the domestic economy, or even in conventional military forces. Similarly, leaders who were once part of rebel groups that fought for national independence or to overthrow a ruling regime, such as past leaders Muammar Gaddafi of Libya or Mao Zedong of China, are also more likely to seek nuclear weapons. Such leaders are also deeply fearful of and sensitive to threats, if they have fought a bloody war to seize control of their countries. Former rebels also tend to be distrustful of international alliances and promises of protection from other nuclear weapon states, rendering ineffective two common tools the international community uses to dissuade a country from going nuclear (see below).

External threat and domestic political leadership aside, countries that are more disconnected from the international community – and which do not seek economic integration through trade and globalization – are also more likely to consider acquiring nuclear weapons. These are countries that are more isolated from the rest of the world, which generally makes them both more fearful and less tractable to efforts by the international community, such as economic sanctions, to deter them from pursuing nuclear weapons.

Persuading Countries Not to Pursue Nuclear Weapons

Despite facing significant international threats, there are several reasons why a country might not pursue nuclear weapons. Some of these reasons relate to the difficulty of acquiring nuclear weapons, some relate to how countries think about investing in national defense, and some are driven by extensive efforts by the international community to convince countries not to pursue nuclear weapons.

Due to a belief in the cost of nuclear war and fear that nuclear proliferation would make nuclear war more likely, the international community has created a substantial set of "sticks" (costs) to use against countries that pursue nuclear weapons, and "carrots" (benefits) for those countries that refrain from doing so. The infrastructure for these carrots and sticks includes treaties such as the Nuclear Non-Proliferation Treaty (NPT); agreements such as the Nuclear Suppliers Group and Missile Technology and Control Regime; the US-led Proliferation

Security Initiative; and efforts to generate economic costs for pursuing nuclear weapons, such as sanctions imposed by the United Nations or individual states.

For example, countries that ratify the NPT agree not to pursue nuclear weapons and in exchange gain access to peaceful nuclear technology, the ability to develop nuclear power plants (as described below, Article VI of the NPT also commits nuclear-armed ratifiers to pursue nuclear disarmament over time). Countries found in violation of their NPT obligations are subject to economic sanctions.

These economic sanctions can impose large costs on a country's economy. In 2012, for example, the United States and the European Union convinced the Society for Worldwide Interbank Financial Telecommunication (SWIFT) to disconnect Iran's banks from the SWIFT system, following evidence of Iranian NPT violations. The SWIFT system is a cooperative that provides secure communications for banks and financial companies. Access to the SWIFT system is necessary for banks to convert currency from one denomination to another, among other things. Cutting off the access of Iran's banks to the SWIFT system made it much more difficult, and less lucrative, for Iran to sell oil, the key commodity whose sale is necessary for Iran's economy. Some believe that the pressure placed on Iran's economy by the SWIFT sanctions, in particular, was one reason that Iran returned to the negotiating table and eventually agreed to restrictions on its pursuit of nuclear weapons in the Joint Comprehensive Plan of Action adopted in October 2015.

There is also a variety of carrots that particular countries, or the international community, offer to countries that do not pursue nuclear weapons (also see the discussion of nuclear proliferation below, **page 353**). An important way that the United States attempts to dissuade allies such as Japan and South Korea from pursuing nuclear weapons, for example, is through a practice known as **extended deterrence**. In extended deterrence arrangements, which are often part of broader alliances between countries, one country agrees to protect another country from attack by promising to commit its military forces in defense of that country. In the nuclear age, extended deterrence functionally means a country like the United States promises to use its nuclear arsenal in defense of a country like Japan. By extending its nuclear "umbrella" over Japan, the United States thus makes Japan less likely to want to pursue nuclear weapons of its own. The country providing the extended deterrent guarantee benefits because it does not want its ally or potential ally to acquire nuclear weapons.

That said, extended deterrence is not completely without risks. Some fear that providing nuclear protection might actually embolden the nonnuclear ally to consider becoming more aggressive itself, as the nuclear alliance will deter attacks on its homeland if aggressive moves backfire. In the 1950s, the United States considered these risks in relation to its alliance with Taiwan, concerned that extending the American nuclear pledge to Taiwan might encourage Taiwan to launch attacks against its bitter rival, China.

How do these carrots and sticks play out in shaping whether countries pursue nuclear weapons? Most prominently, the economic penalties from pursuing nuclear weapons significantly raise the cost of pursuing what is already an exceptionally expensive weapon. Pursuing nuclear weapons requires more than just snapping your fingers. Nuclear weapons are expensive and time-consuming to build. The Manhattan Project in the United States cost billions, and at its peak employed 130,000 people, meaning that by 1945 or so, almost one in every 1,000

Americans was working on building the world's first atomic bomb. By the mid 1990s, the United States had spent over $400 billion on developing nuclear weapons. The cost of building nuclear weapons comes, in part, from the large number of facilities required to develop weapons-grade nuclear material. Domestic production is necessary because acquiring weapons-grade nuclear materials, enriched uranium or plutonium-239, is difficult. As Marty McFly famously says in the 1985 movie *Back to the Future*, "You don't just walk into a store and buy plutonium." Producing weapons-grade nuclear material is extremely expensive and time-consuming – and still requires acquiring raw uranium to start. Nuclear materials are rare and highly controlled, as are the technologies used to develop them, such as centrifuges. The Nuclear Suppliers Group and the US-led Proliferation Security Initiative aim to make these supply problems even more acute, focusing on preventing these materials from spreading. Countries seeking to acquire the materials or expertise to enrich uranium or develop plutonium, unless they are willing to pay the costs of economic sanctions, have to operate on the grey or black markets to acquire materials or spend years or decades developing indigenous expertise – probably both.

The Barriers to Nuclear Acquisition

The points above not only explain why some countries pursue nuclear weapons while others do not; they also illustrate why many countries that pursue nuclear weapons stop well short of actual acquisition. The expense of acquiring nuclear weapons in the first place, especially when added to the cost imposed by the international community for pursuing them, has frustrated many countries with an interest in nuclear weapons. Those costs, especially for less technically advanced economies that lack the built-in engineering infrastructure necessary to design and build nuclear weapons, can lead to failure.

New countries that acquire nuclear weapons also often get help in the form of assistance from abroad, some legal via dual-use technologies, and some illegal, via black and gray market transfers. One example of this is the network created by Pakistani engineer A. Q. Khan, which enabled Pakistan to get nuclear assistance from China and led to collaboration between Libya, North Korea, and Pakistan. Clandestine and open transfers of knowledge and technology have fueled nuclear proliferation from the beginning. The Soviet Union, after all, arguably was able to acquire nuclear weapons in 1949, rather than several years later, due to information it received from atomic spies in the United States and Britain during World War II. Thus, when countries do not get access to these information networks, moving from nuclear pursuit to nuclear acquisition can become more difficult.

A second factor that makes it difficult to move from pursuing nuclear weapons to acquisition comes from the complexity of managing the number of moving pieces required to build deliverable nuclear weapons. The development of the weapons themselves, as well as delivery vehicles, represents a huge project management challenge. Some believe this is one reason why autocratic countries such as Iraq and Libya have failed to acquire nuclear weapons – domestic political regimes built on fear, secrecy, and promoting people based on family or personal loyalty, rather than merit, have more trouble with projects of this scale and complexity.

It is important to recognize, however, that the barriers to acquisition of nuclear weapons may be declining over time in small but important ways. The technology is old, and the basic designs for nuclear devices have become well known over the decades. Moreover, because older versions of nuclear devices still have great relevance for international politics, investments in nuclear weapons are cumulative. With most weapons, investing a small amount every year will not yield a useful military technology simply because by the time the capability is completed, it will no longer be useful. For example, a country that sought to replicate the HMS *Furious*, the first aircraft carrier, deployed in 1917, would essentially be producing a floating target. It would not provide a militarily relevant capability.

Nuclear weapons are different. North Korea proved that a country can essentially put its nickels in a jar every year and eventually develop a nuclear weapon that transforms the regional security environment. It is a testament to the uniqueness of nuclear weapons that North Korea's small nuclear arsenal has triggered so much international action despite the fact that North Korea's weapons and delivery systems are much less sophisticated and reliable than those of the United States or other more advanced nuclear weapons states.

These incentives and barriers may also interact with broader shifts in domestic political regimes and the global economy. The ability of the international community to impose economic costs and promise economic or security benefits to states for not pursuing nuclear weapons depends on the interest of states in engaging with the global economy. The more dependent states are upon trade and global economic interaction, the larger the leverage the international community has over a state – and the less likely a state is to pursue nuclear weapons in the first place, because of its fear of losing the economic benefits of access to the international system.

Extended deterrence commitments have also served to cause countries to abandon the pursuit of nuclear weapons prior to their acquisition. Since the Korean War, the United States has maintained a large military presence in South Korea as part of an alliance. In 1970, the United States began withdrawing 24,000 troops from South Korea as part of a wider pullback from the region connected to US public opposition to the ongoing Vietnam War. Concerned about the threat posed by North Korea's extensive conventional military capabilities and chemical weapons arsenal, South Korea commenced two waves of nuclear activity. In the first wave, South Korea began clandestine actions towards acquiring nuclear weapons. When the United States discovered these activities, US Secretary of State Henry Kissinger threatened to withdraw US protection from South Korea as well as impose economic costs. South Korea backed down.

However, a few years later, during the Carter administration, the United States announced that it was planning to remove all US troops from South Korea by 1982. In response, South Korea began more explicitly developing nuclear weapons. This second wave of pursuit ended when the United States reversed course and pledged to keep US forces on the Korean peninsula and the US nuclear umbrella over South Korea. What is stopping a technically advanced country like South Korea (or, for that matter, Germany, Taiwan, or Japan) from developing nuclear weapons is a lack of will, rather than a lack of expertise. Extended deterrence provides a critical disincentive for nuclear proliferation.

Nuclear Deterrence and Coercion

The destructive power of nuclear weapons in comparison with other weapons naturally raises questions of what they can be used for in international politics. As stated above, fighting against a nuclear-armed state raises the cost of war, because of the ability of nuclear weapons to destroy a country (or an army, if thinking about the effects of tactical nuclear weapons). Many believe that nuclear weapons raise the costs of war to such a high level as to protect countries with nuclear weapons from attack, functionally giving them invasion insurance. This provides nuclear-armed states with a powerful defensive edge that can protect them from threats. This is nuclear deterrence, the idea that the potential threat of nuclear retaliation prevents large-scale attacks against nuclear-armed states or their allies. Deterrent activities in general are those designed to preserve the status quo.

When two nuclear-armed states face each other and both have second strike nuclear capabilities, both therefore have the ability to destroy each other even if the other side strikes first. This condition of MAD, according to many scholars and policymakers, makes war between nuclear-armed states much less likely than it was prior to the nuclear age, and is an important reason why the Cold War between the United States and the Soviet Union never escalated into World War III. The 1962 Cuban Missile Crisis was arguably the closest the United States and the Soviet Union ever came to nuclear war. Nuclear deterrence helps explain why the Cuban Missile Crisis did not lead to nuclear war.

The Cuban Missile Crisis occurred in October 1962, and it began when the United States discovered that the Soviet Union was in the process of deploying nuclear weapons capable of hitting the United States on the territory of its ally Cuba, just 90 miles (about 140 kilometers) from Florida (see Map 11.1). During an escalating crisis that included a blockade of Cuba by the United States Navy, many feared that a global nuclear war was imminent – the type of war that would end both the United States and Soviet Union, if not the world. United States President John F. Kennedy and Soviet leader Nikita Khrushchev, however, eventually came to an agreement, though secret at the time, whereby the Soviet Union would remove its nuclear missiles from Cuba in exchange for the United States withdrawing nuclear missiles it had deployed in Turkey (a NATO ally of the United States) and pledging not to invade Cuba.

That even this extreme crisis did not escalate to nuclear war may have been luck, but it also reinforced for both countries, and the world, the danger of a global nuclear exchange. Both the United States and the Soviet Union attempted to avoid escalation because the costs were thought to be too high.

Critics argue that nuclear deterrence between the United States and the Soviet Union does not explain the failure of the Cold War to escalate. Scholars such as John Mueller argue that the weariness of the world with regard to war after World War II, conventional military deterrence, and the satisfaction of the United States and Soviet Union with the status quo better explains the long peace during the Cold War than nuclear weapons (Mueller 1989). Another qualification is that though nuclear weapons might be useful in deterring the use of nuclear weapons, they do not deter aggression at lower levels of intensity, such as more moderate conventional attacks, as it is not credible to threaten the annihilation of the adversary over minor transgressions. Nuclear use against minor transgressions is especially incredible if

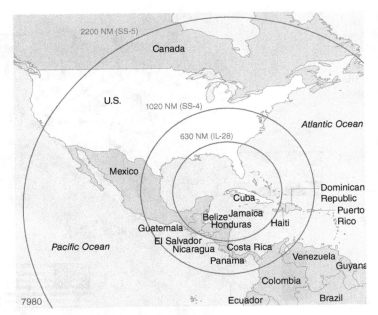

Map 11.1. Map of the range of Soviet nuclear missiles that were being deployed in Cuba, 1962. The White House was very concerned that the missiles could reach as far as Washington, DC, and the US military command would receive very little warning after the missiles launched and before they reached their targets.
Defense Intelligence Agency.

the attacker is itself a nuclear power, as then one would be risking one's own destruction in nuclear retaliation for launching nuclear attacks over lesser clashes. This idea that nuclear weapons provide stability at higher but not lower levels of violence intensity has been termed the **stability–instability paradox**.

We will return to the debate about nuclear deterrence below, in the discussion of the third big question about nuclear weapons, that of nuclear proliferation.

What other relevance do nuclear weapons have, beyond providing invasion insurance? There is a debate about the role of nuclear weapons as tools of coercion and **nuclear compellence**. In contrast to deterrence, which involves efforts to leverage the potential use of force to preserve the status quo, compellence means actions or threats to force an adversary to act. Compellent threats are those designed to change the status quo, rather than to prevent a change to the status quo.

When Nuclear Weapons Are Useful for Coercion

In theory, nuclear weapons can aid efforts to persuade adversaries to change their behavior, because they raise the expected costs of conflict for any country facing a nuclear-armed state (Kroenig 2020). Nuclear weapons should be especially effective when a country with nuclear weapons is facing a country that does not have nuclear weapons. One example of the coercive relevance of nuclear weapons comes from the early Cold War. After World War II, Germany was split into four zones: three occupied by Britain, France, and the United States that would eventually become the democratic country West Germany, and one occupied by the Soviet Union that would eventually become the Communist country East Germany. Berlin, though located entirely in the Soviet-controlled eastern zone, was split as well, with a western-occupied

Map 11.2. After the Soviets blockaded West Berlin (the black city inside the Soviet-controlled red zone), the US, Britain, and France airlifted in supplies to the beleaguered civilians (1948–1949). The American, British, and French zones eventually unified to become the nation of West Germany, with West Berlin as part of West Germany. The Soviet zone became the nation of East Germany, the capital being East Berlin, the red city. Wikipedia.

half and an eastern-occupied half. In 1948, the Soviet Union blockaded the western side of Berlin in an attempt to take control of all of Berlin. They made it impossible to bring supplies into the western part of Berlin by road or rail. In response, the United States and its allies began to airlift supplies into West Berlin (see Map 11.2).

Simultaneously, however, the United States leveraged the power of its nuclear weapons monopoly. United States President Harry Truman sent B-29s, the same class of planes that had been used to bomb Hiroshima and Nagasaki, to Britain and to Guam, a US territory in the Pacific. The move was widely seen as an implied nuclear threat to Josef Stalin, the leader of the Soviet Union: give up the blockade of West Berlin, or the conflict could escalate. And a conflict that escalated could involve a nuclear attack on the Soviet Union. The Soviet Union eventually backed down and pulled back the blockade, accepting the existence of a western island of control in the middle of a Communist territorial sea. While the nuclear capabilities of the United States were only one part of the American response, the case illustrates the potential coercive potential of nuclear weapons.

Nuclear weapons could also have utility for coercion and compellence due to the potential to use them in **brinkmanship** strategies, or what Nobel Prize–winning economist Thomas Schelling (1960) called "[T]he threat that leaves something to chance." Brinkmanship occurs when a country threatens another country in part by suggesting that, if the target does not back down, the conflict could escalate in uncontrollable or accidental ways. Brinkmanship attempts to leverage the risk that a conflict could escalate, and that the threatening state might not be able to control that escalation, which could result in the use of nuclear weapons against the target. An example of a brinkmanship move is when the United States raises the Defense Readiness Condition (DEFCON) of its military forces. DEFCON 5 represents a normal or steady-state level of readiness, while DEFCON 1 would reflect the beginning of a nuclear war. The DEFCON level has only been raised to DEFCON 2 twice, during the Cuban Missile Crisis in 1962 and during the 1991 Persian Gulf War at the beginning of Operation Desert Storm. Raising the DEFCON level illustrates how seriously the United States takes a given situation, communicating to a potential target that if it does not change its behavior, escalation is possible.

One problem with brinkmanship strategies, however, is that they are inherently risky. Explicitly leveraging the risk that a conflict could escalate into a nuclear war means being willing to run that risk – or the threat will be seen as not credible. There is also tension between the interest of leaders in maintaining direct control over a crisis, and threatening something that could lead to a conflict spiraling out of control. The desire of leaders to have control over a conflict can also make brinkmanship signals less credible, since the target might not believe the threat.

When Nuclear Weapons are Not Useful for Coercion

That said, some believe that nuclear weapons are not very useful for coercion and compellence (Sechser and Fuhrmann 2017). One reason is that compellence is much harder than deterrence in general – it is easier to convince someone not to do something (deterrence) than to convince them to stop doing something (compellence). The challenge with using nuclear weapons for coercion and compellence, however, lies in the very thing that makes them so useful for deterrence – the enormous consequences of a nuclear war. For a threat to be credible, an adversary has to believe that a country will actually carry out the threat. When two countries have nuclear weapons and can destroy each other, the threat to escalate to the nuclear level if a target country does not change its behavior can lack credibility because of the ability of the target to respond in kind. The target country will not believe the threat because it does not believe the threatening country would put its own survival at risk.

What about a situation where only one country has nuclear weapons, such as the Berlin Crisis of 1948? In these situations, the explicit or implied threat of a nuclear attack if a country does not change its behavior can often seem disproportionate, like threatening execution as punishment for getting a speeding ticket. Similar to the dynamics in the stability–instability paradox, disproportionate threats are seen as less credible. As a result, the types of situations where a country with nuclear weapons is likely to try to leverage them to coerce another country are generally those where the issue is of large importance for the nuclear power. The challenge is that such issues are likely to be of large importance to the target of the challenge, meaning the target country is less likely to back down.

Nuclear Proliferation and International Stability

One of the largest questions surrounding nuclear weapons is whether the continued spread of nuclear weapons to additional countries will increase or decrease international peace and stability. This process is known as **nuclear proliferation**. Kenneth Waltz, one of the most promin-ent political scientists of the last fifty years, argued for decades that the continued proliferation of nuclear weapons would enhance international stability. In contrast, many others, especially Scott Sagan, argue that nuclear proliferation is destabilizing (Sagan and Waltz 2012).

Which of these perspectives is correct, and what does it mean for efforts by the international community to stop nuclear proliferation?

Nuclear Proliferation Would Increase International Stability

The case for more nuclear proliferation is rooted in the idea that precisely due to fear of the cost of nuclear war, as outlined above, the more states that have nuclear weapons, the more states will find it difficult if not impossible to engage in aggressive actions such as war. The risk of nuclear retaliation for an attack will discourage states from starting lower-level crises, due to the fear that the conflict will escalate. Given the interest that governments have in protecting their citizens, no government would want to subject its people to the risk of nuclear attack.

According to this perspective, it would be stabilizing, rather than destabilizing, for a country such as Iran to acquire nuclear weapons. Right now, Iran feels vulnerable because it views itself as threatened by the nuclear arsenals of the United States and Israel. This leads to insecurity on the part of Iran's leaders, who fear an attack (however unlikely). By acquiring nuclear weapons, Iran would feel less insecure, and it would raise the costs of any potential conflict if an attack did occur. A reduction in Iran's perception of insecurity might also make Iran's leaders less likely to engage in other destabilizing activities, such as supporting terrorist groups, and make them more likely to want to cooperate in the Middle East in general. Thus, conflict would become less likely.

The stabilizing effect of nuclear proliferation is magnified by the difficulty in using nuclear weapons for offensive attacks. A state could not use nuclear weapons on a piece of territory it wished to conquer, because the use of nuclear weapons would destroy that territory to such an extent that conquest would no longer be worthwhile. As President Eisenhower remarked in 1954 regarding the outcome of a nuclear "victory" over the Soviet Union, "Gain such a victory, and what do you do with it? Here would be a great area from the Elbe to Vladivostok . . . torn up and destroyed, without government, without its communications, just an area of starvation and disaster . . . I repeat, there is no victory in any war except through our imaginations" (quoted in Jervis 1989, 4).

Moreover, because nuclear weapons are so powerful, states tend to take care of them responsibly, reducing the risk of accidental or unauthorized nuclear use. Further, countries like the United States can always assist new nuclear states by providing them with safety-enhancing technology such as security locks on weapons (technology referred to as permissive action links), which makes unauthorized use of even a stolen weapon less likely. Indeed, after the Cold War, many in the United States and around the world were concerned that the disintegration of the Soviet Union might mean Russia would be unable, due to the cost and security requirements, to maintain full control over its nuclear arsenal. The United States passed a law called Nunn–Lugar in response, which funded a variety of activities to prevent parts of the former Soviet arsenal from ending up on the black market, available to the highest bidder. These funds were used in part literally to cut into pieces Soviet nuclear weapons and their delivery systems (see Figure 11.5).

Figure 11.5. Swords into plowshares: a Russian shipyard worker cutting into pieces a Soviet nuclear submarine as part of the American Nunn–Lugar Initiative, 1996. The US government may have provided this worker with the blowtorch he is using, and may have paid his salary. Todd P. Cichonowicz, U.S. Navy.

Nuclear Proliferation Would Decrease International Stability

In contrast to Kenneth Waltz and a small number of other scholars, most believe that nuclear proliferation is dangerous. Scott Sagan, prominently, argues that one reason it is dangerous is that every new nuclear state increases the risk of accidental nuclear war. While states can reduce the risk of nuclear accidents through measures such as taking their nuclear missiles off high alert or separating the missiles from the nuclear warheads, some risk of an accident that leads to the use of a nuclear weapon will always exist. The Cold War period was full of near misses. For example, American and Soviet early warning radars sometimes suggested that the adversary was about to launch or had launched its nuclear missiles. If any false warning had been heeded by the national leadership, the world might have faced the horrifying reality of an accidental nuclear war.

One example comes from the late Cold War (Aksenov 2013). On September 26, 1983, a Soviet military officer named Stanislav Petrov noticed a surprising signal on the early warning system he was responsible for monitoring – something he had never seen before. The computer system designed to alert the Soviet Union that the United States had launched a nuclear attack was showing that such an attack had started, and the United States had launched five nuclear missiles at the Soviet Union. Petrov knew what was at stake: a nuclear exchange between the United States and Soviet Union would kill hundreds of millions of people and potentially end human civilization as we know it. There was no ongoing crisis and no reason to think that the United States was about to launch an attack. If Petrov reported to his superiors that an attack was underway, the Soviet Union could have rapidly retaliated by launching its own nuclear missiles at the United States. But what if the computer system was wrong? What if there was an error? In that case, it would be the Soviets striking first, and the United States would undoubtedly strike back. Petrov hesitated – and instead of reporting to his superiors that an attack was underway, he reported an error in the Soviet tracking system. That is how close the world came to World War III. There were other near-misses as well. For example, during the

Cuban Missile Crisis, one Soviet submarine believed it was under attack by the United States and it had authorized to launch nuclear missiles in response. But Soviet naval officer Vasiliy Arkhipov had the power to veto the nuclear launch, which he did, realizing the submarine was not under attack.

Another risk from nuclear proliferation has to do with the way the uneven pace of nuclear proliferation could influence international stability. It is possible that Waltz and others are correct that in stable, symmetrical pairs of states such as the United States and Soviet Union, nuclear weapons can deter war. What happens, however, when one state has nuclear weapons and the other does not? A state that can threaten to destroy its adversary and that does not face retaliation may be more prone to aggression, and certainly more capable of leveraging its arsenal for coercive purposes. Or if one state in a rivalry is in the process of acquiring nuclear weapons, the other state may be motivated to launch a preventive attack before its rival secures an operational nuclear arsenal. Given the long and uneven nuclear acquisition timelines of countries such as Israel, India, North Korea, and South Africa, further nuclear proliferation is likely to occur unevenly as well. In that case, conflict could become more likely rather than less.

Another worrying dimension concerns what individuals are likely to lead new nuclear states. As described above, former rebels and personalist leaders may be especially likely to pursue nuclear weapons. Because these leaders tend to be more revisionist, meaning they are more likely to try to leverage newfound capabilities for aggression, their acquisition of nuclear weapons may pose grave risks to international peace.

The configuration of the international security environment at present is another reason why many worry about the consequences of nuclear proliferation. Even if nuclear weapons are only useful for defensive purposes, countries that acquire nuclear weapons become harder to coerce. For status quo powers such as the United States, which generally seek to sustain the international system rather than change it, more states acquiring nuclear weapons could make it harder for the United States to use nuclear coercion to maintain international order.

Unstable countries with nuclear weapons present another potential risk rising from nuclear proliferation. Specifically, one of them may experience domestic instability in a way that makes nuclear weapons available to separatist groups or terrorists that might not be restrained in their use of the capabilities.

The debate about whether nuclear proliferation might actually enhance international stability, as opposed to making nuclear war more likely, is difficult to resolve. The non-use of nuclear weapons in general presents a significant challenge for policymakers. Those that make policy surrounding the potential use of nuclear weapons do so under a large degree of uncertainty, as our knowledge of the actual causes and consequences of nuclear use remains limited. And uncertainty makes decisionmaking harder.

The Role of Arms Control

The final question about nuclear weapons this chapter addresses is: Can **arms control** agreements and other measures designed to halt the spread of nuclear weapons make nuclear war less likely? If so, how and under what conditions?

Nuclear Arms Control Agreements

Since the dawn of the nuclear age, as the world realized the unique destructive power of nuclear weapons, leaders have attempted to come up with ways to reduce the risk of nuclear war. These efforts started shortly after Hiroshima and Nagasaki. In 1946, the United States, then the only country in the world with nuclear weapons, proposed giving control over atomic research, including nuclear power, to the just-created United Nations, and turning over its nuclear weapons to the United Nations as part of the agreement. The proposal was called the Baruch plan, named after Bernard Baruch, the US representative to the United Nations Atomic Energy Commission. The Baruch plan never came to fruition – the Soviet Union rejected it in part due to concern that the United States and its allies had too much control in the United Nations, and Moscow was unconvinced that the United States really would give over its nuclear arsenal to an international organization. The mere effort, however, shows that interest in international agreements to reduce the risk of nuclear war quickly followed the invention of nuclear weapons.

The 1962 Cuban Missile Crisis shocked the United States and the Soviet Union into thinking more seriously about ways to ensure that the Cold War did not escalate. What followed was the first treaty involving nuclear weapons, the Limited Test Ban Treaty in 1963, which "prohibits nuclear weapons tests 'or any other nuclear explosion' in the atmosphere, in outer space, and under water" (US Department of State 1963). More arms control agreements followed the Limited Test Ban Treaty. For example, in 1972, as part of the Strategic Arms Limitation Treaty, the United States and Soviet Union agreed for the first time to restrict their deployment of nuclear missiles, slowing down the nuclear arms race.

The United States and the Soviet Union/Russia have signed several treaties in the subsequent decades designed to restrict the scope of their arsenals, including:

- The Strategic Arms Reduction Treaty (START, 1991): Russia and the United States agreed to reduce substantially their strategic nuclear arsenals. It followed the reduction in US–Soviet tension in the late 1980s.
- The Intermediate Nuclear Forces Treaty (INF, 1987): This treaty required the United States and the Soviet Union to eliminate all missiles with ranges of 500–5500 kilometers, with the goal of reducing nuclear tension in Europe. Russia and the United States withdrew from the treaty in 2019.
- New START Treaty (2010): The original START agreement expired in 2009, which led to renewed negotiations during the Obama administration and the completion of an extension, reducing the total size of the US and Soviet arsenals even further. However, in February 2023 Russia announced that it was suspending its participation in this treaty.

The world came together multilaterally to complete the Nuclear Non-Proliferation Treaty (NPT), already referenced above, in 1968. The NPT legitimizes the nuclear arsenals of five countries: China, France, Great Britain, the Soviet Union/Russia, and the United States, and prohibits other signatories from acquiring nuclear weapons. Note that this also means that countries that have subsequently acquired nuclear weapons are not in compliance with the NPT. In return for legalizing the arsenals of the existing nuclear weapons states, non–nuclear states received two key concessions. Article IV of the NPT commits the nuclear weapons states to sharing peaceful nuclear technology, such as the ability to use nuclear fuel for power plants, with NPT signatories in good standing. In Article VI of the NPT, the five nuclear weapons states agreed to gradually pursue a world without nuclear weapons, e.g., to commit to eventually eliminating their nuclear arsenals. A key element of the NPT was providing a legal instrument to reassure the Soviet Union that West Germany would not attempt to acquire nuclear weapons.

The NPT has been the cornerstone of what is now called the nuclear nonproliferation regime, a cluster of efforts taken by many countries to reduce the risks of nuclear war. Other critical parts of the regime include:

- The Nuclear Suppliers Group (NSG, 1975): This is an agreement (rather than a treaty) between forty-eight states to not export materials that could help a country build nuclear weapons.
- The Missile Technology Control Regime (MTCR, 1987): The MTCR is an agreement among thirty-five countries to restrict the export of missiles and missile production facilities that could help a country develop long-range missiles that could deliver weapons of mass destruction. Long-range missiles are defined as those that can travel at least 300 kilometers and carry a payload of at least 500 kilograms.
- The Seabed Treaty (1971): The Seabed Treaty prohibits countries from placing nuclear weapons or other weapons of mass destruction on the ocean floor.
- The Comprehensive Test Ban Treaty (CTBT, 1996): Extending the scope of the Limited Test Ban Treaty of 1963, the CTBT prohibits all nuclear weapons tests. While the United States was one of the leading states in the CTBT negotiations and was an early signatory of the CTBT, the United States Senate has not ratified the CTBT. The treaty will not come into force until the United States and a few other key states have ratified it.

Some believe that the catastrophic consequences of nuclear use, both the destructive force of the blast and the subsequent radiation, have created a norm against using nuclear weapons, holding that the actual use of nuclear weapons is morally unacceptable. This taboo against nuclear weapons, it is argued, is the real reason why nuclear weapons have not been used since 1945 (Tannenwald 2007). But others believe this norm is not yet strong enough to reduce nuclear danger. To strengthen the norm, a number of nonnuclear states negotiated and adopted the Treaty on Prohibition of Nuclear Weapons (TPNW). The TPNW bans all signatories from developing, testing, producing, acquiring, possessing, stockpiling, using, or threatening to use nuclear weapons. The treaty was opened for signature in September 2017, and entered into force in January 2021. No countries with nuclear weapons, or that are protected by an extended deterrence umbrella by a nuclear-armed state, have signed the treaty. TPNW advocates argue that, as more countries sign, it will delegitimize nuclear weapons in the international community and eventually place more normative pressure on nuclear-armed states to eliminate their nuclear arsenals. However, skeptics believe the important role of nuclear weapons for deterrence explained above mean that the treaty will never build the normative momentum necessary to shift how powerful countries view nuclear weapons.

How Useful Is Arms Control?

One measure of the success of nuclear arms control is the difference between the world today and the world predicted by John F. Kennedy in 1963. Kennedy predicted that fifteen or twenty states could have nuclear weapons by 1975. As of this writing, nine countries have nuclear weapons. Another measure is the size of the nuclear arsenals of the two countries with the most nuclear weapons, the United States and Russia. From a peak of tens of thousands of strategic nuclear warheads each, both countries have agreed to reduce the number of deployed strategic nuclear weapons in their arsenals. As of September 2021, Russia declared it was deploying 1,561 strategic nuclear warheads, while the United States declared that it was deploying 1,393 strategic nuclear warheads (these numbers include weapons that are not deployed as well as those slated to be dismantled). Given those reductions, and the limited scope of proliferation compared to the world predicted by Kennedy, there is a prima facie case that arms control has at least somewhat succeeded.

These treaties are used in combination with various carrots and sticks to create the most comprehensive regime in human history designed to prevent the spread of a weapons system. A country seeking to acquire nuclear weapons but avoid international sanction could, of course, withdraw from the NPT (as North Korea did) or never sign (mimicking India, Israel, and Pakistan). Such legal maneuvering by a country might reduce one avenue for the international community imposing economic sanctions and other restrictions on a potential proliferator. The problem for that potential proliferator is that many other avenues for sanctions and coercive measures exist even outside of those mandated by international treaties and agreements. From multilateral, non-treaty measures, such as the SWIFT bank access restrictions imposed on Iran (described in a previous section), to unilateral economic sanctions, to multilateral economic sanctions imposed by the United Nations Security Council, the international community has made the acquisition of nuclear weapons both costly and difficult.

That said, there are some who argue that the success of nuclear arms control is exaggerated. Countries generally make decisions based on their national security interests, and it is not surprising that the countries most likely to seek nuclear weapons have been those that felt most threatened – and that believed nuclear weapons were absolutely necessary for their security. Some say it is also inappropriate to give too much credit to arms control for stopping proliferation, as the global proliferation track record might look much worse but for two other factors.

First, the extension of extended deterrence guarantees by the United States to NATO allies, Japan, South Korea, and Taiwan undoubtedly reduced the incentive for those countries to acquire nuclear weapons. Second, some potential proliferators such as Iraq and Libya have fallen short for reasons that had as much to do with their own domestic bureaucratic struggles as with costs imposed by the international community. Thus, a critic might argue that, despite the time and money spent on nuclear arms control, it is traditional foreign policy and domestic politics that have made the biggest difference in preventing widespread nuclear proliferation.

CASE STUDY

North Korea

Issues surrounding nuclear weapons touch on a large set of topics in international relations. This case study focuses on a topic of great importance for the world today – North Korea's nuclear weapons program. Applying this chapter's points to the case of North Korea helps explain why North Korea has pursued nuclear weapons, why it has acquired them, and why it would be so hard to convince North Korea to give up its nuclear weapons through a diplomatic bargain.

Background

North Korea's nuclear weapons program dates back to the first Korean War. Perhaps in reaction to American threats to use nuclear weapons during the war, in December 1952 North Korea created an Atomic Energy Research Institute, established a degree of cooperation with the Soviet Union concerning atomic energy, and began investing in nuclear energy. In 1959, the Soviet Union agreed to assist North Korea in constructing a nuclear power plant at Yongbyon. (For a good timeline of North Korea's nuclear activities, see the Nuclear Threat Initiative website on North Korea: www.nti.org/learn/countries/north-korea/nuclear,) After decades of research, pursued intensely at some points, North Korea's nuclear activities came to the attention of the international community. North Korea signed the NPT in 1985 as well as a joint declaration with South Korea in 1991 agreeing to denuclearize the Korean Peninsula (as part of a deal involving the withdrawal of US tactical nuclear weapons from US military bases in South Korea). Denuclearization in this context referred to the removal of all nuclear weapons, or the potential for nuclear weapons, from the peninsula.

Throughout the early 1990s, a back-and-forth with the international community ensued whereby North Korea began denying access to Yongbyon and other facilities to international inspectors, which led to growing suspicion that North Korea was producing weapons-grade plutonium at Yongbyon. As fear of North Korea acquiring nuclear weapons grew, the United States considered, but rejected, a preemptive military strike on North Korea's nuclear facilities. The continuing crisis led to negotiations and then a deal between the international community and North Korea. The deal was called the Agreed Framework and it was signed on October 21, 1994. North Korea agreed to suspend activities at Yongbyon and allow international inspectors back into the country in exchange for a commitment by the United States and an international consortium to build light water nuclear reactors in North Korea (which could not be used to produce weapons-grade plutonium or enriched uranium).

From the beginning, there were disputes about whether each side was upholding its end of the bargain. North Korea claimed that the United States was too slow to begin constructing the reactors and lifting economic sanctions that isolated North Korea. The

(cont.)

United States and its allies argued that North Korea was not being totally transparent with the international community about the nuclear materials it had already produced.

The Agreed Framework fell apart in 2002 amidst accusations from both sides. For the international community, the revelation that North Korea had an ongoing, secret uranium enrichment program provided clear evidence of North Korea's continuing interest in nuclear weapons. After the collapse of the Agreed Framework, as North Korea ramped up its nuclear development activities, it was only a matter of time before it acquired nuclear weapons.

From October 2006 through September 2021, North Korea tested nuclear weapons six times. Countries such as the United States often detect and measure the nuclear tests of other states by tracking seismic events that occur due to unnatural causes. North Korea is now believed to have several locations throughout its territory dedicated to the development and testing of nuclear weapons and the missiles that carry them (see Map 11.3)

Why North Korea Wants Nuclear Weapons

What does this historical account tell us about why North Korea wanted nuclear weapons in the first place, and how does that fit with our understanding of nuclear proliferation in general?

One reason North Korea wants nuclear weapons is its high level of threat perceptions. Rightly or wrongly, North Korea fears the prospect of attack from the United States and its allies, especially South Korea, meaning it wants nuclear weapons to provide invasion insurance or deter attacks such as airstrikes. Especially given the perception that North Korea's conventional military capabilities have declined relative to those of the United States and South Korea, nuclear weapons thus become more important for providing security for the Kim Jong-un regime. Consistent with the logic of Thomas Schelling discussed above, they provided bargaining leverage.

Another possible reason has to do with North Korea's greater strategic goals. While the conventional balance of power does not favor it at present, North Korea also has had longer-term goals of reunifying the Korean Peninsula under North Korean rule. North Korea might attempt to threaten the United States and its allies with nuclear weapons to try to keep them out of a future war with South Korea. The idea for North Korea is to decouple the United States from South Korea by putting the United States homeland at risk. Betting that the United States will not want to risk losing an American city to protect Seoul, North Korea could seek to use its nuclear capabilities, combined with long-range missiles, to generate more tension between the United States and South Korea and make South Korea more vulnerable to North Korean aggression. This threat was made very real in January 2018, when the US government reported an alert of an incoming North Korean missile attack onto Hawaii. If you were in Hawaii on that day, you would have received the very frightening warning message displayed in Figure 11.6. It was a false alarm.

(cont.)

Map 11.3. Nuclear weapons and missile testing sites are present across North Korean territory, demonstrating the government's commitment to these programs. (2018 data.) Jackson, *On the Brink: Trump, Kim, and the Threat of Nuclear War* (Cambridge University Press).

How did North Korea succeed in building nuclear weapons where so many other states have failed? After all, as described above, the international community takes extensive measures to try to stop countries from acquiring nuclear weapons. In the North Korean

(cont.)

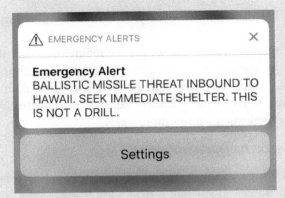

Figure 11.6. An actual cell phone warning of an incoming North Korean missile attack sent to all cell phones in Hawaii, January 13, 2018. Fortunately, it was a false alarm.
Apple Inc.

case, these measures included not just the Agreed Framework, but also many years of inspections, economic sanctions, and other cost-imposing measures. Why did those measures fail?

North Korea is an economically and politically isolated country, especially outside its links with China. Because North Korea is not well integrated into the global economy, it is less vulnerable to the "sticks" the international community uses to dissuade states from pursuing nuclear weapons. The threat of economic sanctions and a loss of access to international markets will generally only have limited effects on North Korea.

North Korea is also less interested in the "carrots" the international community uses to convince countries to give up their nuclear pursuits. North Korea's isolation, which keeps its population poor and relatively uninformed about the rest of the world, is part of how its leader, Kim Jong-un, stays in power. This makes them less vulnerable to economic pressure, particularly because North Korea's leaders have demonstrated a willingness to let hundreds of thousands of North Koreans starve to death rather than give in during a crisis. Greater exposure to the outside world could also generate threats to Kim Jong-un if trade and economic activity created new centers of wealth that then lobbied for political power. Thus, the benefits of trade and integration are simply less attractive to North Korea than they are to other countries.

These factors, however, explain why North Korea did not abandon its pursuit of nuclear weapons. They do not explain how North Korea was able to get over the hump and finally produce a nuclear weapon. One reason North Korea succeeded was that it had help. The A. Q. Khan network mentioned above facilitated a deal whereby Pakistan provided gas-graphite nuclear reactor technology to North Korea in exchange for North Korean missile technology. Another reason North Korea succeeded has to do with something people sometimes forget about nuclear weapons. If you strip away the international community's efforts to prevent proliferation, nuclear weapons technology is over seventy years old, long-range missile technology was first developed over fifty years ago, and knowledge of the core scientific and engineering concepts underlying nuclear

(cont.)

weapons and long-range missiles has disseminated widely. It is thus not that surprising that North Korea succeeded.

North Korea's leaders also maintained tight control over the regime in a way that let them monitor the development of the program. In contrast to other authoritarian regimes, such as Iraq and Libya, which were repressive but had trouble monitoring progress on their nuclear programs, North Korea's leaders were able to effectively track progress and strategically invest to make acquisition more likely.

Persuading North Korea to Give up Its Nuclear Arsenal

Are there scenarios where North Korea might be willing to give up nuclear weapons? The arguments presented in this chapter suggest that a deal with North Korea where it gives up its nuclear weapons is very unlikely. President Donald Trump's 2018 diplomatic efforts to persuade North Korea to scale back its nuclear weapons program produced no solid results. North Korea believes it has learned important lessons from history that mean it should not give up its nuclear weapons. Saddam Hussein of Iraq pursued, but never acquired, nuclear weapons. In 1981, an Israeli preventive military strike against Iraq's Osirak facility set back Iraq's nuclear program. In response, Iraq continued developing nuclear weapons in secret, pursuing paths such as electromagnetic isotope separation to enrich uranium (essentially pursuing a development path similar to the United States in the Manhattan Project). That program, too, was shut down following US-led Operation Desert Storm in 1991. Despite its continued interest in nuclear weapons, Iraq proved unable to move forward much after 1991, and the pursuit ended permanently when Saddam Hussein was deposed in the US-led invasion of Iraq in 2003.

Muammar Gaddafi of Libya voluntarily gave up his pursuit of nuclear weapons shortly after the invasion of Iraq. In 2010, as a civil war broke out in Libya during the Arab Spring, Gaddafi was deposed in part due to military attacks led by the United States and its allies. The lesson North Korea has learned from these cases is that giving up your nuclear weapons puts your country at risk. Thus, North Korea is unlikely to give up its nuclear weapons unless there is some way for the United States and the rest of the world to credibly promise North Korea that it would not be at risk of subsequent attack or invasion.

The discussion in this chapter of the way nuclear weapons provide invasion insurance because of the ability to hold an adversary's territory at risk of destruction also explains why North Korea is seeking to develop long-range missiles that could hit the United States. Since the United States, from North Korea's perspective, represents the greatest threat to North Korea's existence, North Korea needs to have the ability to generate costs for the United States.

To some extent, the many US citizens and 30,000 US troops living in South Korea represent potential targets that North Korea could already strike in case of a conflict. The

(cont.)

threat that North Korean conventional artillery and chemical weapons pose to US troops and citizens in South Korea is one reason the United States did not launch a preemptive strike against North Korea's nuclear facilities in 1993, and it is one reason most analysts believe the risk of war between the United States and North Korea remains extremely low.

But North Korea likely has increasingly viewed that artillery and chemical capability as insufficient to deter the United States and South Korea, because the American conventional military edge is growing. Thus, North Korea has sought not just nuclear weapons, but long-range missiles that allow them to potentially hit a city in the continental United States. The logic is that the cost of losing a city in the continental United States is so large that it would deter any US military action against North Korea.

The North Korea case also helps put the notion of mutually assured destruction in context. The United States government has consistently rejected the idea of allowing North Korea to acquire an ICBM capable of striking the United States, in part because legitimizing North Korea's nuclear missile arsenal would legitimize the continued existence of the North Korean regime. That being said, North Korea having a nuclear missile capable of hitting an American city would not mean the United States and North Korea have a mutually assured destruction relationship. The reason has to do with the asymmetry in the size of the nuclear arsenals possessed by the United States and North Korea, as well as the asymmetry in missile technology and other conventional military capabilities. North Korea's use of nuclear weapons against the United States would undoubtedly lead to US retaliation and the destruction of the Kim Jong-un regime. North Korea, even if it acquires the ability to launch an ICBM armed with a nuclear warhead against the United States, will lack the ability to completely destroy the United States government. That means the relationship cannot be characterized as mutually assured destruction in the way the relationship between the United States and the Soviet Union was during the Cold War.

However, even if the relationship does not evolve into mutually assured destruction, greater North Korean nuclear and missile capabilities could still create a deterrence relationship between the United States and North Korea that North Korea would view as a positive. Even though the United States would have the ability to destroy North Korea if North Korea ever launched a missile at the United States, the United States might itself be deterred from attacking North Korea due to the risk that North Korea could retaliate and destroy even one US city.

Thus, debates about the implications of North Korea's nuclear and missile capabilities help illustrate not just concepts surrounding the drivers of nuclear proliferation, but concepts surrounding deterrence and the potential for conflict escalation between nuclear-armed states.

QUANTITATIVE STUDY

Does Nuclear Extended Deterrence Make Allies More Likely to Start Wars?

This study examines the way some states provide extended deterrence guarantees to allies in an attempt to protect them as well as to discourage them from acquiring nuclear weapons of their own.

Some worry that a downside to extended deterrence is that it might make the allies, those countries receiving protection from a nuclear-armed state, more likely to start conflicts. After all, if these countries know that a powerful state with nuclear weapons is protecting them, they could become more aggressive, knowing the protection granted to them by the nuclear-armed state can bail them out of any trouble.

Political scientists Rupal Mehta and Neil Narang investigated this question through quantitative analysis (Narang and Mehta 2019).

Research Question

Do nuclear umbrellas, or extended deterrence, create a moral hazard that makes war more likely?

Theory and Hypotheses

Alliances can make weaker states act more aggressively, figuring that their more powerful ally will save them from any negative consequences of their action. (This is a form of what economists sometimes call the "moral hazard problem".)

Hypothesis 1: Nonnuclear client states protected in an alliance by a nuclear weapon state are more likely than states that lack a nuclear patron to initiate a conventional militarized interstate dispute (MID).

Hypothesis 2: Nonnuclear client states protected in an alliance by a nuclear weapon state are more likely than states that lack a nuclear patron to escalate a conventional militarized interstate dispute (MID).

Data

The data set includes all pairs of countries in the international system from 1950 to 2000. Each unit of analysis is a dyad-year, such as France–Germany 1957.

Dependent Variable

The dependent variable focuses on militarized interstate disputes (MIDs). A MID is just what it sounds like, a clash between countries in which there is at least a risk of armed conflict, if not actual violence. It includes relatively minor incidents, like one country making empty threats against another, as well as full-blown wars, like World War II. Among all the dyad years in the data set, in some cases one side initiates a MID against another state. Hypothesis 1 predicts that a state is more likely to initiate a MID against the other state in the dyad if the first state enjoys a nuclear extended deterrence relationship. Hypothesis 2 states that nuclear-protected states are more likely to escalate MIDs, that is, they are more likely to get involved in MIDs that are more serious and violent. Fortunately, the MID data set the authors use categorizes the intensity of MIDs, enabling them to test Hypothesis 2.

Independent Variable

The main independent variable measures whether one of the countries in the dyad received an extended deterrence commitment from a nuclear-armed state in a given year. Alliance data come from the Alliance Treaty Obligations and Provisions data set (Leeds et al. 2002).

Control Variables

To account for other potential factors that might influence the probability that a militarized dispute happens or escalates, the authors include a number of control variables, including whether or not the two countries have a rivalry, the military balance of the two states in the rivalry, whether the dyad members are democracies, and whether the two members of the dyad are near each other.

Results

The quantitative analysis shows that the probability of MID initiation rises 2.5 percent if a dyad member has a nuclear-armed alliance partner. However, the results also show that this effect drops off once the authors consider the escalation of a militarized dispute. Specifically, countries with nuclear-armed allies are *not* more likely to initiate disputes that lead to war or even the reciprocated use of military force – meaning a conflict in which both sides use military force. The results also show that countries with nuclear-armed allies *are* more likely to initiate militarized disputes in which their adversaries back down, rather than reciprocate the dispute. The analysis confirms that these effects are statistically significant, increasing the confidence of the authors that alliances with nuclear-armed states may make disputes more likely and may make countries fear a state with a nuclear-armed ally more. However, these alliances do not make escalation or war more likely. In sum, the data provide support for Hypothesis 1, but not for Hypothesis 2.

Figure 11.7 is a vertical bar chart. The bars show the average probability of different categories of militarized disputes. The top of the bar represents the top of the 95 percent confidence interval, and the bottom of the bar represents the bottom of the 95 percent confidence interval. So the total size of the bar encompasses the likely effect. Those bars that are either completely above or completely below zero are statistically significant. The five categories in the figure refer to all militarized disputes (blue, on the left), and then different levels of militarized disputes.

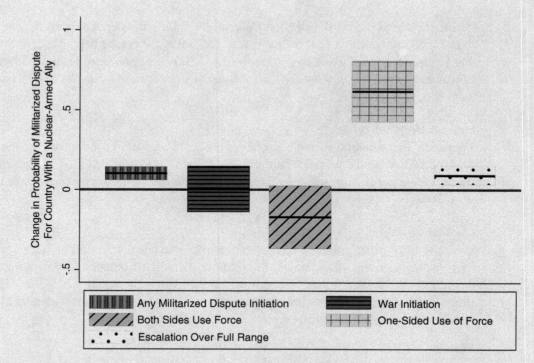

Figure 11.7. Probability of a militarized dispute for countries with a nuclear-armed ally.
© Mehta and Narang 2017.

Conclusion

The study demonstrates that fear that alliances with nuclear-armed states might encourage aggression should not be overstated. Having a nuclear-armed ally makes a country more likely to initiate MIDs, but not more likely to initiate MIDs that escalate to war.

SUMMARY

The topic of nuclear weapons is a critical one for international relations and foreign policy. This chapter makes a number of points, including:

- Nuclear weapons are considered unique in the international security environment due to their destructive power in comparison with other weapons.
- Nuclear weapons are expensive and time-consuming to build, but because even older types of nuclear weapons are still important, investments in them are cumulative.
- Countries are more likely to want to build nuclear weapons when they are in a threatening international security environment, and especially when they have a rival that has nuclear weapons.
- Countries with nuclear weapons attempt to develop second strike capabilities, so they can strike back even if another nuclear state launches a first strike against them. Second strike capabilities help reduce tensions and prevent crisis escalation.

- Nuclear weapons help protect nuclear states from attack because of the ability of a nuclear-armed state to destroy anyone who attacks. The utility of nuclear weapons for coercing other states is more contested.
- Most scholars and policymakers believe nuclear proliferation is dangerous because the more countries have nuclear weapons, the greater the chance that nuclear weapons will be used. Some, however, believe that nuclear weapons enhance international stability by discouraging attacks against nuclear-armed states.
- The international community has developed an extensive set of carrots and sticks to prevent nuclear proliferation, including arms control agreements such as the NPT, the threat of economic sanctions, and extended deterrence guarantees.

KEY TERMS

Nuclear weapons
First strike capability
First strike instability
Second strike capability
Mutually assured destruction
Nuclear triad
Strategic nuclear weapons
Tactical nuclear weapons

Nuclear deterrence
Extended deterrence
Stability–instability paradox
Nuclear compellence
Brinkmanship
Nuclear proliferation
Arms control

REVIEW QUESTIONS

1. Are nuclear weapons unique in comparison with other weapons? If so, what makes them unique?
2. What is the difference between deterrence and compellence?
3. What factors make countries more likely to build nuclear weapons?
4. What are extended deterrence guarantees and why do nuclear-armed states sometimes offer them to nonnuclear states?
5. How important are formal arms control agreements, such as treaties, in explaining why more countries have not acquired nuclear weapons?
6. What are first strike capabilities? What is first strike instability? What are second strike capabilities and why do nuclear-armed states attempt to acquire them?
7. How useful are nuclear weapons for defensive purposes? How do nuclear weapons provide "invasion insurance," and what is the stability–instability paradox?
8. Are nuclear weapons useful for coercion and compellence?
9. What reasons are there for thinking that further nuclear proliferation would increase international instability?

DISCUSSION QUESTIONS

1. Do you think the international community should encourage the spread of nuclear weapons to countries involved in dangerous rivalries, like Taiwan, South Korea, Iran, and Saudi Arabia?

2. How worried do you think the international community should be about North Korea's nuclear weapons program?
3. Do you think the world would have been a safer and more secure place after 1945 if nuclear weapons had never been invented?

ADDITIONAL READING

Berkemeier, M. and M. Fuhrmann (2017). Nuclear weapons and foreign policy. In W. R. Thompson (ed.-in-chief). *Oxford Research Encyclopedia of Politics*. Oxford: Oxford University Press, 1–25.

Braut-Hegghammer, M. (2016). *Unclear Physics: Why Iraq and Libya Failed to Build Nuclear Weapons*. Ithaca, NY: Cornell University Press.

Eden, L. (2004). *Whole World on Fire: Organizations, Knowledge, and Nuclear Weapons Devastation*. Ithaca, NY: Cornell University Press.

REFERENCES

Aksenov, P. (2013, September 26). Stanislav Petrov: The man who may have saved the world. www.bbc.com/news/world-europe-24280831

Brodie, B. (1965). *Strategy in the Missile Age*. Princeton: Princeton University Press.

Dunn, F. S. (1946). The common problem. In B. Brodie (ed.). *The Absolute Weapon: Atomic Power and World Order*. New York: Harcourt Brace, 5–17.

Gavin, F. J. (2012). *Nuclear Statecraft: History and Strategy in America's Atomic Age*. Ithaca, NY: Cornell University Press.

Jervis, R. (1989). *The Meaning of the Nuclear Revolution*. Ithaca, NY: Cornell University Press.

Kroenig, M. (2020). *The Logic of American Nuclear Strategy: Why Strategic Superiority Matters*. New York: Oxford University Press.

Leeds, B., Ritter, J., Mitchell, S., and Long, A. (2002). Alliance treaty obligations and provisions, 1815–1944. *International Interactions* **28**(3), 237–260.

Lieber, K. A., and Press, D. G. (2017). The new era of counterforce: Technological change and the future of nuclear deterrence. *International Security* **41**(4), 9–49.

Mueller, J. (1989). *Retreat from Doomsday: The Obsolescence of Major War*. New York: Basic Books.

Narang, N. and Mehta, R. N. (2019). The unforeseen consequences of extended deterrence: Moral hazard in a nuclear client state. *Journal of Conflict Resolution* **63**(1), 218–250.

Rhodes, R. (1986). *The Making of the Atomic Bomb*. New York: Simon & Schuster.

Sagan, S. D. (1996/1997). Why do states build nuclear weapons? Three models in search of a bomb. *International Security* **21**(3), 54–86.

Sagan, S. D. and K. N. Waltz. (2012). *The Spread of Nuclear Weapons: An Enduring Debate*, 3rd edn. New York: W. W. Norton.

Schelling, T. C. (1960). *The Strategy of Conflict*. Cambridge, MA: Harvard University Press.

Sechser, T. S. and Fuhrmann, M. (2017). *Nuclear Weapons and Coercive Diplomacy*. Cambridge: Cambridge University Press.

Tannenwald, N. (2007). *The Nuclear Taboo: The United States and the Non-use of Nuclear Weapons since 1945*. New York: Cambridge University Press.

US Department of State (1963). Treaty banning nuclear weapon tests in the atmosphere, in outer space and under water. https://2009-2017.state.gov/t/avc/trty/199116.htm

12   Drone Warfare

SARAH E. KREPS

Introduction

In the last two decades, unmanned aerial vehicles, or drones, have gone from a battlefield sideshow to a central feature of war. Although a number of countries have used drones in combat (for drone use in the 2022 Ukraine War, see online Ukraine module), and many others are trying to catch up, the United States' reliance on drones since the 9/11 terrorist attacks has been the most visible example of both the prospects and perils of drones.

American decisionmakers have come to rely on drone strikes for different reasons. Drone strikes have yielded a number of tactical successes, killing suspected militants who might otherwise aim to kill Americans or their allies' citizens or troops. The operational advantages – persistent surveillance over a target in ways that help distinguish between combatants and civilians – can minimize civilian casualties, even if not eliminating them altogether. Drones mean little risk to service personnel. Against the backdrop of these advantages, it is not surprising that the American public has been enamored with drone strikes, Congress has been relatively silent, and presidents of both parties have made this a signature feature of their foreign policies. Since 9/11, the United States has conducted hundreds of counterterrorism strikes with drones, including in Pakistan, Yemen, Somalia, and Niger.

Reliance on drones has risks. Even if drone strikes kill some suspected militants, they can be used as a propaganda tool to recruit new terrorists, thereby undermining the very purpose they are intended to serve. Moreover, one of the appeals of drones is that American troops are not killed, but the flip side is that avoiding American casualties has made American decisionmakers more willing to use force, in more countries.

Other countries have observed the relative ease with which countries with drones, notably the United States, use military force, and have raced to acquire the technology. Even nonstate actors have recognized the value of these weapons and have developed rudimentary drones that they can use on the battlefield.

This chapter walks through how we got here by asking and answering several core questions. What are drones? How are they being used, and how might they be used? Do drone strikes work? Are drone strikes legal and/or ethical? Are drone strikes popular? Has the use of drone strikes been undemocratic, in the sense of expanding executive power?

What Are Drones?

Talking about the history of drones requires thinking first about what we mean by a drone. The term is confusing in part because several other names have been used to refer to the same thing: unmanned aerial vehicle, remotely piloted aircraft, unmanned aerial system, and uninhabited system, among others. What all of these names refer to is a flying platform that does not have a pilot on board. But lots of platforms fly and do not have a pilot on board, such as model airplanes, balloons, rockets, and cruise missiles. Generally, these fall outside the traditional understanding of drones, which is that they are power-driven, two-way, and not model aircraft.

The modern drone has a lineage that dates back to the nineteenth century. In 1849, Austria attacked Venice with 200 explosive-laden unmanned aerial balloons. The Austrians maneuvered the balloons over Venice based on the wind direction, and then detonated the explosives with a long copper wire and battery apparatus. Unfortunately for the Austrians, some of the balloons blew back over Austrian lines, but the concept of remote maneuvering of aircraft, with the intention of doing damage to the adversary and minimizing damage to yourself, was made clear.

The aerial revolution continued with the advent of the airplane in the early twentieth century: the Zeppelin blimp was able to engage in scouting and tactical bombing runs in World War I, while the Kettering Bug, an early experimental, unmanned vehicle, was a precursor of the modern cruise missile. This "flying bomb" deployed the same dolly-and-track system used for the Kitty Hawk's flight in 1903, and used a gyroscope for guidance. After reaching its target, the Kettering Bug would detonate its explosives through impact, making it a rudimentary cruise missile.

Between the wars, the British developed the Queen Bee, which explains the etymology of the term "drone," a remote-controlled aircraft used for training anti-aircraft crews. These target drones became the basis for later aircraft such as the US-made Skeeter.

During World War II, the Germans developed the V-1 rocket, an unmanned missile system. The United States and its allies countered with drones that could destroy launch sites, flying into the ramps used to launch the rockets, though such drones took off with two-person crews that would bail out after setting the course for the target. In the postwar period, particularly during the Vietnam War, the United States exploited sensor technology to create the Lightning Bug, an unmanned reconnaissance aircraft.

The Lightning Bug was a forerunner to the better-known **Predator** (also known as the MQ-1), which had its debut in the Balkan Wars in the 1990s as an unmanned reconnaissance aircraft (see Figure 12.1).

It was only after the 9/11 terrorist attacks that the United States made the decision to arm the Predator, which brought the modern drone its fame. The United States used a Predator for the first armed drone strike in Afghanistan in October 2001. For about fifteen years the United States relied heavily on the Predator, which carried two missiles. In 2017, it retired the Predator, which had been increasingly replaced by the **Reaper** (MQ-9). The Reaper, shown in Figure 12.2, doubled the missile count of the Predator, flew faster, and therefore was a more

Figure 12.1. MQ-1 Predator drone, flying a combat mission over Afghanistan, 2008. The drone is armed with Hellfire missiles which can strike ground targets. Though the drone is shaped like an airplane, note that there is no cockpit for a human crew, as the drone pilot flies the drone from the ground, in an airbase.
Lt. Col. Leslie Pratt, Public domain, via Wikimedia Commons.

Figure 12.2. MQ-9 Reaper drone. The Reaper is a more capable aircraft than the Predator, able to fly about three times faster, and able to carry about fifteen times more bombs and missiles, in weight.
United States Department of Defense.

effective counterterrorism tool. Terrorism is defined by Title 22 of the US Code as "premeditated, politically motivated violence perpetrated against noncombatant targets by subnational groups or clandestine agents" (quoted in Legal Information Institute n.d.; see chapter 8). A counterterrorism strike then entails using drones to target individuals suspected of engaging in these acts of violence.

The first use of a drone for counterterrorism outside an area of active hostilities took place in Yemen in November 2002 when the United States used a Predator to strike the individuals suspected of conducting the 2000 bombing attack on the US Navy destroyer USS *Cole*, an attack that killed seventeen Navy personnel and injured thirty-nine others. That drone strike notwithstanding, in the early 2000s the use of drones for counterterrorism remained limited. During the Bush administration, the United States conducted about fifty strikes against suspected terrorists in Pakistan, Somalia, and Yemen. The Obama administration conducted that many in its first year, and steadily increased the number of drone strikes during its eight

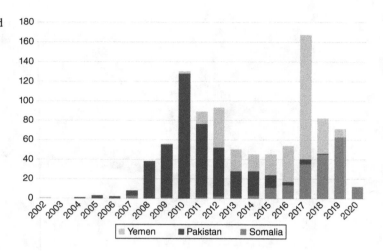

Figure 12.3. Possible and confirmed drone strikes per country per year. The y axis is the count of possible and confirmed drone strikes.
Bureau of Investigative Journalism.

years in power. By the middle of his administration, President Obama acknowledged, "The very precision of drone strikes, and the necessary secrecy involved in such actions can end up shielding our government from the public scrutiny that a troop deployment invites. It can also lead a president and his team to view drone strikes as a cure-all for terrorism" (Obama's speech on drone policy 2013).

President Trump continued the policy of drone strikes, allegedly loosening some of the restrictions stipulating that there be "near certainty" that civilians would not be injured or killed (Savage 2021). He also presided over one of the most high-profile strikes since the killing of Anwar al-Awlaki, an American citizen killed in Yemen in September 2011 (Shane 2015). In January 2020, the United States used a drone to target Qassem Soleimani, the leader of the Iranian Quds Force, a clandestine unit of the Iranian Revolutionary Guard Corps, in Baghdad. Advocates of the strike argued that Soleimani was actively developing plans to target Americans in the region. Opponents critiqued the strike as an example in which drone strikes were potentially going down a slippery slope of targeting specific individuals associated with the government or military of an adversary state (U.S. drone strike in Iraq kills Iranian military leader Qasem Soleimani 2020).

Figure 12.3 shows the evolution of counterterrorism drone strikes from 2002, from the first incident to 2017. While the use of drones started out slowly, with just one strike in 2002 in Yemen, it increased quickly beginning in 2008, spiking in Pakistan in 2010. Drone strikes in Pakistan have tapered off considerably, whereas their use in Yemen has increased. Unfortunately, the war in Yemen has made it difficult to parse whether the strikes are specifically drone strikes, since they are accounted for generically as "airstrikes," but it is clear that drone activity in Yemen picked up as it was declining in Pakistan.

Why Turn to Drones?

Several factors make drones attractive for battlefield use. From an operational standpoint, they have at least two related advantages. One is that drone missions do not face the limitations of humans who need to sleep and eat. To be sure, humans operate the drone, but they can do so from 8,000 miles away in an air-conditioned trailer in Nevada. They do the job as shift work, trading off with colleagues while the aircraft remains in the air, refueling when necessary. Contrast this experience with the B-2 Stealth bomber pilots who flew bombing missions in the Balkan wars of the 1990s. The United States decided to keep the aircraft based in Missouri so it would not have to relocate maintenance facilities abroad or compromise the security of the aircraft. In so doing, the pilots conducted missions of unprecedented duration, thirty-hour flights from the United States to the Balkans and back. The consequence was that pilots were strained by the long flight, which consumed the lion's share of the thirty hours, and then were limited in terms of the operation once they did reach the target area, since their safety was increasingly compromised by the long duration of the mission. More to the point, it was precisely these uncharacteristically long missions that made them so exceptional. Typical crew rest requirements stipulate a twelve-hour maximum flight duty period for pilots, with at least ten continuous hours of restful activities (and eight hours of uninterrupted sleep) in the twelve hours prior to the mission. Meeting these restrictions of crew rest creates challenges and inconveniences that are not posed by the use of drones.

Second, beyond better circumventing the crew rest restrictions, drones themselves have longer "legs" than many aircraft. The F-16 fighter jet that can strike targets can only fly about four hours before refueling. By comparison, the Predator and Reaper can fly almost thirty hours without refueling, which gives them an ability to "loiter" (fly in circles over a battlefield) for long periods to better collect intelligence, find targets, and help ensure that the target is a combatant instead of a civilian. Drone operators do clock out after twelve hours, but they can hand over the controls to the next shift, leaving the aircraft in the air to continue its mission.

Third, drones allow leaders to use military force in foreign countries in ways that would be taboo with aircraft with pilots on board or deployed troops. Although the Pakistani government has criticized American drone strikes, others have said that the strikes almost necessarily have the tacit approval of the Pakistani government. No such plausible deniability would be possible with American boots on the ground or American pilots in the cockpit.

Fourth, and perhaps most importantly, drones offer enormous domestic political advantages. One of the lessons brought home by the Vietnam War was that casualties erode public support for war, and that without public support, maintaining the war effort is far more difficult. If the public is less supportive of war when there are casualties, then why not find a way to reduce the casualties and eliminate the constraints that public opinion imposes on the use of force? That is exactly what drones do. They can provide an enormous political advantage by offering the ability to use force without risking casualties and a way to claim that the country is not at war. The alternative strategies, whether airstrikes launched from piloted craft or the deployment of ground forces, all involve some degree of risk, exposure, and attention compared to drones. Manned airplanes can be shot down, soldiers can be killed. Extended occupations and counterinsurgencies eventually generate wariness. The decision to withdraw from Afghanistan in 2021 after two decades of conflict highlights the political challenges of sustained troop commitments and heightens the political appeal of drone strikes, which shield the government from public scrutiny because they do not involve casualties for the country that uses them.

The balance of political risk became clear during the several instances in which presidents used special forces to kill militants. Some of those troops were killed in action, leading to negative media attention and follow-up drone strikes. In the first week of his administration, President Trump approved a commando strike in Yemen, which resulted in the death of one of the soldiers who conducted the raid and proved the value of airstrikes as the less costly alternative. The raid generated enormous negative media attention. A publicized trip by the president to Dover Air Base to be present when the body returned home became a concrete reminder of the human costs of war. No other commando raids appear to have been attempted the rest of that year. On the other hand, during 2017, there were more than 100 airstrikes in Yemen, evidence of these being seen as the less costly alternative.

Consistent with this logic, drones have been very popular among the public, which sees them as an effective counterterrorism tool that does not put American service personnel at risk. Polls taken between 2011 and 2015 suggest that the policy has generated high levels of support. Support in these polls has never dropped below a majority of Americans and has generally hovered around 65 percent, so at first glance Americans seem enamored with the approach. However, question after question asks whether Americans support drone strikes "to target suspected terrorists," taking as a given that the strikes are legal, ethical, or indeed manage to target terrorists. One study found that when the questions were formulated differently, and raised the issue of whether drone strikes were hitting the right targets in ways that were legal, support for strikes dropped considerably, in some cases by more than 25 percent. The support for drone strikes is dependent on a lack of public information about the specifics of the program and tends to assume that the strikes are legal and an effective approach for counterterrorism. Part of that information gap is due to drones being a form of **hybrid warfare**: part covert, irregular warfare and part overt, conventional. Since the planning and execution of the operation takes place in the shadows, the public has little information about the program, certainly not on a consistent basis. Levels of public support are not dislodged by arguments opposed to the program and remain relatively high. But these are key assumptions about drone strikes to be explored, not ignored. Let's take a closer look.

Do Drone Strikes Work?

Especially since the 9/11 terrorist attacks, scholars and policymakers have tried to figure out how to prevent terrorist groups from planning and carrying out attacks and have generally outlined three main ways to do that. One is through intelligence and law enforcement strategies. These approaches involve anticipating potential terrorist attacks by listening to exchanges of potential terrorists, piecing together information about the time and location of a specific terrorist attack, and then either preventing the attack or capturing the suspected terrorists. These were generally the approaches that were used prior to the 9/11 attacks, but were quickly seen as insufficient for incapacitating or preventing terrorist attacks.

Another possible strategy involves winning over the hostile population through a counter-insurgency, "hearts and minds" approach. The 2006 British counterterrorism strategy high-lighted the importance of "engaging in the battle of ideas – challenging the ideologies that extremists believe can justify the use of violence, primarily by helping Muslims who wish to dispute these ideas to do so" (Countering international terrorism: the United Kingdom's strategy 2006). This approach is based on the assumption that the populace can be the basis of support for a friendly partner or, conversely, a pool of opposition. Which direction these individuals of interest are pushed in depends on whether they feel alienated or befriended. The idea of winning hearts and minds had its roots in early counterinsurgency wars in Malaya and Vietnam, when winning over the local populations seemed to be easier if outside forces treated locals with respect rather than antagonism.

Presidents since 9/11, however, have assumed that the United States is at war, must win, and must use all tools available to prevent another terrorist attack. Intelligence and hearts and minds strategies might be enablers for that war footing, but are not sufficient in and of themselves, or at least are longer-term solutions. As former President Barack Obama summarized in a 2015 speech, "Countering violent extremism is not simply a military effort. Ideologies are not defeated with guns; they're defeated by better ideas – a more attractive and more compelling vision ... this larger battle for hearts and minds is going to be a generational struggle" (Obama 2015).

As part of its war footing, the US government has embraced a policy of **decapitation**, or removing the leader of a terrorist organization either through capture or, in its more extreme form, through the practice of "targeted killing" where the individual is eliminated through force. History provides examples of decapitation by both capture and killing. During the Cold War, Germany used intelligence to capture members of the Baader–Meinhof gang, a leftist terrorist organization. The Turkish National Intelligence Agency, supported by the American Central Intelligence Agency (CIA), arrested a member of a Kurdish militant group in 1999, removing that group's influential head. Israel has used the lethal-force version of decapitation for targeting Palestinian militants, Russia has killed Chechen leaders pushing secession, and Pakistan has used the approach to target militants in its tribal regions.

Proponents of decapitation, especially targeted killing, argue that extremist groups take their inspiration, organization, and mobilization from the leader, so removing the leader will render the organization powerless. At the least, without leadership the group will atrophy and be incapacitated from its original function of planning and carrying out terrorist attacks. One of the reasons decapitation can work is that it saps terrorist organizations of their energy and effectiveness. It does so by making it difficult for leaders to function in a normal fashion. As soon as leaders communicate with their associates, they will become targets. To avoid being targeted, they need to stay underground and low-profile, which makes them ineffective as terrorist leaders.

Detractors argue that the practice is counterproductive, in part because of potential **"martyrdom effects."** The logic is as follows. When a leader is killed by a drone strike, he or she becomes a martyr and, in turn, a recruiting tool to bring individuals off the sidelines to take up arms. The martyrdom effect is arguably most intense as more civilians, or at least individuals who could be cast as innocent, are killed. The seeming recklessness and impunity of the strikes, not to mention the need for drone bases abroad that might be cast as an occupation and at least create foreign policy issues in terms of maintaining good relations in the countries where drone bases are maintained, then magnifies the recruitment dynamic, creating more terrorists sympathetic to their cause. Meanwhile, the organization simply reconstitutes itself and can continue organizing and carrying out terrorist attacks. Alternatively, the removal of a leader may weaken that organization but spawn or mobilize a splinter organization that, drawing on the martyrdom of the former leader, emerges even stronger and more dangerous. After the removal of bin Laden, for example, al-Qaeda as an organization was less vital in its original form but the vacuum allowed another organization, the Islamic State (IS), to gain prominence and thrive, and IS proved to be as lethal in its techniques as al-Qaeda, or more so. For these reasons, former American Commander in Afghanistan Stanley McChrystal concluded that the United States cannot "kill its way out" of struggles against terrorists (Thrall and Goepner 2017).

Until the advent of drones, countries that carried out targeted killings typically conducted them with manned aircraft. Israel, for example, had not infrequently used fighter planes to target senior Hamas leaders in their homes. The United States, however, had treaded more lightly when it came to targeted killing until drones came onto the scene. In place since 1981, Executive Order 12333 prohibits the assassination of foreign leaders. Certainly, the United States had to finagle its way around the order when it attacked the Libyan leader's residence in 1986, arguing that it was degrading Libya's military capabilities rather than targeting the leader himself. In most cases, the ban appeared to impose meaningful constraints, such as in 1989 when the United States restricted its involvement in a Panamanian coup out of respect for the ban. In 1998, when the United States targeted Saddam Hussein's residence, it again claimed that it was not targeting the leader but sending a signal. The United States had several plots to kill bin Laden before 9/11, and in 1998 targeted affiliates of bin Laden's network in Afghanistan, but had stopped short of targeting bin Laden, when it appeared to have a chance in 2000, because of concerns about civilian casualties and discord within the Clinton administration about the legal basis for targeting. After 9/11 and with the ability to use drones, the United States no longer had to put up such pretenses. The United States has shrouded the policy in secrecy, while also leaning on expressions of self-defense, almost fully rendering the ban on assassination a thing of the past.

Whether the decision to embrace targeted killings through drones was wise remains a subject of controversy. In many respects, the debate about drone strikes is an extension of the debate about targeted killings. For drone strike advocates, drones have offered an approach to counterterrorism that is well suited to keeping Americans safe. President Obama asserted that the United States uses drone strikes because we live "in a dangerous world with terrorists who would gladly blow up a school bus full of American kids if they could" (quoted in Coates 2016). The director of the CIA during the Bush administration, Michael Hayden (2016), defended the Obama policy, saying "to keep America safe, embrace drone warfare."

As with the approach of targeted killing, drone strikes rely on a decapitation theory that goes as follows: If strikes eliminate the head of the militant organization, the head of a branch of the organization, and/or other militants around a leader, they will degrade the effectiveness of the organization. For example, in 2017, the United States used a Reaper drone to kill the Haqqani network commander, Abu Bakar, at the Pakistan–Afghanistan border. In addition to the leader, the strike killed about twenty other suspected extremists. Using this approach, the United States has killed a number of high profile militants. In its report of drone strike data, the

Obama Administration reported that drone strikes had killed about 2,500 militants in Pakistan, Somalia, and Yemen and about 100 civilians.

Similar to targeted killings, drone strikes can also have a secondary effect of disrupting militants' communication and training. As long as they know drone strikes are a possibility, militants seek to avoid detection by shunning electronic devices and not meeting in large numbers. Captured jihadist tip sheets in Mali advise militants to be silent, avoid wireless contacts, and avoid meeting in groups. Doing so may help militants avoid being killed by a drone strike, but it also hampers their effectiveness, since militants cannot send orders or train when they are out of communication or not engaging in training.

Again tracking the decapitation debate, detractors of drone strikes have said that drones may hit many of the intended targets, many of whom may not be savory characters, but over time such strikes are ineffective for two main reasons. One is that even if an organization is decapitated, producing some short-term counterterrorism gains, any benefits are fleeting since the organization can simply replace the dead leader with a new one. Leaders are dispensable, or at least not irreplaceable. Even worse, the strikes may spawn scores of new replacements by acting as a recruitment tool. Al-Qaeda routinely broadcasts drone strike footage to support claims of indiscriminate targeting and bullying by a much more powerful country.

As evidence of the backlash that drone strikes can create, in which a strike radicalizes local individuals who then join the militant organization, consider the estimated number of al-Qaeda in the Arabian Peninsula (AQAP) members in Yemen in 2012 compared to 2010, before an escalation of American drone strikes. In an earlier estimate, the Obama administration had identified several hundred AQAP members. By 2012, the estimate had increased to a few thousand. In the meantime, the United States had increased the number of drone strikes in Yemen, lending plausibility to the positive feedback loop of drone strikes, in which the sense of martyrdom creates blowback and increases rather than decreases the militant ranks (Zenko 2013).

Thus, the debate revolves around short- versus long-term advantages, or tactical versus strategic gains. In the short term, drone strikes may be tactically effective because they are capable of striking and killing militants suspected of planning terrorist attacks. Critics of the policy acknowledge that removing these individuals might confer short-term, tactical gains. Over the long term, however, the leaders who were killed can simply be replaced, and the strikes may produce more terrorists, individuals brought off the sidelines by the antagonism toward drone strikes.

Are Drone Strikes Legal? Are They Ethical?

Beyond the question of whether drone strikes actually work is the question of whether they are legal or ethical. The answer, as with the question of effectiveness, is a matter of some debate. The Obama White House defended drone strikes as "legal, ethical, and wise" and an approach that would work "to mitigate ongoing actual threats, to stop plots, to prevent future attacks and, again, save American lives" (RFE 2013). The previous section addressed the question of their wisdom, or effectiveness. This section outlines the arguments about first the legality and then the ethics of drone strikes.

To start, there is no legal prohibition against drones themselves. Members of the international community have come together on other issues, such as chemical weapons, to assemble a treaty prohibiting the use of chemical weapons in war. No such treaty exists prohibiting drones. Thus drones, in the narrowest sense, cannot violate international law since there is no treaty prohibiting the use of drones or drone strikes.

Since drones are not themselves prohibited, the question turns to the circumstances under which they are permitted. The United Nations Charter was drafted in the 1940s largely in response to the types of invasions that had prompted World War II, by both Germany and Japan. It included a strong territorial norm embedded in Article 2 (4), which "prohibits the threat or use of force and calls on all Members to respect the sovereignty, territorial integrity and political independence of other States." States cannot simply use force wherever they want in the world. Limited circumstances can permit deviations from those norms. One is under Article 51, which permits the right of individual or collective self-defense. Another is through UN authorization, which typically takes place through Chapter VII of the UN Charter dealing with threats to peace and security. These types of questions about whether states are allowed to resort to force are termed *jus ad bellum* questions in international law.

A separate set of considerations involves how force is used once countries are involved in a war. This refers to **International Humanitarian Law (IHL),** which seeks to regulate the conduct of conflict, limiting the effects to those actively engaged in hostilities and protecting civilians who are not. International Humanitarian Law includes several core principles that affect how states use force, the two main ones being distinguishability and proportionality. Article 48 of the 1977 Additional Protocol I requires that "the parties to the conflict shall at all times distinguish between the civilian population and combatants," and target the combatants rather than civilians. Article 51 of those protocols, repeated in Article 57, states that "launching an attack which may be expected to cause incidental loss of civilian life, injury to civilians, damage to civilian objects, or a combination thereof, which would be excessive in relation to the concrete and direct military advantage anticipated, is prohibited." Taken together, these principles acknowledge that civilian casualties may occur in war, but that states need to ensure that the harm to civilians is outweighed by the military advantage of the strike.

The debate about the legality of drones has hewed closely to these two main aspects of international law. In terms of the recourse to force, critics argue that counterterrorism strikes violate these territorial integrity norms and are not permissible. The argument is most salient outside the context of active combat operations. For example, in cases such as Libya, the United States had the legal basis offered by a United Nations Security Council Resolution, which authorized the country to use military force. In such contexts, drones operate much like any other platform. The legal concerns generally arise when they are outside a setting of active combat operations. As the earlier figure shows, by 2017 the United States had conducted almost 600 counterterrorism strikes since 9/11, specifically in Pakistan, Somalia, and Yemen. Critics have argued that such strikes violate the territorial norms embedded in the UN Charter. Echoing this strand of concern, in early 2013, a coalition of nongovernmental organizations submitted a formal letter to President Obama asserting that drone strikes in Pakistan were a violation of sovereignty and therefore not legal under international law. Drone strikes have also raised questions about their treatment of civilians and therefore whether they are compatible with IHL. Drone strikes invoke both the principles of distinction and proportionality. Adjudicating whether a target is militant or civilian is difficult, of course, because none of the individuals targeted wear uniforms, and many individuals have roles as both civilian and combatant. Early counts, however, suggest that about 5–10 percent of total fatalities were civilians (Columbia Law School Human Rights Clinic 2012).

Amnesty International conducted an interview-based study and was unable to identify connections to the Taliban for many of the victims in Pakistan. Women and children were often the victims of the strikes. Moreover, evidence suggested that the United States engaged in "double tap" strikes, in which it conducts a strike, people move in to treat the wounded, and it then engages in a second strike to target those people around the scene of the first.

Moving to weigh in on this debate either in favor of or against the legality of drone strikes, the United Nations assigned two sets of **rapporteurs**, or individuals called upon to report on specific investigations, to offer their analyses. In 2014, after a year-long study of drone strikes, the United Nations Special Rapporteur on Human Rights documented thirty instances in which 300 civilians in total were killed by drone strikes, which was cast as a violation of proportionality. The report did not denounce drones in principle, but questioned whether they were being used in compliance with the principles of IHL, and urged greater transparency regarding the facts underlying the strikes.

Whether drones are ethical raises a related set of arguments as to the legal questions. The camp opposed to drone strikes on ethical grounds has questioned the premise that the use of force is necessary at all, and in particular whether having drones makes it seem that force is necessary when it is not. Arguments about the "**moral hazard**" of drones suggest that the risk-free nature of drones makes the use of force more likely. A moral hazard is a phenomenon in which lowering the risk actually creates incentives for people to engage in riskier behavior. For example, despite most skiers now wearing helmets, the incident of head injuries in skiing has not gone down and one suspected reason is that skiers have simply taken more risks, assuming they will be protected by their helmets. Applied to drone strikes, this means that since a country that has drones is shielded from risk – drone operators may experience Post Traumatic Stress Disorder (PTSD) from watching the video feed (Lowe and Gire 2012) but not casualties – it will be more likely to consider using force than if it has to conduct a strike with special forces on the ground, when some of those ground forces could potentially be injured or killed. In short, the moral hazard argument suggests that drones have lowered the threshold for using force.

Decisionmakers themselves have repeatedly made observations consistent with this moral hazard logic. Stanley McChrystal, the former commander of US and NATO forces in Afghanistan, observed that drones lower the political risk for using force, make them more palatable, and therefore make the use of force more likely. Former Secretary of Defense Robert Gates expressed a similar sentiment: that drones allow decisionmakers to mistakenly see war as "bloodless, painless, and odorless," thereby lowering barriers to conflict (quoted in Zenko and Kreps (2014, 10). President Obama offered a comparable viewpoint in an interview toward the end of his presidency: "The truth is that this technology really began to take off right at the beginning of my presidency ... I began to realize that the Pentagon and our national-security apparatus and the CIA were all getting too comfortable with the technology as a tool to fight terrorism." The realization, he observed, unleashed a "big process" that led to "higher standards about when they're used" (quoted in Friedersdorf 2016), an implicit nod to the moral hazard argument that the ease of drones had lowered the threshold for using force. Because the costs feel low, the barriers to their use are also low, increasing the prospects for conflict not just where the United States has used drones but in Nagorno-Karabakh, Syria, and Ukraine (Lyall 2020).

Proponents of drone strikes have argued that if the use of force is necessary, drones may be the most humane tool to use. Not only do they not risk the pilot's life, but they can be more accurate and therefore minimize casualties compared to alternatives. Drones can loiter over a target for long periods, identify terrorists more accurately, divert attacks should a noncombatant wander onto the scene, and, having collected this information systematically over the preceding weeks and months, employ precision weapons when operators are certain that they will avoid civilian casualties. They are, according to proponents, the least bad form of force to use for counterterrorism. Moreover, drones are preferable compared to ground forces that can be seen as unhelpful occupiers or can engage in less than heroic behaviors with local populations.

Drone Strikes and the Separation of Powers

The section above makes reference to international law but sidesteps the question of domestic law and checks and balances. Embedded in the institutions of many democracies, however, is the **separation of powers** in wartime. Different branches of government have different responsibilities that check the power and influence of the others. Perhaps the clearest manifestation of those principles is the *Federalist Papers*, published in 1788 by American statesmen. *Federalist No. 47* outlines the importance of different branches of government: "The accumulation of all powers, legislative, executive, and judiciary, in the same hands ... may justly be pronounced the very definition of tyranny" (Madison 1788). In other words, the president should not be the judge, jury, and executioner. With this prospect in mind, the United States Constitution aimed to distribute wartime powers. Article I grants Congress the power "to lay and collect taxes ... for the common defense," declare war," "raise and support armies," and "make rules for the government and regulation of the land and naval forces." Article II designates the president as the "Commander in Chief of the Army and Navy of the United States." While these powers are admittedly ambiguous, the basic gist was to ensure the separation of powers and to vest war-*authorizing* powers in the hands of the legislature with Article I but grant war-*making* authority to the president in Article II.

The common lament is that Congress cedes its wartime checks to the president, rather than using its constitutionally granted powers of appropriations, investigations, or floor debates to constrain the president and influence public opinion. Indeed, by some accounts the power of the presidency in international affairs has been increasing since World War II, or even before, with some historians citing Teddy Roosevelt's acquisition of the Panama Canal Zone in the early twentieth century, and others citing Lincoln's concentration of powers in the executive branch during the US Civil War. At various points in the last century, that power has seemed to be particularly out of balance, and the Vietnam War produced one of those moments, as well as concerns about an imperial presidency.

Responding to those concerns about unchecked powers, Congress proved able to reassert itself, but mainly as a reaction to public pressure arising from unease at the blood or treasure being expended. Growing losses in the Vietnam War, for example, put pressure on the legislative body to compel the president not to prolong the war. In 1973, the House voted to cut off funds for military operations in Laos and Cambodia, and President Nixon signed an appropriations bill that precluded the use of funds for combat activities in Southeast Asia. Congress also passed the 1973 War Powers Resolution, aiming to rein in what it saw as overweening executive power after the Vietnam War. Under the legislation, the president would be required to notify Congress within forty-eight hours of committing military forces, and was prohibited from maintaining forces for more than sixty days without congressional authorization.

Presidents, at least at the outset of contemporary wars, have frequently downplayed the importance of Congress in the context of wartime constitutional authority. In the run-up to the 1991 Persian Gulf War, for example, President George H. W. Bush repeatedly stated that he did not need congressional authorization, even though he did eventually obtain it. Congress ultimately followed the UN Security Council's lead in authorizing the use of force, but the episode reinforced emerging concerns that the War Powers Resolution, meant to restore the wartime separation of powers after Vietnam, had become a dead letter. As a further nail in the coffin of the War Powers Resolution, during the 2011 Libya war, President Obama asserted that he did not need congressional authorization because the United States did not put boots on the ground and was thereby not bound by the War Powers Resolution, despite the fact the War Powers Resolution makes no such specification about boots on the ground versus air power, but rather "hostilities" more generally.

Indeed, the use of air power, and especially unmanned air power like drones, has caused many of these longtime debates about checks and balances to resurface. One major change after 9/11 has further fueled the concentration of powers in the executive. On September 14, 2001, Congress approved the **Authorization for the Use of Military Force (AUMF),** which granted the president the power to use force against al-Qaeda "and its associated forces" responsible for conducting or supporting the 9/11 terrorist attacks. For President Bush, the group in question was al-Qaeda. As the counterterrorism war evolved, the question of who could fall under the associated forces designation became more complicated, however. Did the IS, which did not exist on 9/11, but was being targeted by drone strikes in Somalia, count as an associated force? One view said yes, because the group has splintered, and the AUMF should account for the splintering of the original group. Another says that the AUMF was too expansive to begin with, has outlived its original purpose, and should be rewritten more narrowly to constrain the executive. This view suggests that Congress has given up its constitutional responsibility and was obliged to reassert itself. On the specific question of drone strikes, critics of the "imperial presidency" viewed this campaign as a new front that should require new authorization, but also more transparency on the process and more oversight. Members of Congress, however, have had little incentive to act aggressively on the issue, in large part because drones do not provoke a backlash from their constituents. In part because members of the military do not die in war because of drones, members of Congress have few reasons to scrutinize and rein in their use.

Evidence suggests that Congress has been relatively inert when it comes to asserting itself on drone policy. Its most visible gesture of oversight was a filibuster by Senator Rand Paul, who spoke on the floor of the Senate in March 2013 to oppose the nomination of John Brennan, the chief architect of the drone policy, to be director of central intelligence. In that respect, public legislative debates about drones have generally followed a **"focusing events"** model of oversight, relying on particular episodes, scandals, or publicly visible incidents as catalysts for a hearing, in that case the nomination of a particular individual who required Senate confirmation. In 2020, following the Trump White House's decision to kill a top Iranian general with a drone strike, the Congress passed a resolution limiting Trump's ability to attack Iran without congressional approval, but Trump vetoed the resolution, and the Senate lacked the two-thirds majority necessary to override the presidential veto.

To be fair, legislative engagement may simply be taking place behind closed doors. Diane Feinstein, a former member of the Senate Armed Services Committee (SASC), has indicated that her committee has nearly daily meetings about the use of armed drones for counter-terrorism, but oversight that happens behind closed doors does not make the process itself any more transparent. One of the major roles of Congress is to educate the public, and closed-door meetings cannot serve that function.

In a number of interviews, Obama referenced the way in which congressional silence could be construed as support, allowing the policy to go unchecked. As he put it, "it matters to have Congress with you, in terms of your ability to sustain what you set out to do" (Goldberg 2016). In a similar vein, Obama noted that "without Congress showing much interest in restraining actions with authorizations that were written really broadly, you could end up with a president who can carry on perpetual wars all over the world, and a lot of them covert, without any accountability or democratic debate" (quoted in Friedersdorf 2016). Based on Obama's own account, lack of legislative interest enables the perpetuation of policies, whereas its presence can offer a constraining function. In sum, the use of drones has reduced the apparent cost of war, or at least the cost to the United States, which takes the wind out of the sails of Congress when it comes to oversight. The turn to drones then reinforces the long-term trend toward the imperial presidency, interrupted only briefly by episodes such as post–Vietnam War oversight, and accelerated after 9/11 by the passage of the broad powers embedded in the AUMF.

Drone Proliferation and Its Consequences

As the United States began using drones with more frequency and in more locations in the years after 9/11, the rest of the world took notice. Drones appeared to provide an answer to terrorism without incurring as many of the costs or constraints. It is not surprising that around 2011, at the peak of the United States' use of drones, the *New York Times* reported alarmingly, "Coming Soon: The Drone Arms Race" (Shane 2011). The author offered a narrative of a Chinese air show that showcased twenty-five Chinese-made drones, an ominous image of the future.

The future, however, had already happened. Countries were already using drones. At that point, Israel had used drones against Hezbollah in Lebanon and Hamas in Gaza, and the UK had used US-made drones against the Taliban in Afghanistan. And other countries were interested in following their lead. By 2016, according to a study by the Center for New American Security, a Washington, DC, think tank, thirty countries had acquired some form of armed drone, and ninety countries and nonstate actors had secured unarmed drones that could be used for surveillance collection. Essentially any country with a security threat near its borders and the economic capacity to acquire drones is in pursuit of drones or has already acquired them. This includes, though is not limited to, China, Israel, India, Pakistan, Turkey, and Iran.

If all of these countries are acquiring drones, what are the implications for regional and international security? The answer is, it depends on the context. For the same reasons that the United States came to rely on drones for counterterrorism strikes, other countries may find drones useful for those purposes. They do not risk their soldiers' life or limb, are effective in targeting individuals suspected of planning terrorist attacks, and are unlikely to be shot down since terrorist havens typically do not have strong anti-air defenses. Israel's use of drones in the Sinai peninsula fits this logic. The Israel Defense Force has relied largely on drones to keep Palestinian militants in check while not needing to mobilize and maintain public support for a major ground campaign. Similarly, countries might be inclined to use drones in the context of border disputes, either in an intra- or interstate scenario, and thereby escalate tensions. Border disputes are potential flashpoints for conflict, and the introduction of drones could inflame those disputes by providing an apparently low-risk way to probe borders, since no human life is at stake. But in locations such as East Asia or the Middle East, where tensions and the prospect for miscalculation and misperception run high, an aircraft crossing the border – especially when the rules of engagement on whether it is legal or appropriate to shoot down a drone are unclear – could become the match that ignites conflict. In early 2018, a drone originating in Syria entered Israeli airspace. Israel proceeded to shoot down what appeared to be an Iranian drone, escalating to also include strikes on command and control centers that had been used to launch the drone. Syria responded by shooting down a manned Israeli aircraft, producing a further escalation against Syrian and Iranian targets in Syria. The incident raised concerns with how drones could indeed offer a new avenue for interstate conflict escalation.

Just as drones might be viewed as a low-cost way to test the waters in interstate territorial disputes, they might be convenient tools for leaders looking to control contested areas within their boundaries. Turkey, China, and Russia all have areas within their territories where groups (e.g., Kurds, Uyghurs, and Chechens) have sought to gain control. Drones can provide government with lower-risk ways to rein in these domestic populations and assert control of territory.

Drones are less likely to be useful in interstate conflict. Drones in their current form fly low and slow and are easy targets for reasonably sophisticated air defenses. Indeed, the incursion of drones across disputed territories might be destabilizing and escalate conflict between two countries – for example, China and Japan in the South China Sea – but those drones would have little value if war actually broke out. As former head of Air Combat Command, General Mike Hostage, warned, drones are "useless" in contested airspace because of their vulnerability. He continued, "Today ... I couldn't put a Predator or Reaper into the Strait of Hormuz without putting airplanes there to protect it" (Schogol 2015). The use of drones in the Middle

East, and the frequency with which they have been shot down, points to the vulnerability of drones in these heavily defended regions. However, as Iranian drone strikes on Israeli targets, Israeli drone strikes in April 2021 on an Iranian tanker, and the possibility of Iranian drone attacks on US forces/Saudi shipping in the Persian Gulf suggest, countries may nonetheless find the prospect of a drone shoot-down, even if it is more likely, to be less controversial than risking the same thing happening to an aircraft with pilots on board (BBC News 2018a).

As the discussion above suggests, drone warfare is not categorically binary in the sense of occurring or not or being transformative or not. Rather, its use and value are contextual. Often drones are used in conjunction with conventional forces to increase operational capabilities, providing insights through their video surveillance footage of combat zones to minimize casualties on the part of both friend and foe. They can be used on their own to conduct targeting (Gallagher 2017; Kindervater 2016).

Because of their battlefield utility and relative affordability, drones have democratized the ability to use military force. Although the most advanced drones are out of reach for most actors, the accessibility and affordability of lower-level commercial drones, even purchased on the Internet, mean that terrorist groups and less developed militaries can acquire and use drones. Groups such as IS have embraced drones as a way to create uncertainty and disruption on the battlefield. All that is required is an extremely rudimentary drone, duct tape (or retrofits in some way), and an explosive device, whether a grenade or a homemade explosive. The result is an airborne Improvised Explosive Device (IED). The IS news agency has promoted video footage of drones dropping airborne IEDs onto targets. The development has not gone unnoticed by the United States military, which has committed at least $700 million to counter-act the threat. Countering these flying IEDs represents a difficult technical problem since the drones are small and difficult to detect (Schmitt 2017). A US Army publication from 2016 cited drones as "the most challenging and prevalent threat platform" and one that was "a logical choice for enemy use" (quoted in Aftergood 2016).

The affordability of drones also makes them an obvious tool for less advanced militaries. In 2018, Palestinians in Gaza created explosive-equipped kites to fly into Israeli space and then detonate remotely or simply drop material to start brush fires. The device merged new with old concepts: the balloon concept from more than a century ago with the more modern version of an improvised explosive device. Israel responded with an equally innovative measure, using amateur drone racers to intercept and shred the kites so as to render them useless.

Similarly, groups in Yemen that appear to be supplied by Iran have been using rudimentary drones. The drones have the serial numbers consistent with the Ababil 2 drone that has been seen in Iran, and have the same configuration as the Iranian-made Ababil drone family. The Islamic State (or ISIS) had an underground factory in Mosul, Iraq, which produced simple drones as well as other insurgent weapons, such as IEDs. Parts of a drone from that factory are displayed in Figure 12.4.

The ease of access also makes drones a potential tool for domestic terrorism. Diane Feinstein, Democratic Senator for California, coded drones as "a perfect assassination weapon" (quoted in Zenko and Kreps 2014, 12). The target could be a high-level individual or a group of people. Indeed, in 2018, Venezuelan President Nicolas Maduro survived an assassination attempt via a drone, blaming Colombian opponents for the attack

Figure 12.4. Parts of a drone captured in 2017, in an underground factory run by the Islamic State in Mosul, Iraq. Note the crude construction and materials in comparison to the high-end engineering and design of the Predator and Reaper drone. However, even simple and inexpensive drones like this one can be effective and deadly. Martyn Aim/Getty Images.

(BBC News 2018b). Drones offer some appeal in this context of assassination for two reasons. One is that drones can transgress the typical security barriers erected to prevent vehicles from transporting explosives. They simply fly over the barriers. Drones already proved that concept of circumventing barriers when an individual was arrested for flying a drone over the gates of the White House. In this case, the drone was merely menacing; but armed with a chemical or biological agent or an explosive, it would become lethal, and in any case can produce the type of psychological shock that is a goal of terrorism. Relatedly, whoever operates the drone can put off detonating until a moment when either the right person or a large number of people would be present. Contrast that dynamic with having to pre-position an explosive device and bank on serendipity that the right person or people will walk by for the device to maximize damage.

If drones have potentially destabilizing effects on national security, why is their proliferation not being contained? One view is that the technology actually is being controlled. The United States and many other countries are part of the Missile Technology Control Regime (MTCR), a group formed in 1987 to restrict the transfer of nuclear-delivery vehicles, which included drones. The regime restricts the export of drones that can fly beyond a certain range (300 kilometers) and payload (500 kilograms). By and large, the United States has adhered to these restrictions, transferring armed drones like the Reaper to the UK, Italy, France, and the Netherlands only.

Another view says that the drone genie is out of the bottle, the MTCR is full of loopholes, and drones will continue to proliferate. This view suggests that the technology is relatively cheap and accessible, which means that efforts to control its spread are bound to be futile. Equally problematic, two of the big drone manufacturers, China and Israel, are not part of the regime and have supplied many other countries who seek the technology. So even if the United States has been relatively careful about which countries it exports to, other countries will not only fill the gaps but gain the industrial benefits.

The reality is likely more nuanced, or somewhere in between. The relatively inexpensive drones used by groups like the IS are nearly impossible to contain, since the hardware can be bought online and retrofitted with an improvised explosive. These can be disruptive on the battlefield or, in terms of domestic terrorism, strike "soft" targets such as outdoor shopping malls, easy and undefended locations with large numbers of people. Armed drones like the Reaper are, however, being controlled in large part because the technology is too advanced for most countries. For decades, for example, Russia has tried to develop a Reaper-like drone but failed, and theirs is not exactly an underdeveloped military, pointing to the challenges that face other countries trying to acquire the technology.

The Future of Drones: The Four S's

Although current-generation drones have their limits, the future will see many of their current deficiencies being addressed. Those improvements can be classified as the four S's: size, swarms, stealth, and speed. The previous section hinted at the way that size could play as an advantage when it comes to drones, and indeed, less can be more when it comes to size. Smaller drones can better evade detection and can therefore be better equipped to reach their target. Nano-drones, which are the smallest-scale drone, take that logic to the next level. They are the size of insects and many of them are named after insects because of their size and resemblance. Figure 12.5 below shows a Black Hornet, a nano-helicopter used by the German, Norwegian, and British militaries. It collects video to provide awareness of enemy movements, has night vision capabilities, and is small enough to fit in a pocket.

The United States and its allies are experimenting with a range of these insect-resembling nano-drones. The United States has tested the mosquito drone, which can fly into buildings and spy, with video technology embedded in the drone. Europe has developed a drone that resembles a bee and embeds an impressive array of ultraviolet, video, and audio sensors. A US Air Force video touts micro air vehicles as a tool of the future for creating situational awareness in urban warfare. The system can be air-dropped or hand-launched, enter into buildings, hide in plain sight by simply seeming like an insect, and use micro-sensors to generate information about the

Figure 12.5. Black Hornet nano-helicopter.
Richard Watt/MOD.

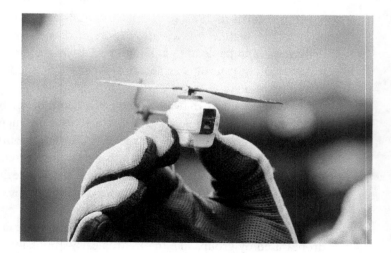

adversary. The idea was popularized in the movie *Eye in the Sky*, which showed British and American intelligence launching a micro-drone that flies into a building and collects footage of a suicide bomber preparing his device. The video enables intelligence officials from afar to send in a larger drone to do the day-to-day surveillance and the eventual strike.

A maneuver that can be employed in conjunction with smaller drones is the second main future development: the use of swarms. The logic here is that the whole is greater than the sum of its parts. A small drone by itself might not be very effective, but flying in formation with other drones can overcome one of the main deficiencies of drones: their vulnerability to air defenses. When drones fly together, they can confuse the radar systems, which suddenly do not know where to focus. Even if 90 percent of the drones are shot down, 10 percent make it through and can persevere to their target. Since the drones cost about $1,000 each, they are relatively disposable.

A third likely development of drones that will address current deficiencies is better stealth. The medium-altitude drones that the United States has typically used for its strikes have what is called a large radar cross section, which means that they are easily detected by radar systems. Industry is in the process of developing new designs that improve the stealthiness of current drones. China has been developing new low observable drones. The United States allegedly operated a stealth drone that was shot down in Iran, suggesting that perhaps it was not a complete success at being stealthy. The United States also appears to have developed a more advanced stealth aircraft, but one that conducts intelligence, surveillance, and reconnaissance missions rather than lethal strikes. The ability to be useful in heavily defended airspace is its claim to fame, and this appears to be one direction in which countries are going to give drones more utility in interstate situations where drones would either be off limits or too vulnerable to be useful.

A fourth future development is speed. The Predator, the first combat drone deployed, had a cruising speed of about 84 miles per hour, which made it vulnerable to being shot down. The Reaper benefitted from a more streamlined design and more power, increasing its cruising speed to 230 miles per hour. Although this is an improvement, speed is still a limitation. Next-generation drones, however, may look different. One avenue of change involves transforming existing fighter planes like F-16s into unmanned drones. The United States military is already looking to transform its manned planes into combat drones. It is also investigating new laser weapons and hypersonic missiles that can maneuver more quickly and with more agility than current weapons, another way of evading anti-air systems. All of the templates for unmanned combat vehicles assume that the airplane will go much faster than current systems.

One future scenario involves a combination of most of the above advancements. Imagine a $100 million stealth airplane launching a flock of $3 million drones that then fly as a swarm to overwhelm air defenses, fire hypersonic missiles that can evade air defenses, or conduct surveillance missions. Although the drones would not be expendable, they would be far more inexpensive and numerous than the F-35, and without the risk of pilot fatality, while also being faster – current prototypes have a top speed of 650 miles per hour – and more maneuverable than the current-generation drones.

In discussions about the future of drones, the question of autonomy often arises. Drones, of course, are by definition semi-autonomous in the sense that they fly without a person in the cockpit. But a human is behind every decision to fire a weapon. Skeptics believe that the future might look different, namely that it would bring more autonomy to the weapons. Nongovernmental and international organizations, following the lead of Tesla founder Elon Musk and others, have taken an interest in banning "**killer robots,**" the label the movement has used for fully autonomous weapons that fly and shoot missiles. The UN has considered the ban as part of the UN Convention on Conventional Weapons, having met since 2014 to discuss how they would ban fully autonomous systems from use in combat.

But what does autonomy actually mean and how can it be banned in practice? By some accounts, a heat-seeking missile would be an autonomous weapon because it is programmed in advance, then launched and travels until it finds its heat-based target. A preprogrammed system like the Tomahawk missile is not vulnerable to hacking because, once programmed, it flies directly to its target. But these systems already exist. Perhaps more to the point, cruise missiles do not violate the spirit of the proposed ban on automation, in that there is still very much a person in the loop in terms of making targeting decisions.

The United States is also exploring autonomy through artificial intelligence. As the commander of US Army Futures Command asked, "is it within a human's ability to pick out which [targets] have to be engaged" when there are hundreds of individual decisions to make and people may not make decisions quickly enough? Indeed, some scholars have argued that autonomous weapons could make more ethical decisions than humans, who have been shown to mistreat the enemy and face cognitive limits because of the emotional and physical pressures of war (Umbrello et al. 2019). Others are more pessimistic. Paul Scharre of the Center for New American Security, a Washington think tank, worries about a slippery slope. If algorithms are decisions about combatant versus civilian, what will stop them from actually pulling the trigger? Those pressures will be especially salient if American adversaries deploy these fully autonomous systems and face an asymmetric disadvantage. Russia and China are also moving toward more autonomy. Groups such as the Islamic State of Iraq and Syria have used drones for targeting, and investment in autonomous systems will inevitably lower the cost of these technologies in ways that make them accessible to these terrorist groups (Knight 2021).

Perhaps raising further skepticism about autonomous systems, the USA and UK have concluded that they are not yet prepared for a full ban on autonomous weapons, even if they have no plans to use them. The thinking is similar to the United States' decision not to ratify the Comprehensive Test Ban Treaty, which prohibits nuclear tests. Even if the United States is not conducting nuclear tests, and has no plans to do so, it aims to maintain strategic flexibility rather than outright prohibit certain actions. On the other hand, not banning autonomous weapons leaves the door open to their eventual use in ways warned of by the "slippery slope" kinds of arguments. Autonomy could first be used to achieve objectives that help civilians in combat. Automation, for example, could allow an unused missile to self-destruct if it does not hit its target, rather than later encountering an innocent civilian. Moving in the direction of more autonomy, combined perhaps with a country like Russia or China making the move toward full autonomy, would make it difficult for the United States to avoid the same move.

CASE STUDY

Drone Strikes in Pakistan

This case study provides a systematic examination of the country where drones have been used most for counterterrorism, Pakistan. The "drone war" first attracted attention because of the frequency of strikes in the tribal regions of Pakistan. This case study focuses on a number of questions about those strikes: which insurgent groups have they targeted, why are they seen as a threat, where exactly are the groups and strikes located, why might drones be necessary, what are the civilian fatalities, and how have outside groups such as nongovernmental and international organizations responded to these strikes?

Why Conduct Drone Strikes in Pakistan?

Answering the question why the United States reached peak drone strikes in Pakistan requires going back to the time before the 9/11 attacks. According to the 9/11 Commission Report that investigated the cause of those events, in 1996 Osama bin Laden, the head of al-Qaeda, moved from Sudan to Afghanistan. After the Soviets withdrew from Afghanistan in the late 1980s, the CIA also left the country, except for two CIA employees who were later murdered but who had reported bin Laden's support for the Taliban. He had funneled considerable amounts of resources to the group, putting it on the map as a potential concern. Secretary of State Madeline Albright had labeled the group "despicable," and the US ambassador to the UN led a delegation to Afghanistan in April 1998. He asked the Taliban, which governed Afghanistan, to expel bin Laden, but the Taliban responded that he represented no threat to the United States. During the late 1990s, the United States created a capture plan for bin Laden, and conducted a series of strikes in hopes of prompting the Taliban to turn over bin Laden, but did not take systematic action to remove the Taliban until after the 9/11 attacks.

What had been a nuisance before 9/11 took on more urgency after the attacks. The United States engaged in a military conflict to dislodge the Taliban from Afghanistan and defeat al-Qaeda. In December 2001, with the Taliban having fallen, Hamid Karzai was selected to lead the Afghan Interim Administration, and the International Security Assistance Force was established to help provide security and reconstruction for the Afghan people. Meanwhile, however, the United States turned its attention toward Iraq, and had few troops in the country. The United States and UK conducted scores of strikes in Afghanistan as part of its "**light footprint**" in the country, meaning few boots on the ground and instead relying on airstrikes, many of which were conducted with drones.

In the wake of Coalition military operations in Afghanistan, the Taliban retreated from major cities and appeared defeated. The group, however, reconstituted itself as an insurgency in 2002, and while it had fewer safe havens in Afghanistan, it took refuge in the tribal regions in Pakistan. Map 12.16 is a map of Afghanistan and Pakistan, with a particular focus on Taliban strongholds. The most significant concentration of Taliban

(cont.)

Map 12.1. Taliban presence in South Asia. National Counterterrorism Center.

influence was in the southeastern part of Afghanistan and northwest region of Pakistan, called the **Federally Administered Tribal Areas (FATA).** The area is thickly forested, mountainous, and difficult to govern, making it semi-autonomous and a perfect staging ground for planning terrorist attacks.

From this perch the Taliban could now hope to confront US forces in Afghanistan, especially as it regrouped and the United States turned its attention to Iraq by 2003. In 2009, the BBC found that only 38 percent of northwestern Pakistan was under government control, the rest a haven for Taliban and al-Qaeda leaders like bin Laden. This region also contained a militant force committed to planning and carrying out attacks. It was in this region that the United States conducted its first drone strike.

In 2004, the George W. Bush administration authorized an armed Predator to strike a local Taliban commander, Nek Mohammad, who had been associated with a plot to kill General Pervez Musharraf, the president of Pakistan. The strike succeeded and also allegedly killed Nek Mohammad's brothers, sons, and suspected militants. In the years thereafter, the strikes were relatively few. In the last year of the Bush administration, however, strikes began to increase, coinciding with increases in the numbers of American troops in Afghanistan and American casualties. In the 2008 presidential campaign, Barack Obama foreshadowed his hawkishness on the question of drone strikes and warned that if the Pakistani government did not stop the planning and execution of

(cont.)

terrorist attacks emanating from its territory, the United States would take action unilaterally. Obama warned that "if we have actionable intelligence about high-value terrorist targets and President Musharraf won't act, we will" (Mazzetti and Schmitt 2010). Once he took office, President Obama did just that, escalating the use of drone strikes in Pakistan.

The initial increase in strikes attracted little attention. One reason is that the US government did not disclose information about the program, only hinting at it in 2010. Not surprisingly, the media was also largely silent on the subject. Not until the strikes started increasing at faster rates in 2009 did the media start paying more attention to the topic. Arguably the first groundbreaking coverage came in a 2009 article in the *New Yorker*, which documented the strike against Baitullah Mehsud, conducted by the CIA.

Baitullah Mehsud, the leader of the Taliban in Pakistan, could be seen reclining on the rooftop of his father-in-law's house, in Zanghara, a hamlet in South Waziristan. It was a hot summer night, and he was joined outside by his wife and his uncle, a medic; the remarkably crisp images showed the uncle administering an intravenous drip to Mehsud, who suffered from diabetes and a kidney ailment. (Mayer 2009)

The article goes on to describe the video feed, captured by the infrared camera, and the stable image the CIA could pick up when its drone launched two Hellfire missiles that killed him, his wife, his father-in-law, mother-in-law, military aide, and seven bodyguards.

The account of the strike publicized President Obama's burgeoning drone campaign. Within the first two years, he had conducted almost eight times as many strikes as during the last year of the Bush administration, 375 for the Obama administration compared to 49 in the Bush administration. From 2004 to 2016, the United States conducted 425 counterterrorism strikes in Pakistan, more than 70 percent of all drone strikes during that period.

The official rhetoric from the United States is that drone strikes are intended to prevent terrorists from striking Americans on home soil. Former President Obama's earlier quote suggested that drone strikes in Pakistan were aimed at preventing the Taliban from striking American school buses. This may be the case, and indeed the United States intervened in Afghanistan to root out the Taliban so it would not allow Afghanistan to be a safe haven for terrorist groups like al-Qaeda motivated to launch attacks on the United States. The story with Pakistan, however, was different. The United States conducted few drone strikes in Pakistan during the first eight years of war in Afghanistan. Rather, it focused its military efforts on eliminating the Taliban in Afghanistan.

Accounting for the increase in drone strikes requires reflecting on what changed around that time. One of the most significant changes was the troop surge. In 2009, after the first eight years of its war, the United States conducted a review of the Afghanistan campaign. The review revealed that the United States was not losing or winning, but could improve its prospects if it had more troops in the country. The United States carried out a troop

(cont.)

Figure 12.6. Relationship between drone strikes in Pakistan and increased US troop fatalities in Afghanistan.
Bureau of Investigative Journalism and iCasualties. org.

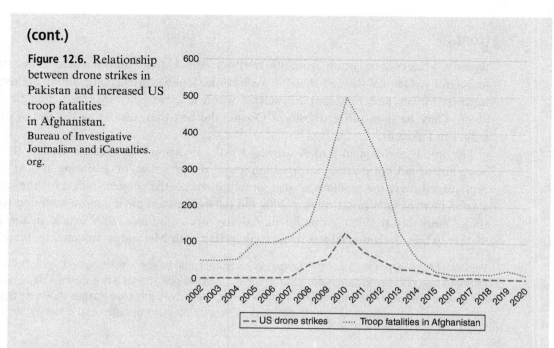

surge that it hoped would trigger a course correction. When American troops started increasing in 2008–2010, however, attacks against them also started increasing.

Drone strikes in Pakistan were as much an effort to put a stop to attacks against American soldiers across the border as they were to prevent that area from becoming a safe haven for terrorist strikes. Indeed, the FATA is quite disconnected from anything outside the region, which makes it difficult to carry out long-distance transnational terrorist attacks from the semi-autonomous tribal region. Perhaps more persuasive is the tight correspondence between American troop fatalities in Afghanistan and the frequency of drone strikes. Figure 12.6 shows that as American soldier fatalities in Afghanistan increased, drone strikes did as well, suggesting a "force protection" story, or the protection of soldiers in neighboring Afghanistan. Also consistent with this story is that as fatalities declined again in 2014, drone strikes tapered off too.

Civilian Casualties in the Pakistani Drone Strikes

Drone strikes in Pakistan brought the drone program to light because of both the number of suspected militants killed and the number of civilians killed. According to the Bureau of Investigative Journalism, between 2004 and 2017 the United States killed about 2,500 people in drone strikes, although some groups claim that these numbers are under-counted. The aspect that drew the most criticism was the rate of civilian casualties. Although the peak year for both drone strikes and fatalities was 2010, when there were approximately 128 strikes that killed about 755 people, those casualties peaked in 2006, when almost all of the total fatalities were allegedly civilians. That year, there were two drone strikes. The larger of the two and the one accounting for the civilian fatalities

(cont.)

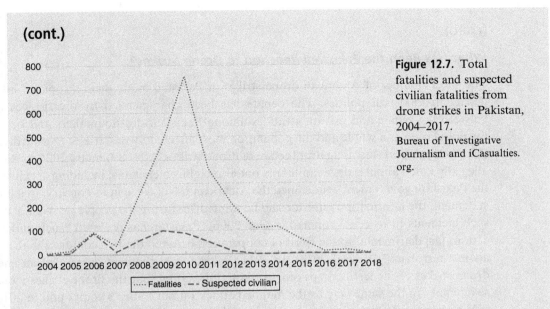

Figure 12.7. Total fatalities and suspected civilian fatalities from drone strikes in Pakistan, 2004–2017.
Bureau of Investigative Journalism and iCasualties. org.

occurred in October. It intended to strike al-Qaeda's second-in-command, Ayman al-Zawahiri, in a madrassa, a Pakistani religious school. The strike killed about eighty students (including sixty-nine under the age of seventeen) who were either in school or being used as shields for militant activity. Al-Zawahiri was not present but the strike appeared to kill Matiur Rehman, who had masterminded a plot to use airliners as suicide devices in the UK. As Figure 12.7 suggests, the ratio of civilians to total fatalities was quite high in some years, in particular between 2006 and 2011, when about 12–23 percent of total fatalities were civilians. Soon thereafter, the United States instituted a new policy stating that it would not strike unless it had near certainty of zero civilian fatalities. After this policy was adopted, the casualty rate did decline considerably and the level has indeed been close to zero in recent years.

In 2016, the US government released a number for civilian casualties for all of the counterterrorism strikes (Pakistan, Yemen, and Somalia), stating that it was just 116. Almost all observers suggest that this official figure vastly understates the rate of civilian casualties. For example, in Pakistan alone, most estimates by nongovernment organizations point to about 425. In contexts where civilians and combatants co-mingle, and combatants do not wear uniforms or insignia, the difference between civilian and combatant can be difficult to parse, which explains the discrepancies between government and nongovernment or UN estimates. Nonetheless, almost all observers agree that casualty levels have declined considerably, in large part because of greater attentiveness to avoiding casualties, whether due to stricter adherence to international law or the view that more casualties would eventually backfire and make the terrorism problem worse.

(cont.)

What Has Been the Pakistani Reaction to Drone Strikes?

The sheer number of American drone strikes in Pakistan made them a topic of intense debate in Pakistani politics. The debate has been characterized by divergences both between the public and private attitudes among Pakistani decisionmakers and between the population as a whole and the population most affected by the strikes. Outwardly, the Pakistani political class is against the use of drone strikes. After a January 2006 strike that allegedly killed about a dozen militants but also eighteen civilians, including six children, the Pakistani government condemned the American use of force in its country. In a public statement, the information minister said he wanted "to assure the people we will not allow such incidents to reoccur" (quoted in Gall 2006). Pakistan has declared "such unilateral actions [as] detrimental to the spirit of cooperation between the two countries in the fight against terrorism" (Yousaf 2018). In 2011, Pakistan's parliament demanded an end to drone strikes on its territory, passing a resolution stating that the drone strikes violated sovereignty in the same way as the manned attack on bin Laden's compound in 2011.

Whether the Pakistani official public condemnation is sincere or merely for public consumption is an unresolved debate, in part because the observed behavior would look the same whether the government was actually opposed to the strikes or merely posturing. On the one hand, given the frequency of strikes, the government is almost compelled to speak out against the violations of sovereignty to appease the public's apparent antagonism toward drone strikes and indignation that it looks like its own military cannot handle the counterterrorism job. On the other hand, it is almost unimaginable that Pakistan has not granted at least tacit approval for the strikes. Perhaps the United States could carry out a handful of strikes without approval, but hundreds would be impossible. All the while, the Pakistani government benefits from the drone strikes as a means to combat militants that threaten its own leaders. A number of accounts have pointed to a bargain between the Pakistani government and the United States: one that allows the CIA access to Pakistani airspace for drone strikes that Pakistan approves and that also happen to target enemies of the Pakistani government. Meanwhile, the United States has also provided precision weapon-equipped helicopters and night vision capabilities to improve the Pakistanis' intelligence collection, but mostly these were helpful by eliminating mutual enemies.

In some ways, it is immaterial whether or not the Pakistani government actually supports the strikes, because its outward gestures suggest opposition. That opposition rides on a related set of questions about whether the Pakistani public supports or opposes drone strikes. The conventional wisdom, consistent with the outward opposition by the government, is that the public is against drone strikes, and at least some forms of evidence suggest that the strikes are unpopular. In 2010, a Pew Global Attitudes survey indicated that 90 percent of Pakistanis agreed that the strikes "kill too many innocent people," although that number receded to 67 percent by 2014. Two out of three Pakistanis oppose

(cont.)

the strikes and only 3 percent approve (30 percent did not have an opinion), although at least two-thirds of Pakistanis had not heard about the drone strikes in 2010. Of those who had, however, 93 percent registered their displeasure (Pew Research Center 2010, 2014).

An alternate view suggests that in the areas that matter – in Waziristan, where several attacks have occurred – many Pakistanis view the drone strikes as a legitimate way to control terrorism. According to interviews conducted by the BBC, individuals reported that they "prefer the drone attacks to army ground operations, because in the operations we get killed and the army doesn't respect the honor of the men or women" (Maqbool 2010). Better-educated Pakistanis who had access to a wider range of news sources were more likely to favor drone strikes, suggesting that there is variation when it comes to the in-country support for the drone strike policy.

The popularity of strikes is worth considering because they can be an input to the overall effectiveness of strikes. If strikes are unpopular, they may contribute to the public backlash and recruitment of new terrorists as predicted by martyrdom arguments. However, the evidence is mixed, so the quantitative study that follows seeks to unpack more systematically the question of consequences. Have drone strikes in Pakistan been effective? This study addresses the question of why and where drone strikes might impact terrorism, and examines it with empirical evidence.

QUANTITATIVE STUDY

Do Drone Strikes Reduce Terrorism?

The premise of counterterrorism strikes is that they kill suspected terrorists and reduce the threat of terrorism. Opponents of drone strikes have pointed to American officials saying that the number of militants in Yemen went from hundreds in 2010 to thousands by 2012, a period punctuated by drone strikes (Zenko 2013, 10). The assertion conflates correlation with causation. Or rather, reverse causality, questioning whether a spike in militants causes a spike in drone strikes. Yet a decisionmaker wants to know the causal effect of drone strikes. At some point, if drone strikes were creating more terrorists than they were killing, they would no longer make sense.

The reason why studying this connection between drone strikes and terrorist activity represents a difficult social science proposition is that drone strikes are not randomly distributed. They are not as likely in Switzerland as in Pakistan. Asserting that there are no terrorists in Switzerland because there are no drone strikes reverses the causal arrow. Maybe there are no drone strikes because there are no terrorist plots coming out of Switzerland. Similarly, the reason for the increase in militants in Yemen may not be the drone strikes; it may be that there were more drone strikes because the number of militants in Yemen was increasing. The political scientists Patrick Johnston and Anoop Sarbahi pursued that question using data on drone strikes and terrorism in Pakistan between 2007 and 2011.

Research Question

Do drone strikes increase terrorist violence, decrease terrorist violence, or have no effect?

Theory and Hypotheses

As noted earlier in this chapter, drone strikes could actually create more terrorism. The most straightforward way they do that is by radicalizing the local populations. Underlying this logic is that drone strikes alienate local populations, making individuals in those populations more susceptible to recruitment by terrorist groups. These groups might then have a larger base of human and material resources to draw upon in order to plan and carry out terrorist attacks (Johnston and Sarbahi 2016). Another mechanism through which a drone strike might increase terrorism is by fomenting rivalry among potential successors. These competing individuals or factions might seek to establish their "street cred" by carrying out attacks.

Hypothesis 1: Drone strikes increase the likelihood of terrorist violence.

Alternatively, drone strikes may decrease terrorist violence because they disrupt the organization, efficiency, and capabilities of terrorist networks. Seeking shelter from attacks drives terrorist planning literally underground and prevents them from using communications that would draw attention to their location. Terrorists cannot plan attacks when they are hiding from attacks. Therefore, the second hypothesis is as follows:

Hypothesis 2: Drone strikes decrease the likelihood of terrorist violence.

While it may appear as though violence declines, terrorist activity may simply relocate to other areas with less drone activity. If this is the case, then drone strikes would not address terrorism but rather simply move it elsewhere, for example to mountains or areas with heavy tree cover that could shield groups from drone strikes. If this is the case, then the following would find support:

Hypothesis 3: Drone strikes increase militant violence in surrounding areas.

Data

The data included all drone strikes in the FATA region between January 2007 and September 2011. Data were sorted based on the district in which the drone strike occurred in order to analyze potential variation. Since the hypotheses also implied the potential for dislocation, it was also important to collect data on terrorist violence in areas within twenty-five kilometers of the location of the drone strikes.

These particular data risk selection effects: drone strikes may increase because terrorism in an area is going up, but the observable outcome of drone strikes being correlated with terrorist violence might give the false impression that drone strikes are causing terrorism. However, in practice, decisions about when and where drone strikes will occur do have a somewhat random element to them. The weather on a given day, bureaucratic considerations like whether the government has signed off on a strike, and accessibility of the target all affect the decision to launch a drone strike. Each of these factors makes the strike a quasi-random event so that the concerns about causality are mitigated.

Dependent Variable

The outcome variable of importance consists of the number of militant incidents or attacks in a given region and week. It also includes the number of individuals killed or wounded in attacks in a particular area and week to give a sense of intensity of the terrorist incident.

Independent Variable

The main independent variable is the number of drone strikes in a particular region and week.

Results

Empirical analysis shows that while violence increased in 2007–2009, drone strikes followed rather than preceded that violence. Violence appears to have prompted the drone strikes rather than the other way around, which supports hypothesis 2 above, rather than hypothesis 1 which would have led to expectations of an increase in violence. Escalation in the drone war followed terrorist violence rather than the drone war causing terrorist violence. Further analysis shows that the frequency and lethality of attacks declined rather than increased in the wake of drone strikes. Going even further, the analysis shows that killing more militant leaders decreased the incidence of violence. Specifically, drone strikes were responsible for a five-percentage-point decline in terrorist attacks. Whereas, on average, there were 0.88 attacks per week between 2007 and 2011, weeks with a drone strike had about 0.68 attacks on average.

It may be simply that the violence shifted regions. To analyze that possibility, the radius of the region's "neighborhood" was expanded from twenty-five kilometers out in increments of twenty-five kilometers. Yet the evidence does not suggest any "spillover" effects in which proximate areas received the brunt of the effects.

Conclusions

This analysis shows that in the context of Pakistan, drone strikes reduced the incidence of terrorist violence in the region, at least in the short term. It does not address the question of whether drone strikes have an effect on cross-national terrorist activity – for example, planning of terrorist attacks that might have an impact on American interests – which is the stated objective of these strikes. The finding might also be confined to the context of Pakistan rather than generalizable to Somalia and Yemen, which have very different structures of government, militant activities, and underlying civil conflicts. Indeed, this study is part of an ongoing debate about the effectiveness of drone strikes against militant and terrorist violence, in which other works have sometimes offered different perspectives (Gartkze and Walsh 2022; Rigterink 2020). As with other areas, the accumulation of careful studies will over time provide an increasingly accurate and nuanced account of the effects of drone strikes.

SUMMARY

This chapter has made several points about drones. Those points include:

- Drones are remotely operated aircraft that states and nonstates are increasingly using in combat.
- The earliest hints of drones can be found in balloons, rockets, and reconnaissance drones.
- The frequency with which the United States uses drones for counterterrorism has shined the spotlight on the United States, but many other countries have combat drones and many more are acquiring the technology.
- Whether drones are transformative as a battlefield technology depends on the context where they are being used, with the largest impact on counterterrorism and for nonstate actors.

- Drones have been a popular instrument of war because they can skirt the limitations of human pilots so that soldiers or pilots do not become casualties of war.
- Proponents of drones argue that drones are an effective tool of counterterrorism, but detractors have questioned whether those gains are only short-term and whether the strikes create more terrorists than they kill and thus are counterproductive.
- The technology has raised questions about whether drones are legal or ethical, and arguments exist on both sides of that debate.
- The future of drones is likely to mean advancements in autonomy, even if not full autonomy, and improvements in stealth, speed, swarms, and size (i.e., smaller may be better).

KEY TERMS

Predator
Reaper
Hybrid warfare
Decapitation
Martyrdom effects
International
   Humanitarian Law
Rapporteur

Moral hazard
Separation of powers
Authorization for the Use of Military Force
Focusing events
Killer robots
Light footprint
Federally Administered Tribal Areas

REVIEW QUESTIONS

1. What is the history of drones or drone-like devices on the battlefield? What can current drones do that early variants did not?
2. What countries have used drones in combat? The United States has used drones against targets located in which countries?
3. What are the operational and political advantages of drones that have made them attractive to decisionmakers?
4. What is the current international regulatory regime that deals with the transfer and export of drones, and has it worked to contain the proliferation of armed drones?
5. What are the arguments in favor of the effectiveness of drone strikes for counterterrorism? What are the arguments against? How do these relate to debates about decapitation strategies?
6. How might nonstate actors use armed drones and to whom do they pose a threat?
7. Are drones legal under international law, and do they present ethical concerns?
8. What is the future of drones? What types of developments are likely and how will these affect how they are used on the battlefield?
9. What has been the Pakistani reaction – on the part of the government and its citizens – to American drone strikes?
10. Have drone strikes in Pakistan increased or decreased the incidence of terrorist violence in the regions where the strikes have taken place?

DISCUSSION QUESTIONS

1. Under what circumstances would you support the use of drone strikes? For example, would you require very high confidence that no civilians would be killed, approval from the host government where the strikes take place, and/or congressional approval?
2. Do you think the president should be given significant independent authority over the use of force, including drone strikes, or do you support stronger congressional checks on presidential power?
3. Do you support the eventual deployment of fully autonomous weapons (called "killer robots" by some), weapons that are controlled by computers?

ADDITIONAL READING

Byman, D. (2013). Why drones work: The case for Washington's weapon of choice. *Foreign Affairs* **92**(4), 32–43.

Cronin, A. K. (2013). Why drones fail. *Foreign Affairs* **92**(4), 44–54.

Horowitz, M., Kreps, S., and Fuhrmann, M. (2016). Separating fact from fiction in the debate over drone proliferation. *International Security* **41**(20), 7–42.

Jordan, J. (2019). *Leadership Decapitation: Strategic Targeting of Terrorist Organizations*, Stanford: Stanford University Press.

Kaag, J. and Kreps, S. (2014). *Drone Warfare*. New York: Polity.

Plaw, A. and Fricker, M. (2012). Tracking the predators: Evaluating the US drone campaign in Pakistan. *International Studies Perspectives* **13**(4), 344–365.

Strawser, B. (2013). *Killing by Remote Control: The Ethics of an Unmanned Military*. New York: Oxford University Press.

REFERENCES

Aftergood, S. (2016, October 25). Defending U.S. forces against enemy drones. https://fas.org/blogs/secrecy/2016/10/drone-defense

BBC News (2018a, April 13). Iranian drone was sent to Israel "to attack." www.bbc.com/news/world-middle-east-43762193

BBC News (2018b, August 5). Venezuela president Maduro survives "drone assassination attempt." www.bbc.com/news/world-latin-america-45073385

Coates, T. (2016, December 21). "Better is good": Obama on reparations, civil rights, and the art of the possible. *The Atlantic*. www.theatlantic.com/politics/archive/2016/12/ta-nehisi-coates-obama-transcript-ii/511133

Columbia Law School Human Rights Clinic (2012). Counting drone strike deaths. https://web.law.columbia.edu/sites/default/files/microsites/human-rights-institute/files/COLUMBIACountingDronesFinal.pdf

Countering international terrorism: The United Kingdom's strategy (2006). https://assets.publishing.service.gov.uk/government/uploads/system/uploads/attachment_data/file/272320/6888.pdf

Friedersdorf, C. (2016, December 23). Obama's weak defense of his record on drone killings. *The Atlantic*. www.theatlantic.com/politics/archive/2016/12

Gall, C. (2006, January 15). Airstrike by U.S. draws protests from Pakistanis. *New York Times*. www.nytimes.com/2006/01/15/world/asia/airstrike-by-us-draws-protests-from-pakistanis.html

Gallagher, K. (2017, October 26). Drone intelligence gives military and defense users the insight to act. www.simulyze.com/blog

Gartzke, E.. and Walsh, J. I. (2022). The drawbacks of drones: The effects of UAVs on escalation and instability in Pakistan. *Journal of Peace Research* **59**(4), 463–477.

Goldberg, J. (2016, April). The Obama doctrine. *The Atlantic*. www.theatlantic.com/magazine/archive/2016/04/the-obama-doctrine/471525

Hayden, M. V. (2016, February 19). To keep America safe, embrace drone warfare. *New York Times*. www.nytimes.com/2016/02/21/opinion/sunday/drone-warfare-precise-effective-imperfect.html

Johnston, P. B., and Sarbahi, A. K. (2016). The impact of US drone strikes on terrorism in Pakistan. *International Studies Quarterly* **60**(2), 203–219.

Kindervater, K. H. (2016). The emergence of lethal surveillance: Watching and killing in the history of drone technology. *Security Dialogue* **47**(3), 223–238.

Knight, W. (2021, May 10). The Pentagon inches toward letting AI control weapons. *Wired*. www.wired.com/story

Legal Information Institute (n.d.). 22 U.S. Code § 2656F. www.law.cornell.edu/uscode/text/22/2656f#d_2

Lowe, M. S. and Gire, J. T. (2012). In the mind of the predator: The possibility of psychological distress in the drone pilot community. *Modern Psychological Studies* **17**(2), 2–7.

Lyall, J. (2020, December 16). Drones are destabilizing global politics. *Foreign Affairs*. www.foreignaffairs.com/articles/middle-east/2020-12-16

Madison, J. (1788). *Federalist No. 47, The Particular Structure of the New Government and the Distribution of Power among its Different Parts*. www.congress.gov/resources/display/content/The+Federalist+Papers?loclr=twloc

Maqbool, A. (2010, July 22). America's secret drone war in Pakistan. *BBC News*. www.bbc.com/news/world-south-asia-10728844

Mayer, J. (2009, October 19). The predator war. *New Yorker*. www.newyorker.com/magazine/2009/10/26/the-predator-war

Mazzetti, M., and Schmitt, E. (2010. September 28). C.I.A. steps up drone attacks on Taliban in Pakistan. *New York Times*. www.nytimes.com/2010/09/28/world/asia/28drones.html

Obama, B. (2015, July 6). Remarks by the President on progress in the fight against ISIL. https://obamawhitehouse.archives.gov/the-press-office/2015/07/06

Obama's speech on drone policy (2013, May 23). *New York Times*. www.nytimes.com/2013/05/24/us/politics/transcript-of-obamas-speech-on-drone-policy.html

Pew Research Center (2010, July 29). America's image remains poor: Concern about extremist threat slips in Pakistan. file:///C:/Users/dreiter/Downloads/Pew-Global-Attitudes-2010-Pakistan-Report.pdf

Pew Research Center (2014, August 17). A less gloomy mood in Pakistan. www.pewresearch.org/global/2014/08/27

RFE (2013, February 6). U.S.: Drone strikes "legal, ethical, wise." www.rferl.org/a/us-drone-strikes-legal-ethical-wise/24894199.html

Rigerink, A. S. (2020). The wane of command: Evidence on drone strikes and control within terrorist organizations. *American Political Science Review* **115**(1), 31–50.

Savage, C. (2021, May 6). Trump's secret rules for drone strikes outside war zones are disclosed. *New York Times*. www.nytimes.com/2021/05/01/us/politics/trump-drone-strike-rules.html

Schmitt, E. (2017, September 23). Pentagon tests lasers and nets to combat a vexing foe: ISIS drones. *New York Times*. www.nytimes.com/2017/09/23/world/middleeast/isis-drones-pentagon-experiments.html

Schogol, J. (2015, March 17). Predator UAV lost over Syria. *Air Force Times*. www.airforcetimes.com/news/your-air-force/2015/03/18

Shane, S. (2011, October 9). Coming soon: The drone arms race. *New York Times*. www.nytimes.com/2011/10/09/sunday-review/coming-soon-the-drone-arms-race.html

Shane, S. (2015, August 30). The lessons of Anwar al-Awlaki. *New York Times*. www.nytimes.com/2015/08/30/magazine/the-lessons-of-anwar-al-awlaki.html

Thrall, T. and Goepner, E. (2017, June 26). Step back: Lessons for U.S. foreign policy from the failed War on Terror. *Cato Institute*.www.cato.org/policy-analysis/step-back-lessons-us-foreign-policy-failed-war-terror

Umbrello, S., Torres, P., and De Bellis, A. F. (2019). The future of war: Could lethal autonomous weapons make conflict more ethical? *AI & Society* **35**(1), 273–282.

U.S. drone strike in Iraq kills Iranian military leader Qasem Soleimani (2020). *American Journal of International Law* **114**(2), 313–323.

Yousaf, K. (2018, January 25). Drone strike sparks Pak-US diplomatic spat. *Express Tribune*.https://tribune.com.pk/story/1618046

Zenko, M. (2013, January). Reforming U.S. drone strike policies. *Council on Foreign Relations*. www.cfr.org/report/reforming-us-drone-strike-policies

Zenko, M., and Kreps, S. E. (2014). *Limiting Armed Drone Proliferation*. New York: Council on Foreign Relations.

13 Environment and Conflict

CULLEN S. HENDRIX

Introduction

Every society, from the most technologically advanced to hunter-gatherer tribes deep in the Amazon, must meet two very basic challenges every day. The first is to provide at least 7.5 liters of potable freshwater to each person; this constitutes the World Health Organization's bare minimum for survival. The second is to provide each person with 2,100 calories of food, a value the World Food Programme calculates as meeting the minimal requirement for sustenance. These challenges are absolutely fundamental; they are the challenges that must be met over and over, day after day, in order to pursue any other goals.

For these reasons, the fates of even the inhabitants of the wealthiest countries on Earth are intimately tied to the environment, at both the local and global scale. In the developing world, this dependence is even more profound. Many households must produce their own food for sustenance, and ownership or access to land and water is a precondition for survival.

Because these resources are both vital and finite – there is only so much fresh water and arable land – they are valuable. And precisely because they are valuable, they have been fought over at least since the dawn of the Neolithic era some 12,000 years ago. In more modern times, concerns over access to arable land – land suitable for planting crops – were motivating factors behind Nazi Germany's expansion into Eastern Europe and the Soviet Union. In contemporary times, climate change and drought, or a shortage of water due to a period of prolonged abnormally low rainfall, have been identified as the sparks that started the Syrian Civil War in 2011. Yet most of the time, access to renewable resources like fresh water, land, and food is secured through peaceful means. This chapter will identify the specific conditions under which meeting these fundamental resource needs prompts violence, and how conditions of plenty can be conflict-prone as well.

This chapter answers a series of questions about environmental conflicts. What are environmental conflicts? When and where do they arise between states and within states? How do conflicts of all types affect the environment? Finally, how will climate change affect environmental conflict, and what can be done to mitigate these effects?

What Are Environmental Conflicts?

Environmental conflicts are disputes over access to or control of renewable resources such as farmland or pastures, water, livestock, or fisheries. Environmental conflicts can involve a very diverse set of actors, ranging from sovereign states and rebel groups – the core actors in state-based conflicts – to herding communities, farming cooperatives, community organizations, tribal groups, militias, and private businesses. This chapter focuses on conflicts *between* states – interstate conflicts – and conflicts *within* states – civil conflicts.

Renewable resources are resources that naturally replenish themselves – fish spawn, cattle reproduce, and lakes and rivers naturally recharge themselves from springs or runoff. However, these resources can collapse – a drastic and long-lasting reduction in the size of the resource – if they are overused. Alternately, these resources can dwindle due to pollution. Some renewable resources are **common-pool resources**, a type of resource available to many actors for consumption, and each actor's consumption of the resource reduces its availability for others to consume. If the resource is consumed at a rate at or below which it can be renewed, then the common pool resource endures. The numbers of bison, a large North American herd animal killed for meat, endured for centuries because native Americans did not hunt bison beyond the bison's natural ability to replenish their populations.

Resource collapse is often the result of a **tragedy of the commons**, when a common-pool resource is consumed faster than it can be replenished. In the canonical example, an entire community are free to graze their cattle on an open pasture; the famous Boston Common was originally used in this fashion. Each member of the community receives 100 percent of the benefit of use (grazing their cattle), but the costs (less forage for other animals) are imposed on the whole community. In turn, each member has an incentive to overuse the resource, leading to too many cattle, overgrazing, and destruction of the pasture.

Take the example of the Atlantic cod fishery off the shores of Newfoundland, historically one of the most productive and economically valuable in the North Atlantic Ocean (Figure 13.1). By the early 1960s, the fishery had been sustainably harvested for several centuries by small-scale local fishers and migratory fleets. In the 1970s, larger industrial fishing vessels armed with sonar and navigation systems began trawling the waters, leading catches to nearly double in less than a decade. However, these large catches undermined the ability of the fish to reproduce, causing the population to collapse by the early 1990s. To this day, the fishery has never rebounded to its pre-1970 level of productivity despite moratoria on fishing, leaving smaller-scale local fishers out of work and entire communities in flux (Hilborn 2012).

Because the most obvious solution to the tragedy of the commons is to restrict use, many environmental conflicts are over usage rights: who is allowed to make use of the resource and how much they are allowed to harvest. With many resources, this is done through communal or private property rights. Others, such as marine fisheries, are governed by country's territorial waters and exclusive economic zones (EEZs), which demarcate the maritime "territory" within which a country claims exclusive rights for fishing, drilling, and other economic activities. Like other territorial claims in the international system, these claims are subject to international law but ultimately enforced through the threat or use of force.

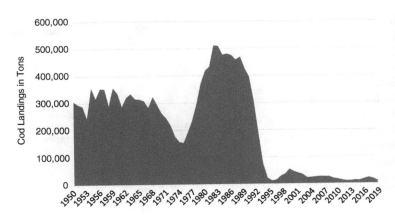

Figure 13.1. The rise and fall of the Atlantic cod fishery, 1850–2019. The graph shows how the excessive fishing of the late twentieth century has resulted in a tragedy of the commons, overconsumption of a common pool resource drastically degrading a renewable resource.

Food and Agricultural Organization of the United Nations, FAO Fisheries & Aquaculture.

Because most renewable resources are rival goods – land I use to farm corn is not available for you to graze your cattle on; water I use to irrigate my crops is not available to water your livestock – competing claims on these resources are omnipresent. However, violent conflict over them is not. Most of the time, competing claims are handled through market transactions, decided by law, or adjudicated through the courts or international treaties. The United States and Canada have an ongoing dispute over the international boundary of the Beaufort Sea in the Arctic Circle, which may hold vast untapped fisheries and natural gas deposits. But these competing claims have been handled peacefully through bilateral negotiations. Nevertheless, environmental conflicts have been a source of armed conflict both between and within states, and climate change may intensify competing claims and resulting conflicts in the future.

Environmental Conflicts and Interstate Conflict

Renewable resources often cause conflict between sovereign states. Broadly, the three main environmental claims that lead to conflict are (1) territorial claims, (2) claims over shared freshwater resources like rivers and lakes, and finally (3) maritime claims involving seas and oceans. While most of these claims are settled peacefully, they have been a cause of conflict in the past – and will continue to be into the future.

Population Growth and Territorial Claims

Territorial conquest – the desire to conquer and hold territory and that territory's economic assets – has been the central motivation to wage war for millennia. While the motivations have always been multiple, access to arable land has been chief among them. The Neolithic transition to sedentary agriculture (~10,000 BCE) facilitated explosions in the size and complexity of human communities, but also introduced concerns about the population outstripping the food supply.

Thomas Malthus (1766–1834), an English clergyman and economist writing at the dawn of the Industrial Revolution, was perhaps the first to clearly state the problem and link it to

Figure 13.2. The Malthusian relationship between the food supply, which grows linearly, and human population, which was thought to grow exponentially. Though neither claim has been borne out in the centuries since Malthus published his theory, it continues to motivate thinking about environmental conflicts. Created by chapter author.

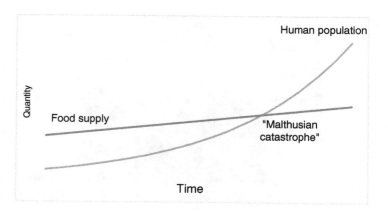

conflict. He observed that while human populations grow at an exponential rate (i.e., in percentage terms, with a compounding effect over time: 2, then 4, then 8, then 16 …), the food supply, at least in eighteenth-century England, appeared to increase only linearly (2, then 4, then 6 …), as more land was brought under cultivation. Figure 13.2 depicts the difference between exponential population growth and linear growth of food supply. At first, the difference between exponential and linear growth is small, and food supply is more than adequate. Over time, however, the difference is huge.

The implication is straightforward: human population will outpace its food supply, resulting in competition for ever-diminishing shares of resources. Human populations would be kept "equal to the means of subsistence" (Malthus 1798, 12) by means including potentially disease, starvation, and violent death – a "Malthusian catastrophe."

Though Malthus did not explicitly link food shortages with political violence, the term "**Malthusian**" has come to describe those who argue conflict occurs when the population's resource needs surpass the **carrying capacity**, the maximum sustainable population of a given ecosystem or environment, sparking distributive conflicts. In more modern times, this logic has been expanded to include not just basic necessities – food and water – but competition over natural resources that are rivalrous in their consumption – water my cattle drink is not available for others' cattle to drink, for example – and are either nonrenewable (coal, oil) or exhaustible due to overexploitation (farmland, rivers). The Malthusian perspective holds that countries will attempt to take territory by force when they begin to confront these constraints.

Malthusian catastrophes occur often in the animal world because animals do not have agency over either their reproductive habits or the food supply. With respect to humans, however, Malthus appears to have been wrong on both counts. Human population growth is not exponential and is anticipated to level off by the mid twenty-first century. Moreover, the food supply has increased faster than population since the 1800s. Despite this, Malthusian concerns have spurred conflict in the past, especially when circumstances in the international system amplified them.

That said, war is often a last resort to satisfy a country's resource needs because it is extremely costly. Many countries have populations that far surpass their own carrying capacity, and few resort to conflict to get the resources they need. Most trade for them, importing these resources from abroad. Major powers (and economies) China, Japan, and the United Kingdom are net food-importing countries, meaning they are at least partially reliant on food sourced from abroad to meet their domestic needs.

Territory is in most instances the ultimate divisible good. It can be split up a virtually infinite number of ways, making negotiated settlements easier. States typically only take the costly step of fighting when conditions in the international system restrict trade in either food or other important resources. Territorial conquest was commonplace under mercantilism – an economic system that prevailed from the sixteenth to eighteenth centuries under which European powers sought to minimize trade with their rivals – because it was one of the only mechanisms for Europe's empires to satisfy their resource needs.

Similarly, in the twentieth century, territory and population concerns became fused with nationalism and imperial ideology in Nazi Germany and Imperial Japan. In Germany, the concept of *Lebensraum* ("living space," and the need for the German people to expand territorially to accommodate their numbers) was central to Nazi ideology and used to justify Germany's annexation of Austria (1938), territorial expansion into the Sudetenland (1938), and invasions of Poland (1939) and the Soviet Union (1941). Similarly, Japan's annexation of Manchuria (1937) was in part the result of Japan's high population density and need to expand its agricultural base. Both of these campaigns occurred against the backdrop of the Great Depression, during which global trade had nearly come to a halt. In this context, war was deemed necessary to satisfy resource demands.

Transboundary Rivers and Lakes

Fresh water is obviously the most critical of renewable resources. In addition to being necessary for sustaining human, animal, and plant life, it is also a critical input for power generation. Hydropower, or electricity generated by hydraulic pressure via dams, is the world's leading source of renewable energy and accounts for roughly one-sixth of all power generation. Globally, demand for water is massive, yet it is uneconomical to transport water long distances. Thus, most countries and populations are reliant on surface water – water that collects in lakes, rivers, and wetlands – and groundwater accessed via wells to satisfy their water needs.

Surface water resources are often **transboundary,** meaning they are shared by two or more countries or jurisdictions within a country. For example, the Nile River (see Map 13.1) originates in Ethiopia and Uganda but crosses the territory of South Sudan and Sudan before making its way to Egypt, the most populous country in the Nile basin (basin being the land a river flows across or under and from which rainfall drains into the river). Because of its desert landscape, Egypt is also the country most dependent on the river for fresh water. North America's Colorado River is transboundary both in the international and domestic senses. The Colorado River flows from the United States into Mexico, and within the United States flows from Colorado through the states of Utah, Arizona, Nevada, and California.

Both the Nile and Colorado River basins create upstream/downstream relations between states. Upstream/downstream relationships are those where one country is entirely upstream and can control how much water flows to the downstream country via dams. In the Nile, Ethiopia and Uganda are the upstream countries, while South Sudan, Sudan, and Egypt are the

Map 13.1. The Nile River basin, an example of a transboundary water river that has upstream/ downstream dynamics. Wikipedia.

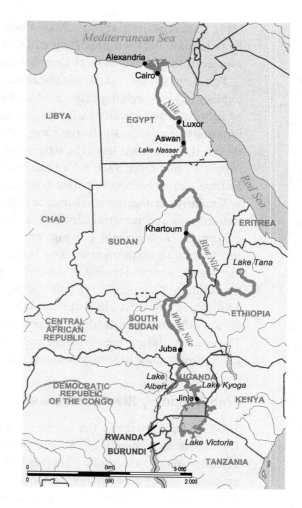

downstream countries. This contrasts with situations in which the sharing countries each have direct access to the resource. Both Canada and the United States have direct access to Lake Superior. Upstream/downstream relations are typically more conflict-prone than those in which sharing countries have direct access. When both countries have direct access, there is no potential to cut off the flow.

Most shared water resources are governed peacefully, especially when countries use international river treaties – formal agreements that specify how river resources are to be co-managed and how disputes over usage rights are to be resolved. These agreements typically specify how states will cooperate to monitor water levels, manage and render judgments regarding any usage disputes that arise, enforce the results of those judgments, and often create permanent commissions staffed with scientists and bureaucrats from member countries to carry out these tasks. The most famous of these commissions is the Permanent Indus Commission, which is composed of Indian and Pakistani officials and which co-manages the Indus River. Despite the history of conflict between the two countries, the commission has been in effect and operated continually since the 1960s, even during periods of active armed conflict between the two countries. This is a good example of how international institutions can facilitate cooperation, even among rivals.

Conflicts over shared water resources, **water wars**, typically arise when one country attempts to unilaterally divert the flow of the transboundary resource and restrict the amount flowing to downstream or other users. Especially in arid regions, where alternative sources of water like rainfall are lacking, these moves can spark conflict. This stress is likely to increase under climate change as many regions become even more arid over time.

The most famous water war was the **Six Day War** (1967) between Israel and Egypt, Jordan, and Syria. Concerns over water were a major cause of the conflict. Former Israeli Prime Minister Ariel Sharon (2001, 166) wrote in his memoir: "People generally regard June 5, 1967, as the day the Six Day War began. That is the official date, but in reality it started two and a half years earlier on the day Israel decided to act against the diversion of the Jordan River."

The Jordan River flows from headwaters in Syria and Lebanon to the Sea of Galilee, also known as Lake Tiberias, and on to the Dead Sea in the south (Map 13.2). Historically, the Jordan River has supplied a large share of both Israel's and Jordan's fresh water. The salience of the Sea of Galilee for Israel increased substantially after Israel began construction of the National Water Carrier in 1949, a system of aqueducts and reservoirs designed to siphon water from the Sea of Galilee and deliver it to Israel's more arid central and southern regions.

These withdrawals would mean less water flowing downstream into Jordan, which at the time controlled both the west and east banks of the Jordan. Both Jordan and Syria objected. Tensions flared in 1953 when Syrian artillery fired on an Israeli construction team that had begun construction for the intake of the National Water Carrier in a demilitarized zone established at the end of the 1948–1949 Arab–Israeli War. A US-brokered agreement over shared use of the water, the Johnston Plan, was negotiated in 1955 but ultimately not ratified by Jordan and Syria.

In late 1964, Jordan, Syria, and their allies in the Arab League decided to take unilateral action against Israel's siphoning from the Sea of Galilee, and began construction on projects that would divert flow from the Sea of Galilee's headwaters. This would reduce Israel's overall freshwater resources by nearly 10 percent. Israel responded to this plan with force in 1965, using airpower, artillery, and tanks to destroy Syrian earthmoving equipment. These actions were the ones referenced by Ariel Sharon, and would come to be viewed as one of the major proximate causes of the Six Day War.

The Six Day War ended with Israel's occupation of the West Bank of the Jordan River, the Sinai Peninsula, and the Golan Heights. Control of the Golan Heights allowed Israel unfettered access to the Sea of Galilee. Today, however, Israel is much less reliant on the Sea of Galilee than in years past. One way to lessen conflict over shared resources is to make them less vital to national interests. Israel achieved this by investing in desalination plants, facilities that convert salt water into fresh water, which now produce more freshwater than Israel consumes. These investments, along with conservation efforts, have radically lessened Israel's dependence on the Sea of Galilee.

The Six Day War is the most prominent example of a water war. However, it is hard to argue water was the only cause of the conflict. The competing claims on the Jordan River may have heightened tensions, but Israel, Jordan, and Syria were already among the "most likely" cases of

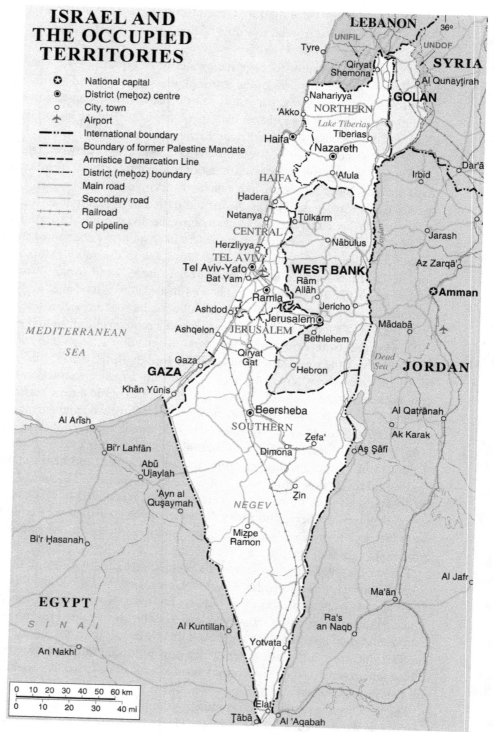

Map 13.2. Map of Israel and the Occupied Territories. Israel captured the Golan Heights in 1967, giving it control of significant headwaters of Lake Tiberias, an important source of fresh water for both Israel and neighboring Jordan. Wikipedia, which indicates it is a modification of a United Nations map.

conflict: a democracy (Israel) confronting autocracies (Jordan and Syria), with extremely limited economic linkages, and a history of past conflict (the Arab–Israeli Wars of 1948 and 1956). Other factors – like Egypt's closing of the Straits of Tiran, a shipping corridor linking Israel's port of Eilat on the Red Sea to the Indian Ocean – could be viewed as triggers as well. Many most-likely cases for water wars – the Six Day War; conflict between India and Pakistan over the Indus River – are most-likely cases for conflict for reasons that have nothing to do with water.

Maritime Claims

As we discussed earlier, states have territorial claims that exist beyond their land territory, extending into both territorial waters and their exclusive economic zones. These waters are not just important for shipping and navigation, they provide access to valuable resources. Fisheries are the most obvious, but since the 1960s developments in offshore oil, natural gas exploration, and drilling technology, maritime claims have become even more valuable. Motivations related to both renewable and nonrenewable resources are at play in China and Japan's dispute over the Senkaku Islands in the East China Sea. Though the islands are uninhabited, they provide access to rich fisheries and potentially vast hydrocarbon deposits.

Fisheries-related conflicts are among the most common types of small-scale interstate conflict today. Markets can deliver fish across borders to consumers, but profits from fisheries only accrue to those with access to them. This creates strong domestic lobbies for expansion of fishing rights claims. Many fish are migratory, and their migration patterns have no regard for human territorial claims. Often, this results in fishers following fish out of their own waters and into the waters of other sovereign states.

Fisheries-related conflicts typically take the following form: One country attempts to enforce a maritime boundary that is not recognized by the "foreign" fishing vessels of another. Upon interdiction or boarding by the "home" country's navy, the "foreign" fishing vessels then call on the navy of their home country for protection, precipitating a standoff between the navies of the two countries. These conflicts are typically initiated by privately owned vessels rather than state actors, and driven by economic, rather than food security–related, interests.

The classic examples are the **Cod Wars** of the mid twentieth century. British fishing vessels had been fishing the cod-rich waters off the coast of Iceland for centuries. In 1958, Iceland unilaterally expanded its exclusive fishing zone from four nautical miles (nm) (roughly 7.4 km) to twelve (22.2 km) in order to provide Icelandic fishers with exclusive access to the highly lucrative fishery. This move was protested by Iceland's NATO allies on the basis of prevailing international law – a 1956 decision by the Organization for European Economic Cooperation – recognizing only the four nm exclusive fishery limit. Great Britain announced its fishing fleet would continue to fish within the expanded Icelandic waters under protection of several warships, leading to confrontations between Icelandic and British warships. Similar skirmishes occurred in the 1960s and 70s, but with just a single fatality resulting. Thus, the term "Cod War" is a bit of a misnomer. Still, it is an example of an environmental conflict between "least likely" belligerents: two democracies and alliance partners. The dispute was finally resolved in 1976 with Iceland claiming a 200 nm Exclusive Economic Zone; six years later, the 200 nm EEZ would become standard per the United Nations Law of the Sea.

Environmental Conflicts and Civil Conflict

Civil conflicts are conflicts between state and nonstate actors within a state's borders; internationalized civil conflicts are civil conflicts that involve several sovereign states fighting against nonstate actors (see Chapter 7). A recent example of an internationalized conflict is the conflict between ISIS and the governments of both Iraq and Syria. Communal conflicts are conflicts between nonstate actors that do not directly involve the state. Communal conflicts are often much smaller in scale and somewhat harder to classify, as they may involve groups ranging from armed criminal organizations to ethnic and tribal militias.

There are two common types of environmentally linked civil conflict: conflict over claims to renewable resources, i.e., distributive conflicts, and conflicts related to environmental degradation.

Distributive Conflicts

Distributive conflicts are conflicts over claims to renewable resources – over who has a right to use, or in some cases own, a resource. These rights can be individual or collective. For example, I may, as an individual, own my home and the land on which it sits. I have individual rights and claims on that land. However, some lands are held communally, with members of a given community having rights to that land as a collective that can then assign rights within the community. For example, the *ejido* system in Mexico assigns usage rights to land for farming to collectives whose members do not own the land but have exclusive usage rights to particular parcels within the *ejido* that they can pass along to their children. They have usage rights, but the land is owned by the collective in the sense that the collective can decide to sell it. Communal ownership structures mean that one community member's use or misuse of the resource affects something of value owned by the collective, making it more likely the entire community will be involved in conflict over it.

Distributive conflicts can take multiple forms. The most common relates to communal conflict over usage rights to renewable resources like land, water, or cattle. One example is the Samburu–Turkana range war (1996–2015) in northwest Kenya. The Samburu and Turkana are ethnic groups that have semi-nomadic, pastoral lifestyles. This semi-arid region is home to many cattle herders, who move their herds in search of forage (food) and water. Because both forage and water are rival in their consumption, conflict often erupts over access rights. In addition, because the cattle themselves are a valuable resource, cattle raiding – armed theft of cattle – is another cause of conflict. This raiding activity occurs most frequently just after droughts, as herders seek to replenish their herds thinned by starvation and related diseases. These raids are most often conducted by young men related through kinship. Thus, these bands are organized and armed but do not pursue political aims, which makes their raids distinct from state-based armed conflict.

A second class of distributive conflicts is **"sons of the soil" conflicts**. These are conflicts between ethnic groups that consider themselves indigenous – the original inhabitants of a given territory, but not necessarily "native peoples" such as Native Americans or Aborigines– and recent migrants from other regions of the country. Migrants come in search of land, often at the prompting of the central government. Central governments may believe it is their responsibility to "nation build" and integrate ethnic homelands. Governments may also be responding to demographic pressures in other parts of the country and seek to ease overcrowding there by encouraging the landless to move.

Competition for resources between "locals" and migrants sparks low-level decentralized conflict, often taking the form of ethnic rioting: outbreaks of violence targeted at either locals by recent migrants or vice versa, that can spiral, with initial attacks being met with ever larger tit-for-tat responses fueled by a desire for revenge, fear of being attacked and wanting to take the initiative, and even rumor. Eventually, state forces intervene, typically taking the side (or at least appearing to take the side) of their co-ethnic recent migrants. At this point, many sons of the soil conflicts become civil wars, with locals taking up arms to try to secede or gain greater regional autonomy.

The Sri Lankan Civil War (1983–2009) is a prominent example of a sons of the soil conflict. Sri Lanka is a small island country off the southern coast of India. Upon gaining independence from Great Britain in 1948, the country was very dependent on farming and fishing for employment, with much of its rapidly growing population clustered in its central and southern provinces. Sri Lanka is made up of two primary ethnic groups, Tamils (20 percent) and Sinhala (75 percent). After independence, the Sri Lankan government – then dominated by Tamils – empaneled the Gal Oya Development Board to address overpopulation in some provinces by relocating landless farmers to Tamil-dominated areas in Sri Lanka's eastern province. These relocated peasants were almost all Sinhalese. In 1956, the Sinhala-dominated Sri Lankan Freedom Party (SLFP) won elections on largely ethnic grievance–based appeals, and on increased perceptions among Tamils that their lands were being colonized from within.

Events of that year illustrate how these small ethnic conflicts can spiral:

[W]hen the Official Language Act was still being debated, a Tamil burned a Sinhalese shop, and the shop owner shot three Tamils who were watching the shop burn. Tamils then went to the Batticaloa–Amparai road and stoned Gal Oya Board trucks. One of the truck drivers went to Amparai and reported that a Sinhalese girl had been raped by Tamils. This rumor was sufficient to induce general assaults on Tamils. That night there were assaults by members of both groups against the other. The next day a rumor spread that a Tamil army was moving into the area, and this created a panic. By the third day, Tamil colonists in Gal Oya headed back to their home villages, and returned in large numbers with guns ... Through it all the police force was ineffective, in large part because its members were afraid of the mobs.

Despite the fact that moderate Tamil leaders negotiated a compromise with the government as to who would get preference for settlement in the newly irrigated lands, under demographic challenge, Tamil-organized protest groups, parties, and self-protection (or provocation) militias began to form. (Fearon and Laitin 2011, 202–203)

This vignette is a very clear example of spiraling conflict, with small-scale attacks followed by increasingly violent responses.

The Sinhala government's placement of an air force base in the eastern province only enflamed Tamil fears of internal colonization and displacement. As ethnic rioting spiraled out of control, Tamils began fleeing to other Tamil-dominated areas in the north, with many men and women deciding to join rebel forces. By 1983, the Liberation Tigers of Tamil Eelam

Figure 13.3. The brutality of the Sri Lanka Civil War. This 2016 protest, seven years after war's end, seeks to draw attention to the 22,000 people, mostly Tamils, still missing from the war. Many were abducted by government forces using "white vans," snatched off the street or from their homes, never to be heard from again. ©LAKRUWAN WANNIARACHCHI / Stringer/AFP/ Getty Images.

(LTTE) began open rebellion against the Sinhala-dominated government. The conflict would ultimately claim between 60,000 and 100,000 lives, with tens of thousands more missing (see Figure 13.3), before ending in 2009 with the LTTE's defeat.

Environmental Degradation and Conflict

Some environmental conflicts are not about claiming a larger share of resources but rather preventing damage to existing resources. Industrial and mining-led development, although potentially highly lucrative, generally entails significant environmental costs in the form of resource degradation, water pollution, and poor health outcomes. Conflict can ensue when these costs are concentrated in communities that do not receive a large share of those benefits, especially when those communities are ethnically or religiously distinct from the elites who reap the financial rewards. These conflicts typically involve the central government approving – either explicitly or tacitly – of environmentally destructive economic activities. These activities are opposed by subnational actors, leading to conflict with the central government.

Take oil production in the Niger delta of Nigeria. Oil is a central pillar of the Nigerian economy, accounting for nearly 90 percent of exports and 70 percent of government revenues. All of Nigeria's oil production, however, occurs in and around the Niger River delta, which makes up 7.5 percent of the Nigerian land mass and is home to about 20 percent of its population. Vast networks of small pipelines crisscross the landscape and are prone to leaks and sabotage; in the recent past, the region has averaged almost 420 spills per year. These spills foul freshwater resources, destroy important mangrove forests, and damage cropland (see Figure 13.4).

Of course, the oil industry also generates massive economic resources, but most of these resources leave the region and flow to the federal government and transnational corporations like Royal Dutch Shell. Feeling marginalized, activists for the Ogoni and Ijaw – two tribal groups in the region – began protesting local environmental degradation and what they saw to be an unfair distribution of oil riches. These protests began peacefully but were met with

Figure 13.4. Frequent oil spills in Nigeria's Niger Delta have wrought havoc on local livelihoods. These fishing boats have been abandoned due to the pollution of estuaries and mangrove forests that provide habitat for fish.
©Bloomberg Creative/Bloomberg Creative Photos/Getty Images.

repression by the Nigerian government. In 2004, the Movement for the Emancipation of the Niger Delta (MEND) and Niger Delta People's Volunteer Force (NDPVF) began an armed insurrection against the Nigerian government. Their claims revolved around reapportioning a greater share of the oil wealth to affected states and providing more resources to clean up environmental damage. Their campaign wound down in 2009 under a government amnesty plan for former combatants. However, the region continues to be plagued by armed groups motivated by a combination of environmental and economic grievances and, in some cases, greed. These pipelines also make attractive targets for oil theft or payment demands for not sabotaging the pipelines in the first place.

Where Do Environmental Conflicts Occur?

As we discussed earlier, competing claims over renewable resources are omnipresent. Even in wealthy countries, population growth and increased wealth seem to push demand for land, water, and other resources ever upward. However, violent conflict over renewable resources is not inevitable. There are contextual factors that matter in determining whether environmental conflicts become violent. Three contextual factors are most important: (1) state capacity and legitimacy; (2) dependence on rural livelihoods; and (3) **groupness**, or the degree to which individuals in society depend on distinct identity groups, like ethnicity or religion, for their economic prospects, physical security, and as a platform to pursue political power.

First, state capacity and legitimacy are key. State capacity is the ability of the state to mobilize resources and enforce its territorial monopoly on the legitimate use of force. When state capacity is high, these conflicts are almost always channeled through legitimate legal and political institutions, like courts and legislatures, or effectively by strong, professional militaries. Similarly, legitimacy matters for whether these state institutions are viewed as fair and impartial – as when institutions, especially courts, are viewed as legitimate and impartial arbiters of conflict, and the use of violence to settle disputes will be met with criminal charges and punishment. These institutions can provide peaceful channels for resolving conflict and, by imposing punishments for taking the law into one's own hands, dramatically increase the costs of fighting, thus making peaceful outcomes more likely.

In many parts of the developing world, these institutions are either weak – courts and police officers are neither physically close enough to conflicts nor powerful enough to contain them – or viewed with deep skepticism, i.e., they lack legitimacy. In these contexts, disputes often involve participants taking matters into their own hands. Alternatively, disputes may be taken up by informal institutions, like village or tribal elders, who may not be seen as legitimate by all parties. When state institutions, and therefore state capacity, are weak, environmental conflict is more likely to turn violent.

Second, conflict is more likely when renewable resources are central to livelihoods and wellbeing, when people need to "live off the land." Singapore is remarkably overcrowded in the sense that it produces little food and has exceptionally high population density. However, vanishingly few Singaporeans are engaged in farming, with the vast majority involved in manufacturing or services. More broadly, direct access to natural resources like land and water is not central to most livelihoods in the developed world. In countries of the Organization for Economic Cooperation and Development (OECD), like the United States, Germany, and France, only 1 to 3 percent of the population work in agriculture. In contrast, agriculture is the primary source of employment in most developing countries. In Ethiopia, Rwanda, and Uganda, agriculture employs roughly three out of every four people in the workforce; in Nepal, the share is closer to two out of three. Less developed countries typically do not have vast systems of water management and irrigation for agriculture, meaning that agricultural productivity is almost entirely determined by weather conditions. In these predominantly rural societies, direct access to land and water is much more tied to the ability to provide for one's family, making violent conflict over threats to renewable resource access more likely.

Third, strong group identities (or "groupness") make environmental conflict more likely. In societies with high groupness, ethnic, religious, and/or clan identities provide access to economic opportunity and political participation. They also determine who receives political benefits from those in power. These identities tend to be ascriptive, in the sense that they are identities individuals are born into and are relatively hard to change. In many developing countries, these identities form the basis for political office-seeking.

Ethnically homogeneous countries, like the Republic of Korea, and extremely ethnically diverse countries, like Tanzania, are characterized by low groupness. Identities are not highly salient for political mobilization. In contrast, in countries like Iraq (Sunni Arabs, Shia Arabs, and Kurds), Burundi and Rwanda (Tutsis and Hutus in both), and Myanmar (Bamar, Shan, Kayin, Rakhine, Mon, Kachin, Royhinga, and others), political cleavages and patronage networks break along identity-based lines, making groupness high.

Groupness matters for two main reasons. First, in societies with high groupness, individuals are already embedded in communities and networks of action; it is easier to identify one's "team" and facilitate cooperation and coordination, including coordinating to engage in violent activities. Second, identity-based cleavages make it easier for political entrepreneurs – those seeking to further their own interests by promoting conflict – to identify their natural base of supporters and "other" nonmembers of the group. Othering is the process of rhetorically heightening the differences between an in-group and an-out group, dehumanizing the members of the latter to the point that standard, nonviolent norms of behavior do not apply to interactions with them. Othering has been central to the justification for and conduct of mass atrocities throughout history, with prominent examples including Nazi promotion of Aryan features and demonization of Jews, Roma, Poles, and homosexuals, and Hutu agitators referring to Tutsis as "cockroaches." When groupness is high, political entrepreneurs can frame environmental issues like access to land and water as zero-sum conflicts with despised out-groups, facilitating mobilization and legitimizing the use of violence. Indeed, political entrepreneurs can be key figures in heightening groupness, often weaving historical narratives about particular groups in order to mobilize followers to serve their own ends.

Taken together, these factors indicate we should expect to see more violent environmental conflicts in societies with weak state capacity, high levels of dependence on agricultural livelihoods, and high degrees of groupness.

When Do Environmental Conflicts Occur?

We've discussed *where* we might expect to see intrastate environmental conflicts, but *when* should we expect to see them? Malthusian logic would suggest conflicts occur when resources are particularly scarce, such as during a drought or in the aftermath of a natural disaster, like a hurricane or typhoon, that destroys cropland and infrastructure.

For instance, if I am a Turkana herder and my region is experiencing a drought, access to what little forage and water exists is incredibly important: without it, my herd – and with it perhaps my family – will die. Under these conditions, violence may well be my last-best answer. Under more bountiful conditions, however, I would be less likely to put my life at risk to fight for access to a water hole when I could just drive my herd farther along to another hole or to a stream. I have much less risky alternatives.

While this logic is intuitive, it does not tell the whole story. An opposing viewpoint holds that instead of focusing on scarcity as a motive for conflict, scarcity can be viewed alternately as a factor affecting the perceived costs of fighting. Other things being equal, as fighting becomes more costly, actors are less likely to take up arms (see Chapter 1).

As the perceived costs of conflict increase, the range of outcomes that both parties prefer to war increases. These costs can be real, in terms of "blood and treasure," but can also take the form of opportunity costs: the economic and social losses stemming from diversion of resources into fighting. This is known as a "guns or butter" tradeoff: resources spent on fighting are unavailable to spend foraging or working, in the case of individuals, or on disaster relief or crop insurance, in the case of governments. From this perspective, fighting ought to be less likely during periods of acute scarcity. With abundance, society can more easily shoulder the costs of conflict without cutting into the average citizen's quality of life. Rich societies, in turn, might be more likely to wage war, because the costs of war are less painful.

So, which perspective is right? Does scarcity increase or reduce conflict? The evidence is complicated. With respect to communal conflict and more spontaneous forms of conflict, it appears conflict is more likely during periods of abundance and drought than during "normal" conditions. With respect to state-involved conflict, there is some evidence that it occurs more frequently under more abundant conditions. Finally, with respect to interstate conflict, it appears that dryer than normal conditions are pacifying. Research on this topic is still in its early stages and much is left to be discovered.

Conflict Effects on the Environment

With few exceptions, conflict is incredibly damaging to the environment. The effects are both direct, with environmental harm being a goal of military activity, and indirect, with environmental harm resulting from human responses to wartime conditions or as a side effect of preparing for or waging war.

Direct Effects

Warfare is often about imposing costs on one's enemies in order to compel or coerce them to do something: quit territory, change behavior, or provide some sort of tribute or acquiescence. Sometimes it is imposing costs for costs' sake, simply to punish. One way to impose costs is to make habitat unlivable. Historical accounts of "salting the earth" – spreading salt, minerals, and invasive weeds in order to make arable land unsuitable for planting – date back to at least the Assyrian Empire (2500–605 BCE). Though these stories may be more folklore than fact, it has been common practice since the dawn of large-scale warfare for armies to destroy crops and farmland in order to coerce starving populations. In conflicts from the Second Boer War in South Africa (1899–1902) to present day South Sudan, food denial has been used against both combatants and civilians.

Land mines and unexploded ordinance have similar effects. Land mines are a cheap way to set a defensive perimeter or cover a retreat. Especially in the latter circumstance, many of these minefields are never recorded. Despite de-mining efforts, many places are still considered no-go zones for both agricultural and animal grazing purposes. Every day, people and livestock are killed or maimed by land mines that may have been set during conflicts that occurred decades ago.

Harming the environment in order to deny adversaries cover or refuge is a second direct effect. This is especially common in the context of counterinsurgency, where large armies confront small, lightly armed and irregular opposition forces. US campaigns against Iraqi Sunni insurgents in Al-Anbar and the Viet Cong in Vietnam are two examples of counterinsurgency. Because insurgent forces are almost always outnumbered and outgunned, they tend to rely on guerrilla tactics that make use of cover provided by forests, tall grasslands, marshes, and mountains – hence the term "head for the hills," which means to retreat and regroup under the cover provided by mountains.

Frustrated by these tactics, armies sometimes resort to attacking the very environment that provides cover. During Operation Ranch Hand (1961–1972), US airplanes dropped an estimated 20 million gallons of herbicides and defoliants on South Vietnam, destroying 20,000 square kilometers of forest, an area roughly the size of New Jersey. Some of these chemicals, like Agent Orange, were highly toxic and left lasting legacies of cancer and birth defects among the Vietnamese population and among the US servicepersons who handled them. This strategy is not new, however. Julius Caesar's Roman armies would cut down forests during European campaigns in order to protect themselves from hit-and-run attacks, and retreating Soviet armies burned crops rather than allow them to be captured by advancing Germans during Operation Barbarossa in World War II. Deliberate destruction of the environment is part of some war-fighting strategies.

Indirect Effects

Some of the indirect effects are straightforward. War-fighting invariably destroys some of the surrounding environment: tanks leak diesel fuel and rip up surface vegetation, armies forage for food and fuel, harvesting food and plants as they go, and bombs destroy both their intended targets and surrounding ecosystems. Depleted uranium, a dense material used for tank armor and armor-piercing bullets and shells, may be leading to increased rates of cancer and birth defects in some regions of Iraq where it was deployed.

Even preparations for conflict can have deep and lasting environmental consequences. During the Cold War, nuclear powers conducted 423 above-ground and over 1,400 underground nuclear tests, releasing radioactive material into the atmosphere and the ground. Just storing and maintaining these nuclear arsenals comes with significant environmental costs.

Similarly, the carbon footprint of modern, mechanized warfare is huge – and has grown larger over time. During World War II, the US military consumed roughly one gallon of fuel per soldier per day; by 2006, that number was up to sixteen. On a daily basis, the US military was consuming as much gasoline as the entire country of Sweden. Outside of nuclear aircraft carriers and submarines, most weapons of war are not alternative-fuel vehicles. War is incredibly energy-intensive, and most of this energy comes from burning fossil fuels.

Other indirect effects are by-products of how human populations try to cope with war. First, wars almost always displace people, leading to unsustainable coping strategies. This is true of both large-scale interstate wars and civil conflicts, but the effects are even more pronounced for civil conflicts, as many governments and rebels resort to "draining the sea" – forcibly depopulating areas where the enemy is thought to be active, in order to separate insurgents and/or government sympathizers from combatants. Refugees often wind up inhabiting marginal lands with few economic prospects – if they weren't marginal, they'd be inhabited already – making them dependent on humanitarian assistance and unsustainable foraging strategies for food, shelter, and energy. For example, refugees from the Rwandan civil war in the Democratic Republic of the Congo (DRC) deforested roughly thirty-eight square kilometers, an area about one-third the size of San Francisco, within three weeks of their arrival in and around the city of Goma near the Rwandan/DRC border. Former Rwandan rebels pushing into DRC were implicated in the slaughter of already endangered highland mountain gorillas, for bushmeat. These foraging practices harm both ecosystems and the wildlife they support.

Second, war promotes unsustainable harvesting practices. Wartime often causes breakdowns in social order and the rule of law, undermining faith that usage rights will be enforced and protected. When this happens, people who normally have incentives to take the long view and carefully tend to their herds, fields, or orchards instead worry that they will not have access to them in the future, and thus overharvest them in the present. Surveyors found after the US invasion of Afghanistan in 2001 that half the country's natural pistachio woodlands had been cut down in order to sell wood or hoard it for future use. Given how long pistachio trees take to mature, it was the early 2010s before those orchards could be regrown and returned to production. Conflict leads to unsustainable and shortsighted harvesting practices that can undermine the long-term viability of the resource.

Finally, these same breakdowns in order and the rule of law provide opportunities for illegal activities. In wartime, insurgents, local warlords, and often members of the military are able to make substantial fortunes trafficking in illegally harvested resources. These resources include everything from conflict timber – exotic, sometimes endangered hardwoods – to "conflict fish," rhino horn, and ivory. These resources have received less attention than conflict minerals – nonrenewable, highly lucrative minerals like diamonds, gold, and tungsten – but their over-harvesting can lead to biodiversity loss and permanent changes in ecosystems.

There are a few exceptions: circumstances where conflict helps to preserve the environment. Interstate wars sometimes create a "no man's land," where human activity is limited due to fighting or defensive perimeters. In these conditions, some ecosystems can flourish.

During World War I, Germany and Great Britain sought to enforce naval blockades on one another and used surface craft and submarines to police the waters of the North Sea. Sailors both naval and merchant came to fear the dreaded German U-boats, which could attack seemingly without warning from below the surface. Fearful of being sunk, many fishing vessels stayed in port. Once the war ended in 1918, European fishers reported significantly higher catch rates and significantly larger fish – both signs of a flourishing population. Freed for years from fishing pressure, the fisheries of the North Sea grew larger and healthier (Heidbrink 2018). Another example can be found in what is perhaps the most dangerous territory on Earth: the demilitarized zone (DMZ) between the North and South Korea. The roughly 4 km–wide, 238 km–long zone has become a conservation haven for several endangered or vulnerable species, like red-crowned cranes and white-naped cranes (Kim 2013). However, the conservation-promoting effects of conflict are not to be overestimated. By and large, conflict is as destructive to the environment as it is to the human populations that wage it.

Climate Change and Conflict

How does climate change fit into this picture? Climate change is perhaps the most vexing challenge facing the international community today. It will affect lives and livelihoods every-where by changing weather patterns, spurring migration, placing strain on infrastructure and social safety nets, and changing the geography of food production worldwide.

Given these expected changes, will climate change spur conflict? This question began gaining traction in the US national security community in the early 2000s, largely in response to news coverage linking drought and desertification to the armed conflict in the Darfur region of Sudan. UN Secretary General Ban Ki-moon (2007) was among the voices saying the Darfur conflict "began as an ecological crisis, arising at least in part from climate change." More recently, climate change has been implicated in the Syrian Civil War, possibly the gravest humanitarian disaster of our time. Are we facing a future of endemic conflict resulting from climate change?

It is very hard to know. Our understanding of the human impact of climate change lags behind our understanding of the physical impact for several reasons. First, forecasting human impacts requires scientists to move out of comparatively deterministic hard sciences like physics, chemistry, and biology, and into the less deterministic disciplines of the social sciences: sociology, economics, political science, and anthropology. We have yet to develop models that accurately predict future economic growth or where wars are likely to occur, for example. People are complicated and, as a result, the interactions between them are more highly variable, historically contingent, and context-specific than for their counterparts in the physical world.

Second, humans are bad at anticipating the technological solutions we devise to overcome problems posed by our physical environment. Paul Ehrlich's bestseller *The Population Bomb*, published in 1968, predicted that India was headed for mass starvation. However, *The Population Bomb* appeared at about the same time Norman Borlaug was introducing high-yield strains of wheat and rice to the subcontinent, sparking a Green Revolution that substantially boosted food production, helping India become self-sufficient in the production of grains by the mid 1970s, averting a food crisis. Our present forecasts about the human effects of climate change are limited by our inability to imagine the future fruits of human ingenuity.

We face this question with a host of unknowns. Still, we can look at the historical record for some guidance as to how climate change might contribute to conflict in the future. We will discuss three main mechanisms: (1) climate "shocks" resulting in violence, (2) climate change spurring migration and leading to host–migrant conflicts, and (3) climate change causing food price spikes with destabilizing effects. Via these mechanisms and others, scholars believe that under a business-as-usual climate scenario of a 4°C increase above historic global temperatures, the risk of climate-induced violence will increase fivefold, up from the estimated 5 percent average effect over the past century (Mach et al. 2019).

Climate "Shocks" and Violence

Human societies have proven remarkably adaptable to a host of different climates: think of the Inuit who have adapted to the bitter cold climate of the Arctic Circle, or the Bedouin nomadic peoples who survive in the arid and extremely hot Sahara Desert. This is because given stable climatic conditions, humans can adapt their agricultural, foraging, and food and water management systems accordingly, seemingly no matter how harsh that stable state might be. However, what happens when formerly stable conditions change rapidly?

Climate change will result in a decline in the predictability of climatic conditions. The term global warming refers to a general increase in average temperature, but the increase in mean temperatures will be accompanied by an increase in the variance as well – more years of unseasonably cold and warm temperatures. Similarly, annual rainfall totals are anticipated to decrease in many parts of the globe but their variance will increase as well – more droughts *and* more flooding. Figure 13.5 depicts these changes graphically: the grey line represents a "new normal" in which the mean of, say, temperature has increased, but so has its variability. This

Figure 13.5. Shifting means and variances. The black line represents the baseline. The grey, dashed line represents the "new" normal. Note that while the mean of the distribution has increased, i.e., moved to the right, the variance has increased as well, with more observations "in the tails" taking on extreme values. This schematic can be applied to rainfall, daily temperature, and the magnitude of cyclonic storms. Created by chapter author.

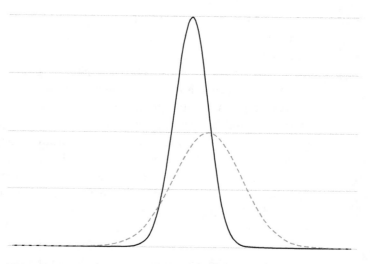

means more days/months/years will be far from the mean; what used to be a once-in-100-years occurrence will occur much more frequently, as we are already seeing with flooding and cyclonic storms like hurricanes and typhoons. For example, the United States experienced at least twenty-four once-in-500-years rain events from 2010 to 2017, including Hurricane Harvey which devastated the Houston area (CBS News 2017). Later in this chapter we will discuss the drought that preceded the Syrian Civil War, a drought that was probably the worst Syria had experienced in 900 years.

These kinds of rapid, year-to-year deviations from normal climatic conditions are called climate shocks. When climatic conditions deviate greatly from normal – i.e., stable expectations – conflict becomes more likely. This is true both of positive deviations – too much rainfall, overly hot temperatures – and negative deviations – too little rainfall (drought), overly cool temperatures. These shocks can result in temporary shortages, flooding, or crop failures that threaten livelihoods and result in distributive conflict between producers – like cattle raiding – and between producers and consumers of food. That is, these shocks can give rise to the kinds of temporary scarcity that spur conflict through mechanisms discussed in previous sections.

Climate Change, Migration, and Conflict

One strategy for adapting to climate change is migration, either within or across national borders. This is true of both longer-term changes in human habitat due to changes in climate, like sea level rise in low-lying areas of Bangladesh, and of short-term shocks, like the mass out-migration that occurred after Hurricane Katrina in New Orleans. Some countries, like the low-lying island state of Mauritius, may become effectively uninhabitable due to sea level rise. If livelihoods become completely unsustainable due to changes in climate, human populations have no choice but to move.

Of course, moving means moving somewhere else. Though most migrants are peacefully welcomed to their new environs, migration can spark conflict in several different ways. One is distributive conflict over land resources, similar to the sons of the soil conflicts discussed earlier.

An example of this is the Chittagong Hill Tracts conflict in Bangladesh. Because of overpopulation and recurrent flooding in and around Dhaka, the capital, the Bangladeshi government began encouraging migration by Muslim Bengalis from its central region to the Chittagong Hill Tracts, a less densely populated region primarily inhabited by Buddhists and Hindus. This in-migration resulted in a long-running insurgency by the armed wing of the United People's Party of the Chittagong Hill Tracts (1975–1997), a Buddhist- and Hindu-dominated movement seeking regional autonomy.

In the short term, these migrations place significant strain on government services and infrastructure in receiving communities. Over the long term, migrants typically boost the economies of their receiving communities. However, large migrations can tax existing government programs and safety nets, especially if these migrants come in large numbers over a short time, as is typically the case following natural disasters like hurricanes or floods. When government policies fail to provide for these populations, protests can provoke violent crackdowns and lead to conflict. (See case study: The Syrian Civil War, p. 426)

Again, context will matter greatly for whether migration will spark conflict. In more developed countries with adequate resources for addressing migrant needs and in countries with low groupness, these migrations are unlikely to spark conflict. However, in poor countries with high groupness, conflict is much more likely.

Climate Change and Food Price Spikes

A third mechanism by which climate change may contribute to conflict is via its effects on food prices. Climate change will reshape the geography of global food production, with many countries near the equator seeing large declines in crop yields due to rising temperatures and less rainfall, while higher-latitude countries will see increasing productivity as more land becomes cultivable and growing seasons become longer. As countries near the equator will see their populations grow much more rapidly than higher-latitude countries, the locus of global demand will shift as well. In these circumstances, global food trade will be vital to meeting global demand, and prices in global markets will increasingly determine local prices paid by consumers.

At the same time, climate change will make extreme weather events like droughts and floods more frequent in these northern latitudes, leading to more frequent food price shocks, or rapid increases in food prices. High food prices can be extremely politically destabilizing, and were among the grievances that fueled the Arab Uprisings of 2010–2011. Interestingly, it was not local drought in the Middle East and North Africa that caused these spikes, but rather droughts and wildfires in Russia and floods in Australia – both major food-exporting countries – that caused crops to fail and sent prices spiraling. Thus, global markets are an important vehicle for reducing long-term vulnerability to climate change but can also transmit the destabilizing effects of a local shock in a food-exporting country throughout the globe.

Addressing climate change will be one of the major challenges facing the globe in and beyond your lifetime. Thankfully, most adaptations to climate change will be peaceful and benign, if not even beneficial. However, climate change is likely to exacerbate existing environmental conflicts and create new ones via the mechanisms described in this chapter.

CASE STUDY

The Syrian Civil War

The Syrian Civil War has so far claimed over 500,000 lives and displaced nearly 11 million refugees and internally displaced persons. However, the role of environmental factors in the conflict is hotly contested. Some view it as a climate-caused conflict; others think climate change and drought had little to do with the outbreak of violence. This case study presents three perspectives on the causes of the conflict in turn: (1) the Malthusian, or environmental determinist, narrative; (2) a revisionist narrative, which counters that the case for environmental causes is overblown; and finally (3) a synthetic perspective that attempts to bridge the differences between the two. In doing so, it highlights how environmental factors can be important in creating grievances but focuses our attention also on the contextual factors – and government responses – that determine whether these grievances will result in conflict. Finally, it requires us to think critically about what we mean when we say climate change "caused" a particular conflict.

The Malthusian Narrative

In 2011, Syria was not considered a likely candidate for falling into civil conflict. The country had experienced nearly thirty years of political stability – albeit brutally imposed – under the al-Assad dynasty, with power transferring to Bashar al-Assad after his father, Hafez, died in 2000. Though the country is predominately Sunni Muslim, the al-Assad family is Alawite, an offshoot of Islam that considers itself a separate religion. Syria is comparatively poor, with GDP per capita ranging from \$725 to \$2,060 between 1994 and 2007, though it had been experiencing rapid and sustained economic growth in the early 2000s. Syria had been considered a militarily capable state and had a vast security apparatus used largely to squelch domestic protest and jail political dissidents. Though Syria was much less agriculturally dependent than most states in sub-Saharan Africa or South Asia, 50 percent of the population still lived in rural areas.

From 2006 to 2011, Syria experienced one of the worst long-term droughts in the history of the Fertile Crescent, with climate scientists calling it the worst "in the instrumental record" (Kelley et al. 2015) (see Figure 13.6). Further analysis would link the drought to climate change, arguing that climate change had made this type of extreme drought more likely. Particularly agriculturally dependent regions like Hasakeh in the northeast saw 75 percent of crops fail and herders lose 85 percent of their livestock. These losses left 1–1.3 million Syrians food-insecure and made rural life unsustainable. Fleeing the drought-imposed hardship, more than 1.5 million people – mostly agricultural workers and family farmers – moved from rural areas to cities, slums, and camps in and around Syria's major cities: Aleppo, Damascus (the capital), Dara'a, Deir ez-Zour, Hama, and Homs. Many of these migrants were young men accustomed to farm work who found their employment prospects dim in these urban centers. Successful farmers and farmhands became unskilled, lowly paid laborers almost overnight.

(cont.)

Figure 13.6. Cracked earth at the bottom of what is normally a water reservoir, outside a monastery in Syria.
©Thomas Halle/ Moment Open/Getty Image.

This rapid mass migration placed significant strain on these urban centers, especially as food prices skyrocketed across the Middle East and North Africa. Taking cues from the Arab Spring uprisings in neighboring countries and angered by spiraling food prices related to Russia's drought and wildfires, some of these displaced young men began protesting the al-Assad regime, demanding the release of political prisoners in March 2011. These demonstrations began peacefully but escalated to violent clashes as the security forces responded in heavy-handed manner. By July of 2011, these clashes had erupted into a full-blown insurgency. The fighting continues as of 2023, having drawn in ISIS rebels as well as the United States, Russia, and Turkey, among others. (See Chapter 7 for an in-depth treatment of conflict dynamics there.) The massive refugee crisis created by the conflict strains both neighboring countries and relations within the European Union.

In this narrative, the causal chain linking climate change to conflict is relatively straightforward: climate change results in a historic drought, which leads to crop and livestock failure, which leads to rural hardship and migration to urban centers, which leads to dissatisfaction with the government and employment prospects, which leads to protest and violent repression, which leads to dissidents taking up arms.

This perspective has become dominant in policy circles, with figures like then–US President Barack Obama and then–US Secretary of State John Kerry linking the Syrian Civil War to climate change. President Obama said climate change–related drought "helped fuel the early unrest in Syria, which descended into civil war" (Obama 2015), while Secretary Kerry noted "it's not a coincidence that immediately prior to the civil war in Syria, the country experienced its worst drought on record" (Kerry 2015).

The Revisionist Narrative

The revisionist narrative of the Syrian Civil War places very little emphasis on climatic conditions. Rather, in explaining the conflict's onset it points to factors like authoritarian

(cont.)

rule, political marginalization, and the removal of subsidies that had served to prop up the rural economy. To explain the specific timing, this account looks to the demonstration effect of young Syrians seeing fellow Arabs protesting authoritarian rule across the region during the Arab Spring.

The revisionist narrative points also to some weak links in the causal chain outlined earlier. First, the revisionist narrative does not deny the historic magnitude of the drought for the Fertile Crescent as a whole. But it does counter that the meteorological data is not clear-cut on the magnitude of the drought for Syria, and that data from many Syrian weather stations do not demonstrate a drying trend over the latter half of the twentieth century. That is, climate change does not appear to be making northern Syria, the area most affected by the drought, more arid and more drought-prone. Under this interpretation, climate change did not make the drought worse or more likely to have occurred in the first place.

Second, the revisionist narrative contends that drought was not the main cause of the crop failures that made rural life intolerable. Drought certainly affects crop yields, or the amount of crop harvested from a given piece of land in a season, but it is far from the only factor. For one thing, irrigation can break this relationship. And since much of the area around Hasakeh is irrigated, it was not entirely dependent on good rains for good harvests. Instead, the revisionist narrative counters that crops failed due to severe late-season frost and, more importantly, removals of subsidies on inputs like fertilizer and water that tripled farmer costs essentially overnight. That is, crops failed not because of drought, but because of misguided policy changes and a late-season freeze that had nothing to do with the drought itself.

Finally, the revisionist narrative doubts the importance of drought-related grievances and drought-affected participants to the initial uprising. For example, protesters in Dara'a presented thirteen demands to the local administration in March 2011. None had anything to do with drought or drought relief. Rather, they focused on issues like security sector reform, removal of the town governor, reinstatement of women teachers who were expelled for wearing the *niqab* (a face-covering veil), and lowering fuel prices. Additionally, there is little evidence to indicate that displaced rural dwellers were active in organizing or attending the protests. In Dara'a, recent migrants neither participated in protests in large numbers nor were targeted for arrest or beatings. Once the protests began, many fled the city to avoid being caught up in the conflict. Thus, the link between environmental grievances and protest activity is suspect.

The revisionist narrative looks elsewhere than the environment to explain why Syrians were angry with their government: longstanding issues like authoritarian rule, human rights abuses, and exclusionary patronage networks built around religious identity (i.e., high groupness); and proximate "sparks" like surging food and fuel prices and the demonstration effect of Arab Spring uprisings in neighboring countries.

(cont.)

An Attempt at Synthesis

How can we reconcile these two perspectives? One puts environmental factors front and center; the other barely assigns them any weight at all.

First, we should note that to claim any particular conflict was "caused" by climate change is exceedingly difficult. Dissidents almost always have multiple motivations, such as revenge, greed, and ideology, and these motivations are both stated and unstated. Second, as we know, contextual factors, like dependence on agriculture for livelihoods, patterns of exclusionary ethnic rule, and low levels of economic development, affect whether a given climate "shock" results in violence. The drought that affected Syria also affected neighboring Jordan, Lebanon and Cyprus, yet widespread violence did not occur there. Even if and when climate matters, it matters in a specific political, social, and economic context that must be taken into account.

Third, whatever the cause of crop failure – be it drought, frost, or subsidy removals – its impact was much larger in a more agriculturally dependent country like Syria than it would have been in an OECD country, where fewer than three in 100 people are farmers. Renewable resources – and access to them – are still a central part of the story linking declining rural livelihoods to surging urban populations.

Finally, this case points out the importance of choice: in times of crisis, governments can use policy levers to ease the pain associated with environmental or market-based shocks. Facing rising discontent in urban centers, the Syrian government responded the way most authoritarian governments do: by cutting back on social services for rural dwellers and attempting to concentrate benefits on urban ones. This strategy ultimately backfired, as it heightened grievances in rural areas and encouraged migration to the cities.

So, did climate change "cause" the Syrian Civil War? Most research in this area – such as the study discussed in the next section – finds that climate shocks raise the probability of a large-scale event (like conflict onset) occurring relative to some baseline, or increases the frequency with which smaller-scale events (protests, individual battles or skirmishes, cattle raids) occur. That is, climate shocks are probabilistically causal in the sense that they make *some*thing more likely. They are not deterministically causal in the sense that they are wholly responsible for the outcome. These relationships emerge from the study of hundreds if not thousands of cases using quantitative methods. Claiming that climate change is the cause of a particular conflict takes on the air of a necessary condition – if not for the climate shock, the event would not have occurred. This claim, though, is almost always very difficult to make.

QUANTITATIVE STUDY

Does Drought Cause Conflict?

The previous section applied the concepts in this chapter to a single case: the conflict in Syria. Another way to evaluate social scientific arguments is to test them using quantitative data. This section walks you through the motivation, design, and results of one such study.

While much of the chapter focused on types of environmental conflict and the political, economic, and social contexts in which they are likely to occur, relatively less was said about when conflict is likely to occur. One question is whether conflict is more likely or more prevalent in times of scarcity or in times of plenty. The standard Malthusian argument would hold that conflict should be more likely in times of scarcity, such as during droughts, as actors fight for the dwindling remains of the pie. However, there is an alternative perspective – the abundance argument – that holds conflict is more likely during conditions when actors' basic needs are being met, freeing up resources to invest in higher-order activities like addressing political and economic grievances through violence. One can spin stories and cite examples to support either argument. The Syrian Civil War followed a historic drought. Alternatively, the East African drought of 2011–2012 appeared to significantly weaken al-Shabaab, the Islamist militant group, and undermine its campaign against the government of Somalia: drought forced farmers and herders to flee the rural al-Shabaab strongholds, undercutting the economic base of the movement and making it harder for it to sustain its forces. That is, there is case-based support for both scarcity and abundance arguments. In a situation like this, the best option is to analyze large amounts of data containing thousands of observations of conflict and peace and see whether one effect dominates the other.

In 2014, Idean Salehyan and Cullen Hendrix (2014) designed a quantitative study to test these hypotheses. We will take each element of the study in turn.

Research Question

Is political violence more likely to occur in conditions of environmental scarcity or abundance?

Theory and Hypotheses

As discussed earlier in this chapter, there is an open discussion over whether violence is more likely in conditions of abundance or scarcity. The Malthusian perspective holds that resource scarcity and environmental shocks generate grievances and fuel conflict over resource distribution as people fight directly over control of resources needed for survival. The abundance perspective holds that organized political violence, like armed conflict, will be more likely when basic resource needs are met, freeing up actors to invest effort in political activities.

However, as also discussed earlier, we don't believe these relationships will hold under all circumstances. Rather, the authors argue that for these mechanisms to operate, environmental conditions need to be the primary determinant of wellbeing. That is, the relationship – in either direction – should be contingent on the society being economically dependent on agriculture and having low levels of economic development. They expect the correlation between climatic conditions and political violence will be present in poorer, more agriculturally dependent societies and not in wealthier, less agriculturally dependent societies.

Hypothesis 1 (Scarcity hypothesis): Organized political violence is positively associated with drought and water scarcity, i.e., less water, more conflict.

Hypothesis 2 (Abundance hypothesis): Organized political violence is negatively associated with drought and water scarcity, i.e., more water, more conflict.

Hypothesis 3 (Conditional scarcity hypothesis): Organized political violence is positively associated with drought and water scarcity in less developed, more agriculturally dependent societies, but not in more developed, less agriculturally dependent societies.

Hypothesis 4 (Conditional abundance hypothesis): Organized political violence is negatively associated with drought and water scarcity in less developed, more agriculturally dependent societies, but not in more developed, less agriculturally dependent societies.

Data

The data for this study come from a sample of 165 countries, analyzed from 1970 to 2006. The units of observation are countries across calendar years (country/years), for a maximum of 5,432 observations. Each country/year – i.e., Kenya in 2002, Kenya in 2003 – is an observation.

Dependent Variable

Because political violence is a broad concept, this study includes several different measures of the dependent variable. First, civil conflict incidence is a variable that has a value of 1 if an armed conflict occurred in a country-year, 0 otherwise. Data are from the Uppsala University Conflict Data Program/Peace Research Institute, Oslo (UCDP/PRIO) Armed Conflict Database. UCDP/PRIO defines armed conflict as "a contested incompatibility which concerns government and/or territory where the use of armed force between two parties, of which at least one is the government of a state, results in at least 25 battle-related deaths" (Gleditsch et al. 2002). Second, the study uses annual counts of battle deaths as a proxy for conflict intensity. As rebel organizations grow in size and capability, the authors argue this will be reflected in their ability to inflict losses on the battlefield. Third, they use annual counts of terror attacks. Finally, they use annual counts of the deaths caused by these attacks. Each dependent variable is analyzed separately.

Independent Variables

The main independent variables are various measures of rainfall and temperature that serve as proxies for environmental abundance or scarcity. The Palmer Drought Severity Index is a measure of drought, including information on precipitation, temperature and soil conditions. Higher values correspond to more precipitation and more lush vegetation. In separate regressions, they include measures for rainfall and temperature, normalized to each country's observed means and variances. This accounts for the fact that what would be an exceptional drought in the Congo (twenty centimeters of rain in a given year) would be considered a very good year in an arid country like Somalia.

Recall that the authors argue the environmental-conditions/conflict correlation should be confined to poorer, more agriculturally dependent countries. In order to test this, the authors split the sample into richer and poorer countries. They also split the sample to look at African and Asian cases separately, as these two world regions are the most agriculturally dependent.

Control Variables

Because humans don't control the rainfall or temperature in a given year, control variables are not really necessary. We can thus estimate the measures of rainfall and temperature as if they were assigned as random, as in an experiment. That said, just to be sure, some models in the study include controls for political institutions, population and population growth, the presence of a large youth population, oil wealth, and other factors known to affect the incidence of political violence.

Results

The statistical analysis provides some support for H2, the mobilization hypothesis: wetter conditions correspond to a greater incidence of conflict occurrence. The evidence for the conditional mobilization hypothesis, H4, however, is much stronger. The correlations between environmental abundance and conflict are much stronger for African, agriculturally dependent, and poorer countries. In Africa, a one standard deviation increase in precipitation from the mean is associated with a 32.4 percent increase in the likelihood of conflict.

Conclusions

This study is part of a large debate on the impacts of climatic conditions on conflict. In contrast to much of that debate, which focuses on Malthusian concerns, this study indicates that times of relative plenty, rather than times of scarcity, are more conflict-prone. Additionally, climatic conditions can affect conflicts that are in no obvious way "about" resource scarcity, as they make conflict itself more or less costly for rebels.

SUMMARY

This chapter has demonstrated these primary points:

- Renewable resources can be degraded if consumption is unrestricted
- Water is a key cause of conflict, both over water boundaries and water shortages
- Population growth can put stress on resources, making interstate conflict more likely
- Civil conflicts can arise over communal access to resources and "sons of the soil" dynamics
- Individuals sometimes resort to violence in an attempt to stop environmental degradation
- State capacity, a rural economy, and "groupness" can all make conflict over resources and environmental stress more likely
- Violent conflict can itself affect environmental quality
- Climate change can worsen conflict

KEY TERMS

Carrying capacity
Cod Wars
Common-pool resources
Environmental conflict
Groupness
Lebensraum
Six Day War

"Sons of the soil" conflicts
Thomas Malthus
Malthusian
Tragedy of the commons
Transboundary
Water wars

REVIEW QUESTIONS

1. What are renewable resources and how do they relate to environmental conflicts?
2. What is the tragedy of the commons, and how is it typically avoided?
3. Territorial conquest was especially common during the mercantilist era and the Great Depression. Why?
4. What are sons of the soil conflicts?
5. What is groupness, and why does it matter for intrastate conflict?
6. What kinds of countries are most prone to environmental conflict?
7. When are those countries most prone to environmental conflict?
8. How does conflict typically affect the environment?

DISCUSSION QUESTIONS

1. Why is it hard to foresee the implications of climate change for war and peace?
2. Do you think climate change caused the Syrian Civil War?
3. What can individual nations and the international community do to reduce overconsumption of common pool resources?

ADDITIONAL READING

Bale, R. (2016, August 29). One of the world's biggest fisheries is on the verge of collapse. *National Geographic*. [Blog.] www.nationalgeographic.com/animals/article/wildlife-south-china-sea-overfishing-threatens-collapse

Busby, J. (2022). *States and Nature: The Effects of Climate Change on Security*. Cambridge: Cambridge University Press.

Daoudy, M. (2020). *The Origins of the Syrian Conflict: Climate Change and Human Security*. Cambridge: Cambridge University Press.

Hendrix, C. and Noland. M. (2014). *Confronting the Curse: The Economics and Geopolitics of Natural Resource Governance*. Washington, DC: Peterson Institute.

Snyder, T. (2015). *Black Earth: The Holocaust as History and Warning*. New York: Tim Duggan Books.

Vivekananda, J. et al. (2019). *Shoring up Stability: Addressing Climate and Fragility Risks in the Lake Chad Region*. Berlin: Adelphi Research.

REFERENCES

Ban Ki-moon (2007, June 16). A climate culprit in Darfur. *United Nations Organization*. www.un.org/sg/articles/articleFull.asp?TID=65&Type=Op-Ed

CBS News (2017, September 8). "Five-hundred-year" rain events are happening more often than you think. www.cbsnews.com/news/what-does-500-year-flood-really-mean

Fearon, J. D. and Laitin, D. D. (2011). Sons of the soil, migrants, and civil war. *World Development* **39**(2), 199–211.

Gleditsch, N. P., Wallensteen, P., Eriksson, M., Sollenberg, M., and Strand, H. (2002). Armed conflict 1946–2001: A new dataset. *Journal of Peace Research* **39**(5), 615–637.

Heidbrink, I. (2018). The First World War and the beginning of overfishing in the North Sea. In R. P. Tucker, T. Keller, J. R. McNeill, and M. Schmid (eds.). *Environmental Histories of the First World War*. Cambridge: Cambridge University Press.

Hilborn, R. (2012). *Overfishing: What Everyone Needs to Know*. New York: Oxford University Press.

Kelley, C. P., Mohtadi, S., Cane, M. A., Seager, R., and Kushnir, Y. (2015). Climate change in the Fertile Crescent and implications of the recent Syrian drought. *Proceedings of the National Academy of Sciences* **112**(11), 3241–3246.

Kerry, J. (2015, November 10). Remarks on climate change and national security. https://2009-2017.state.gov/secretary/remarks/2015/11/249393.htm

Kim, K.-G. (2013). *The Demilitarized Zone (DMZ) of Korea: Preservation, Conservation, and Restoration of a Unique Ecosytem*. Berlin: Springer.

Mach, K. J., Kraan, C. M., Adger, W. N. et al. (2019). Climate as a risk factor for armed conflict. *Nature* **571**(7764), 193–197.

Malthus, T. R. (1798). *An Essay on the Principle of Population*. Cambridge: Cambridge University Press

Obama, B. (2015, May 20). Remarks by the president at the United States Coast Guard Academy commencement. https://obamawhitehouse.archives.gov/the-press-office/2015/05/20

Salehyan, I. and Hendrix, C. S. (2014). Climate shocks and political violence. *Global Environmental Change* **28**, 239–250.

Sharon, A. (2001). *Warrior: An Autobiography*. New York: Simon & Schuster.

Index

CPSIA information can be obtained
at www.ICGtesting.com
Printed in the USA
LVHW021225150723
752577LV00011B/1235